THE TALL SHIPS PASS

THE TALL SHIPS PASS

by

W. L. A. DERBY

The Story of
THE LAST YEARS OF DEEPWATER
SQUARE-RIGGED SAIL

*embodying therein the History and detailed Description of
the Finnish Four-Masted Steel Barque*

'HERZOGIN CECILIE'

Illustrated by 96 photographs and
with drawings reproduced from the
original scale-plans of the barque

With an Introduction by
BASIL LUBBOCK

NEW EDITION

DAVID & CHARLES REPRINTS

ISBN 0 7153 4952 X

First published in 1937 by Jonathan Cape Limited
Second edition published in 1970

Printed in Great Britain
by Latimer Trend & Company Limited, Whitstable, Kent
for David & Charles (Publishers) Limited
Newton Abbot   Devon

CONTENTS

LIST OF ILLUSTRATIONS

[Except where otherwise stated, photographs are of 'Herzogin Cecilie'. Where no acknowledgment is made photographs were taken by the Author].

ILLUSTRATIONS

ILLUSTRATIONS

THE PLANS OF 'HERZOGIN CECILIE'
(*Redrawn by Mr. T. H. Simpson*)

SCHEDULES

INTRODUCTION

IN these days of mechanical transport the sailing vessel must appear to modern youth as archaic and inefficient a form of progression over the sea as the horse-drawn vehicle — to quote the official phrase — over the land.

To many the square-rigger must seem but a windmill for present-day Don Quixotes to tilt at, in their desperate attempts to preserve the memory of their bad old days and bad old ways. Such, one would think, must be the verdict of the young of both sexes, who suffer from that latest of germs — the speed germ. Yet even the most mechanically-minded and greatest sufferers from irritable unrest find that there is a peculiar charm in sail. Your machine and its driver tend to become more and more automatic and so the very uncertainty of the wind-jammer, with her unending combat against the forces of nature, the wind and sea, provides an irresistible attraction to the machine-ridden and the adventurous-minded.

The rebellion against the automatons of this mechanical age is steadily growing. We see it everywhere. Let me give an instance. When I first knew those two yachting rivers, the Hamble and the Crouch, a few, smart, professionally-run yachts shared their empty reaches with the sturdy craft of the crabbers, oyster-dredgers and local trawlers. Nowadays, though, alas, the fishermen are almost extinct, the yachts have so grown in numbers that it is very difficult for a stranger to find a berth.

The wish, however, to escape from the mechanical drudgery of the daily round is not the only reason for the vast fleet of yachts of all sizes and rigs which now crowd every river and port in the United Kingdom.

The British above all other nations, except, perhaps, those of the Vikings, have the love of a ship in their blood. We have inherited through generations of seafarers a sea and ship sense — perhaps scientists would call it a sea-gene — which makes us peculiarly sympathetic to all books dealing with sea life. Most British boys begin by showing an interest in books which deal with pirate schooners; by the time they have reached manhood the schooner has often found a rival in their affections in the shape of a clipper ship or a Cape Horn grain-carrier, to which last category *Herzogin Cecilie* belonged. There is, however, a good deal more than the purely romantic in the life of such vessels.

Of all the works of man, the ship alone possesses an individuality, a character — one might almost venture to say a spiritual entity or soul. And this is the reason for the devotion shown by seamen for particular craft. This devotion *Herzogin Cecilie* has aroused in the hardened breast of many a deepwater seaman; thus, this valuable addition to the bibliography of sail will, I am sure, give great pleasure to many an old shell-back as well as to the large host of admirers of that famous old barque.

Basil Lubbock.

PREFACE

And now and then one of the dwindling number
Of proud square-riggers lifts there, slim and tall,
The wonder of her spars above them all.

IT is sometimes said that the decease of the deepwater windjammer has been responsible for an unwarranted flood of sail literature. Even to the enthusiast in such matters, there is much truth in this allegation, for so many voyages have been described, and so many biographies penned, that it would seem the saturation point has already been reached.

I feel, therefore, that some justification, in fact almost an apologia, should be advanced on behalf of yet another addition to that plethora of books, even though, as I believe, the subject is in this case approached from a new angle.

I first set foot on the deck of *Herzogin Cecilie* when she was discharging a cargo of Australian grain at Millwall Dock. That locality, known as the Isle of Dogs, was a fitting environment for the sailing vessel of this twentieth century, for it has a history rich in the memories of bygone sail. Thereabouts was the home of the grand East Indiamen of 'John Company', and there, in an adjacent dock, were berthed, in later days, the renowned Blackwall clippers.

Rarely enough nowadays, however, can square-rig be seen in London River. The four, tall, white-trucked masts, with their delicate tracery of running and standing rigging etched against a summer sky, stood out that day on the horizon like an oasis in the drab, monotonous desert of roofs and chimneys which forms the purlieus of Dockland.

Herzogin Cecilie was a familiar name even then. It had figured in the Press on several occasions in the preceding few years as that of the soi-disant 'winner of the grain race', and a book had been written describing one of those passages.

I knew that she was a big, steel, four-masted barque, built in Germany thirty years before: that, until the War, she had been the crack cadet-ship of the Norddeutscher Lloyd, and that for a dozen years she had tramped the world under Finnish colours as the flag-ship of the last fleet of deepwater sail.

15

PREFACE

So I went down to Blackwall to see what a real windship was like. Until then my sea-going had been confined to steam, and my knowledge of commercial sail as it exists to-day had been gleaned from hearsay, from books and pictures, and from the business view-point of Lloyd's.

The sum total of the general impression thus acquired concerning the surviving square-riggers visioned a trade doomed by decay, senility, and parsimony, the fruits of a long, and now lost, battle against steam. In place of decay I found beauty and grace; for senility, trim seaworthiness; for parsimony, a strong, well-found barque.

Later I was to realize how fortunate I had been in choosing for my initial acquaintance with sail one of the finest vessels of her type then afloat. On that summer evening she looked, at any rate to outward appearance, from her polished teak and gleaming brass on deck to her powerful and lofty top-hamper, the very antithesis of the toilworn, weather-beaten windjammer for which I was prepared.

When, shortly after, I sailed aboard her, studied her long and honourable record, and came to know those who managed and manned her, that casual first impression was confirmed rather than belied. Subsequently, I sailed in or examined in detail several other units of the little group of windjammers, most of them owned by Finland, which represent the final venture under sail, but in no case did I find the peer of *Herzogin Cecilie*.

Gradually this study of the last of the old tall ships became an absorbing work, and soon I began to realize the great number of devotees the subject still possessed. Few among the younger generation of to-day have seen, or now ever will see, a real sailing vessel, and yet all over the world it seems that ship-lovers, both old and young, are reading about, modelling, photographing, and following the movements of the few deepwatermen still in active commission.

There was much to learn, a host of queries to be answered, and numerous economic issues to be understood before the full story of this swansong of sail could be pieced together. I could discover no exhaustive text-book dealing with the vessels and the period in question, and many and varied were the sources of information which supplied answers to a thousand questions.

Thus was this book born, as the outcome of that research. Had it been feasible for the task to be undertaken by a true 'shell-back' its value might have been thereby enhanced, but the English sailor of the sail has gone, never to return, and it remains, perforce, for an amateur to record the results of his investigations, believing that they may prove of some interest and benefit to both contemporary and future enthusiasts in such matters.

When deploring the dearth of reliable information about famous bygone vessels, Mr. Keble Chatterton, in the preface to his recent *Ship Models*, says: 'Speaking of Columbus's *Santa Maria* and Drake's *Golden Hind*, it is one of the scandals of history that only the barest details of these ships have been handed down. It is the old story of not deeming it worth while to narrate for the future that which is constantly before the eyes of the present generation.'

Obviously *Herzogin Cecilie* must occupy a humbler niche in the great sea-gallery than those famous craft to which Mr. Chatterton refers, but even of her the same comment may become true. It is conceivable that in days to come this closing period in the centuries-long era of sail propulsion may evoke an interest similar to that now shown in the many previous chapters of that glorious story.

My object and hope in compiling this present record is that it may help, in some small way, to meet that need if and when it arises. For the present, although intended primarily for the student of sail history, and especially for the model maker, I trust that it may also be of some general interest. In consequence, while endeavouring throughout to be accurate and precise, I have tried not to be too highly technical. If, at times, the expert finds redundant detail and explanation or, at others, a striving for simplicity, I tender a plea for indulgence on behalf of the layman.

The greatest care has been taken to check and verify every detail and figure, and to avoid the inclusion of unauthentic matter or of fictitious embellishment. No responsibility is assumed, however, for any statement of fact: I should indeed be grateful for any correction or additional information from authoritative sources.

Mr. Basil Lubbock, the great historian of the sailing ship, has up to the present gone no farther in his published researches than the pre-War West Coast nitrate trade. His *Log of the Cutty Sark*, in conjunction with Doctor Longridge's splendid technical treatise on the construction of that famous clipper, enables one to know her intimately, to model and rig her accurately from scale plans, and to learn every detail of her story.

PREFACE

Mr. Masefield's *Wanderer of Liverpool*, and Mr. Laing's *Sea Witch*, describe in detail two other splendid bygone vessels. In Volume II of his monumental work, *The Last of the Windjammers*, Mr. Lubbock deals briefly with the earlier career of some surviving square-riggers, among them *Herzogin Cecilie*, and he gives the hull and sail plans of several barques of like type but of earlier date.

In recent years many descriptive accounts have been written of contemporary voyages made aboard one or other of the big sailers still engaged in the Australian grain trade. Mr. Alan J. Villiers was the originator and chief exponent of such literature, and his works have been deservedly popular. His practical experience is extensive: he served before the mast in *Lawhill*, *Grace Harwar*, and *Herzogin Cecilie*; he sailed for two years aboard *Parma* as her part owner, and then became Master and owner of the square-rigged, world-cruising yacht, *Joseph Conrad*. His *Falmouth for Orders* describes an actual voyage in *Herzogin Cecilie*, and contains much information and many illustrations of that barque.

No single book or combination of books can, however, be found presenting a detailed, accurate, and complete exposition of the commercial windjammers of this decade, embracing within that scope the economic issues which have been responsible for the development, design and survival of such vessels, and for the conditions under which they trade.

This is the ground which I have endeavoured to cover. In addition, I have included something of the life and work in deepwater sail to-day, of those who operate, command and man the last of the square-riggers, and of the cargoes which even now offer a livelihood to the windjammer.

The technical aspects of square-rig are dealt with by concentrating on a description (by text, photographs and scale-plans) of one particular vessel, *Herzogin Cecilie* — for fifteen years the most outstanding vessel in that final odyssey of sail, the story of the Erikson Fleet.

I commenced my task in 1934, and in point of fact the description of the barque was the first section to be completed. It was, naturally, written in the present tense, for *Herzogin Cecilie* was then sailing regularly in the Australian grain trade.

The unfortunate and inexplicable casualty, on April 25th, 1936, when she drove ashore near Bolt Head, is still fresh in the memory of all ship-lovers. No greater proof could be evidenced of the abiding affection of a sea-minded nation for a form of transport to which, in the past, much of Britain's maritime supremacy and colonization had been due, than the public interest aroused in this country by the stranding of *Herzogin Cecilie*. Offers of help, both pecuniary and practical, came from all over the country, and, during the many weeks which elapsed before she succumbed to stress of weather, private enterprise came within measurable distance of saving her.

But it was not to be, and I had to consider the effect of the loss in relation to this book. For me, however, perhaps because she had for so long filled my thoughts and my leisure, *Herzogin Cecilie* refused to die. I spent several hours aboard her just before further damage quashed all hope of salvage, and I decided then that, whatever her fate, her description should read as though she were still the 'proud square-rigger' of the verse that heads this Preface. Therefore, whereas Book One and the last three Chapters of Book Two (her history) are tensed correctly, the intervening, descriptive Chapters retain, in the main, the form in which they were conceived.

The grim struggle for survival waged with success during the last decade by a score or so of second-hand sailing vessels, mainly the property of one ex-captain, is a sea epic in itself. There is no hope of victory, no incentive in the future outlook, only the sure knowledge, shared by all concerned, of ultimate extinction. Lightly manned by young boys, uninsured, toilworn after an already long sea life, these old-fashioned craft are menaced by every reduction in grain freights, for the Australian grain trade offers them their only regular employment, and on that one trade alone depends their continued existence. So far they have managed to eke out a living, but this last brave effort of sail is drawing rapidly to its close.

Herzogin Cecilie, unlike some of her surviving contemporaries, was to the end a staunch, sound, seaworthy vessel. For her type and generation her lines were good, her equipment and accommodation lavish, and her sailing qualities far above the average, but to dub her, as others have done, a 'clipper' is mere journalese and quite unjustifiable. I have sought no unwarranted glorification on her behalf. My lily is ungilded, and no attempt has been made to include any extraneous narrative or imaginative matter.

In planning the completed picture of *Herzogin Cecilie* one of the greatest difficulties lay in deciding what to omit. To catalogue every minute detail of her hull, for example, would not only make tedious reading, but even be unreadable to any but the technical expert. I have, I believe, incorporated a sufficiency of plans and photographs to cover the whole area of her hull, decks, and top-hamper in both pictorial and scale detail. Consequently, my intention is that the four chapters which comprise the construction and lay-out of the barque should be regarded as complementary and subservient to the illustrations and drawings, supplementing and amplifying the latter in respect of colour, alterations, cause and effect, and so forth. For model-making I think that an intelligent use of pictures and prose will fulfil every need without, in either case, being redundant.

Perhaps the best indication of the method of approach to those chapters is for the reader to imagine himself inspecting *Herzogin Cecilie*, say, in dock. No pictures or plans would be necessary on such an occasion, but the services of a guide, versed in the history of the vessel and in the whys and wherefores of this or that, might increase the pleasure of the visit, and serve to explain how, when, and why she was so designed and fitted out.

A further problem has been to avoid the pitfall of repetition. For example, a certain casualty may have given rise to a definite structural alteration, and in dealing with the latter the former has, however briefly, to be mentioned in an explanatory sense. Nothing is more vexing or confusing than to encounter the same incident in differing contexts. Only the barest references to the vessel's history, therefore, are made in the technical chapters, to be amplified in greater detail in their correct context elsewhere.

So many people have helped me with information that it is not possible to enumerate and to thank them individually. My especial thanks, however, are due:

To Mr. Alan J. Villiers, not only for his encouragement of a project which encroaches somewhat on his own preserves, but for his permission (and for that of his publishers, Messrs. Geoffrey Bles Limited), to use any suitable material from his several books; to Messrs. Rickmers Rhederei, A.G., of Hamburg, for supplying copies of the builders' plans and an early photograph of *Herzogin Cecilie*; to Mr. W. L. Leclercq of Amsterdam, for a detailed part copy of the barque's log, together with other supplementary data of her post-War history; to Mr. Percival

Marshall (publisher of, amongst other works, *Ships and Ship Models*), and to Mr. J. P. Taylor (Editor of *Shipbuilding and Shipping Record*) for advice and guidance in technical matters; to Mr. A. A. Hurst (now serving aboard *Moshulu*), Mr. B. H. Jones (Assistant Librarian at Lloyd's), Mr. T. B. Duncan, and Mr. W. J. Russell for their several contributions toward the progress of the work; to Mr. A. S. Calder and Mr. C. H. Tinker, of Messrs. H. Clarkson & Company Limited (London Agents of the Erikson Fleet), for copious information regarding the business side of windjamming; to the Intelligence Staff of Lloyd's, for placing at my disposal their remarkable system of records; to Messrs. Appleby & Son, Ship Chandlers, for particulars concerning the fitting out of a sailing vessel.

Unknowingly, the authors of the books listed in the Bibliography have contributed much to the birth and growth of this chronicle. Particularly am I conscious of the inspiration and assistance derived from the many works of Mr. Basil Lubbock, to whom I am also indebted for his kindness in writing an Introduction.

When they heard that the net author's royalties from the sales of *The Tall Ships Pass* was to form a donation to the 'Flying Angel' (The Missions to Seamen), many people kindly offered photographs free of reproduction or copyright fees: Mr. A. S. Herring and Mr. A. A. Hurst, who both possessed extensive collections of hitherto unpublished pictures of sail, allowed me to choose therefrom at will; Mr. Adrian Seligman, Mr. R. A. Beazley, and Mrs. G. Greenacre each contributed a number of photographs.

In the List of Illustrations, the source of every picture used has been acknowledged, but I should like to add that both the *Western Morning News*, and Captain F. C. Poyser of the Nautical Photo Agency, supplied several pictures free of cost; while 'Fox Photos' afforded me privileged treatment.

For permission to incorporate short extracts from her sea-poems, and one prose excerpt, I am indebted to Miss C. Fox Smith, that veritable 'Kipling' of the sailing vessel, of whom Joseph Conrad wrote: 'In her I verily believe the quintessence of the collective soul of the latter-day seaman has found its last resting place, and a poignant voice before taking its flight for ever from the earth.' Messrs. Philip Allan & Company Limited, and Messrs. Methuen & Company Limited, as publishers for Miss Fox Smith, were kind enough to endorse her permission.

PREFACE

If, for some readers, this book supplies answers to any of the many questions for which I have sought solution, or fosters, in others, an affection for those relics of the past, the old windjammers, I shall be well satisfied.

W. L. A. D.

'Warley'
Beckenham
1937

BOOK ONE

THE PASSING
OF THE DEEPWATER
SQUARE-RIGGER

CHAPTER I

FIFTY YEARS OF SAIL
DEVELOPMENT

PART ONE: WOODEN CLIPPER TO STEEL FREIGHTER

They passed — like Summer clouds they passed,
As fleeting and as fair:
The shapely hull, the soaring mast,
The speed beyond compare.

IT is perhaps difficult to realize that the true clipper-ship, the fruit of centuries of maritime experiment, was conceived, born, flourished, degenerated and passed away for ever, all within the span of an average lifetime.

Although that short period has been ably dealt with in full detail by several eminent authorities, some account of the economic causes which contributed to the development and decline of the big steel barque is a necessary prelude to this book.

So closely related are many points in the management and voyagings of the last of the commercial windjammers to the exigencies of competition that, to appreciate their continued existence, some familiarity with what might be called their genealogy is almost essential.

The commercial charter, by which the great East India Company had since 1600 held the prerogative of Indian trade, was abolished in 1813, but it was not until 1833 that Lord Grey's Act terminated the like restriction of the China trade and entirely closed the Company's monopoly. In anticipation of the end their famous fleet of armed merchantmen was disbanded by private sale between 1830 and 1834.

1833
The end of the Eastern monopoly

Gone for ever were the slow and ponderous dignity, the semi-naval discipline, and the vast profits of the ships of 'John Company', but these vessels were to form the nucleus of many new and more minor maritime enterprises, and their design continued to influence the ideas of British shipbuilders for the next twenty years.

Old tradition dies hard: 'frigate-fashion' was deeply engrained into the conservative principles actuating British designers. As late

1848
'Frigate-fashion'

27

as 1848 the new Tyne-built merchantmen, *Blenheim* and *Marlborough*, were counterparts of contemporary naval frigates; in fact, in scantlings, design, and general stoutness they were almost identical with a 40-gun Ship of the Line.

With enormous jib-booms, heavy overhanging sterns pierced by many windows, little or no sheer, 'kettle-bottomed', full in the bilge and with blunt and rounded bows, such vessels were strong and sturdy craft, but great speed was as yet a quality neither expected nor sought by English shipowners. The sides of the hull of an Indiaman had, however, less 'tumble-home' than was customary in the warships of the period, and some of them were almost wall-sided.

The Blackwallers of the early fifties

The famous Blackwall frigates of the early fifties, hard-wood, copper-fastened, East India passenger ships, owned by Green, Wigram, Smith, Somes, and Dunbar, maintained the old, unstinted precepts of management and manning known as 'Blackwall fashion', which characterized the Indian trade for many years, and rarely extended on quite so lavish a scale to any other Colonial trade under sail.

The stately Blackwallers were splendid examples of the solidarity and perfection of English craftsmanship, and when, in 1855, Laing of Sunderland delivered *La Hogue* to the order of Duncan Dunbar of London, the supreme development of the frigate-type merchantman was reached.

These vessels, although still subject, by reason of their hull lines, to considerable leeway, improved greatly upon the lengthy passages of their predecessors, the Indiamen of the Company, whose invariable habit had been to shorten down to topsails each nightfall. Neither the trade value of speed, coupled with an ability to sail well when close-hauled, nor the means by which these desirable attributes might be attained were then appreciated by the designers of our sailing vessels.

1844
The early American clippers

History leaves little doubt that, by 1850, the United States of America led the world in the art of building fast and beautiful hulls. Unhampered by tradition or custom, American designers were inspired rather by the graceful lines of visiting French vessels than by the heavier, blunter, English types.

America had made considerable commercial use of the privateers built for the war with England of 1812-1814, vessels which, by their superior speed and handiness, had been remarkably successful in action against slower opponents. Although their rather coffin-shaped, round-bottomed hulls bore scant likeness to the sharp, narrow lines of their successors, it was for these little New England vessels, mostly schooner or brig-rigged, that the word 'clipper' was first coined.

Round about 1840 a number of small vessels, ranging from 100 to 300 tons burthen, both English and American, were engaged in the Chinese opium trade. It was practically smuggling, and called for swift, well-handled craft of light draught.

The success of these two classes of vessel emphasized the benefits accruing from superior speed, and, in 1844, Smith and Dimon of New York launched the *Rainbow*, whose unorthodox, hollow bow lines created quite a furore in shipping circles. She was the first true extreme clipper-ship, and was quickly followed by a host of lovely craft.

Between 1844 and 1845 the little American *Natchez*, under Captain Waterman, made the outstanding passages of seventy-one days from New York to Valparaiso and seventy-eight days from Canton to New York. Three years later, Smith and Dimon's *Sea Witch*, regarded as the fastest and most beautiful vessel of her day, lowered those same two passages by two and three days respectively.

A long series of Navigation Acts, passed between 1381 and 1660, had encouraged, by the exclusion of foreign competition, the ships, seamen, and commerce of Great Britain. While such protection was in force no goods might be imported into England or her dependencies in other than English bottoms or in those of the producing country. The gradual repeal of these Acts, culminating, by 1849, in their entire withdrawal in respect of ports abroad, removed the whole of the deep-water trade restrictions. The resultant Free Trading exposed the importation of tea and silk from China, a country with no export facilities of her own, to intensive foreign competition. In 1854 a like protective measure governing British coastal trade was also discontinued.

1849
The repeal of the Navigation Acts

American vessels, crossing the Pacific in search of further lucrative employment after an outward passage from the Atlantic seaboard, now began to encroach on the China trade. The *Oriental* was the first American clipper to bring tea to England after the cessation of the Navigation Acts, and she secured, in 1850, nearly double the freight offered to British tonnage. By their superior speed American ships between 1850 and 1855 skimmed the cream of this valuable business,

29

earning greater profits than our own slower bottoms could command, and causing thereby great consternation among London and Liverpool shipowners.

In 1852 the fastest passage of the year, and one of the best ever accomplished under sail from China, was made by the American clipper *Witch of the Wave*, for she reached England in ninety days.

These early American clippers were rarely of a greater tonnage than 1,000 gross, but the discovery, in 1847, of gold in California gave a tremendous fillip to American shipbuilding. The trans-Continental traverse from the populous Eastern States to the Golden West was, in those days, a long, toilsome and hazardous journey by wagon-train, the 'schooner of the prairies'. So great was the 'get-rich-quick' incentive that multitudes were willing to pay dearly for the alternative of a quick sea-passage to San Francisco, via the Horn. In the twelve months prior to the gold-strike only four sailing vessels arrived at San Francisco from the Atlantic ports, while in 1849 no fewer than 775 vessels sailed for the new Eldorado, and 91,000 persons made the passage.

American ships held the monopoly of this new transportation as, at that time, vessels of any other nationality were precluded by law from operating between two American terminal ports.

1850
The California clippers The urgent demand was for larger and faster craft, and, by 1850, the ever famous California clippers were opening the eyes of a surprised world to the possibilities of a new era in sail design.

In his excellent book, *In the Days of the Tall Ships*, Mr. R. A. Fletcher gives the following table of American tonnage launched for the California trade: 1850 — 13 vessels, 1851 — 31, 1852 — 33, 1853 — 51, 1854 — 20, 1855 — 13, 1856 — 8, 1857 — 4, — a grand total of 173.

With a registered tonnage of 1,500 to 2,500 tons, and built of soft-wood, most of these new clippers were long, very fine-lined (especially at entrance and delivery), and, with a beam-to-length ratio of as much as 6·7, they made all other merchantmen of their day seem squat and stocky by comparison. Setting, as they did, immense sail plans embracing many innovations in 'flying-kites', there was nothing then afloat which could live with the Yankee clippers in the strong winds for which they were primarily designed; while in general weatherliness they were years ahead of all contemporaries. The records set up by these extreme clippers during the decade which followed have never

facing: THE BEAUTY OF BELLYING CANVAS

been surpassed in all the long history of sail.

It is a sore temptation to anticipate a later chapter by digression into the fascinating bypath of clipper performance. How, for instance, *Flying Cloud*, in 1851, on her maiden passage, sailed the 17,597 statute miles from New York to San Francisco in eighty-nine days twenty-one hours, an average of 222 statute miles per day: or how the peerless *Lightning* established, in 1854, the record for all time for one day's sailing.[1] Her log states that during her maiden voyage from Boston, Massachusetts, to Liverpool she was, on March 1st, running in a strong southerly gale, '18-18½ knots, lee rail under water, and rigging slack'. Between noon on February 28th and noon on March 1st she ran 436 nautical miles. Again, between March 18th and 19th, 1857, when running her Easting down in 42° S., outward bound to Melbourne, she covered 430 nautical miles from noon to noon. These phenomenal runs exceeded by almost 100 miles the best day's run then logged by steam.

The magic nomenclature and magnificent performances of the superlative creations of that master builder, Donald McKay of East Boston (born at Shelburne, Nova Scotia, in 1810) — *Staghound* (1850) his first out-and-out clipper, *Flying Cloud* (1851), *Sovereign of the Seas* (1852), *Great Republic* (1853), *James Baines*, *Lightning*, and *Donald McKay* (1854) — vie in the history of sail with the names of such great captains as James Nicol Forbes, Charles Porter Low, Lauchlan McKay (a younger brother of the builder), Anthony Enright, and many another splendid seaman, who drove those big clippers as vessels had never before been driven.

Donald McKay, the master builder

McKay's designs were essentially suited to strong winds; built to utilize to the full the heavy weather of the North and South Atlantics, in light airs they were definitely inferior to the daintier, more yacht-like, British tea-clippers of a later date.

When still a young man, Donald McKay had established a reputation by the vessels which he had built for the North Atlantic packet service: the *St. George* of the Red Cross Line and Enoch Train's *Joshua Bates* were two of McKay's best-known packets.

The Atlantic packets

As far back as 1816 this regular Transatlantic passenger trade had been started by the beamy 500 tonners of the American Black Ball Line, whose average crossing was in the neighbourhood of forty days, the passage from East to West often occupying three months. By the

[1] For correction of this claim see *Champion of the Seas* on pages 51 and 284.

31

time the later clippers had reduced the east-bound passage to a minimum of thirteen days, steam competition was offering a ten- to twelve-day crossing in either direction with a regularity unapproachable by sail.

It seems a long step from Samuel Cunard's little barque-rigged, side-wheeler *Britannia* (230 feet in length and 1,154 tons gross) which in 1840, by her west-bound record passage of 2,755 miles in fourteen days eight hours, averaged 8.19 knots, and became the first holder of the Trans-Atlantic Blue Riband, to the *Queen Mary* (80,773 tons) which in 1936, at an average speed of 30.63 knots for 2,939 miles, crossed the Atlantic in three minutes under four days.

It is probable that few shipowners of the 'fifties, either in New York or Liverpool, visualized the imminence of the total eclipse of sail. At any rate, they were still then eager for improved sail tonnage, and the small packet ships were superseded by American-built semi-clippers of anything from 1,000 to 1,500 tons. Between 1843 and 1844, McKay built several successful ships for the Red Cross and the White Diamond Packet Lines, vessels which were the forerunners of his larger and more famous extreme clippers.

1849
The Australian
goldfields

The rush by sailer to the Pacific Coast diggings only endured until 1857, for a railway across the Isthmus of Panama with steamer connections at its terminal points so shortened the journey from New York to San Francisco that the clippers after a few years lost much of their former prerogative in passenger transport.

The discovery of gold in Australia in 1849, however, reproduced in England an equivalent demand for an identical type of tonnage — large, fast, passenger clippers — and Liverpool shipowners, by the charter and purchase of suitable American bottoms, set out to reap the golden harvest of the stampede to the new diggings. Some idea of the scale of emigration at the time is given by the increase in the population of Bathurst, N.S.W., from 70,000 persons in 1850 to 333,000 in 1855, a direct result of the finding of local gold deposits.

The Australian run was, for many years to come, to remain in the hands of the sailing vessel, and, as will be seen, was one of the last regular trades to succumb to the encroachment of steam.

1853
James Baines
of the Black
Ball Line

In 1853 James Baines of Liverpool chartered McKay's *Sovereign of the Seas*, and a year later ordered from the same builder two big clippers, of 2,500-3,000 tons register, for the Black Ball Line. This famous fleet (not to be confused with an earlier American packet line of the same name) had been started with the New Brunswick ship *Marco Polo*. The new clippers, *Lightning* and *James Baines*, the fastest vessels then afloat, earned undying fame for their designer, and great profits for their enterprising owner, by accomplishing between them, under the British flag, a remarkably consistent series of outstanding performances.

The Australian gold rush reached its height in 1856, some ten years before the zenith of the China clipper, at a time when beamy teak and oak vessels were the P. & O. liners of their day, and when the Atlantic packet service was still vested largely in American interests.

The boom period in American clipper-ship building, however, endured for only the bare decade between 1848 and 1858. America was the fortunate possessor of unlimited reserves of soft-wood in close proximity to her shipyards. In the early 'fifties her ships were, ton for ton, cheaper to build than anything which Britain could produce, confined as we were to the hard-woods — teak, oak, and the like — for hull construction.

1858
The decline of the soft-wood clipper

On the other hand, as against its higher prime cost, a hard-wood hull was far more durable, and, in the long run, more economical than the soft-wood type. Moreover, the intensive driving to which the American clippers were subjected militated against longevity: it was found that five years was about the effective average lifetime of these big, soft-wood ships. After two or three round voyages they tended to become strained, leaky, and water-logged, with a consequent liability to cause damage to cargo, combined with depreciated sailing qualities.

Often the greatest feats of these Yankee fliers were accomplished during their maiden voyages, and they soon became unprofitable propositions.

The prior claim of naval needs had partly denuded our own forests of oak, and much of our commercial shipbuilding at this time was carried out in selected hard-woods imported from the Continent and from India. The cost of importation increased the expenses of construction, and, oak supplies not being inexhaustible, British builders were forced to turn their attention to the possibilities of metal as an alternative to wood. The building of wooden clippers reached its zenith about 1856, by which time several iron sailers had been launched, but there was a lengthy interim stage of composite construction before iron became the general medium.

33

Teak, which, because of its oily nature, was able to resist the ravages of water and weather to a remarkable degree, had long been a favourite material for the outer planking of hulls. When wood gave place to metal for hull construction, teak continued in use for deck fittings, for which purpose it is still employed to-day.

The end of American supremacy in sail

For some years after the outbreak of her Civil War in 1861, America was too occupied by her own internal troubles to keep the lists in the wider field of competitive international trade. American superiority in clipper-building waned, and never recovered its former status: for the remainder of the century the British windjammer was to represent all that was best in sailing-vessel construction.

The United States, with its enormous coastline, its lack of colonial possessions, and its protective shipping legislation, continued for many decades to operate a large local, sailing mercantile marine. Although it entailed a circumnavigation of South America, the long traverse from Atlantic to Pacific could be classified as coasting, and remain, as such, largely an American monopoly. American shipbuilders continued to favour wood as a general medium, though they produced many fine steel vessels.

The splendid history of the later host of magnificent 'Down Easters' (so fully recorded by Mr. Lubbock in his treatise of that name) is familiar to all students of sail matters, but, in the wider sphere of general world trade under sail, American domination had, to all intents and purposes, ended by the close of the fifties.

1860 The 'China Birds' and composite construction

Of all the merchantmen that ever sailed the seas none were better built or more carefully finished than the tea-clippers of the sixties. No expense was spared, and they were furbished up and fitted out like the great yachts they were. They were no slavish copies of the American model, but a distinctive type with marked innovations of hull and sparring evolved to meet a definite need.

Copper and iron cannot be employed in juxtaposition because of galvanic action. Copper sheathing for ship bottoms, with its remarkable freedom from marine growth and the protection it afforded from the ravages of the teredo or ship-worm, had always been a feature of the wooden clippers. In the transition period from all-wood to all-metal hulls, the difficulty was overcome by wooden planking copper-sheathed below the water-line and bolted to iron frames, beams and stringers; keel and sternpost, however, being of wood. *Tubal Cain*, 787 tons gross, launched in 1851, was the initial experiment in this class of construction.

In general the British composite extreme clippers were of smaller tonnage than the soft-wood American vessels, rarely exceeding 1,200 tons gross. Although they never quite equalled the great sailing records set up by McKay's wonders, they were better all-rounders, and well suited to the lighter winds which characterized the China tea trade for which they were primarily designed. Like all fine-bowed craft, they were wet ships, especially in a head sea, but they were amazingly efficient in working to windward, and their supreme quality of 'ghosting' along in faint breezes had never been attained by their American predecessors.

Many of the later tea-clippers, notably *Thermopylae* (1868) and *Cutty Sark* (1869), added to these distinctive attributes the ability and strength to carry all plain sail under the gale conditions which prevail in high latitudes like the 'Roaring Forties', a feature which was to stand them in good stead when, in after days, they entered the Australian trade.

The first composite tea-clipper was launched by Robert Steele & Company of Greenock in 1863. By 1870 the China tea trade, which twenty years before had threatened to become almost an American perquisite, had passed entirely into British control. The period between 1865 and 1870 saw the halcyon days of this profitable employment of British clipper ships.

In 1866 the great Tea Race took place, when *Ariel*, *Taeping*, and *Serica* ran a triple dead-heat, all three vessels docking on the same Thames tide.

The largest composite sailing vessel, and undoubtedly the most comfortable, was *Sobraon*, launched in 1866 by Hall of Aberdeen, for Lowther Maxton & Company, her registered tonnage of 2,131 earning for her the soubriquet of 'The Great Sobraon'. She was unique in that she was intended originally for a steamer, but was completed as a sailer. In 1873 she was bought by Devitt & Moore, and until 1891 was one of the best liked passenger vessels in the New South Wales trade. The Government of that State retained her until 1911 as a reformatory ship in Sydney Harbour.

So magnificently were these composite clippers made that, when the Federal Government had *Sobraon* surveyed for a training-ship, she

1866
'The Great
Sobraon'

was found, after forty-five years afloat, to be as sound as a bell. Although she was to spend many years at moorings in Rose Bay, she was re-christened *Tingira*, a name meaning 'The open sea'. In her jubilee year, 1916, she was paid off from official service, and became the club-house of a philanthropic enterprise.

A few months ago, at the ripe age of seventy, this famous craft was advertised for sale 'in excellent condition'. It was anticipated that she would, at long last, go to the ship-breakers, but an examination of the hull disclosing that it was still perfectly sea-worthy, efforts are now being made to get *Sobraon* to sea again, equipped with auxiliary power, as a coasting pleasure-cruiser.

It is indeed fortunate that, owing to the initiative and care of Captain Dowman, the present generation can still see and enthuse over *Cutty Sark*, the only other survivor of the old racing clippers, as, restored to much of her original glory, she lies to-day in Falmouth Harbour.

The early seventies – the passing of the tea-clipper

The general high standard of tonnage competing in the tea trade was the main reason for the withdrawal, in 1867, of the tonnage bounty which, previously, had been earned by the first ship home, and which had been so great an incentive to racing. In the middle sixties, when tea was retailed in London at five shillings per pound, freights had soared to as much as £7 per ton, but they now receded rapidly. In 1871 a maximum freight of £3 per ton was the best fixing obtained by sail, and so great was the influx of steam through the newly opened Suez Canal that only three clippers loaded at Foochow that season. By 1876 all the first teas were secured by steamers, and only £2 per ton was offered for the later loading among the few sailers participating at the time. The predominance of the tea-clipper had waned for ever: a few Britishers continued for some years to carry China tea to American ports, a striking contrast to the inverse position of twenty years before, but the majority were diverted to other seas and other cargoes.

*1870-76
The iron clippers*

Although iron is a heavier medium than wood, an iron hull, because of the comparative thinness of its plating, is only about three-quarters the weight of a wooden hull of equal strength and equal outward dimensions. Also, that same diminution in the material employed enlarges the internal carrying-capacity of the said hull without impairing its buoyancy.

The stolid conservatism of many British shipowners gave rise to

36

widespread and bitter opposition to the general employment of iron, but when the invention of anti-fouling bottom composition offered a part solution to the drawback of corrosion and marine growth, much of the adverse criticism ceased.

The first iron tea-clipper was the *Lord of the Isles*, built by John Scott of Greenock. Once established, the new construction soon ousted the old, and between 1874 and 1876 the extreme iron clipper ship reached its highest development. Enduring as were some of the composite vessels when compared to their wooden predecessors, the iron ships of this period were among the strongest and most durable vessels ever built.

The history of the iron ship *Katherine* gives a good idea of the great and effective longevity of the type. Fifty years ago — 1887 — she was launched at Glasgow by Barclay, Curle & Company for R. & J. Craig's famous County Line, with a gross tonnage of 2,495. As the four-masted full-rigger *County of Linlithgow*, she flew the Red Ensign until 1906, when Craig's sold her to Philippine owners, who rechristened her *Katherine*. To-day she is still trading regularly in the Mediterranean, under the Greek flag, although converted for the carriage of bulk oil, de-sparred, and fitted with Bolinder oil engines of 348 n.h.p. The remarkable thing is that after all her toil and vicissitudes she still retains unimpaired her Lloyd's Classification of 100 A1, a striking tribute to her strength and quality.

Another of Barclay, Curle & Company's products, the iron barque *County of Inverness*, 1,796 tons gross, launched in 1877, is still afloat as the steamer *Nemrac*, under the Estonian flag. For twenty years she flew Craig's house-flag, and then was sold to Shaw, Savill & Albion of London. In 1933 she passed her fifth 'Number One' survey by *Lloyd's Register*, and retained the 100 A1 classification to which she had conformed fifty-six years before. 'Good iron — good ships!'

Harbinger, launched in 1876 by Steele of Greenock, for Anderson, Anderson & Company, was the supreme effort of that gifted designer in the production of fast, iron, passenger ships, and, incidentally, she was one of the last sailers to carry on the old tradition of 'Blackwall fashion' in management.

The New Zealand emigrant trade, which developed between 1870 and 1873, was a factor largely responsible for the success of this popular type of vessel. The New Zealand Shipping Company was inaugurated in 1873 by the ordering of four first-class, iron full-riggers for passenger-cum-cargo purposes, and in the spring of 1874 3,000 emigrants left England for New Zealand.

The threat of steam competition The day was now fast approaching when the sailing vessel, in her passing, was of necessity forced to become both larger and more economical if she were to continue as a commercial proposition, for the era of high speed as a prime factor occupied a remarkably short period in the long history of sail.

The early marine engine was prodigal in its fuel consumption, and the successful development of the steamer was a gradual process governed to a great extent by the price of coal and by the need for the provision of adequate rebunkering facilities. Before the days of the Suez Canal, steamers employed on the Eastern run were confined, by the necessity for carrying enormous quantities of bunker coal, to the transport of passengers, mails, specie, and such small bulk commodities as silk.

The first Anglo-Indian steamship, the *Enterprise*, of 470 tons and 120 nominal horse-power, had in 1825 voyaged from London to Calcutta in 113 days, at an average speed of a little under nine knots.

1869
Suez By 1842 the P. & O. Company had commenced a regular steamer service to India, via the Cape of Good Hope, but it was not until the opening of Suez in 1869 that steam dealt to sail the first of a succession of punishing blows in the long and bitter fight which was to end in the ultimate extinction of the deepwater windjammer. The Suez route reduced the Far Eastern run by almost one-half, but it was of little benefit to the sailer by reason of its high dues and the unsuitable weather conditions of both the Red Sea and the Mediterranean. As soon as sufficient new coaling stations were established, the steamer abandoned to sail the old traverse round the Cape, and by the reduction in her bunker spaces was enabled to carry larger and more valuable cargoes at an economical rate.

The rise of steam was slow, but once the element of intensive competition was introduced it represented an ever-growing menace, whose repercussion on the design and management of the sailing-vessel finally produced, in *Herzogin Cecilie* and her twentieth-century contemporaries, sail's last dying challenge to the victor.

Sail tonnage reached its zenith in 1868 when its aggregate volume totalled 4,691,820 tons as against the 824,614 tons of steam then in existence. By 1873, however, a bare four years after the advent of Suez, steam had more than doubled itself in reaching the figure of 1,680,950 tons; while those five years had reduced sail's total to 4,067,564.

Although the Canal made little difference in distance on the Australian voyage, 1876 found sail and steam in fierce competition for the Antipodean passenger traffic, for Wigram's steamers and the early Orient liners were making the Sydney run in round about fifty days against the sixty-five to seventy of the fastest sailers.

1876
Competition for the
Australian
passenger trade

The rapid growth of trade between Great Britain and her Colonies, however, provided at this date plenty of employment for all concerned. Vast quantities of jute, wool, and grain were offering for shipment, and Colonial expansion filled both the cabin and steerage accommodation of the outward-bounder.

In no phase of our history is the inestimable value of vast colonial possessions more marked than in the story of the growth of Britain's great mercantile marine during the second half of the nineteenth century. The commercial development of the hitherto untapped resources of the more distant Colonies, and the vast emigration traffic which populated them, produced a boom in shipping which placed Britain far ahead of any other contemporary, and earned for her the proud title of 'Carrier of the World'.

Ever since Columbus demonstrated the existence of a New Hemisphere, and thereby made possible a Spanish Empire overseas, the successful expansion from country to empire has been directly measurable in terms of nautical endeavour, for colonization is entirely dependent upon sea transport. As the greatest of all Empires, Britain's debt to the 'sailor of the sail' is illimitable. Without minimizing the accomplishments of steam, nevertheless it is true that, for the most part, steam has consolidated holdings which had been discovered and first exploited by the sailing vessel.

When it is realized that McKay's first big clipper *Staghound* earned $80,000 over and above her prime cost in her first year's trading (New York — 'Frisco — Canton — New York), or that, in 1851, a wooden ship carrying 1,800 tons of cargo from New York to San Francisco earned no less than $78,000 in freight, while in 1852 — 1853 the *Sovereign of the Seas* received for her maiden voyage $84,000 for the transport of 2,950 tons of merchandise, it is easy to imagine the inducement that the clipper trades had offered to shipowners in the days when such profits were the direct reward of speed.

The great profit
of the early clippers

It was the custom in the heyday of the clippers for their captains to be financially interested in the ventures undertaken. American owners allowed to their more successful Masters a commission of five per cent on the profits, while in the China tea trade, English captains fought for the handsome bounties which rewarded the winner of the annual race home to the London and Liverpool markets. It is said that the famous Captain Anthony Enright demanded, and received, from James Baines & Company, £1,000 a year salary, exclusive of other perquisites, for his command of *Lightning* in the fifties, a figure which was then, of course, of far greater relative worth than it would be to-day.

Once the steamer, with her greater earning facilities, entered the lists against sail these pecuniary inducements became a thing of the past, and sailing-vessel owners were faced with the twin issues of increasing the carrying capacity of their vessels and, at the same time, reducing operating costs.

1880
*The medium
clipper*

To the extreme clipper, cargo capacity had always been subsidiary to speed. As has been shown, such ships, originally evolved by the need for rapid conveyance of passengers and specie, had developed into carriers of such light weight, easily stowed cargoes as tea and silk, small in bulk but of high intrinsic value.

It became obvious by the early eighties that these graceful, stream-lined hulls were unfit, by their very fineness, to compete against the full-sectioned steamer, although, of course, a good turn of speed was still an essential. Some radical change in hull design was indicated, and the immediate need was met by the introduction of the medium, iron clipper.

These vessels were both larger and more capacious than their yacht-like predecessors. In them were combined the fine bow and stern lines of the extreme clipper and the longer and fuller midship-section demanded by large holds. They were best exemplified in the famous British 'liner' fleets of sail of the ensuing period, carriers of fair-sized general cargoes, with provision for a big complement of both cabin and steerage passengers.

These big, medium-lined semi-clippers proved to be excellent passage makers. They traded in company with many of the older and smaller ex-China clippers which had been compelled to seek employment in the harder but still lucrative sphere of Antipodean trade.

By 1884, for example, *Cutty Sark*, launched in the year that saw the opening of the Suez Canal, had become a regular unit of the

Australian wool fleet, and she only returned again under British colours to Eastern waters on one occasion when, in 1886, she loaded a cargo of scrap-iron for Shanghai. Scrap-iron was a queer cargo for an ex-tea-clipper, and the voyage, via the Cape, occupied no less than 124 days. *Cutty Sark* proved, however, over a ten-year period, a remarkably successful wool carrier, accomplishing the finest performances of her long career when, in competition with the iron medium clippers, she raced home from Australia round the Horn.

In his *Colonial Clippers* Mr. Lubbock covers the period now under review in the greatest detail, and, like all his works, that book can be recommended as the best guide to a detailed study of a particular phase in the story of commercial sail.

It is a temptation to enthuse over the twenty years between 1870 and 1890, for in many ways it was then that sail propulsion reached the peak of its achievement. Great and unbeaten as had been the individual performances of the extreme wooden and composite clippers, it was during these later decades that organized regularity and general reliability characterized the work of a multitude of splendid sailing vessels. The ideal 'all-round' sailing vessel was never evolved by any one particular trade, nor by the stressing of any one quality. The medium-sharp, general merchantman, the successor of the clipper, represented the highest average development of sail.

1870-90
The Glorious Era

Whereas the clipper had placed a premium on speed at the expense of capacity and reasonable economy, the later vessels in the British Colonial trades (and their American prototypes the 'Down Easters') merged the benefits of speed, handiness, capacity, and low operating costs into an economic success, for they proved capable of carrying any and all cargoes on any of the world's sail routes.

As in all other spheres of development and evolution, competition bred efficiency: Watson Brothers' 'Bens' — Thomas's 'Cambrians' and 'Counties' — Newton's 'Dales' — Lyle's 'Capes' — the 'Sierra' fleet of beautiful, iron full-riggers — Fernie's 'Omene' Line — the Waverley clippers — the lovely 'Lochs' — such fleets and their owners set a standard of sustained perfection which well merited the title of 'Glorious Era' by which this period will always be remembered.

It is an era which cannot be dissociated from some remembrance of the great shipbuilders who graced it — W. H. Potter & Sons, and T. Roydon & Sons, of Liverpool; J. Reid & Company, and Russell, of Glasgow; the Whitehaven Shipbuilding Company and a dozen other famous firms who were largely responsible for Britain's undoubted supremacy in mercantile sail affairs at that time.

1885
*The introduction
of steel*

The last great boom in the building of iron medium clippers was between 1882-1884, for round about 1885 the steel vessel was coming into fashion. A steel hull was found to be approximately fifteen per cent lighter in weight than an iron hull of equal dimensions, and steel superseded iron so completely that in the closing decades of the sailer, or in fact from 1890 onwards, steel hulls were almost universal. In theory, the size of a steel hull was unlimited, but in actual practice unhandiness provided a reasonable check on dimension. In confined waters, for instance, the larger the vessel the more dependent she was on tug assistance, always an expensive matter.

1900
*The big steel
freighters*

Prior to 1890, sailing vessels of over 2,500 tons gross were uncommon, but gradually the urgent dictates of the ever-advancing power of steam forced the designers of sailing vessels to concentrate on capacity. The short, straight midship section of the medium clipper was extended farther and farther fore and aft, until, finally, there emerged the long, steel, wall-sided, box-like carriers of the early twentieth century.

They were immensely strong, serviceable vessels, if withal sometimes lumbering and unwieldy. Except at bow and stern the worst of them differed little in hull design from the steamers, which were now fast ousting sail from trade after trade until, finally, it was only in the carriage of comparatively imperishable cargoes of solid bulk, such as nitrate, guano, coal, timber, and grain, that the windjammer was to find a livelihood.

The majority of the cross-sections of a vessel of this type were of equal dimension, and her large square holds, strongly bulkheaded, held a great tonnage of cargo. As near unlovely as a sailing vessel could ever be, wet, sparsely manned, brutes to steer, many of them deadly slow, they waged a gallant but losing battle, facing certain defeat and ultimate extinction once the Panama Canal rendered obsolete the old Cape Horn Road.

But the survey has progressed a little too rapidly. It must not be presumed because a windjammer was large, steel built, and launched after 1890, that she was of necessity a mere lumbering 'wagon'.

Many beautiful, big, steel barques graced those last hard days of the long struggle. Macvicar, Marshall & Company of Liverpool, the

'Bank' line of Andrew Weir & Company of Glasgow, John Hardie's later vessels, the last of the 'Sierras', and scores of other ownerships were represented for almost another twenty years by well-run sailers.

The earlier marine engines were, by modern standards, so comparatively inefficient and so wasteful of coal that the longer ocean passages under sail were the last to succumb to the stranglehold of steam competition. As late as 1880 both mails and passengers were conveyed to and from Australia largely by sailing vessels, while the Antipodean cargo traffic was still carried, almost exclusively, in the holds of the sailer. It has even been claimed that, unless the new compounding principle had introduced its radical changes in the steam-engine, sail might have continued for many years to be the main method of long distance deepwater transport, because the problem of bunkers would otherwise have proved insoluble. *Australian wool and American grain*

The remunerative homeward wool trade was held until well into the nineties, and large fleets of magnificent medium clippers raced home with each season's clip. In 1891, for example, seventy-seven windjammers loaded full cargoes of wool at Sydney for the London sales, held during the first quarter of each year, and captains and owners taxed to the utmost the capacity of their vessels.

The lovely medium clipper *Mermerus*, one of the fastest of the iron colonial ships, screwed into her holds 10,000 bales of wool representing a total value of £130,000. By detailed personal attention to the screwing process, Captain Woodget of *Cutty Sark* is said to have increased the capacity of his famous old composite clipper from 4,289 to 5,304 bales.

Grain from the West Coast of North America was another active trade which remained for a long period in the hands of the sailer. In 1882, 550 sailing vessels loaded a total tonnage of 1,250,000 tons of Californian and Oregon wheat and barley for shipment to European ports via the centuries-old route round the Horn.

A great blow was dealt to the sailing vessel in 1897 when Lloyd's Underwriters fixed a large and general increase in insurance rates on sail tonnage, a burden which forced many famous owners to commence, by foreign sales, to disband their fleets. *1897 Increase in insurance rates*

'But the steam come up and the sail went down,
And them tall ships of high renown
Was scrapped, or wrecked, or sold away....'

*Steam versus sail
in practice*

It must always be borne in mind when comparison is drawn between sail and steam that, although the fast sailing vessel could, and can occasionally still, reel off a speed greater than that of a modern tramp steamer, she cannot maintain anything like the same average of speed. Nor can she, moreover, utilize the direct tracks of the steamer, for her journeyings are based on the prevailing wind-belts, and the passage from B to A may take double or treble the time of that from A to B, and demand an entirely different itinerary en route. The difference between the east-bound and west-bound passages of the old Atlantic sailing packets is a striking example of such discrepancy in time and route.

To make her fast passages the windjammer must arrange, or be fortunate enough, to sail at specific seasons of the year, and even then the ultimate arrival date is, as always, dependent on 'God and the Wind', for she is alike at the mercy of protracted calm and fickle winds.

The tramp steamer's advantage is even greater on the shorter voyages and in confined waters, but, taking an average of all trades and seasons, the annual carrying-power of a modern cargo steamer is at least treble that of a sailer of the same cargo-capacity, owing to the ability of the former vessel to complete a greater number of round voyages in any given period. The mechanical regularity and the non-dependence on weather conditions of the steamer enable her to maintain more even supplies of commodities to the world markets; also her charters are more readily fixed in view of the comparative certainty of her arrival date at any given loading port.

The dependability of the modern steamship was never attainable by sail, although, throughout the fifty years or more which I have surveyed so briefly, many owners of sail fleets, by the dispatch of vessels at stated and regular intervals (at any rate on the outward half of the voyage), merited the title of 'liner' concerns. Monthly passenger and mail services to Australia were a feature of many fine sail-liner fleets, but, in the main, the tally per ship rarely exceeded one round voyage each twelve months.

*The twentieth-
century
Britain abandons
the building of
sail tonnage*

By the opening years of the twentieth century Great Britain's interest in sail tonnage as a commercial proposition had very largely ceased. From an aggregate of 3,851,045 tons in 1880, her holding had dropped by 1910 to 1,101,494 tons. Admittedly, as already pointed out, many windjammers, good, bad, and indifferent, flew the old

'Blood an' Guts' up to and during the Great War. A few of them even survived to sail in post-War years.

The War years of 1914-1918 depleted the world's quota of sail tonnage at an amazing rate. Although freights were high, risks were correspondingly great, and the sailer proved an easy prey to raider and to submarine.

During the two or three immediate post-War years, the artificial boom in shipping, created by the temporary revival of trade, induced great activity in shipbuilding circles, and the resultant, and, as it proved, unwarranted over-production of steam tonnage left little room for the small quota of sailers which survived the War.

The twentieth century sailer had never been more than a cargo tramp, and the advent of the fast cargo liner, which has now so successfully encroached upon trades which formerly were the prerogative of the tramp, soon compelled the owners of steam tramp tonnage to enter actively into many rough trades which had, up to then, been relinquished to the sailer.

In the inevitable slump which followed the short post-war boom, most of the famous old ownerships in the world of sail were forced to discard their remaining windjammers, and by 1923 Lloyd's Register evidenced only twenty-eight British-owned sailing vessels of 1,000 tons and over. A few British owners, here and there, carried on with a vessel or two, but gradually they, too, were faced with the apparent financial impossibility of making sail pay its way.

Such a firm, for instance, was John Stewart & Company of London, whose long participation in the story of sail came to an end in 1927 by the sale of their *William Mitchell* to German ship-breakers. The final voyage of this vessel under British flag — Tocopilla to Ostend with nitrate in 1927 — was the last passage ever made by a British full-rigger manned by a British crew.

'William Mitchell' – the last British full-rigger

Sir William Garthwaite's four-masted barque *Garthpool* then became the only British deepwater square-rigger in active commission, and it was largely through sentiment that he persevered with her. She was the last Britisher to participate in the South Australian grain trade under sail. So bad were grain freights by 1928 that, to keep her at sea, her last two grain cargoes were purchased by Garthwaite for his own account, a merchant-adventure which, as it turned out, did yield him a small profit on his gamble.

'Garthpool' – the last British square-rigger

45

Garthpool was built in 1891, as *Juteopolis*, for Messrs. Charles Barrie of Dundee by W. B. Thompson & Company of the same city, and was successively owned by the Anglo-American Oil Company, and George Windrum & Son of Liverpool, before Sir William Garthwaite acquired her just before the War. She was wrecked on Ponta Reef, Boavista Island, Cape Verde, on Armistice Day, 1929, when outward bound, and so ended Britain's participation in deepwater windjamming.

Garthpool's Red Ensign, the last to fly at the gaff of a big British square-rigger, is preserved in the museum on board the training-ship *Worcester*.

The French subsidy schemes Because of a series of lavish shipping subsidies, France, in 1910, owned almost as many sailing vessels as she had done thirty years before. Regular State aid and protection were given to French shipping for the first time in 1881. One of the most extraordinary experiments was the introduction, from 1899 to 1902, of a bounty per net ton for every 1,000 miles sailed or steamed, provided that a periodical call was made at a French port. Thus it was even possible for a vessel to show a good profit from a protracted ballast voyage. The scheme provided a remarkable stimulant to the building of sail tonnage and enabled French vessels to accept very low freights and yet to pay handsomely.

By 1901, for example, France's total sail tonnage had in eight years increased by roughly forty per cent, this at a period when world figures for sail were decreasing annually. The subsequent restriction, however, of this governmental encouragement was too great a burden for private enterprise to shoulder, and except for the nitrate fleet of Antonin Dom Bordes et fils of Bordeaux, France's quota of sailers soon disappeared from the seas. At the outbreak of War in 1914, the Bordes Fleet consisted of forty-six sailing vessels with a total cargo capacity of 163,160 tons.

Germany's part in sail history Up to the middle of the nineteenth century, Germany possessed little in the way of a deepwater mercantile marine. She then came into some prominence by the purchase of both American wooden and British iron vessels. With these for inspiration her builders produced a large number of fine craft which were employed almost exclusively in her own trades, and were manned, under German law, entirely by her own nationals. Coupled with an insistence on the sail training of all ship's officers, Germany continued to operate and even to build sail tonnage on a successful commercial basis for years after most other nations had relegated it to an obscure corner of their marine programmes. In 1914, 107 big sailing vessels (total net tonnage 212,500) were registered at Hamburg: forty-eight of them were four-masted barques and thirty-eight were full-rigged ships. At this time the German Mercantile Marine had attained to a grand total, steam and sail, of over five million tons.

Under the Versailles Treaty Germany ceded to the Allies all her merchant shipping of a gross tonnage of 1,600 or over, half of the tonnage between 1,000 and 1,600, and a quarter of her fishing fleet. These penalties, coupled to her actual losses during the War, reduced Germany's mercantile holdings, by 1920, to an aggregate of less than 700,000 tons, and in the *débâcle* her large quota of deepwater square-riggers of pre-war days entirely disappeared.

In the post-War years Finland was concerned with the acquisition, at break-up prices, of good, second-hand sail tonnage. She had never, from the deepwater standpoint, been a producer of her own vessels, and from 1920 onwards, when the ports of Europe were congested with idle, unwanted sailers, she acquired a serviceable fleet of big vessels at a most moderate cost. The above-mentioned operation of Reparations had thrown a mass of ex-German sail tonnage into an already overstocked market, and the Finns had a wide choice at their disposal.

Finland acquires a windjammer fleet

The ex-German training barque *Herzogin Cecilie* was one of Finland's best bargains, for, after a long period of voluntary internment in Chile, she had been handed over to France, who, although being loth to accept a German offer of repurchase, was only too glad to find a ready buyer elsewhere for this fine, steel four-master.

Finland has had small cause to regret her gamble in sail. She has run these old vessels and profited by them in a fashion little short of miraculous, but that is a story which must be reserved for its rightful place in this book.

It may seem somewhat strange that the story of a foreign barque has been selected as the subject of an English book, but the lamentable facts remain that, not only was the last, big, British-owned square-rigger (*Garthpool*) wrecked eight years ago, but that, of the few British-built sailers still afloat under foreign flags, none is worthy to rank with *Herzogin Cecilie* in condition, sailing qualities, or in interest of record. On the other hand, during this twentieth century both Germany and Finland have done so much to lengthen the era of commercial sail, and

The part played by Germany and Finland in the extension of the sail era

their vessels have had such signal success in their voyagings, that those two nations may be justly regarded as the leaders of that last chapter in the story of the windjammer.

Although, apart from training-ships, Germany's present quota of deepwater sailers is but two — *Padua* and *Priwall* — an examination of those which now belong to Finland, a country which owns to-day the large majority of the world's total sail tonnage, reveals almost one-half to be of German origin. Three were built by Rickmers of Bremerhaven (the builders of *Herzogin Cecilie*) — *L'Avenir*, *Penang*, and *Winterhude*; while four — *Penang*, *Pamir*, *Passat*, *Pommern* (besides the smaller Baltic trader *Pestalozzi*), formerly flew the house-flag of Laeisz of Hamburg. Of these four only the first three were actually built in Germany.

Gustaf Erikson and Ferdinand Laeisz

Two shipowners will go down together to posterity as the outstanding figures of the final decades of sail history. One is Captain Gustaf Erikson of Mariehamn, Finland, owner of *Herzogin Cecilie* since 1921, and the man who, for more than twenty years after sail ownership had become obsolete elsewhere, has maintained in constant commission, and operated uninsured, a fleet of sailing vessels. I shall deal later with his remarkable career and unique flair for sail management.

With him must be bracketed Herr Ferdinand Laeisz of Hamburg, founder in the seventies of the famous 'Flying P' line of nitrate-carrying sailers, a fleet which, to quote Mr. Lubbock's own words, 'were worthy to be compared with the best of our British sailing ship lines at the height of our shipping prosperity'. It represented one of the most successful and meritorious attempts ever undertaken at establishing a 'liner' schedule with sailing vessels.

For two decades before the War the Laeisz vessels, aided by the firm's own efficient craft organization at the Chilean nitrate ports, maintained a regular service between Europe and the West Coast, via Cape Horn, making, on the average, per ship, three round voyages every two years. It was a gruelling trade, demanding strong, serviceable, well-found, well-manned sailing liners. In strength, capacity, and speed, the 'P' fleet represented, at a time when the windjammer was being ousted for ever from the seas, the zenith of sail's effectiveness and a sustained perfection which sail-driven craft never achieved in any other service.

48

facing: BECALMED OFF THE SCILLIES IN 1930

Some of these latter-day, big, steel freighters, like *Herzogin Cecilie* and the Laeisz liners, put up performances which by comparison — due allowance being made for cargo-capacity, free-board, longevity, and personnel — were as meritorious as any in the annals of sail. Nor were such performances mere isolated efforts accomplished more by luck than judgment, for it was in the very consistency by which a service was maintained that the Laeisz fleet demonstrated its ascendancy.

When I reach the question of *Herzogin Cecilie's* own log, the tabulation of both comparative speed and distance will bear witness to the surprising fact that, with the sole exclusion of the great feats of the big American racing clippers of the fifties, the German nitrate traders were capable of sailing qualities fit to rank with those of any of the great host of their predecessors under canvas.

Mr. Frank C. Bowen, in his introduction to Mr. Alan Villiers' *Herzogin Cecilie* book *Falmouth for Orders*, writes:

'The old clipper ship men would look down in disdain on a big steel cargo carrier like *Herzogin Cecilie*, yet she has most of the virtues of the old clippers with the addition of good earning powers, and at least some claim to habitability. The observer of the future indeed is likely to regard her and her consorts as the finest development of sail, and to dismiss the famous clippers as being something akin to freaks, although the latter satisfied a particular purpose and bred magnificent seamen.'

The short career of the extreme clipper, as a distinct type, is directly traceable to the development of an uneconomic design at the behest of speed. The prevalent belief that the clipper ship represented the peak of sail design is the result of much over-enthusiastic literature on the subject of the remarkable feats of those vessels.

The ideal sailing vessel could not be developed within the narrow requirements of any single employment. To place a premium on one qualification to the exclusion of others does not indicate any lasting improvement in type. On the combined grounds of technical plus economic perfection, sail design did not attain to its zenith until the sailer was forced into world-wide competitive trading.

The War cost Herr Laeisz his whole fleet, which, in 1914, had *The post-war 'P' fleet* totalled fourteen vessels. Some were captured and others interned, and at the end of hostilities the enforcement of Reparations scattered the 'P' liners among the Allied flags.

49

Laeisz, however, was prepared to build up once more. He repurchased six of his vessels from their new owners, who were well satisfied to receive cash for craft which, at that time, were 'white elephants' to the shipping profession in general. He commissioned two new vessels in the post-War period — *Priwall* in 1920 (her keel had been laid down in 1917), and *Padua* in 1926 — but the invention of artificial nitrate, the opening of the Panama Canal route, and the world-wide surplus of cheap steam tonnage combined in time to kill the import of Chilean nitrate to Germany by sailers.

It is interesting to look back on the nitrate trade of twenty-five years ago. The Panama Canal was still in course of construction, and steamer and sailer alike came home from Chile round the Horn.

The insurance rates ruling at the time in the London market were indicative of the high repute in which the 'P' vessels were held. The rate on nitrate by fully-classed steamers of not exceeding fifteen years of age was 37s. 6d. per cent. On approved sailing vessels with the same age-limit the rate was 42s. 6d. per cent, but Laeisz was granted a special rate of 38s. 9d. per cent, only 1s. 3d. per cent above the premium asked for a good class steamer. The French sailers of Messrs. Antonin Dom Bordes et fils, Laeisz's great rivals, were also singled out for special treatment, cargo in their bottoms being rated at 40s. per cent; this at a time when other French and all Italian windjammers were subject to a substantial increase on the general tariff.

Gradually throughout the long post-War period of financial stress in Germany the second Laeisz fleet was depleted and dispersed, many of them passing to the Finns, until the two survivors, *Padua* and *Priwall*, found their only livelihood in the Australian grain trade, a trade which was, at the time, the main *raison d'être* of the Erikson Fleet. However, it is pleasing to be able to record that in 1936 the Laeisz flag was once more to be seen on the 'Flaming Coast', for, after many years' interval, both *Padua* and *Priwall* again secured nitrate charters. These two barques are, unquestionably, the finest trading square-riggers afloat and are maintained in the true 'P' tradition.

The firm of Laeisz is not dependent to-day on the activities of its two remaining sailing vessels, as it operates five fruit-carrying steamers on the Cameroons run and two 6,000 ton steamers in general trading.

Some of the Laeisz vessels were of enormous dimensions, and it is interesting to note that *Preussen*, a steel, five-masted, full-rigger of over

5,000 tons gross, was launched by Rickmers' great rival and former pupil, J. C. Tecklenborg of Geestemunde, in 1902, the year of the birth of *Herzogin Cecilie*.

It is also an arresting commentary to remember that in 1902 the first wireless message was transmitted across the Atlantic. A new era overlapped the old. Long-range wireless, destined to prove so great a boon to navigation and to safety at sea, coincided with the last days of sail construction.

After launching *Herzogin Cecilie* and *Preussen*, perhaps the finest products of their respective genius for sail design, both Rickmers and Tecklenborg concentrated mainly on the building of steamers. In fact, the world over, the construction of big sailing vessels for commercial purposes had practically ceased, although as late as 1926 Tecklenborg 'came back' to produce for Laeisz *Padua*, probably the last big trading windjammer which will ever be built.

The end of sail construction

Germany, in an attempt to keep up her sail tradition, is said to be contemplating the ordering of two or three four-masted barques of about 2,500 tons register. As the intention is for each barque to provide accommodation for about 150 passengers, they should, presumably, be confined to pleasure cruising, and, in consequence, are likely to be fitted with some form of auxiliary motive power.

November, 1937. Copies of the weekly news-sheet issued aboard the clipper *Champion of the Seas* came to light recently in Australia. One of them contained an extract from the report of her Master, Captain Alex Newlands, concerning her maiden voyage to Melbourne in 1854 for the Black Ball Line of Liverpool. It stated that between noon on Dec. 12 and noon on the following day she logged 465 nautical miles when between Latitude 47°S. and 49°S. Running eastward, the difference in Longitude represented 43 minutes of time, and so noon to noon was 23 hours 17 minutes. This means that she sailed throughout at a mean speed of 20 knots. It eclipses the claim made on page 31, that the all-time record for one day's sailing was *Lightning*'s 436 miles on Feb. 8 of the same year when eastbound in the North Atlantic. Both these fine ships were built by Donald McKay of East Boston.

There ain't no racin' clippers now, nor never will be again,
And most o' the ships are gone by now, the same as most o' the men,

Like the ships that made a forest on the 'Frisco waterside,
The slashin' big fourmasters from the Mersey an' the Clyde
An' the Yankee skysail yarders with their plankin' scoured like snow
Loadin' grain at 'Frisco — forty years ago!

The evolution of the full-rigger

For the sake of clarity I have avoided reference in the foregoing survey of hull development to the kindred subject of alteration in rig, although the two issues are closely allied in regard to both cause and effect.

The term 'ship', like 'clipper', is frequently misapplied. Its original significance was not concerned with rig but merely denoted a vessel of the largest size then extant. Gradually it came to be used as the description of one particular type of vessel only — a full-rigged sailer having three or more masts. These masts, three, four, or even five in all, must be square-rigged, i.e. be crossed from deck to truck by a varying number of yards instead of only setting booms, schooner fashion.

Although at the latter end of the fifteenth century four-masted vessels were comparatively common, the sailing vessel did not progress, as seemed probable, toward the standardization of quadruple masting, but rather, by the close of the following century, toward an increasing area of square sail, with a consequent diminution of fore-and-aft canvas. The primitive six-sail equipment of the square-rigger of the early sixteenth century comprised a sprit-sail, fore and main courses with single topsails, and a lateen mizen.

Many of the larger galleons of Elizabethan times were square-rigged on their fore and 'mayne' masts, but carried fore-and-afters on the 'mison' and 'bonaventure'. (Nautical terminology was not improved when, in later days, the resurrected bonaventure was renamed jigger.)

During the seventeenth century this fourth or aftermost mast disappeared from general usage, the mizen set a square topsail, and so, gradually, was evolved the full-rigger of the eighteenth century.

Ship-rig was eminently suited to the days of merchant convoys and fleet tactics, for the requisite regulation of speed in company could be controlled by backing the square-sails on the mizen. The Navy continued to use this rig to the end of the sailing era, and a man-of-war remained a three-masted and square-rigged vessel right up to the adoption of steam. The design was retained also by most of the faster, deepwater, commercial vessels long after convoy days had ended, more or less as a matter of tradition.

The patent-truss method of lower-yard attachment, which, about 1845, replaced the old chain slings, conferred a decided benefit upon the square-rigger.

It supported the yard at some distance from the mast and so enabled a greater angle to be obtained by bracing. This, in turn, made it possible for a vessel so equipped to sail closer into the wind.

Upon the advent of the big, racing clipper, the plainness of contemporary square-sail plans was enhanced by the addition of a host of extra sails, many of them mere canvas 'gadgets', and of little real practical value.

At the same time the new-fangled, long, fine bows of the American *Jibs and* wooden clipper necessitated the stepping of the foremast in a more *jib-booms* afterly position than had been the custom on the blunt, rounded foredeck of the frigate type merchantman who carried her greatest beam well forward.

The experiment had marked success, and it encouraged the setting of an increased volume of head sails, jibs and the like. This, in turn, led to the lengthening of the bow-sprit by the provision of a jib-boom and later, of a flying jib-boom. So a spar which, in the first place, was merely a 'sprit' for housing an outboard grapnel and which, by the sixteenth century, had been given a little square-yard on which a spritsail could be set, became not the least important item of a clipper's tophamper. It was later to recede again, in the day of the big steel barque, to its original singleness of form, although never to its original purpose.

Since in the days of the Indiaman and the Blackwaller it was con- *Sail carrying* sidered to be a breach of good seamanship if any canvas or gear were *in clipper days* carried away, precautionary measures were taken at the first likelihood of such loss developing.

The men who extracted the last possible knot of speed from the clippers were of a very different calibre, and were no like economists in gear aloft. Their practice was to hold on to their canvas until the last minute, for, with the big crews of the time, sail could be reefed, or brailed and furled, at very short notice. The loss of spars and gear was a common-place event, and many a slim, lofty, new clipper limped in under jury-rig as a result of reckless over-driving during her maiden voyage.

The extreme clipper of gold-rush or tea-trade fame was almost invariably a three-masted full-rigged vessel. Barque-rig was much in the minority and confined principally to the coasting trades, although, strangely enough, the largest wooden sailing vessel ever built — McKay's ill-fated *Great Republic* of 1853 — was a four-masted clipper barque. She was also the first vessel to be fitted with a deck engine for her halliard winches and her pumps.

Having already defined a 'ship', it is perhaps consistent to explain that a barque or, to revive an old Yankee term, a shipentine, is a three-, four-, or five-masted vessel, square-rigged on all but the aftermost mast, this being equipped, schooner fashion, with gaff and boom, and setting no square-sail at all.

Metal hulls lead to over-sparring

The adoption of metals for the construction of both hull and top-hamper encouraged a general and necessary increase in the size of the sailing vessel. Maximum dimension was, however, governed by the combined limitations of balance, handiness, and manning.

By the seventh decade of the nineteenth century, a fine period in shipbuilding, there was a growing and decided tendency toward over-masting. Longer hulls induced heavier sparring, for the old clipper precepts of hard driving and sail-carrying were indulged in under the severe weather conditions of Easting latitudes by vessels which were far more heavily laden and of lower freeboard than their predecessors.

About 1875, when the iron clipper-ship was the favourite type of new vessel, it was realized that, in spite of iron and wire, the three-masted full-rigger carried so much weight aloft that she was by no means the perfection of either balance or economy and that, at times, she could be decidedly difficult to handle.

The return of the 'bonaventure'

When, after a relatively short period of ascendancy, the extreme clipper hull was superseded, on economic and competitive grounds, by the medium-lined type with increased length and tonnage capacity, a fourth mast was required, if the correct out-spacing and balance of top-hamper were to be unimpaired. Where masts were set too far apart, yards of excessive diameter and length were entailed if the drift between the masts was to be filled with canvas. Ship designers thereupon

54

facing: THE MIZEN

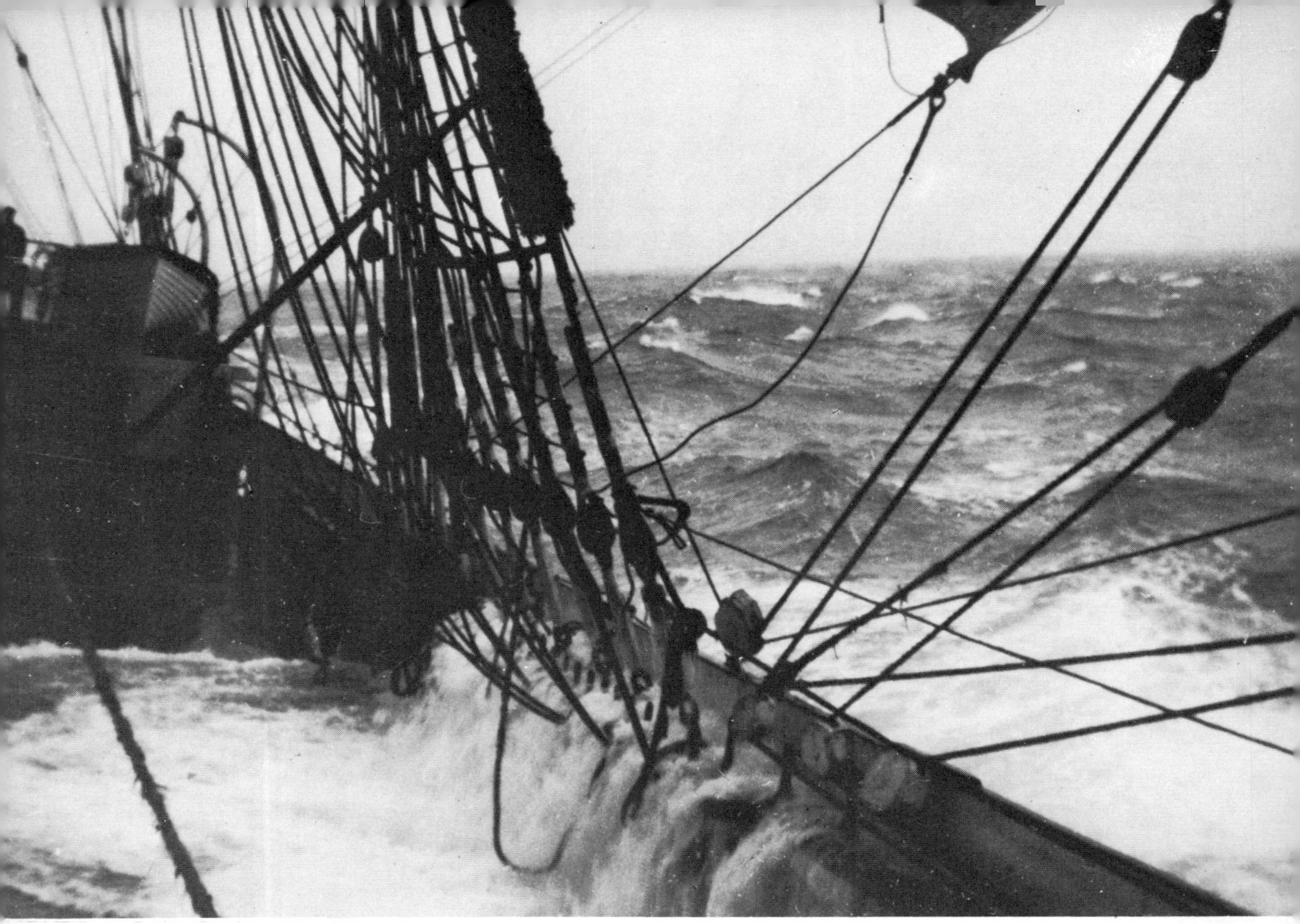

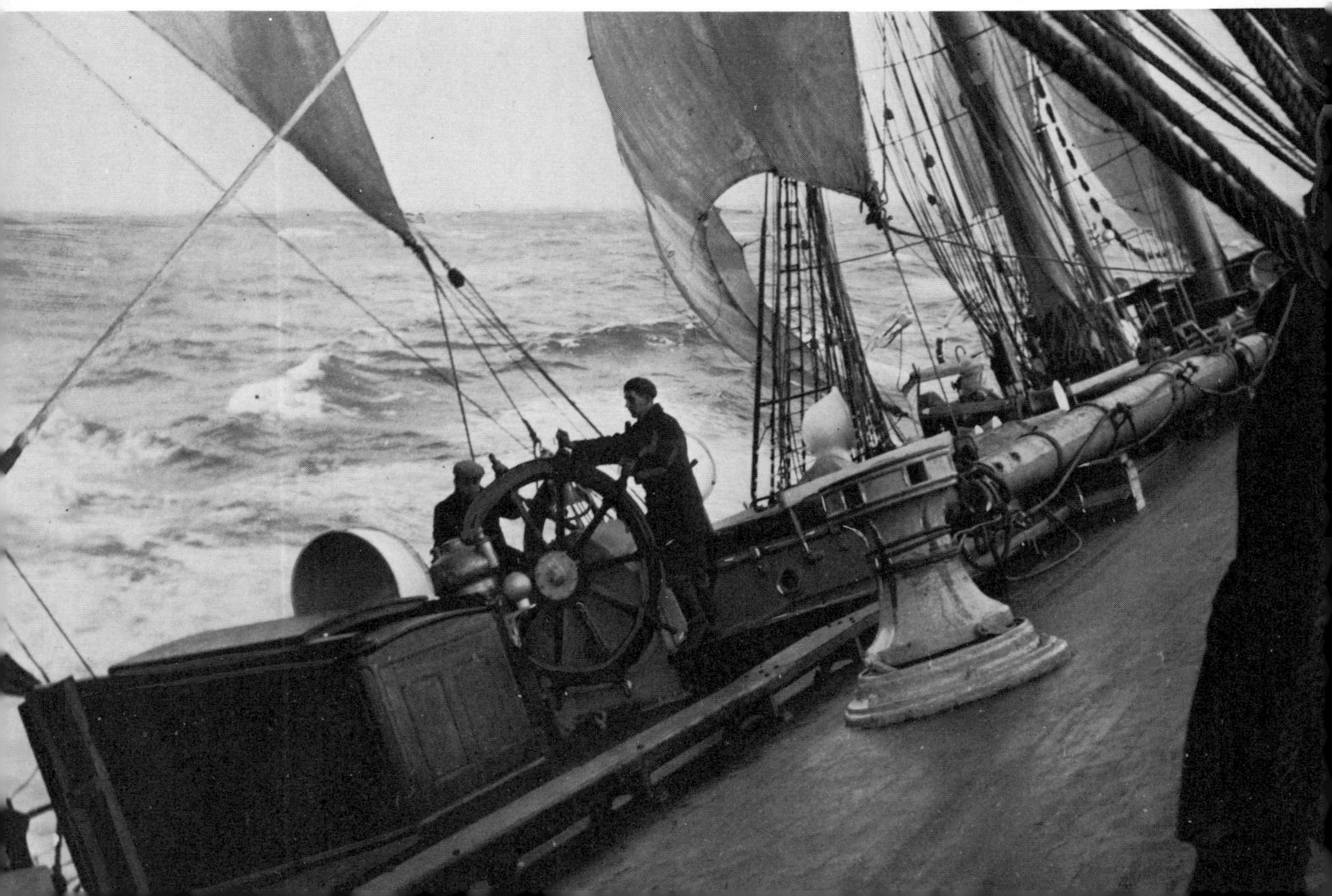

turned their attention to the four-masted full-rigger. This type of vessel proving expensive to run, difficult to steer when under full canvas, and none too easy to work, was soon followed by the four-masted barque, which needed fewer spars, less canvas, and less gear.

The new abbreviated rig was found, in general practice, to be almost as fast as full-rig, without demanding so large a personnel to handle it, and so, after a lapse of more than a century, the old bonaventure was reborn under the utilitarian guise of the jigger.

The first big, four-masted barque, if the unorthodox *Great Republic* is excepted, was the *Tweedsdale*, launched in 1875 by Barclay, Curle & Company, who, two years later, built the barque *County of Inverness* of which mention was made in Part One of this chapter.

The four-masted barques of the nineties

By 1890 most vessels of over 2,000 tons were barque-rigged, although right on into the middle eighties designers had continued to experiment with the alternative of the big full-rigger. Many smart and handy three-masted barques were built during this period, and, though of smaller capacity, they proved to be highly satisfactory in the essential quality of economic operation.

The full-rigger did not, of course, suffer any immediate eclipse, the change-over being gradual in the extreme. Many of them were converted into three- or four-masted barques, sometimes being cut down aloft in the process by the removal of their royals, a transformation known by the expressive term of 'baldheading'.

Grace Harwar, built at Glasgow in 1889, was the last full-rigger to be in active commission. She was broken up in 1935, after long service under the Finnish flag.[1]

Incidentally, the four-masted barque, provided she carries royals, presents, I think, a more handsome and better proportioned ensemble than the full-rigger, once the 2,000 ton mark is exceeded.

As was explained in the first part of this chapter, the advent of the Suez route for Eastern trade, combined with the greater carrying capacity and fast improving machinery of the steamer, spelt extinction to the fine-lined, uneconomic clipper, and brought about the birth of the utilitarian, steel, sailing freighter.

Besides increasing the size of his holds, the owner of sail tonnage had

[1] It is reported that the American full-rigger *Tusitala* is to put to sea again for a trading voyage from New York to the Philippines. She has been laid up at New York for four years. *Tusitala* is a beautiful model of a ship. She was built in 1883 by Steele of Greenock, and as the *Inveruglas* was, for years, well known in the Australian wool trade.

acing: Top. 'WINTERHUDE' IN THE SOUTH ATLANTIC

Bottom. WINDJAMMER WEATHER

to cut down his running expenses in proportion to his reducing freights and more uncertain charters. No longer possible were the large crew and the lavish upkeep of the clipper ship, and sail plans, therefore, now assumed more uniform proportions.

The 'Flying Kites' of the past

Gone were the bonnets, water-sails, moon-rakers, save-alls, and jib o' jibs, beloved of the captains of the crack clippers, who, it is said, on occasion even set the sails of the lifeboats as they lay fast on the weather skids.

By 1880 all 'flying kites', with the exception of skysails, had passed out of fashion for new tonnage. Even the familiar studding-sails, the popular sideward extensions of the basic square-sails, disappeared. The great height of top-hamper remained for a while, a legacy of the clipper, but in general the tendency, as the sailer grew bigger, stronger and more lightly manned, was for her sail-plan to become squarer, that is, for the length of the upper yards to approach more nearly that of the lower yards. It is interesting to note that in 1880, when she deserted the China tea trade for the more arduous Australian wool run, *Cutty Sark's* sail plan was cut down by the removal of her skysail and the shortening of her masts and yards. Many years later, when she had passed to the Portuguese, she was degraded to barquentine-rig. Captain Dowman restored her to full ship-rig in 1922. James Baines' wooden clipper *Marco Polo*, whose unpleasing hull lines gave little indication of her remarkable speed, was sold to J. Wilson & Company of South Shields, in 1871. They put her into the Mediterranean coal trade, having reduced her yards and converted her from ship to barque.

The new-fangled top-hamper of the big steel barque

The long graceful bowsprits, jib-booms and flying jib-booms, which had been necessary for the great clouds of head canvas set by those same old-timers, degenerated gradually into the one-piece stump bowsprit of the large steel barque. Steel-wire shrouds and stays, set up by rigging-screws from inboard ring-bolts, superseded hempen standing-rigging with its lanyards and outboard channels. Flexible manila rope took the place of the harsher and more unyielding hemp for light running-gear, while such innovations as brace and halliard winches and steam capstans dealt with the great strain of the heavy steel yards and with the chain and wire gear of the lightly-manned four-poster.

Another measure of economy lay in the provision of inter-changeable yards for the fore, main and mizen masts of a steel barque. In addition, the old-fashioned single topsails and top-gallants had entirely given place to the more easily handled double or upper and lower type, first introduced, in 1841, by Captain R. B. Forbes. Double topsails were in service aboard the huge American clipper *Great Republic* in 1853, but another fifteen years elapsed before the first appearance of split topgallants. The bands of reef-points by which the working area of a big sail, given the necessary man-power, could be controlled and reduced, are no longer to be seen in any of the few remaining windjammers.

Mr. R. C. Leslie in the preface to his delightful book *Old Sea Wings, Ways and Words in the Days of Oak and Hemp* (written in 1890, but recently republished by Messrs. Chapman & Hall) writes:

Mr. R. C. Leslie
on the passing of
oak and hemp

> ... the introduction of steel spars and wire rope has so greatly changed the work, not only of fitting out but of keeping a ship's gear in repair at sea, that a modern rigger working among iron masts and yards, in turn supported by steel-wire shrouds and stays, with much of the running rigging of chain, has far more of the smith or engine-room artificer about him than of the old seaman-rigger ... it follows that few of the hands even on board a large sailing ship, especially Englishmen, are now able to turn in a dead-eye, strop a block, or point a rope, in the old 'ship-shape Bristol fashion'.

Be that as it may, the demise of oak and, in part, of hemp at the introduction of steel gave to the windjammer a new lease of life and strength.

The great strains to which the wooden spars, rope standing-rigging and planked hulls of the earlier clippers, both hard- and soft-wood, were subjected during long periods of 'cracking-on', together with the ever-present hazard of fire, did not make for long life. As has been seen, their employment did not demand the economical preservation of worn-out tonnage, for, in their day, large profits rewarded speed, and capacity was subsidiary to sailing qualities. Their ultimate successors had to pay for themselves by producing over long periods, in return for a reasonable expenditure in upkeep, a steady, hard-earned, though small profit, without undue wear and tear or depreciation.

By the close of the nineteenth century European shipwrights had evolved a more or less standardized pattern of strong, steel, four-masted barque, designed to carry maximum loads of all type commodities to and from anywhere in the world, at a reasonable speed, but needing, by

The final stage
– the big four-
posters of this
century

tonnage comparison with earlier sailers, only meagre crews. These vessels were the outcome of centuries of experiment in the harnessing of wind-power to propulsive uses: their development was hastened, and ultimately stopped, by steam competition. Lacking the daintiness, the handiness and the sweet lines of their speedy progenitors, they nevertheless represented, at their prime, sail's epitome of combined strength, seaworthiness, economy and longevity.

The big American schooners

Actually, the most extreme point in the saving of labour was gained in the evolution of the big schooner. Confined mainly to the American coastal trades, such vessels reached the amazing total of seven masts, all fore-and-aft rigged.

Five-masted schooners of 2,500 tons had appeared in 1898, and six-masters, of up to 3,000 tons, by 1900, but when in 1902 the steel schooner *Thomas W. Lawson*, of 5,218 tons and 395 feet in length, was launched at the Fore River Yard, Quincey, Massachusetts, some difficulty arose as to the nomenclature of her seven masts. The terms coined for the purpose were fore, main, mizen, jigger, spanker, driver, and pusher. Such vessels combined immense carrying-capacity with minimum running costs, for, in proportion to their size, the personnel needed was astonishingly small.

Thomas W. Lawson, the only seven-master ever constructed, cost $250,000 and was fitted with steam winches for sail manipulation, and with steam steering-gear. Each of her masts was of equal height, a 135-foot steel lower-mast capped by a 58-foot pine topmast. She carried a crew of only sixteen men. In 1907 she was chartered for a Transatlantic cargo of case-oil: weather-bound off the Scillies in December, she dropped anchor, but subsequently turned turtle, all but two of her complement being drowned. A fine model of this freakish craft may be seen in the Science Museum, London.

When the German iron four-masted barque *Columbia*, of 2,518 tons gross, was re-rigged in 1904 as the six-masted barquentine *Everett G. Griggs*, of Vancouver, her crew was reduced from twenty-eight to seventeen.

Five-masted square-riggers

Although in the last decades of sail history a few very big steel full-riggers were launched, they were regarded as being so unorthodox that they can hardly be classified as a type. Judging from their histories they would appear to have been over-sparred, as, for one reason or another, most of them were fated to be short-lived in the service of the sea.

Their records lead to the conclusion that four masts, barque-rig, and a gross tonnage of not more than 3,000, represents about the effective general limit in sail development, although the Laeisz five-masters *Preussen* and *Potosi* were striking exceptions.

In 1906, four years after building *Herzogin Cecilie*, Rickmers of Bremerhaven launched the last sailing vessel constructed at their famous yard. She was for their own account, for shipbuilding and shipowning were their allied interests. Rickmers themselves described the new vessel as 'the last supreme effort of the sailing vessel to hold its own on the highways of the world', and the shipping world in general followed the career of the giant *R. C. Rickmers* with close attention.

Auxiliary sailers

She was a steel, five-masted, auxiliary barque of 5,548 tons gross, 441 feet in length, with a carrying-capacity, including bunkers, of 8,000 tons. Her 1,000 h.p., coal fired, auxiliary engines gave her a speed, under power alone, of seven knots when loaded and eight knots when in ballast; while, with such a huge spread of canvas, she proved a fine performer when wind-driven.

The 'R. C. Rickmers'

Many attempts have been made to extend the lifetime of deep-water sail by coupling it with mechanical motive power, but, in most cases, the combination has been unsuccessful.

The reasons which contributed to the failure of *R. C. Rickmers* to fulfil the high hopes of her owners are applicable to other similar experiments. Engines and coal occupied valuable cargo space; an engine-room staff increased the pay-roll; the profit of saved days was swallowed up by the cost of fuel; finally, the big barque did not prove to be independent of tug assistance in confined waters.

The prime asset of the windjammer — that of economy in operation — is negatived to a great extent by the installation of machinery sufficiently powerful to render her independent of her canvas. Low-powered auxiliaries for landfall use alone have proved, on the other hand, to be hardly worth fitting and maintaining, because the retardation of sailing speed, due to the inevitable drag of a screw, negatives any advantage gained in manœuvrability.

By 1914, Rickmers had disposed of all their sail tonnage except *R. C. Rickmers*. Running costs made her unsaleable, and Herr Paul Rickmers converted her into a cargo-carrying training-ship to provide personnel for his steamer fleet.

Her first voyage in this new capacity was to Cardiff, in ballast, to load a cargo of coal. While there, War broke out. She was seized by England, her crew and apprentices interned, and, renamed *Neath*, she flew the Red Ensign for three years until, by the irony of fate, she was sunk off the Irish coast by a German submarine while on passage from Mauritius to England with sugar.

The Vinnens

In recent years, however, another German firm, Messrs. F. A. Vinnen & Company of Bremen, appear to have evolved a more successful type of auxiliary sailer. These unorthodox craft are five-masted steel schooners, setting square topsails and topgallants to fore and mizen, and sometimes, in addition, a shallow-cut, square foresail. They are engined by submarine-pattern Diesels.

Five of these hybrid vessels were built by Krupps at Kiel between 1921 and 1922:

Adolf Vinnen, while on her maiden voyage, was wrecked on the Lizard in February 1923; *Susanne Vinnen* was sold to Italy, and became the training-ship *Patria*; *Cristel Vinnen* in 1934 was converted to a fully-powered motor-ship. The two other vessels — *Werner Vinnen* (1,859 tons gross) and *Carl Vinnen* (1,827 tons gross) — however, still trade as auxiliaries, usually between Europe and the east coast of South America, although, in the past, both of them have carried home grain from Australia. Their nominal horse-power is ninety-seven, and, presumably, their semi-schooner-rig is easily handled by a small crew, and their oil engines occupy less space in proportion and run more economically than did the powerful, coal-fired engines of *R. C. Rickmers*.

'Magdalene Vinnen'

In pre-War days Vinnen's owned a fine, steel, four-masted barque of 3,350 tons gross — *Magdalene Vinnen*, built as *Dunstaffnage* in 1892 by W. H. Potter & Son of Liverpool, for Macvicar, Marshall & Company. Vinnen's sold her to the Italian Government, and she was broken up in 1925, by which time a new *Magdalene Vinnen* had made an appearance.

This vessel, which on several recent occasions has participated in the Australian grain trade under sail, is a very different and much more orthodox type than the Vinnen schooners. Built and engined by Krupps in 1921, she is a four-masted steel barque of 3,476 tons gross, with auxiliary oil engines of 128 n.h.p. The engine-room is situated well aft; she has a big midship section occupying one-third of her total length of 329 feet; and possesses the unusual feature of a carrying

facing: LAST OF THE FULL-RIGGERS. 'GRACE HARWAR' FROM 'HERZOGIN CECILIE', 1933

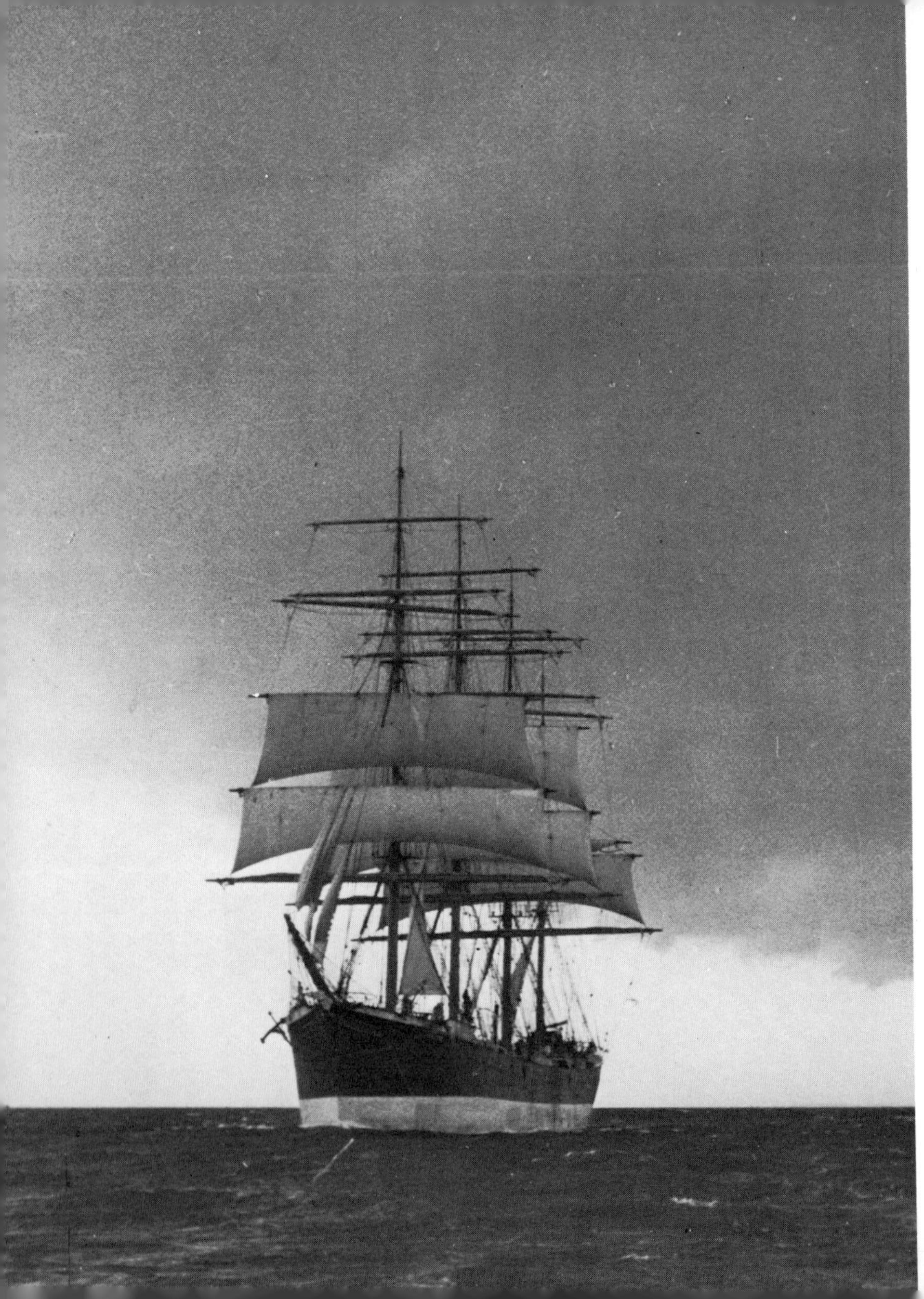

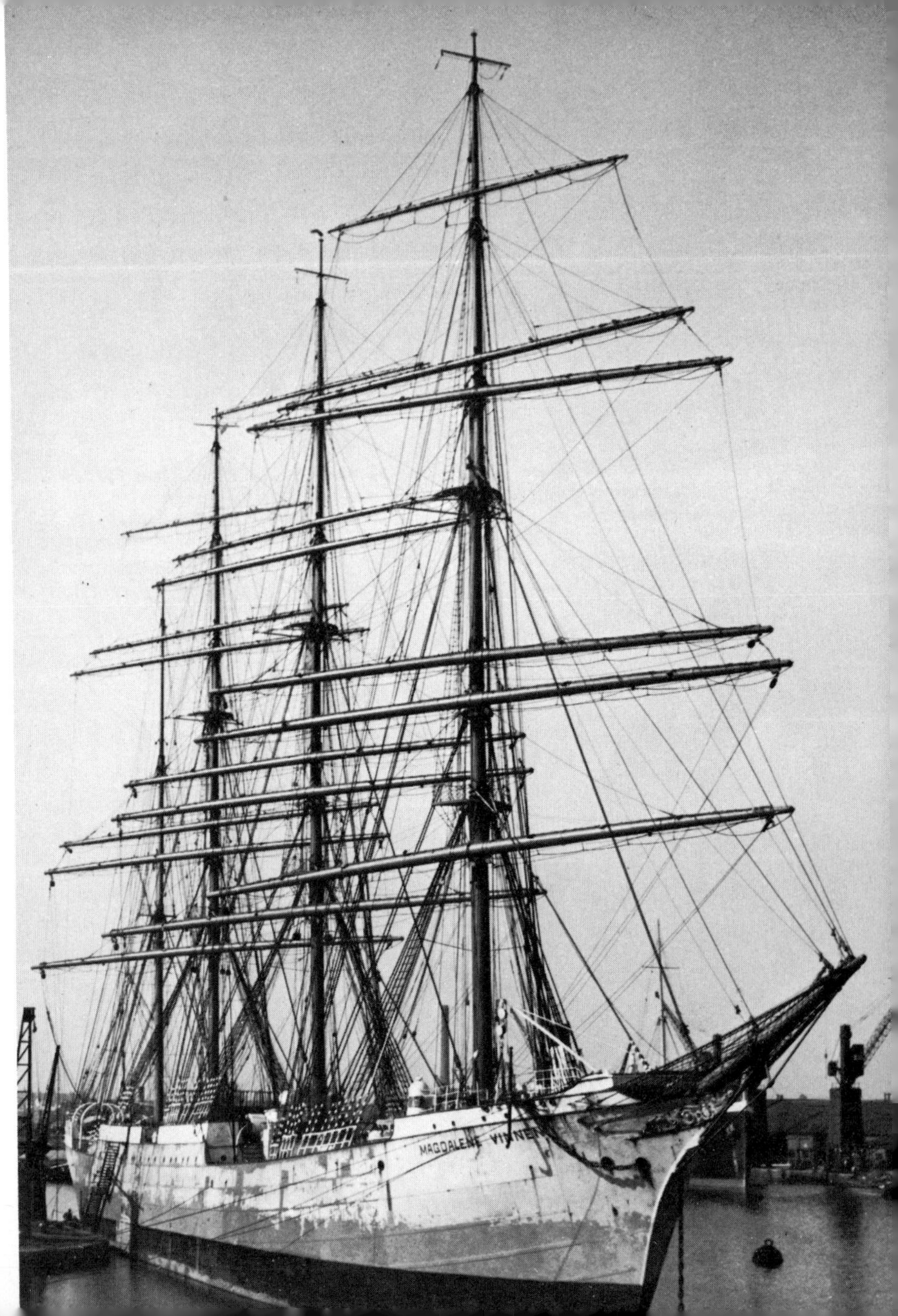
MAGDALENE

capacity of 5,000 tons in a single hold, divided throughout its whole length by a longitudinal steel bulkhead to prevent the shifting of bulk cargo.

In 1936 Vinnen's sold her to the Norddeutscher Lloyd Company of Bremen as a sail training-vessel. The purchase aroused considerable comment in shipping circles. It will be of interest to see, in view of the dearth of freights available to sail, whether the new venture takes the form of a purely training scheme or whether an attempt is made to combine training with cargo carrying, as the Norddeutscher Lloyd did, so successfully, before the War with *Herzogin Cecilie*. (See page 415.)

Auxiliary versus windjammer in the grain trade

On long ocean voyages the auxiliary vessel shows little saving in time to offset the extra expense of operation. In this connection it is interesting to compare the passages made since the War by true square-riggers in the Australian grain trade with those accomplished by auxiliary sailers on the same run.

For the sixteen consecutive seasons between 1921 and 1936 inclusive, the average of the best annual passage each year under sail alone works out at ninety-six and a half days from loading port to first port of arrival. During this period auxiliary vessels competed in eight of the sixteen years, the average of their eight fastest passages being one hundred and three days.

The best post-War passage under sail was that of *Parma* in 1933 — eighty-three days from Port Victoria, South Australia, to Falmouth. The quickest auxiliary passage to the Channel was made in 1934, when *Magdalene Vinnen* made landfall at Plymouth, ninety-one days out from Port Victoria. The longest auxiliary passage since the War was the one-hundred-and-twenty-seven-day voyage of the *Werner Vinnen* from Adelaide to Dungeness in 1923.

The cruise of the 'Seeadler'

The remarkable story of the punitive expedition of the German auxiliary full-rigged ship *Seeadler* has been told in a book called *The Sea Devil*. It is a story which will always remain an epic of the sea, a successful and daring feat of seamanship undertaken in most chivalrous fashion by a fine seaman.

Since sail played so large a part in this voyage, which in the main followed the old Cape Horn Road of the west-bound windjammers, and as the raid resulted in the destruction of half a score of big, Allied windships, a brief résumé of the facts will make a fitting conclusion to this account of the development and decline of square-rig.

61

facing: Right. THE AUXILIARY BARQUE 'MAGDALENE VINNEN'

Left. 'PONAPE' IN BALLAST, 1936

Late in 1914, off the north of Scotland, a British cruiser intercepted a full-rigged vessel flying the American flag. She was the *Pass of Balmaha*, built by R. Duncan & Company in 1888, 1,571 tons gross, and then on a voyage, ostensibly, from New York to Archangel with a cargo of cotton. Suspicious of her real destination, the cruiser put a prize crew aboard, and ordered the windjammer to proceed to Kirkwall for investigation. A few days later, when nearing Kirkwall and under the British flag, *Pass of Balmaha* was captured by a German submarine, and taken into Cuxhaven.

After the Battle of Jutland she was fitted with powerful auxiliary engines and a full modern armament, and, extraordinarily well camouflaged as an innocent Scandinavian tramp sailer, she left Germany in 1916, under the command of Graf Felix von Luckner, the Sea Devil of Lowell Thomas's book. He had re-named her *Seeadler* — 'Eagle of the Sea'.

Successfully she ran the gauntlet of the blockade round the north of Scotland, and on January 9th, 1917, when off the Azores, sank her first victim, the British steamer *Gladys Royal*. In two hundred and twenty-four days *Seeadler* covered 30,000 miles before she was wrecked on Mopelia Island in the Society Group, South Pacific.

During this time von Luckner sank fourteen vessels and captured one. Nine of these sinkings took place in Atlantic equatorial latitudes off the Brazilian coast. Four months later, in mid-Pacific, also near the Equator, three vessels were sunk in close proximity. Among *Seeadler's* fifteen victims were three British cargo steamers, two British barques (one, the *Pinmore*, loaded with nitrate, was a vessel in which Graf von Luckner had served, before the mast, in his younger days), five big French square-riggers, and three American four-masted schooners.

The elimination of these fifteen Allied vessels cost only one life, that of a seaman in the British steamer *Horngarth*, and von Luckner demonstrated his regret by committing the body to the sea with full naval honours.

In March 1917, two hundred and eighty-seven prisoners were transferred from the overcrowded *Seeadler* to the captured French barque *Cambronne* (one of Dom Bordes' nitrate fleet), which von Luckner spared in order that the prisoners should be landed in safety at Rio de Janeiro.

CHAPTER II

THE SURVIVAL OF SAIL

PART ONE: THE AUSTRALIAN GRAIN TRADE
UNDER SAIL

I often think how sad that time will be
When no wind lifts a sail on any sea.

IT has become inevitable that the few remaining commercial deepwater sailing vessels should be linked, in public opinion, with the
carriage of grain. The progression of events, which, after forcing
upon her a strictly utilitarian specification, drove the windjammer from
the seas, has already been explored. From a racing clipper, designed
specifically for the carriage of valuable commodities, she became, in
her heyday of development, a general carrier of all forms of imperishable merchandise, handling, in addition, much of the long-distance
passenger traffic of the world. 'Imperishable' is here used, of course,
in a comparative sense, but it is a quality which, in itself, has had a
great bearing upon the obvious inability of the sailing vessel to adapt
herself to modern requirements.

So accustomed have we become, in this country, to the unfailing
provision of imported produce of all kinds, that the vast and recent
improvement in the transport of perishable foodstuffs is apt to be overlooked or taken for granted. The principle of refrigeration, for example,
has benefited humanity to an incalculable extent during the last half-
century, and to-day the fruits of the world are as commonplace and as
cheap in the Home markets as is our own local produce. One of the
most striking lessons taught by the late War was our utter dependence
upon the unrestricted sea-transit of foodstuffs. More than one-half of
the beef and mutton and ninety per cent of the dairy produce consumed
in Great Britain to-day are imported by steamer. Sail, however, has
played no part in the widespread economic changes brought about by
the new methods of chilling, freezing, ventilating, and otherwise preserving in their raw state fruit, meat, dairy produce, fish, vegetables,

Refrigerated
transport

63

and the like. In 1861, a Lancashire emigrant, Thomas Sutcliffe Mort, established the first freezing plant in the world at Sydney, New South Wales. In 1876 he installed a form of refrigeration into a sailing vessel, but it proved a failure in practice, and the now vast import trade in Australian frozen meat was, from its inception, almost entirely dependent upon steam conveyance. The first successful shipment to Europe was in 1877, and in 1880 the steamer *Strathleven* brought home London's first consignment. Shaw Savill's sailer *Dunedin* inaugurated the import of frozen mutton from New Zealand, by carrying home a cargo in ninety-eight days in 1882, and for a short period New Zealand meat was imported under sail.

So soon, however, as British engineers, shipbuilders, shipowners and merchants realized the almost illimitable prospects held out by refrigerated transport, steamers so equipped were built, or converted, in increasing numbers.

In its infancy the new-born trade was far from reliable, and it was not until low-temperature research and mechanical experiment made better preservation possible that refrigerated freight became established on a basis lucrative to producer, carrier and distributor alike.

Sail's unsuitability to perishable cargoes Although refrigerating plant, originally an integral part of the general propulsive machinery of a steamer and operated from the main boilers, has become a more or less separate entity, at no stage in its development was its successful installation or operation suitable to the windjammer.

Now that the art of preservation embraces such a highly perishable item as soft fruit, speed and regularity of carriage are almost as essential as dependability of method, and the modern fruit-carrier, designed and equipped for one specific purpose, would seem already to have attained almost perfection in a difficult and scientific trade.

The relative uncertainty and slowness of the sailer precluded her from any chance of participation or competition in the new vistas thus opened to the steamer. Even were time not so vital a factor, the installation and maintenance of merely the simplest satisfactory freezing plant could not be considered practicable in vessels whose only remaining chance of existence lay in cheapness of operation. No, where foodstuffs were concerned, the deepwater windjammer was limited to those few varieties which were more or less immune from deterioration.

Dried and salted fish, for example, is still brought under sail to the

Latin countries of Europe and South America, where it is one of the staple articles of diet, by schooners from Newfoundland. Grain travels as well in sailing bottoms as in the holds of a steamer. Tea, coffee, cocoa, rice, sugar, canned goods, and even certain livestock are all suitable for extended carriage under sail, but, in her declining years, the windship was concerned with commodities rather than with the foodstuffs for which market conditions demanded steam transit with its greater speed and dependability, even though its freights were higher. Jute, oil, timber, coal, nitrate, guano, wool, hides, pig-iron, machinery, piece goods, cotton, and general merchandise filled the manifests of the big, steel, sailing carriers of the nineties and the early years of the present century.

The harness cask, the hencoop, the sheep pen and the pigsty are still to be found aboard the trading windjammer of to-day, although the custom of carrying a cow has long since lapsed even in unchanging sail. Its place has been taken by condensed milk, and, although these old craft derive no benefit from refrigeration even for their personal requirements, modern methods of canning vegetables, fruit, fish, meat, etc., have alleviated to an extent some of the old-time privations of a dilatory passage under sail.

Perhaps at this point it would be as well to clarify the series of expressions employed to indicate the period and the vessels with which this book is mainly concerned. *The scope of 'The Tall Ships Pass'*

Sail, in the deepwater sense of the term, has almost reached its nadir, and not even her most sanguine admirer can visualize any resuscitation of the big, commercial windjammer. Yachts, barges, fishing and coasting craft there are, and will continue to be, a'plenty under canvas. Small barques and schooners still ply in fairly large numbers around the Baltic shores, the coasts of Italy, and other localized venues. Many fine sail training-vessels of various rigs, possessing in most cases auxiliary power, still keep the seas, but the cargo-carrying square-rigger, in the true deepwater sense of the term, has almost vanished, never to return.

This book is concerned with those few survivors of that genre which are in active commission to-day, and with them alone. To them are intended to apply such phrases as 'the last of the windjammers' or 'the surviving square-riggers', and they are the tall ships whose passing has provided a title.

Of all the forementioned trades which in pre-War days provided a livelihood to the square-riggers of this century, only one is active to-day. Admittedly, after the War quite a number of cargoes of wool, nitrate, coal, coke, guano, and the like were shipped in sail, but only grain, and South Australian grain at that, now offers regular freight to the windjammer. (I except, of course, in this generalization the return in 1936 of Laeisz' two barques *Padua* and *Priwall* to the West Coast nitrate trade because it does not denote the reopening of that trade to sail in general; again, as regular employment only is referred to, the statement is not contradicted by the very occasional cargo of guano or timber still secured by the sailer.)

The reasons for this present limitation to one localized commodity are partly economic and partly geographic. There are certain factors which can still operate in favour of the windjammer and which have enabled her, for a time, to withstand in certain spheres the pressure of steam competition. The principal points by virtue of which she may be said to gain some advantage over the steamer are:

(*a*) Antiquated loading facilities which still prevail in some out-of-the-way loading ports, and which involve the steamer in costly waste of time;

(*b*) The outward ballast voyage involved by the poverty, inaccessibility, or lack of import trade of such loading places, a less expensive preamble to freight-earning in the case of the sailer than the steamer;

(*c*) The possibility of profitable speculation by the sale and resale of certain cargoes is sometimes increased by a lengthy passage, which, in addition, where a cargo is not needed in any urgency, offers the further benefit of free warehousing;

(*d*) The fact that the lower rate of freight payable for cargo carried in sailing instead of in steam bottoms rather more than offsets the higher cost of insuring that cargo;

(*e*) The existence of certain 'rough' cargoes which do not demand speedy transit, whose tardy arrival causes no loss of seasonable market, which need no precautionary measures in the nature of controlled temperature of the holds during the voyage, which stow well, easily, cheaply, and in bagged form, and, finally, of which a full cargo can be obtained at a single loading port and carried direct to a single port of discharge.

66

A combination of all, or at any rate of the majority, of these reasons is applicable to very few commodities, but to the export of Baltic timber, the transport of guano, and the import to Europe of Chilean nitrate and South Australian grain they are, in the main, peculiarly apposite.

In her declining years the hard-worked, sparsely manned, sail freighter could no longer 'tramp' the big ports of the world with any certainty of picking up chance cargoes, for all too many steamers were so engaged. She had to be 'fixed' in advance to load a definite consignment or, failing that, sail out in ballast to one or other of the out-of-the-way localities whose local export trade had not yet been entirely absorbed by the ubiquitous steamer, places where the cheaper freight and low overheads of the sailer still enabled her to maintain a foothold.

Such a trade, for instance, is guano, one of the most unpleasant cargoes in the world to load and to carry. Actually a bird excrement, it is worked as a mineral, and may be described as an earthy nitrate. It is found at such distant spots as Lobos Island off the coast of Peru, at Nauru Island and the Solomons in the South Pacific, and at the Seychelles Group in the Indian Ocean. No outward cargoes can be obtained for such destinations, although in the case of the guano islands of the Indian Ocean the trade can, on occasion, be combined successfully with a timber cargo from the Baltic to South or East Africa or a cargo of patent fertilizer to Mauritius. In general, therefore, a guano charter, like Australian grain or Chilean nitrate, entails a lengthy, prior, ballast passage.

The guano trade under sail

The loading of this unsavoury product can prove a protracted and sometimes dangerous matter. Frequently, it is carried out by craft, the vessel herself lying offshore at an open anchorage and compelled betimes, by weather conditions, to abandon loading for a while and to stand away out to sea. In the old days, especially at Lobos where the guano was loaded by girt-line, it was usual for the deposits to be quarried by the crews of the loading vessels.

There is no short cut for the guano-laden windjammer. Even if climatic conditions were more suitable, her low freight prohibits the use of the big canals. The homeward-bound sailer from Lobos must circumnavigate the entire continent of South America via Cape Horn to reach Europe; while from the Seychelles she comes home round the Cape of Good Hope (unless, as is often the case, her cargo is consigned to New Zealand).

To-day, the Seychelles is the last of the guano areas available to the windjammer, and, at the time of writing, the barque *Winterhude* is outward-bound from London, in ballast, to load a cargo of Seychelles guano for New Zealand. It is to be hoped that she will be more fortunate in her loading than was the four-masted barque *Olivebank* in 1928.

'Olivebank' at
St. *Pierre*, 1928

Owing to a slow outward journey, *Olivebank* arrived at Assumption Island too late to fulfil her guano charter. Proceeding to Mahé, she received orders to sail to the little islet of St. Pierre, 180 miles NNE of Madagascar, where another cargo was available for New Zealand consignees. Eighty-four negro workmen and the white manager of the island joined *Olivebank* at Mahé.

It transpired that the loading jetty was on the western point of St. Pierre and exposed at that time of the year, July, to the prevailing south-west wind. *Olivebank* was compelled to anchor in 12 fathoms, a ship's-length off a lee shore. Such was the conformation of the sea-bed that, whereas her port anchor, with 80 fathoms of chain out, found apparently good holding ground, the starboard anchor, after 45 fathoms had been let run, rolled off a subterranean shelf and hung straight down on its chain. Just as the first two boatloads (about eight tons of guano) were loaded by the negroes, ballast being discharged overside simultaneously, *Olivebank* was badly shaken by the slipping of the port anchor, which fell into such deep water that it now hung suspended at the end of 480 feet of cable. A providential set of the current carried the barque offshore, but she was compelled to sail well to the eastward of Mahé again before she could beat back to St. Pierre. The islet was sighted, for the second time, fourteen days later. On this occasion *Olivebank* found good anchorage with both anchors in 5 fathoms, and was able to complete her loading.

St. Pierre is a round coral islet, one mile in diameter. Stripped of its bird-deposit, there remains only bare coral, for there is little or no vegetation and the only denizens are rats.

The guano sacks are sent down a chute from a small pier into craft because of the swell which runs almost continuously. Many vessels have dragged or lost their anchors on the steep sea-bed of this precarious roadstead, and some, less lucky than *Olivebank*, have driven inshore.

68

In 1906, the Norwegian barque *Norden,* when fully laden with guano, was carried ashore and there was only one survivor from the wreck.

Grace Harwar loaded guano at Juan de Nova (Mozambique Channel) in October 1931, *Passat* at Assumption Island in October 1932, and *Winterhude* at the little Seychelles islet of St. Denis in November 1932. Then, for four years, guano was transported only by steam; *Winterhude's* present charter may prove to be the last occasion upon which sail will take part in the trade.

A second trade which remained open to the sailer later than most was the import of Chilean nitrate to Europe. It has now passed into the hands of steam, but as late as the first decade of this century the roadsteads of the 'Flaming Coast' attracted large numbers of fine square-riggers. *Herzogin Cecilie* was employed in this trade, and in Chapter One I have said something of the great French and German fleets which, in those days, made sail history by their wonderful nitrate passages. Although a number of windjammers, including some of the Erikson vessels, secured nitrate charters after the War — *Herzogin Cecilie,* for instance, making three successive voyages to the West Coast between 1922 and 1924 — comparatively few such cargoes have been carried by sail during the last dozen years.

The export of Chilean nitrate by sailer

In addition to the shortening of the steamer route brought about by the Panama Canal, a large proportion of West Coast nitrate is now carried as parcels by liners instead of, as heretofore, in the form of full cargoes by tramp steamers. Also, the modern tendency with full cargoes of nitrate is to ship in bulk, in place of bags, a method of stowage which operates against the windjammer.

In the days before the present amalgamation of buying, selling, and shipping interests, with a controlled distribution from large European stocks, nitrate was a seasonable commodity. Low and high season values differed considerably and offered opportunities to individual speculators. A cargo shipped in sail at the tail end of the season had an advantage over a similar cargo forwarded by steam because the storage charges in Europe, pending renewed agricultural demand, were minimized by the extra two months occupied by the windjammer in making the homeward passage from the West Coast via the Horn.

Artificial nitrate has reduced considerably these Chilean exports. It has been calculated recently that, although in 1935 the exportation of nitrate from Chile touched a higher level than in any year since 1931, she supplied only fifteen per cent of the world-consumption for 1935 as against, roughly, ninety per cent in 1913. So, the march of progress, in closing yet another door to the sailer, leaves but one opening through which the fast-dwindling quota of tall ships can envisage regular employment and earn the bare livelihood which, to-day, justifies their continued survival.

The Great Australian Bight and Spencer Gulf Before passing on to an explanation of the way in which, by the successful exploitation of certain economic factors, one solitary owner continues to make sail pay its way in the carriage of grain from Australia, some geographical features of that trade must be made clear.

Indenting the southern coast of the Australian Continent is a vast, concave, shallow bay, 1,600 miles in length, known as the Great Australian Bight. In the Bight the Continental shelf extends seaward for roughly 200 miles from the coast before the ocean floor reaches, in Jeffrey's Deep, a maximum depth of 3,000 fathoms. It is an area dreaded by the sailor for its sudden storms, its paucity of safe anchorages, and its inhospitable and barren shores hedged about by submerged reefs. The nomenclature of this coastline, a legacy, in the main, of the days when the seaman cartographer was dependent on sail alone, gives a vivid idea of his experiences in the locality: Cape Arid, Cape Catastrophe, False Bay, Anxious Bay — such are typical names from the charts of the Bight.

At the extreme eastern end of the great bay, a long narrow inlet runs north-eastward for 180 miles into the hinterland of South Australia, reaching a head about five miles above Port Augusta. It is known as Spencer Gulf, having been so named by Captain Matthew Flinders, R.N., of H.M.S. *Investigator*, who charted this area. Spencer Gulf is entered between Cape Catastrophe and Cape Spencer, which are about forty-eight miles apart. Captain Flinders named Cape Catastrophe in memory of the Master, a midshipman, and six of the crew of H.M.S. *Investigator* who were lost there by the swamping of a small boat in bad weather. The Gulf is navigable over its greater portion by vessels of large size, and vessels of moderate draught can lie even as far north as Port Augusta. Every year, round about Christmastide, at the height of the golden harvest of the South, the last of the big square-riggers foregather in Spencer Gulf to load grain.

The small ports of this quiet backwater have no import trade, and the sailer has only her ballast to discharge on arrival. A few of the square-riggers are, wholly or in part, water-ballasted, but where solid ballast is carried, much of it has to be dumped overside by the crew, near the entrance of the Gulf. The residue, solid or water, is retained as stiffening until the vessel reaches her loading berth. There, 500 tons or more of grain displaces the remaining ballast, which, in the case of rubble, must then be discharged at special ballast-grounds adjacent to the anchorage before the vessel completes with cargo.

Now and again one or other of these square-riggers may have shortened and made profitable the long, empty, outward voyage from Europe by taking a cargo of Baltic timber to Lourenco Marques or Beira, and ballasting there for Australia. However, such freights, which make a big difference to the year's trading yield, are getting more and more rare owing to steam competition, and, in general, the homeward grain freight entails sailing an equivalent outward distance in light trim.

There are several causes contributing to the suitability of Spencer Gulf as the last venue for deepwater sail. From there the windjammer has the option of two comparatively clear homeward routes over something like 15,000 miles of open seaway, her choice being dictated, sometimes, by weather conditions. On leaving the Gulf she can go eastward through the Bass Strait between Tasmania and Victoria, or even go below Tasmania, and, passing well to the southward of New Zealand, take the grand old 'Sailor's Way' round Cape Horn. Alternatively, she can run westward to the Leeuwin, then across the Southern Indian Ocean, and into the South Atlantic by way of the Cape of Good Hope. There seems to be, in recent years, a growing tendency to select, when possible, the latter route in preference to the Horn.

The alternative homeward routes from South Australia

The South African route is, in actual mileage, about 1,200 miles the shorter of the two, but passages thereon are apt to be more protracted because of the quieter conditions which prevail, at any rate during the summer period, on the first half of the homeward passage. The two routes converge in South Atlantic equatorial latitudes, and from thenceforward the only divergences from a broad but common track are such as may arise through force of circumstance or from a variance in destination.

'Cape Stiff' knows no more the homeward-bound windjammer from the grain ports of Western North America, for steam, via Panama, has captured that trade in its entirety. The gale-swept path of 55° or 60° S. is almost as denuded of shipping to-day as it was in Captain Cook's time, or even in those far-off days of 1578 when Drake's *Golden Hind*, the first known vessel to sight Cape Horn, proved that Magellan's Strait was not merely a channel through a great southern continent, and so established the conjunction of the Atlantic and Pacific Oceans. The dreaded Cape, actually the most southerly island of the Tierra del Fuegan archipelago, was named after the town of Hoorn by Schouten, the Dutch navigator, in 1616.

Argentine grain, loaded under the finest of modern facilities at ports whose import trade is almost as prolific as their export, is also carried entirely by steam.

The great grain areas of the world are closed to sail transport, with the sole exception of the South Australian wheat belt, for which Spencer Gulf provides a natural outlet under conditions less favourable to the steamer than to modern sail.

The outports of Spencer Gulf

There are no large towns or up-to-date ports in all its 180 miles length, but, here and there along the shore, are small outports, some of them hardly even villages — a few shacks, a general store, a post-office, a wooden jetty, and, in season, a huge dominating stack of wheat by a shallow, sandy, treeless shore: such settlements are little known to the outside world.

The jetties, a great feature of the local loading methods, vary in length according to the depth of water offshore, Spencer Gulf being subject to large tidal variation. Port Germein, near the head of the Gulf, has the longest cargo jetty in South Australia, and possibly in the world. It is over a mile in length, floored with sleepers, and, apart from a handrail on one side and a single rail-track on the other, is quite bare. The water at the outer end is of just sufficient depth to permit one big windjammer at a time to berth alongside at all states of the tide.

In the spring of 1936 *Killoran* was compelled to lie for forty days off Port Germein, waiting her turn to load. *Ponape*, *Winterhude* and *C. B. Pedersen* had all been chartered for that same port, and as the quickest time in which they could, one by one, be handled and dispatched was approximately three weeks apiece, *Killoran's* sailing was delayed until April 10th. When, at the end of 1936, the grain charters for 1937 were arranged, an extra sixpence per ton was obtained by

facing: HOMEWARD BOUND. 'THE HEEL (
A HULL THROUGH HISSING SPRA

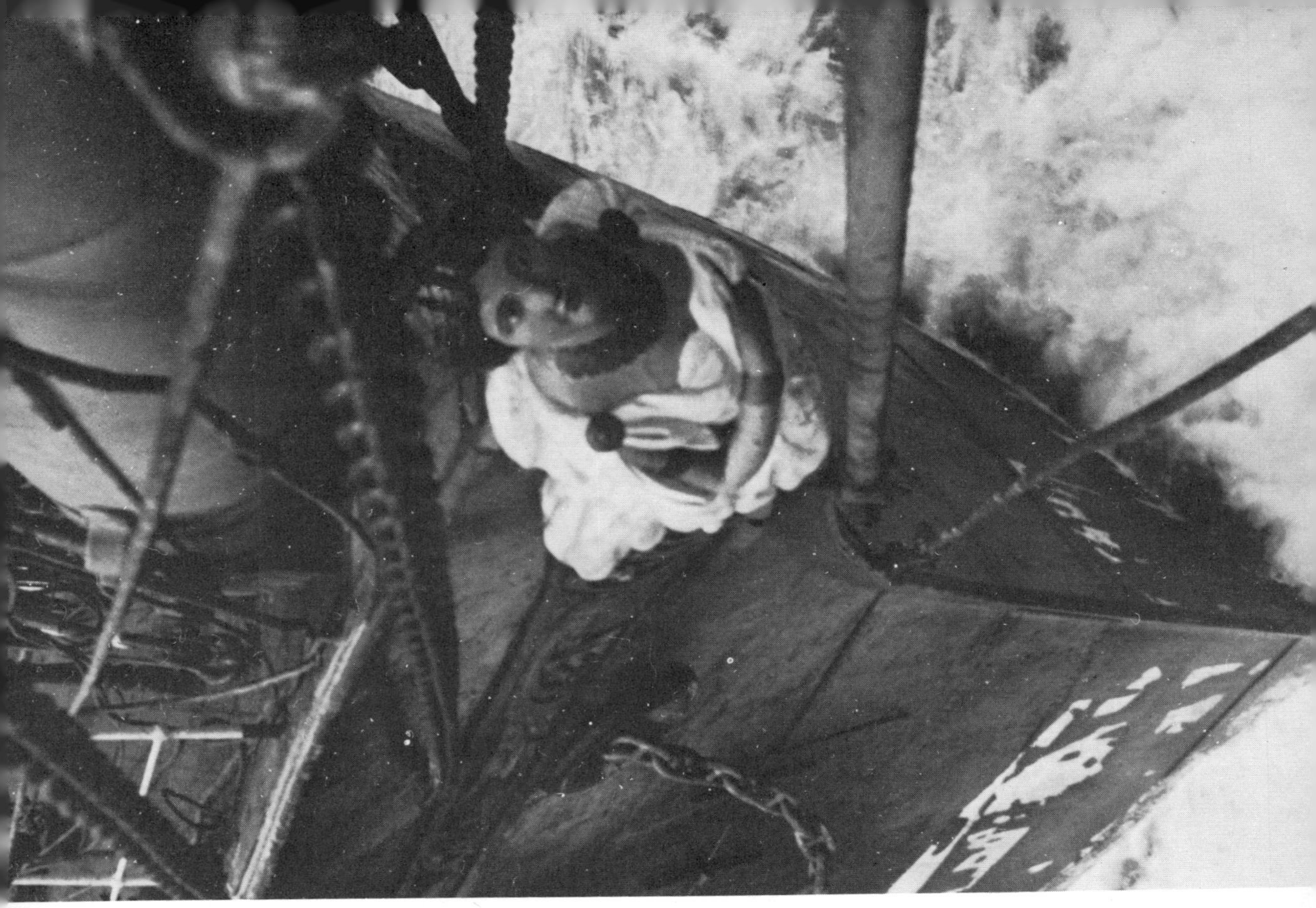

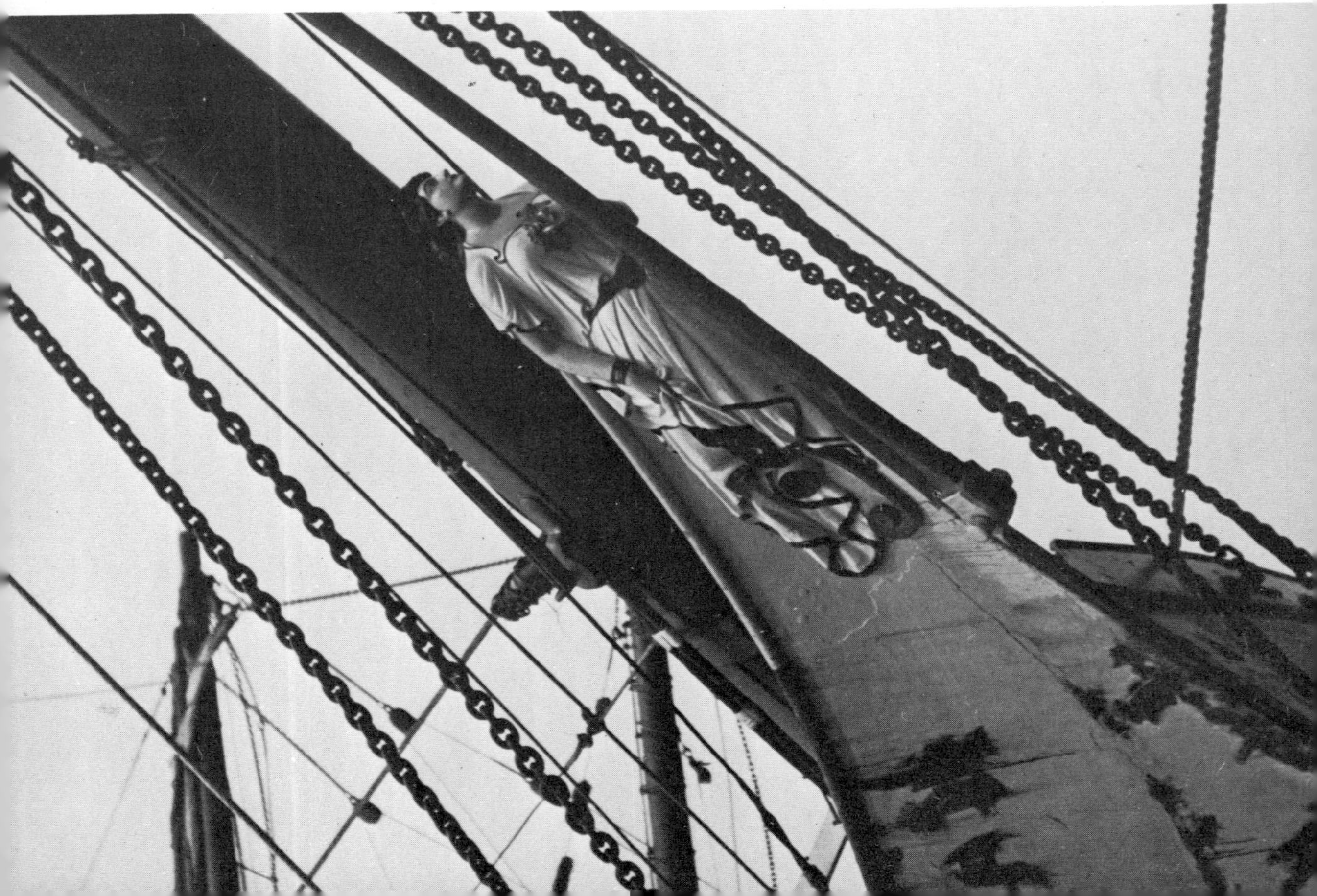

any vessels fixed to load their grain cargoes at this slow and difficult little place.

At Port Lincoln, however, closer to the entrance to Spencer Gulf, the pier is comparatively short, for this township possesses, as the chief port to the Eyre Peninsula, a good, landlocked harbour. Port Lincoln is only twelve hours by steamer from Adelaide, and, in the summer, its population of about 2,000 is augmented by many holiday-makers.

At these two loading ports, and also at Port Augusta, Port Pirie and Wallaroo, the square-riggers berth at the jetties, and load from trucks and from lighters moored alongside. At others, such as Port Victoria and Port Broughton, a different and more dilatory method has to be adopted. The windjammer anchors away offshore, sometimes several miles out, and the grain, which has been carted or railed from the vast farms of the adjacent back-blocks, is ferried out to her by local ketches and schooners. These old craft, many of them fitted with oil auxiliaries, hold up to 100 tons of wheat apiece. They are sometimes loaded direct by the farm hands who have transported the grain to the port and thereby saved the expense of a lengthy transit by rail to Adelaide. The sailer's own tackle is used for swinging the bags inboard from the ketches, but although the actual stowage is in the hands of the charterers' own stevedores, loading charges, which vary with the berth in question, are a charge on the shipowner. It is usual for the inward-bound windjammer to call at Port Lincoln or Port Victoria in order to ascertain at which of the Gulf ports they are to load; also to undergo a visit from the doctor and customs authorities. Early in 1934 ten square-riggers made landfall at Port Victoria within twenty-four hours of each other. Such a gathering must have presented a unique and magnificent spectacle, commonplace enough elsewhere in the past great days of sail, but one which, in all probability, may never again be seen.

Apart from its harvesting, grain is not a product dependent on season. No markets are lost by failure to make a fast passage. The free warehousing afforded by the long voyage under sail, allied to the saving of transhipment expenses, can even operate in favour of the windjammer. These cargoes are nearly always sold and resold, sometimes several times over, before the vessel calls at her orders port to ascertain the final destination of her grain. The sailer may prove a belated but popular arrival from the view-point of the speculator who has made her the basis of a successful gamble on a fluctuating grain

The South Australian grain trade under sail

73

market. The outcome of these transactions is dependent upon the market value of grain. The sailer offers the best speculation when her cargo has been arranged on a rising market because then there is every possibility that, by the time her average passage of four months is ended, the cargo will have appreciated in value. If, however, she load near the peak of the market, depreciation is then the most probable alteration in grain prices.

Grain is considered to be a light cargo, and it carries so well and needs so little attention or special precaution that, broadly speaking, it is imperishable, and so is as little affected by the 120-day average passage of the windjammer from Australia as by the shorter period in the holds of a fast steamer.

The difference in time between sail and steam transport on a long voyage, especially through latitudes of strong wind, is, sometimes, less than might be imagined. In the autumn of 1936, for example, a good-class, modern, British tramp steamer of 5,000 tons gross, and 652 n.h.p., laden with grain from Port Lincoln, arrived off the Isle of Wight fifty-three days out. The steamer route being several thousand miles shorter than that of the windjammer, which has to seek and keep to favourable wind-belts, this represented an average speed of 8 knots for about 10,500 miles. The quickest homeward Australian passage made under sail since the War is eighty-three days, Port Victoria to Falmouth, accomplished by *Parma* in 1933. She sailed about 15,000 miles on that passage, the actual distance made being 14,555 miles, and her average sailing speed was about $7\frac{1}{2}$ knots. In 1936 *Herzogin Cecilie* came home in eighty-six days and *Passat* in eighty-seven. The discrepancy between tramp steamer and tramp sailer is not always so great, after all, if due allowance be made for the difference in distance covered.

To the sailing vessel, securing, in general, but one cargo every twelve months, tardy loading is immaterial. The cost of food and wages for her small personnel (in her case an astonishingly low figure) is the principal extra expense accruing from time spent in Spencer Gulf, apart, of course, from port charges and harbour dues, which are on the same basis for her as for a steamer. She sails from Spencer Gulf in January or February, and reaches a port of discharge in England sometime between April and June. After three weeks or so discharging, she sails northward, in ballast, to her home port, there to refit at leisure

74

before voyaging out again to Australia in the late autumn. Consequently, it matters little to her if she takes three, four, or even six weeks to load her grain. On the other hand, loading time is a very much more serious item where a steamer is concerned. The high overheads, wage bills, port expenses, and demurrage of the steamship make unwarranted delay a serious matter for her owners. In these highly competitive times she must load rapidly if she is to be profitable. Use must be made of the giant elevators or the travelling cranes of a modern port, and loading must, when possible, be carried out simultaneously through several hatchways. She may be on time-charter or have subsequent cargoes already fixed for her by her owners, in which case a few days' delay in the loading of the present cargo might involve her, later, in heavy penalty for, or even in the cancellation of, such commitments.

Such are some of the reasons which have so far combined to permit the continued participation of the big windjammer in the export of South Australian grain, a participation now threatened, amongst other difficulties, by the increasing adoption of the bulk method of shipment as opposed to bagging. The latter method is eminently suitable to the loading facilities of Spencer Gulf, and to carry out the necessary interior conversion which would fit the holds of the sailer for bulk stowage at more up-to-date berths would be an expensive matter.

It must not be presumed that the Spencer Gulf trade is by any means entirely in the hands of sail, for that is far from correct. A fairly large number of steamers and motor-ships now load wheat each season at Port Lincoln, Wallaroo, and Port Pirie, but sail does still secure practically the whole of the grain which is shipped from the smaller Gulf ports.

The Charter Party for Australian Grain Cargoes in Sail (1935)

The Charter Party for Grain Cargoes in Sail (1935), drawn up by the Australian Grain Shippers' Association, is an interesting document, and some familiarity with its contents is necessary in order fully to understand sail's only remaining employment.

Loading and discharge

The Charter Party, embodying in all twenty-five clauses, forms a mutual agreement, for one passage, between the charterers and the owner of the vessel. The charterers agree to give loading instructions within twenty-four hours of the notification of the vessel's arrival in Australia. Various places are mentioned to which they may then direct her, but 'Smoky, Streaky and Tumby Bays and Port Thevenard in South Australia' are specific exclusions owing to their unsuitability. At Tumby Bay, for instance, there is a mean depth of only eighteen feet of water at the outer end of the jetty. *Viking* was allowed to load 1,500 tons of grain there in 1936 by special arrangement in the charter; she completed her full cargo subsequently at Wallaroo.

The vessel must proceed to dock, wharf, or anchorage, or 'as near thereunto as she may safely get', and load a cargo 'not exceeding what she can reasonably stow and carry'. The tonnage of grain mentioned in the charter party is provisional, in so far as it provides the charterers with a fairly accurate indication of the carrying capacity of the vessel. A ten per cent margin on this figure is stipulated in the document as a maximum and minimum limit, and this allows the Master to adjust the trim of his vessel to her best advantage.

From her loading berth the windjammer is 'forthwith to proceed to Queenstown, Falmouth or Plymouth for orders to discharge in any one safe port' in Great Britain or Ireland, or on the Continent between Bordeaux and Hamburg, or in Norway and Sweden (Moss-Malmo limits), or in Denmark.

She is consigned to the owner's agents at the port of discharge, there to 'safely lie, always afloat' during unloading. Cargo must be brought to, and taken from alongside, the vessel at charterers' expense. Should they require the bags to be cut open in the holds, for purposes of discharge by suction pipes, they must bear the cost of so doing. This cutting of bags is sometimes the cause of trouble during loading. The contents of a certain number of bags, maybe a thousand in all, are used to fill up the crevices in stowage and so render the cargo a solid, unshifting mass. The more loose grain thus employed, the easier the work of the stevedores in cramming to capacity the lower holds, but as the liability for excessive damage to bags falls upon the shipowner, indiscriminate slitting must be carefully controlled by the Mate of the windjammer.

Freight is payable on net delivered weight, that is, minus the weight of the bagging — known as the tare. The 50,000 or so bags, which constitute the 4,000-ton full cargo of a big sailer, entail the free transport by the shipowner of roughly 50 tons of sacking. Freight is payable concurrently with discharge, and is subject to two months' discount, at five per cent, on the total earned.

Lay-days   A certain period, known as the lay-days and usually comprising twenty to twenty-five 'weather working days', is allowed for loading in Australia, and for delay at the orders port in U.K., the period varying with the size of the cargo. Seven days are reserved for 'order' purposes. The remainder, which apply to loading, represent a maximum of eighteen times twenty-four working hours, or over four hundred working hours in all. Taking an eight-hour working day on the part of the stevedores, these eighteen loading lay-days could, if required, extend to cover eleven weeks of five working days per week, or fifty-four calendar days (excluding Sundays). In no case are the charterers allowed to detain the vessel at her orders port in U.K. for longer than seven days (Sundays and holidays excepted) unless they pay demurrage, of from £25 to £30 per day according to the tonnage of the vessel, for a further period, limited to ten extra days in all. 'Dispatch money', the opposite of demurrage, and the means by which the owner reimburses the charterers for unused lay-days, is not customary in sailing vessel charters.

Then follows a clause which, should the owner or his agents fail to advise the charterers of the date of sailing from Australia, penalizes him by the addition of five extra lay-days. This clause is usually deleted from the charter party.

No other cargo may be carried without the charterers' consent, but they may sublet the whole or any part of the vessel's cargo space without prejudice to the agreement. They can demand the production of a surveyor's certificate as to the pre-loading condition of the vessel, but they agree to provide sufficient stiffening of grain to enable all ballast to be discharged at the grounds.

Charterers' privileges

A commission of five per cent on the gross freight is due to the charterers on completion of loading. Their liability then ceases, lien on the cargo being thereafter vested in the owner for freight, demurrage, or detention. The option of cancelling the charter in the event of the non-arrival of the vessel by a specific loading date, and in seaworthy condition, closes the contract, except for the stipulation that all moneys payable under it are to be settled in English currency or in the equivalent.

Freight is an infinitely variable factor, governed very largely by supply and demand. For example, the anticipated failure of the American wheat crop will undoubtedly cause important repercussions in many commodity markets, and, as it is coincident with accounts of

Freight of Australian grain

harvest damage in Russia, and a shorter Canadian crop than usual, it is fairly evident that shipowners interested in the carriage of grain must look principally, in the near future, to Australia and the Argentine. During the last year (1936) the price of Australian grain has risen from £6 10s. to £8 10s. a ton, with prospects of yet further early appreciation. Italy's re-entry into the market as an importer of grain has helped to produce this inflation. Consequently, it now seems likely that the fourteen square-riggers, which should comprise the 1937 grain fleet of sail, can voyage outward in ballast this autumn with a fair hope of finding reasonable homeward freights awaiting their arrival.

Every variation of one shilling per ton in the freight of Australian grain produces a difference of £200 (less commissions) on the earnings of a barque whose cargo capacity is a net 4,000 tons. Freights can and do vary from year to year by many shillings. The total annual freightage of the present Erikson Fleet is affected by something like £2,500 to £3,000 by an alteration of only 1s. per ton in the price paid for the carriage of grain.

A ten-year survey of freights rates It is interesting to review the position of the last ten years in the matter of freightage of South Australian grain by sailing vessels. The following examples are indicative of the freights ruling for the 1926-7 season: *C. B. Pedersen* 35s., *Gustav* 45s., *Greif* 47s. 6d., *Garthpool* (the last Britisher to participate in the trade) 41s. per ton.

By 1930 the market slumped to such an extent, because of a poor crop, that, whereas *Herzogin Cecilie* secured 22s. 6d. and *Archibald Russell* 22s., *C. B. Pedersen* accepted a record low freight of 16s. 6d. from Melbourne. This was, however, not quite so bad as it sounds, for, like several other windjammers in the trade at the time, she had carried a cargo of Baltic timber out to Melbourne. Some of these vessels had to shift round in ballast from Melbourne to Spencer Gulf, where higher homeward freights were obtainable. *C. B. Pedersen*, by the way, on the homeward passage was so badly damaged by a hurricane 200 miles west of the Horn that ultimately she took the unusual course of using the Panama Canal.

Penang was offered a similar low freight, but as at that wage the voyage entailed a loss of several shillings per ton on the charter, she, like Lundqvist's barquentine *Mozart*, came home again in ballast. *Olivebank* stayed out in Australia until the following season, laid up after repairing extensive damage incurred on her outward trip. The

78

facing: Right. OFF CAPE HORN, 1933 (FROM 'OLIVEBANK')
Left. 'THE DUCHESS CECILIE'

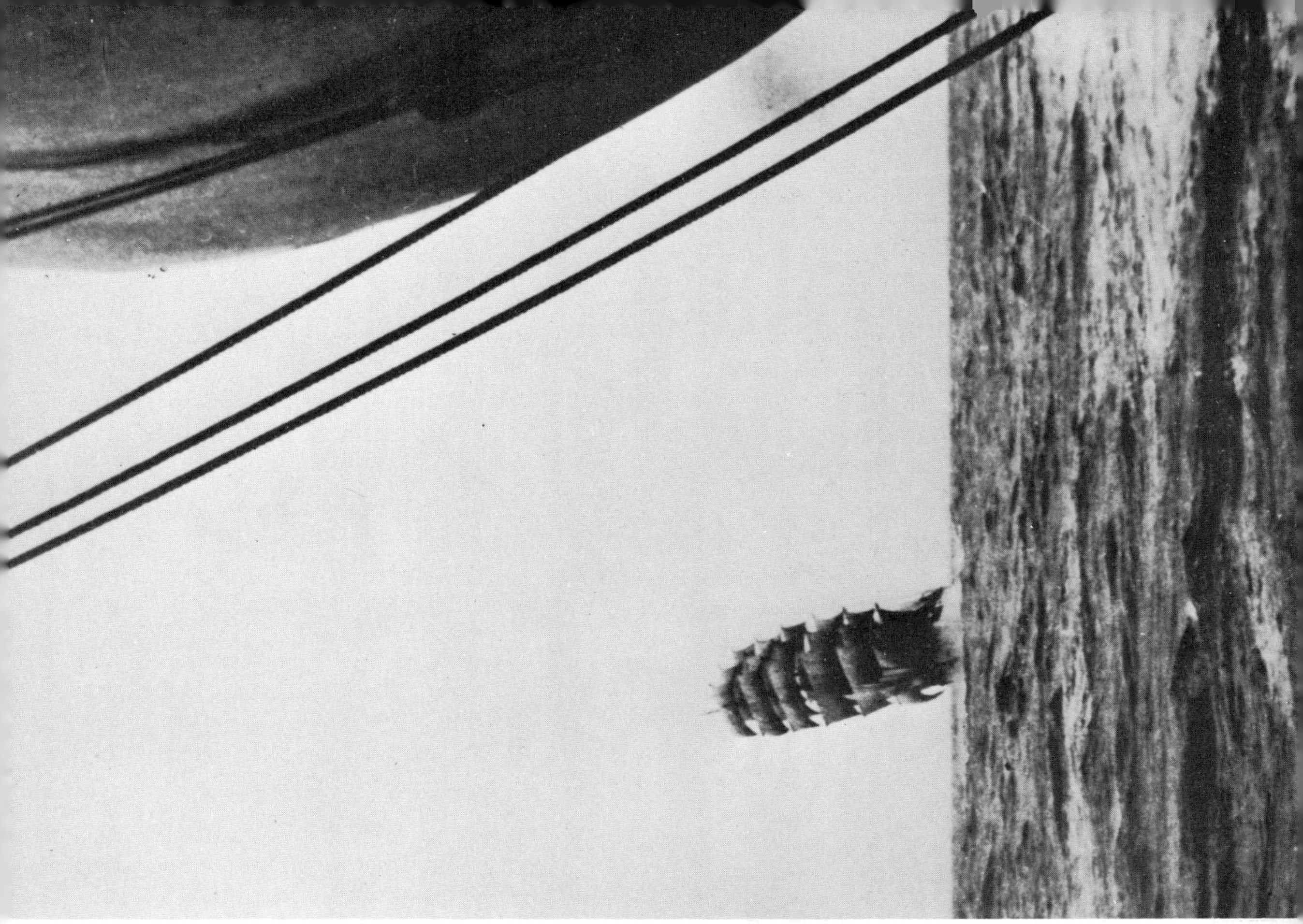

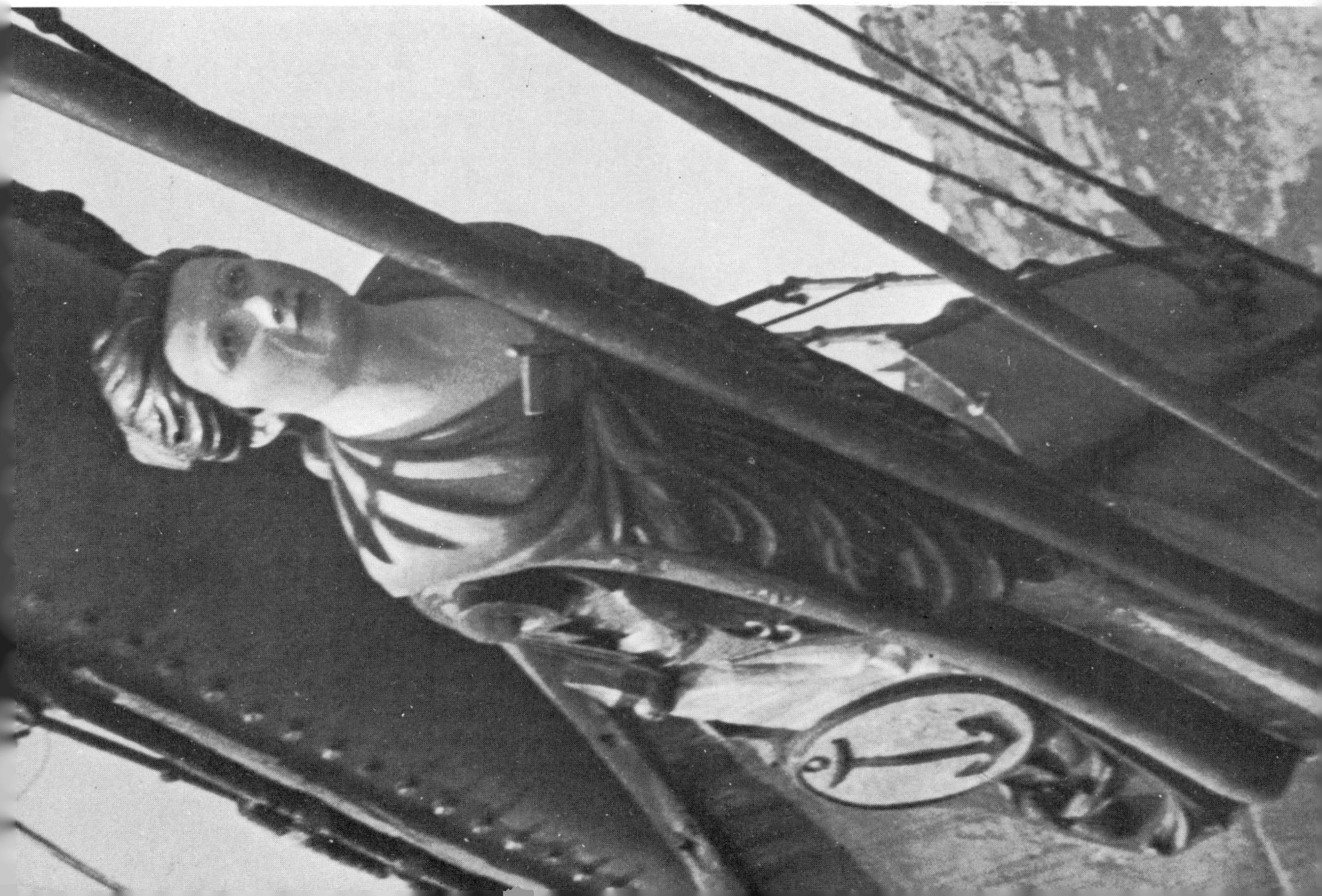

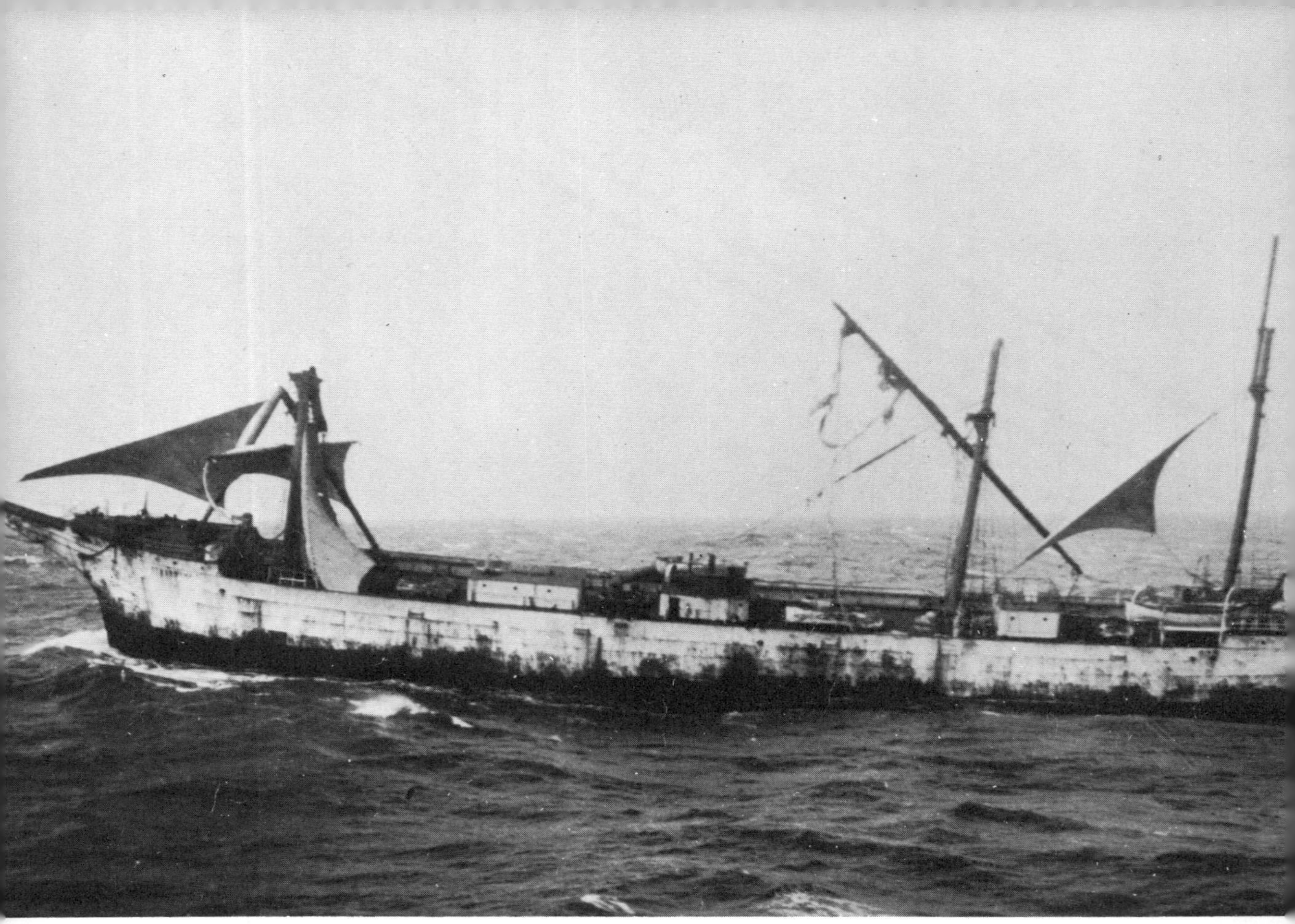

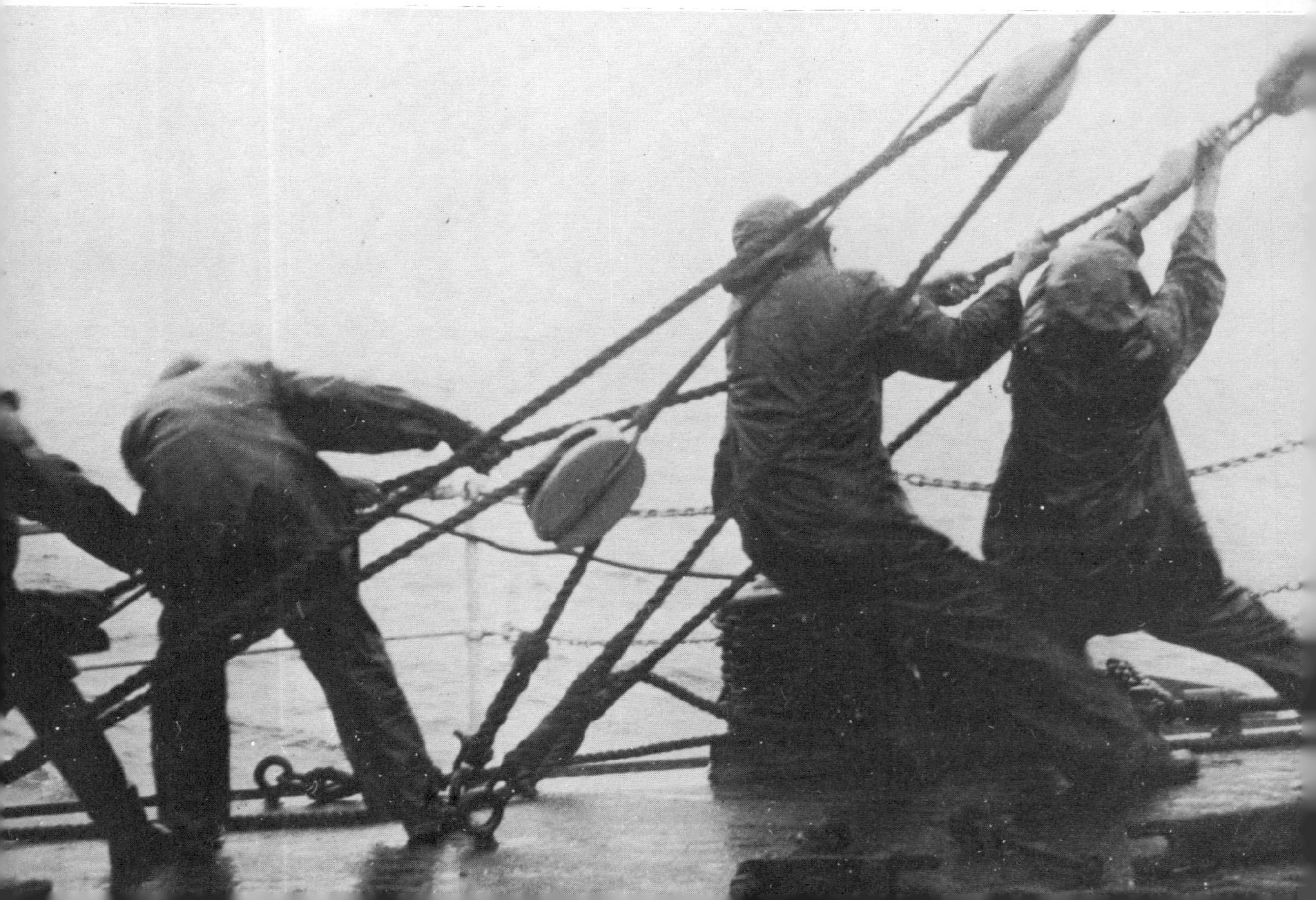

beautiful old Swedish barque *Beatrice* (ex *Routenburn*) brought home from Melbourne the first cargo of wool for many years to be carried in sail, and, it now seems, the last ever to be so transported.

1931 showed much improvement, several vessels securing 30s. and *Herzogin Cecilie* 31s. 1932 was quite a peak year in recent chartering. *Favell*, for a small cargo of 2,200 tons, earned a freight of 34s. 6d.; *Archibald Russell* carried 3,800 tons at 33s. 9d., *Herzogin Cecilie* 4,250 tons at 32s. 6d., and *Melbourne*, for a cargo of 3,500 (fated to remain undelivered) received 31s. 6d. The variations over any one year are due to a number of reasons: date of fixing, size of cargo, popularity or otherwise of vessel, cancellation date, etc., all having some bearing on the rate; the larger vessels, especially those which, by their previous performances, are well spoken of in the trade, are the easiest to fix.

The average fixing for sail in 1933 dropped to 27s. 6d. and by the time the earlier charters for the following year were arranged a further reduction of 1s. per ton had occurred.

1935 showed, at 24s. 9d. — 25s. 6d., another general drop of 1s. for the early fixings. *Pamir*, *Ponape*, and *Mozart*, the later arrivals, found an even greater slump, for they secured only 19s. 6d., while *Parma* had to be content with 19s.

In December 1935 the decision of the Argentine Grain Board to increase the price of new wheat and linseed had an immediate and very radical effect on the Australian market. In four days thirty-five bottoms were fixed on the Baltic for homeward grain from Australia, and sixpence premium was offering for any tonnage which could agree to a January cancellation clause. Australian chartering jumped to the position of the most active of all homeward markets; a corresponding slump being manifested in tonnage demands for the River Plate. Steamers were, of course, the subject of most of this activity, but seventeen windjammers obtained Spencer Gulf charters for U.K. ports, fourteen of them being Erikson vessels.

The average sail freight was 25s. 6d., the lowest being 25s. 3d. and the highest — *Moshulu*, making her maiden voyage under the Erikson flag — 26s. Australian grain at that time being round about £6 10s. per ton value, *Moshulu's* big cargo of 4,850 tons was worth more than £30,000, and entailed a freight of over £6,000. Steamers, loading at the larger ocean ports, were receiving from 27s. to 28s. per ton for

cing: Top.   'HOUGOMONT', OFF SPENCER GULF, UNDER JURY-RIG, 1932

Bottom.   ACTION!

bagged cargoes of 7,000-8,000 tons. By October 1936 steam tonnage was conceded 28s. 3d. bulk, and 30s. 9d. bags, for immediate sendings of South Australian grain. Autumn shipments represent a clearance of existing stocks, but the increase in rate is a pointer toward good prices for the carriage of the new season's crop.

This gradual upward trend to a more stable basis, with, as already mentioned, fair prospects of activity for the ensuing season, is heartening to those to whom, be it for business reasons or through mere sentiment alone, the preservation of square-rig means much.[1]

According to the above figures, however, freights for 1936 were approximately 8s. per ton lower than in 1932, and about 15s. less than they were ten years ago. How long the grain trade under sail can continue the fight is entirely problematical. These statistics should serve, however, to emphasize the skill and initiative demonstrated by those who, in the face of ever-increasing difficulties, have, by a combination of astute chartering with personal management, enabled the Erikson Fleet to keep the seas as the last fleet of deepwater sail in existence.

The necessity for mobility

In a decade when a larger percentage than ever before of the world's steam tonnage is idle and unproductive, and during which trade has reached what, it is profoundly hoped, will prove to be its lowest ebb, it is no mean feat to operate sail as a business proposition.

One of the prime essentials to success is mobility. The windjammer must, at all costs, avoid long periods of inaction. She must be ready and willing to accept any freight which proffers even the smallest margin of profit, and be prepared, if necessary, to undertake a speculative ballast passage to secure it.

The foregoing notes on chartering must not convey the misleading impression that the profits of the grain carriers are based upon advance chartering. Much of the fixing takes place while the windjammers are on the high seas, outward-bound, and quite often they arrive before their cargoes are arranged. If Captain Erikson was not prepared

---

[1] December, 1936. Apropos of the forecast advanced for 1937 sailings, the author is pleased to be able to record that his optimism was justified. An average rise of no less than 3s. 6d. per ton is shown by the sail-charters arranged during the last few weeks. All the windjammers were fixed at prices between 28s. 9d. and 29s. 3d. except the last arrival in Spencer Gulf, *Olivebank*. She secured the excellent rate of 31s. for 4,000 tons (Feb.–March loading). (*See note C on page* 415.)

Steam tonnage, which in November obtained a freight of 30s. bulk and 32s. 6d. bagged, has risen to the remarkable figures of 43s. bulk and 45s. 6d. bagged for the carriage of South Australian wheat.

sometimes to take the chance of sending his entire fleet to Australia in ballast, a possible total of 200,000 miles per annum of unproductive sailing, in the hope that all, or most of them, would earn a homeward freight, he might just as well abandon entirely his now unique business.

The chartering and, in fact, all the business side of the Erikson regime except the actual management of the vessels and their crews, is conducted from London by the one firm in existence to-day which, among other activities, deals with the chartering of sail. The marine superintendence of the fleet is carried out at Mariehamn by a small office-staff directed by the owner himself, who also pays periodical personal visits to his London agents. The survival of sail to the present day is as much due to the agency of Messrs. H. Clarkson & Company of Bishopsgate, London, who have been associated with Captain Gustaf Erikson ever since he started sail-owning in 1913, as to the supervision and foresight of that remarkable personality himself. As practically all the Australian grain cargoes shipped in sail are for delivery to British consignees, it is a pleasing sidelight on the history of sail that the preservation of the windjammer is dependent on British merchants, English management, and Empire produce.

The London Agents of the Erikson Fleet

To stand a chance of being a profitable undertaking a modern square-rigger must make good regular passages, be possessed of a large carrying capacity, keep down maintenance expenses for canvas, gear, etc., to a minimum, and, through the medium of a small inexpensive crew, undertake the major part of her conditioning. Finally, and perhaps the most important point of all, she must run without sustaining casualties or incurring liabilities, for to-day the commercial sailer is compelled to be independent of insurance protection. That, however, is a subject which will be enlarged upon in its proper context — the story of the Erikson Fleet.

THERE are only two places in the wide world where it is still possible to see the grand old panorama of a number of big square-riggers grouped together. One, Spencer Gulf (in particular Port Lincoln and Port Victoria) has already been dealt with; the other, Mariehamn, capital of the Finnish archipelago of Åland (pronounced Awland), and the last home of deepwater sail, should furnish a more colourful picture, as there is much of interest to record about a locality whose principal title to contemporary fame rests in its sailing vessels.

A brief résumé of Åland history

The Swedish subjugation of part of what is now known as Finland, between A.D. 1150 and 1300, was followed in 1660 by the acquisition of its whole coastline. Between 1721 and 1809, however, the entire territory was conquered by Russia, and, from thenceforward until the overthrow in 1917 of the Russian Empire, the principality formed an autonomous Grand Duchy, the Tsar of Russia being Grand Duke of Finland. But, despite several attempts, Finland was never Russianized, nor did its people ever consider themselves Russian nationals. In 1809 Russian troops, attacking in winter across the ice, captured Åland, the largest of a group of islands lying in mid-Baltic between Sweden and Finland. The whole of this archipelago was ceded by Sweden to the Tsar, Alexander I of Russia, under the subsequent Treaty of Frederikshamn.

In 1854, England then being at war with Russia, Admiral Napier sacked and burned Bomarsund, the ancient fortress of Åland. Bomarsund, of which the ruins still remain, was never rebuilt, for the newly established town of Mariehamn, named after the Tsarina Marie, now became the capital.

During the Great War a large Russian garrison was maintained in Finland. These troops became disaffected when the Kerensky Government was overthrown, and allied themselves to the local Communist party. In 1918, however, after six months' bitter civil war, Finland overcame the Bolshevist regime and won independence.

When peace was restored, Sweden laid claim to the Åland Islands.

Her candidature, based on the close affinity existing between her own people and the population of Åland, was supported by a referendum taken in the islands. Although the religion and many of the customs of Åland were Finnish, in language, manners, and sympathies these island folk were, and still are, far more Swedish than Finnish. Finland, however, strongly resisted the suggested annexation, and the dispute was submitted for arbitration to the League of Nations. In 1921, the League, by its initial settlement of a major territorial dispute, placed the islands under Finland's jurisdiction. They remain, nevertheless, self-governing; the inhabitants are exempt from military service, and no Finn from the mainland may become a landowner in Åland until he has been domiciled there for at least five years.

Although the Swedish names of Åland and Mariehamn are in general use in the islands, the small Finnish-speaking population and the Finns of the mainland use, instead, Ahvenanmaa and Maarianhamina.

The geography of Åland

The territory of Åland embraces about three hundred separate islands, in addition to many thousands of rocky islets. Only about eighty of the islands are inhabited, and of the total population of something under 30,000, two-thirds reside on Åland itself, an island eighteen miles in length and intersected by several long fiords. Rock, of glacial boulder formation, is a characteristic of the landscape: it crops out as high pine-clad bluffs along the shores of the larger islands, and forms the substrata to a meagre top-dressing of soil on the low-lying areas. The islands are farmed wherever ground permits; hardy cereals are raised, and cattle pastured, during the short, warm summer. An Åland farm may consist of a group of small islets, where boats take the place of farm carts. On the larger islands dense pine-woods cover the untillable areas, but here and there, where soil is more plentiful, the countryside is strangely English in appearance. In Åland there are hundreds of windmills, every hamlet boasts its elaborate, jingling maypole, and many of the little wooden churches have tall, bulbous, Byzantine spires.

The produce and the people of Åland

Meat, fish, hides, wood, dairy produce, sea-birds' eggs and eider-down are the chief exports, but the inhabitants of the sea-girt territory are essentially seafaring folk, veritable descendants of the Vikings, whose blood would still seem to run salt through Åland veins, for from this Swedish-Finnish stock is drawn a large part of the personnel of the last of the windjammers. The sea offers a ready livelihood to the young

Ålanders, and a surprisingly high percentage choose it as their first profession.

Being, in the main, of Swedish extraction, the hardy Åland folk use Swedish as the general tongue, although, by law, Finnish is taught in the schools. They are a quiet, careful, hard-working, frugal people, old-fashioned and unsophisticated in many ways. Few modern communities lead a simpler or healthier life, for living is very cheap and amenities, by comparison with other countries, few. Åland is only frost-free between May and September, and men and women alike toil hard during that period to glean the harvests of their meagre acres. Rye, barley, hay, flax, and vegetables are the principal crops, and are stored to meet the exigencies of a long, hard winter.

The story of sail in Åland

For hundreds of years these islands have maintained a mercantile marine of their own. The wood, the flax, the cargoes, and the sailors were there, in close proximity, and little Åland-built sailing craft carried fish, timber, cheese and so forth to the markets on the adjacent mainland, centuries before the registry of 'Mariehamn' was displayed on the counters of big square-riggers lying at Circular Quay, Sydney, in the roadsteads of Chile, along the 'Frisco waterfront, or berthed in London River.

The trading methods of Åland farmers furnished an early example of co-operative industry. They amalgamated in the building and rigging, on the spot by local labour, of little, wooden brigs and schooners, using home-felled timber and home-grown flax. Each shareholder supplied a man toward the crew, and was responsible for his food and keep for the season's trading. Loaded with the produce of the participating farms, these vessels traded successfully along Baltic shores.

Once the excellent harbour of Mariehamn was developed as the centre of Åland industry, the scope of trade increased. Vessels became larger and ventured farther afield and the next step lay in the acquisition of second-hand foreign tonnage.

The secret of the apparent backwardness, even in quite recent years, of the Finnish mercantile marine is said to lie in the lack of cheap capital available in that country. Because new and modern steam tonnage entails the expenditure of considerable capital, Finnish owners are still content to work with older vessels, which, although they may entail relatively high expenses for repairs, can be obtained for an attractive initial outlay and involve little capital depreciation. During the closing decades of the last century many fine old barques, ships, and schooners passed from America, France, England, and Germany, where the pinch of steam competition was already becoming a very real threat, to Åland owners, who, at that time, knew little and cared less about steamers.

The capital investment was small, the shareholders many; depreciation was avoided by purchase at practically scrap value, and the repair and renovation of such vessels was a local speciality; provisioning was simple and cheap, and the supply of suitable personnel more than adequate. An Åland syndicate, it appeared, could turn a vessel to profitable account when in other countries she would be considered as a liability, and, with many big iron and steel square-riggers in active commission, Åland assumed, in time, a humble part in the wider sphere of deepsea world trade. In 1914, three-score or more big square-riggers were owned in Åland, besides a host of short-sea traders. At that time, of course, they all flew the Russian flag, and, in consequence, suffered heavily in the terrible years that followed. Eight vessels were lost in one month (May, 1917), and although, as an outcome of the War, Finland gained her freedom from the Russian yoke, she forfeited all chance of recouping her War losses, which, prior to the emergence of the Soviet Republic, had been covered by Russian State Insurance.

However, under the new flag of Finland, Ålanders continued to concentrate largely on sail, and, because of their economic advantages, cheap labour, and self-husbanding principles, were again successful in the management of the many big windjammers which gravitated to the Blue-and-White ensign during the post-War European shipping slump. Strikes and labour disturbances were not among the problems to be faced by owners like Lundqvist, Anderson, Wennstrom, and Erikson of Mariehamn, for there were always plenty of young men willing and eager to ship deepwater. The feats accomplished with sailing vessels by their small, young crews of to-day, crews who handle successfully tonnage designed to carry twice or three times the present personnel, render ample proof of the quality of seamanship and hardihood inbred into such material by generations of sea-going ancestors.

Situated at the southern extremity of Åland Island, Mariehamn possesses a fine, sheltered harbour, whose entrance, opening due south, is well marked, and has a depth of sixty feet of water. Being ice-bound

Mariehamn harbour

85

from January to April, the port is kept open to traffic by a powerful ice-breaker. The harbour, in shape like an hour-glass, has a large outer basin and a longer, narrower, inner sector, to which access is obtained through a neck guarded by rocky, pine-clad heights. There is hardly any rise and fall owing to the tidelessness of the Baltic, but pilotage is compulsory. The hard bed of the inner harbour falls away so sheerly that vessels of considerable draught can moor along the wooden quays in natural berths that need no dredging.

The home-coming of the big square-rigger

Given favourable wind, it is the practice of the big windjammer, homeward bound in ballast, to sail right up to her moorings by the town. She drives through the narrow outer entrance, a stone's-throw from the low, rocky promontories which hedge it about, and glides across the smooth water of the outer lagoon, keeping, by nice judgment, sufficient way on to carry her through the intervening neck and down the mile-long fairway of the inner port, where, on the starboard bow, can be seen, nestling in a forest, the roofs of the little wooden houses of Mariehamn. The harsh rumble of an anchor chain through a steel hawse-hole, the steady clank of capstan-pawls as the tall square-rigger is warped in broadside to the quay for the last few score feet of the 40,000 to 50,000 miles she has traversed since leaving Mariehamn ten months or so ago, and the wanderer is home from the sea.

Mariehamn is a gay little place in summer when the square-riggers are in. Trim and ship-shape after the customary spring-clean of the homeward voyage, gleaming with new paintwork, varnished teak and polished brass, and with their canvas tightly gasketed to a neat harbour-stow or unbent altogether and stored away below decks, the old wind-jammers, gay with bunting for fêtes or celebrations, make a beautiful picture. Some are berthed along the quay, others anchored in mid-harbour or moored to the pines which, on the far side, come down to the water's edge.

It happens but rarely that the entire quota of Åland deepwater-men is present at Mariehamn. One or other of its units may have been fortunate enough to secure an outward timber charter for South Africa, in which case she proceeds to Kotka, Uuras or Trangsund to load her cargo. Another may, by reason of a protracted grain passage, be so late in discharging that, if she is to make Spencer Gulf again in time for the next grain crop, she must dry-dock in England and sail straight out on the old Southern trail once more.

86

In general, however, the procedure is for the inward-bound grain sailers to call at Falmouth or Queenstown about April, May, or early June, anchoring out in the Roads until they receive orders to proceed to a port of discharge selected by the final purchasers of the grain. Falmouth and Queenstown have always been the favourite order ports of the windjammer because they have large, safe, easily reachable bays: no harbour dues accrue to vessels lying therein, and, normally, no tug assistance is required for arrival or departure. Occasionally, however, a sailer is towed from order port to port of discharge if the charterers require her presence there by a definite, proximate date. London, Hull, Ipswich, Belfast, Dublin, Cork, Liverpool, and Glasgow are among the most usual final destinations, and sometimes two or three vessels go to the same port. For instance, out of the sixteen vessels which discharged in the United Kingdom this summer (1936) two went to Ipswich, three to Glasgow, and no fewer than five to London.

'Order' and discharge ports in Great Britain and Ireland

Discharge occupies, on the average, about three weeks, and then, with a minimum of ballast (for summer conditions in home-waters do not necessitate full ballasting) the square-riggers sail home to Marie-hamn. Some go round the North of Scotland, some come up-Channel, but they all converge on the Skaw and go down Copenhagen Sound, for the expense of the Kiel Canal is unnecessary. So, about July or August they foregather at the home port, where any overhaul or refit is undertaken by their own personnel under the seamanlike eye of the owner. It is said of Captain Gustaf Erikson that he knows personally every man and boy in his employ, and he most certainly knows his vessels from truck to keel.

The summer ballast voyage

Serious repairs go to Nystad, to the Erikson slipway and shipyard, but, unless the vessels have been dry-docked at the grain discharge port, it is usual for them to call for that purpose and for stores and for compass adjustment at Copenhagen, when again outward-bound.

The possibility has just been mooted that, in years to come, Marie-hamn harbour may no longer shelter the Erikson Fleet for the short annual period of inaction, for, at the time of writing, both *Olivebank* and *Archibald Russell* are laid up at Gothenburg. It is rumoured that Captain Erikson is considering the change-over to Gothenburg, as a summer base, in order to avoid the long and none too easy passage from the Skaw to Mariehamn and back. Although as yet unconfirmed, the proposition has aroused much interest in Gothenburg, a port already in

Gothenburg and the Erikson Fleet?

annual touch with the grain trade under sail through the participation therein of the Swedish training-cum-trading barques *Abraham Rydberg* and *C. B. Pedersen*.

The Mariehamn
of to-day However, to return to the gay little Mariehamn of summer days. The beautiful, landlocked harbour is dotted thickly with a shoal of smaller craft: little white passenger-steamers from Stockholm or Åbo, cities only a few hours' steam away; scores of yachts of all types, for Åland is a yachtsman's summer paradise; fishing vessels, timber-trade sailers, and, as a fitting background, a group of tall square-riggers, whose towering spars are reflected in the mirror of the placid lagoon.

Mariehamn is little more than a village: it straggles across a narrow, forested tongue of land between two fiords. The main thoroughfare, 'Esplanad-gatan', is a shady boulevard about half a mile in length, having a harbour at either end, for at its eastern extremity is a smaller anchorage used mainly by yachts. Hereabouts stands the one large hotel, built of wood like most Åland structures. A comfortable little guest-house (and I speak from grateful experience) faces the wind-jammer quay. Indicative of the low cost of living in Åland is the fact that one can live at this guest-house, and live well, for five shillings a day inclusive. Mariehamn is quaintly primitive and entirely unspoilt. It smacks of Switzerland in its brightly painted, deep-eaved chalets, with their gay flower-boxes and sheltering pines. Motor cars are few, for most of the local transport of this northern Venice is by water.

There are, however, many sights in Mariehamn peculiar to a maritime community, and uncommon elsewhere in the world: a school for sea-cooks, a State school of navigation (free, except for the provision of books), a collection of the figureheads of famous bygone wind-jammers and a private museum of sailor-made models of many of the post-War square-riggers. Here also, at a moment's notice, can be obtained for the asking the entire crew, from Master to boy, of a deepwater square-rigger. Last but not least, for in his unique business lies the cause of little Mariehamn's present publicity, here is the residence of Captain Gustaf Erikson, managing-owner of the only fleet of big windjammers in existence to-day.

Gustaf
Erikson Gustaf Erikson was born sixty-four years ago, of seafaring parentage, at Lemland in the Åland Islands. From childhood he was bred to the sea, and by the age of nine was 'boy' aboard a little barque in the North Sea timber trade. A sea-cook at thirteen, he was, in turn, A.B. and

88

facing: AN 'ONKER' BARQUE; 'LINGARD', 193?
(AN UNTOUCHED PHOTOGRAPH)

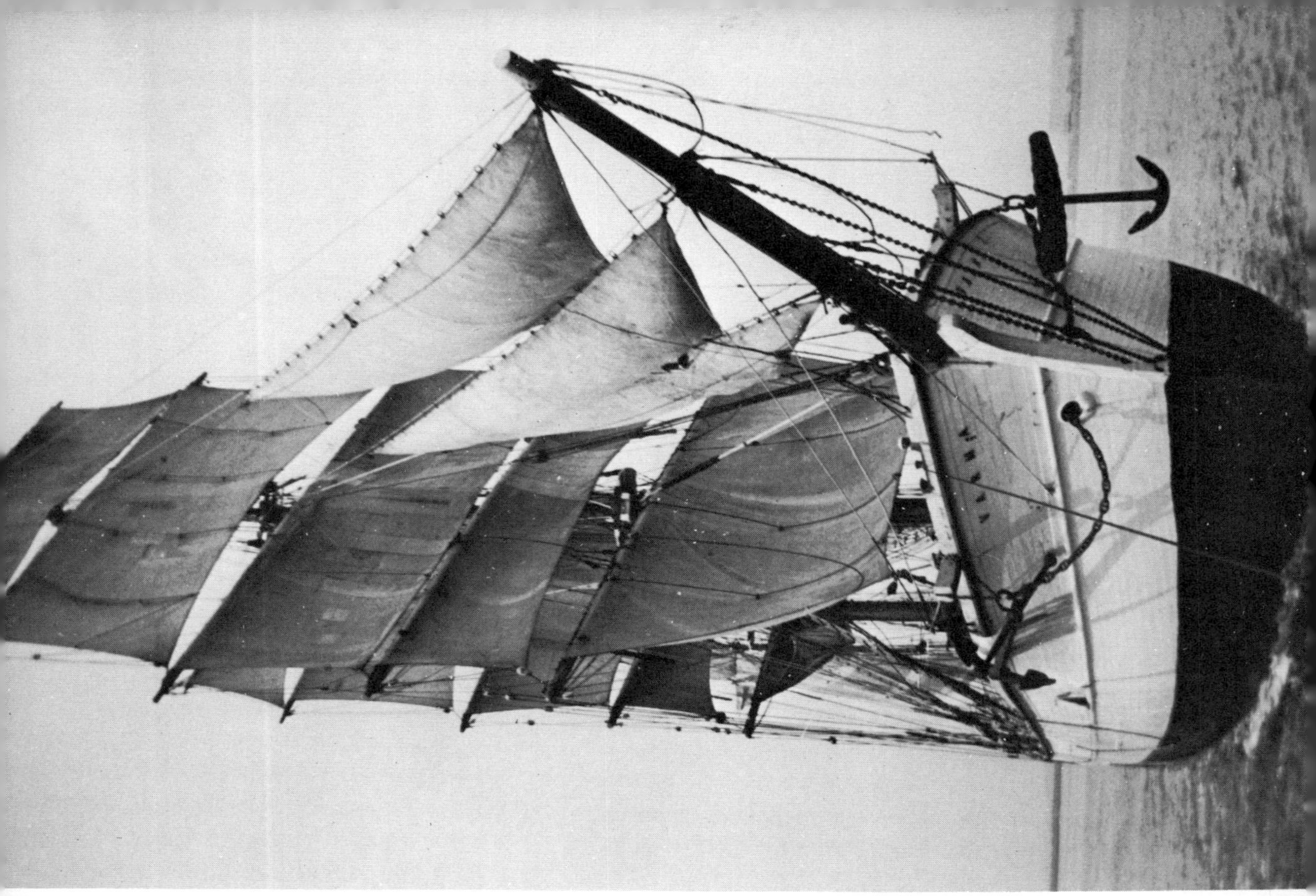

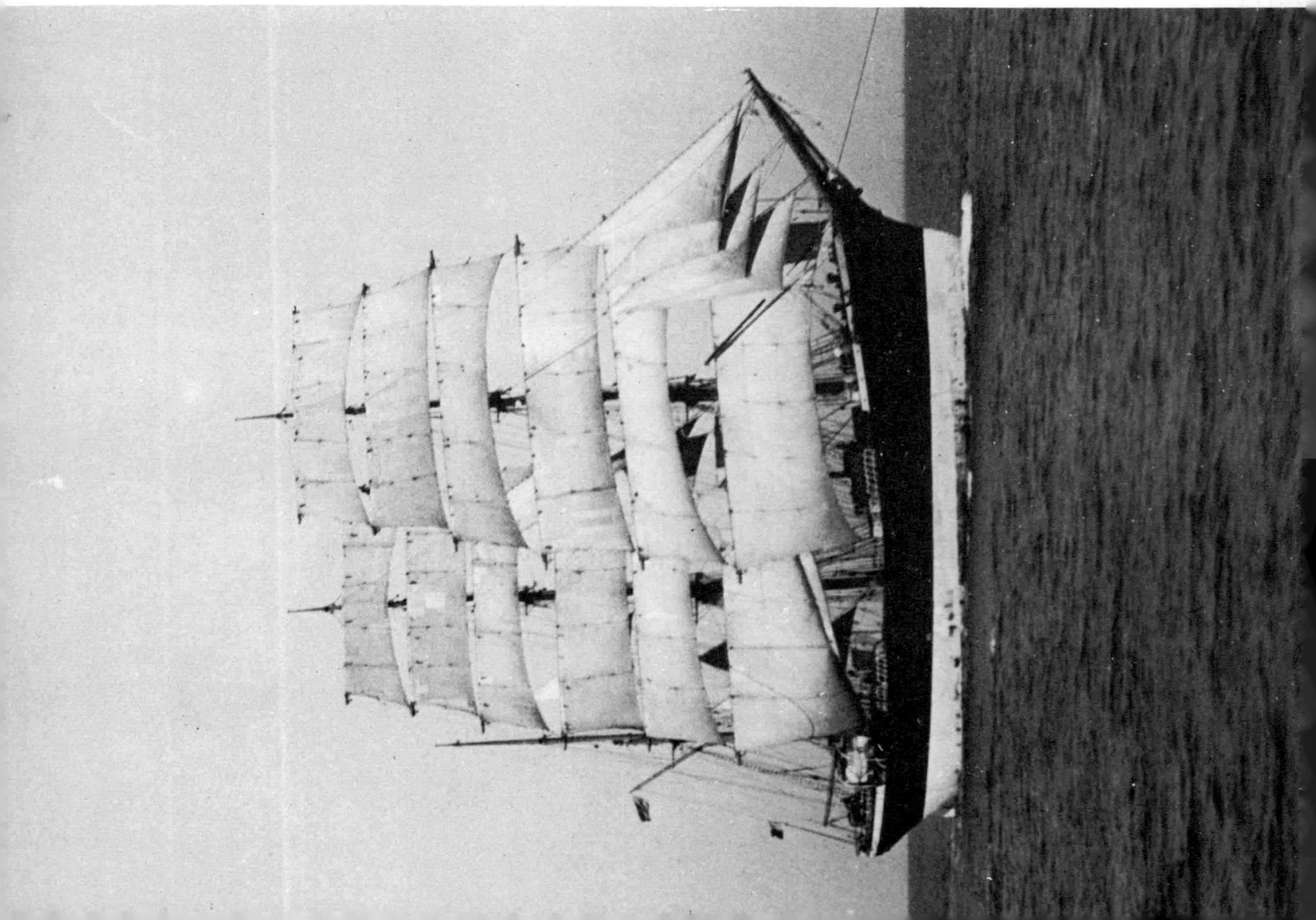

bo'sun, and when only eighteen became Mate of a timber carrier. A year later he rose to command, his first charge being *Adele*, but the short-sea trades did not hold him for long. Within two years he shipped deep-water, and spent the next five years as a Mate in foreign-going square-rig. From 1902 to 1913 he was Master of several vessels in different trades, his last command being the Finnish iron barque *Lochee*, 1,753 tons gross, owned in Nystad (on the mainland). Then, at the age of forty-one, he relinquished command for ownership and settled down at Mariehamn.

Toward the end of 1913 Captain Erikson bought the German four-masted iron ship *Renée Rickmers*, and renamed her *Åland*: she was a vessel of 2,066 tons gross, built by Russell & Company at Port Glasgow in 1887. In August 1914, during the maiden voyage under her new colours, she drove on to a reef near New Caledonia and became a total loss. With no knowledge of the War which had broken out since her departure, *Åland* stranded quite close to a light which, as a precautionary War measure, had already been extinguished. It was an unfortunate start to Captain Erikson's deepwater ventures.

The inauguration of the Erikson Fleet

Another Erikson vessel lost by War perils was the *Borrowdale*, built in 1868 by W. H. Potter & Sons at their Liverpool yard, famed for its fine sailing vessels.

Both these casualties were doubly severe as, like so many Åland vessels of the period, they were covered by the Russian State Insurance scheme, and the owner was unable to recoup himself. Payment of such claims was delayed, until, finally, the success of the Revolution negatived all hope of ultimate recovery from Russia.

In 1915 a compatriot of Erikson, A. M. Troberg of Mariehamn, possessed a fleet of nine square-riggers — *August*, *Borrowdale*, *Garnet Hill*, *Isabel Browne*, *Lawhill*, *Margareta*, *Professor Koch*, *Prompt*, and *Thomasina*. Gradually, throughout the War, this fleet was disbanded by loss or sale, until, by 1920, it had disappeared entirely. Captain Erikson bought *Borrowdale*, *Professor Koch*, and, after the War, *Lawhill*, from Troberg, and in 1916 he secured the full-rigger *Grace Harwar* from Stenius of Helsingfors.

Professor Koch, a steel barque of 1,543 tons gross, 100 A1 at Lloyd's, was launched at Glasgow in 1891 by Russell & Company. Like *Grace Harwar*, she rendered yeoman service to her new Marie-hamn owner. Both vessels survived the War, having during those

acing: Right. THE WOODEN BARQUE 'VARMA', 1934

Left. 'PENANG', 1933

hazardous days earned good freights which helped to offset Gustaf Erikson's irrecoverable losses. They continued in active commission under his flag, *Professor Koch* until 1922 and *Grace Harwar* until 1935.

Tjerimai, a small, Amsterdam-built, composite barque of 1,011 tons gross, was another War-time addition to the growing fleet. She had been launched in 1883, and already flew the Russian flag when Erikson acquired her. She lasted him until 1928, when, at the ripe age of forty-five, she was lost in collision with the Dutch trawler *Christina Catharina* in the North Sea. Her crew were saved but the Master lost his life in the accident.

The post-War purchases

It was, however, upon the advent of the widespread shipping slump, which was generated by the short fictitious boom of the immediate post-Armistice years, that Captain Erikson displayed his peculiar ability and acumen. When the shipping world had written off sail as an impracticable proposition in view of the great mass of unemployed steam tonnage, this one man set out to build up a fleet of square-riggers. Many even among his fellow countrymen participated in the almost universal discard of sail which now took place; but Erikson bought where others sold. He obtained good class second-hand tonnage at literally scrap prices, and the service which the majority of his vessels have rendered him has proved how judicious was his selection. As personal supervision was the foundation of his system of management, he restricted his buying to reasonable limits, and spread it over a considerable period, but, in addition to hulls, he built up an invaluable reserve of sails and gear by bidding for the outfit of many vessels destined for the ship-breakers. For instance, when in 1933 the Shaftesbury Homes bought Laeisz's *Peking* to replace the old *Arethusa*, Captain Erikson secured many useful deck fittings, such as winches and the like, and a supply of gear, for which *Peking's* new owners had little use, but which to him were treasure-trove.

The following is a chronological list of Captain Erikson's post-War purchases of deepwater sail tonnage, together with the source from which the vessels were acquired.

1919	*Lawhill*	From A. M. Troberg of Finland	Still afloat
1920	*Woodburn*	„ Nystad	Hulked, 1926
1921	*Herzogin Cecilie*	„ France	Wrecked, 1936
1922	*Loch Linnhe*	„ J. Lundström of Nystad	Wrecked, 1933
1923	*Pommern*	„ The Greek Government	Still afloat
1923	*Archibald Russell*	„ J. Hardie & Co. of Glasgow	Still afloat
1924	*Killoran*	„ J. Hardie & Co. of Glasgow	Still afloat

1924	*Hougomont*	From J. Hardie & Co. of Glasgow	Dismasted, 1932
1924	*Olivebank*	,, Norway	Still afloat
1925	*Winterhude*	,, Hemsoth of Hamburg	Still afloat
1925	*Penang*	,, Nurmeinen of Helsingfors	Still afloat
1928	*Melbourne*	,, The Altona Co. of Hamburg	Sunk in collision, 1932
1929	*Ponape*	,, H. Lundqvist of Mariehamn	Broken up, 1936
1929	*Viking*	,, The United Shipping Co. of Copenhagen	Still afloat
1931	*Pamir*	,, F. Laeisz of Hamburg	Still afloat
1932	*L'Avenir*	,, Cie. Maritime Belge	Still afloat
1932	*Passat*	,, F. Laeisz of Hamburg	Still afloat
1935	*Moshulu*	,, C. Nelson & Co. of San Francisco	Still afloat

When a list of the Troberg Fleet of Mariehamn in 1915 was given *Nomenclature* it may have been noticed that most of the vessels bore English names. The retention of the foreign name is quite a common practice among Finnish shipowners who deal largely with second-hand tonnage. For example, *Grace Harwar*, *Woodburn*, and *Lawhill*, each owned by more than one Finnish firm, kept their original English nomenclature throughout their existence. Only once since the loss of *Åland* (ex *Renée Rickmers*) has Captain Erikson coined a new name for one of his purchases. In cases where a vessel had borne several different names he has restored the title under which she had gained the greatest credit. Thus, after a period as *Caledonia*, *Olivebank* regained the name she bore when one of Weir's Bank Line. *Ponape*, which in the interim had been *Bellhouse*, was rechristened with her former Laeisz name. Either no change was made, and, in consequence, *Herzogin Cecilie*, *Killoran*, *Archibald Russell*, *Passat*, *Pamir*, and others previously mentioned, kept the name under which they had been launched, or else a former name was resuscitated. The single exception since the loss of the *Åland* was *Gustav* (ex *Austrasia*), which Captain Erikson converted into *Melbourne*. It is a curious thing that within four years she too, as will be related, was sunk with the loss of many of her personnel.

To attempt to recount the history of all these vessels would need a book in itself, besides which, much of the ground has already been covered by Mr. Lubbock, Mr. Villiers and others. A few notes, however, on the ex-Britishers of the fleet may be of especial interest:

Grace Harwar had the distinction of being the last full-rigged ship *'Grace Harwar'* in active commission, and in 1935, at the end of her long career, she was *last of the* the oldest square-rigger then trading deepwater. A ship of 1,816 tons *full-riggers*

91

gross, she was launched in 1889, forty-seven years ago, from the yard of William Hamilton & Company at Port Glasgow. Her original owner was W. Montgomery of London. *Grace Harwar* had the short poop and long, open main-deck of the typical 'lime-juicer' of the eighties, and, although never a maker of record passages, her long period of continuous service showed her to be a well-built ship. She retained to the last her full original sail-plan, setting three royals above double topgallants (single on the mizen); she had no mechanical devices for sail handling.

Under the command of the well-known Captain T. C. Fearon, who died in 1931 at the age of seventy-five, *Grace Harwar* came home round the Horn in 1911 minus her entire bowsprit. She had been caught in a terrific hurricane, which devasted Iquique and Coquimbo, and had been blown down on to a French steamer. The collision carried away her bowsprit and figurehead, and she lost her starboard bower anchor and cable. (The figurehead was never replaced, ornamental scroll-work being substituted.) When the weather abated and the debris had been cleared, the forestays were set up short to the bows, and, with a single jib and a fore-topmast staysail as her entire head canvas, Captain Fearon navigated her home.

In 1913 *Grace Harwar* was sold to Russia, and three years later was bought from Helsingfors by Captain Erikson, for whom she traded safely throughout the War. Her final round voyage — ballast out in 1934 and a grain cargo from Spencer Gulf in 1935 — was the best of her post-War performances, for she was eighty-one days from the Downs to Port Lincoln and ninety-eight days back again from Port Broughton to Falmouth. The latter is, perhaps, the more meritorious passage, for any windjammer of to-day 'breaking the hundred home' is doing very well indeed. After this passage she was sold to Firth of Forth ship-breakers for £2,150.

Mr. Villiers relates a *macabre* yarn about this old full-rigger. One of her earlier Masters took his wife to sea with him. From time to time quarrelling and screams were heard emanating from the saloon: later on in the voyage the lady died, at a time when the crew were somewhat out of hand, and they lost no time in accusing the Master of murder. To prove his innocence he pickled the corpse in salt in a harness cask, and so brought it home for a post-mortem.

'Lawhill' *Lawhill*, built in 1892 as a sister-ship to *Garthpool*, was one of

Captain Erikson's most fortunate acquisitions, for she has been perhaps the most consistent profit-earner of the fleet. In 1899 Captain Barrie of Dundee sold *Lawhill* to the Anglo-American Oil Company of London, and in 1911 she was bought by G. Windram & Company of Liverpool. In 1914 she passed to Åland, A. M. Troberg of Mariehamn operating her until 1916, when, with a passage of 122 days from Wallaroo, she reached Brest unscathed through the height of the submarine menace. Troberg considered the risk of sending her to sea again unjustifiable, and she lay idle at Brest from 1917 to 1919, when Erikson bought her.

Although rather an ugly model of a barque, she deserves her soubriquet of 'Lucky *Lawhill*' because of her comparative freedom from serious casualty and her surprising aptitude for securing good freights. She is now, however, long past her prime and cannot be considered as a strong vessel in comparison with more modern barques like *Passat*, *Pamir* or *Viking*.

From the foregoing schedule of his fleet it will be noticed that Captain Erikson bought, in quick succession, three British-built vessels from the same owners, J. Hardie & Company of Glasgow. This purchase emphasizes the striking contrast between the inability, through force of circumstances, of even experienced British owners of the time to maintain sail as an economic proposition, and the results achieved with the same vessels under the more advantageous conditions prevailing abroad.

Archibald Russell, the first of the three ex-Hardie vessels to pass to Finland, has the joint distinctions of being the last square-rigger to be built at a British yard for British owners, and the only big windjammer ever fitted with bilge-keels. These keels are said to steady her with the wind abaft the beam, but to cause her to sail much farther off the wind when beating up. Scott Russell of Greenock, her builder, inserted a clause in her bill of sale to the effect that her name, a family one, must remain unchanged. This rendered her one of the few exceptions to Hardie's general practice of naming their fleet after British successes in the Peninsular Campaign, e.g. *Albuera*, *Corunna*, *Hougomont*, *Nivelle*, *Saragossa*, *Talavera*, etc. *Archibald Russell* is a good-looking barque, and, despite her thirty-one years, still in sound condition.

'Archibald Russell'

Hougomont, except for the absence of bilge-keels, was a sister-barque to *Archibald Russell*. Her story, together with that of the ill-fated *Melbourne*, must be reserved until Erikson's casualties are reviewed.

93

Killoran, a three-masted barque, has had, on the whole, an eventful career, but in April 1926 she only just escaped total loss. She was forty days out from Newcastle, New South Wales, with coal for Callao, running under foresail and lower topsails only, in very heavy weather, when the foresail split badly. It was not possible to replace it under the prevailing conditions, and the loss rendered her almost unmanageable. It was terribly cold, a big sea was running, and she yawed wildly, taking aboard much water. Oil was seeped overside until supplies were exhausted, but it afforded little mitigation. Suddenly *Killoran* was pooped over the stern by a big sea which smashed in the poop skylight, destroyed a lifeboat, gutted the galley, and did much other minor damage; but, worst of all, it carried away wheel, binnacle, and the helmsman, who was never seen again. *Killoran* steers from the after end of her poop, and in those days she had no protective wheel-house, a deficiency which has since been met by the installation of one which formerly sheltered the helmsmen on *Hougomont* (condemned in 1932). Out of control, *Killoran* broached-to, and what canvas she had set at the time blew out. Then her coal cargo shifted, and she lay over on her beam ends. An attempt to keep her head to sea, by streaming a sea anchor, failed, and it was only after a period of the utmost peril and by the herculean efforts of her personnel that complete disaster was avoided.

In 1933, when *Killoran* was weighing anchor off Copenhagen, she damaged the Barjeback-Charlottenlund telegraph cable. The Danish Postal Authorities were, it is reported, awarded 50,000 Kronen as compensation by the Courts.

Killoran is the prettiest of the three Erikson three-masters, and her hull is in excellent preservation. She has a very graceful sheer-line, upsweeping both fore and aft, and her feminine figurehead is the finest example of such adornment in the Fleet.

Olivebank, after twenty-one years under British ownership, was sold to J. Henschien of Norway in 1913. Five years after the Armistice she was resold to Christiania owners, and became the *Caledonia*. Her chequered career of many misfortunes would seem to justify the appellation of 'Unlucky *Olivebank*' which has attached itself to her.

On one occasion, early in her long history, she was towed into 'Frisco with only her jigger-mast standing: the other three masts had gone by the board during a typhoon on the passage from Shanghai, and it had taken the crew five days to clear the wreckage. In 1909 she

facing: 'TALL SHIP'. 'KILLORA▮
IN THE KATTEGAT, 19

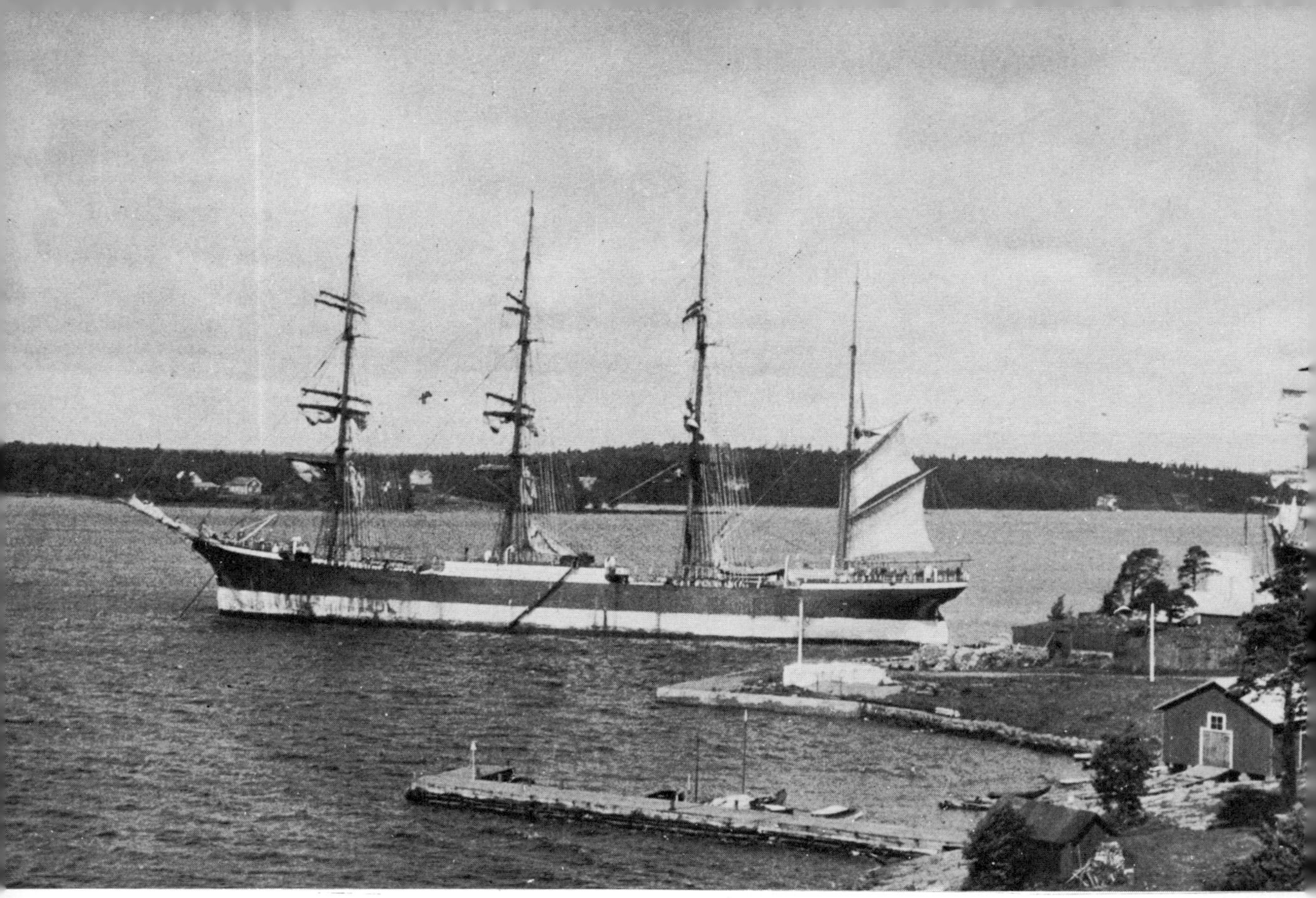

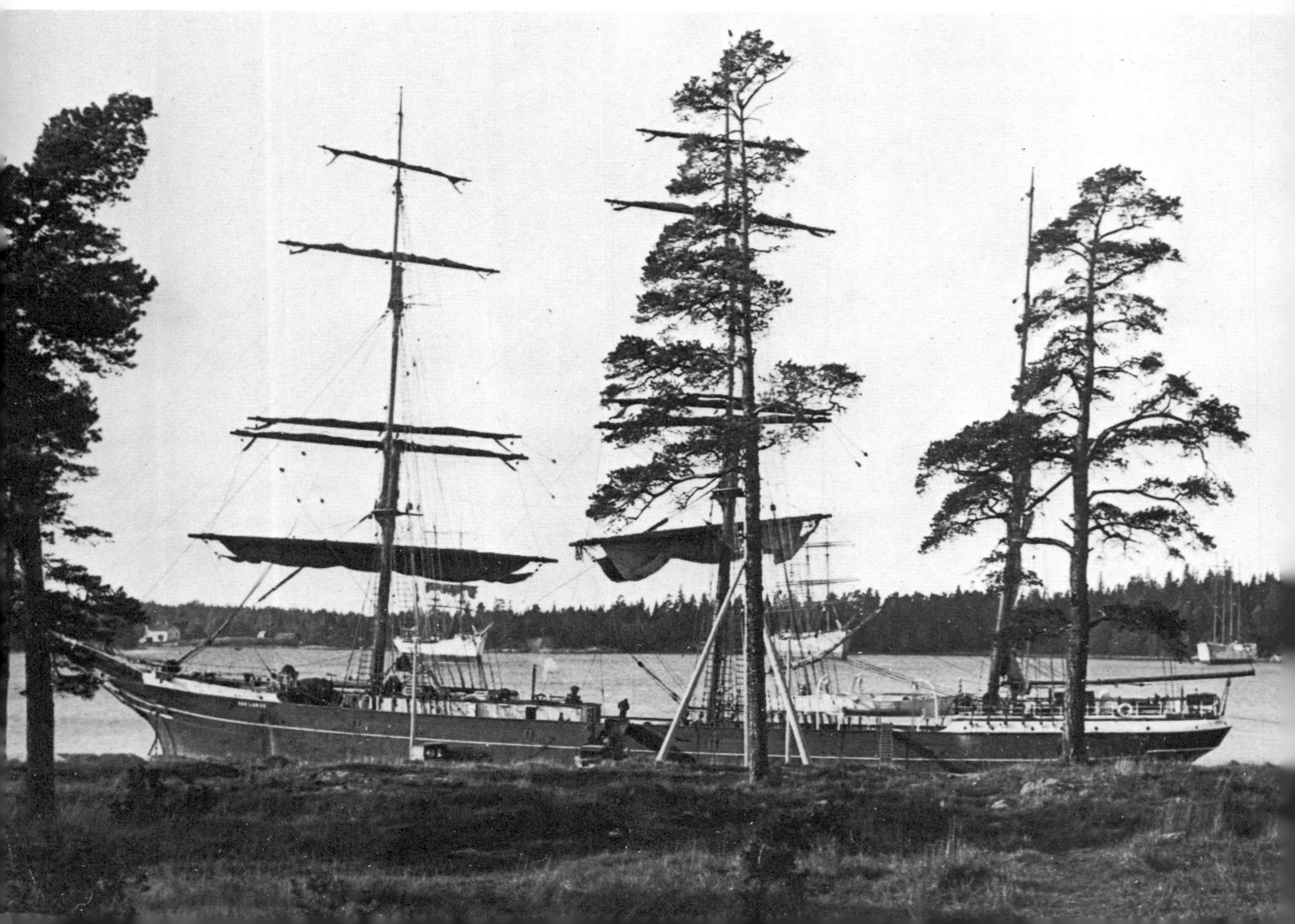

was again crippled, this time by a squall off Sydney Heads when wearing ship, and, after being assisted into Newcastle, New South Wales, spent six months there refitting. In February 1911 *Olivebank* caught fire in Santa Rosalia harbour when discharging a cargo of patent fuel and coke: the afterpart was entirely gutted, and, owing to the amount of water pumped into her, she grounded, listed to port, and finally slid off a bank into deep water. The inrush of water extinguished the fire but caused an explosion which blew off the after hatches. Cofferdams were constructed, pumps installed, and she was refloated, discharged and repaired. On June 29th, however, while anchored in the Roads awaiting orders, she was struck by a sudden hurricane: the anchors dragged, and she drove, stern on, toward a breakwater. A seaman was killed but the barque escaped, for the gale blew itself out as quickly as it had arisen. Stern damage, the denting of a few bottom plates, and a set-up rudder were the total damages sustained.

Olivebank has many slow passages to her discredit, but her appearances at Lloyd's as an 'Overdue' have, so far, not been followed by a 'Missing' paragraph.

Olivebank left Port Lincoln on April 24th, 1926, to fulfil a guano charter at Assumption Island in the Seychelles. Her Master intended to sail westward on the direct route round Cape Leeuwin, but owing to the presence of contrary winds in the Bight he turned eastward, and on May 4th reported from Queenscliff, at the entrance to Melbourne Bay, that he was proceeding into the Indian Ocean through Torres Strait. This north-about alternative was a most unusual and risky course for a big windjammer to take, and *Olivebank* is believed to be the largest sailer ever to adventure it. Passing inside the Barrier Reef, she entered the Arafura Sea via Thursday Island, and reached Mahé in the Seychelles on June 27th.

C. B. Pedersen, 650 tons smaller, came home in ballast via Torres and the Cape of Good Hope in 1935, but she did not take the inside passage. She had attempted the Horn route home, but meeting adverse winds to the south of New Zealand, turned northward up the eastern seaboard of Australia. The ensuing passage through narrow and tortuous channels like Basilisk Pass has been described by seamen as one of the finest examples of seamanship on record.

On the ensuing passage back to New Zealand with her guano, *Olivebank* was posted 'Overdue' at Lloyd's. After dry-docking at Auckland,

95

cing: Top. 'PASSAT' AND 'PENANG' AT MARIEHAMN, 1934

Bottom. MARIEHAMN, 1930. 'OAKLANDS' (FOREGROUND), 'LINGARD', 'GRACE HARWAR', AND 'BALTIC'

New Zealand, a grain cargo from Port Lincoln followed, and, with the exception of *E. R. Sterling* (an account of whose dismasting is to be given), she made the worst grain passage of the 1927 season, arriving at Queenstown 167 days out. The best passage — 98 days — was made that season by *Herzogin Cecilie*. By a margin of three weeks this passage of 167 days was the most lengthy of *Olivebank's* ten post-War grain runs, and it cost the lives of two of her crew. Subsequently £4,000 was spent to enable her to pass the survey for reclassification by *Lloyd's Register* at the end of 1927.

In 1928 *Olivebank* carried a coal cargo from Swansea to Luderitz Bay, South-west Africa, proceeding thence round the Cape of Good Hope, to again fulfil a guano fixing at Assumption Island. Owing to a delayed passage in ballast she arrived at the Seychelles after her cancelling date had expired, and the charter was lost. She went on to Mahé, and was fortunate in hearing that another cargo awaited her at St. Pierre. Her subsequent experiences at that little island have already been related.

Shortage of provisions, the outcome of her protracted loading, gave rise to a shocking outbreak of beri-beri sickness (a form of scurvy, due to lack of vegetable foods) during the ensuing passage to New Zealand. With her young and scanty crew depleted by this scourge, she underwent a severe gale near New Amsterdam Island. Her cargo shifted, but somehow they got her to an even keel once more, and struggled on. Three months after leaving St. Pierre, and after making abortive attempts to reach Fremantle, Albany and Port Adelaide, she finally made landfall at Port Phillip Heads, Queenscliff, where medical attention and fresh provisions were obtained. One of the crew died just prior to arrival, and another succumbed shortly afterwards.

Notwithstanding her many bad passages and her forty-four years of voyaging, *Olivebank* still possesses quite a good turn of speed. For her five consecutive homeward runs with Australian grain since 1932 she has an average of 111 days, the best passage being 104 days in 1933. Undoubtedly she was unfortunate in her earlier Masters, for, under the command first of all of Captain J. M. Mattson and then of her present Master, Captain Lindvall, the old barque has manifested a new lease of life and sailed steadily and well. Captain Lindvall graduated to her poop from *Herzogin Cecilie*, where he had been Mate under Captain Sven Eriksson.

'*Pommern*'   *Pommern* (ex *Mneme*), another British-built barque, has held her present name since 1906 when she was sold by B. Wercke & Sohne of Hamburg to Ferdinand Laeisz. By the action of Reparations she passed to the Greek Government, from whom Erikson bought her shortly afterwards.

For those who have an abiding affection for the true type of deep-waterman, *Pommern*, although she sets no royals above her topgallants, is one of the handsomest of the surviving fourposters. Like *Archibald Russell*, she is graced by that fine, sweeping curve, imparted by an unbroken sheer-line, which is possible only in vessels having a long open main-deck, a short poop, low-built houses and no midship section. Among the existing square-riggers *Olivebank* also complies with these conditions, but, because of her greater size and fuller lines, she lacks the lower freeboard and more rakish appearance of the two smaller vessels.

Although, as a product of Italian yards, *Ponape* does not come under the heading of ex-Britishers, she is well worthy of comment because, in her later days, she was perhaps the finest model of a real 'old-timer' afloat. She looked particularly well under full canvas, especially when laden to her marks, because of the perfectly balanced placing of her four masts. With a dead-weight capacity of 3,450 tons against a gross tonnage of 2,342, her hull lines and sheer were pleasing to the eye, but perhaps because of that very grace of line, allied to the fact that she was not a water-ballast vessel, she was never among the best profit-earners of the Erikson Fleet. In the fight to keep deepwater sail at sea there has now come a time when vessels must pay or be scrapped, and in September 1936, *Ponape* was sold for £3,400, with delivery to Latvian shipbreakers at Libau (Liepaja). Captain Granith, who had commanded her for several years, had the unwelcome task of sailing her down from Nystad to Libau.

'Ponape'

Laeisz changed her name from *Regina Elena* to *Ponape* when he bought her in 1911. She was captured during the War by H.M.S. *Majestic*, while on passage from Iquique to Hamburg, and sold to James Bell & Company of Hull, who placed her, as *Bellhouse*, under the Norwegian flag. From 1923 to 1929, when Erikson bought her, she was operated by Captain Hugo Lundqvist of Mariehamn.

Captain Erikson is especially proud of the two fine ex-training barques *Viking* and *L'Avenir*, which he added to his fleet between 1929 and 1932. They are of similar design to *Herzogin Cecilie*, and as the

'Viking', 'L'Avenir', and 'Herzogin Cecilie'

97

full specification of the last named is to follow there is no need, here, to describe her two prototypes. For the same reason no details have yet been given of the purchase by Erikson of *Herzogin Cecilie*. Sufficient now to say that, for a minimum outlay, Erikson secured a splendid vessel, and one which at once became, and so remained for fifteen years, the flag-ship of his fleet. By her performances she earned much distinction and publicity, both for herself, her Captains and her owner.

Viking was built at Copenhagen, by the firm of Burmeister and Wain, as a Danish cadet-ship. After the tragic and, so far, unsolved fate of the great steel auxiliary five-masted cadet-barque *Kobenhavn* (which left Buenos Aires for Melbourne on December 14th, 1928, and was never heard of again), Denmark, deciding to dispense with big, cargo-carrying, cadet-vessels in favour of the smaller, purely training type, sold *Viking* to Captain Erikson.

L'Avenir, a strange name for a passing type, since it means 'The Future', was launched by the same builders and for the same purpose as *Herzogin Cecilie*, but on behalf of the Belgian Government. Erikson's opportunity came when Belgium replaced her by an auxiliary barquentine having no facilities for cargo. *L'Avenir* made several Australian grain passages under Belgian colours, one of which — 110 days in 1926 — was the best passage of that season.

The ex-Laeisz
vessels
'Passat',
'Pamir' and
'Penang'

Laeisz of Hamburg who, as mentioned in Chapter I, repurchased after the War six of his former 'P' fleet, was later compelled to relinquish those vessels, and Captain Erikson thus obtained such fine additions to his fleet as *Passat* and *Pamir*, which, with *Pommern*, *Penang*, and *Ponape*, brought, by 1932, his tally of big ex-Laeisz vessels up to five.

Great strength, both of hull and top-hamper, allied to a big cargo capacity, was always a feature of square-riggers constructed by German yards for the nitrate trade. Both *Passat* and *Pamir* have proved to be extraordinarily consistent makers of good grain passages since they became of Finnish registry. *Passat*, with an average of $100\frac{1}{2}$ days for her four passages to date, and *Pamir* with an average of 104 for five passages, head the performance tables of recent years. *Passat* in particular, as yet only twenty-one working years of age — if War years be excluded — and the youngest vessel in the Erikson Fleet, is a very sturdy, powerful barque, still fit for many years of hard work. All her accommodation is amidships, inbuilt as an integral part of the hull, and she is well equipped with winches for handling her exceptionally strong gear and heavy sparring.

A certain confusion arose because two vessels named *Albert Rickmers* were launched by the same builders. The first, a four-masted iron barque of 2,395 tons gross, built in 1895, became, in 1899, *Herzogin Sophie Charlotte*, a training vessel for the Norddeutscher Lloyd. The second, now the 2,019 ton three-masted barque *Penang*, was launched as a steel full-rigger in 1905. Rickmers operated the latter vessel themselves until 1911, when she was sold to Laeisz, and renamed. She was owned successively by Balhinaur of Bremen, Grimen of Hamburg, and Nurmeinen of Helsingfors, before being added, in 1925, to the Erikson Fleet. Although the criticism has been passed that by her conversion to a barque her hull became disproportionate to her top-hamper, she is, as may be seen from the photographs, a graceful and attractive vessel. She still carries the hatted bust of Herr Albert Rickmers at her prow.

The Erikson Fleet, however, is not limited to big grain-traders, for at the present time a dozen or more smaller craft fly the Erikson flag. So far, their owner has never abandoned the export trade of Baltic timber, that hard school in which so much of his extensive knowledge of sail matters was obtained by practical experience.

The 'onker' trade

In these days it is not a very lucrative business for sail, this 'onker' traffic as it is called, for it embraces only firewood and the like. The better side of the wood trade, which includes bigger timber, deals, battens, boards, scantlings, poles, props, etc., is now handled by steamers, British vessels carrying a large proportion.

Mr. Frank Bowen states that the origin of this curious term 'onker' was the 'onk-urr, onk-urr' of the windmill deck-pumps, which were fitted to the leaky old wooden vessels in whose hands the trade rested in the past, and to whom continuous pumping was a necessity.

Competition between Finland and the Soviet has cut such freights to a disastrous extent, and has adversely affected the entire timber trade; in fact, now that Russia has lifted the temporary embargo which she had placed upon timber exports, it is possible that the sailers' days in this trade are numbered. On one occasion in recent years, when the embargo was still in force, three of the grain traders — *Lawhill*, *Parma*, and *Mozart* — each made an intermediate, summer passage with full cargoes of Baltic firewood to the United Kingdom, a strange employment indeed for a Cape Horner'.

The trade term 'firewood' is a little misleading, as under that heading are included the short, residual lengths of timber left over from the completion of an order for bigger grades, and used for making boxes, tables, chairs, and so forth.

The smaller vessels of the Erikson Fleet

Among the smaller Erikson units there are some vessels of considerable interest to the student of sail. *Pestalozzi*, for instance, a recent purchase, is an iron barque of 1,047 tons gross, built by Blohm and Voss (the builders of *Pamir* and *Passat*) at Hamburg in 1884 for Laeisz, in whose arduous trade she, notwithstanding her size, rendered good service. She brings the total quota of ex-'P' vessels under the Erikson flag to-day to five. (See footnote opposite.)

It does not seem necessary to particularize about the several smaller barques, employed mainly in the Narrow Seas, which have, at one time or another, passed through Captain Erikson's hands, but which have, in the interim, been lost, sold, or scrapped. Such were *Lalla Rookh*, *Lingard*, and *Carmen*, all three well-known North Sea traders a few years back. The decease of the iron barque *Loch Linnhe*, however, is so recent, and she served Erikson so well, that she merits some comment. Built in 1876 by G. Thompson of Glasgow for Messrs J. & R. Wilson of that city, she started life as a full-rigged ship of 1,460 tons gross. Captain Erikson bought *Loch Linnhe* fourteen years ago, after she had undergone several changes of ownership. In her final years she was employed principally in the 'onker' trade, but, although small by modern standards, she carried Baltic timber to Melbourne in 1925, and also spent some time in the West Indies logwood trade. In November 1933, when returning in ballast from London to Mariehamn, she ran on to a skerry, known as Flisskär, near Kokar, forty miles to the southeast of Mariehamn. It was early morning; a severe snowstorm was raging and her rockets were unobserved. Not until 5 a.m. on the following day were the crew able to reach, by boat, the pilot station at Uto. Later they returned to the wreck, and found the old barque lying upright and with her masts still standing. Her bottom, however, was torn open, she was full of water, and so exposed to southerly gales that salvage was impracticable.

Kylemore was until November 1936, when she was sold to Hamburg buyers, the most ancient of the whole fleet, having been built by John

Reid of Port Glasgow in 1880. She is a steel barque of 1,229 tons gross, and, although fifty-six years old, her full Lloyd's 100 A1 class still holds good.[1]

In the matter of age it is interesting to note that Mariehamn possesses the two oldest sailing vessels making regular appearance in *Lloyd's Daily Index*. They are not owned by Captain Erikson. *Frideborg*, a composite barquentine of 510 tons gross, originally the tea-trader *Cleta*, was built by Gardner of Sunderland in 1866. No doubt, at three-score years and ten, she makes good use of the windmill pump which she now carries. *Sverre*, of 404 tons gross, was composite built as a steamer in 1872, and rebuilt as a barquentine in 1920. *Alastor*, an iron barque of 850 tons gross, owned at Hango in Finland, and built in 1875 by Mounsey & Foster at Sunderland, almost ranks with the other two ancients. Despite her great age, she is still 100 A1 at Lloyd's, and is one of the trimmest vessels in the 'onker' trade.

The oldest sailing vessels in Lloyd's Index

Erikson's wooden barque *Varma* (or *Warma*, as she is given in the Registers) is a picturesque, bluff-bowed, little vessel. She was built at Nystad in 1922, and, with a gross tonnage of 718, her dimensions are 201 × 35 × 17 feet.[1]

The remainder of the fleet consists of a rather heterogeneous collection of three small auxiliary vessels and several wooden barquentines and schooners of local build, including the four-masted schooner *Dione*. Captain Erikson owns two somewhat unorthodox motor vessels of about 450 tons gross, *Sweden*, of Swedish origin in 1920, built of wood and driven by Bolinder oil engines, and *Vera*, also oil powered, built, of composite materials, at Norrkoping in 1918. He also operates his own tug, *Johanna*, and his own shipyard, with a slipway, at Nystad.

Besides the Erikson contingent, there are, also, a few other big square-riggers still engaged in active trading, and the following list embodies every such vessel in commission at the end of 1936.

A complete list of all big square-riggers now in commission

There are several still serviceable big barques laid up on the west coast of the United States. One or two other old sailers are used by American film concerns, and a number of other sailing vessels are in use in different parts of the world for training purposes only. In 1921 the number of sailing vessels visiting Australian ports, in various trades, was given as 304, of which 68 loaded homeward grain cargoes. By 1922 this total had dropped to 138, and only 7 loaded grain. Again, in 1930,

[1] *Pestalozzi*, *Varma* and *Kylemore* all went to Continental shipbreakers early in 1937.

THE BIG TRADING SQUARE-RIGGE

(in order of g

(Particulars f

Name	Flag	Formerly named	Rig	Registered Tonnage			Classification So
				Gross	Under-deck	Net	
Priwall	German		4-mast barque	3,185	2,849	2,834	Germanische Lloyd
Passat	Finnish		,,	3,137	2,759	2,585	Lloyd's
Moshulu	Finnish	*Kurt*	,,	3,116	2,881	2,911	American R — now Ll
Padua	German		,,	3,064	2,713	2,678	Lloyd's
Lawhill	Finnish		,,	2,816	2,696	2,540	Lloyd's
Pamir	Finnish		,,	2,799	2,528	2,365	Lloyd's
Olivebank	Finnish	*Olivebank Caledonia*	,,	2,795	2,639	2,427	Lloyd's
L'Avenir	Finnish		,,	2,754	2,200	1,871	Bureau Veri
Viking	Finnish		,,	2,670	2,324	2,154	Lloyd's
Pommern	Finnish	*Mneme*	,,	2,376	2,203	2,114	Germanische Lloyd
Archibald Russell	Finnish		,,	2,354	—	2,048	British Cor tion
Abraham Rydberg	Swedish	*Hawaiian Isles Star of Greenland*	,,	2,345	1,984	1,966	Lloyd's
C. B. Pedersen	Swedish	*Emanuel Accame Ferm Elsa Olander Svecia*	,,	2,142	1,929	1,843	Lloyd's
Penang	Finnish	*Albert Rickmers* (full-rigged ship)	3-mast barque	2,019	1,871	1,743	Germanische Lloyd
Winterhude	Finnish	*Mabel Rickmers Winterhude Selma Hemsoth*	,,	1,980	1,805	1,709	Bureau Veri
Killoran	Finnish		,,	1,817	1,675	1,523	Lloyd's

F THE WORLD IN DECEMBER 1936

nnage and excluding auxiliaries)

oyd's Register for 1936-7).

ilt	Builder	Owner	Length	Breadth	Depth	P.	B. or H.	F.	Code Signal letters
			Dimensions (in feet)			Superstructures P = Poop-deck B = Bridge-deck, i.e. midship section F = Fo'c'sle H = Large deckhouse			
20	Blohm & Voss, Hamburg	Laeisz (Hamburg)	323	47	26	30	B.65	38	DIRQ
11	Blohm & Voss, Hamburg	Erikson (Marie-hamn)	323	47	26	53	B.69	36	OHQR
04	W. Hamilton, Glasgow	Erikson	335	46	26	20	B.65	32	OHZD
26	Tecklenborg, Weser-munde	Laeisz	320	46	25	53	B.65	31	DIRR
02	Thompson, Dundee	Erikson	317	45	25	42	B.48	33	OHQA
05	Blohm & Voss, Hamburg	Erikson	316	46	26	16	B.66	36	OHQP
02	Mackie & Thomson, Glasgow	Erikson	326	43	24	40	—	28	OHQM
08	Rickmers, Bremerhaven	Erikson	278	45	26	170	—	38	OHPZ
07	Burmeister & Wain, Copenhagen	Erikson	294	46	24	201	—		OHRU
03	Reid, Glasgow	Erikson	310	43	24	37	—	32	OHQW
05	Scott's, Greenock	Erikson	291	43	24	41	—	36	OHPC
02	Connell, Glasgow	Thulin (Stock-holm)	261	43	23	72	B.53	28	SIMN
01	Continental Iron Company, Pertusola	Pedersen (Gothenburg)	289	40	25	48	H.128	36	SIYN
05	Rickmers, Bremerhaven	Erikson	265	40	24	48	—	42	OHQS
08	Rickmers, Bremerhaven	Erikson	285	40	24	45	—	38	OHRV
0	Ailsa S.B. Company, Troon	Erikson	261	39	23	46	—	30	OHPW

a year of bad harvests (see notes on freights for 1930), only 7 sailing vessels secured charters, and another carried wool. By 1934 the grain fleet had risen to as many as 22, including one auxiliary vessel, but, according to the foregoing schedule, the total for 1937, if every available deepwater windjammer, including the two Laeisz representatives, should secure a grain cargo, cannot exceed 16.

It would seem then that the last days of the big square-rigger are to be numbered, apart from other contributory causes, by the lifetimes of the present vessels, because there are so few possibilities of depletion, by loss or break-up, being made good. The Laeisz barques, *Padua* and *Priwall*, sole survivors of a once great fleet of sail, may, conceivably, one day fly the Erikson flag; one or other of the handful of old windjammers laid up in America might, like *Moshulu*, Captain Erikson's latest purchase, prove worth recommissioning. Few of the sail-training vessels of to-day are economically suitable for use as traders, owing to their limited capacity and to the fact that most of them have auxiliary engines. Finally, it is reasonably certain that no new sailing vessels of the requisite type will ever again leave the stocks, and so, when the tall ships of this book pass, deepwater sail will be but a memory, and the Erikson Fleet one of the legends of maritime history.

Analysis of the sail quota of 1937

There are one or two comments worth detailing in regard to the 1937 schedule. All the vessels shown therein are built of steel: five of the sixteen date from the last century, the oldest, *C. B. Pedersen*, from 1891. Only two, the Laeisz barques, are of post-war construction. Thirteen are four-masted barques, the other three being three-masted barques, for not one full-rigger is left in commission. Every vessel holds the classification of one or other of the leading Register Societies, and the ten which are classed by *Lloyd's Register* are all, still, 100 A1. Seven are British built, seven German, one Italian, and one Danish. Germany owns two, Sweden two (these four barques being used, in part, as cadet-ships), and the remaining dozen are all registered at Mariehamn as the property of Captain Erikson.

'Moshulu'

Moshulu must be considered fortunate in her emergence from a forced retirement of eight years at Seattle, for it seemed unlikely that she would ever go to sea again. A large sum was needed to get her into good trim. She had to be re-rigged completely, the work being undertaken by personnel sent out to Seattle from Finland, and supervised by Captain Boman, formerly Master of *Grace Harwar*.

104

One vessel in the list merits a little space if only because she is the sole sailer still afloat ever to have borne the proud title of 'Skysail-yarder'. When called the *Hawaiian Isles*, *Abraham Rydberg* set skysails on main and mizen. She is now the last four-masted barque to retain the old-fashioned, big, single topgallant-sails. As *Star of Greenland* she formed part of the famous Star Fleet of the Alaska Packers' Association, trading on the west coast of North America. Of all that fine fleet of by-gone days *Abraham Rydberg* is the only representative in commission to-day. In 1929 Sweden bought her from the Alaska Packers, since when she has carried a large and regular complement of young cadets, who, as crew, learn practical seamanship under trading conditions. The present owners of *Abraham Rydberg* are not concerned primarily with passage-making. The cadets are there to serve a certain minimum apprenticeship in sail, and for this purpose long voyages are advantageous. Again, as a training vessel she is kept always in meticulous condition, and as Captain S. Tamm, who commanded her for many years, once wrote: 'You cannot keep a vessel in good shape and have her battered about in trying to make a record passage in stormy weather.' The Horn route home is very hard on a sailing vessel, especially if she be manned partly by unskilled labour, and *Abraham Rydberg's* management think more of the uninterrupted training routine, which is attainable only under fine-weather conditions, than of unnecessary exposure to hardship. Consequently, it is quite usual for this barque to choose the alternative way via the Cape of Good Hope, and she makes no attempt to qualify for the lead in what is so often miscalled the 'Annual Grain Race'.

This barque is now, in part, supported by an endowment fund which, many years ago, was instituted by a Swedish shipowner named Abraham Rydberg. The Society's first vessel was the little brig *Gustavus Adolphus*; she was followed by a full-rigger bearing the name of the donor of the fund; the present training-vessel is the third to perpetuate his name. *Abraham Rydberg* is usually ahead of the windjammer time schedule because, between her Australian voyages, she spends less time in port in Europe than do the Erikson vessels. It is her general practice to sail outward from Gothenburg a full month before any of the other vessels in the trade leave home. This enables her to complete her loading and to quit Spencer Gulf in early January, sometimes weeks before the slower vessels among her competitors have arrived in Australia. As a result, notwithstanding her unhurried homeward passages, *Abraham Rydberg* has on several occasions in recent years been hailed, quite erroneously, by the Press as the 'Winner of the Grain Race' because she has happened to be the first windjammer of the year to reach English waters. The length of the passage, of course, is the only decisive factor for comparative purposes, and is, in her case, always improved upon by later arrivals. So far her best homeward passage was 107 days in 1934, and she has never yet accomplished the shortest passage of the year.

'Parma'   Because, only as recently as September 1936, she was sold for conversion into a coal-hulk, *Parma* could not be included in the foregoing list. I feel, nevertheless, that she deserves some mention, especially as she figures elsewhere in this book. She was launched in 1902 at Port Glasgow, by Messrs A. Rodger & Company, for the Anglo-American Oil Company Limited, of London. Ten years later, Laeisz bought her for £15,000, and employed her in the nitrate trade until 1914. She was interned at Iquique for six years, then allocated to England, and repurchased by Laeisz. In 1930 she was laid up at Hamburg for a year, and then passed into Finnish hands, being operated by a syndicate, one member of which was Captain Ruben de Cloux, past Master of *Herzogin Cecilie*. He took command, and she made several successful voyages in the grain trade, one of which, 83 days in 1933, was the finest passage from Australia under sail since the War.

Parma, with a gross tonnage of 3,047, possessed a large carrying capacity and a fine turn of speed. Except for a run of ill-fortune, she might still be in commission. In 1935, when leaving Barry, she incurred a net loss of about £300 for a fouled anchor, which necessitated her return to Barry Dock, the anchor being salved later. A collision with the dock-wall at Glasgow, when entering to discharge her 1936 cargo, brought a heavy bill, for, besides damage to her bows of, roughly, £700, she had to meet a liability of £150 for repairs to the dock. *Parma* held the distinction among Finnish square-riggers of being partly protected by insurance, but the conditions of her policy — total and constructive total loss, general average and salvage charges only — were of little help to her owners in such circumstances. Although she was not due for reclassification until 1937, she needed, in addition to the bow repairs, about £200 in minor renovations, and her owners deemed it wise to sell *Parma* as she lay, for £3,350, rather than spend nearly £1,000 on reconditioning her. As narrow as that is the margin to-day between profit and loss from sail tonnage, and thus yet another of the tall ships passed. It is understood that, when she has been stripped down to a bare shell, *Parma* will be towed out to Haifa.

It is hoped that the following notes on the identification of the wind-jammers of to-day will prove useful to any readers who may have the good fortune to encounter one or other of those barques at sea under sail. No claim is made for completeness in regard to any individual vessel. As some of the details are dependent on memory, aided by photographs, I cannot even vouch for their absolute authenticity, but a combination of the facts given about any one vessel can apply, *in toto*, to that vessel alone and to no other at present in commission. In years gone by, such descriptions would have been quite inadequate, in view of the large number of windjammers then in existence. Those ranks are so depleted that it is possible to give sufficient data to provide an infallible means of identification between the eleven vessels catalogued.

The identification of the last of the windjammers

Unless otherwise mentioned, they are four-masted barques, setting single spankers, double topgallants, and royals. In each individual barque her fore, main and mizen masts are of approximately equal height. Nationality and code-signal letters appear in a previous table. Colour is apt to be a changeable factor. At the present time *L'Avenir* and *Viking* are white-hulled, with white or light-coloured sparring. *Abraham Rydberg's* upper plating is grey, and she has white boot-topping and white topsides. All the others are black above the water-line, and, generally, their spars are yellow-ochre or brown. Without exception, deck-houses, midship-sections and the like are white-painted.

Unfortunately, five out of the sixteen surviving deepwater sailing-vessels are so much alike that, although to the seaman's eye there are a host of minor discrepancies, it is not possible to specify enough major points to provide a sure means of differentiation at a distance.

Pamir, Passat, Moshulu, Padua and *Priwall* are all big black-hulled craft with large midship-sections, bowsprit-netting, double spankers, double topgallants, and royals. They all steer from amid-ships. *Padua* and *Priwall* fly German colours, and carry a small wire-less pole at the head of the mizen topgallant mast, a feature which is absent in the three Finns. To the eye there appears little difference in tonnage, and there is a total variation of only four feet in the length of

107

AN IDENTIFICATION TABLE O

Name	Peculiarities of rig	Outstanding deck-erections, etc.
Abraham Rydberg	Single topgallant sails Triangular mainsail and cross-jack Rather square aloft Pole spanker with no gaff topsail	Midship section and forward deck-hous Flying bridges to poop and foredeck Extensive poop
Archibald Russell	———	Deck-house forward of mainmast Smaller house abaft mizen Flying bridge fore and aft Good sheer-line
C. B. Pedersen	Triangular mainsail and cross-jack Mizen mast shorter than fore and main masts	Long, high deck-house forward; sma house amidships. Both housing lifebo
Killoran	Three-masted barque with double top-gallants and royals	Deck-house aft of foremast Small bridge joined to the poop by a sh catwalk
L'Avenir	Triangular mainsail and cross-jack Prominent wireless spreader half-way up jigger topmast Lower masts and topmasts in one piece	Very long poop-deck having a short rai sector and a donkey-house between mainmast and the break of the po High boat-skids forward of mizen
Lawhill	Baldheaded, i.e. minus royals Lower masts and topmasts in one piece Topgallant masts stepped abaft the top-mast caps	Short midship section with donkey-ho on after end Flying bridge to poop, crossing boat-s Full hull lines
Olivebank	———	Big deck-house aft of foremast and smaller houses Very short poop, commencing at jigg mast No flying bridges Full hull lines
Penang	Three-masted barque Double topgallants and royals	Deck-house between fore and main m Boat-skids forward of good-sized poop No flying bridges
Pommern	Baldheaded	Big deck-house between fore and m and smaller house forward of poop Good sheer-line
Viking	Small wireless spreaders at main, mizen and jigger trucks	Very long poop deck with no raised se Foremast rises from well-deck High boat-skids forward of chart-hous Yacht-like stern, with no vertical cou
Winterhude	Three-masted barque Baldheaded Double spanker	Deck-house between fore and main m

E LAST OF THE WINDJAMMERS

Figurehead	Bowsprit netting	Steering position	Wheel-house
Yes	Under forward part only	Aft	No
Yes	No	Aft	Yes
No	No	Aft	No
Yes	No	Aft	Big
No	No	Amidships, with spare wheel aft	No
Yes	No	Aft	Yes
Yes	No	Aft	Yes
Yes	Yes	Aft	No
Yes	No	Aft	No
No	Yes	Aft	No
No	Yes	Aft	No

the raised midship-sections of the five craft. *Moshulu* and *Pamir* have much shorter poop-decks than the other three vessels, but there is nothing to choose between the area of any of the five fo'c'sle decks.

The Erikson creed

In *Seadogs of To-day* Mr. Villiers quotes these words of Captain Gustaf Erikson's:

'I love those ships. I have spent my life in them and for them I will keep on. When I go, they go, but while I stay, they stay. I will never be a steamship owner. I may be forced to sell or to give up some of my ships, but I shall keep all those I can while I live.

'How can I keep on? Because I never have a holiday; because I look after them all, personally; because I do not let others do anything I can do myself; because I keep always a good lot of young chaps in them who are trained, in them, to become officers; and because not one of them is insured. I cannot afford to have them insured. If I had to pay the rates the underwriters ask, I would have to give them up, every one. If I lose my ships I lose everything.

'But I have been Mate and Master too. I have my ships brought home whenever they have to lay up in Europe, and I climb the rigging and go out along the yards myself and do my own surveying. I see that they are free from rust, that the gear is good and the rigging sound, that the masts and yards will carry their sail round the Horn and anywhere else I send them.

'Australian harvests spoil, steamers take the guano, port charges are impossible, tugs regard the sailing ship as easy prey, and, in all but the most outlandish port, it is asking for loss to allow my ships to go. If they be lost, everything is lost, for I get nothing.'

Hull insurance

The compulsion to dispense with hull insurance in order to produce a profit from the operation of sail is, as he indicates above, a most vital factor in Gustaf Erikson's scheme of management. The burden of the risk which he thereby accepts is heavy, for, besides acting as marine-superintendent of the fleet, Captain Erikson, it must always be remembered, has taken no partners into his unique business.

This principle of uninsured operation applies solely to the ship-owner's own interests and liabilities in regard to hull and freight. The insurance of Employer's Liability in respect of the crew is compulsory by Finnish law, and is covered under a Government scheme, which,

facing: CAPTAIN GUSTAF ERIKSON IN 1931

Gustaf Erikson

however, embraces no protection for loss of life or personal injury inflicted on third parties.

The cargoes carried by the Erikson vessels are, as the property of the shippers, the consignees, or the charterers, the subject of separate insurance by the interested parties, the policy passing with the goods in the event of resale during the voyage. The shipowner, as a common carrier, is not responsible for the fortuitous loss, by perils of the sea and so forth, of goods placed in his charge, providing that he exercises due diligence and takes normal precautions to ensure safe delivery. This matter of cargo insurance has played its part in the decline of wind-jamming, for, among the many economic issues which it governs, the cost of insurance can be a major factor in deciding the manner, the route and the means by which goods shall be transported. *Cargo insurance*

A few years before the War the rate charged in London to cover full cargoes of Australian grain to U.K. and/or the Continent in sailers owned by British, German, Norwegian or Russian firms, or by approved Italian owners or by Dom Bordes of France, was 30s. per cent on the value of the cargo for vessels up to 15 years of age; 40s. per cent up to 25 years; 50s. per cent up to 30 years; and 70s. per cent up to 35 years. Frenchmen (other than Bordes) were 50s. per cent up to 20 years, etc. At that time the corresponding rate for good steamers was 10s. per cent to U.K., Havre, or Antwerp, and 12s. 6d. per cent to other Continental ports not north of Hamburg.

To-day, because of improvements in navigation, and through a general trend in market conditions, the steamer rate is just about one-half of the above rates, whereas that for barques of 25 to 30 years of age (the average age of the present Erikson Fleet) is still, roughly, the same as it was a quarter of a century ago. In other words, it now costs eight to ten times as much, in general, to insure Australian grain in sail as in steam, the difference being reflected in the lower rate of freight paid to sail tonnage.

This differentiation is not due wholly to the actual difference in the risk, but, like freight, is partly the outcome of supply and demand. **When, as now, there are only sixteen possible risks of the one type to** be insured, underwriters cannot make a well-balanced book from them, for one loss might wipe out all the premium earned by the coverage of sail cargoes over a considerable period. Suppose, for example, that the average cargo per vessel be 4,000 tons of grain valued at, say, £20,000.

111

Then, the total consignment carried by all the sixteen existing wind-jammers would be worth £320,000, which, at 50s. per cent, would produce a total premium of £8,000 gross, or less brokerage, etc., about £7,500 net to underwriters. The total loss of any one vessel would involve the insurance market in a payment of £20,000, the equivalent of the entire premium accruing from sail in three years.

Owing to the loss in 1936 of *Herzogin Cecilie*, and of almost her entire cargo, it is probable that the insurance premiums for the 1937 grain cargoes under sail will be increased. Thus, the repercussions of one loss impose an added burden on the remaining windjammers, for a rise of 20 per cent in the insurance cost of their future cargoes would mean, at the present price of grain (about £8 10s. a ton), advancing the difference between the coverage of steam and sail to the equivalent of nearly 5s. per ton of grain. (December, 1936. Rates have been put up by 10/-%).

Maritime hazards   There are, of course, many other happenings besides actual total loss which bring claims under the cargo policies, but they are often a more serious matter for the vessel than for her contents. Now that wooden hulls are a thing of the past fire is not a serious hazard in the grain trade, collision, stranding and dismasting being the most prolific sources of expense to the uninsured owner of sail tonnage. It is almost essential for the modern windjammer to avoid such eventualities if she is to be worth maintaining. Even a slight stranding, not severe enough to involve new plating, may necessitate heavy expense for dry-docking and survey. More serious stranding, as in the case of *Herzogin Cecilie*, can easily develop into total loss, for the intending salvor of an uninsured sailing vessel is in a curious position to-day.

His remuneration is based on the arrived damaged value of the property salved, and, nine times out of ten, the only value possessed to-day by the hull of a salvaged but badly damaged sailer would be its value as scrap. Consequently, unless the salvage of the cargo offers to the salvor sufficient inducement in itself for him to undertake the job, it is unlikely that he will commit himself to any great expenditure in respect of the hull.

The theory that a windjammer encounters her greatest perils round about landfall is equally as true to-day as in the past great days of sail, and is reflected in the list of post-War casualties to sailing vessels. It is still the custom for some of the many underwriters interested in cargoes under sail to reinsure their commitments on what is known as the '12°

West' basis. This means that they transfer their liability elsewhere, by the payment of a reinsurance premium of less than half that which they received for the entire voyage, from the time that the vessel passes the longitude of 12°W. and so enters the area where stranding and collision are most likely to occur, and where lurks fog, the most dreaded, by seamen, of all forms of weather.

Under the 'Rules of the Road at Sea' it is the duty of steam to give way to sail, and a windjammer is rarely held liable for collision by a Court of Inquiry, provided that her lights were in order at the time. On the other hand, it would appear, in view of the large number of accidents which have taken place in the congested waters of the English Channel, to be fatally easy for a steamer to underestimate the speed of the big sailing vessel running up or down Channel before a fair wind. The steamer is by no means always at fault. A windjammer carries no lights above deck level, and only the port and starboard lights from her fore-deck lighthouses show ahead: these, being set a trifle inboard, may be only partly visible to an oncoming steamer unless the two vessels are approaching each other at a considerable angle.

The precincts of the Channel have proved to be a veritable grave-yard for the nitrate sailers of Laeisz's 'Flying P' Line. The great five-master *Preussen* was lost in 1910 on her way down Channel. The Newhaven-Dieppe steamer *Brighton* attempted to cross her bows instead of running under her stern, and the two vessels came into violent collision. A south-east gale increased the peril of the disabled windjammer, and although a pair of tugs did their utmost to bring her into Dover, she drove ashore under Shakespeare Cliff, and became a wreck.

Windjammers in collision

In 1912 *Pisagua*, loaded deep with nitrate, collided with the P. & O. liner *Oceana* off Newhaven. The steamer sank in shallow water, and, after her specie had been removed by divers, she was blown up. *Pisagua*, badly damaged, was repaired at Dover, but Laeisz subsequently sold her to Norway.

A third Laeisz sailer to be lost by collision in home-waters was the 3,000 ton four-masted barque *Pangani*. When outward-bound she was run into off Cap la Hogue by the steamer *Phryne*, and sank almost immediately, with a loss of all but four of her personnel.

In 1928 the French steamer *Daphne* ran across the bows of the outward-bound *Passat* (then a Laeisz barque) when twenty miles south-west of Dungeness: the steamer was cut down, and sank in ten minutes.

In 1929 the Russian four-masted training-barque *Tovarisch* (George Duncan's old steel full-rigger *Lauriston*, of 2,301 tons gross, built at Belfast in 1892) ran down and sank the Italian steamer *Alcantara* in the Channel.

Erikson's *Lawhill*, outward-bound in ballast from the Baltic, sank the Polish steamer *Niemen*, in thick weather, late in 1932, ten miles NW. by N. of the Skaw, an even more crowded and confined locality than the English Channel.

Abraham Rydberg, laden with grain, was coming up-Channel in 1936 when, at midnight on Sunday, May 10th, she was run into by the British steamer *Koranton*, bound south from Newcastle. The barque was hit near her fo'c'sle head, sustaining damage to the plating of her port bow. In swinging round, the steamer carried away some of *Abraham Rydberg's* main back-stays, and the main topmast collapsed in the way of the doublings, snapping its yards. *Koranton* was practically unhurt, but the sailer was later towed from London to Blyth for repairs. While in tow, near Tilbury, one of her cadets fell from aloft, and was killed.

The Erikson post-War record
Until the wreck of *Herzogin Cecilie*, underwriters had not suffered a major loss on cargo carried in any of the Erikson windjammers, trading deepwater, during the eighteen years which have elapsed since the War. In that period three, in all, of those vessels were totally lost, but only one — *Herzogin Cecilie* — seriously affected the insurance market. In her case, not only did Erikson lose one of his finest vessels without reimbursement but, also, that part of her freight which would have been payable on arrival, and which, likewise, was uninsured. Of her total gross freight of £5,400 for that passage, about £1,400 had been paid in advance at Port Lincoln, and was not returnable: the remainder, due at the discharge port of Ipswich, was forfeited by her non-arrival.

Distance freight'
An interesting point arose in this connection: under Finnish law the principle of 'distance freight' is admitted, whereby the shipowner is entitled to freight based on the distance he has carried any cargo which may be landed or salved elsewhere than at the destination named in the charter-party. In the case of *Herzogin Cecilie* — lost when her voyage was almost completed — Captain Erikson could, had Finnish practice applied, have claimed almost the entire freight attaching to that part of the cargo which was saved, but limited to the net proceeds of such grain after deduction of salvage expenses. Although a Finnish vessel, *Herzogin*

Cecilie had, however, an Australian charter-party for cargo which was consigned to a British port, and she was wrecked on the English coast. In such circumstances salvage is governed by British law, which does not recognize 'distance freight'.

Of his two other major post-War catastrophes, which both occurred in 1932, the first vessel, *Hougomont*, was in ballast when fatally dismasted in Australian waters. The second, *Melbourne*, sunk in collision off the Irish coast, was fully laden with grain, but the cost of the hull and a large part of the cargo claim were reimbursed by the colliding steamer, whose owners admitted liability for the fatality. A full account of these two casualties will follow in due course.

The long period of successful trading which Erikson enjoyed between 1919 and 1932, when vessels like *Lawhill*, *Archibald Russell*, *Grace Harwar* and *Herzogin Cecilie* were earning steady and regular freights without undue deduction for repairs, besides enabling him to build up his fleet doubtless aided him to withstand the financial misfortunes of succeeding years. It may, perhaps, be presumed that the dangerous corner of non-insurance was turned by the luck of those older vessels and by the skill of those who manned them. Having so completely dispelled the spectre of capital depreciation by astute and timely purchasing that the question of writing down his assets year by year did not arise, Captain Erikson built up a system of maintenance based on personal supervision and governed by the tenets of wise economy. It is, however, sound, well-judged economy and not parsimony, for under no consideration does he send a vessel to sea in other than a seaworthy condition, and his Masters are under strict orders to avoid unnecessary risks.

The Erikson method

Naturally, when dealing with vessels already twenty-five or thirty years old, wear and tear take a steadily mounting toll. Following, in a practical fashion, the sea-tradition of the bygone days of sail, the Erikson captains and officers cherish to the best of their ability those old windjammers; but, no matter how great the care lavished upon them by a meticulous owner and a proud Master, a time is bound to come when further outlay is uneconomic, and break-up becomes the only solution.

Wear and tear and break-up

At reasonable scrap prices this fate represents, from the owner's point of view, the most satisfactory ending to worn-out tonnage. In the past Finnish owners reckoned that the profits of the first three or four years of successful trading should reimburse them for the purchase price of a big second-hand square-rigger. To-day, when half the voyaging is in ballast, that period has lengthened, but once the windjammer has paid for herself, future net earnings represent clear profit. If at the finish of her useful sea life she then brings even £1 per ton as scrap metal, she can surely be regarded as a profitable investment, always supposing that she had traded without serious casualty. *Grace Harwar* was a very good example of such a history. (May, 1937. Scrap is now £3 per ton.)

The beginning of the end?   Concurrent with the penning of this Chapter in September 1936, comes the notification of the sale of two more of the square-riggers, *Parma* and *Ponape*. Captain Erikson also gave consideration recently to an offer he received from Messrs Lauritzen of Denmark for the purchase of *L'Avenir* as a training-ship.

Is this the beginning of the end? Only one man can answer this question, the man who to-day owns just three-quarters of the survivors of deepwater commercial square-rig. Mayhap the heavy loss which he incurred in respect of *Herzogin Cecilie* and her freight has turned the scale between profit and loss, for she is the fifth of his bigger vessels to go within five years: in 1932 *Melbourne* was sunk, and *Hougomont* dismasted and scuttled; in 1935 *Grace Harwar* was broken up; in 1936 *Herzogin Cecilie* was wrecked, and *Ponape* broken up. At this rate of depletion the fleet, as such, cannot continue much longer, for those five years have seen only one replacement of tonnage (*Moshulu*).

Three other square-riggers, all owned in Finland, have been broken up during that short period — *Favell* in 1934, *Mozart* (the last barquentine to trade to Australia) in 1935, and *Parma* in 1936. Out of a total of twenty-three big windjammers trading in 1932, over one-third have disappeared in the succeeding five years, and only one resurrection of laid-up tonnage has taken place. Sixteen are in commission to-day, of which twelve are owned by Gustaf Erikson. In very truth, the tall ships pass!

Dismasting   The owner of sail is, in a way, more concerned with a vessel's condition aloft than with that of the hull, because, apart from collision and stranding, dismasting is his most dreaded casualty, it now being almost synonymous with total or constructive total loss. The principle of constructive total loss has been likened to a shilling which, having fallen into an inaccessible location, requires the expenditure of several shillings' worth of labour to recover it. So with a square-rigger crippled by the loss of her top-hamper: in most parts of the world to-day, apart from salvage expenses, it would cost more than her low market value to refit her, and the owner must realize what he can by selling her as she lies, usually for scrap.

A case in point was the Finnish training-cum-trading four-masted barque *Fennia* (ex *Champigny*). She was dismasted in 1927 off the Horn on a voyage from Cardiff to Valparaiso. She reached Port Stanley, in the Falklands, but repairs were impracticable at that lonely spot, and, the cost of towage to a suitable port being prohibitive, her hulk remains to this day as a store-ship at Port Stanley.

The final dismasting of Erikson's *Hougomont* was one of the most spectacular events in the story of latter-day sail. It was said of *Hougomont* that she had been more frequently in serious trouble than any other windjammer of her generation. She was a deep-framed, four-masted barque, built in 1897 by Scott's of Greenock for John Hardie & Company of Glasgow. In 1902, when homeward-bound from San Francisco to Liverpool, she drove ashore in the Solway Firth. With her hatches stove in and her topgallant masts down, she had every appearance of a total loss, but the Liverpool Salvage Association refloated her, and she was repaired and re-masted. She was posted 'Missing' at Lloyd's in 1908, when 80 guineas per cent was quoted for her by the 'Overdue' market. Three months after leaving Coquimbo for Tocopilla (both West Coast of South American ports) she arrived, however, at Sydney, New South Wales, having been prevented, by head winds, from making Tocopilla. In 1914 she was once more badly ashore, this time in thick fog outside New York, but was again refloated, and repaired.

Hougomont was at sea throughout the War, and then in 1924, after she had been laid-up at St. Nazaire for three years, Hardie's sold her to Erikson. She was partly de-sparred for the third time in 1928, off the Portuguese coast when outward-bound to Melbourne, and was towed into Lisbon, where she lay for a month refitting. Four years later the end came. She left Gravesend on December 31st, 1931, but did not pass Prawle Point until February 2nd, 1932; surely a record for delayed progression at sea. Much of this period was spent beating around the North Sea in winter gales, and it was followed by a collision in the Channel, *Hougomont*, however, being exonerated from blame. At 1 a.m. on April 21st *Hougomont* was in Latitude 39° 34' S., Longitude 126° 53' E., in the Great Australian Bight, 530 miles south-west of Cape Borda (Kangaroo Island). She was then 111 days out from London and was

The dismastings of 'Hougomont'

117

making her way to Spencer Gulf to load grain. As the westerly wind was freshening and a big swell running, the Second Mate ordered the watch to make fast royals and fore and mizen upper-topgallants, so as to lessen the excessive rolling of an empty vessel. Suddenly, without warning, a vast, black pall of cloud raced toward the barque, the barometer falling to an alarming extent. The Master was called, and all hands were ordered to relieve *Hougomont* of the remaining upper canvas. Before this could be carried out the vessel was struck by a cyclone, whose velocity was afterwards estimated as being about 100 miles an hour. The fore-topmast was the first item to go, and in its collapse it brought down the mainmast and much of the mizen rigging. The fore-mast buckled just below the foretop; the mainmast snapped six feet from the deck; and the mizen gave at the head of its topmast. Two men had reached the foot-ropes of the mizen upper-topgallant yard when the squall hit the barque: this spar snapped like a withered branch, throwing the men backward. They were, however, flattened against the standing-rigging by the tremendous wind long enough for them to secure a hold, and they reached deck uninjured. Two other men, one of them a Graduate of Yale working his passage for the sake of the experience, were also in the rigging, but they slid down the back-stays to safety. The suddenness of the collapse was terrifying. *Hougomont*, borne down by the dead weight of broken top-hamper dragging overside, assumed a dangerous list, and all on board expected her at any minute to fall on to her beam ends and capsize. Loose wires and lengths of chain-sheet were flaying about like whips; heavy blocks were swinging wildly from the loose gear, threatening to brain those on deck. The most imminent danger lay in the suspended wreckage of the fore-topgallant mast, the fore-topmast and the mainmast: this mass crashed against the starboard side of the hull with every roll, and, it seemed, must soon pierce the steel-plating. The fore-yard, one of the heaviest of the spars, had buckled in the centre, and now, with its yard-arms against either bulwark, formed a gigantic and menacing triangle; while the cross-jack yard was completely cock-billed. Every soul of the twenty-five aboard, Master, Mates and crew, made superhuman efforts to save themselves and the vessel. The squall, passing as quickly as it had come, left in its wake a turbulent sea, and *Hougomont* rolled so violently that, notwithstanding her list, she dipped each rail alternately. With chisel, hammer, axe and saw the crew strove to release her from the encumbrance pounding overside.

Somehow, tackle was passed around the wreckage of the foremast to take the strain while the steel-wire rigging was severed. Up aloft, one of the mizen yards, its braces carried away, was swaying wildly between mizen and jigger; two boys were sent aloft to control it and prevent it from falling to the deck. To the relief of all concerned, the hatches were found to be undamaged, and when the carpenter sounded the wells and reported that the old barque, despite her thirty-five years at sea and her many vicissitudes, was making no water, matters looked more hopeful. By 10 a.m. *Hougomont* was freed from much of the encumbering debris, but, suddenly, the fierce rolling brought down the weakened mizen and part of the jigger. The Third Mate missed death by inches when a falling spar smashed the lifeboat which he was engaged in provisioning. This left only one lifeboat intact, although, in the sea that was running at the time, abandonment was almost an impossibility. Another spar crashed into the poop-deck, and also destroyed the standard compass. The uncontrolled spanker-boom had crushed the wheel-house, while the gaff-boom yawed from side to side: two men went aloft on the jigger to deal with these spars.

By 1.15 p.m., after nearly twelve hours' continuous toil under appalling conditions, the barque was placed on an even keel again, and the exhausted crew had their first spell. All that now remained of *Hougomont's* tophamper were the three jagged stumps of fore, mizen and jigger lower-masts, the cross-jack being the only yard *in situ*. Some forty feet or so of the mainmast, which had broken just above the deck, lay across the starboard bulwark, projecting overside at right angles to the hull. The galley was gutted, the living quarters a welter of sodden rubbish, but the decks were clear, the hull was sound and the immediate danger past.

Now followed a truly remarkable feat of seamanship, one which probably saved *Hougomont's* owner many hundreds of pounds in salvage charges and brought the barque into port without any loss of life.

Captain Ragnar Lindholm, hampered by the loss of his standard compass, set about getting *Hougomont* under control. Work was started on a jury-rig at about three in the afternoon. The stump of the foremast was stayed to the uninjured bowsprit, and an inverted staysail set, peak downward, on this new forestay. A reserve royal-yard was mounted on the foremast, a royal being set from it. Inside the fore lower-shrouds, which were still taut, was spread a staysail, another being stretched on the remains of the jigger to balance the improvised rig. Under this queer medley *Hougomont* limped onward on her course, and actually attained to a maximum speed of four knots. The first news of the mishap was relayed by the Australian steamer *Kooliga* on the morning of April 25th, but all offers of assistance were refused by the crippled barque. Later, when twenty miles WSW. of Cape Borda, and making for Port Lincoln, *Hougomont* was spoken by the Weir motor-vessel *Forresbank* who proposed towage; but, with the signal 'All well, no assistance required', she sailed onward alone. (See photograph, page 79.)

The wind, which since the squall had been in her favour, turned, on April 28th, to a dead muzzler, when Cape Borda was only fifteen miles distant, and *Hougomont* was compelled to head seaward again. Borda Light, however, had seen her, and the news was wirelessed to Adelaide. A tug went out in search of what promised to be a nice fat salvage job, but could find no trace of the disabled barque. Seventeen days after the dismasting *Hougomont* made landfall again, eleven miles north of Borda, and by the following morning, May 8th, was safely in the shelter of St. Vincent Gulf, where, 129 days out from London, she dropped anchor at Adelaide Semaphore.

The efforts of her personnel merited a happier fate than that which fell to the lot of *Hougomont*. She was damaged too severely, by this her fourth dismasting, to warrant reconditioning at the estimated figure of nearly £3,000, even had the necessary spars and gear been obtainable in that part of the world. The alternative of part-repair in Australia, to be completed at Nystad after a long voyage under a better jury-rig, was mooted, but even this expense was prohibitive.

On January 7th, 1933, *Hougomont* was towed for the eighty-four miles from Semaphore Roads to Stenhouse Bay, Yorke Peninsula, by the tug *Wato*: no purchaser had been forthcoming, and so the hulk had been presented, gratuitously, to the Waratah Gypsum Company. After being placed inshore with the bowsprit about 200 yards from the rocks, it was sunk, by gelignite, to form a breakwater for the Stenhouse Bay jetty. Once the hull had settled into its sandy bed, the decks were just awash at high water. Captain Lindholm, Third Officer Ekstrand, and three of *Hougomont's* crew were deputed to conduct the barque to her last resting-place. Before the end every useful movable fitting had been detached, to be carried home to Mariehamn by *Herzogin Cecilie*. Such material forms a valuable reserve, only obtainable under like circumstances.

The two vessels were moored together for the purpose of exchanging ballast from *Herzogin Cecilie* for the salvaged parts of *Hougomont*, this ballast being left in *Hougomont* when she was sunk. *Herzogin Cecilie* sustained slight stern damage from the mooring wires during heavy weather while the barques were alongside each other.

Amongst other salvage *Herzogin Cecilie* carried home several spars (which can be seen, in some of my photographs, lashed along the hatch-coamings), the anchors and the chart-house. During the ensuing winter this house was fitted to *Penang's* poop by her Mate, Mr. Björkholm. *Killoran* benefited by the installation of *Hougomont's* wheelhouse. The figurehead can still be seen, for, after all its adventures, it now rests in the garden of Gustaf Erikson's home at Mariehamn.

Captain Lindholm's bad luck clung to him. On his return from Australia the owner gave him command of *Loch Linnhe*, operating in the firewood trade, but, as already related, within a few months she was wrecked in a snowstorm near Mariehamn.

The story of the last voyage of the American six-masted barquentine *E. R. Sterling* should serve to illustrate the vicissitudes which may beset the windjammer.

The last voyage of 'E. R. Sterling'

She was a vessel which passed through several changes both of ownership and rig. In 1883 Harland Wolff delivered to the Lord Line of Belfast a four-masted iron full-rigger, of 2,518 tons gross, named *Lord Wolseley*. Seventeen years later she became the German four-masted barque *Columbia*, and, in 1903, was dismasted off Cape Flattery and abandoned to underwriters. Sold to Vancouver, and renamed *Everett G. Griggs*, she underwent the metamorphosis to a six-masted barquentine. Captain E. R. Sterling bought her in 1910 for $27,000, and, under his name and his son's command, she traded profitably and successfully throughout the War. After the Armistice Captain Sterling refused an offer of $75,000 for his vessel.

On April 16th, 1927, *E. R. Sterling* sailed from Adelaide, one of that season's seventeen homeward grain sailers bound to Falmouth for orders. All went well until she was off the pitch of the Horn, where fog, ice, snow and a tremendous swell were encountered. The ice danger was not from bergs but from thick drift-ice, which impeded her progress for close on 500 miles. On July 4th, after passing the Falklands, the barquentine met with a terrific gale, and lost her main and mizen masts. She was spoken on August 16th, when 122 days out, 600 miles south of the Equator in Longitude 31° W. About three weeks later, in the latitude of the Cape Verde Islands, she lost her foremast, the Mate sustaining severe injuries. As the aerial also had carried away, no 'S.O.S.' could be broadcast, and the Mate died before the wireless operator was able to repair the damage to his installation. *E. R. Sterling* was, by the way, the first big sailer to be equipped with wireless, this being one of the many improvements which her owner-Master incorporated in a vessel of which he was inordinately proud. Amongst other luxuries she had electric light, a telephone, a pianola and expensive and beautiful cabin-fittings.

The delayed 'S.O.S.' was answered by s.s. *Northern Monarch*, but, in the meantime, the crippled windjammer had been jury-rigged, and was proceeding toward the West Indies. She put into St. Thomas on October 15th, having sailed 2,200 miles under her improvised top-hamper. There were no facilities at St. Thomas for refitting, and she lay there until December 15th. The Dutch tug *Indus* then towed her, via Fayal, to London, where she arrived on January 28th, 1928, 286 days out from Adelaide. Repairs, the bugbear of modern sail tonnage, were economically impracticable, and three months later, her cargo having been discharged, *E. R. Sterling* was towed to Sunderland, where shipbreakers had bought her for £4,000.

The sinking of 'Melbourne'

On the night of July 1st, 1932, Erikson's four-masted barque *Melbourne* was sunk in collision thirty miles to the north of Fastnet Light with the loss of many of her personnel.

Melbourne was built in 1892, as *Austrasia*, by Russell & Company of Port Glasgow for J. & W. Goffey of Liverpool. In 1910 she was sold, for £5,200, to Gebruder Vinnen of Hamburg, and renamed *Gustav*. Erikson acquired her in 1928 from Hermann Engel of Altona, Elbe, and, contrary to his usual practice, bestowed upon her the entirely fresh name of *Melbourne*.

Austrasia was partly dismasted on her maiden outward passage, when running her Easting down. She put back to Rio under courses, staysails and main lower topsails, and from there, under a more elaborate jury-rig, went home to Liverpool for a complete refit. In 1908 she was again at Rio in distress: she arrived with her sails in rags, her Master in irons, and with both Mates incapacitated by wounds. The Master was tried for shooting the Second Mate, but was found insane; four members of the crew received terms of imprisonment for dereliction of duty.

122

facing: 'PASSAT' IN BALLAST, 1935

As *Gustav*, this vessel was one of the many German War-time inter-
nees in Chile. Like *Herzogin Cecilie*, she was afterwards allocated to
France under Reparations, but, by 1921 was again under the German
flag.

One of a grain-laden fleet of nineteen sailers, *Melbourne* left Port
Victoria on March 17th, 1932. She met with bad weather shortly after
quitting Spencer Gulf, and again off the Horn, where, on May 1st, 44
days out, she ran before a fierce south-easter. The barque was swept by
huge seas, her wheel and boat-skids being damaged, poop-ladders
smashed, and the galley flooded. Unusually fickle Trade winds followed,
and a long deviation was necessary to weather the Brazilian coast. When
nearing Queenstown under easy canvas, after 105 days at sea, the lights
of a steamer were sighted some distance off. It was a night of drizzling
rain, a high sea, fresh south-west breeze, and moderate visibility. The
two vessels were on opposing courses, and each saw the other's lights
clearly. The tanker — *Seminole* of the Anglo-American Oil Company,
bound from Clyde to Baton Rouge — altered course to cross *Melbourne's*
bows. Then, owing, it is said, to an incorrect order from the officer of the
watch (for her Master was below at the time), she again changed direction, intending perhaps to pass astern of the windjammer, but, instead,
struck the latter full on the port bow. Cut down to the water-line,
Melbourne sank within a few minutes, her masts collapsing above her as
she went down. Several of the crew were in their bunks and failed even
to reach deck. The tragedy was heightened by the sacrifice of three
lives in a vain attempt to save the Master, who was making his last voyage
before retirement. Forgetting, in his agitation, the absence of the poop-
ladders, which had not yet been repaired, he fell from the poop on to
the main-deck, breaking both his legs. While trying to rescue him the
First and Third Mates and the bo'sun were engulfed by the sinking
vessel and drowned. The steward and six sailors also perished, and of
the remaining fifteen of *Melbourne's* small complement who were landed
at Queenstown by a tug, one died later in hospital.

Seminole, which sustained forepeak damage below the water-line,
acknowledged her responsibility for the collision by reimbursing a major
part of the loss sustained in respect of hull, freight, and cargo of *Melbourne*,
besides the other liabilities incurred. The insured value of *Melbourne's*
cargo was in the neighbourhood of £25,000, including profit and advanced freight. Although the assessment of the damaged value of the

grain on arrival was considerably less than this figure, it is believed that *Seminole's* repayment to the cargo owners alone was close on £16,000.

Collision liabilities

Where the circumstances of a collision at sea are such as to bring it under English jurisdiction, the damages recoverable from the wrong-doing vessel are those which are directly consequent upon the accident. They include the loss or damage of the other vessel and her cargo, the freight at risk, passage-money if any, crew's effects, loss of life or personal injury to her crew, demurrage (compensation for the loss of use of the vessel during repair), the repatriation expenses of her crew and passengers, surveyors' fees, salvage charges, etc. At Common Law the liability of a shipowner, in respect of a collision for which his vessel alone is to blame, is unlimited. Limitation proceedings, based upon the tonnage of the vessel at fault, may, however, be undertaken (under the Merchant Shipping Act of 1894) in order to confine this liability to a figure of £8 per ton for material damage, or to £15 per ton should loss of life be involved. Loss of life has a prior claim up to £7 per ton of the £15, any balance not satisfied ranking, *pari passu*, with property damage for the remaining £8 per ton. Where one vessel alone is to blame, the liability for damage rests solely with her, but if the blame be divisible, the liability is apportioned in accordance with the degrees of fault. In Norway, Germany, France and many other maritime nations, the general limit of total liability is the damaged value, at date of arrival, of the blameworthy vessel, plus the amount of her freight then at risk. Should the vessel, although at fault, be sunk by the collision, and so possess no arrived value, she avoids responsibility.

Consequently, if the case be governed by English practice, collision can prove a serious matter for the uninsured owner of a guilty sailing vessel because her low market value, of far below even £8 per ton, may be swallowed up several times over, by her liabilities, before limitation point is reached. A foreign shipowner, possessing no impoundable property in this country, might not take advantage of the option of limitation, because the only means by which the claim against him could be enforced would be by the subsequent arrest, in British waters, of the vessel at fault or, in certain cases, of other units of the same fleet. Action for collision must be instituted in English Courts, by the issue of a writ within two years of the accident. A foreign vessel which has caused injury to British property or subjects in any part of the world is then liable to detention if found within the three-mile limit of the

United Kingdom, in order to compel her owner to abide the issue of any judgment given against him. As already pointed out, however, because steam must give way to sail at sea it is unusual, providing her lights were in order at the time, for the windjammer to be held at fault to-day. On the other hand, again by reason of her low value, her entire claim, including the cargo damage, should fall well within the scope of the liability of the average steamer, even if the latter's limitation proceedings are successful. On the whole, therefore, English law is likely to operate in a windjammer's favour rather than the reverse.

So many other, and fortunately less dangerous, pitfalls, besides the major hazards of wrecks, dismasting, fire and collision, beset the path of the last owner of a fleet of deepwater sail, that it is all the more remarkable that he can still tread that path without the protection of insurance. The fact remains, however, that the cost of such protection would be so prohibitive that, unless he sold his windjammers and turned to steam, he could not continue as a shipowner. *Minor accidents*

If the 1931-32 round voyages to Australia were any criterion of the normal experiences of the windjammers it would hardly be possible for the Erikson Fleet to go on. In addition to the total loss of *Melbourne* and *Hougomont*, many of the grain vessels encountered very bad April weather in the South Pacific. *Archibald Russell*, *C. B. Pedersen* and *Pamir* were battered severely. *Pamir's* spanker-boom broke adrift and played havoc with her poop, the helmsman being injured and the saloon flooded. In 160°W., 53°S., on the night of April 5th, *Parma* broached-to, lost much canvas and her steering compass, had her midship-house gutted, and very nearly foundered. *Melbourne*, in the same weather, incurred the deck damage which was later to be the cause of the death of her Master and his attempted rescuers. These five barques had all left Spencer Gulf within the space of one week, but two earlier departures — *Killoran* and *Herzogin Cecilie* — received heavy-weather damage during their homeward passage.

All this wear and tear means heavy expense, for to retain her classification and to continue as an asset rather than a liability to her owner, the windjammer must be maintained in a sound and seaworthy condition.

In Chapter IV of Book Two I intend to quote details of the normal upkeep in the way of gear and canvas incurred by *Herzogin Cecilie*. To give some idea of the requirements of a big barque, it may be stated *The upkeep of a wind-jammer in canvas, gear and stores* here that on the average, in ordinary wear and tear, she used up annually about two tons of new Manila rope and between 8,000 and 10,000 square feet of Standard flax canvas. At to-day's prices, her complete suit of thirty-five sails would cost, new, about £2,000, and would involve in maintenance between £300 and £500 worth of fresh canvas every year.

Captain Erikson obtains practically all his supplies of canvas, gear and paint in the United Kingdom. The stores and provisions are purchased in Denmark, except in the case of vessels sailing to Australia direct from British ports.

It is only permissible, or even possible, to generalize in matters of expense, all figures mentioned being merely indicative; but, according to the London ship-chandlers, the upkeep of a steel four-poster of about 3,000 tons gross entails, on the average, the following annual expenditure:

Provisioning (excluding fresh-water): £500, plus small replacements and additional purchases in Australia; flour, for example, is, by reason of its cheapness, bought in Spencer Gulf.

A foreign vessel using Australian ports must pay duty on the stores broached during her stay, although they were purchased in Europe. Consequently, it is cheaper to buy locally sufficient provisions for immediate needs, especially now that the exchange rate is so favourable.

Paint (for use on board): White-lead, red-lead, mast-colour, boot-topping, etc. (two tons or more in all), £90 — £100.

Manila rope, plus small stuff — spunyarn, ratline, and the like — (about 2 tons in all), £70 — £100.

Wire rope, including wire seizing, etc., (1 — 1¼ tons) £80 — £100.

In addition, there are such sundries as linseed oil (4 barrels), Stockholm tar, pitch, oakum, wooden and iron bars for shrouds and ratlines, leather casing for rigging-screws, and so on. Altogether the chandler's account for provisioning and outfitting such a vessel for a year's voyaging is somewhere between £800 and £1,000, excluding canvas.

Bottom painting

In bygone days many devices were adopted, to protect the bottoms of wooden vessels from worm and weed, before copper sheathing became general. For instance, at one time large-headed iron nails were implanted all over the under-water area. A mixture of coal-tar and hair was found to be moderately effective, but, in the eighteenth century, this was superseded by a dressing of tallow. Despite the use of modern preventatives, marine growth will still accumulate at an alarming rate on the under-water area of a steel hull, especially if the craft remain for long periods at a time in tropical waters, and its presence will greatly impair her sailing qualities.

Unless special circumstances intervene, the Erikson vessels are dry-docked once every year. In addition to docking expenses and, when they fall due, survey fees for reclassification, it costs about £40 per vessel for bottom-painting. One coat of anti-rust composition is followed by two coats of anti-fouling paint; the area between light and load lines has an undercoat of anti-corrosive before it is painted.

Such figures may give some idea of the outlay required to keep a sailer in commission, but there are any number of other expenses entailed by her trading.

Loading charges for grain (variable according to method employed, but round about 2s. 6d. per ton in Spencer Gulf), pilotage, port charges, discharging, towage and charterers' commissions are all chargeable to the vessel's account. The cost of discharging grain in the United Kingdom varies with locality and system. At the London elevators, like McDougalls Ltd. of Millwall Dock, or Joseph Rank Ltd. of Victoria Dock, powerful suction-pipes do the work, and all that must be done by hand is the slitting of the bags to release their contents at the mouth of the pipe. The cost for this type of discharge in London is 1s. 7d. a ton. Where, however, the bags have to be slung out by hand, as, for instance, at Cork and Ipswich, the charge rises as high as 2s. 3d. a ton. Hull has a special Railway Company's rate of 8d., plus cost of crane-age, and, therefore, from Erikson's point of view, is one of the most economical ports of discharge. *The cost of loading and discharging grain*

The total bill for discharge, towage, light-dues, pilotage, ballast, water and all the score or so minor disbursements incurred by a wind-jammer docking in the United Kingdom, to unload, say, 4,000 tons of grain, vary from about £1,200 to £1,800, according to the port concerned.

Captain Erikson has found by experience that the square-rigger possessed of large carrying-capacity is a far better proposition than a smaller or more fine-lined vessel. The smaller barques may cost less in wages, stores and upkeep than the big four-masters of 4,500 tons or *Carrying-capacity* more capacity, but the saving is disproportionate to the loss of freight on, maybe, 1,000 tons of grain. Many of the dues and charges for which a trading vessel is liable are based upon her net registered tonnage. A hull designed as a floating warehouse with, in the case of a windjammer, all its propulsive power above deck and all its living quarters on deck, can accommodate a large bulk of cargo in relation to its net tonnage. Of this class are such square-riggers as *Lawhill* and *Olivebank*. With a net tonnage of 2,540, the former can load 4,800 tons of grain; of 2,427 net register, the latter carries 4,300 tons. Although in every other respect these two barques were the inferior of *Herzogin Cecilie*, she, for a net tonnage of 2,584, could only take a maximum grain cargo of just under 4,300 tons. Thus, her dues would be approximately the same as those of *Lawhill*, although her cargo was the smaller by 500 tons; while *Olivebank*, carrying an equal cargo to *Herzogin Cecilie*, would be rated for port-dues on a basis of 157 tons less.

The reasons for such discrepancies, which, from that point of view only, made *Lawhill* and *Olivebank* more economical freighters than *Herzogin Cecilie*, was because the latter was intended for a different purpose. The two British barques were freight-earners, purely and simply, and built to compete with steam. In the case of the German barque the consideration of carriage was allied to the provision of adequate accommodation for a large number of cadets. In addition, her hull was designed to sail well and to look well, a certain amount of capacity being sacrified to obtain graceful lines.

The economy of water-ballast

Again, the vessel which is wholly, or in part, ballasted by water is at a considerable economic advantage over her rubble-ballasted sisters in an employment where to-day, more than half the voyaging is in light trim. Literally, solid ballast is money thrown away, since ultimately it must all be jettisoned overside if a full freight is to be earned. At the present time four of the twelve Erikson square-riggers are water-ballast barques, *L'Avenir*, *Viking*, *Penang*, and *Winterhude*, *L'Avenir* taking, in addition, about 100 tons of solid ballast for trimming purposes. To some extent *Herzogin Cecilie* outset her slight disadvantage in carrying capacity by reason of the fact that she was ballasted, in part, by water.

The length of sailing time taken en route is another factor in determining the trade value of a particular vessel. The old saying 'More days, more dollars' is still true, and the better consistent passage-makers in the Fleet thereby reduce the owner's expenses for food and wages.

In September 1931, when Great Britain abandoned the Gold Standard, Finland re-stabilized her Mark currency by co-relating it to the Swedish Kroner, Sweden having followed our example. Against a former par sterling value of 193, the Fin-Mark now stands at 226 to the Pound. Although the standard of living in Finland has improved in recent years, it is still astonishingly cheap in comparison to that of the adjacent Scandinavian countries. Low as the Finnish maritime wage-scale seems to us, the sea is there looked upon as one of the better-paid occupations, and is considered to be preferable to agriculture or to manual labour ashore. Finnish shipowners, particularly of steam tonnage, have had little difficulty in obtaining sufficient local personnel, and where, as in Erikson's case, the earnings of their vessels are payable in sterling and the wage bills in Fin-Marks, considerable benefit is derived from the existing monetary standards. The subject of wages must be reserved for a following chapter, but, as a very rough estimate, the average annual wage-bill of the Erikson Fleet would be something like £800 sterling per vessel if no apprentices were carried. Apprentices represent a double gain, for, besides the saving effected in wages, their premiums are a distinct asset.

The effect of currency exchange

The employment of English chartering-agents, who also act for him in the handling of all accounts relevant to the transport of cargo (whether incurred in Australia or England) is a great advantage to Captain Erikson under present conditions. Details vary so greatly and for such diverse reasons that it is impossible to do more than generalize in the matter of expenses. With the Australian pound at 125 to £100 sterling the various bills for stevedoring, port dues, Consular charges, extra stores, etc., which an Erikson windjammer incurs each year in Australian waters, vary between £1,200 and £1,500 sterling *in toto*, according to the tonnage of the vessel and the system of loading employed. As the entire freight is payable in sterling the Australian expenses to-day are, in terms of freight, reduced by 20 per cent.

The foregoing indications, rough though they must of necessity be, should serve to show how vital it is for the uninsured windjammer of to-day to obtain at least one good annual freight and to run without unduly severe repair accounts.

A full cargo of 4,500 net tons of Australian grain, at a carriage rate of 30s. a ton, produces a gross freight of £6,750 sterling. Taking rough averages of the expense items already referred to — £800 wages, £900 stores and gear, £400 canvas, £1,400 in Australia and £1,500 in England — they involve a total outlay of about £5,000 sterling to earn that £6,750. This is without dry-docking, reclassification, and other similar items, besides the provision of a sinking fund to provide for major exigencies. A few years ago, it was said (although I hold no brief for the statement) that Captain Erikson calculated, if all went well, on clearing an average annual profit of something like £800 per vessel.

Every one of the sixteen square-riggers trading deepwater to-day is fully classed by a Registration Society, ten of them holding the 100 A1 class of *Lloyd's Register*. The maintenance of an old sailing vessel in such condition that she complies with the top-class requirements of any of the big classification societies is no light task. The severity of the necessary periodical surveys increases with the age of the vessel. Although Lloyd's 100 A1, the **100⚓** of the Germanischer Lloyd and the equivalent insignia of the various other societies are the finest recommendation that a craft can possess, the attendant inspections are the most rigorous which she can undergo. Once a vessel has held such distinction over a long period it would be prejudicial, in the eyes of those who contemplated her hire, for the owner to allow the class to lapse or, worse still, to be withdrawn because of his non-compliance with the strict rules of such societies. Also, not only would this considerable saving in expense have a detrimental effect on the insurance rates for cargoes in sail, but the owner would be judged, in shipping circles, to have lowered the standard of his tonnage, even though he might continue to expend the same care on its upkeep.

Besides exchange, there are two items which help to lighten, by a little, Captain Erikson's task. From each of a number of apprentices whom he carries, he receives a premium of £50 sterling or its equivalent in other currencies. This is for the period of one year or a round voyage, after which the boy is entitled, if found suitable, to take a position as deck-boy or ordinary seaman at current wages. During his apprentice year he receives 100 Fin-Marks (approximately 10s.) per month from the owner, i.e. about 10 per cent of his premium is returned as wages. Further details of the indentures of an Erikson apprentice will be included in the next chapter.

Captain Erikson has not overlooked the lucrative sideline of passage money. After a long period of oblivion sail-travel has been resuscitated by a limited number of enthusiastic sea-lovers, who, chosing the more spartan joys of a windjammer instead of the amenities of a luxury liner, count themselves well rewarded by the unforgettable experience of seeing the sea, in all her moods, her beauty and her wrath, mastered after the fashion of their forefathers. Few, however desirous, can afford the time, or maybe the means, necessary for a deepsea passage under square-rig; but for those able to indulge their ambition, it is easy enough to arrange matters through the agents for the Erikson Fleet in London, Copenhagen, Amsterdam, Stockholm, or Australia.

Passengers in sail

Several vessels in the Fleet have quite extensive and almost luxurious vacant quarters, and each of the others can provide accommodation for at least one supercargo.

The class of housing offered below the long poop-decks of *Viking* and *L'Avenir*, or in the midship sections of *Passat* and *Pamir*, enables the passenger in sail to live under conditions of comparative comfort, although, of course, in really bad, cold weather windjamming always entails a varying degree of hardship for all on board.

It is necessary for the intending passenger to be signed on in the articles as a member of the vessel's company, although work is only undertaken at the individual's own pleasure and at his own risk; but that subject will be alluded to again later.

A flat rate of 10s. sterling per day, inclusive, is charged. No special arrangements are made beyond the provision of a berth, which is rendered as comfortable as circumstances will permit, and the same food as supplied to the officers.

The outward passage from Copenhagen to Australia averages 90 to 100 days, the homeward passage to England being 100 to 120 days or even more. Consequently, a passenger making the round trip would pay the owner about £100 and would have, approximately, seven months at sea plus the loading period in Australia. This sum, less an allowance for food, is clear profit to the owner, and three or four passengers, therefore, represent quite a fair increase in the annual earnings of a square-rigger.

A certain number of passengers travel out to Copenhagen or

Mariehamn when the Erikson Fleet makes its short, homeward, summer, ballast trip from the discharge ports. In this case 12s. 6d. a day, with a minimum fare of £12, is charged. Numbers, however, are restricted by the passenger-carrying regulations in force in this country and by the extra dues incurred by vessels using our ports for purposes other than trade. In every instance it is compulsory for a passenger to give Captain Erikson a written undertaking, backed by that of a guarantor, relieving the owner of all liability in the event of accident, damage and loss, or for medical treatment or expense of repatriation.

A remarkable incursion into the sphere of holidaying under sail was made a year or two ago by Captain Erikson when he commissioned *L'Avenir* for temporary pleasure cruising in the Baltic, thus employing profitably her usual short summer period of inaction. She was advertised to make a number of trips from Mariehamn, each of seven or eight days in duration, during July and August, and, in order to maintain this schedule, she was accompanied by a tug. Accommodation was provided for about seventy people, and, for the time being, *L'Avenir* was equipped with an orchestra, a swimming bath, and (shades of Cape Horn!) deck-games, a dance floor and a bar. The fares ranged from 165 Swedish Kroner, 1st class, to 95 Kroner, 3rd class. Rumour has it that, for once, her Master and his crew welcomed with considerable relief *L'Avenir's* subsequent departure upon her lawful business!

The fate of 'Herzogin Cecilie' – sentiment outweighed by common sense

Although, in theory, the art of modern sail management implies, perhaps even demands, on the part of the owner a certain amount of sentimentality, in practice it is a business which leaves little room for the exercise of unwarranted sentiment. This attitude was demonstrated when *Herzogin Cecilie* was ashore at Salcombe. Erikson loved that barque, which, since 1922, had been his favourite and his flag-ship. For years she had been commanded by one of his most trusted and successful Masters, Captain Ruben de Cloux, and she must have repaid her low purchase price at least twice over during fourteen years of constant employment. Yet, when the end came, her owner, faced by a heavy loss of freight and, in his judgment, by the unavoidable loss of a fine barque still fit for another ten or even twenty years' trading, did not permit sentiment to override the dictates of experience.

As a strictly business proposition *Herzogin Cecilie* appeared to be an almost certain constructive, it not an absolute, total loss. Her owner refused to commit himself to a salvage contract whose chances of success were disproportionate to the risk of increasing an already heavy loss by the share of salvage charges attaching to the hull. Owing to the apparently critical position of the barque, no offers were forthcoming for salvage on a 'no cure, no pay' basis, the customary method under which a salvor's remuneration is dependent upon the success of his work and established by subsequent arbitration. The other and less common form of agreement would have been for the owners of hull and cargo to participate in the cost of salvage on a stipulated basis, taking thereby the risk of financing one or more abortive attempts to save their property. Even had immediate salvage operations on the latter basis proved successful, the subsequent repair bill would have been large, and so, if the Erikson Fleet was to continue, the owner had to reconcile himself to the desertion of one of his finest vessels. But I anticipate my concluding chapter, in which the story of those unhappy months at Salcombe, and of the unavailing efforts of private enterprise, will be set out in full.

The recommissioning of old second-hand sail tonnage by foreign owners is sometimes derided in these mechanized days. Perhaps the foregoing presentation, incomplete in scope as it may be, of the difficulties with which such ventures are surrounded, will serve in some small way to enhance the reputation of an owner who, unaided by insurance, has built up and maintained a fleet of sail through one of the worst and longest slumps in the history of shipping.

CHAPTER III

'THE SAILOR OF THE SAIL'

AS HE EXISTS TO-DAY

These are the chaps that toiled together
In Trade and Doldrum and black Horn weather:
Scoured and holystoned, reefed and furled,
Watch and watch round the whole wet world,
Hauled and sweated at sheets and braces
With sun in their eyes or the sleet in their faces,
Fought and fisted the frozen canvas
On footropes jumping like bucking horses.
These are the men that sailed and manned,
Worked her and drove her from land to land.

So long as the word 'sailor' remains in the English vocabulary, so long will live the work from which that word was derived. The original significance of the term is now a thing of the past, for the 'sailor' has become a 'seaman', but the debt which we, as a nation, owe to the bygone sailor of the sail will not lightly be forgotten.

In the appended Bibliography a fairly comprehensive list is given of books dealing with the closing phases in the history of square-rig, and of others which have the present-day windjammer as the setting for their narratives. In the Introduction I gave some explanation why I was adding to such literature, and in planning this Chapter I allowed for the fact that much of the suitable subject-matter had already been adequately covered.

A composite description of life under sail to-day

With no intention to belittle the many other works of a like nature, I suggest that in the perusal of four or five particular narratives, embracing a diversity of view-points, there will be gained a comprehensive idea of the conditions of life in deepwater sail to-day.

In London, in October, 1933, a young Englishman shipped aboard *Lawhill*, as an apprentice, for a round voyage to Australia. R. B. Sheridan, son of Clare Sheridan and nephew of Mr. Winston Churchill, was only nineteen years of age when he wrote *Heavenly Hell*, but his book is an excellent piece of work, describing his experiences in full detail, and with a wealth of colour.[1]

In 1932 Claude Muncaster signed-on as an ordinary seaman aboard *Olivebank*, then lying in Melbourne, for a passage round the Horn to Cardiff. As an artist his object was to depict on canvas one of the last of the windjammers, and, as a member of the crew, to have personal experience of life before the mast. In *Rolling Round the Horn* he states that his hope was to make 'some permanent record of those ill-paid, ill-fed, and much suffering seamen who belong to the grand tradition of rope and canvas'.

Mr. Sheridan and Mr. Muncaster have sketched a composite picture of fo'c'sle life under present conditions which may well act as a deterrent to others who, possessing glamorous and romantic (but mistaken) notions, contemplate a like experience.

Mr. Villiers' several books, in which he describes his ventures before the mast in *Grace Harwar* and *Herzogin Cecilie*, and on the poop of *Parma*, are too well known to require description. He loves the life, and the life suits him. In consequence, he is more concerned with the spectacular side of the work, and with the thrill, the beauty, and the history of the windship, than with the hardship and sordidness which are the almost inseparable accompaniment of life in such craft.

Little more than two years ago Commander C. M. Butlin, D.S.C., R.N., was a passenger from Port Germein to Falmouth in *L'Avenir*, a barque which, in hull-design and accommodation, approximated closely to *Herzogin Cecilie*. In his *White Sails Crowding* the oft-told story of the Cape Horn run gathers new interest by reason of the way in which the daily happenings are linked, by a nautical expert well read and well informed in many kindred subjects, to a wealth of diverse, but always relevant, data.

A passenger has greater scope and far more opportunity for observation and inquiry than a member of the crew, and in the 139 days which he spent aboard *L'Avenir*, Commander Butlin amassed a store of information which later was to form a valuable record of 'most of the game' as seen by an onlooker.

If the foregoing volumes be read as complementary they should give an adequate idea of the personnel and the work aboard the Erikson

---

[1] At the age of 21, Mr. Sheridan died, after an operation for appendicitis, at Constantine, Algeria, in January 1937.

Fleet. Where one narrator discounts, another emphasizes; and the four observers, seeing the same motif from different angles, depict between them a satisfying portrait of the conditions prevailing in vessels which, if they are to exist at all, must do so by the 'blood and sweat unending' of those who man them.

Therefore, although the prime object of this book is to preserve, while the subject-matter is still extant, a comprehensive record of the closing era of square-rig, it has been thought sufficient to confine this Chapter to a few unembellished facts concerning the manning of the windjammer, the routine of working her, and the subject of apprenticeship in sail. With the addition of a few biographical notes, and an account of a round voyage to Australia by the Master of *Pommern*, these should supplement the needs of the reader, who can, if desired, obtain elsewhere a more general impression, replete with local colour.

Sail – now the prerogative of youth

In days gone by the true 'shell-back' of the fo'c'sle was often content to spend his whole life in the service of sail, with little prospect of advancement. To-day, deepwater windjamming is the prerogative of youth alone. The deck of a sailer serves in numerous instances merely as a stepping-stone toward the bridge of a foreign steamer, and many of the youngsters who man these last square-riggers are graduates to wider spheres of life afloat. The small pecuniary inducement which such craft can afford to offer is insufficient to attract and retain older men either to their fo'c'sles or their poops, for, as the years pass and the windjammers decrease in number, the chances of future promotion in sail become more remote. Apart from these reasons, it is doubtful, now that the old breed of 'sailing-ship sailor' has passed away for ever, whether a more mature crew could handle these big 'sailing work-houses' (as they have been dubbed) with the success of the boyish personnel upon whom sail-trading to-day depends. The vitality, endurance and irresponsibility of youth, coupled with its power of recuperation and its sense of adventure, form a combination which rarely breaks down under the stress of an experience calculated to make or break those who undergo it. In actual fact few of the youngsters who to-day ship in square-rig fail to make good under physical and mental strain which might incapacitate and disgust a more mature man.

These boy crews have proved to be a most fortunate post-War experiment, for in this solution of the labour problem lies one of the secrets of the success of the Erikson Fleet. They consist of a wide admixture of nationalities: Swedes, Finns, Ålanders, Englishmen, Australians, Danes, Belgians, sometimes even Americans, fill the fo'c'sles of the Åland square-riggers. *Moshulu* for her present passage out to Australia has no less than six English-speaking young men among her crew, there being three Australians, one Canadian, and two Englishmen aboard.

The German aspirant for a Mate's ticket must have had at least fifty months' service before the mast, of which period a minimum of twenty months in sail is compulsory. Herr Hitler recently decreed that German youth must train in German tonnage, and he thus terminated the steady quota of German boys who in the past were to be found aboard many of the Erikson vessels, and who furnished some of the finest material available for the manning of that Fleet.

The crew of a modern windjammer vary widely in type: some are rough and uneducated, and will never rise above the fo'c'sle, whereas others are of good social standing, and, if windjammers endure, may yet be Masters of sail. In due course, a proportion may become steamship officers or graduate to a pilotage service, while others aspire to Naval rank.

To a minority the windships and everything connected therewith are anathema. Others regard time spent in sail as a necessary evil, an unavoidable rung on the ladder of promotion. A few are serving therein because the appeal of the deepwater square-rigger cannot be denied, while fewer still, like, for instance, Mr. Sheridan, 'do it for fun'. In general, however, one and all, seamen, apprentices or afterguard, have the sea-salt in their blood and the fearlessness and vigour of youth on their side.

Now that Finland's holding in steam is increasing steadily, and at long last there is a promise of a widespread revival in sea-borne trade, it is said that the problem of manning the Erikson windjammers tends to be less easy than of yore. The trend is setting more and more in favour of employment in steam rather than sail, presumably owing to the better prospects held out by the steamer. Trading under sail is waning, and although it is hoped that for many years to come the square-riggers will continue to carry their grain, it is obvious that the opportunities for advancement which they can offer must, by degrees, become more limited. In those cases where service in sail is made a stipulation for commissioned rank in steam, the growing tendency is for the candidate to gravitate from the one to the other at the earliest possible opportunity. The dearth of capable officers for the windjammers is likely to be more acute than the possible shortage of unskilled foremast hands, for once a man has passed as Mate the newer profession becomes the more attractive.

The social drawbacks of service in sail

To find any contentment at all in windjamming the sailor must love the sea for itself alone, because, considering the thousands of miles he travels, he sees but little of the world ashore. Nowadays his foreign venue is, usually, Spencer Gulf, a locality which offers few worth-while inducements to shoregoing. In the Antipodean grain trade under sail there are no ports of call, in fact it is quite usual for no land to be sighted throughout such passages. Occasionally a stay of a few hours may be made in the offing of the lonely island of Tristan da Cunha, whose inhabitants are only too glad to visit any vessel which may pay them a call. This landfall serves the useful purpose of providing a check on the windjammer's chronometers. The islanders, old and young, throng out in small boats, and a brisk trade develops on the windjammer's deck. It makes a strange scene, for it is as if the pages of history had been turned back for several score years. The visitors, in their queer, almost uncouth, garb, seem to fit perfectly into the background formed by a type of vessel which has in many essentials remained unchanged for generations. The basis of trade is by barter, fruit, vegetables, fresh meat, fish, sea-birds' eggs, sheepskin mats, dressed penguin skins, berets made from feathers, and other curios galore being exchanged for books, papers, tinned provisions, clothing, etc.

Apart from such rare experiences, the crews of the grain-ships, sailing 30,000-40,000 miles in the course of a year, see less of the world than falls to the lot of the passengers on even the shortest of pleasure cruises. Although the vessels lie for three or more weeks at a port of discharge in the United Kingdom the boys see little or nothing of our country. Except at week-ends, they work all day until 5 p.m., and not until nearly 7 p.m. are they ready to go ashore. If their vessel be discharging at great ports like London, Liverpool or Glasgow, few of them ever penetrate beyond the wide precincts of dockland. In London, for example, the windjammers very often berth in Millwall Dock, in which case 'Charlie Brown's' public-house in Limehouse, at the entrance to the Isle of Dogs, is as far Cityward as many of the crew will get. This rendezvous, with its astonishing exhibition of curios, is, nowadays, an interesting and innocuous haunt of sightseers. All its old, grim reputation is a thing of the past, and the adjacent dance-floor is a favourite spot for the boys from the square-riggers.

At smaller ports, like Ipswich, Dublin, or Belfast, the barques berth closer to the centre of the town, and in more attractive and convenient surroundings. They are then likely to receive a far larger number of visitors, especially of the fair sex, and sometimes generous hospitality may be extended toward the crew by interested residents.

Having completed discharge, the barques sail direct to Mariehamn or Gothenburg, and the outward call, next passage, at Copenhagen is of too short duration to be classed as a visit.

It is a regrettable feature of a sailor's life that, as a general rule, whether he be in sail or steam, he sees only the more sordid and less pleasant aspects of many of the ports he visits. The famous 'Flying Angel' and the other like Missions which, irrespective of his nationality or rank, offer him a warm and ready welcome, are worthy of interest and support. Without doubt, such amenities are really appreciated, especially by the better type of young seaman. *The Missions to Seamen*

The subject of manning is a wide and interesting field for research, following, as it has always done, the same dictates of competition and economy which have determined the development and decline of the square-rigger. *Crews of the nineteenth century*

In 1815 the East Indiaman *Earl of Balcarres*, of 1,417 tons, carried a complement of 138 persons, including the Commander, 6 officers, surgeon and assistant, purser, 6 midshipmen, gunner and his mate, master-at-arms, armourer, butcher, baker, poulterer, caulker and his assistant, 2 coopers, 2 stewards, 2 cooks, 8 boatswains, 6 quarter-masters, sail-maker, 7 servants for the afterguard, 78 seamen, and 4 supernumeraries or supercargoes.

The famous clipper-ship *Sobraon*, built in 1866, registered tonnage 2,131, carried in her prime, in the Australian passenger trade, a personnel of 69: Master, 4 officers, 8 apprentices, carpenter, sail-maker, bo'sun, donkeyman, 2 bo'sun's mates, 26 able-bodied-seamen (A.B.s) 4 ordinary-seamen (O.S.), 2 boys, 16 stewards and 2 stewardesses.

Some of the members of *Sobraon's* complement served aboard her for periods which must constitute records in such matters.

Captain J. A. Elmslie commanded her for 24 years; John Cameron was her carpenter for the whole of her career in the Australian trade under the British flag, 1866 to 1891; James Farrance, A.B. and then bo'sun, was in her for 16 years; and Thomas Routledge cut her sails for 10 years. Such were the 'shell-backs' of the Glorious Era of Sail, competent craftsmen wedded to the sea and to the service of its finest craft.

Donald McKay's wooden clipper *Sovereign of the Seas*, launched in 1852, 2,421 tons register, was manned by 106 men — Master, 4 officers, 2 bo'suns, 2 carpenters, 2 sail-makers, 3 stewards, 2 cooks, 80 seamen and 10 boys.

Miss Fox Smith has committed to verse the crews of two famous types of sailer in the following lines:

'She had midshipmen, topmen, and gunners and all,
And forty prime shellbacks to heave and to haul,
A bosun to pipe, and a fiddler to play,
The stately Blackwaller, bound Eastward away.'

'They had tough-nut skippers as hard as nails
To crack 'em along in the Cape Horn gales,
And hard-case shellbacks thirty-two
There used to be in a Blue Star crew,—
To man the capstan, and raise the shout
At tacks and sheets when she went about,
And brassbound reefers eight or nine
In them tall ships of the Blue Star Line.'

By the seventies the manning of sail had assumed smaller proportions. The iron full-rigger *British Ambassador*, a 'lime-juicer' of 1,794 tons register, built in 1873, was manned by the Master, 3 Mates, bo'sun and mate, sail-maker, carpenter, donkeyman, 24 A.B.'s, 4 O.S., 2 cooks and 2 stewards, making 41 all told, and in addition she carried 6 apprentices in her half-deck.

1910
The cadet barque 'Medway'

As the question of apprentices will be coming under review, mention may be made of the well-known trading cadet carrier *Medway*. She was a steel four-masted barque of 2,511 tons gross, built in 1902. Devitt and Moore added her to their fine fleet in 1910, and under their training scheme she carried a full half-deck of 26 cadets; with the Master, 4 Mates, carpenter, sail-maker, bo'sun, doctor, instructor, stewards, cooks and 18 seamen, her total complement was 56.

facing: AT THE STARBOARD MAIN-BRACE

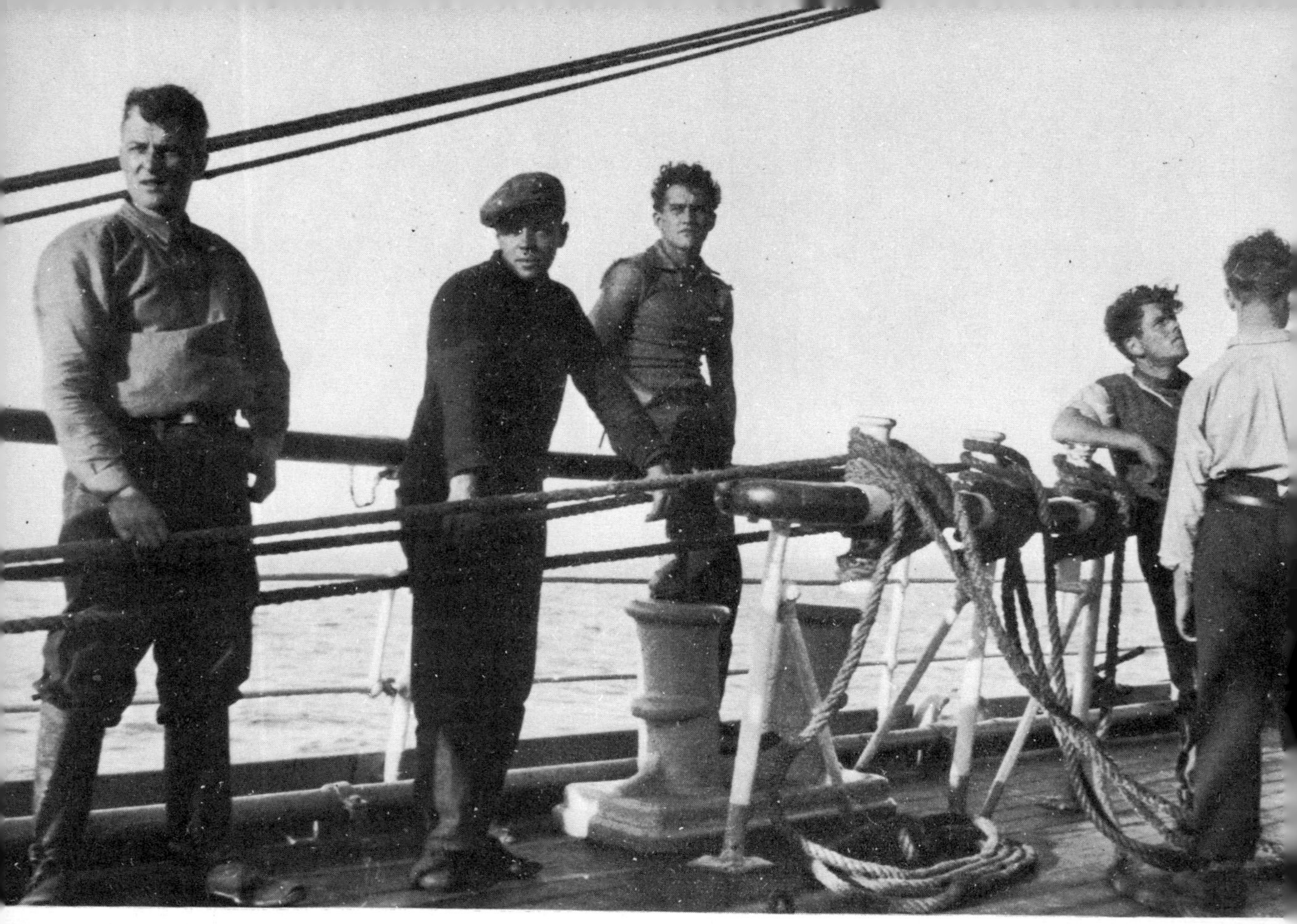

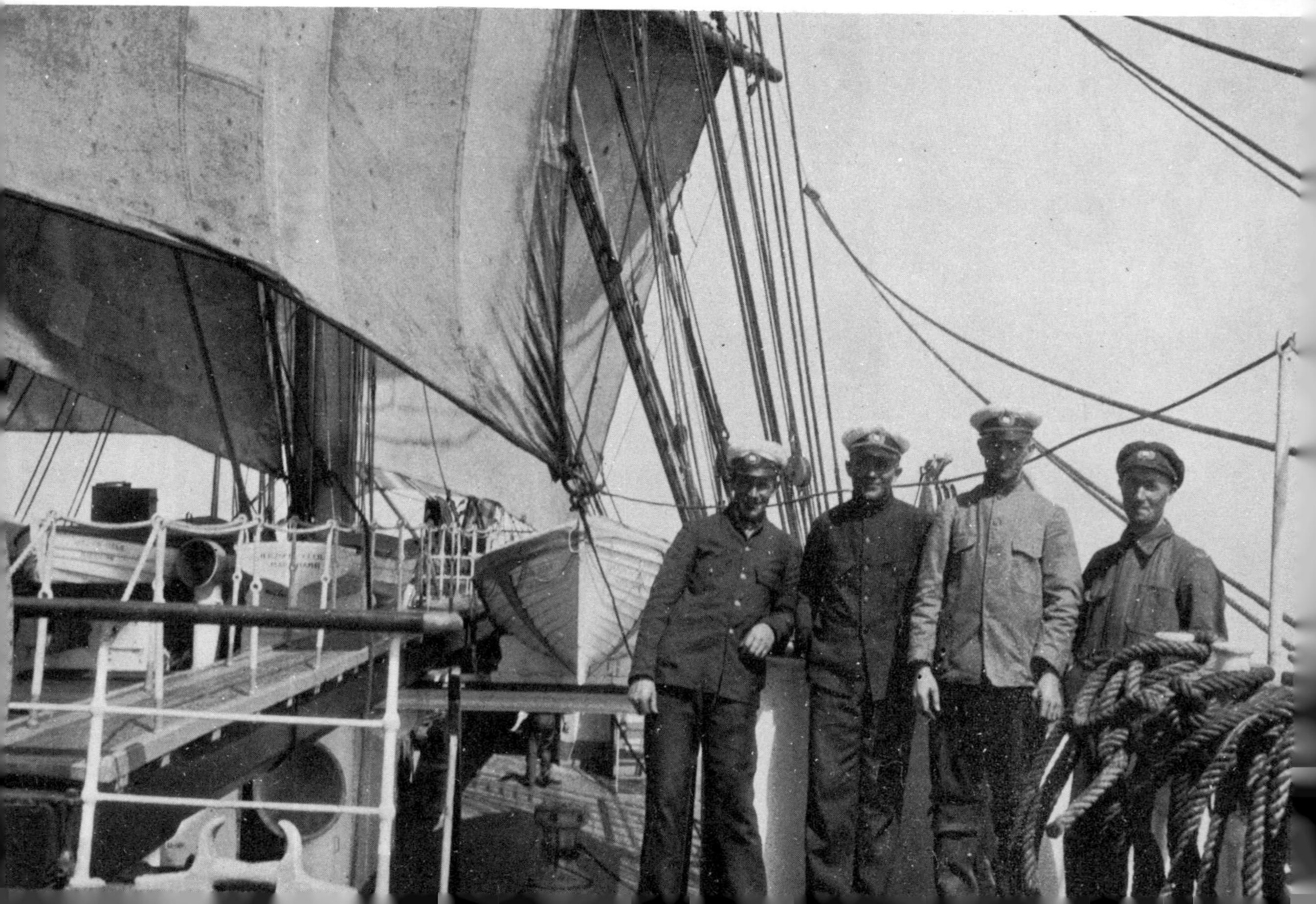

Laeisz's great steel five-masted barque *Potosi*, in her heyday perhaps the finest sailing vessel in the world, and of which much is to be said in a later chapter, accomplished her wonderful feats in the nitrate trade with an average personnel of just over 40 men. Built in 1895, she had a cargo capacity of 6,000 tons, and, when under full canvas, set 24 square-sails and 18 fore-and-afters. Her usual crew consisted of the Master, three officers, 2 bo'suns, sail-maker, carpenter, blacksmith, cook, steward, 16 A.B.s, 14 O.S., and 3 or more apprentices. Considering her size, the area of her canvas, and the arduous trade in which she was engaged, this personnel seems relatively small in comparison with that of the above-mentioned vessels; although when regarding the size of the crews of Finnish sailers of this decade, *Potosi* seems almost over-manned. *'Potosi' – the great five-master*

Parma, with a gross tonnage of 3,047, and a cargo capacity of nearly 5,000 tons, was sailed in 1930 by a total crew of 30. In her fo'c'sle were 2 Australians, 1 Englishman, 1 American (a yachtsman) and 11 Germans, the rest of the hands being Finns. Seven of the German youths were first-voyage apprentices; the other four were experienced A.B.s who had several times previously rounded the Horn under the Laeisz flag. *Priwall* and *Padua*, the last of the 'P' Fleet, at that time were laid up, and a number of their hands had signed on with Gustaf Erikson. *Crews of Finnish square-riggers*

In 1932 *Parma's* complement numbered 29 — Master, 3 Mates, sail-maker, carpenter, cook, steward, 4 A.B.s, 7 O.S., 7 apprentices and 3 boys, half the bunks in her fo'c'sle being unoccupied.

A few years ago *Grace Harwar*, a full-rigged ship of 1,816 tons gross, made a passage home from Australia with only 19 persons on board — Master, 2 Mates, sail-maker, carpenter, 6 A.B.s, 2 O.S., 4 boys, cook, and mess-boy.

As *Herzogin Cecilie* is to figure so largely in this book, a few facts in reference to her manning will not be out of place here. Built as a cargo-cum-cadet vessel for the Norddeutscher Lloyd Company, she was equipped to house a large personnel, and was not provided with the mechanical adjuncts to manual labour which helped to lighten the work aboard many of her purely trading contemporaries. For her maiden voyage she was manned by a complement of 88 as against the 56 carried by Devitt and Moore's *Medway*, a vessel of similar purpose but of rather smaller tonnage. The total of 88 was made up as follows: the Commander, 4 officers, surgeon, 2 school-masters, cook, steward, 13 *The manning of 'Herzogin Cecilie'*

acing: Top. 'SAILORS OF THE SAIL', 1933

    Bottom. MATES OF 'HERZOGIN CECILIE', 1933. CHIEF MATE, L. LINDWALL, ON LEFT regular seamen, 6 third-year cadets (drafted from a sister training-vessel, and rated as A.B.s) and 59 other cadets. During later voyages under the German flag, this total was, at times, increased to nearly 100 all told. 600 cadets served aboard *Herzogin Cecilie* between 1902-1914. The cadets paid the equivalent of £40 per annum for keep and tuition, and, if satisfactory, were rated as full seamen in their third year. A boy received sound training in practical and theoretical seamanship, and, after passing a stiff examination, could sign on as 4th Officer of a Norddeutscher steamship.

After the War, however, upon becoming a hard-worked member of the Erikson Fleet, the same barque, carrying identically the same big sail-area, was worked by a crew of, on the average, one-third the number of the German personnel of earlier days. In 1928, for example, she carried her grain home from Australia to Europe with a crew of 26, 19 of whom were before the mast. They were the Master, 4 Mates, steward, cook, 7 A.B.s (who included in their work the duties of bo'sun, carpenter, sail-maker and donkeyman), 3 O.S., 3 boy-ratings and 6 apprentices. Of the 26, 14 hailed from Åland, 6 were Swedes, 3 Finns, 3 Germans, one Englishman, and one Australian. Excluding Captain Ruben de Cloux, the average age of the officers was 25, and that of the crew a month or two under 19. The youngest aboard, an apprentice, was only 15, and two of his companions were 16 years of age.

In 1932, she had, by modern standards, the quite full complement of 32, 23 of whom were before the mast. Her Master was Captain Sven Eriksson, aged 28, and he was served by 3 Mates, steward, cook, sail-maker, donkeyman, carpenter, 3 A.B.s, 9 O.S., 10 apprentices and a ship's-boy. In addition, because one of the four passengers was a lady, *Herzogin Cecilie* ascended to the dignity of employing a stewardess. The majority of the photographs depicting scenes on board *Herzogin Cecilie*, which appear in this book, were taken in 1933 when the big, white barque was carrying 30 men, and, again, a stewardess. Besides Captain Eriksson and 4 Mates, there were a cook, pantry-boy, 3 'idlers', and 20 foremast hands, among whom were several apprentices. This tally, however, included one officer and a few of the crew of *Hougomont*. They were being repatriated after the loss, by dismasting, of their own barque in Australia (vide Chapter II, Book One).

Sometimes it happens that when a vessel is making her maiden voyage for Gustaf Erikson she is given a relatively large crew, in order that much of the necessary reconditioning work may be undertaken at sea.

No reflection on the Erikson regime is intended by the foregoing comparisons between bygone standards of sail-manning and those in force to-day. The Finnish sailers may be lightly manned, but they are never undermanned to an extent which would affect their safety at sea, and although apprentices and other first-voyagers may be carried, such unskilled labour is always leavened by a reasonable number of young, but experienced, able-bodied seamen.

As an example of a modern system of combining organized training in sail with the earning of freight, the Swedish barque *C. B. Pedersen* may be instanced. For her general participation in the grain trade she is manned by the Master, 3 officers, wireless-operator, sail-maker, carpenter, cook, steward, 4 seamen and 25 apprentices, the average age before the mast usually being below 20 years.

'C. B. Pedersen' and 'Abraham Rydberg'

Abraham Rydberg carries about 45 cadets, who each pay a £40 premium for a single round voyage to Australia. They receive full instruction from the afterguard in seamanship, and are paid a small wage. Navigation is taught at shore-schools. The only regular hands carried are the bo'sun, carpenter and sail-maker. The normal watches are divided into two sub-sections, each boy taking, in consequence, a spell on deck of one-half the ordinary length.

In recent years the controversial subject of sail-training has been the topic of considerable and heated discussion in Great Britain. Now that the Manning Committee of the Shipping Federation has decided to adopt, without qualification, the report of its Advisory Committee, little more remains to be said. That report definitely negatived both the necessity and the practicability of a revival of general sail-training as a grounding for the personnel of our own Mercantile Marine. It is a decision which, albeit, largely from sentimental motives, many people may deplore. The dictates of progress must be obeyed, but the regret remains.

Sail-training to-day

The majority of the other maritime nations of the world continue, in a greater or lesser degree, to supply the necessary facilities for sail-training to either or both their naval and mercantile services. Some of them stipulate for such preliminary experience as a condition of future commissioned rank. The vessels used for the purpose to-day make an imposing array.

Denmark possesses two fine auxiliary sailers, the *Danmark* and the new full-rigger *Georg Stage*; Norway, the ex-German auxiliary barque *Statsraad Lehmkuhl* and the full-rigged school-ship *Sörlandet*; Sweden, the naval training-ship *Af Chapman* and the two freighters-cum-school-ships *C. B. Pedersen* and *Abraham Rydberg*. In addition to several apprentice-carrying windjammers in the Australian grain trade, Finland has a national training venture in the *Suomen Joutsen*, or 'Swan of Finland', an appropriate name for a beautiful craft. Russia owns the four-masted barque *Tovarisch*, which has not, however, put to sea in recent years. Poland has the 1,600 ton auxiliary full-rigger *Dar Pormorza*. To replace the handsome old *L'Avenir*, to-day under the Finnish flag, the Belgian Government built the auxiliary barquentine *Mercator*. Last year Brazil took delivery, from Messrs. Vickers of Barrow, of the big, Diesel-engined, four-masted barquentine *Almirante Saldhanha*. The Argentine sail training-ship is the *Presidente Sarmiento*. Spain, Yugoslavia and Greece all operate auxiliary sailers for cadets. Italy runs a trio of school-ships: two of them, *Amerigo Vespucci* and *Cristoforo Colombo*, both naval units built in 1931, are big auxiliary vessels of over 3,000 tons, and, except for their double topsails, resemble closely the old-time 'Seventy-fours'; the third vessel, *Patria*, was in former days the German auxiliary trader *Susanne Vinnen*. Japan maintains four fine steel auxiliary four-masted barques, two of which were built as recently as 1930. Working in conjunction with training establishments on shore, they make, under the auspices of the Education Department of the Government, frequent cruises to Australia and the South Pacific. The Portuguese cadet-ship *Sagres*, a smart, well-kept, steel barque with most attractive lines, is a frequent visitor to northern waters. Originally German, a War internee, she still relies entirely on sail power and is commanded by a naval officer of high rank. The German School-ship Association (D.S.V.) of Bremen, founded in 1900, operates the steel full-rigger *Schulschiff Deutschland* exclusively for training purposes. Their other square-rigger, *Grossherzogin Elisabeth*, was, after retiring from active commission, moored close to the Nautical College at Finkenwarder. The three-masted auxiliary barque *Gorch Fock* provides sail training for German naval cadets.

Each of the two Laeisz four-masters, *Padua* and *Priwall*, carry a half-deck of about 40 apprentices, who pay 600 Marks for their first voyage, and 400 for a second; third-voyagers may be rated as ordinary seamen, in which case they earn between 50 and 60 Marks per month, but only about one man in four is thus promoted.

It is stated that the big auxiliary four-masted barque *Kommodore Johnsen* (ex *Magdalene Vinnen*), the latest recruit to the ranks of sail-training vessels, will carry 60 cadets. Her new owners, the Norddeutscher Lloyd Company, are to equip her with wireless direction-finding apparatus and an echo-sounding device. It is understood that instruction will be given in every phase of practical seamanship, and that English and Spanish are to be included in the curriculum. In addition to the Commander and five officers, this fine vessel will have on board a doctor, a language master, and two engineers.

Four of the United States of America — Massachusetts, New York and Pennsylvania on the Atlantic seaboard, and California on the Pacific coast — conduct nautical school-ships. When, quite recently, the Pennsylvanian vessel, *Annapolis*, visited London, her Commander, Captain J. Hines, U.S.N. (retired), stated that, although sail-handling was incidental to the general instruction given, there was nothing, in his view, which taught alertness to a young man more than a knowledge of sail: it gave him a better 'weather eye' and increased promptness in action. Consequently, *Annapolis*, a schooner-rigged steamer of 1,010 tons displacement, loaned to the State by the United States Navy, proceeds whenever feasible by wind-power alone. She carries 90 boys, who undergo a two-year period of tuition, after which they can sit for an examination before the Federal Steamboat Inspectors in order to qualify as certificated engineers or third mates. The object of the scheme is to maintain a steady supply of young mercantile officers equipped, by practical sea experience, in the fundamentals of their chosen career.

The trading square-riggers of the Erikson Fleet are held in high esteem as a training-ground for young Swedish and Finnish seamen. Under Finnish regulations, only those windjammers incorporating certain specified accommodation, which allows the apprentices to be segregated in separate quarters, may carry apprentices. *Viking*, *L'Avenir* (and, in her day, *Herzogin Cecilie*), because of their extensive poops, represent the ideal type for this work. *Pamir* and *Passat*, with roomy midship-sections, and one or two of the other barques having several large deck-houses, are also suitable, but smaller craft, like *Penang*, in which most of the crew live under the fo'c'sle head, do not take apprentices.

Apprenticeship in the Erikson Fleet

145

Sometimes the payers outnumber the paid, as in the case of *Archibald Russell* in 1932, when, out of a crew of 24 before the mast, there were only four wage-earners.

The old days of the 'brass-bounder' and the half-deck have no parallel in these present windjammers. In almost every particular the Erikson apprentices form an integral part of the general personnel. No distinction is made in work, food, or treatment, except that the more unpleasant and monotonous jobs are apt to fall to the lot of those who have paid a premium for the privilege. Even the practice of having the apprentices aft for periodical instruction from the Master in navigation and its kindred subjects is now dropping into disuse, for, by the indentures, the owner does not bind himself to provide any other tuition than that of practical seamanship. It is a hard school; the pupils assimilate their knowledge by painful experience, and it may be the intention that the opening clause of the 'Conditions for the Acceptance of Apprentices in Finnish Sailing Vessels' shall imply a warning. It reads: '... applicants should not be less than 16 years of age ... and should be of strong constitution.' Two doctors' certificates are called for, one of which must state 'that the work of a seaman will not be harmful to the applicant'. The boy's character must be vouched for by a clergyman. The apprentice is expected to produce proof that his parents or guardians assent to his sea-going, and these persons must be prepared to guarantee any expense to which the owner is put by the desertion or misconduct of the boy. Should an apprentice decide that he is unsuited to the life, or should he be discharged for offences against discipline, he must find his own homeward travelling expenses; but if he die, or be incapacitated, a pro-rata repayment of his premium is claimable. If, owing to sickness, he be left at a foreign port, the medical expenses and cost of repatriation fall, under Finnish law, to the owner's account. The boy must provide his kit, bedding, oilskins and so forth, and is charged with the cost of the certificate which is his due upon completion of his indentures.

The risk of desertion   In due course, when the apprentice is rated as an ordinary seaman, a deposit of 5,000 Fin-Marks (say £25) has to be provided against the risk of desertion. A like sum is required from every seaman in the fleet, because the not uncommon happening of 'French leave' in Australia involves the owner in a fine of £100, plus £25 to cover the expenses incurred by local authorities in locating the unlawful immigrant.

Captain Erikson's agents in Australia have to give a bond in respect of any such delinquent. As this bond is only released if and when the absentee is apprehended (and repatriated at the owner's expense), it may not be liquidated for a considerable period.

The wage scale in force to-day in the Åland windjammers may seem low in comparison with the pay of seamen in other, bigger countries, but, as already pointed out, allowance must be made for the wide difference in living standards, etc. An ordinary seaman receives 450 Fin-Marks (£2) a month, and an able-bodied seaman an additional 100 Fin-Marks. The positions of sail-maker, donkeyman, bo'sun and carpenter carry increased pay, a sail-maker, for example, getting up to 800 Fin-Marks a month. The highest-paid member of the crew is the steward, who is reputed to earn more than the Chief Mate! In this case it is probable that prevailing rumour includes, and exaggerates greatly, the various perquisites appertaining to such employment. All the world over, the mercantile profession, considering the risks run and the responsibilities incurred, is too poorly rewarded, and, to judge from their wages, the officers of a windjammer rank low on the general wage scale. For what is surely one of the hardest and loneliest jobs in all the Seven Seas, the Master of a Finnish barque receives the equivalent of between £15 and £20 per month, according to the size and type of vessel. It is understood that, in some cases, this salary has fallen to as low a figure as £12. The handling of a square-rigger may be a dying and almost useless art, but it still demands a high standard of seamanship, coupled with constant watchfulness.

The wages of windjamming

Even if the considerable extra risk entailed by life in sail be discounted, it will not be surprising if the difficulties of supplying the Erikson Fleet with competent officers increase as the years go by. Another reason acting as a deterrent is the long absence from home involved by participation in the grain trade. The minimum period of a voyage from Åland to Australia and back is nine months, and it may be that two consecutive round voyages will elapse between a windjammer's visits to Mariehamn.

Finnish regulations require an initial period of three years in sail, followed by nine months at a State navigation school, before the intending officer can sit for his certificate as 2nd Mate, a post which carries a salary of about £5 a month. Aspirants to further promotion must return to sea for two years, and then re-enter school to qualify as Chief Mate.

Finnish promotion

147

This position must be held at sea for at least one year before the final course, for a Master's ticket, can be undertaken. Such a system is calculated to produce competent officers who have all graduated 'aft from the hawse-hole', and, although the minimum period in which a seaman could qualify for command would seem to be about nine years, the early age at which the young Ålander first goes 'deepwater' accounts for the fact that many of the Erikson Masters have achieved their rank before the age of thirty.

Many Ålanders are gifted linguists, and, as a command of English is one of the qualifications required for officership, it is not unusual to find that, besides the Master and the Mates, quite a number of the crew are able to converse in more or less fluent English. In general, the Erikson Masters have an excellent command of our language. This is a great asset to passenger-carrying, because the majority of the few who to-day travel in sail for pleasure are English-speaking people.

The passenger in sail

Such an undertaking needs careful consideration, for it is not by any means 'everybody's meat'. Lasting keenness is a prime essential. It is of little avail to allow boredom to develop on a passage which may take one out of sight of land for three months at a stretch. The best method of avoiding monotony is to take a regular part in the work of the vessel, although whether to the extent of keeping watch is a matter for the individual concerned. Of course, by joining one of the two watches a more intimate personal knowledge of the crew and of their life is obtainable. Bad health, or even a liability to recurrent sea-sickness, are perhaps the greatest of deterrents in view of the total absence of qualified medical aid. The food is apt to become insipid and mono-tonous, although on the better vessels there is abundant provision of surprisingly good quality, and always plenty of fresh white bread. It is no pleasure-cruise in the commonly accepted meaning of the phrase. A portable gramophone will be the orchestra, a swill under the pump the swimming-bath, the sport will consist in a long pull at the braces or a fight up aloft with wet, bellying canvas. The reward, however, will be a grand and wonderful experience, of a kind which in a few years' time may never again be possible. The enthusiastic amateur can be promised his fill of hard work, and all the unchanged, epic beauty, magic and thrill of a bygone era.

The occasional Britisher to be found serving among these Northern crews is usually there for one of two reasons: as seaman or apprentice, he is probably under the urge of a genuine craving to see at first hand and before it is too late, life before the mast on a windjammer. Apart from these adventurous young men, any other Englishman in sail is almost certain to be preparing for the position of pilot.

The Pilotage Committee of Trinity House, under the governance of the Elder Brethren, still demands that its Channel Pilots shall be master-mariners, qualified to take charge of a square-rigger by having served for not less than a year, and at a rank not lower than that of 2nd Mate, in a sailing vessel of over 250 tons. Except in the case of what is known as 'choice work', the Channel Pilots serve on a rota system, taking in turn whatever type of craft requests their services. Consequently any one of a half-score of the Dover Pilots, who at the time happen to be on duty in the pilot-cutter cruising off Dungeness, may find himself scrambling up a Jacob's-ladder to the poop of a big inward-bound barque; he will remain in charge until he hands the vessel over to his colleague, the River Pilot, at Gravesend, ninety miles away.

Sail qualification for Channel pilotage

The harrowing little tale which follows was told by a late colleague of the man concerned — a pilot on the Harwich Station, whose luck it was one day during the War to board a London-bound sailing vessel. The craft was of a type which has now disappeared, a Scandinavian ice-drogher, a slow, unwieldy vessel, packed with blocks of ice for the provision markets. It was a hard, thrifty trade, and to the skippers of such vessels the expense of tug assistance was anathema. For nearly two weeks she beat about the mouth of the Thames, waiting for a fair wind to take her up-river. The 'old man' was deaf to all protestations from the unfortunate pilot, who no doubt was living, meanwhile, under conditions of great discomfort and on execrable food. At last, late one afternoon, the wind changed, and the clumsy old tub lumbered away up toward the Nore. In those perilous days there were certain parts of the estuary where, by order of the Naval Authorities, no vessel was permitted to anchor. As luck would have it, the light breeze died away completely when the windjammer was in the vicinity of a restricted area. Probably she was in some danger of drifting with the tide into shoal water, but, at any rate, the skipper announced his intention of lying where he was until the calm ended. The pilot implored him to close with the offer made by the Master of a tug, who, scenting a job, had kept in the offing. It was a comparatively short tow to Gravesend, where the River Pilot was to take over, but no amount of argument was

149

of avail, and down rumbled the anchor chain. Some time later a naval patrol-vessel picked up the stationary craft in the beam of her search-light, and through a megaphone inquired, in no measured terms, 'what the . . . those in charge thought they were up to'. The unhappy pilot pleaded that no power on earth would make the skipper spend a penny on towage. Back came the immediate request to pass a hawser aboard, and, rubbing his hands for joy over the prospects of a free tow, the skipper complied. To his consternation, however, he found himself being towed, not westward to his destination but eastward, back past the Nore! Daylight found the drogher once again at the scene of her previous futile efforts to approach the mouth of the Thames, and many weary days elapsed before the pilot, over whose outraged feelings it is perhaps best to draw a veil, went ashore at Gravesend, a sad and disillusioned man.

It is rumoured that in the near future the stipulation of sail exper-ience for candidates to pilotage may be allowed to lapse. In days gone by, many men, still living, served their time in British sailing vessels prior to entering the service of steam, but, where the succeeding genera-tion is concerned, the opportunites for compliance with the qualifica-tion demanded by Trinity House are very limited. For a number of years the only suitable opening for the embryo pilot, who wished to spend his year in sail under the British flag, was provided by the little barquentine *Waterwitch*, built at Poole, Dorset, in 1871. Many officers served as mates aboard this old-fashioned coaster, but sometimes, when there was a waiting-list for such berths, a candidate would elect instead to ship aboard a Finnish square-rigger for a round voyage to Australia.

Waterwitch is now, however, laid up, and for sale, at Par, Cornwall, and so long as the present requirements are in force the young intending pilots have no option but to 'ship foreign'. As, by law, Finnish vessels must be officered by Finnish nationals, the British applicant for a 2nd Mate's discharge from sail serves only in the capacity of a supernumerary officer aboard a windjammer already adequately staffed.

Races and languages in the Erikson vessels

It is not often that the present-day sailor of the sail remains for long in one fo'c'sle: the general opinion of the Erikson employees is that two voyages in the same vessel are sufficient.

The pure-blooded Finn from the interior of the Finnish mainland comes of Mongol stock. He is apt to be regarded as somewhat of a foreigner by the Ålanders and the Swedes, who dislike the readiness

150

with which the Finn will, at the slightest provocation, whip out the knife, known to him as 'Finland's Saviour', and which is carried universally aboard the square-riggers. Where numbers permit, the Finns may be put together in one watch, and the Ålanders and the Swedish boys in the other.

Although both English and German are sometimes used, Swedish is the 'Lingua Franca' of the Erikson Fleet, and, except in conversation, pure Finnish is rarely heard. A certain number of English expressions have crept into daily usage, and 'Orlright' is common parlance in the windjammer.

A few of the Swedish terms employed to-day in sail are:

Kapten	= Master
Förste styrman	= Chief Mate
Andre styrman	= 2nd Mate
Tredje styrman	= 3rd Mate
Båtsman	= Bo'sun
Kock	= Cook
Timmerman	= Carpenter
Matros	= A.B.
Lättmatros	= O.S.
Yungman	= Boy
Styrbord	= Starboard
Babord	= Port
'Looa'	= 'Helm up'
'Falla'	= 'Helm down'
'Dikt'	= 'Hard over'
'Alla man på däck	= 'All hands on deck'
'Bi de vind'	= 'By the wind'
'Stag vända'	= 'Tack ship'
'Rund vända'	= 'Wear ship'

The watch system

The system of watches in operation aboard the Erikson square-riggers is designed to prevent a man being on duty for a like period on two consecutive days. It is held to be superior to the older system of short dog-watches, instituted to break the continuity of the 'four hours on and four off' division of labour afloat. (It is now reported that one of the oldest traditions of the sea, the separation of a crew into port and starboard watches, is passing into history in the annals of British shipping. With the coming into operation of the National Maritime Board Agreement, all deck-hands on foreign-going vessels of 2,500 tons and over will, in future, through the institution of a third watch, work the equivalent of an eight-hour day. The change completes the severance of present-day life at sea from the conditions which governed it in the days of sail. For the first time in history the seaman will have eight hours of uninterrupted sleep. Thus he enters upon a basis of employment undreamed of by the 'shell-back', working conditions at sea on a par with those on shore.)

Ship's-work (by which is meant all tasks on board except those, such as steering and sail-handling, concerned directly with the navigation and progress of the vessel) lasts from 6 a.m. to 6 p.m. The duties of sailing the vessel go on, of course, without cessation, and, at any time of the day or night, one or both watches may be called upon to brace yards, to shorten or to set canvas, and so forth.

The following table shows how the ingenious Finnish method operates over a period of 48 hours. The two forms of employment are shown in juxtaposition:

	Port Watch				Starboard Watch			
	On Watch	Hours on watch	Ship's-work	Hours at work	On watch	Hours on watch	Ship's-work	Hours at work
1st day	Midnight—4 a.m.	4	—	—				
					4 a.m.—8 a.m.	4	6 a.m.—8 a.m.	2
	8 a.m.—1 p.m.	5	8 a.m.—1 p.m.	5				
					1 p.m.—7 p.m.	6	1 p.m.—6 p.m.	5
	7 p.m.—midnight	5	—	—				
2nd day					Midnight—4 a.m.	4	—	—
	4 a.m.—8 a.m.	4	6 a.m.—8 a.m.	2				
					8 a.m.—1 p.m.	5	8 a.m.—1 p.m.	5
	1 p.m.—7 p.m.	6	1 p.m.—6 p.m.	5				
					7 p.m.—midnight	5	—	—
Total		24		12		24		12

Thus, taking, for example, the time-table of a hand in the starboard watch during the above period, it will be seen that he is on watch for twenty-four out of the forty-eight hours, the remainder, weather permitting, being for sleep, etc. For half his total time on deck he is engaged in ship's-work, chipping, painting, washing down, repairing rigging, and similar jobs, but, like his leisure hours, all such work is subservient to the actual handling of the vessel. His longest period off duty is the six hours from 1 p.m. to 7 p.m. on the second day, the other free times being four, five, five and four hours, respectively. His watches on deck are similar in duration, six hours on the first afternoon being the longest stretch of duty. His quota of ship's-working hours total to seven during the first day, against a single-period of five hours on the next day. In fine weather, the week-ends, from 1 p.m. on Saturday until 6 a.m. on Monday, are usually free from tasks other than the actual management of the vessel.

Fo'c'sle meals are arranged to fit in with the above system of watches, the last half-hour before going on watch and the first half-hour of the free watch, respectively, being thus occupied. The meals are—

Food – past and present

<blockquote>
Breakfast at 7.30 and 8 a.m.
Dinner at 12.30 and 1 p.m.
Supper at 6.30 and 7 p.m.
</blockquote>

In addition, there are 'coffee' periods at 3.30 p.m. (to break the long spell of the afternoon watch on deck) and, usually, about 5.30 a.m. (for the watch who have turned out at 4 a.m.). There is, however, no break in the long forenoon watch.

Throughout the history of sail the subject of food has been a byword, and the sea-cook has been the most vilified member of the windjammer's personnel. In such matters it is only possible, of course, to generalize. Although, in past days, much unnecessary hardship was due to deplorable provisions, many of the better-class owners of sail tonnage were punctilious about the standard of living on board their vessels. Apart from such notable exceptions, British windjammers, as a whole, had a bad name in the matter of food, for unscrupulous owners took full advantage of certain substitute rations which were allowed under the Board of Trade scale. So much of the feeding trouble arose from the practice of letting the steward do the provisioning that it led to the saying that 'stewards built houses for captains to rent'.

It is customary for the steward to have charge, under the Master's control, of the victualling arrangements of an Erikson windjammer, and, in general, the meals are not so bad as might be anticipated, considering that the best sea-cooks would chose a berth in steam in preference to sail. The food varies more than a little between one vessel and another, and depends to a great extent upon the cook. When passengers are carried, especially in cases where half a dozen or more are making a short trip in home waters, extra provision is made, and the meals served are often of surprisingly good quality, the menus being well varied from day to day. On the other hand, the sameness of the food during a long, deepsea passage is one of the drawbacks of life under sail, for the difference between the dishes prepared for the crew or for the after-guard lies very largely in the supply of a few extra delicacies, most of which are, of course, tinned.

Cleanliness is a Scandinavian trait, and most of the Erikson sea-cooks keep their galleys extraordinarily spruce considering the difficulties and lack of space with which, at times, they have to contend. The cook is the hardest-worked person aboard a windjammer: his day begins soon after 4 a.m. and lasts perhaps until 9 at night. In fine weather, Sunday, a slack day for the crew, demands a full day's work from the unfortunate cook.

Although most of the actual ingredients are, to say the least of it, passably good, and the quantity supplied is sufficient for the needs of the vessel, it is true that the general standard of fo'c'sle meals is unappetizing and monotonous. Many of the outlandish dishes of bygone days have fallen into disuse by now, but it may be of interest to detail one or two of the better known:

Burgoo or loblolly = Porridge, spliced with molasses
Cracker hash = Pounded biscuit mixed with chopped meat, water and slush from the galley, and then baked
Lobscouse = Salt-horse (beef ?), ship's-biscuit and potatoes, boiled into a wet hash
Dandy-funk = Powdered biscuit, grease and molasses, mixed to a paste and baked on a plate
Dog's-body = A baked paste made from cold pea-soup and pulverized biscuit, and covered with slices of salt pork
Sea pie = Alternate layers of potato, salt meat, onions and flour paste
'Strike-me-blind'
    or = Rice, boiled with molasses
'Tar-and-maggots'

Nowadays the main ingredients of meals aboard a Finnish sailer are salt-horse, i.e. unboned beef pickled in a brine cask, and made up into a moist hash with potatoes; salt pork, often boiled in with the pea soup; fruit soup, a thick, greyish, glutinous liquid made from dried fruits, which is much more appetizing when hot than its appearance suggests; stockfish, a solid block of dried and salted cod, which can be portioned with a sharp chopper, and which needs much soaking and stewing before it is edible. These constituents are augmented by plenty of excellent brown and white bread, usually fresh-baked twice a week, rice, potatoes (at every meal), brown ship's-biscuit, tinned salmon, sugar, tinned butter, etc.

The killing of a pig is one of the outstanding dietary events of a long passage under sail, for, besides pork, it provides two delicacies(!) which are much appreciated by the Finnish crews — liver pudding and blood pancakes, the latter being eaten with jam!

The cabin extras consist of such items as sardines, canned fish-balls, cheese, prunes, condensed milk, beetroot, pickles, etc., but on a long passage there are no fresh vegetables other than potatoes.

It takes a little while to become accustomed to the method of making tea: a quantity of leaves are stewed in a little water until all the goodness (and the tannin) have been extracted; thereafter the procedure is as with spirits — two fingers of this black tea-essence are topped up with boiling water to taste.

Fresh fish, of course, is always most welcome, both bonito and porpoise being quite eatable. Every opportunity is taken, when circumstances permit, to catch a supply, or even to buy or barter for a sack of fish from any trawler which may come alongside.

A protracted diet of preserved or highly-salted food can have injur- *Health* ious consequences. Indigestion and constipation are rife, for, however unpalatable the frequent salt stews may be, the long spells of hard work engender a hunger which is oblivious to the palate, and which must be assuaged in a minimum of time. Painful sea-boils, of which the proximate cause is the chafing of the skin by wet oilskins, are largely traceable to the food. Mention has been made in a previous chapter of the fatal outbreak of beri-beri sickness which attacked the crew of *Olivebank* during one of her more extended passages. On the other hand, however, the bad old days of stinking harness-cask and weevily biscuit have no parallel in the last of the deepwatermen, whose stores, rough and unappetizing as some of them may be, are, for their type, of decent quality. The high general standard of physical development evident in the average young crew of these vessels, and the almost surprising lack of serious illness, bear sufficient witness both to the beneficial effects of the life itself on those who can stand its hardships, and to the fact that the food is at least sufficient in both quantity and nourishment to let a healthy youth thrive upon it. The officers scan a new crew carefully between Mariehamn and Copenhagen, the first short leg of the outward passage to Australia; anyone whose health or physical constitution indicates a liability to sickness, malingering or incapacitation is paid off at Copenhagen, and his berth filled by a more suitable seaman.

After the first week or two at sea it is almost impossible to have an outbreak of any infectious sickness; simple cases of broken bones, etc., come within the province of the Master, who must, perforce, include the duties of a doctor among his many responsibilities.

The division of work

The crew of a windjammer are divided into two watches: the port watch work under the Chief Mate, and the starboard watch under the Second Mate. In the matter of ship's-work the port watch are responsible for the port longitudinal half of the deck area, and are also in charge of the head sails and all the foremast canvas and gear. The starboard watch deal with the starboard side of the decks and the rest of the square-sail area.

Unless weather conditions are unusually severe, the bo'sun, carpenter, sail-maker and donkeyman, known, quite unjustifiably, as the 'idlers', are day-men, that is to say, instead of serving in the watches they work all day and rest at night.

Any spirit of rivalry between the respective watches is fostered by the Mates as being productive of better work. The division of labour is adhered to most meticulously. In washing and painting jobs, for example, it is quite a case of *lèse majesté* for the port watch to clean and repaint the whole of a cargo winch, because one half of the structure lies on the starboard side of the centre-line of the vessel, and is, therefore, in the province of the starboard watch.

A brief survey of a day in the life of a sailor may help to clarify the general procedure. There are three regular duties which go by rota — the helm, the look-out and the 'policeman'. Usually they are undertaken in spells of one hour at a time. The first two are self-explanatory; the 'policeman' acts as 'fag' for the officer of the watch, and is responsible for keeping the binnacle-lamps in good order, for rousing out the watch below at the appointed time, and for answering every note of the officer's whistle. One blast calls the 'policeman' only, two blasts mean that the whole watch then on duty are required, and a three-whistle signal brings all hands on deck.

For a few minutes imagine that you are a sailor in the port watch of a big, heavily-laden four-masted barque, homeward-bound from Australia. It is many days since she left the rigours of Cape Horn astern, and, on this fine night in March, she is sailing steadily northward toward the Equator, is just beginning to feel the beneficent influence of the SE. Trades, and all hands are looking forward to the most pleasant period of a long passage. It is midnight, and the look-out, up forward on the fo'c'sle head, has just struck 'eight bells' on the big bell in answer to the eight strokes sounded by the helmsman. The 'policeman' has roused out your watch, and all hands, except the helmsman, the look-out and the 'idlers', muster below the break of the poop, the two watches gathering on their respective sides of the deck. As soon as the 2nd Mate has made certain that the tally is complete, he gives the order to relieve wheel and look-out, and then hands over to the Mate, who has just come from his cabin in the poop for his four-hour spell on deck with the port watch. It happens to be your trick at the wheel, and, after repeating aloud the course given by the departing helmsman, you settle down to an hour of steering, a pleasant and none too arduous job on a night like this. In the meantime the free watch, who have been on duty since 7 p.m., have turned-in for their four-hour rest. At the end of your turn as helmsman comes another period of duty, an hour as look-out. The third task on the rota, that of 'policeman', happens to fall due at 3 a.m., and so when, at 3.30, 'one bell' is struck, you enter the starboard fo'c'sle to turn out the other watch for the 4 a.m. muster. As there are ten men in the port watch it will be some time before your next trick at the wheel comes round again on the rota. The Mate dismisses the watch, and you go below to sleep until breakfast time, 7.30 a.m. At 6 a.m., after morning coffee, the ship's-work commences, in which, from 8 a.m. until 1 p.m., you will be engaged without cessation. One of the first tasks is the sounding of the wells, water-ballast tanks and bilges. This is the duty of the carpenter before he goes to his 'shop' under the fo'c'sle head. For the watch on deck there are multifarious tasks; water to pump and coal to fetch for the cook, pigsties and latrines to be cleaned, lamps to be filled and trimmed, chipping rust, painting, washing, decks to be scraped and oiled, teakwork to be scrubbed and varnished and brass to be polished. Up aloft, gear needs overhauling, buntlines want

A good day in the life of a sailor of the sail

157

slacking-off, and fresh robands are required here and there along the jack-stays. There are new blocks to strop, and chafing gear to make and fit. Every now and again two whistles from the Mate bring the whole watch from their work to brace the yards to a slight change of wind, or to set more canvas as the freshening breeze promises a good day's sailing. At 1 p.m. the starboard watch come out from dinner, and now, if the present fair weather holds, you are free until 7 p.m., to eat, sleep, read, or get on with that ambitious model of the barque which you plan to finish by the time Falmouth is reached. At 6 p.m. all working gear is stowed away, for the ship's-work is over. While you are having your tea, preparatory to a long five-hour period on deck until midnight, the starboard watch are cleaning themselves in readiness for dismissal at the first of the three musters of the coming night at 7 o'clock.

Cleanliness　　Personal cleanliness aboard a windjammer is very largely consequent upon the collection and storage of rain-water in auxiliary containers, because the vessel's fresh-water supply, however adequate, is jealously guarded and strictly rationed. An exaggerated idea of the dirt and squalor of sail can be obtained from works of fiction, or even from the aspect of windjammers during working hours in port. Such matters depend almost entirely on the particular 'crowd' in occupation at the time, but given that the quarters themselves are reasonably water-tight and in sound condition, the average young Swede, German or Ålander will do his best to keep them as habitable as circumstances allow. Naturally the oldest and dirtiest of clothing is good enough for hard, rough work, or for painting, tarring-down and chipping, but, after working hours in port, or off watch in good weather at sea, these boys welcome a thorough scrub down, a clean change of clothes (even though it be just a shirt or sweater, dungarees and canvas shoes) and a decent fo'c'sle in which to eat and sleep.

The other side of the picture　　The foregoing sketch of a day under sail may give quite a favourable impression of the life to those who love the sea. But only the more pleasant aspects of the work have been touched upon: it can be very different under more severe conditions of weather. There are many, many, days on the long passages to or from Australia when all ship's-work is impossible, and when life is a cruel round of wet, cold and bitter hardship. For weeks together, clothes are never dry, cuts and sores will not heal, and the grim toil at sheets and braces or up aloft on ice-covered yards with frozen canvas becomes almost unendurable. There are two

158

facing: TRIMMING THE FOREMAST YARD

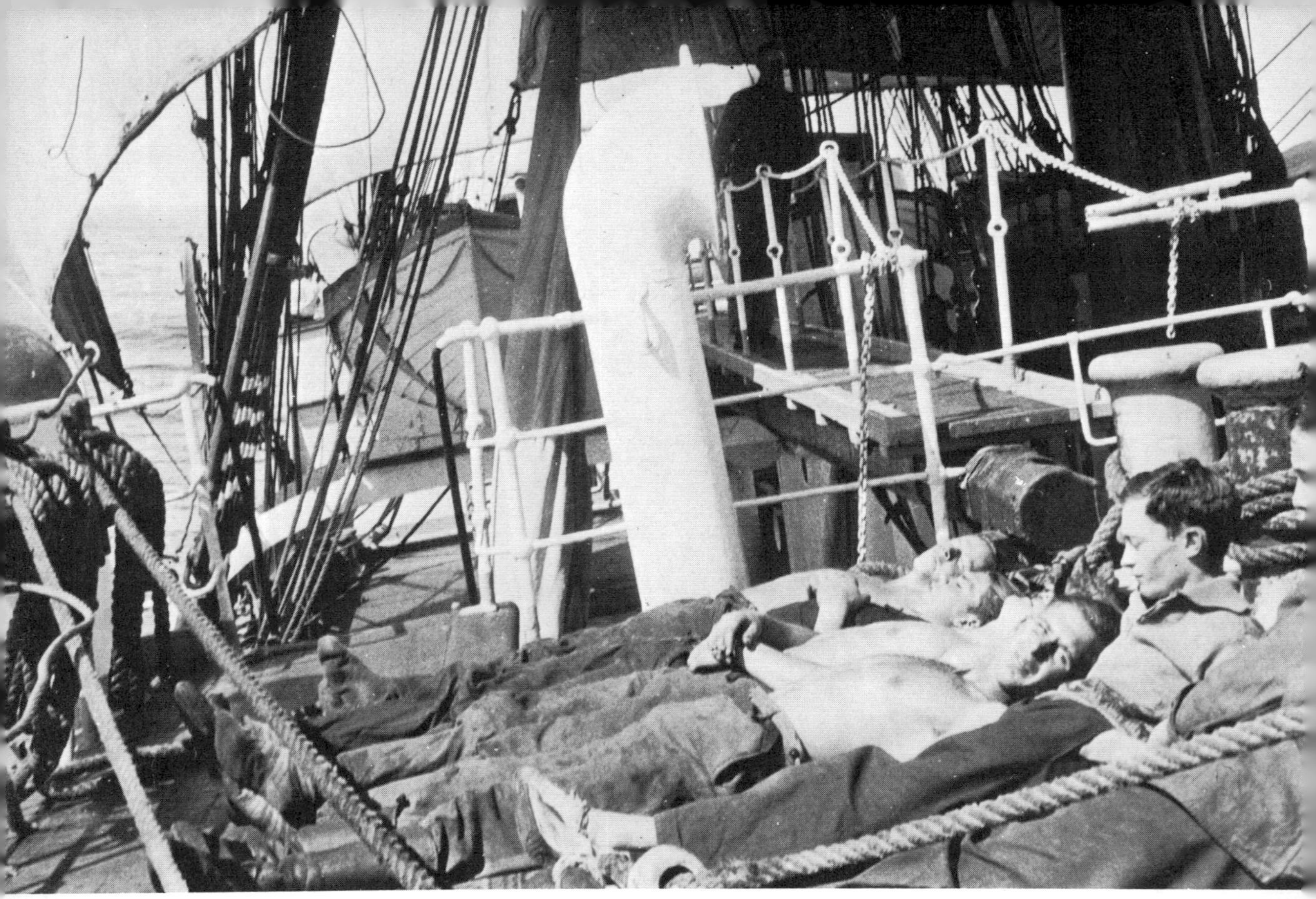

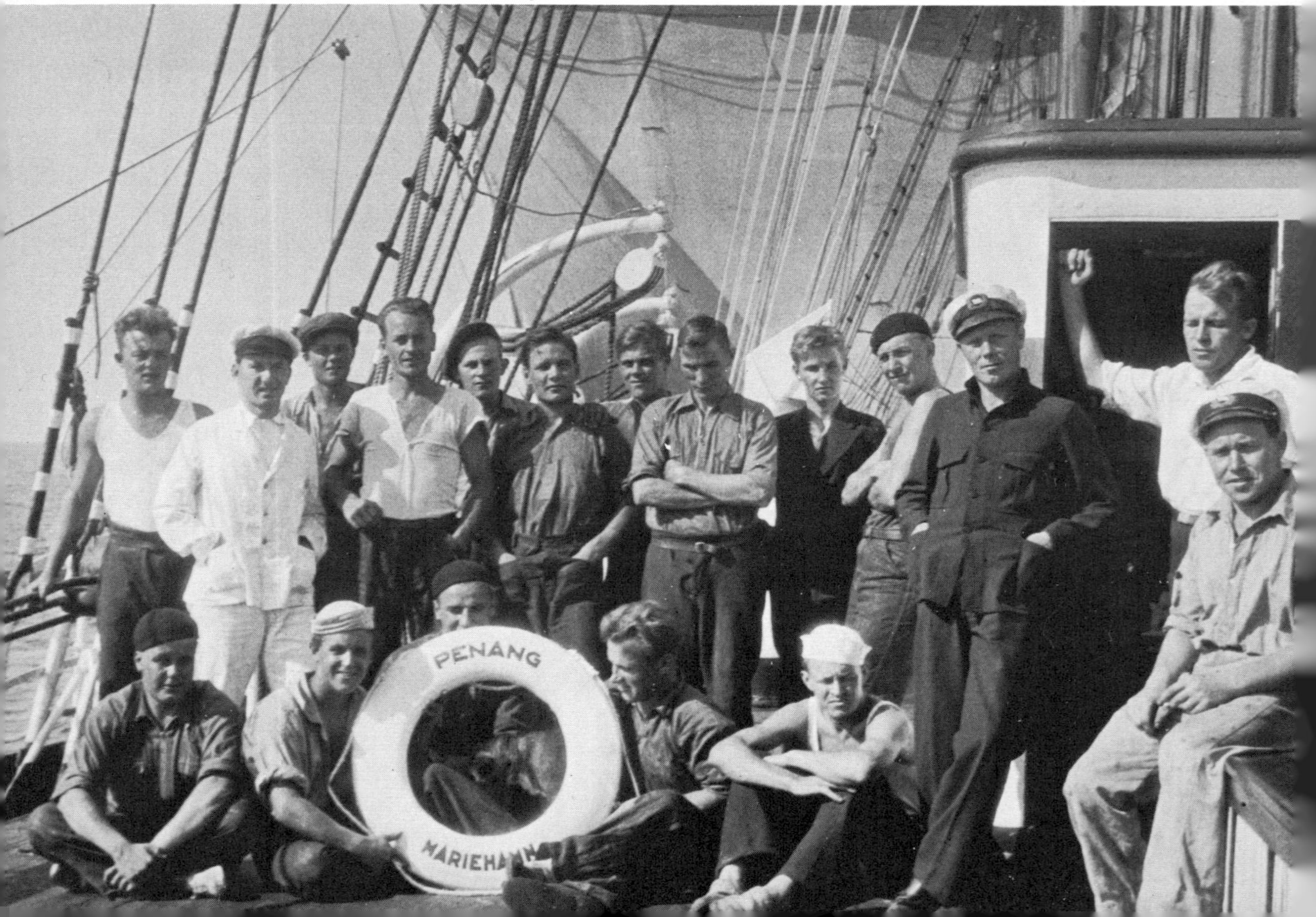
PENANG
MARIEHAMN

jobs of particular unpleasantness, 'knacker roost' (rust chipping below decks), and the discharge overside, in Australian waters, of stone-ballast. A lurid description of both tasks will be found in Mr. Sheridan's *Heavenly Hell*. During the outward passage to Australia, Mr. Sheridan spent 232 hours down in the lower holds of *Lawhill* removing a five-year accumulation of rust from her bilge-frames, by the light of a paraffin lamp. His account of this work is qualified to dissuade others from seeking a like employment.

Rust is one of the bugbears of a steel sailing vessel, and any departure from a constant programme of clearing away the oxidization, rubbing down, and then repainting, may lead to infinite trouble, and cause the vessel to show signs of neglect in a very short time.

Sail-changing According to the size of the crew, the amount of work to be done, and the particular sector of the passage, extra daymen may be appointed from among the A.B.s, and taken out of the watch system to help the regular 'idlers'.

Besides spare canvas, every square-rigger carries at least two complete working suits of sails, the one of stout-grade, newish canvas for use in latitudes of strong winds and severe weather, the other a suit of light 'tropical rags', well-worn and much patched, for equatorial and northern summer conditions. The change-over takes place at least twice on each outward or homeward Australian passage, and for this task it is usual to divide practically the whole crew into two shifts of day-men. Each mast is taken in turn, and a competitive spirit is engendered in the manning of a complete mast by one shift, who are encouraged to excel the other party in the time taken to send down the old canvas and bend the replacements. If a donkey-engine can be utilized the entire sail-area of a big four-poster can be changed in two days, but, with capstans and manual labour alone, it may take far longer.

The Mates The condition of the entire top-hamper, and of all the running and standing rigging, is the particular responsibility of the Mate, who, as a rule, is a seaman to his finger-tips and a complete master of his trade. He is the Captain's right-hand man, and, as such, ranks far above the 2nd Mate. It is usual for the 3rd Mate to be attached to the port watch, under the Chief Mate, and many of the more unpleasant of the executive duties of the vessel fall to his lot. The distinctions of rank are, at times, more loosely observed in the windjammer than is the general custom at sea. To run a big square-rigger with a small, young crew entails the

cing: Top. IN THE FREE WATCH

Bottom. PERSONNEL OF 'PENANG', 1934. CAPTAIN MATTSON AT THE DOOR; CHIEF OFFICER O. BJÖRKHOLM IN UNIFORM officers sharing in part of the work, as well as directing it. This is especially so in the handling of sails and running gear in bad weather, for not only the extra power but also the encouragement of active skilled leadership are alike invaluable.

Sometimes a certain amount of camaraderie and fraternization is in evidence between the officers and the crew. It varies considerably according to the vessel and the men concerned. It is understandable that, where the afterguard have, to a man, graduated through exactly the same hard school as the boys they control, some reasonable amount of licence and free speech is permissible. So long as the position is not abused, this state of affairs tends to promote general good-feeling on board, although obviously it has its pitfalls. By age-old custom, the Master is in an aloof and lonely position.

Entry to the quarters of the afterguard, both to poop-deck and to cabin accommodation, is forbidden to the crew without permission. The old rule is still observed, that a man coming aft along the poop, to the wheel or for other duties, must keep to the leeside of the deck, leaving the weather-side clear for the officer of the watch.

Deck-oiling In place of the older method of scouring all the deck-planking to an even whiteness by scrubbing it with wet sand and a 'bible' (a wooden block wrapped in sail-cloth), or by constant holystoning, the Åland square-riggers have their decks dressed with a mixture of linseed oil and turpentine. For a short while this treatment yields a very treacherous surface, especially in wet weather, but, besides preserving the wood, it produces a dark, uniform, waterproof finish which wears well and needs little attention. The poop may be holystoned after the oil has soaked in, in order to preserve its smartness. The gleaming, snow-white decks beloved of fiction writers may be regretted, but, like many other measures adopted to-day in square-rig, the more utilitarian result achieved by oiling is in accordance with the scale of manning.

The annual spring-clean Now that 'clean' cargoes, such as grain and timber, are her only freights, the ideal of cleanliness is readily attainable aboard the wind-jammer, always providing that the necessary impetus and initiative are forthcoming from the afterguard. It is customary aboard the Erikson vessels for the latter half of the homeward passage from Australia to be devoted, as far as possible, to a thorough and painstaking overhaul and spring-clean. By the time they reach Mariehamn they present a picture to delight the eye of any true sailor. The test of the work comes when the owner, as is his invariable habit, arrives on board to make a personal inspection. His critical eye, trained by years of practical seamanship, is quick to detect any flaw in hull or rigging, and to note any trace of inferior workmanship.

To an uninsured owner the condition of his tonnage is of the greatest importance, for, if he allow reasonable economy to deteriorate into unseaworthiness, or even into a measure of dilapidation, the risk of loss entailed thereby falls on his own shoulders. The Masters and Mates of the Erikson barques take great pride in the appearance and condition of their charges, and to their constant care is very largely due the general soundness of the hulls and the top-hampers of the fleet. After countless hours of washing with a solution of caustic-soda and soft-soap, repainting, chipping, scraping, tarring-down, etc., the windjammers look trim and spotless from truck to water-line, from bowsprit to counter. At least to outward appearance, there is little reasonable criticism on the ground of their general upkeep.

The shanty-man has no place in the daily life of modern wind- *The music* jamming, perhaps because the work is too hard to encourage his services. *of sail* I believe that a fiddler plays the capstan round aboard the well-manned *Abraham Rydberg*. Most of the grain carriers boast several gramophones with a distressingly limited selection of well-worn records! Some kind of orchestra enlivens the fo'c'sles of many of the barques, and at times, quite good singing may be heard from the free watch. Apart, however, from the grunted 'A-ha, A-ho, A-hay, Kom-op, Vast' which accompanies the heavy toil at braces or halliards, work is carried on in comparative silence, and is not stimulated by any organized shantying.

The following account is taken verbatim from Mr. Villiers' book about *Herzogin Cecilie* (*Falmouth for Orders*). At the time (1928) he was serving before the mast.

'In *Herzogin Cecilie* there was a concert in the starboard fo'c'sl on the night that we came around Cape Horn. All the boys were there, and the ship's orchestra played beautiful, sad Finnish music, and Swedish, and German. Schmidt of Weimar was the leader with the violin, of which he was a master, and his players were Fyhrqvist with another violin, Nyman with a mandoline and Ringe with his drums. What a memorable concert it was down there! Schmidt, his body swaying with the motion of the ship and the light of the fo'c'sl lamp falling fitfully on his face, standing there with his violin, leading his little orchestra with the ability of a genius — I never heard such music on a ship before as Schmidt could get from that orchestra; it was lifeless without him — Fyhrqvist beside him, playing as if he loved it (as he did); Nyman swaying on a form with his back crouched against the fo'c'sl table; Ringe struggling with the drums in his bunk, with the photographs of his home and his ships around him. Lying in their bunks, huddled on their sea-chests or on the forms, the boys gathered round and listened. The lamp swayed from side to side with the roll of the ship; outside was the roar of wind, and the pelting of rain overhead, and the swish of water on the fore-deck; and now and then there came the thunder of a sea smashing on the steel side so close, and the whole ship shuddered violently. What did we care? We listened to the music, and thought. And predominant in our thoughts was the knowledge that Falmouth was not just a name upon the map any more. For we had come around Cape Horn.'

Fo'c'sle conditions
In most sailers each man serves in rotation, and for the period of a week, as the 'fo'c'sle man' of his particular watch. His duties are to keep the living-quarters as clean and as tidy as possible, and to give them at least one thorough scrubbing during the week. It is also his job to fetch from the galley the kids and mess-tins containing the whack of food for the watch, to wash up the tin plates, etc., and to clean down the table after meals.

It was announced recently in the Press, that the following accommodation for the crews would be embodied in two big refrigerated steamers which are being built on Clydebank for the New Zealand trade: each man will have a separate cabin 'hung with curtains to match the bedspread'; panelled in hardwood, each room will contain an oak bed, book-case, writing bureau, easy chair, wardrobe and wash-hand basin, 'in a restful colour-scheme'. Times have certainly changed!

A windjammer's fo'c'sle offers little individual privacy, for the life is almost entirely communal. The short, broken hours of rest, and the stark publicity of practically every word and action, can be a greater mental hardship to some than the physical strain of the work itself or than the rigours of the outward life. His six-foot-by-two, coffin-like bunk is the young sailor's only private domain, and, in consequence, each such recess reflects in a very short time the character of its owner. The interior atmosphere of a fo'c'sle varies from vessel to vessel, even from voyage to voyage. I have been in fo'c'sles which were neat, clean, and almost picturesque, with scrubbed floors, scoured tables, and with coloured curtains to each bunk, the whole interior being well-painted and rustless. Others more nearly resembled sties than human habitations, where table-tops bore an ever-thickening scum of grease, where floors were foul with refuse, and where the rusty, sweating walls and foul bunks harboured many denizens besides their lawful occupants.

Naturally during long spells of bad weather, when watch after watch is broken by the triple whistle for 'All hands', when rough food has to be eaten hurriedly at odd intervals, when dripping oilskins, wet sea-boots, and every kind of sodden clothing cumber the walls, and when cuts, bruises, sea-boils, sheer physical weariness and lack of sleep combine to fray tempers and stretch patience to the uttermost, little heed can be paid to living conditions. It is in the long, fine spells of the Trades or of the summer North Atlantic and Baltic that the difference between one fo'c'sle and another is manifested, and when, given a decent 'crowd' forward, such quarters can be made tolerably comfortable.

In the course of a long passage under sail a bunk becomes the depository of a heterogeneous array of oddments. The following description of what lay behind the curtains of a certain lower-tier bunk aboard *Penang*, was noted down in 1934. The curtains themselves are an important fitting because they provide that modicum of privacy which can mean so much. At head and foot of the bedding, which consists of a thin mattress and some blankets covering the bottom boards, is a wooden shelf with a deep rim or fiddle. On one shelf, chocked so securely that it will not carry away in the roughest weather, is a half-completed model of a three-masted barque: masts, yards, and shrouds are in position, but the rigging and painting are unstarted. On the outer wall of the rectangular recess, or, in other words, on the painted steel-plating of the vessel's hull, is stuck a little picture-gallery of photographs, some personal and others from magazines. Alongside a few well-worn books on the other shelf is a large cigar box: it contains several curios — the vertebrae of a shark which, when threaded on to a metal rod, will be transformed into a walking-stick; a couple of tie-pins made from dried shark's-eyes; and some weed and a weird little fish from the Sargasso, preserved in a bottle of spirit. Reposing also on this shelf are a fancy mat woven out of dyed spun-yarn, a pipe, matches, a pocket lamp, and a queer souvenir, the skull and beak of a Cape Horn albatross, boiled, scraped and varnished. The rest of the occupant's belongings, in the nature of shore-going kit, etc., are stowed away in a wooden sea-chest, with plaited beckets, which is cleated down securely to the deck, a canvas sea-bag being wedged between the chest and the bunk boards. Oilskins are kept in a special space just outside the door of the fo'c'sle.

Model making at sea

In the ensuing chapters, which will describe *Herzogin Cecilie* in detail, I shall have largely in mind the needs of model-makers. The models made on board the windjammers are of considerable interest, and sometimes display genuine artistry. The construction of miniature sailing vessels is the most common hobby among the boys who man the Erikson Fleet, and the results achieved are truly amazing considering the conditions under which the work is carried out. Naturally not one such model in a hundred approaches, in actual finish, to the standard of the best class of shore work, but somehow there always seems an atmosphere of reality about a model made at sea by a sailor, which is missing from its shore-built prototype.

It is a curious fact that this hobby follows the dictates of a form of fashion. One seaman starts a model. He decides that it shall be of water-line type mounted on a putty sea, overall length about two feet, showing the vessel riding to anchor under bare poles. By the end of the passage, five out of the other six models which were started subsequently will portray a similar type. The carpenter of *Penang* had a flair for making those attractive little hanging models which depict a vessel under full sail, and are framed, behind glass, in a replica of a lifebuoy or a steering wheel: in consequence, there was only one orthodox model aboard *Penang*, but nearly every bunk in her fo'c'sle was decorated with a hanging model. The ship-in-a-bottle type is hardly ever attempted on board. Although the boys reproduce copies of clipper ships, galleons, and even yachts, as well as of the barques in which they serve, the work is usually on a fairly big scale. Except for the small, framed variety, their facsimiles are not less than a foot, and sometimes as much as three feet, overall.

Remarkable ingenuity is shown in the utilization of oddments, and some astonishing adaptations and improvisations are invented. Yarn is unravelled and retwisted to varying thicknesses. Lead-foil, tin cut from boxes, bristles of every kind of brush, odd pieces of wire, needles, pins, matches and the works of old watches and alarm-clocks are hoarded jealously by the model-maker. His work is finished off with ship's paint. The hobby provides a constant source of criticism and argument on board, for the sailor is almost more concerned with accuracy than with finish.

The rigging of a model made at sea reaches a very high standard, and, in correctness, is often superior to the type made ashore and based on drawings or photographs. There are many examples in which not only is all the standing and running rigging *in situ*, but every foot-rope, stirrup, jack-stay and ratline is correct. In such creations the yards can be trimmed by miniature braces, or hoisted by proper lifts and halliards. It is not uncommon to see models in which the rudder is controlled by steering tackles rove to the tiny wheel, and in which the anchor-capstan can be turned by a minute winch below the fo'c'sle head. Some are even fitted with electric light, and rigged so meticulously that wherever wire or chain is used aloft in the vessel herself, such gear is reproduced correctly in the replica. Usually, the yards are left bare of canvas owing to the difficulty of portraying sails, either set or stowed, in a natural manner.

The more elaborate copies take a couple of voyages to complete, and, nowadays, they find a ready market at quite high prices. One of the chief problems is to preserve them undamaged during the voyage. The usual expedient adopted is to make a wooden case with one side hinging outward, and to install a deep cradle if the model is a complete hull, or nailed wedges if it is of water-line variety.

It is little short of miraculous that these beautiful and accurate miniatures can be produced from the rough materials available, and in surroundings which are hardly conducive to delicate and meticulous workmanship. Unknowingly, the boys who to-day fill in their spare time by fashioning the out-of-date vessels in which they serve are doing valuable work by preserving, in a correct form, the characteristics of a type of craft which may, within a few years, have vanished for ever and live only in pictures and in such models.

In Joseph Conrad's great classic *The Mirror of the Sea* appears the oft-quoted sentence: 'Ships are all right, it's the men in 'em.' It is to the boys in the fo'c'sles and the men on the poops of the last of the windjammers that much of the credit for the successful survival of a handful of square-riggers is due.

*Captain
Ruben de Cloux*
The names of Captain Ruben de Cloux and Captain Sven Eriksson will receive frequent mention when the history of *Herzogin Cecilie* is recounted. The following are brief biographies of those two Masters, who, between them, commanded that barque for almost all her fifteen years of service under the Finnish flag. Ruben de Cloux was born in Åland in 1884. As his name indicates, he comes of Belgian stock, his forebears having emigrated to Åland in 1662. His father was a sailor-farmer, a combination typical of the islands in which he lived: he owned a farm, ran a small coaster, and, in addition, was a pilot. At ten years of age, Ruben went to sea as cook of a small local sailing vessel. After a short spell ashore for schooling, the boy then shipped, at fourteen years of age, in the 1,000 ton barque *Wolf*, and obtained his first taste of deepwater life during a passage of 151 days from the White Sea to Port Natal. Wanderings all over the Seven Seas followed before *Wolf* eventually arrived back in the Baltic. De Cloux left her at Stockholm, passed through navigation school, and secured a Mate's ticket. In this capacity he spent two years in the barque *Ocean*, and then, having married, he crossed Siberia, and was employed for a season in the salmon fisheries of Kamchatka. In 1913, as Mate of a steamer, he forsook sail for a while, but soon returned, to command a small barquentine in the Baltic trade. Early in 1915 de Cloux went deepwater again, as Mate of the big four-poster *Lawhill*, owned at that time by A. M. Troberg of Mariehamn. He remained in her until 1917, when, as a result of the submarine blockade, her owner decided to lay her up at Brest. From then until the end of the War Captain de Cloux was Master of an American tug operating from Bordeaux, and engaged in salvage and towage work.

Captain Gustaf Erikson bought *Lawhill* in 1919, and placed de Cloux in command. For several years he sailed that barque successfully and well, and then, as elsewhere related, was instrumental in the purchase of *Herzogin Cecilie* from France. He was appointed to command and, in 1922, at Fredrikstadt, *Herzogin Cecilie* loaded her first cargo for Captain Erikson. Eight years later, again at Fredrikstadt, de Cloux handed her over to his young Chief Mate, Matthias Sven Eriksson. For those eight years Captain de Cloux sailed *Herzogin Cecilie* with conspicuous success. During a well-earned holiday, in 1924, the barque made a round voyage to Chile under the command of Captain Grönlund, who had been Mate under de Cloux.

166

Among his fellow Masters, Captain de Cloux is credited with the gift of a 'wind-troll', for he is reputed to possess an almost uncanny foresight in anticipating weather conditions and in utilizing this preknowledge. With extraordinary accuracy he could prophesy that infinitely variable figure, the length of a passage under sail. Undoubtedly these forecasts were based on a vast and detailed knowledge of all likely exigencies, and of such factors as season of departure, trim, time out of dry-dock, capabilities of personnel, weather lore, condition and power of top-hamper, and all the many details which affect the progress of a sailing vessel.

At the age of forty-five Captain de Cloux relinquished command in order to buy and manage a small Åland farm, and, after thirty-five years of sea-wandering, to settle down in peace with his wife and family. He vegetated for just one year, and then accepted command of the barque *Plus*, a frequent visitor to London with cargoes of firewood.

The next change was in the direction of ownership, for he became one of the shareholders of a Finnish syndicate formed to operate the big four-masted *Parma*, of which he was appointed Master.

Late in 1933, after, as a last example of his wizardry, bringing *Parma* home from Port Victoria to Falmouth in eighty-three days (the shortest sail passage in the grain trade since the War), de Cloux retired from sail, although still retaining a financial interest in the barque. He became part-owner, with Captain Wennstrom, of the steamer *Bodia*, which for some time traded under his command between the Baltic and this country.

On December 4th, 1936, *Bodia* was wrecked on the coast of Norway near Rundo. She was proceeding northward from Ostend to fulfil a time-charter. Very severe weather was encountered and during a violent snowstorm her steering-gear broke down. She drifted inshore; her anchors failed to hold and her side was torn open when she struck. Captain de Cloux got a lifeboat away, but three men, out of *Bodia's* complement of twenty, were drowned in the attempt. The weather was so bad that rowing was of little avail, but after several hours of bitter exposure, the seventeen survivors were found by a pilot-cutter, which towed the boat to safety.

During the eight years which elapsed between Captain de Cloux's first departure from Australia in *Herzogin Cecilie* and his last arrival at Falmouth in *Parma*, he made, on four occasions, the best grain passage of the year, under sail, twice with *Herzogin Cecilie* and twice with *Parma*.

In 1932 nine of the fourteen Erikson Masters of deepwater sailing craft had served under, and been trained by, de Cloux. By wind-jamming standards he was an old man, for he was thirty-eight when he first took command of *Herzogin Cecilie* and forty-nine when he gave up windjamming; but sufficient has been said to give an idea of the qualities he exhibited during his many years in sail. He was one of Gustaf Erikson's most trusted captains, and a worthy representative of that fine old-fashioned type of seaman, the Master-Mariner of Cape Horn square-riggers. A broad, immensely strong man, with huge, gnarled hands and a lined, weather-beaten face, he is capable of undertaking any conceivable task connected with square-rig. He is a first class sail-maker, a fine navigator and seaman, a sail-carrier of great judgment, yet never reckless. In Åland it is said that Captain de Cloux has never lost or seriously injured a man through any defect in the rigging of his vessels, and in his sailing days he was reckoned, from the view-point of the fo'c'sle, as the 'safest' skipper in his profession.

He contributed much toward the building up of the fortunes of the world's last fleet of deepwatermen, and, by all who take an interest in the passing of those vessels, his name will always be linked with that of his beloved *Herzogin Cecilie*.

Captain Sven Eriksson

Matthias Sven Eriksson was only twenty-five when, in 1929, he succeeded Captain de Cloux as Master of *Herzogin Cecilie*. He had, however, been her Chief Mate for the previous twelve months. He is related to Hugo Lundqvist, a sail-owner of Mariehamn, and as a youth he made, in 1921, a round voyage to Australia on Lundqvist's barque *Prompt*. Two years later, Sven Eriksson became Mate of a Baltic schooner, and afterwards entered the service of Gustaf Erikson. He served aboard the Erikson schooners *Baltic* and *Estonia* before going deepwater again in the three-masted barque *Killoran*.

It was, however, in *Herzogin Cecilie* that he found his *métier* and realized his ambition. She had the quality of invoking a varying degree of affection in many hearts, but in none more so than that of this, her last master. Captain Eriksson was intensely proud of the big white-hulled barque, and he gloried in her strength and her speed. Under his care, until the end, she remained an example of what unremitting attention can produce, for at her best, with the stains of travel and the

facing: BENDING THE MAINSAIL TO ITS GEA

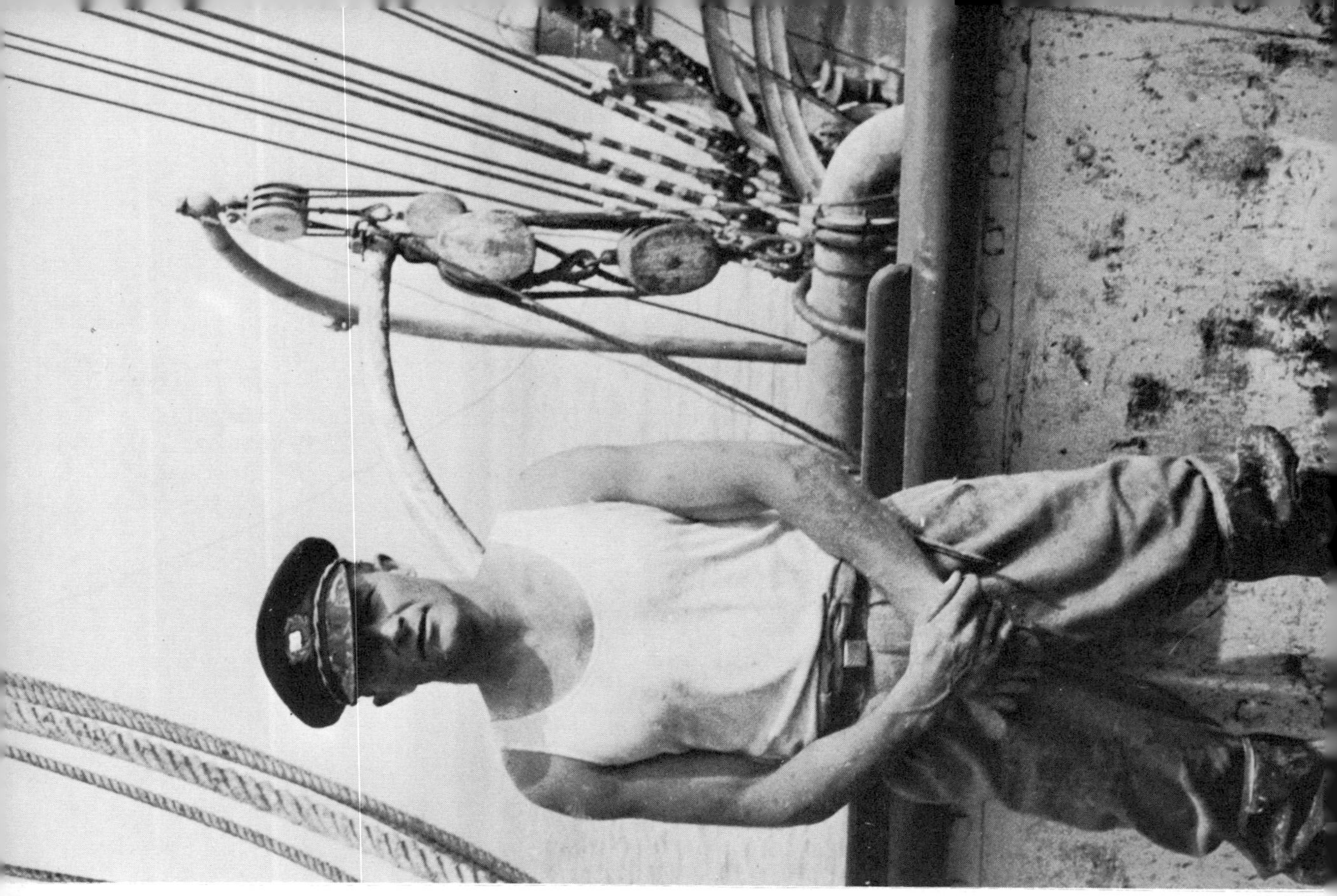

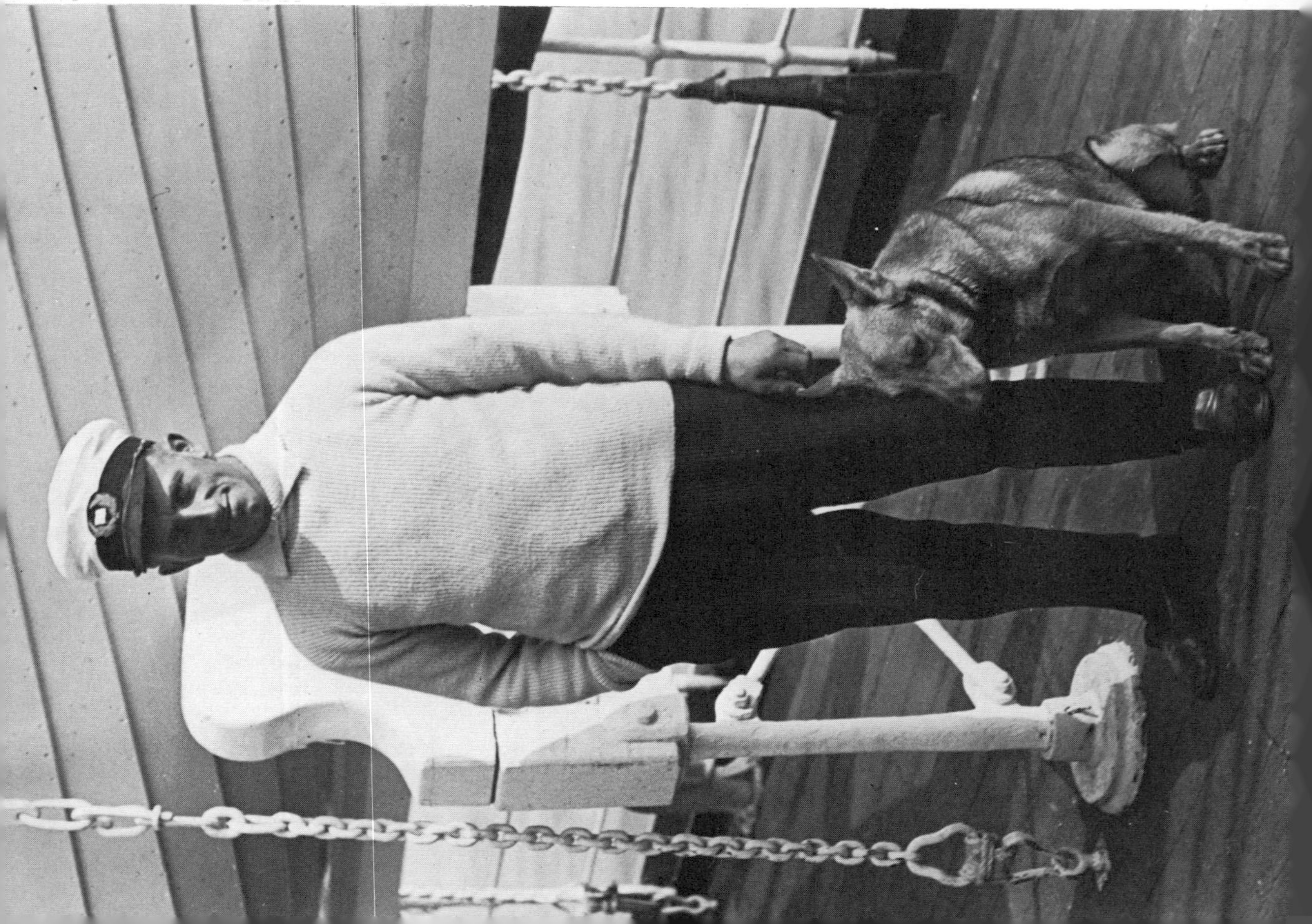

dirt of discharge removed, she more nearly resembled a great yacht than that doomed relic of the past, a sailing freighter. Those who know him feel that to him, above all others, the wreck of *Herzogin Cecilie*, at Salcombe in the Spring of 1936, was bitter tragedy.

There was no outward similarity between the two Ålanders who had command of *Herzogin Cecilie*. Sven Eriksson's trim, spare build belies, at first sight, his great physical strength, a legacy of his graduation through the rough school of the sailer's fo'c'sle. He acquired the reputation of being a strict taskmaster and disciplinarian to his crews, and he did not fraternize with his officers to quite the same extent as did some of his colleagues. The more or less like origin, age and training of most of the Masters and Mates of the Åland windjammers does not create the same barriers of etiquette between Master and Mate, or, for that matter, between Mate and crew, as are common to other maritime communities. On the other hand, the routine of duties on board does not involve the regular participation of the Master except in the matter of the navigation, although it demands his constant surveillance. Captain Eriksson had a fixed habit of making the rounds of his vessel at least twice during every day, and he kept a practical and unrelenting eye on all work in progress.

To those who visited his floating home, Sven Eriksson was a pleasant host, and in him the Scandinavian traits of courtesy and enduring friendship were very evident. No one could have been kinder, under trying circumstances, than was Captain Eriksson on the occasion of my last visit to *Herzogin Cecilie*. She was then at Starehole Bay, near Salcombe, and in a parlous condition. The wet grain was gassing so badly in her holds that the work of discharge, absolutely vital to ultimate salvage, was almost at a standstill and dependent on volunteer labour. The long weeks of anxiety which had elapsed since she first went ashore at Sewer Mill Cove had taken an obvious toll of the health of her young Master, and yet, perhaps because they appreciated that my visit was underlaid by a very real affection for their unfortunate vessel, both Captain Eriksson and his English wife did all they could to satisfy my many inquiries, and, later, to ensure that I received a personal souvenir of *Herzogin Cecilie*.

In return for the care which her Master lavished upon her, *Herzogin Cecilie* had responded by giving him of her best. In 1931 she attained to her highest recorded speed, 19¾ knots through the water and 20¾

cing: Right. MR. ELIS KARLSSON, MATE OF 'HERZOGIN CECILIE' 1933-1936

Left. CAPTAIN SVEN ERIKSSON, MASTER OF 'HERZOGIN CECILIE' 1929-1936, AND PAIK knots over the ground. This is very nearly the greatest speed ever logged under sail. In the same year, with ninety-three days to Falmouth, she had the fastest homeward passage of the grain fleet. It was, however, during that final, ill-fated round voyage, which was to end on the rocks of Devon, that *Herzogin Cecilie* excelled herself, for not only was her outward ballast passage of eighty-three days from Copenhagen to Port Lincoln the best of her seven such passages in post-War days, but by reaching Falmouth in eighty-six days on the ensuing grain passage she again beat all the other windjammers, and produced the shortest of her eleven runs in that trade under the Finnish flag.

Pommern's round voyage to Australia in 1932

The following account of a recent round voyage to Australia in *Pommern* is unique in that it is the work of the Master of an existing windjammer. Notwithstanding the large number of narratives which had been written on the same subject, it is understood to be the only contemporary description yet published of a year's work under sail from the view-point of a Captain. It was written, at the request of Mr. Ernest R. Clayson, by Captain Granith, as a contribution to *Sea Breezes*. It is here reproduced in a very slightly abridged form.[1]

Pommern, a steel, four-masted bald-headed barque, of 2,376 tons gross, was launched at Glasgow, in 1903, as *Mneme*. From 1906 to 1914 she was one of the Laeisz 'P' Fleet of nitrate sailers, hence her change of name. Gustaf Erikson bought her from the Greek Government, and she has proved a good and speedy grain carrier. For the round voyage described by Captain Granith, *Pommern* was manned by a personnel of twenty-six. She sailed from Mariehamn, in ballast, on October 2nd, 1932, bound for Port Victoria, South Australia, and was the last of the Erikson fleet, that year, to leave the home port.

Captain Granith's narrative continues:

The outward passage

'After four days out, we anchored at Copenhagen to take on board some stores and water, and then sailed away again in the evening of October 8th. Being favoured by a fresh south-easterly wind, we made an average speed of 14 knots to the Skaw. In the smooth waters around these districts there is great pleasure in sailing these ships, especially with a leading wind, but, unfortunately, head-winds and bad visibility only too frequently occur.

[1] By courtesy of the publishers, The Pacific Steam Navigation Company of Liverpool, and by kind permission of Mr. Clayson.

'During that first night at sea, we passed a score of steamers and smaller sailing craft, but owing to the darkness we were unable to show them what a sailing ship could do under favourable conditions, so the Mates were rather disappointed. When passing the Skaw Lightship the wind hauled more to the east, accompanied by heavy rain squalls, which made it necessary for some of our lighter canvas to be furled.

'Under the prevailing weather conditions, I decided to take the route north of Scotland instead of by way of the English Channel. Once, between the rain squalls, we sighted the Norwegian coast, and a course was now shaped for Fair Island.

'The easterly wind had by this time increased to gale force, sending us along at a very good rate, so that after only 39 hours from Copenhagen we passed that green storm-thrashed piece of land.

'In order to keep well away from the Scottish coast, the course was changed to due west, but as the wind, which has so much to say in these ships, kept backing around to the north and west, we only just managed to steer clear of the coast. Abreast of St. Kilda the wind was SW., blowing fairly hard.

'After heading north-westward, close-hauled for a day, the wind suddenly veered into the NW.; the ship was taken full aback, which caused a certain amount of confusion amongst our untrained crew; but, fortunately, we had the lower courses and all the light sails furled at the time, so with all hands pulling at the braces, we soon had the ship on her course again, heading south. The wind continued to blow a moderate gale, accompanied by occasional hard squalls.

'As all mariners know, north of Scotland is no picnic ground, so with all sails set we were anxious to get away from there as soon as possible. When the squalls struck the ship, she was luffed up in the wind in order to take the greatest part of the strain off the rigging, and when the hardest part of the squall had passed, the ship was put back on her course. This process caused a tremendous clattering and flapping of the sails, but it saved us from clewing them up.

'On the parallel of Cape Finisterre we sighted the four-masted barque *Pamir*, also belonging to Capt. Gustaf Erikson; she left Copenhagen 2½ days ahead of us, and was bound for the same port. We kept her in sight the following day, but we parted again during the night.

171

'The next day offered us a fresh south-westerly gale: the hardest
blow we had experienced during the whole voyage. Still it could not
be termed really bad weather; it did not last very long before it wore
round to the north, and, without further delay, set us right into the
north-east Trade and fine weather.

'For five days we were detained in the Doldrums with light and
unsteady winds — as usual. One day a school of dolphins made an
appearance, and we caught a good many fine specimens, which gave
us a welcome change in our menu.

'During the afternoon of November 5th, we picked up the south-
east Trades, and how glad we were to know that for the next week or
ten days we'd have a steady wind. The only good thing about the
Doldrums is that they offer an excellent opportunity for an inex-
perienced crew to learn how to pull the braces, and to gather rain-
water while waiting for the next shift of wind.

'At daybreak, on November 7th, we sighted another sailing
vessel, astern, and at first we thought she was overtaking us, so we
immediately set about trimming out kites aloft to a T — sheeting
home a little more here and slacking a little there — until nothing
further could be done to them. After a couple of hours it was quite
evident that our early fears were quite unnecessary. We recognised
her to be the three-masted barque *Penang*. We backed our main-
yards until she came abreast, when we exchanged signals, and after
wishing each other " pleasant voyage " continued on our respective
courses. *Pommern* proved to be the faster ship, although the difference
in speed was only slight. We kept *Penang* in sight for three days
before she finally disappeared astern.

'The same day we sighted *Penang* we crossed the Line, and at
4 p.m. Neptune and his Staff paid us a visit. We continue to keep up
this old sea-custom of initiating those members of the crew who
experience their first Crossing of the Line.

'The performance being over, and the boys having washed themselves clean, they felt rather elated at the thought of having been
initiated into the realm of Neptune. The certificate to this effect,
signed by the Master, is much sought after and is taken great
care of, as it is not many who wish to go through this performance a
second time.

'We lost the south-east Trade in latitude 9° S., and on coming to

172

facing: ON THE MIZEN LOWER-TOPSAIL YAR

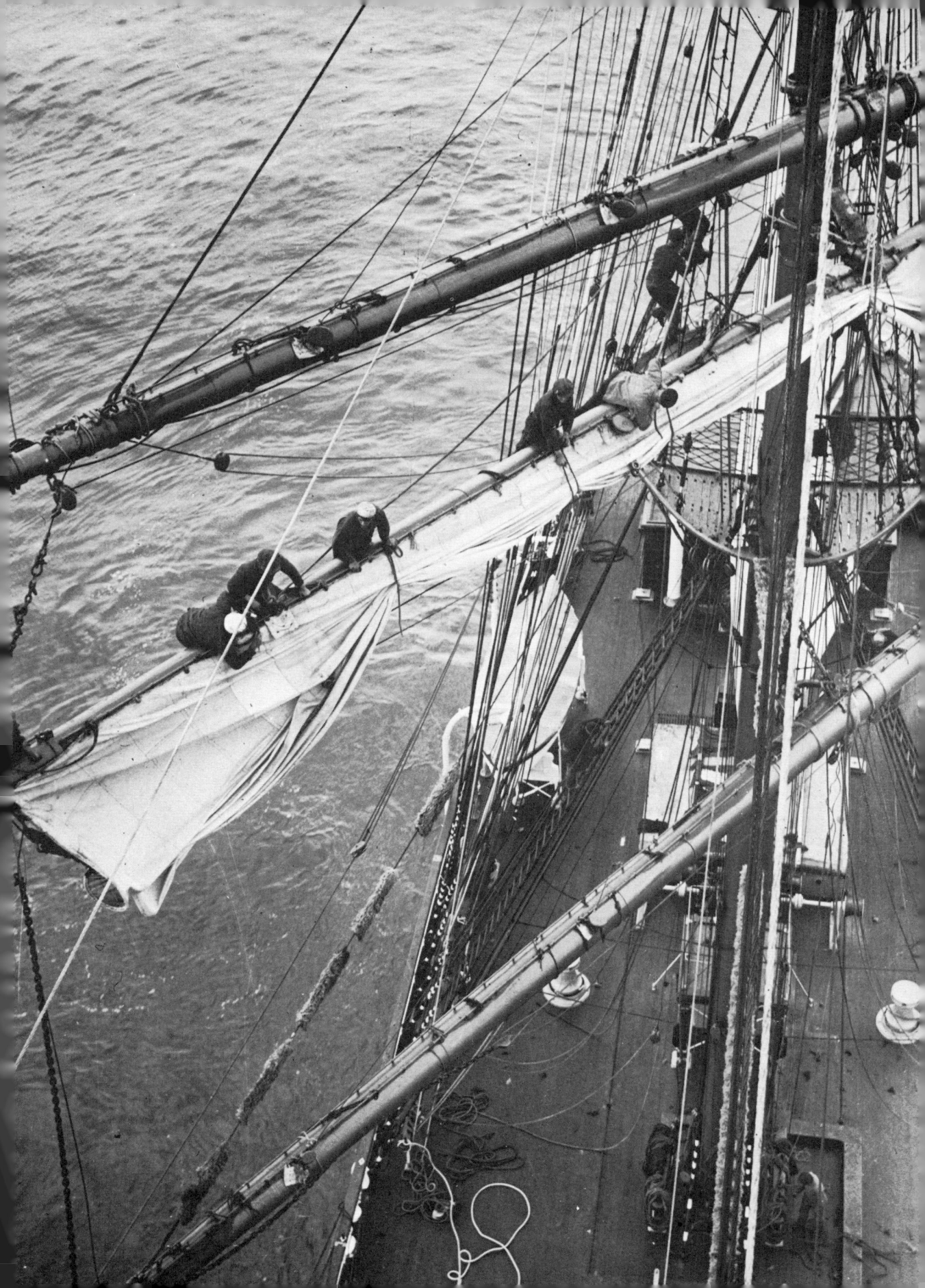

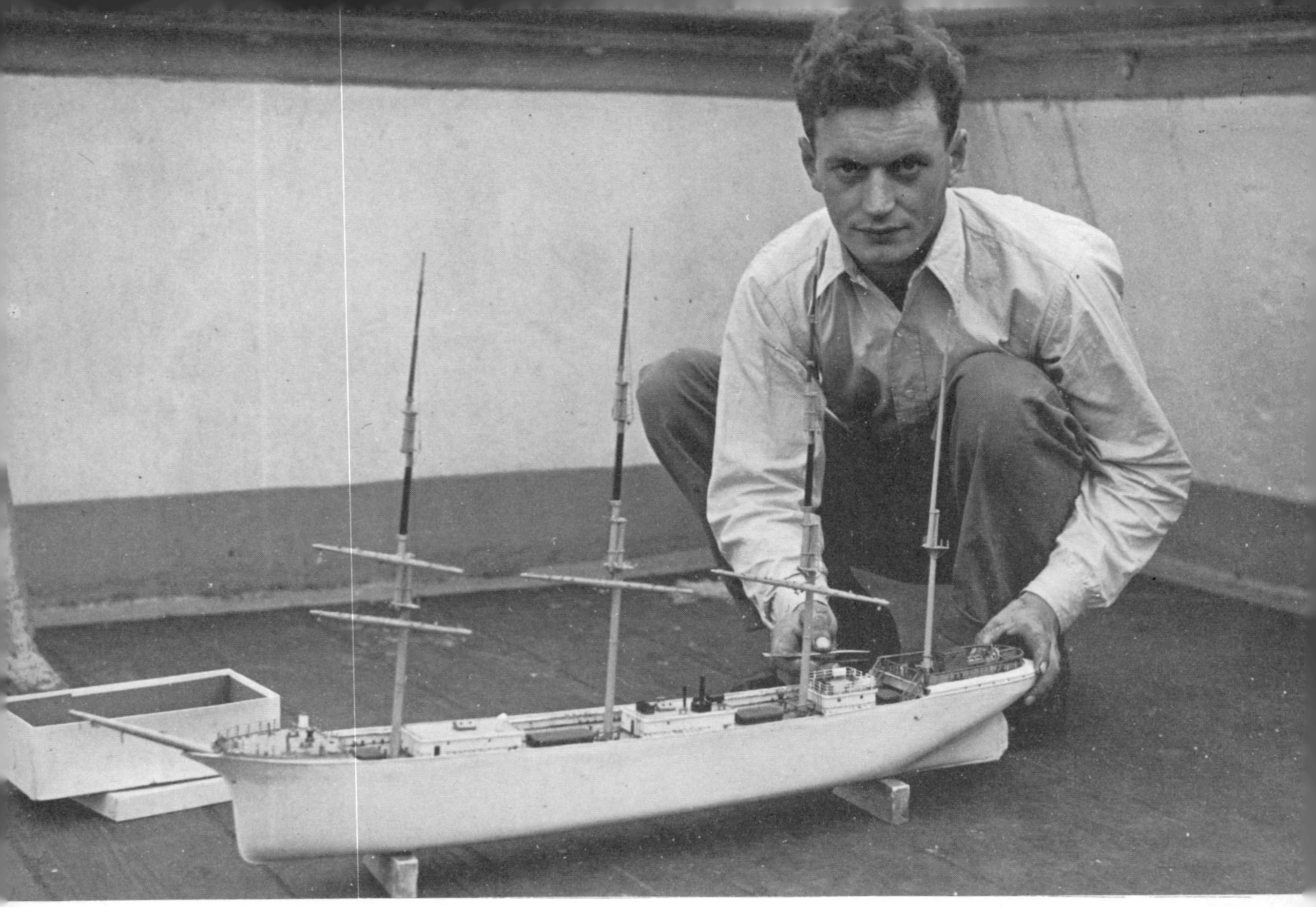

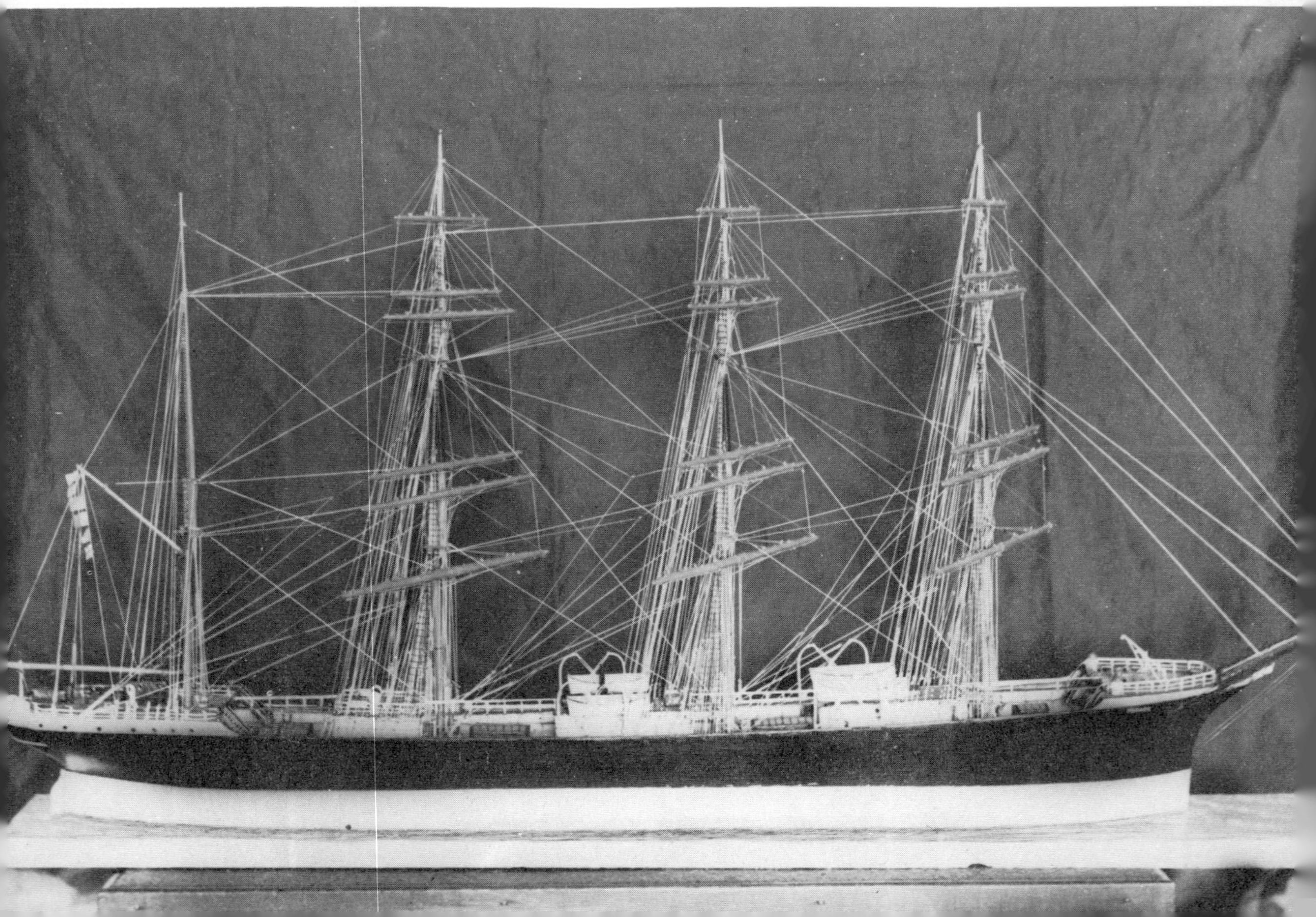

the Calm Belt of Capricorn we again sighed *Pamir* ahead of us; the wind being free we slowly gained on her. Shortly afterwards we were both becalmed for two days, lying idly in a high swell without steerage way. When the wind came up again, from the south-west, we saw, to our disgust, *Pamir* drawing ahead and, finally, disappearing altogether. There was no mistake about it — close-hauled she was the faster barque.

'I intended to sail in sight of the Island of Tristan da Cunha in order to ascertain the correctness of the chronometers, and probably heave the ship to for a couple of hours for the purpose of bartering with the islanders and leaving with them a parcel of books, newspapers and a few other things. They are always very grateful to any ship that comes to stop and exchange greetings, etc., with them. However, thick weather set in and we did not even sight the island.

'We crossed the O. Meridian in 40° S., and, from now on, commenced the best piece of sailing I have ever had the pleasure to take part in. The westerlies blew strong and steady, so that for the first five days we had the following runs: 300, 303, 304, 296 and 304 miles.

'In a squall off the Cape of Good Hope, with all square sails set, the two helmsmen allowed the ship to run up into the wind. I thought for a few dreadful moments that some of our spars must carry away; the topgallant masts bent at a dangerous angle, but fortunately everything held. A third man was now sent to the wheel, and the officer of the watch stood continually by the compass.

'On the parallel of 44° we ran the easting down across the Indian Ocean. The winds only slackened twice during the run down, and then they soon came up strong again from the westerly quadrants — thus it happened that we had only two days' runs below 200 miles.

'In the eastern portion of the Indian Ocean the winds were very steady, and it was here that we made our record run of 330 miles from noon to noon: this distance is by log, and does not include the easterly set of the current.

'Taking an average of our daily runs from O. Meridian till we arrived at Port Victoria, we had made 265 miles for twenty-four consecutive days.

'We made Port Victoria on December 23rd, thus completing the

ng: Top.   R. HUSELL AT WORK ON A FULL MODEL OF 'PONAPE'

Bottom. A SAILOR-MADE WATER-LINE MODEL OF 'PONAPE'

passage from Copenhagen in 75 days 3 hours. (This was the best outward passage, under sail, for that year. — *Author's note*.)

'The same day *Pamir* arrived at Port Lincoln with a passage of 77 days from Copenhagen. (*Penang* reached Port Victoria on the following day — 75 days out from Dungeness. — *Author's note*.)

The homeward passage

'The first windjammer to leave Port Victoria was the German four-masted barque *Priwall*, on January 18th, then followed *Mozart* and *Olivebank* on February 1st; *Viking* sailed away four days later.

'We had rather a slow dispatch, and did not leave for Falmouth (f.o.) until the morning of February 11th, 1933.

'A leading wind soon took us out of the Spencer Gulf, but shortly after reaching open water the wind wore ahead.

'I had intended to take the usual route homeward around the Horn, but as the SSE. wind was a dead muzzler for the Eastern route, I abandoned the idea and after a short attempt at beating, squared-off for Cape Leeuwin.

'After sailing westward for three days, we again struck head-winds. I was by this time quite undecided what to do — to turn back meant loss of time and increased distance; on the other hand, I knew of ships beating against the westerlies for weeks in vain efforts to weather Cape Leeuwin, and then having, finally, to turn east. Thinking this would probably happen to us, I decided that as we had already lost enough time it was as well that we should revert to our original intentions to come around the Horn.

'For several days we had a nasty south-east swell and light westerly winds, so that we were unable to get a proper way on the barque; however, we finally drifted by Tasmania, and on March 3rd we passed Campbell Island (S. of New Zealand). Thence to the Horn we made a smart run.

'Two days before we rounded the Horn, we sighted a wind-jammer on our port bow. At once we set every stitch of canvas hoping that we should be able to catch her, but, unfortunately, rain and darkness separated us before we could identify her.

'On March 24th, forty-one days out from Port Victoria, we rounded the dreaded Cape with the finest weather imaginable, a high and steady barometer and an exceptionally smooth sea. I have been around the Horn more than a dozen times, and I have never passed it under such favourable weather conditions.

'At Easter we enjoyed some eggs, and killed one of four pigs which we had aboard.

'From Cape Horn to the Line, which we crossed on April 20th, took us 26 days. The winds were light, but we were favoured by an unusually strong current setting east.

'Off the Falkland Islands we struck a northerly gale, the hardest blow we had had so far on the homeward run.

'Along this section of the route, between the 50th and 40th parallels, is situated the district I dread more than any other on the Globe. Owing to the numerous icebergs we passed there during our passage in 1927, it is impossible for me to pass through this region without remembering that experience. In that year we had ice constantly in sight for more than 700 miles, with several close calls for collisions.

'I have since sailed six times through this same zone, but without seeing any icebergs at all.

'The Doldrums treated us extremely well this time: the wind was easterly, light but steady. We were fortunate not to strike any dead calms, so close-hauled we slipped through into the north-east Trades without touching a brace.

'Similar conditions were experienced in the Horse latitudes. As soon as we entered the Anti-Trade winds we picked up a fresh SSW. breeze, which became so strong that, on May 13th, we made a record run for the homeward passage — 276 miles.

'Our light canvas was suffering badly, but there was nothing to do except let the sails stay there: if we had touched them they would have surely gone to tatters.

'From the Azores we had only slight winds to the Channel. At daybreak on May 19th we sighted a large sailing vessel ahead of us; at first we thought her to be *Viking*, but as we gained on her we recognised the four-masted barque *Herzogin Cecilie*. She had sailed from Adelaide 17 days ahead of us.

'At noon, Bishop Rock was abeam, our chronometers being more than four minutes out. I rather expected this, as twice during the voyage we had tried to sail within sight of islands, but were unable to see anything of them.

'We arrived at Falmouth Bay at 2 a.m. on May 20th, having made the passage in 97½ days. (Only two other sailing vessels made a better passage than *Pommern — Pamir* with 92 days and *Parma* with 83. — *Author's note*.)

'Thus ended the finest and the most pleasant round trip to Australia and back I have ever made — without a storm or any damages to the ship or loss of valuable canvas.'

BOOK TWO

THE DESCRIPTION AND
HISTORY OF
HERZOGIN CECILIE

CHAPTER I

THE HULL

A song of strength and a song of speed,
Of the dream made true and the word made deed,
In bow and bulwarks and ribs and keel,
An epic in iron an ode in steel.

The
*Norddeutscher
Lloyd and sail
training*

THE news, in the summer of 1936, that the great Norddeutscher Lloyd Company of Bremen had purchased the auxiliary barque *Magdalene Vinnen* for training purposes, was as surprising as it was unexpected, for it is now over twenty years since their flag was set at a windjammer's gaff: she was *Herzogin Cecilie*, for twelve years prior to the War the crack cadet-ship of the Line. *Magdalene Vinnen* has been renamed *Kommodore Johnsen* in honour of one who, after serving in sail, rose to the command of the great Atlantic liner *Europa*, and became the Commodore of the Norddeutscher Lloyd Fleet.

Doubtless Herr Hitler's recent edict forbidding German youth to train in foreign vessels was one of the factors which determined the metamorphosis of the *Magdalene Vinnen*, for the Norddeutscher Lloyd have always believed in the efficacy, if not the necessity, of a sail-trained personnel for their liners. (See notes C and D, page 415.)

As long ago as 1896 it became apparent to the Company that the supply of officers required to man a big steamer fleet was endangered by the decrease of the commercial sailer. German regulations demanded sail-training as one essential attribute of all candidates for a Master's ticket, and so heartily did the Norddeutscher Lloyd endorse this qualification that they decided the time had come when only a private training scheme could ensure the fulfilment of their own demands.

The Grand Duke of Oldenburg, an enthusiastic supporter of this local venture, was elected President of the scheme, and in 1899 the Norddeutscher Lloyd purchased from the builders, Rickmers of Bremerhaven, the iron barque *Albert Rickmers* (2,395 tons gross, and four years old).

As a tribute to the ducal President, the vessel was rechristened *Herzogin* (i.e. Duchess) *Sophie Charlotte*, and she was commissioned for the exclusive purpose of training, under trading conditions, future officers for the Norddeutscher Lloyd steamers.

Rickmers, who were also shipowners on a large scale, had acquired, over a long period of shipbuilding, the reputation for designing speedy craft. *Herzogin Sophie Charlotte* upheld that tradition most worthily: her twenty-one day passage from Hiogo to Portland, Oregon, has never since been equalled under sail power; while 77 days Sydney to Europe and 106 days Honolulu to Bremen are passages of which any clipper might well boast.

The birth of 'Herzogin Cecilie'

The training scheme proved so successful, both financially and in regard to its output of satisfactory personnel, that, although retaining *Herzogin Sophie Charlotte* in active commission, the Norddeutscher Lloyd placed, in 1901, a specific order with Rickmers. They required a high-class, speedy, smart, four-masted steel barque possessing larger cargo-capacity and better accommodation than was available in the earlier vessel. The new barque was launched on April 22nd, 1902, received the Mecklenburg title of *Herzogin Cecilie*,[1] and by June of the same year she was ready to start on a career, to date, of thirty-four years of successful sailing. Her condition to-day reflects every credit on those who designed and built her and on the qualities of material and workmanship which they embodied in her.

So it was to that vexed question, the advisability of training under canvas, that *Herzogin Cecilie* owed her birth and, in some measure, her continued existence. It was a birthright which endowed her with the fair lines, lavish equipment, individual lay-out and excellent sailing qualities which, later, were to single her out from among the surviving commercial sailing vessels of the post-War era as one of the finest square-riggers still in commission.

The term 'clipper'

The descriptive term 'clipper' is subject to frequent misuse; in fact, so often is it misapplied that its original significance has become obscured. It is to-day a common fallacy to designate a vessel 'a speedy clipper' (*vide*, for instance, the annual 'blurb' concerning the so-called 'Grain Race') merely because her lines appear a fraction sharper and shapelier than the general box-like proportions of her twentieth-century contemporaries or because, given a sufficiently strong wind, she may be able at times to sail reasonably well.

[1] Duchess Cecilie of Mecklenburg became, upon her marriage to the eldest son of Kaiser Wilhelm II, the Crown Princess of Germany.

facing: PLAN

CARGO RIGGING CABLES

Dº

CARGO CHAIN Lᴿ FORE PEAK

W.B. TANK

110   120   130   140

AILS

CARGO   CARGO   CARGO

CARGO   CARGO

TUNNEL   TUNNEL

W. B. TANK   W. B. TANK

PUMP RM

50   60   70   80   90   100

"HERZOGIN CECILIE" IN 1902

E PROFILE OF THE HULL AND THE PLAN OF RIGGING AND

PROVISIONS PROVISIONS CARGO

AFT
PEAK CARGO CARGO

W. B. TANK

0 10 20 30 40

0 25 50 75 FEET

TH

THE HULL

Clipper lines

Theoretically, the lines of an extreme clipper attained maximum breadth at only one point in her entire length, that point being situated well forward of the midships mark. From thence, flowing lines swept away symmetrically fore and aft with ever-increasing taper. The underwater lines narrowed steeply to a deep keel, and the bows raked well forward with considerable sheer. In other words, the design was an early and highly successful application of the modern principles of stream-lining. Vessels so endowed were yacht-like in their poise and grace: to the eye they were a pure delight, having that satisfying beauty of creations perfectly suited to the service for which they were designed.

The big American soft-wood clipper *Lightning*, holder of the record for the greatest distance ever sailed in one day, was not only almost as sharp up forward as is the modern destroyer, but was actually concave at the water-line. A cord stretched from her cut-water to a point just abaft the fore-mast, along the load displacement line, showed a concavity of sixteen inches. Her stem raked boldly outward, the bow lines becoming gradually convex, blending harmoniously with the sheer line and cut-water, and balancing perfectly with the fine-drawn clearance of her stern and quarters. (See note, page 51).

The *Sovereign of the Seas*, another of Donald McKay's superb creations, was so sharp in her ends that, although her registered tonnage was 2,421, she could not take, when fully loaded, more than 3,000 tons of cargo. (See note, page 51).

Such were the clippers; slim, exquisitely proportioned racers, the ideal of applied art, designed first and foremost for their sailing qualities.

In point of fact, so wet did the earlier extreme clipper prove in heavy weather, owing to the fineness of her bows, that it became apparent that average speed was, if anything, more dependent on the run of the stern than on sharp cut bows alone, for the former attribute had a marked effect on the ability of the vessel to 'ghost' (i.e. slip through the water) in light winds. Fine stern delivery, like fine bow entry, could be overdone, and was inclined to render a vessel liable to the danger of being pooped over her counter by a following sea.

Clipper trim

The true clippers were, in the first place, built for the rapid transportation of passengers and specie, then for the carriage of specific cargoes whose small bulk was disproportionate to their high value.

Cargoes of this type were stowed by expert stevedores in a scientific

181

manner which permitted the vessel's trim and balance to be adjusted to the finest degree, mere quantity loaded being of secondary importance. So meticulous were the Captains of certain of the 'China Birds', that, after loading to an even keel they would, on reaching the open sea, re-trim by shifting heavy weights about the ship, such as the transfer of lengths of chain cable from the forward locker to an after stowage.

This allied perfection of line and trim enabled the clipper to cut into rather than to smash through the seas, and although when hard-driven, close-hauled, in heavy weather they were often, as the saying goes, half under water, they could sail well in almost every diversity of weather.

It is a well-authenticated fact that passengers aboard *Lightning* were able to dance on the poop-deck when, running her Easting down under all plain sail before the strong prevailing Westerlies and big seas of those latitudes, she was logging a steady fifteen to seventeen knots.

The smaller, daintier, English, composite or hardwood tea-clippers of a subsequent decade could 'ghost' ahead in breezes too light and faint to give their ultimate successors — the big, blunt, steel four-posters — even steerage-way.

With their enormously strong top-hamper of steel spars and wire and chain rigging, however, those same utility 'Cape Horners' of a later day could, naturally, carry canvas under gale conditions which would have proved suicidal to the hemp-rigged, wooden-sparred clipper.

In practice, it is only in really heavy weather that the big sailing vessel of this century has been able to log speeds in any way comparable with those of such famous forerunners.

'*Herzogin Cecilie*' not a clipper

When the subject of speed and performance comes under detailed examination, comparisons will be drawn between *Herzogin Cecilie*, her predecessors, and her contemporaries. At present it is sufficient to say that, although for her age and type she is one of the fastest and most seaworthy sailers afloat, she is not, nor ever was intended to be, a clipper.

Herzogin Cecilie cost 860,000 Marks (at that time, £43,000), and no expense was spared in her specification: she was built to sail, handle and look well, and her occupation rendered her to a large extent independent of her earning powers. Given the carrying capacity and the strength befitting a commercially successful freighter in the arduous West Coast nitrate trade, she was, nevertheless, conceived primarily as the crack German cadet-ship of her time.

THE HULL

Heavy bulk or bagged cargoes, crammed piecemeal into large square holds and forming a solid 'dead' mass incapable of fine trimming, are hardly conducive to a vessel's speed, handiness or 'tenderness', but *Herzogin Cecilie's* designers managed successfully to combine beauty, sea-worthiness and capacious utility in one splendid whole.

It must, however, be once more reiterated that, although her definitely handsome lines did endow her with more grace and better qualities than was possessed by most of her contemporaries, *Herzogin Cecilie* is undoubtedly 'full' in comparison with even the most medium of the true clippers.

For purposes of hull comparison, a rough and ready form of Architect's Block Coefficient can easily be arrived at from a vessel's dimensions.

Block coefficient of hull

Suppose, for instance, that the solid model of a hull is being carved from a rectangular block of wood already cut to the requisite length, depth and width. To produce the light, graceful body of a yacht at least one-half of the block would be trimmed away; whereas for a beamy, full-lined dinghy model barely a fifth of the material would disappear.

The actual fraction of the block which remains, in the form of a hull, is ascertained mathematically by dividing the cubic area of the original block, representing the overall length by breadth by depth of the vessel, into the under-deck tonnage of the finished hull (rendered into cubic feet at 100 cubic feet to the ton).

For example, a hull 200 feet by 40 by 20 (160,000 cubic feet) and 1,000 tons under deck (100,000 cubic feet) would have a coefficient of $\frac{100,000}{160,000}$ or ·625, showing that about one-third of the solid had been cut away. Naturally, when using this method of comparison, equivalent measurements of the respective vessels must be taken. In the following table, dimensions given by *Lloyd's Register* of the period have been used throughout — this being as near to a standard basis as can be attained.

I have calculated the coefficient of a few representative hulls of varying types and periods, all famous craft, several of which will be referred to later, for purposes of comparison, when *Herzogin Cecilie's* history and sailing qualities are under discussion.

Comparison of hull coefficients

Cutty Sark and *Thermopylae*, two of the best-known of the English extreme clippers, need little introduction. They were both composite full-rigged ships.

Sobraon was the largest composite iron and teak full-rigger ever built, and had wrought-iron lower masts, steel topmasts, and steel lower yards. Her story was sketched, briefly, in Book One, Chapter 1.

Lancing, originally built in 1865 as an iron, screw barque, with engines of 1,000 h.p. and a big sail-plan, was converted at Glasgow in 1888, by Robert Napier & Sons, into a four-masted full-rigged ship, and, her engines removed, she became one of the finest and fastest sailing vessels of her time. She was broken up in 1925, the iron hull having lasted out sixty years of sea service.

France, a five-masted steel barque, and the wonderful five-masted steel ship *Preussen* were exceptionally large and powerful 'Cape Horners', running, like *Herzogin Cecilie*, in the nitrate trade during the final transition period of sail versus steam. *France*, built by Henderson of Partick for Antonin Dom Bordes et fils of Bordeaux, was abandoned on her beam-ends when outward bound in 1901. *Preussen*, owned by F. Laeisz of Hamburg, was wrecked after a collision off Dover in 1910.

	Built	Length	Breadth	Depth	Under Deck Tonnage	Coefficient
Cutty Sark	1869	212·5	36	21	892	·55
Thermopylae	1868	212	36	20·9	927	·58
Sobraon	1866	272	40	27	2,089	·71
*Lancing	1888	356	43·8	27·3	2,620	·62
France	1890	361	48·8	25·9	3,725	·82
Preussen	1902	407·8	53·6	27·1	4,788	·81
Herzogin Cecilie	1902	314·1	46	23·8	2,672	·78

* As converted.

The subject of measurement discrepancies will be dealt with in due course, and an explanation given of why, in *Lloyd's Register* for 1935, *Herzogin Cecilie's* dimensions differ from those given above. For the present purpose it will suffice to say that the former are based on Finnish practice, the latter on German. The extra twenty feet in length (334·8) given in the 1935 *Register*, and representing almost the entire overall length of the hull (without bowsprit), makes a striking difference in the coefficient, reducing it to ·71, but it is an unfair basis to adopt for comparative purposes.

Moulded depth (where figures are available) renders, of course, the most representative coefficient of all, because it is the entire depth of the hull amidships from keel to upper-deck, whereas registered depth (as used in the foregoing table) is only the maximum depth of hold.

Herzogin Cecilie's coefficient if arrived at by using overall length (334·8) and moulded depth (27·8) becomes as low as ·62. *Preussen*, on the same data, becomes ·67; *Lancing*, ·58; while the two English tea-clippers are only a fraction over ·50.

Another basis of hull comparison is by the method of 'beam-to-length' ratio, i.e. the figure obtained by dividing the extreme breadth of a hull into its overall length.

The development of beam-to-length ratio

The rounded, tubby, flat-bowed, low-waisted profile of the Elizabethan galleon is familiar to everyone. Such vessels had a beam-to-length ratio of three; in fact Sir Walter Raleigh is said to have expressed the opinion that the best proportions to use in building a 'greate shippe' were 100 feet by 35 feet.

Even the famous *Sovereign of the Seas* of 1,522 tons, built in 1637, conformed relatively to those dimensions. She was designed, by command of King Charles I, as the finest man-of-war and the largest vessel of her time.

Ponderous, slow and unwieldy though they now seem in comparison with the clippers of a later day, the fighting East Indiamen, of glorious historical achievement, raised the beam-to-length ratio from three to four, and it was along the lines of increased length that further development proceeded.

By 1845 the Blackwall frigates had reached a ratio of 4·3 which rose, by 1850, to 4·7.

When American originality and experiment menaced our own sea supremacy by the introduction of the first wooden clipper-ships, it was the slim leanness of the new-fangled design which most impressed the beholder. The attention of the British Government was attracted, and Admiralty draughtsmen were sent down to Green's Dry Dock to take off the lines of *Challenge* and *Oriental*.

The English extreme tea-clippers ran about 5·7 to 6·0 beam-to-length ratio, *Cutty Sark* and *Thermopylae* being, at 5·9, a few points better than their larger American rivals, for *Lightning* and *Champion of the Seas* were 5·5. The longer and stronger iron medium clippers of later date, in the Australian wool and passenger trade, averaged round about 6·3 in the 'sixties, increasing to 6·7 during the two following decades. The dimensions of the giant *Queen Mary* (1,018 feet by 118 feet) give her a ratio of 8·6; while the *Berengaria*, 883 feet in length, reaches a figure of no less than 8·9.

Herzogin Cecilie's ratio works out (taking overall length of hull) to 7·3. The conclusion is not, of course, implied that she is either faster or finer than the clipper of ratio 6. The increased strength of more modern steel construction permits a considerable extension in length, and such figures must always be viewed in conjunction with the under-water design and the block coefficient of the hull.

In my possession is a large model of *Lawhill*, a steel four-masted barque of 2,816 tons gross, and a typical example of an economical, tramping windjammer of the 'nineties. The model shows that, on the water-line, *Lawhill* is 'slabsided' from mizen to foremast, because for over half her entire length her cross-sections are identical. Her bows are blunt, her cut-water at entry almost vertical, and her after-lines rounded and steep.

The lines of 'Herzogin Cecilie's' hull

To my regret, I have been unable to obtain, for inclusion with the appended plans, a body-plan giving the station and buttock lines of the hull of *Herzogin Cecilie*. I believe, however, that a careful study of the photographs in conjunction with the profile and deck plans will meet the deficiency for model-making.

It will be clear, for example, that at tween-deck level *Herzogin Cecilie* tapers in width, to fore and aft, in approximately two-thirds of her length, or, in other words, only for one-third of her entire length are her sides actually parallel and her hull of equal section.

Her stern is cut away in such fashion that its run (i.e. that part of the bottom which rises and narrows in approaching the sternpost) forms a striking example of the shipwright's art. It is not until well forward of the mizen-mast that her great weight is allowed to settle solidly down to the conventional flat bottom and bar keel of the modern freighter. There is a certain fullness, however, noticeable in the forward part of the stern run, below the water-line, which detracts somewhat from the appearance of the hull when *Herzogin Cecilie* is in dry-dock.

Her bow lines

In the bows, she is shapely and symmetrical, with moderate sheer, the graceful curve of a yacht-like forefoot, a good entry and a long, raking uprise from cut-water to figure-head. Far from being bluff-bowed, or, to use an older term, 'apple-cheeked', her hull offers little water-resistance forward of No. 2 hatch, a point midway between fore and main masts. This is sufficiently far aft to eradicate the bumping, smashing motion and progression typical of many of her 'blunter' sisters.

186

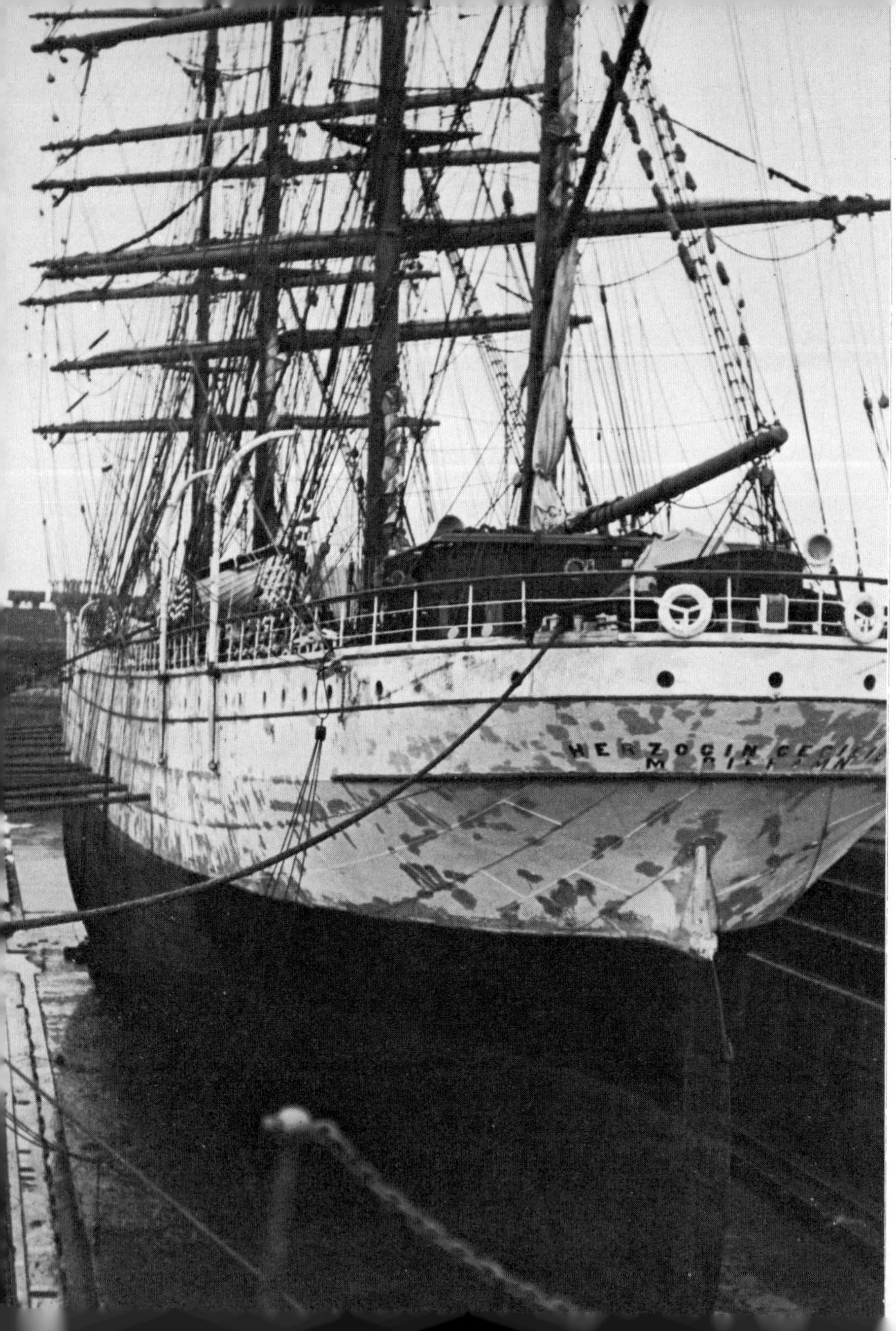
HERZOGIN

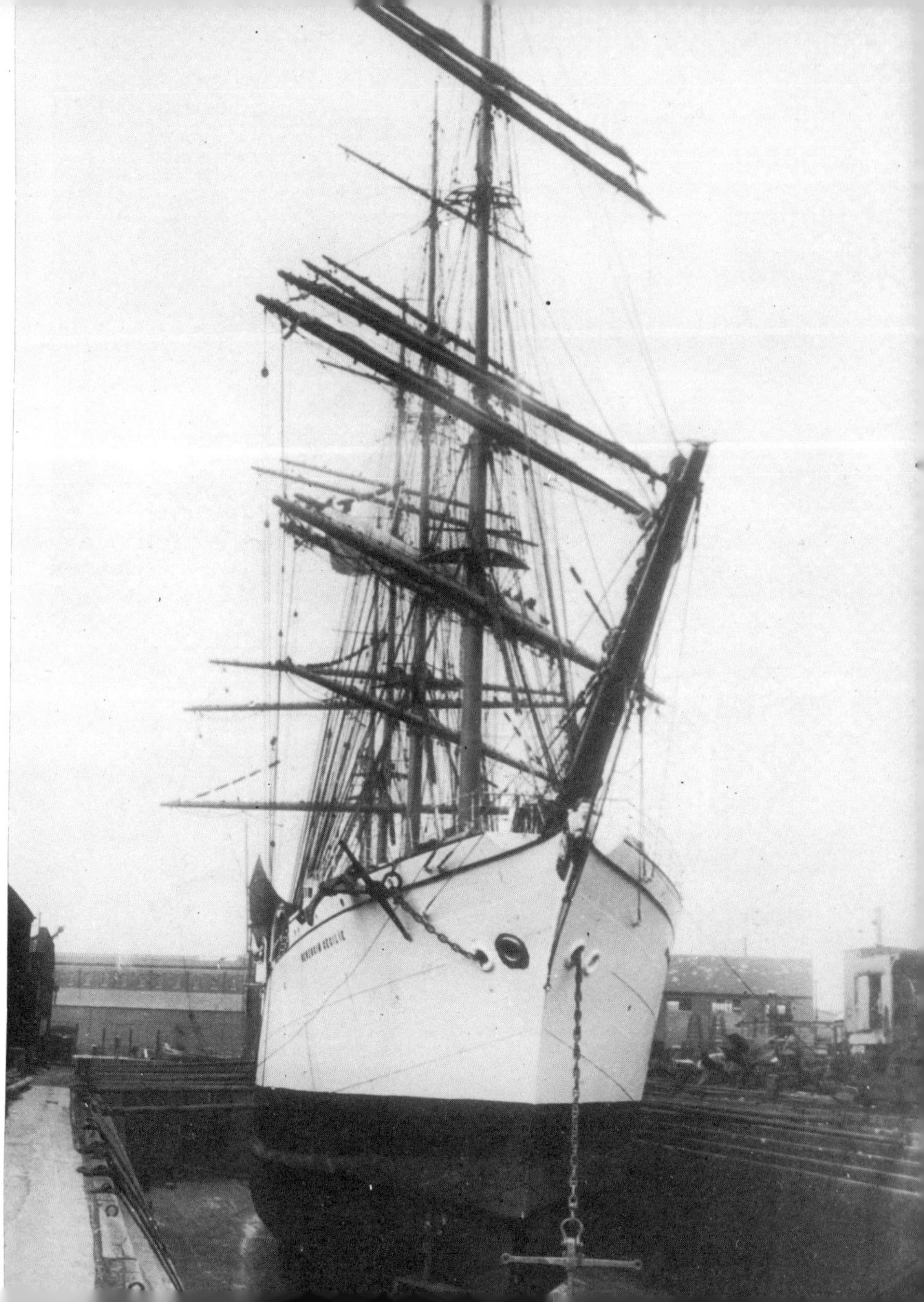

It is a well-established principle of hull design that stern run is of greater importance for speed and steering than is a sharp entrance. The sailing qualities of *Herzogin Cecilie* are influenced more by the efficient clearance of her stern and quarters than by the equally pleasing uprise of her bows. Her easy motion in a sea-way, even in heavy weather, is an outstanding quality, and is attributable to the fact that, when sailing before the wind, big following seas seem to divide and slide away along her sides. Admittedly, in bad weather, any big, steel four-poster is always a brute to steer, but *Herzogin Cecilie's* shapely counter undoubtedly makes for added ease of handling.

Absence of mechanical devices

Conversely, *Herzogin Cecilie* was fitted with few artificial aids to manual labour, her intended complement of crew and cadets being deemed, quite rightly, adequate to man-handle her vast spread of canvas. The small, young crew she now carries under the Finnish flag often have cause to envy the comparative luxury of steam capstans, brace and halliard winches and the like, such as are to be found cluttering the decks of most of the remaining ex-German nitrate-carriers.

A big donkey-engine supplies steam-power to the cargo winches at *Herzogin Cecilie's* hatchways and to the anchor windlass on the fore-deck, and drives the dynamos which govern her electric light supply. All else aboard is, perforce, dependent on man-power alone.

Hull specification

Rickmers gave *Herzogin Cecilie* a very strong hull. She is built throughout of steel, is heavily web-framed, double bottomed, and has three specially strengthened, transverse, water-tight bulkheads extending to the upper-deck. She is a two-deck vessel, both decks being planked over their steel plating. Above the main-deck she has an exceptionally long poop, and a short, conventional fo'c'sle or fore-deck. These superstructures leave only a brief portion of main-deck exposed to form a well or waist.

In later life, when lasting strength had become a far greater asset to the windjammer than mere grace of line, this solidity of hull, matched as it was by an equally powerful top-hamper, was to stand *Herzogin Cecilie* in good stead in the hard fight for profitable existence.

Germanischer Lloyd classification

She was built to the full classification requirements of the *Germanischer Lloyd Register*, and her class has been maintained uninterruptedly by the requisite periodical four-year surveys.

In 1936, *Herzogin Cecilie* drove hard ashore near Salcombe, South Devon (see Book Two, Chapter VI), and there remained, wedged on

acing: Right. IN DRY-DOCK, BARRY, 1931. THE STERN

Left. IN DRY-DOCK, MILLWALL, 1933. THE BOWS

rock, for nearly a month before being refloated and towed to her last berth. No better proof could be given of the remarkable strength and quality of the plating of her bottom and of her lower strakes than was evidenced by the manner in which the thirty-four-year-old hull withstood the enormous stresses set up by grinding rock without and by several thousand tons of swelling grain within.

Herzogin Cecilie spent the War years as an internee. She lay in Chilean waters, and not even the resultant corrosion and pitting of bottom plating (a factor which detracted irreparably from the condition of many of the other German vessels which underwent a like stagnation) could seriously impair or weaken steel of the grade which Rickmers employed for her hull.

The 1935 *Germanischer Lloyd* contains the following entry for *Herzogin Cecilie*:

Number in Register: 98
Flag: Finnish
Signal Letters: OHAU
Type: 4-mast barque

Owner: G. Erikson
Port of Registry: Mariehamn
Captain: S. Eriksson (Appointed 1929)

Classification:  Klasse II 9/30 — i.e. built under Germanischer Lloyd supervision. Top class, subject to submission for survey each four years. Second special survey for renewal of class in September 1930.

B R 9/34. *V B* 7/35. *Belfast* — i.e. Bottom examined and minor repairs carried out at Belfast in September 1934. Class extended to July 1935.

⚓ 1/28 — i.e. Anchors and chains tested, on an approved machine, in January 1928.

Launched: April 1902. *Registered:* Bremerhaven, June 1902.
Built: By Rickmers, Reismühlen.

When dry-docked at Nystad, Finland, in September 1935, *Herzogin Cecilie* underwent a rigorous examination by the *Register* Surveyors. She received a 'clean bill', and the full class was again renewed without modification, Klasse II 9/30, above, becoming Klasse III 9/35 in the 1936 *Germanischer Lloyd*.

According to her builders, the dead-weight tonnage of *Herzogin Cecilie* is 4,200, whereas for cargo purposes her present owner lists her as 4,350.

Measurement discrepancies

Where several different authorities can be consulted, the question of both tonnage and dimension is apt to be confusing. The model-maker, working mainly from the builders' scale plans and aided by the photographs, will pay scant heed to a controversial, perhaps even academic, subject of this nature. But to the student of maritime matters the resultant discrepancy may be of interest, and call for some explanation. The following table shows four different sets, or rather systems, of measurement — metres, for purposes of comparison, having been converted into feet.

	Rickmers		Lloyd's Register 1903 Feet	Lloyd's Register 1935 Feet	Germanischer Lloyd, 1935	
	Metres	Feet			Metres	Feet
Length	94·48	310	314·1	334·8	102·7	336·9
Breadth	14·02	46	46	46·3	14·11	46·3
Depth	7·53	24·8	23·8	24·2	7·37	24·2
Moulded Depth	8·38	27·6	27·8	—	8·46	27·8
Gross Tonnage	3,242		3,242	3,111	3,111	
Net Tonnage	—		2,786	2,584	2,584	
Under-Deck Tonnage	—		2,672	2,672	2,672	

A vessel can be measured in varying ways, either for differing purposes or by different standards. The many shipowning countries of the world maintain bodies, corresponding to our Board of Trade surveyors, to ascertain the dimensions of their own national tonnage. These figures are recorded in an Official Register, from which source they are abstracted subsequently for the purposes of *Lloyd's Register*, a work which embraces the whole of the world's sea-borne tonnage, irrespective of whether the individual units are actually classed by Lloyd's or not.

In 1921, when *Herzogin Cecilie* changed her nationality from German to Finnish, she had to be remeasured under Finnish practice for the purpose of entering her in Finland's national register. In consequence, *Lloyd's Register* particulars, up to then derived from German figures, were amended. The latest *Germanischer Lloyd* entry differs somewhat from each of the other sets of figures, because every Classification Society applies its own system of measurement to vessels wishing to be entered in its records.

The following Board of Trade definitions of ship-dimension will enable computation to be made of *Herzogin Cecilie's* size, under British practice, from the scale plans:

Board of Trade definitions of dimension

> *Length:* As from the fore-side of the stern to the after-side of the sternpost, on the range of the upper deck beams. (In the case of *Herzogin Cecilie* this would exclude the overhang of her counter and the final sheer of the stem, which by their inclusion in the *Germanischer Lloyd* measurements make up the 337 feet shown therein.)

Breadth: The extreme breadth of the outside of the vessel's shell.

Depth: The distance from the top of the beam at the tonnage deck to the top of the floors, or ceiling if fitted, at centre-line (i.e. depth of hold).

Moulded Depth: is greater than registered depth, being the entire depth of the hull amidships from the top level of the keel to the upper deck beam level at the gunwale.

British rules for tonnage measurement

Although to-day the British system of tonnage measurement is adopted, in broad outline, by most European countries, there are minor differences in method of attainment which result in slight discrepancies. British practice is as follows:

Gross Tonnage: The vessel's entire internal volume expressed in units of 100 cubic feet.

Under Deck: The gross tonnage less any enclosed spaces situated above the upper deck (when less than three decks). In the case of *Herzogin Cecilie,* therefore, less the internal area of the space covered by the poop.

Net Tonnage (or Registered Tonnage): The gross tonnage less various deductions for crew space, navigating space, etc., and, in the case of a steamer, propulsion space.

Deadweight Tonnage: The vessel's carrying capacity (in avoirdupois tons) when floating at her load draught, variable in relation to season and trade.

The 1912 poop extension

Before leaving the topic of dimensional variation, one other point must be noticed, in this case arising from structural alteration. *Lloyd's Register* for 1903 shows *Herzogin Cecilie* as having three erections above the main-deck — a poop of 175 feet, a deck-house 18 feet long, and a 46-foot fore-deck or fo'c'sle-head. The present entries in both *Lloyd's Register* and the *Germanischer Lloyd* give only two such superstructures — the same 46-foot fore-deck and a poop-deck of 194 feet. What happened was this: as shown by the builders' plans, the deck-house was actually the donkey-boiler housing, which lay immediately forward of the break of the poop, along the vessel's centre-line. In 1912, the poop-deck was extended to embrace the donkey-room, the new poop-rail running unbroken, 'thwartships, 19 feet forward of its original position.

facing: Top. FULL MODEL OF 'HERZOGIN CECILIE' BY G. SÖDERLUND OF ÅLAN

Bottom. BOWS AND FIGURE-HEAD; TAKEN AT SALCOMBE, 1936

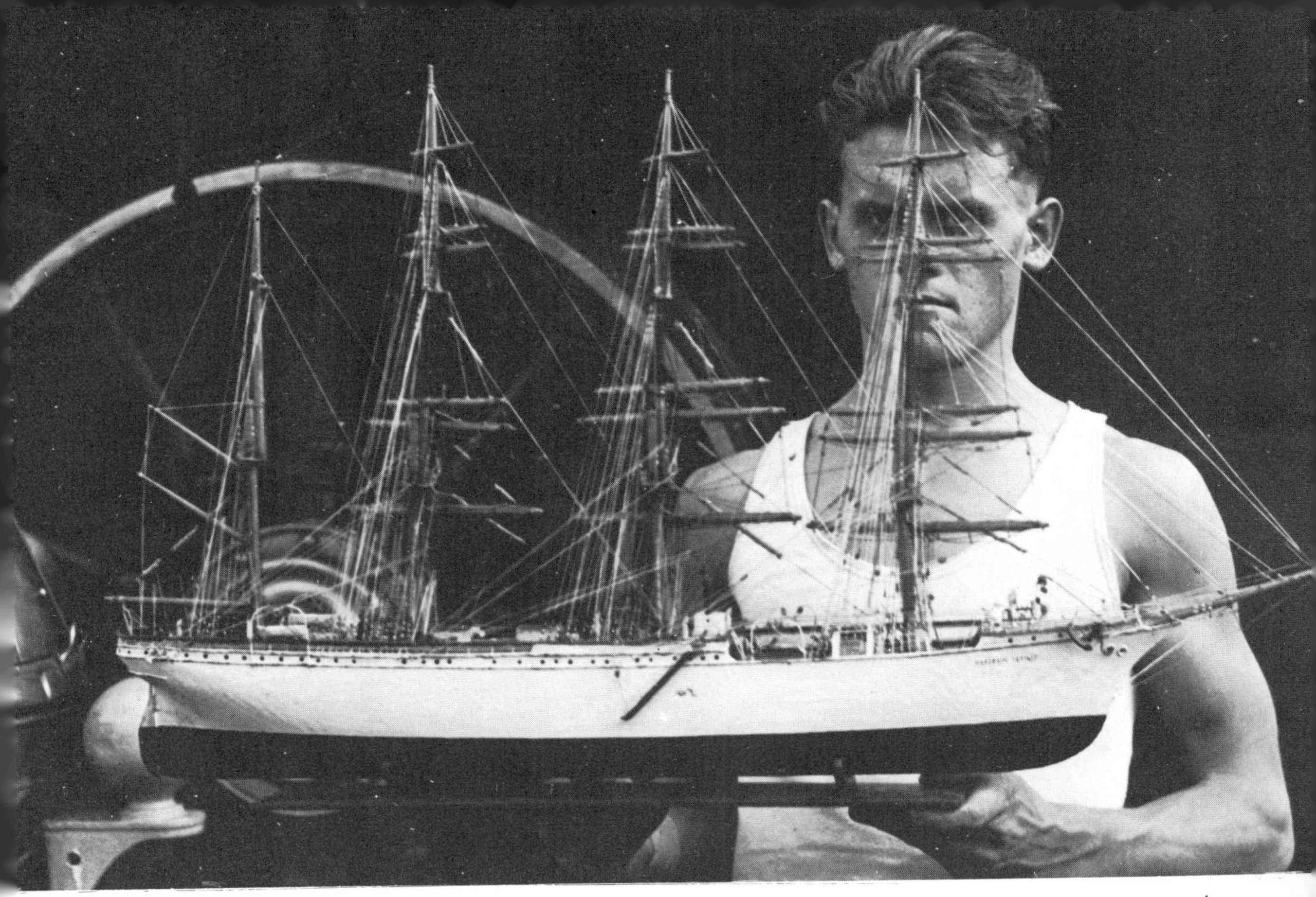

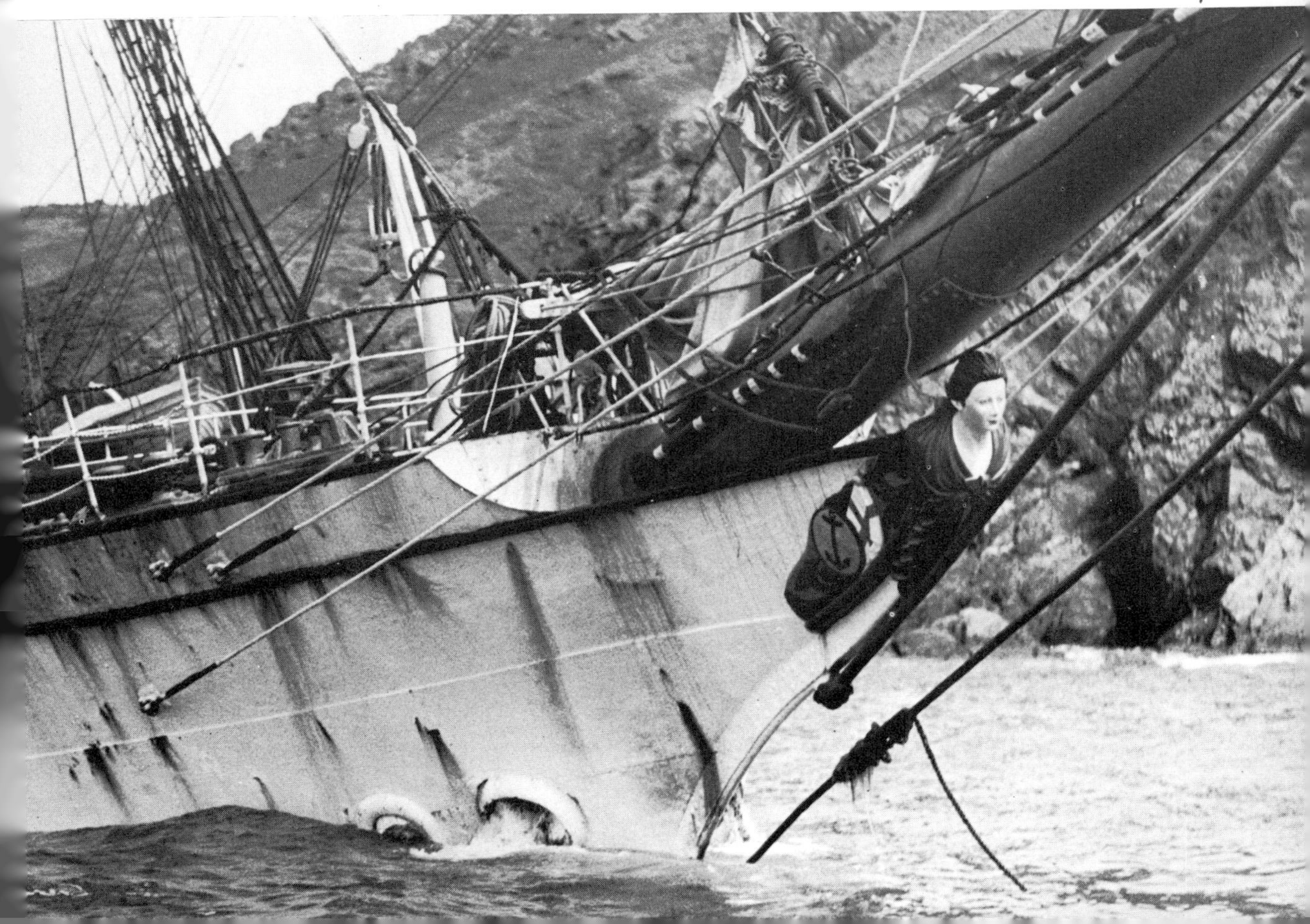

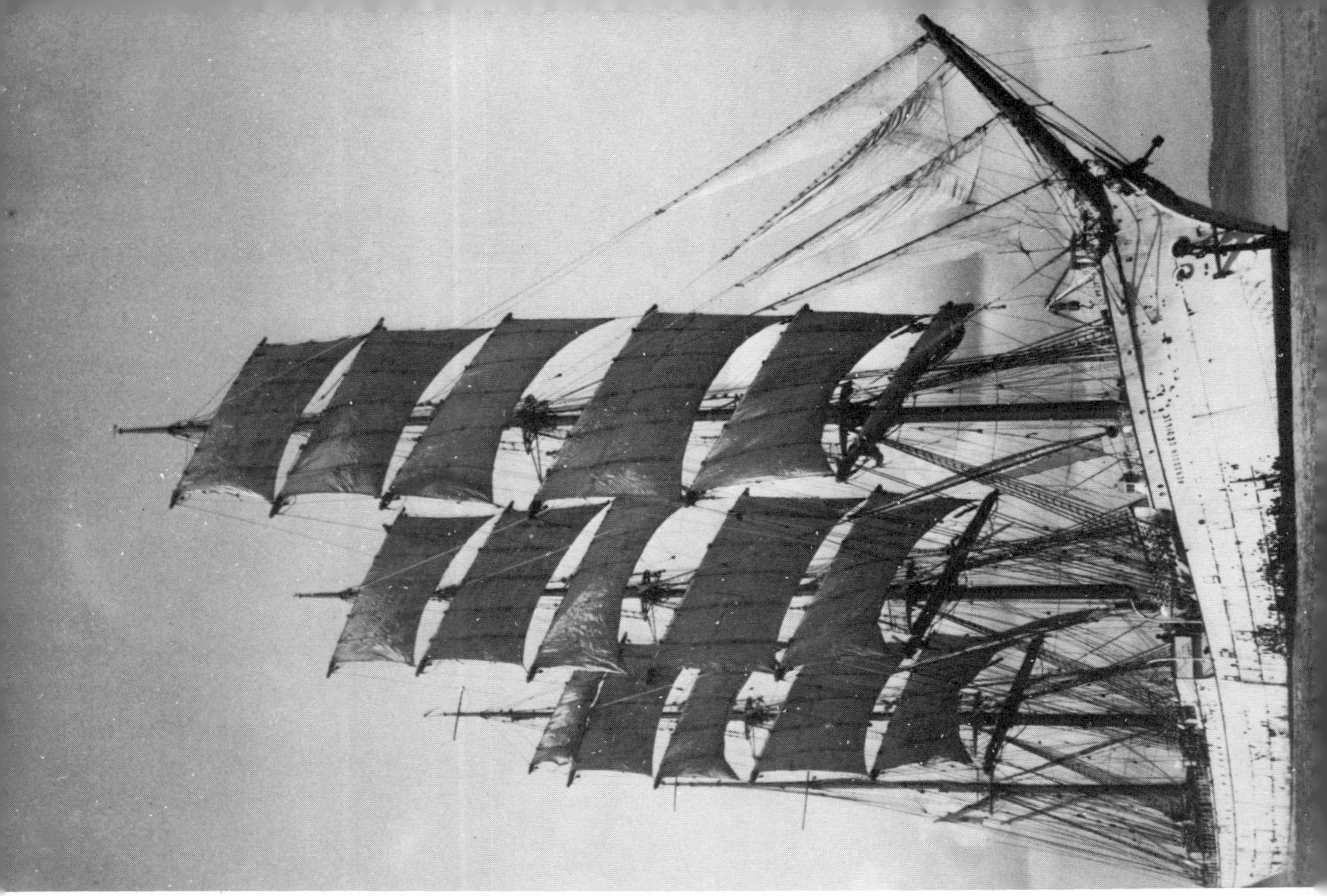

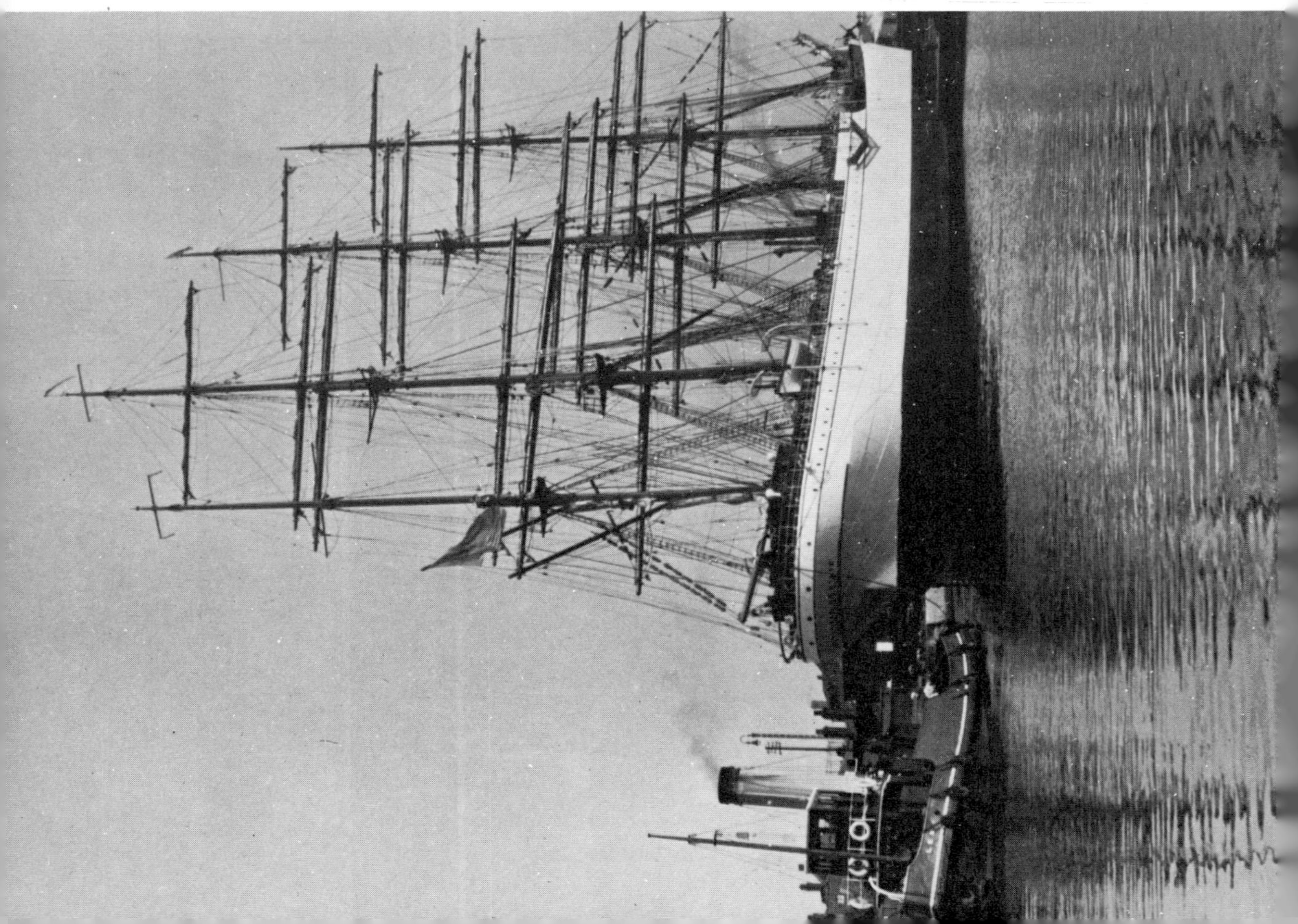

The open rail, which encircled the entire area of the original poop, was substituted in the extension only by steel bulwark plating, presumably for weather protection, since the fore-braces were, at the same time, led to the extension instead of to their old location, the after end of the well-deck.

The new bulwarks

At a distance, this short, isolated length of 'solid' bulwark gives to *Herzogin Cecilie* the appearance of having either an island midship-section or a large 'Liverpool' deck-house, whereas, apart from a donkey boiler-house, she has no superstructures on deck, all the living accommodation being below the long poop.

From the purely aesthetic and non-utilitarian view-points, a poop so extensive that it occupies nearly two-thirds of the entire length of the vessel, is not all that can be desired. In my opinion, the beauty of a broadside view of *Herzogin Cecilie* is marred by the size and squareness of her poop: it ceases, abruptly, well forward of the mainmast, and the short, sunken well between the break of the poop and the fore-deck is oddly angular in profile. This gap breaks up the flowing curve of a continuous topgallant rail, such as was common to the more orthodox, old four-masters with long, open main-decks and low-built deck-houses.

The effect on appearance of an ultra-long poop

The graceful effect of an unbroken, concave sheer-line flowing from bow to taffrail, dipping to so low a free-board between main and mizen that protective netting was needed above the bulwarks in heavy weather to prevent men being washed overboard when hauling braces, was heightened by a parallel sub-band of painted ports. This combination accentuated the steep uprise of the bows, and imparted a rakish appearance to the hull.

An accurate, full model of *Herzogin Cecilie* may prove a little disappointing in its entirety by reason of the heaviness of the long, level poop imparting, in conjunction with the fullness of the midship sections, a rather deep, steamer-like form to the hull when broadside on. In consequence, a water-line model is recommended·for those workers whose reproductions are constructed to delight the eye rather than to present a complete and correct replica.

At sea *Herzogin Cecilie* looks at her very best when loaded to her marks, for ballast trim (never a favourable condition under which to view any vessel), in her case, entails a very definite sacrifice in appearance.

In 1912 *Herzogin Cecilie* was fitted with wireless. The set had a 300-mile transmission radius, the aerial running between spreaders at

Wireless installation

acing: Right. 'FALMOUTH FOR ORDERS'

Left. LEAVING MILLWALL DOCK, 1933

the main-truck and the jigger-truck, over the head of the mizen. A section of the chart-house (at the after end of the poop) was partitioned off as a wireless cabin. To-day the installation is rarely used for transmission, for *Herzogin Cecilie* does not carry a special wireless-operator; the aerial serves mainly for short-range reception on the Captain's private set, or, on occasion, to avoid the necessity of putting into an 'orders' port.

The two Laeisz barques *Padua* and *Priwall* and the two Swedish barques *C. B. Pedersen* and *Abraham Rydberg*, in their dual capacity of freighters and training craft, report themselves by wireless at frequent intervals during their Australian voyages. Among the Erikson Fleet, however, wireless is rarely used and the world hears little of *Herzogin Cecilie* and her consorts during the three or four months between departure and landfall.

Likewise, although in full working order, the luxury of electric light on *Herzogin Cecilie* is now a rare indulgence.

The dynamo house

The dynamos and an attendant paraffin-motor are housed in a small compartment in the centre of the well-deck, underneath the boat-skids. This room, part of which is now a workshop, dates from the installation of the wireless and lighting plants. It is not shown in the builders' plans, its site being there occupied by a spare anchor and a meat-safe. For registration purposes it hardly comes into the category of a deck-house, since it was formed merely by walling-in the boat-platform which now serves as its roof.

Registration numbers

Most of the maritime nations of the world give an official registration number to each unit of their Mercantile Marine. Germany is an exception; Italy and Finland differ from other countries in that each port assigns its own numbers. *Herzogin Cecilie* received her first and only registration numerals — *Mariehamn* 703 — in 1921, when she was sold to the Finns.

Signal letters

In all, she has had three sets of signal letters. Prior to 1934 every country allotted, in assocation with the International Code and upon application from a shipowner, signal letters, to which, to avoid duplication, was added the national flag. *Herzogin Cecilie* hoisted QHLK when she was a German training-ship, changing on her transference to Finland to TPMK. On January 1st, 1934, as the result of proposals made by the British Government, the New International Signal Code was adopted: it abolished duplication and embodied code-signal and wireless call-sign in one four-letter block. *Herzogin Cecilie* then officially became, and still is, OHAU. (See page 257.)

Before turning to a detailed deck survey, two other very vital *Draught* figures must be mentioned — *Herzogin Cecilie's* loaded draught and her ballasting. Her best draught is approximately 23 feet forward and 24 feet aft. Any noticeable variation from this slight trimming-down by the stern has an immediate effect on her sailing qualities. In 1932, for example, it was found that after loading 4,225 tons (gross) of grain at Port Augusta, South Australia, she was drawing 23 feet 6 inches forward and 23 feet 7 inches aft, i.e. was trimmed level. The absence of that extra foot of stern draught had such noticeable effect on the helm that cargo from No. 1 hold was shifted at sea, by the crew, to No. 5, until her bow was given the requisite buoyancy.

For her homeward passage in 1936, when she accomplished the fastest time she had ever made in the Australian grain trade (eighty-six days to Falmouth), *Herzogin Cecilie* was drawing 23 feet 4 inches forward and 24 feet 4 inches aft. Her cargo on that occasion consisted of 52,514 bags of wheat (gross weight 4,295 tons) of which approximately three-eighths was stowed in Nos. 1 and 2 holds and five-eighths in Nos. 3, 4, and 5.

A master is permitted to use, within limits, his discretion in regard *Cargo* to the exact tonnage of cargo which he may think fit to load. The *capacity* Australian Grain Charter Party (Sail), for instance, allows an adjustable margin of ten per cent on the tonnage of cargo indicated therein, in order that the exigencies of trim may be controlled.

A few examples, chosen at random, of actual cargoes carried by *Herzogin Cecilie* are given to complete the notes on tonnage:

> Coke: 3,275 tons.
> Nitrate: 4,351 tons.
> Baltic Timber: 1,363 standards.
> Australian Wheat: 4,295 tons gross, 4,242 tons net.

The 53 tons difference, or tare as it is called, between net and gross represented the approximate weight, at $2\frac{1}{2}$ lb. per bag, of the 52,514 bags in which the wheat was loaded. On nitrate, a cargo so heavy that the bags were stowed pyramid-wise and so filled only a part of each hold, freight was payable on the gross tonnage inclusive of bags. The difference between tonnage loaded of coke, a light-weight cargo of large bulk, and that of grain or nitrate is striking.

Herzogin Cecilie's double bottom is utilized for water-ballast tanks (see builders' plans). On a long deepsea passage without cargo, such as the outward run to Australia, she carries 600-650 tons of water-ballast, plus about 800 tons of sand, gravel, or stone-ballast. The solid ballast is shot, piecemeal, into the lower holds, and trimmed down by the crew. The water-ballast tanks can be utilized for the stowage of additional cargo of suitable type; it is quite usual, for instance, to replace the water by bagged grain for the homeward run from Australia.

Fresh, i.e. river or dock water, is preferable to sea water since it has a less corrosive effect on the tanks. Fresh water is lighter than salt water: the former is usually taken at 36 cubic feet, the latter at 35 cubic feet to the ton. Both dock water and sea water vary slightly in weight according to the locality at which they are obtained, but there is, on the average, a difference of round about $1\frac{3}{4}$ lb. per cubic foot between the two.

Solid ballast also varies in weight: shingle goes about 23 cubic feet to the ton, coarse gravel 19, and 'Thames ballast' 20. All such factors must be taken into account by the Master in deciding the important question of correct ballasting. Sometimes, a certain amount of gravel ballast is needed even when a full cargo is carried. Baltic timber, for example, is a cargo of light weight but of large and awkward bulk, and on one occasion *Herzogin Cecilie* when loaded with between 1,200 and 1,300 standards of timber required, in addition, 400 tons of gravel ballast.

Immediately prior to arrival at loading anchorage or berth in Australia at the completion of a light (i.e. ballast) voyage, the rubble is jettisoned at sea; just sufficient stiffening is retained to enable the vessel to sail the remaining fraction of the journey in safety.

On short 'round the land' trips without cargo, as, for instance, from the grain discharge port in U.K. to Mariehamn, far less ballast is necessary. Gravel ballast is cheaper in Finland, and a saving can be effected by purchasing as little as possible in the United Kingdom. Such passages are made about midsummer, and traverse shallow, sheltered waters. In ultra light trim the vessel rides high, and is subject to far greater leeway or drift; in fact, with such minimum ballasting she would be definitely unseaworthy for more severe conditions of wind and sea. Should any outward cargo, such as timber, be offering in the Baltic the English rubble is discharged, in other words, wasted; if not, extra and cheaper

facing: PLAN

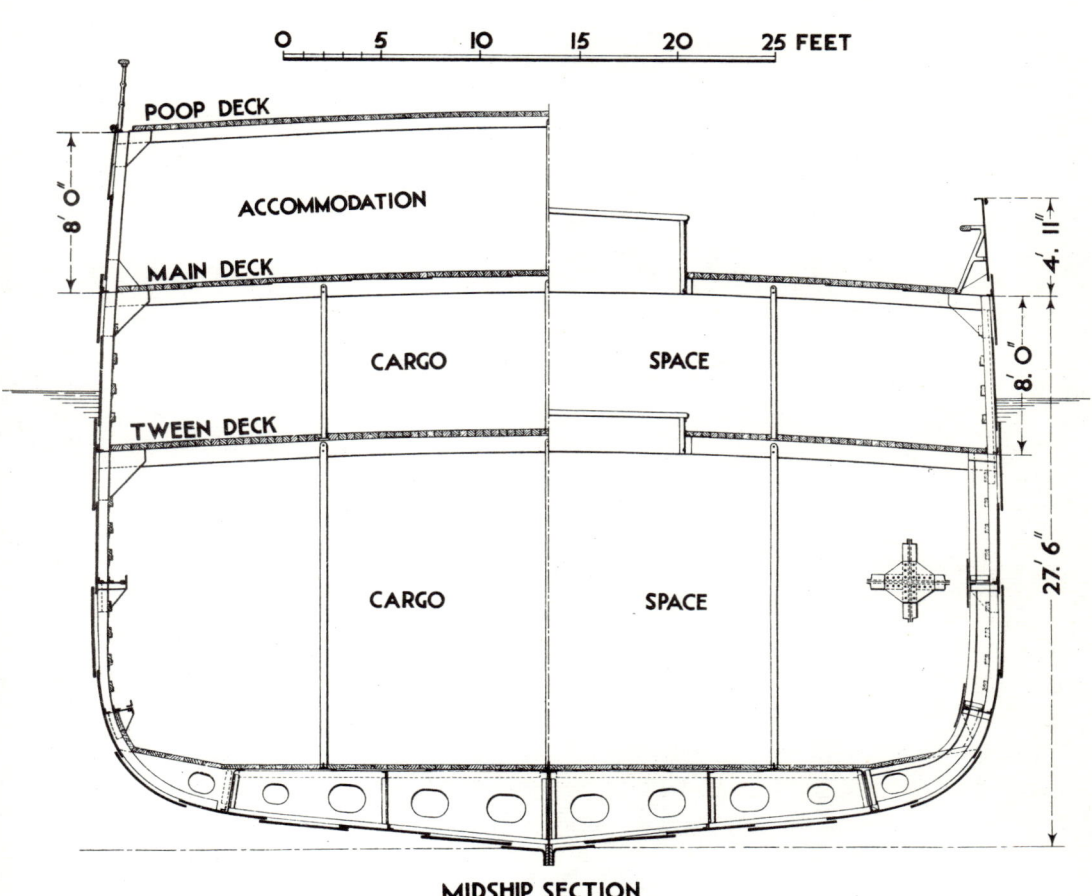

PRINCIPAL DIMENSIONS

LENGTH OVERALL	310′. 0″
LENGTH BETWEEN PERPENDICULARS	308′. 2″
BREADTH	46′. 0″
HEIGHT TO MAIN DECK	27′. 6″

0   5   10   15   20   25 FEET

POOP DECK

ACCOMMODATION

8′ 0″

MAIN DECK

4′. 11″

CARGO   SPACE

8′. 0″

TWEEN DECK

CARGO   SPACE

27′ 6″

MIDSHIP SECTION

"HERZOGIN CECILIE" IN 1902

ballasting is provided before she again sets out on the long, unproductive, empty run to Australia.

The subject of sailing-vessel stability is a most interesting study. *Stability*
It is controlled by three factors, the centres of gravity and of buoyancy,
and the measure of metacentric height.

If a vessel be floating upright in still water the centre of gravity, from
which her total weight acts vertically downward, and the centre of
buoyancy, that is, the upward counter-thrust of the sea itself, may be
visualized as two forces acting equally in opposite directions along a
vertical plane. But should the vessel heel over, the centre of buoyancy
moves in accordance with the unequal under-water distribution of the
hull, and its upward impulse meets the downward pull of gravitation
at a new point known as the metacentre.

The distance between the centre of gravity and the metacentre *Metacentric*
is the metacentric height, and is indicated by the letters G.M. This *height*
sign is prefixed by + (plus) when, being higher than the centre of
gravity, it tends to restabilize the heel, and by — (minus) when, being
below gravitation point, it encourages the vessel to heel over beyond the
safety point, or even to capsize. G.M. is an established and known quantity
in every vessel, and can be regulated by correct stowage or ballasting.

Overlarge G.M., when, for instance, heavy dead weight is carried *'Stiffness'*
low down in the hull, results in 'stiffness', i.e. the vessel is given to
violent rolling but without fear of capsizing, although such excessive
stability may introduce other degrees of danger amounting almost to
unseaworthiness.

Obviously a vessel does not, knowingly, put to sea under negative *'Tenderness'*
G.M. conditions, but when 'tender', that is, when the plus margin is
too small, she will roll less quickly but with a more sickening, hanging
gait, as though she were minded to turn over rather than to return to
the upright.

A big steel sailer like *Herzogin Cecilie* should, when fully loaded,
be neither 'stiff' nor 'tender'; but perfect seaworthiness when in ballast
needs careful consideration because of the larger proportion of the hull
then above water level. In general, the lower in the craft the ballast be
stowed, the greater will be its control on stability.

The carriage of deck-cargo complicates still further the stability
problem, as deck-load, of course, has an immediate effect on the centre
of gravity.

When excessive wind force causes a sailing vessel to heel over to leeward, a point may be reached when gravity assists wind pressure, and only water-resistance prevents capsizing. Then, the lower the centre of gravity is established below the pivotal point of heel, the greater is the capacity for self-righting. The pivotal point of heel can, of course, be lowered by reducing the upper sail area.

The draught, or under-water depth, of a hull is another factor asserting control on stability.

It will be realized that a big, bar-keeled windjammer has none of the adjuncts of her smaller sisters in sail — yacht keels, lee-boards, or centreboards — to help maintain her equilibrium. A deep V-sectioned hull is more 'weatherly' than a shallower draught, round-bottomed design, for, although the latter may offer greater initial resistance to heel, its ultimate factor of safety and its self-righting tendencies are considerably smaller.

CHAPTER 11

'WATCH ON DECK'

I never was in clipper ships when they was in their prime:
The tea fleet an' the wool fleet, they was done afore my time.

The ship I knowed the best was a big Cape Horner
Thrashin' to the Westward round that stormy corner.

When it was Round the Horn and 'ome again, that's the sailor's way,
'Crost the road to Newcastle, back to 'Frisco Bay.

I T is probably difficult for a landsman to appreciate the width of
the gulf which to-day separates the remnants of deepwater sail
from steam as a whole. It is not entirely a matter of propulsion, of
wind-power versus machinery, as it was, say, forty or fifty years ago;
nor of speed, comfort, regularity, economics, or any of the standard
and obvious differences. It is a gulf which, year by year, has grown
wider and wider, the gulf of progress and development, and which, in
improving the one beyond belief, has left the other practically
unchanged.

Steam progress marches with sail's stagnation

The windjammer has never known, and now will never know, the
revolutionary benefits of gyroscopic compasses, direction finders, echo-
sounders, wireless time-signals, and the like. So long as she still survives
she will continue to depend upon much the same aids to navigation as
did her lordly forbears, the clippers. The deviating magnetic compass,
hand and deepsea leads, sextant, and logline have served unaltered, but
for slight minor improvements, for generations of sail navigation.
Dead-reckoning is as necessary an art aboard a Finnish windjammer
to-day as it was on a tea-clipper in the sixties, and her vital
chronometers must still run with unchecked accuracy for three, four, or
even five months at a time if she is to make safe landfall. In fact, life
to-day in the lonely, self-contained, little world of one of these old
vessels is not only a totally different experience from any passage in
steam but, apart from a few, insignificant amenities, it is literally a
reversion to the maritime life and practice of twenty-five, or even fifty,
years before.

197

*The lonely
trade-routes
of the sailor*

With the possible exception of the big Antarctic whaling factory-ships, no other vessels, in these days, are continuously at sea for periods approaching in length the 100- to 130- or 140-day, 15,000-mile, passages of the homeward-bound sailer from Australia via the Horn or the Cape.

Since the advent of the Suez and Panama Canals, the centuries-old wind-routes have reverted almost to the loneliness of Captain Cook's day, for steam pays scant heed to prevailing winds, and the few steamers which still go south-about cut the corner, via Magellan, instead of rounding the Horn itself. It is not uncommon for England to be the windjammer's first landfall after leaving Australia, and such craft rarely 'speak' or even sight another vessel until they reach the North Atlantic.

With one or two exceptions, the sailing vessels are without the boon of wireless telegraphy, with its power for positioning, reporting, timing, weather-lore, life-saving and salvage, and its companionable benefits of news and entertainment. No, the last of the windships plough their lonely furrows up and down the age-old trade-routes between the Hemispheres, as independent of modern maritime development as were their forerunners in sail, and as reliant on 'God and the wind' alone in making their destination. The journeys, the work, the hardships, the dangers, almost the very food, are much the same as they were half a century back, and it is on that note I would like to begin an inspection of *Herzogin Cecilie's* decks and top-hamper.

She and her like were the outcome of centuries of development in the harnessing of wind-power to commercial use, her size and strength the legacy of competition against conquering steam, but there progress stopped short, and to all intents and purposes she remains a typical sail-trader of forty or more years ago.

*The conversion
of 'Herzogin
Cecilie' from
cadet-ship to
freighter*

The model-maker will notice several slight structural differences between *Herzogin Cecilie's* lay-out, both on and below decks, as shown by Rickmers' original drawings and as shown by the sketch-plans which I made in 1933. The biggest change — the poop extension of 1912 — has already been dealt with; most of the others took place in 1921, when she was sold to the Finns. Ruthless minor alterations, particularly in the half-deck space amidships, characterized her transition from crack cadet-ship to the more utilitarian freighter and wage-earner. Even since 1933, further changes have been made, principally below deck, in order to permit the carriage of a few additional passengers.

198

facing: PLAN

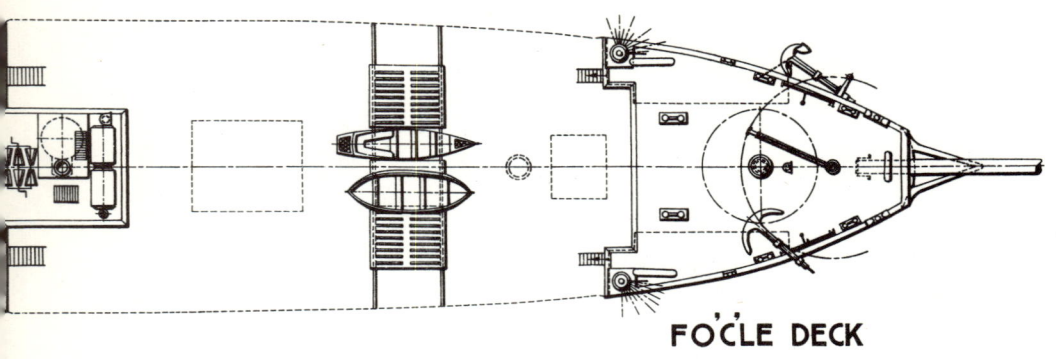

FO'CLE DECK

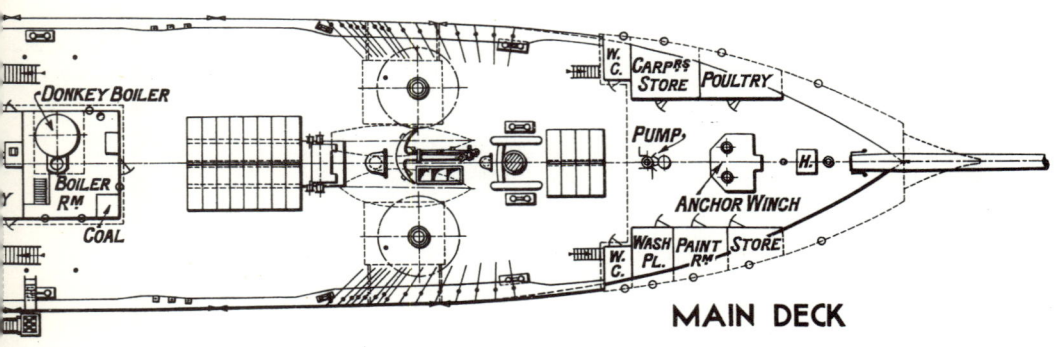

DONKEY BOILER

BOILER
R^M

COAL

W. CARP^{RS}
C. STORE POULTRY

PUMP

WASH PAINT STORE
PL. R^M

W.
C.

ANCHOR WINCH

H.

MAIN DECK

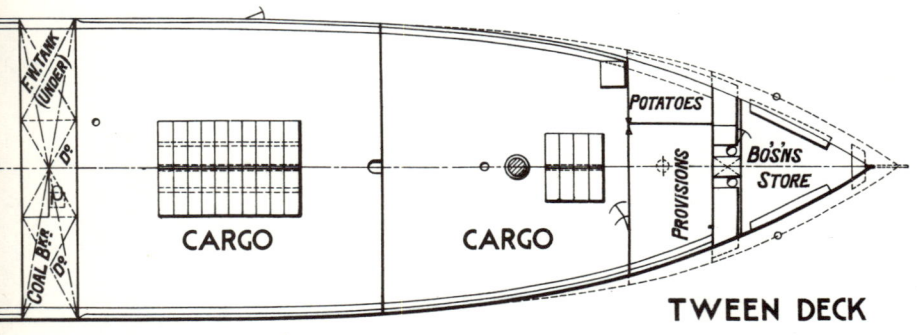

F.W.TANK
(UNDER)

D?

COAL BKR
D?

POTATOES

PROVISIONS

BO'S'N'S
STORE

CARGO   CARGO

TWEEN DECK

" IN 1902

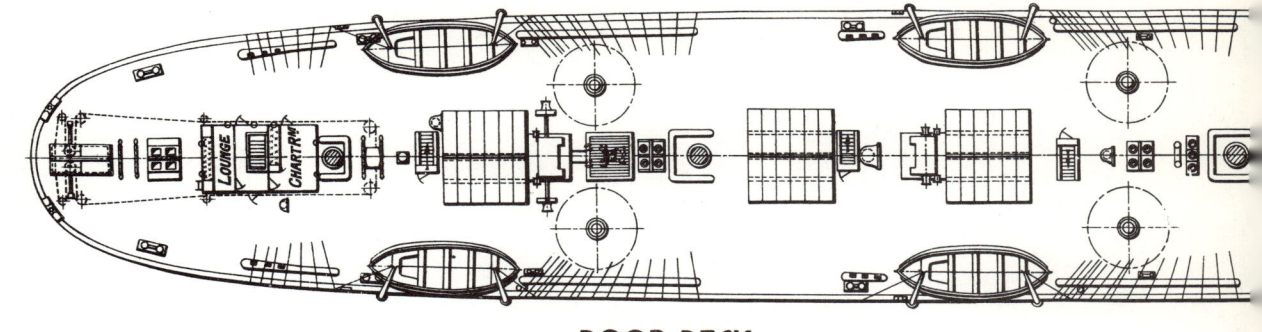

POOP DECK

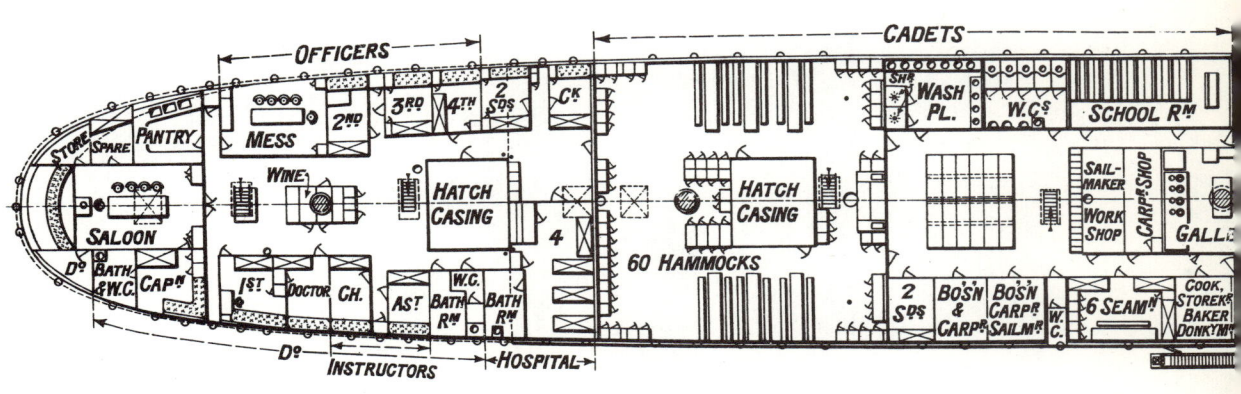

OFFICERS — CADETS

Store · SPARE · PANTRY · MESS · 2ND · 3RD · 4TH · 2 SDS · CK · WASH PL. · W.Cˢ · SCHOOL Rᴹ

SALOON · WINE · HATCH CASING · HATCH CASING · 60 HAMMOCKS · SAIL-MAKER WORK SHOP · CARPᴿˢ SHOP · GALLE

Dᵒ · BATH & W.C. · CAPᴺ · 1ST · DOCTOR · CH. · ASᵀ · BATH Rᴹ · BATH Rᴹ · 4 · 2 SDS · BOˢᴺ & CARPᴿ · BOˢᴺ CARPᴿ SAILᴹᴿ · W.C. · 6 SEAMᴺ · COOK, STOREKᴿ BAKER DONKYᴹ

Dᵒ · INSTRUCTORS · HOSPITAL

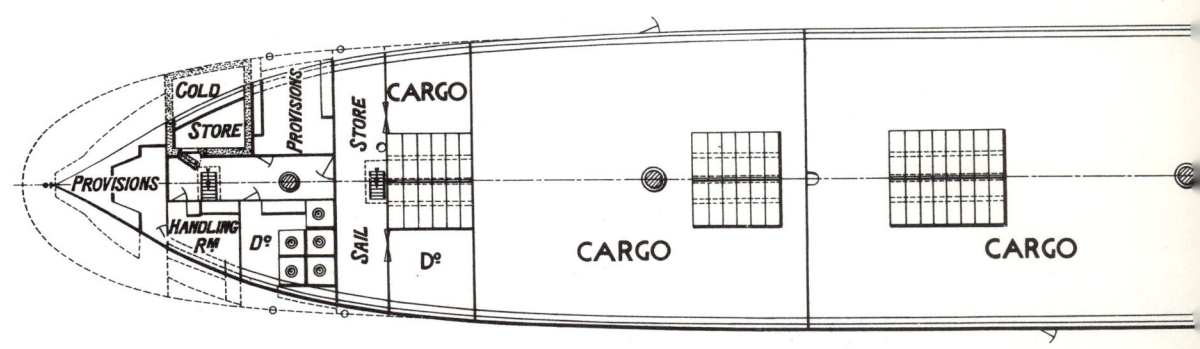

PROVISIONS · COLD STORE · PROVISIONS · SAIL STORE · CARGO

HANDLING Rᴹ · Dᵒ · SAIL · Dᵒ · CARGO · CARGO

"HERZOGIN CECILIE

THE DECKS

ON DECK

The sketch plans and photographs should give a clearer conception of the present (1933) lay-out than any detailed textual catalogue, but some supplementary comment and explanation are needed. The different sections will be dealt with in the following order: Fore-deck, well-deck, poop, forward 'tween-deck space, and, finally, poop 'tween-deck accommodation, lower-deck, and holds.[1]

The Fore-deck. Right at the extreme forward point of the barque — the outer end of her single-piece, steel bowsprit — is nailed a shark's tail, dried and bleached to the colour and almost to the consistency of old ivory by long exposure to sea and sun.

A shark's tail for luck

Shark fishing is one of the few relaxations aboard a windjammer, and every opportunity is taken to hook the hated scavengers of the sea. Once landed, invariably the big fish is brutally maltreated before being killed. Its vertebrae are in great demand among the crew for the manufacture of walking-sticks — made by threading the bone sections on to a thin, metal rod. Pouches are made from the skin, and the fins become valued souvenirs. Be it superstition, tradition, or just custom, the 'sailor of the sail' still believes that a shark's tail at the bowsprit brings luck to his vessel.

Contrary to the usual practice aboard German 'Cape-Horners', *Herzogin Cecilie* is not fitted with safety-netting below the bowsprit. This strong, triangular net, stretching from either knighthead to the bowsprit end, is definitely a great safeguard for men working, in bad weather, on these exposed foot-ropes, and many lives have been saved by its presence. From a purely aesthetic view-point, however — little as that counts against a safety measure — such a fitment would undoubtedly hide and blunt that graceful sweep formed by the merger of bow, figurehead and bowsprit-heel, which adds much to the appearance of *Herzogin Cecilie*.

Bowsprit netting

Little change has taken place on the railed-in fore-deck since 1902, except that nowadays the spare sheet-anchor is housed there, on deck, abaft the windlass drum instead of under the boat skids on the well-deck.

Fittings on the fore-deck

The powerful, steam-driven anchor windlass is convertible to hand gear, if necessary, by using the drum on the fore-deck. This drum has a

---

[1] In the plans, the terms fo'c'sle-deck and 'tween-deck are used, correctly, instead of, as in the text, fore-deck and lower-deck.

This variation has been made for the sake of simplicity and in order that the useful expression 'tween-deck can be utilized for the spaces roofed by poop and fore-deck and floored by the main-deck.

double tier of square sockets arranged checker-board fashion round its upper rim, to accommodate the butts of wooden capstan-bars.

A pin-rail for the jib down-hauls stands between the knightheads. It is flanked by pairs of heavy cable-guides (or fairleads) and bollards for mooring-wires.

The bow-lines of *Herzogin Cecilie* are unmarred by projecting catheads, those ugly, old-fashioned excrescences so reminiscent of the bygone 'lime-juicer'. Once she is well free of land on a long passage, the two bower anchors are hoisted inboard by crane, and cleated down securely on the fore-deck, because the anchors of a windjammer, not being of the modern, stockless variety, cannot be drawn up into the hawse-pipes. The position of the mechanical anchor release-gear, which, with a crane, superseded the old catheads, is shown in the sketch-plan. A number of ring-bolts, not marked in the plans, are let into the fore-deck. They take the blocks of fore-tack or jib-sheets as required.

Lighthouses and Bell

At either side of the break of the fore-deck stands a lighthouse, a squat, cylindrical tower, domed with well burnished copper and protected by two arched bars crossing each other at right angles at the apex of the dome. On the after edge of the fore-deck and midway between the two lighthouses is the big, bronze bell, on which, for thirty-four years, day and night, the hours have been struck. The bell hangs from the cross bar of a pear-shaped framework, and the lanyard attached to the clapper can be reached from the well-deck.

The Waist. Descending from the fore-deck by either of the two companion-ladders, a short, open section of the main-deck is gained: this forms *Herzogin Cecilie's* well or waist. It is bridged, longitudinally, by a narrow, graceful flying-bridge or catwalk, and, laterally, by high-arched boat-skids.

Flying bridge

The railed catwalk, which gives direct access to the poop from the fore-deck, crosses the starboard side of the boat platform. It is not shown in Rickmers' deck-plan, but, on the evidence of the earliest photographs of the barque, it was included in the original specification.

Boat platform

The flooring of the boat platform is in three sections. In the centre, the square, flat roof of the small motor-house cradles two craft, a motor-launch and a little pram or dinghy. On either side of the roof, filling the space between the parallel skids, is a heavy, wooden grating housing, in cradles, a big lifeboat. These two lifeboats were formerly slung in davits (now dismantled) on the poop just abaft No. 3 hatch. In my sketch-plan I have indicated only three of the four boats in order to reveal more clearly the lay-out of the platform itself.

Across the forward wall of the motor-house is a rack holding half a dozen wooden buckets.

A movable set of davits and falls can be erected either to port or to starboard of the well-deck, as required; special sockets are fitted in the respective bulwarks and scuppers, abreast of No. 2 hatch, to take the davit-butts. Both fore-deck and well-deck are fully planked above the deck plating, except, of course, in the scuppers. *Waist davits*

Modellers should note that the decks are not dead level from side to side; they have a slight downward slope, or camber, from the centre-line to either scupper.

The smallest (No. 1) and the largest (No. 2) of *Herzogin Cecilie's* five cargo hatches are situated in the well.

The bulwarks of the well-deck are of the familiar type — high, steel-plated sides capped by a broad gunwale. A heavy pin-rail runs from end to end below the gunwale, broadening considerably at the fore-shrouds, whose lower dead-eyes are located just above the rail. The strops of these dead-eyes are bolted to long, steel shanks slanting, through apertures in the pin-rail, to the outer edge of the scuppers, where the shank-butts are riveted to the top strake of the hull plating. *Waist hatches and bulwarks*

In place of the more usual solid, moulded design of stanchion, the bulwark plating is braced by round-section bars, sloping outward from the underside of the pin-rail to the inner edge of the scuppers. A horizontal, stiffening bar, from the centre of the stanchion to the bulwark, gives added strength.

The waist, the only really wet area of *Herzogin Cecilie's* spacious decks, is drained by four large, square wash-ports, or, as they are sometimes called, freeing-ports. Hinging along the upper edge, they alternately open and close as she rolls, allowing egress to the water shipped aboard over the rail, but clanging down under water-pressure from outside. In the ordinary way they are, of course, unnecessary, and are secured by long, iron bolts fitting into sockets on the inner face of the adjacent plating.

The bulwarks are also pierced by four big, oval hawse-holes, two to port and two to starboard. One pair lies between the forward wash-ports and the lighthouses, the other between the after-wash-ports and the break of the poop. Through them, mooring wires can be led to the adjacent heavy deck-bollards.

Salt-water pipe-line

Just under the fo'c'sle head and close to the bell, is the salt-water pump, whence a large-gauge pipe-line conveys water as far aft as the chart-house on the poop. This piping runs along the port side scuppers: it rises perpendicularly from well-deck level, through the pin-rail, to the height of the poop-deck. At this point a branch pipe, running athwart the wall of the break of the poop just below poop-deck level, enters the boiler house.

The pipe is fitted at intervals with screw-cock nozzles, to which hoses may be attached for the purposes of deck washing or fire fighting. The latter, and sterner use, has, fortunately, never yet been needed.

The Poop. Ascending by one of the two companion-ladders at the after end of the well-deck, the tremendous poop is reached. This stretches for two-thirds of the vessel's entire length. Few sailing craft embodying a 200-foot poop-deck have ever been built, and this lay-out is perhaps *Herzogin Cecilie's* most striking and unusual characteristic.

Two other surviving barques, *L'Avenir* and *Viking*, both ex-training-ships, are of similar design. They, however, are somewhat smaller vessels: *L'Avenir* (according to *Lloyd's Register* for 1936) of 2,754 tons gross and 278 feet in length, has a poop of 170 feet; while *Viking*, 2,670 tons gross, 294 feet long, has a poop-deck of no less than 201 feet. Although magnificent vessels, they are more rounded and blunter in the bows than *Herzogin Cecilie*; the heaviness of the poop design is thereby accentuated, and their general appearance suffers in comparison.

The advantage of a long poop

The long poop lay-out is peculiar to vessels intended for a large complement of crew and cadets, yet needing, nevertheless, the entire hold space below the main-deck for cargo.

Many of the old passenger sailing vessels in the Colonies' trades were given lengthy poop-decks, but as those trades passed into the hands of steam, and the sailer became purely a cargo vessel, the short poop became standardized. Numerous French sailing vessels of a later date had big poops because the Government bounties, by which they were then subsidized, were based on the gross enclosed area and not on net tonnage.

From the point of view of the small crews who man the commercial

202

facing: AFT FROM THE FORE-DEC
ACROSS THE FLYING-BRIDG

windjammer of to-day, crews to whom the labours of Hercules must, at times, seem easy by comparison, a long poop has everything in its favour. For the watch below it provides dry, sheltered, secure accommodation in place of the oft-gutted deck-houses and fo'c'sle of more orthodox barques with long, open, sea-swept main-decks. The deck above can be reached in safety from this midship 'tween-deck fo'c'sle, and food, warmth, and dry clothing obtained from the adjacent galley.

Working conditions on deck are considerably ameliorated by the few, vital, extra feet of free-board supplied by a poop-deck. 'Green' water, taken aboard the poop in heavy weather, disperses rapidly through the open rails which surround almost the entire circumference of that deck, instead of smashing and surging up and down an open main-deck, whose dozen or so wash-ports, in otherwise solid bulwarks, are quite inadequate to drain away one cataract before the next sweeps over the rail. In heavy weather, life-lines and bulwark-netting are essential if men are to work in safety on a flush main-deck.

It has been computed that the steel, four-masted barque *Parma* (3,047 tons gross, and 327 feet in length) could ship as much as 700 tons of water on her open main-deck at one time, when that area was inundated, from rail to rail and from mainmast to jigger, by a big sea.

It was estimated that, since she sank one foot in the water for every 380 tons of cargo loaded, this extra weight of water submerged her load-line by nearly two feet, and so reduced an already meagre free-board by a like amount.

Every inch in draught over and above the fully loaded mark makes an appreciable and vital difference to a vessel's buoyancy, for the deeper she lies the more sluggish she is and the harder to keep on her course, apart from the havoc which the continued presence of several hundred tons of water can wreak to deck fittings and houses.

The Laeisz design

Although *Parma* was at one time under the Laeisz house-flag, she was almost the only 'open' vessel in their fleet. They favoured the three-superstructure lay-out of fore-deck, short poop, and a large and very substantial midship-section. The last was not a deck-house but a platform or bridge-deck, filling the entire width of the vessel. In many cases it accommodated the entire personnel, and, in English parlance, was known as a 'Liverpool house'.

Passat and *Pamir*, and, of course, *Padua* and *Priwall* the most modern sailing freighters in the world, are typical Laeisz bridge-deckers.

cing: FORWARD HALF OF THE POOP-DECK

This bridge deck was the navigation centre: there were situated the chart-house, the wheel, and the standard compass, and thereon the officers kept their watches. It was an area so encumbered by winches, fife-rails, lifeboats, skylights, ventilators, and the like, that there was little spare room. It split the exposed part of the main-deck into two isolated wells of moderate size, but, apart from its congestion, had most of the advantages of a long poop.

With their vast experience of the hardest trade in the world for windjammers, Laeisz would obviously favour the most suitable type of vessel for that trade. It must, however, be remembered that their craft were not built as cadet-ships, although they carried a quota of apprentices, and that, being fitted with every known mechanical adjunct to manual labour, much of the work lay in turning cranks rather than in hauling on running gear. Much less deck-room is necessary for the operation of a brace-winch than would be occupied by a watch of, say, ten men tailing on to the slack of that same brace.

'Lee fore brace'

When commenting on the 1912 poop-extension, I mentioned that the fore braces now lead (via outboard brace-bumpkins) to the poop instead of, as formerly, to the waist. The old dreaded command of 'Lee fore brace', which in bad weather usually meant at least an icy ducking for the unlucky watch, has no like terror for men hauling braces on the drier, high poop-deck.

Miss C. Fox Smith describes this dangerous manœuvre in a poem entitled 'Lee Fore Brace', from which I quote three verses:

> 'There was ten men haulin' on the lee fore brace
> In the rain an' the drivin' hail,
> An' the mile-long greybeards chargin' by
> An' the thunderin' Cape Horn gale;
>
> 'There was ten men haulin' on the lee fore brace
> When a big sea broke aboard;
> Like a stream in spate, a foaming flood
> Right fore an' aft it poured.
>
> 'There was ten men haulin' on the lee fore brace ...
> Seven when she rose at last;
> An' the rest was gone to the pitch-dark night,
> An' the sea, an' the ice-cold blast.'

ON DECK

Except for the handling of jib-sheets and other fore-deck gear, or the foremast halliards, clew-lines, etc., in the waist, *Herzogin Cecilie's* crew are rarely compelled to work in water.

The following quotation from an account, by Captain W. J. Wade, of a homeward passage from Melbourne aboard the grain-laden Liverpool ship *Crown of Italy* (built in 1885), may give some idea of what a hell a heavily-laden, long, open-deck sailer can be in bad weather. It is extracted from Miss Fox Smith's *Ocean Racers*, in which also appears this graphic summary of the closing era of the sailing vessel:

'The last long road'

'It was', she writes, 'a hard, and in many ways a sordid, yet for all that an epic era. Those great iron and steel cargo-boxes, the general traders, ran the Easting down to Australia, or hammered round the Horn against the Westerlies, loaded down with pig iron, rails, Portland cement or Cardiff coals, then over to Newcastle for coal again, and finally back round the Horn crammed to the coamings with grain, nitrate, or tinned salmon. They battered their way through the seas where the clippers had ridden like horses, and were like half-tide rocks in heavy weather. A hard, bitter, man-killing life — yet a kind of sombre splendour gleamed through it, even as through the mud and blood of Flanders trenches. The tea-clipper was in her glory rolling down to St. Helena, a cloud of sail: the wool racers exulted in the wrestle with the "Roaring forties": but it was Cape Horn which was the chief milestone on the windjammer's last long road.'

A very 'wet' ship

Captain Wade says: 'She [the *Crown of Italy*] was the wettest ship I ever sailed in. It was a positive danger to traverse that ship's decks with even a moderate sea running, as she would ship green water and dash men off their feet without the slightest warning. The main hatches were protected by four-inch planks laid down close to each other, running fore and aft, with other planks lying across them, and the whole secured by chains to special ring-bolts fitted in the decks. If it had not been for this protection, I am sure nothing could have saved the hatches from being smashed in by the terrific seas which used to break aboard in the waist with monotonous regularity, and fill the decks flush with the bulwark rails. By means of extra skids on the same level as the boat skids, with planks bolted down to them, a bridge was formed to enable the crew to get fore and aft to work braces, etc., and several times I have seen them swept about even at that height above the decks.'

From the foregoing it would seem that although sail can never be really comfortable, carrying as it must many disadvantages to weigh against the advantages claimed by its devotees, it is undoubtedly true that as regards privation, danger and discomfort, the finest type of modern sailer compares favourably with her predecessors.

Steam power on 'Herzogin Cecilie'

To return to *Herzogin Cecilie*, it will be noticed that the two cylindrical feed-tanks, which supply water to the donkey-boiler, now lie side by side, 'thwartships, on the starboard side of the boiler-house, instead of, as originally, end on to each other forward of the house. This alteration, which took place during the 1912 poop extension, made room for a gangway across the front of the house, linking the two sides of the poop-deck.

Fittingly enough, the only unsightly erections marring the decks of *Herzogin Cecilie* are connected with steam.

Even cargo-winches, when their drums are painted black and white, and their central mechanism clothed in well-tailored canvas jackets, can look neat and be in keeping with the hatches they serve. Smoke-stacks on a sailer, however, are always an eyesore. A short, fat, black stack 'adorns' the roof of the donkey-boiler house, and a long, thin, equally black one, just abaft the mainmast, rises from the galley below. The chimney of the donkey-engine is collapsible: it hinges on its lower rim, and can be cleated down, athwart the roof, when the fires are drawn. The roof is reached by means of a series of rungs bolted to the after wall of the house.

Steam is conducted fore and aft from the donkey by pipes which run along the decks close to the port side of the hatch-coamings. These pipes are protected by angle-section iron casings, and take the steam power as far forward along the main-deck as the gearing of the anchor-capstan, and as far aft along the poop as No. 5 hatch-winch, serving, en route, four other cargo-winches.

The elusive brace winch

From the first *Herzogin Cecilie* was intended to be entirely man-handled when under sail, and, in consequence, was not fitted with either brace or halliard winches. In Rickmers' plans, however, a large brace-winch is shown just abaft the donkey-house. I have been somewhat doubtful as to the advisability of going into such minor discrepancies for fear of becoming merely prolix, but, for the sake of any readers who may contemplate making an accurate model of the barque, and who might be misled by the plans, it was necessary to provide correct detail.

206

facing: THE OPEN MAIN-DECK OF 'POMMER
(NOTE BRACE AND HALLIARD WINCHI

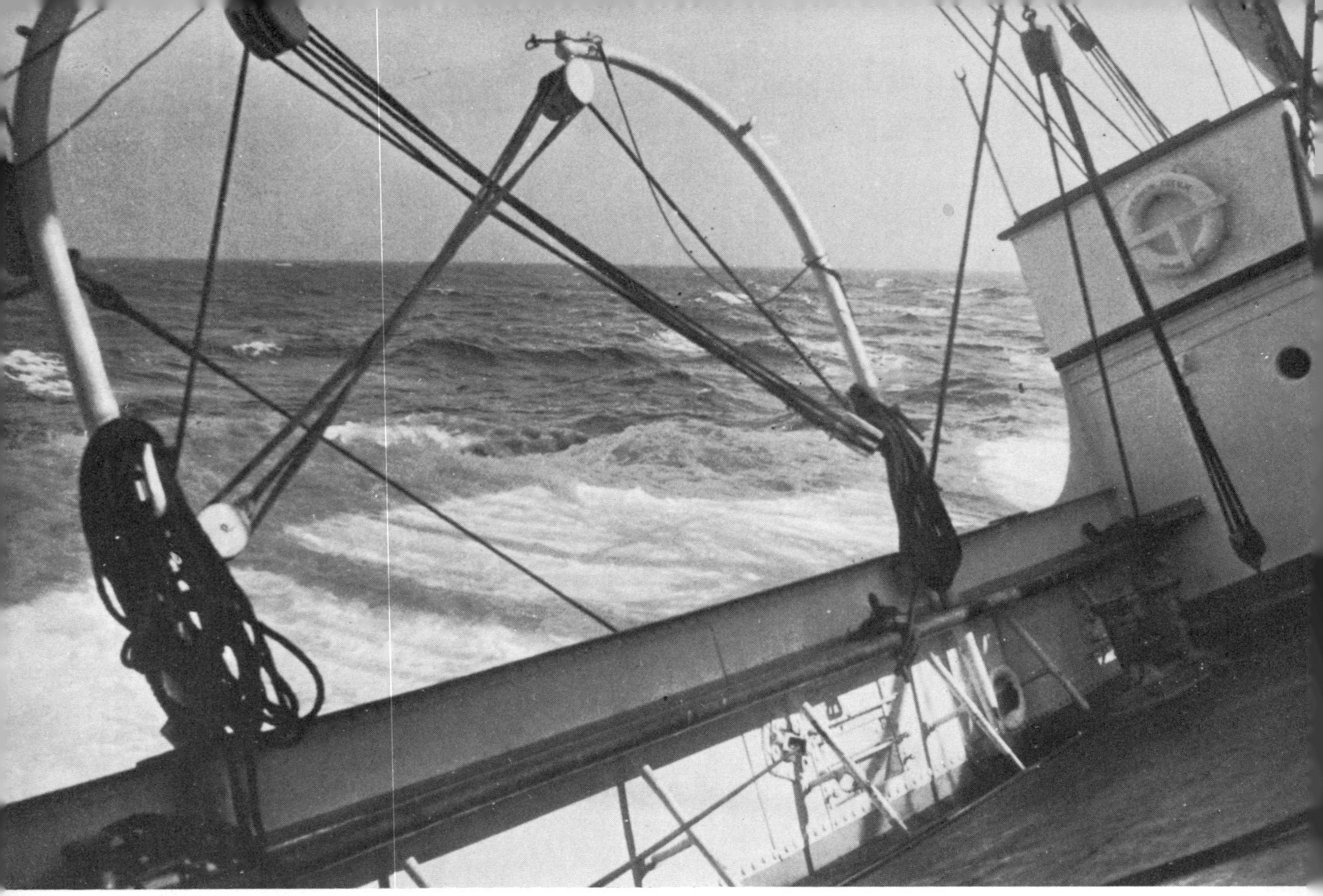

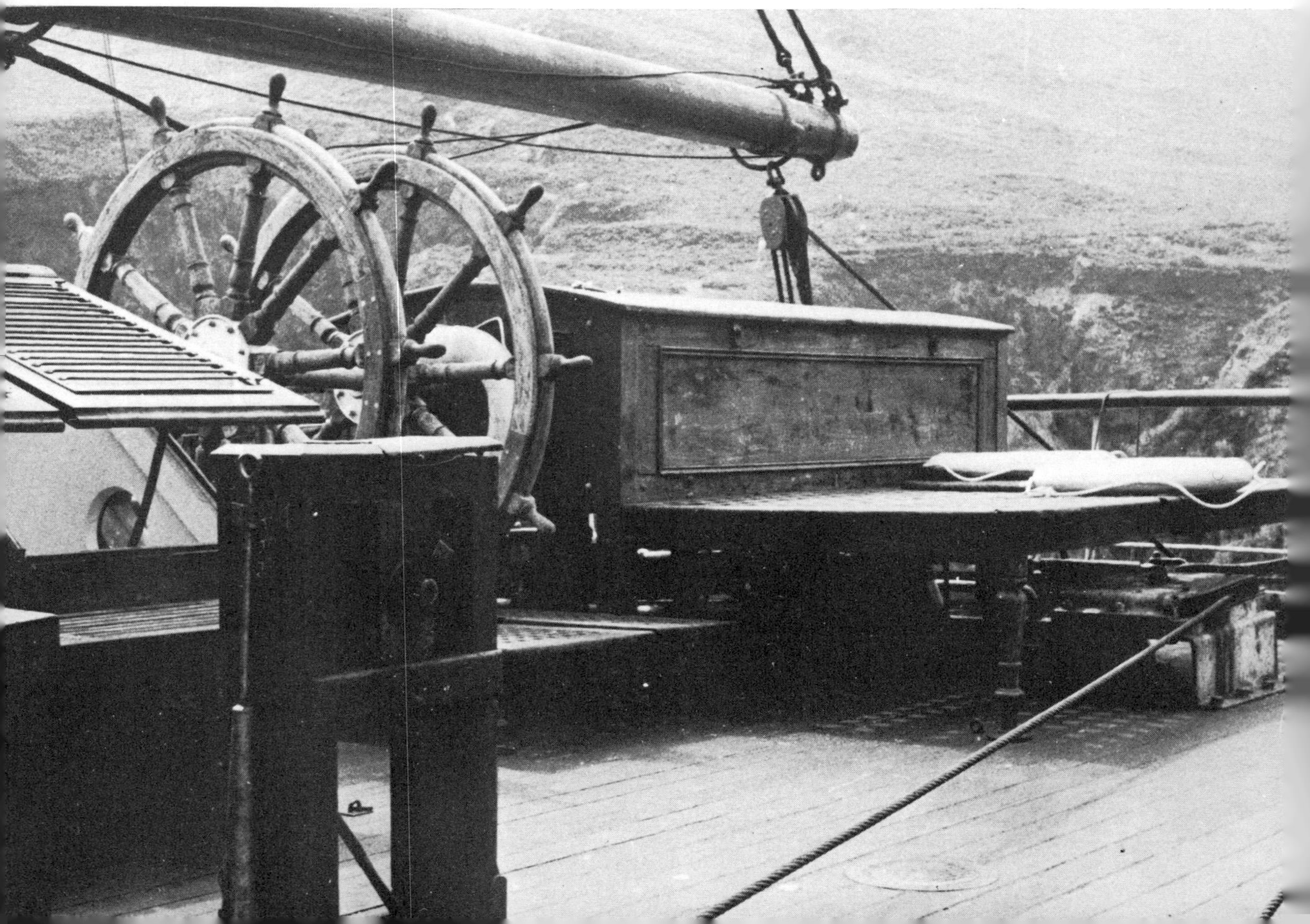

I have been unable to find any trace of that elusive winch: no sign of its installation shows to-day; it is very doubtful whether it ever existed, since one solitary brace-winch aboard a big, heavily-manned, steel four-master would appear incongruous by its very isolation.

Before proceeding further aft on this tour of inspection, it is worth noting the handsome fife-rails round the base of the mainmast, identical with those pertaining to each of the other three masts. Three-sided and made of heavy, teak baulks, these rails are supported at each corner by bulbous, teak pillars socketed into square metal bases bolted to the deck.

Fife-rails

Although several auxiliary sailers have been equipped with steam-steering gear, powered steering is quite unknown to the true windjammer.

Midship steering wheels

A close-coupled pair of six-foot, teak, brass-bossed steering wheels, flanked by high, wooden gratings, lie aft of the mainmast. The reason for double wheels, operating, of course, as one unit, is to enable, in case of necessity, four helmsmen to work at the same time, whereas in normal, fair weather a single helmsman is sufficient. He stands to windward of the wheel, an extra hand being sent to the 'lee wheel' when required. A small brass bell is mounted on the top of the domed gear-casing, which links the two wheels.

The more common location for the steering wheel of a sailing vessel was on the main-deck, just below the break of a short poop or, in later days, at the after end of the poop itself. Steering chains or cables were, in consequence, short, for, especially in the latter position, the wheel was almost directly above the rudder-post. Midship steering control was attributable largely to the introduction of the bridge-deck or 'Liverpool house'.

The helmsman on many of the big, steel full-riggers and barques was protected by a crude but efficient wheel-house, usually a forward-curving, steel arch about eight feet in height with its sides enclosed. The idea was partly psychological, for, although sheltering him from wind and rain, it prevented the man at the wheel from looking backward: in him, as in Lot's wife, a habit to be discouraged. Many a good ship has been lost because her helmsman, unnerved by the terrifying spectacle of big, following seas piling up behind him and threatening to break over the poop, has deserted his post and fled forward for shelter.

cing: Top. WELL-DECK BULWARKS AND BREAK OF THE POOP

Bottom. AT THE TAFFRAIL

The menace of 'pooping'

The menace of being 'pooped' is a very real one to the deep-laden sailing vessel. Scudding before a gale, somewhere South of the Horn, maybe shortened down to storm lower-topsails, foresails and fore stay-sail, continuously awash like a half-tide rock, with betimes only her poop and fo'c'sle-head showing out of the surging welter of broken water, she has little chance of heaving-to without being dismasted. If she be 'pooped' over the stern, i.e., should an extra big sea topple over and break aboard, the probability is that, without some protection, both man and wheel would be swept away. Uncontrolled, she might fall off, broach-to, and, at the best, if her shrouds and stays parted under the strain and allowed her top-hamper to carry away overside, become a mastless hulk, navigable after a fashion under attenuated jury-rig. At the worst, she would go over on her beam-ends, have her hatches stove in, and, ultimately, another 'missing' entry would be posted at Lloyd's.

Herzogin Cecilie once broached-to owing to the shifting of her ballast and it was four days before the herculean efforts of all on board could get her on an even keel. Riding high in light trim, her hatches did not receive a fatal battering, and both they and her standing-rigging held unbroken. (See page 320.)

This was in recent years, but in March 1909, right down in 50° south, when running for the Horn, scupper deep with Australian grain, she was pooped by a tremendous sea. It smashed in the chart-house, flooded the poop accommodation, and threatened her with complete disaster. She was, without doubt, only saved by the fact that she was being steered from amidships. (See page 281.)

Dual steering control

Actually, *Herzogin Cecilie* has two pairs of dual wheels, motion being transmitted from amidships to the steering-gear itself by heavily-greased, steel cables running along the poop-deck through pulleys at the corners of Nos. 3, 4, and 5 hatches.

The reserve pair of wheels stand right aft, immediately forward of the steering-gear casing, and well abaft the chart-house. They, or rather the original pair, were swept away by that same great pooping sea in 1909, but, being unmanned, neither life nor control was lost.

The alteration of the forward wheels

The forward wheels, as shown by Rickmers' plan, were at first located just forward of the jigger-mast (the attendant binnacle being still *in situ* in 1933). They were later moved farther forward to their present position between main and mizen. This entailed the lengthening of the steering-cables to practically 150 feet, and might appear to increase the possibility of cable breakage. In practice, however, they show no weakness, although they are not enclosed in any protective tubing or shield. They can be a fruitful source of minor accidents to the unwary on dark nights and in bad weather. Screw gear, operating through long cables, is positive enough when new, but after a while, when wear develops in the thread, the wheel is prone to kick violently in bad weather.

Like all big four-masted barques, *Herzogin Cecilie* is 'heavy' on the wheel. Such vessels answer much more slowly to the helm than do the smaller, slighter types of sailing craft, and instant tiller reaction is unknown to latter-day square-rig. Although the sweet run of *Herzogin Cecilie's* stern and counter help her to some extent, especially in a following sea — that worst of all 'wheels' — she can be a terrible handful to her helmsmen. Oft-times as many as four, panting, sweating, oil-skinned boys toil together on the gratings around the six-foot midship wheels, but, hard grind though it may be, they at least work in comparative security.

When the present midship wheel position was established, the hooded companion-way leading down from the poop to the crew's quarters in the 'tween-decks had to be shifted a few feet farther forward. It replaced the large, square skylight, which lit the original carpenter's shop and sail-maker's workroom. The present companion opens to starboard through low, double doors: it has an adjustable roof for convenience in fair weather, the higher or starboard half sliding back over the rear half.

The fo'c'sle companion-way

The galley is lit and ventilated by two skylights: the larger of the two stands between the companion-way and the mainmast. It is a rectangular box, roughly the same height as the hatch coamings, and it carries on its after-face a rack of wooden capstan-bars. Its hinged, sloping lid, which contains four glass port-lights, is usually propped wide open. Although, for a windjammer's caboose, *Herzogin Cecilie's* galley is unusually safe and weather-proof, there was one calamitous occasion — at night, down south of New Zealand — when a heavy sea came right over the length of her, sweeping the man from the lee wheel, and cascading down the open skylight on to the cook below. The other skylight, between the donkey-house and the mainmast, is about a foot higher than the larger one, and has two oblong lights in its rectangular lid.

The galley skylights

The standard compass, which is placed immediately abaft the mizen mast, stands on a brass-railed, teak platform, raised six feet above deck level, access being given by a ladder at the after end. A rack of capstan-bars is fitted between the supporting pillars of this platform, both to port and starboard, close to the deck. Beneath the forward end of the platform there is a raised skylight, of penthouse type, with two, round, glass port-lights in each flap. A tall, slender chimney, whose purpose will be given later, stands between the platform and the mizen mast.

The half-deck companion
Rickmers show a companion-way from the cadets' quarters (or half-deck) opening on to the poop where No. 4 hatch-winch now lies. In 1934, when Captain Sven Eriksson made several adaptations to the passenger accommodation, he reinstated the half-deck companion in a slightly different position. It opens, to starboard, between the compass platform and the mizen fife-rail. It is the actual structure, which, as shown in the sketch-plan, stood just abaft No. 5 hatch, and is similar in design to the crew's companion, having double doors and a sloping roof. A new skylight fills the gap in the poop-deck caused by the removal of this companion.

The hatches
The barque has five cargo hatches; two are situated in the waist and three upon the poop, No. 2 having the largest tonnage opening. They are each equipped with a steam winch, and the hatch covers are secured in the normal manner, that is, by hatch-beams running 'thwartship and covered by tarpaulins. The latter are made fast below the hatch coamings by iron battens resting in cleats. Hardwood wedges are driven between bar and cleat, pinning the tarpaulin against the coaming. In addition, each hatch has two heavy beams or hatch-bars laid edgewise, fore and aft, above the tarpaulin. These bars have slotted ends which take long, screw bolts rising from the coamings. Numerous, reversible, steamer-type, cowled air-shafts ventilate the 'tween-decks, holds, pump-room, etc. (*vide* the sketch-plan and photographs).

A further and most vital benefit of a 200-foot poop-deck is the protection which it affords to the hatches, the most vulnerable point of any moderate-sized vessel. Countless ships have foundered because their hatch-coverings have been unable to stand the terrific battering of heavy seas. Once the tarpaulins are torn and the batten-wedges work loose it is not long before one hatch-beam is unseated, and, as the rest follow, water pours down ceaselessly and unchecked through the unprotected aperture.

facing: PORT SIDE OF POOP-DECK, FROM A

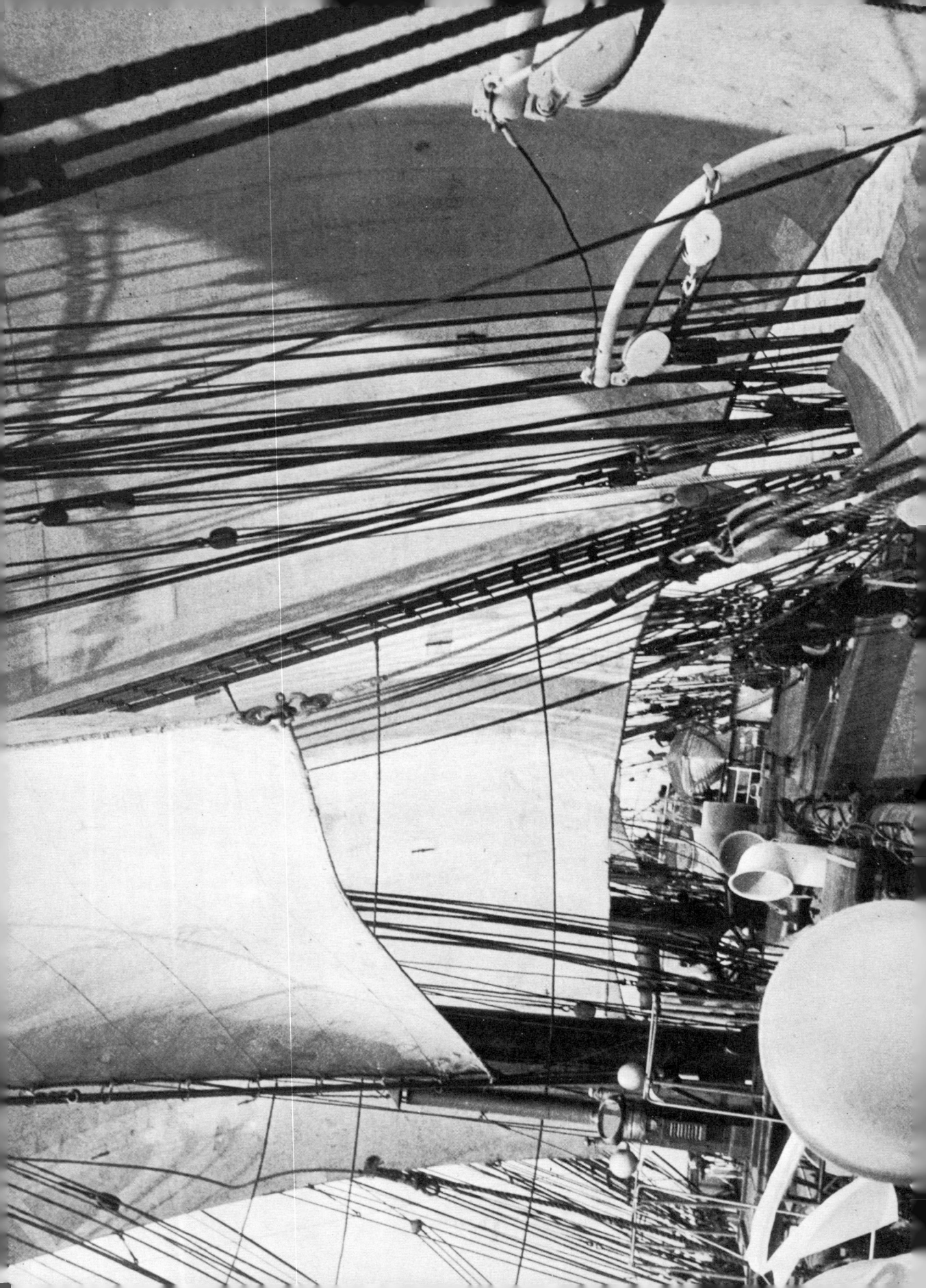

It is conceivable that this could happen only to that pair of *Herzogin Cecilie's* five cargo-hatches which lie in the well-deck. One of these is her smallest hatch, and is partly protected by the break of the fore-deck. The other — No. 2 — may be considered as being the most vulnerable chink in her armour. Even then, the well-deck is so short that this hatch is not exposed to anything like the same stress or weight of water as are any one of the hatches in a long, open main-deck.

The other three hatches — Nos. 3, 4, and 5 — are perfectly protected by the poop superstructure, in that their main-deck tonnage openings are superimposed by poop-deck hatches of a corresponding size.

In the case of Nos. 4 and 5 these dual apertures are connected by square, steel shafts or casings, access to the lower hatch being obtained through a door in each casing at main-deck level. Should the uppermost hatch of either pair be broached, little else could happen but the filling of the casing: the weight of a square, motionless column of water, eight feet in depth, would be insufficient to displace the beams of the lower hatch.

Should No. 3 hatch, on the poop, be destroyed, it is unlikely (although the matter has never been put to the test) that the amount of water which would then inundate the 'tween-deck space, subdivided as that confined area is by transverse bulkheads, could gather sufficient impetus to demolish No. 3 lower hatch and penetrate into the hold.

The two big quarter-boats of *Herzogin Cecilie* are carried, several feet *The quarter-boats* above poop-deck level, in sturdy, metal-legged half-cradles, designed to allow the boats being swung outboard by their davits with the minimum of lift. Only the keel of the boat is actually held, by a deep notch in the cradle, rigidity being obtained by four adjustable chain gripes from boat gunwale to deck.

Herzogin Cecilie's commodious chart-house, at the after end of the *The chart-house* poop-deck, is shown in the modern sketch-plan as being of considerably larger dimension than the original structure. The exact date of the alteration is difficult to trace, but reasonable assumption places it just subsequent to the destructive 'pooping' in 1909, when the back of the old chart-house was driven completely inward and the interior gutted. At any rate, when wireless was installed in 1912 the wider house permitted the inclusion of a special wireless cabin.

The new structure is handsome, beautifully built, and almost

acing: UNDER THE ARCH OF THE CRO'JICK; STARBOARD SIDE OF POOP FROM CHART-HOUSE luxurious in its appointments. It is practically square, flat-roofed, constructed entirely of teak, lighted by large, brass-rimmed ports, and is encircled externally by a brass-mounted, teak handrail set about waist high. Up the starboard side of the after wall an iron ladder gives access to the roof.

The upper hall and the stairway

Two lateral bulkheads divide the interior into three sections, of which the middle one forms a hall having two doors, with high sills, opening to port and starboard on to the poop. Midway between these doors, converging stairways lead down from the upper hall to a small landing, whence a short, balustraded staircase, facing forward, descends the remaining distance between poop and main-deck, and opens into the central hall of the afterguards' quarters.

The 'office' and the chart-room

The foremost of the three sections of the chart-house is divided into two communicating rooms — an 'office' to port, and a chart-room or navigation-room to starboard. The little office is furnished with a settee, a swivel chair, a tall cupboard for signal-flags, and a big, flat-topped writing desk. The desk contains such impedimenta as dividers, rules, scales, and gauges.

Across the forward wall of the navigation-room are a series of long drawers for the storage of charts and a cupboard containing three chronometers. A couple of wall-racks for navigation books, sailing directions, log-books, tables and the like, a rack of rocket distress-signals, a clock, barometer, telescope, binoculars, and the pitch-and-roll recorders complete a severely practical inventory.

One of the most treasured volumes on the book-shelves of *Herzogin Cecilie* is a presentation copy of *Lloyd's Register* for 1933, a gift to Captain Sven Eriksson from a former Chairman of Lloyd's. The barque's name is gilt-embossed on its leather covers, and she is probably the only sailing vessel afloat to possess a like personal distinction.

The wireless cabin and smoke-room

The third and aftermost section of the chart-house contains two compartments. The smaller, to starboard, is the wireless cabin. The large room on the port side is a cosy smoking-room: a table runs down the centre, flanked on the inner side by a long, crimson, plush settee and on the after side by a row of swivel chairs. The doors of the three principal rooms in the chart-house open, for bad weather security, on to the central passage, there being no direct access to the deck. The door of the smoke-room is of sliding type, and, at the far end of this room, is a door into the wireless cabin, which has no other exit.

ON DECK

Just abaft the chart-house stands a large, raised skylight, roofing the *The saloon skylight* Master's private saloon. Like every fitting aboard, it is beautifully made and of solid and handsome design. Built of varnished teak to match the house, it is flanked on either side by a broad ledge or bench, a favourite and pleasant fair-weather seat. The central, penthouse skylight, its glass frames protected by thin, brass rails, is in two sections, each hinged along the upper edge, so that the whole can be clamped wide open when weather permits. An inner shelf or railed coaming forms a draining trough for any water which may be forced through the skylight frames. This shelf is filled with potted geraniums and trailing fern, which flourish prolifically beneath the forcing glass. Hanging on a long chain from the centre of the skylight is a large, gilded, canary cage — the home of the barque's 'prima donna'.

A few feet away from the skylight, on the port side, stands the patent *Sounding machine, log and batteries* sounding-machine in a narrow, rectangular box about three feet in height, encased in a tight-fitting jacket of canvas. A deepsea lead is mounted in clips down the forward edge of the box, which contains several hundred fathoms of line and a mechanical counting device. The latter registers the run of the line, which leads over a reel on the port quarter of the taffrail. The dial of the patent log, or distance indicator, is set on the starboard quarter of the taffrail.

Between the after wall of the chart-house and the end of the sky-light is a narrow strip of deck almost filled by a long case, about two feet in height and covered in canvas, in which are stored a set of wireless batteries.

Between skylight and taffrail lies the steering-gear housing, a big *The steering-gear casing and after-wheels* teak erection with a slightly curved roof. It is extended to either side by gratings, raised about two feet above the deck on turned legs. A lower grating runs across the forward end of the casing: hereon are mounted the after pair of dual wheels, helm movement, in this instance, being transmitted by direct action. They are used only in case of such emergencies as the breaking or jamming of the long steering-cables from the midship wheels. These cables lead into the casing through sheaves below the side-gratings.

The flat gunwale, which tops the poop bulwark-rail, is not stained *The gunwale* and varnished like all other teak fittings but retains its natural pale buff colour by periodic scourings with sand and canvas. Its continuity is broken by gaps abreast the quarter-boats to allow the boats to be swung

213

straight outboard, and by hinged sections at the head of the poop ladders. All attendant fittings, such as hinges, end plates, etc., are of polished brass.

Lifebuoys A pair of circular life-buoys, lettered HERZOGIN CECILIE, MARIE-HAMN, are housed against the poop rail in outboard slings of canvas, one on either quarter of the taffrail. A similar pair are slung high up on the wall of the break of the poop, to port and starboard respectively of the two poop-ladders. Horse-shoe shaped life-buoys are mounted on the flat outer end of the quarter-boat cradles, and there is one also on the forward wall of the donkey-house.

The accommodation gangway When at anchorage or in port, the old, German, accommodation gangway is fitted to the bulwarks, by pins and sockets, just abreast of the mainmast, the bulwarks at this point being steel-plated, not open rails. There is a quaintly naval air about this gangway with its square, white-railed upper platform and long, three-sectioned, hinged ladder. It is not difficult to picture the rigid ceremonial receptions of bygone days when high dignitaries — civil, naval or mercantile — mounted this ladder in order to review the then crack German cadet-ship, whose orderly ranks of smart 'brass-bounders' presented, with the Commander, officers, instructors, petty officers and uniformed crew, a very different appearance to the hard-worked handful of boys of many nationalities who in these days drive the old barque about her lawful occasions.

Colour There only now remains to be catalogued the question of colour (so important to the model-maker) before going below. From her earliest days *Herzogin Cecilie* has been always a white-hulled vessel. Few of the world's remaining sailers are painted white, since, by reason of superior wearing qualities and because rust streaks are less pronounced, black is the more serviceable and customary dress for tramp tonnage, both sail and steam. From an artistic view-point, black imparts a slimmer effect to bulk, but where a hull has reasonably handsome lines, the showier, more distinctive white is much more striking in appearance.

White is predominant aboard *Herzogin Cecilie*: not only the entire hull above the load-line, but the motor-house, donkey-house and its tanks, ventilators, flying bridge, boats, boat-skids, davits, cradles, galley skylight, hatch-coamings, lighthouses, all rails (including pin-rails where not teak), crane, life-belts, the inner side of the well-deck bulwarks and the break of the poop from deck to deck are so painted, for everything consistent with utility is white.

facing: AT THE MIZEN BRACES; SHOWIN
DETAIL OF CHART-HOUSE

No hard and fast ruling can be laid down in respect of the remaining paintwork about the decks: it depends partly on the whim of the Master and partly on the paint in store at the time, but the modeller may like to work to the colour-scheme in vogue in 1933, when most of the accompanying photographs were taken, since it then looked very attractive and quite harmonious:

Winches: Drums –	Black, their circular, recessed, outer faces being white
Mechanism –	(where not jacketed in canvas), grey
Inside of Ventilators	Sky-blue
Capstans –	Medium grey, picked out in green
Bollards, Bitts, etc. –	Medium grey
Steam-pipe Casing –	Black
Scuppers –	On the poop, grey
	In the waist, black*
Brace-bumpkins –	White

* In times past it was customary to paint the scuppers red, a tradition inherited from naval practice where this crude camouflage disguised the sight of 'scuppers running red with blood' during an engagement.

The barque's name on bows and counter, the accompanying raised beading (*vide* photographs), the sheer-line and the beading across the break of the poop at poop-deck level are all picked out in black.

Yards, bowsprit, tops and cross-trees are, invariably, 'mast-colour' — a deep yellow-ochre — with the trucks (the round, bunlike caps which surmount the masts) contrasted by white. The masts are painted in the same yellow-ochre, with the exception of that part of the topmasts which lies between the lower-mast cap and the heel of the topgallant mast. Up and down this section of the fore, the main and the mizen move the collars of the upper-topsail yards, and, in consequence, it is customary to paint it black.

The colour of the top-hamper and rigging

I wish that I could instruct the model-maker to pick out with white the yard-arms, the head of the bowsprit, and that portion of the top-gallant masts above the royals. Such embellishment would, however, be false to the real *Herzogin Cecilie*, although few details set off a sailing vessel to better advantage. In the old days these finishing touches were a favourite form of adornment aboard the smart, passenger clippers. The late Mr. J. Spurling, whose beautiful and authentic paintings of bygone sailers are so deservedly popular, embodies this smartening effect in several of his pictures, and it shows up particularly well in his spirited rendering of Thompson's grand old *Sophocles*.

In general, the standing-rigging is black up to the lower-masthead

cing: Right. FROM THE JIGGER SHROUDS

Left. THE STERN, FROM THE MIZEN UPPER-TO'GALLANT

level and white above it, with the customary smart, white bands on the seizings of the lower shrouds; while, in accurate models, the blocks should be white in the lower rigging, i.e. brace-blocks, etc., and mast-colour farther aloft.

Boot-topping

The boot-topping — a band of contrasting colour occupying the hull space between load-line and light-line — was emerald-green in 1933. This paint is applied over an under-coating of anti-corrosive (i.e. non-rusting) compound. Below the light-line the whole bottom is covered with red, anti-fouling paint as a partial preventative to marine growth, a subject whose effect on sailing qualities is dealt with elsewhere.

Woodwork

All the wooden structures, such as the chart-house, companions, wheels, gratings, saloon skylight, standard-compass platform, binnacle pillars, pin-rails and fife-rails, are of varnished teak, and the accompanying fittings, i.e. binnacle-hoods, wheel-bosses, port-lights and so on, are brass.

Owing to her superior condition, complete equipment, prepossessing appearance and meticulous Masters, *Herzogin Cecilie* repays for careful upkeep to a greater degree than do some of her more plebeian and toil-worn sisters. At the risk of courting criticism on the ground of unjustified exaggeration, I maintain that when in her best trim, with all the stains, dust and wear and tear of a long ocean voyage or of a lengthy stay in port erased, *Herzogin Cecilie's* decks might well vie in neatness and smartness with many a private yacht. All ropes are coiled down neatly on their pins, paintwork is fresh, brass and copper burnished, teak sand-scoured almost to whiteness or gleaming brown under new varnish, standing-rigging is tarred and whitened, canvas covers of boats and winches are scrubbed and restretched, and, for all her age, it is difficult to find dents, chips, abrasions, or indeed much outward sign of thirty-four years' continuous service at sea.

The figure-head

Last, but not least, is that most intimate adornment of a sailing vessel — the carved, wooden figurehead, which represents that Duchess Cecilie by whom the barque was christened thirty-four years ago. This figure-head, like the vessel, has altered somewhat with the passing of the years, for whereas in 1902 it depicted a lady with hair of Nordic fairness, to-day she is raven black.

In 1934 *Herzogin Cecilie* carried home from Australia a lady passenger, Miss Pamela Bourne, B.A., who, later, was to become the wife of Captain Sven Eriksson. She took the 'Duchess' in hand, and I cannot do better than give, in brief, her delightfully feminine description of the result.

'She was not only plain, she was hideous. It began to dawn on me that she wore a mask; this grotesque, pock-marked countenance was not the Duchess Cecilie. I drove my knife into her pitted cheek: the flesh cracked, a wad of paint fell into the sea. There were no less than fifteen coats of paint on that unfortunate creature — yet she was obviously a good and chaste woman. The first layer was gold leaf, glittering yet, a relic of the days when *Herzogin Cecilie* was a German training ship. After I had repainted her face she seemed more pleased with me. The faint flush of her olive cheeks was to her liking. Her blue eyes were bluer than the sea, of which her draperies were a darkling echo. She had small shell-like ears, humorous tip-tilted nose, and her mouth I painted dark red. In her breast nestled the blue-and-yellow flag of the Åland Islands, her adopted home. Gold combs decked her raven hair, which was tied back in a trim queue by orange ribbons. She melted into the ship's slim stem in a formal turmoil of yellow and black scroll-work grouped round the flag of Finland to port and round the flag of Sweden to starboard.'

The renovation of the 'Duchess'

Be it hoped that the effect is lasting, for when I first made the acquaintance of the 'Duchess' she looked a somewhat severe personage, whose highly-coloured, rather raddled features seemed to express disgust at the cumulative efforts of the many successive, keen but amateur, male beauty specialists among her servants.

Only a short length now remains of the original double band of trail-boarding with its moulded scroll-work, which ran some distance aft from the figurehead on either bow. The missing ornamentation was removed in 1921 and was sold, it is understood, in company with other unnecessary fittings. The remainder, in which Miss Bourne incorporated the crew's national flags, surrounds, on either bow, a large plaque still bearing the insignia of the Norddeutscher Lloyd — a dark blue anchor on a white ground. Two lines of black beading run round the fo'c'sle head, one on the upper and one on the lower edge of the top strake, which is pierced by the port-lights of the fore-'tween-deck, the next section of *Herzogin Cecilie* to engage attention.

The scroll-work and beading

217

CHAPTER III

'WATCH BELOW'

A ship in a bottle some sailor had made,
In watches below, swinging South with the Trade,
When the fellows were patching old dungaree suits,
Or mending up oilskins and leaky sea-boots,
Or whitling a model, or painting a chest,
Or smoking and yarning and watching the rest.

Misuse of the term fo'c'sle

THAT triangular area of a vessel's main-deck which is bounded by the convergence of her bows and roofed by the fore-deck, is still referred to by the generic term 'fo'c'sle', an abbreviation of an ancient and self-explanatory title — the forward-castle of the galleons.

On the other hand, fo'c'sle has also come, by general practice, to signify the living quarters of a crew, but, as in *Herzogin Cecilie*, where the crew are berthed amidships, a misleading contradiction in terms arises. Consequently, I propose throughout to use the word fo'c'sle to denote the crew's accommodation under the poop, whereas the area now under discussion is more rightly and properly described as the fore-'tween-deck. For a like reason, I have used the term fore-deck instead of the more colloquial fo'c'sle-head.

The fore-'tween-deck

Rickmers did not intend *Herzogin Cecilie's* fore-'tween-deck to be used for human accommodation, and the various compartments which line its outward-flaring and forward-tapering sides are merely workshops, stores or lavatories.

Lavatories washing accommodation and stores

Beneath either lighthouse, and forming the aftermost compartment on either side, are the crew's lavatories. In the old days the larger, adjacent compartment on the starboard side was fitted with a shower, and provided good washing facilities for the crew. To-day it is used by the starboard watch, but buckets, or the ubiquitous wire-handled margarine cans, serve as basins, and a douche under the near-by salt-water pump or a welcome tropical rainstorm replace the shower-bath. In practice, ablutions are more usually performed in the well-deck, proper baths being an unknown luxury before the mast. The general primitive sanitary arrangements form one of the minor hardships of life under sail.

Adjoining the starboard wash-place are stores for paint, oil, shackles, ropes, blocks, etc. Fresh meat, in the shape of live pigs, resides in temporary wooden sties under the fore-deck, for the former piggery on the port side of the 'tween-deck space is now the carpenter's shop. The remainder of the live-stock, chickens and sheep, are housed in the half-deck. Forward of the carpenter's shop is another large compartment, used originally as a chicken-coop, but which has been subdivided into a wash-place for the port watch and a lamp locker.

The four hawse-holes, through which the anchor cables lead, via a small, square hatch in the main-deck, to the cable-tier below, are closed at sea by stoppers known as hawse-blocks or bucklers, cemented in to make a water-tight joint. *Hawse-holes and windlass*

The pillar supporting the fore-deck anchor-crane stands between the heel of the bowsprit and the powerful, steam-driven anchor-windlass, which is coupled by a massive spindle to the fore-deck capstan above. A bell-mouthed, brass speaking-tube is fixed to the roof of the fore-'tween-deck just above the brake-lever of the windlass. This enables orders to be passed from the fore-deck to the man operating the windlass mechanism.

The poop-'tween-deck

Nothing else in the fore-'tween-deck space calls for detailed comment: facing it across the length of the open waist is the high, straight wall of the break of the poop. This bulkhead is pierced by a row of ports and by three steel doors — the entrance to the fo'c'sle proper on the starboard side, the donkey-room door amidships, and, to port, a high-coamed doorway opening into an alley. *The break of the poop*

This third entrance gives access to the poop-'tween-deck space, an area nearly two hundred feet in length, completely enclosed, and containing the entire living accommodation aboard *Herzogin Cecilie*. The total area is subdivided into four distinct sections: from forward, aft, these sections are (*a*) crew's quarters and galley, (*b*) the old half-deck, now a sail-room, (*c*) the accommodation for officers and passengers, and (*d*) the Master's private suite. I shall deal with them in that order, and shall incorporate between sections (*b*) and (*c*) some notes on the lower-deck and the holds. *The four sections of the poop-'tween-decks*

219

In days gone by the crew of a sailing vessel were housed either in the fo'c'sle proper, that is, up in the bows, or in steel deck-houses situated along the centre-line of an open main-deck. Some of the big twentieth-century 'four-posters' had a built-up midship-section, or island, spanning the full width of the hull, and containing all, or a large part, of the living accommodation. This island split up the open main-deck into two well-decks, rather like the three superstructure lay-out — fo'c'sle, bridge and poop — of the normal tramp steamer. Laeisz, as I have already mentioned, greatly favoured this type of sailing vessel.

Advantage of poop accommodation

Vessels built for the dual purposes of sail-training and cargo-carrying, however, were generally of the long poop design, and although to-day the crew of *Herzogin Cecilie* lead a hard life, with rough food, small wage, and few comforts or amenities, their lot is, because of the superior housing, preferable to that of the crews who man many of the Erikson Fleet.

The more orthodox type of commercial sailing vessel, with a flush main-deck encompassed by high, steel-plated bulwarks, suffered greatly from excess water in heavy weather owing to the inability of the wash-ports to cope with continuous flooding. Almost every account of voyages aboard such vessels deplores the discomfort of flooded deck-houses, the lack of hot food owing to the frequent dousing of the galley fires, and the weeks at a time when the unfortunate crew toiled in wet clothes and slept in sodden bunks.

Contrast this squalor and privation with *Herzogin Cecilie's* quarters. Apart from work in the waist and on the fore-deck, her crew at least labour under reasonably dry conditions, and her helmsmen stand amidships in comparative safety. In addition to this, the crew eat and sleep in dry security, for, in bad weather, the three doors opening on to the waist can be battened and caulked until, with their high coamings, they are permanently water-tight. Egress to the decks is then obtained up the covered companion-way abaft the foremast, and the living quarters cannot be inundated unless a major accident occurs or something be actually stove in. The soi-disant fo'c'sle remains dry and more or less warm throughout the whole voyage and clothes, books, models, etc., can be stowed away in safety. There is a vast and comforting contrast between coming below to a dry bunk and hot food and entering a cold, cheerless deck-house in which every stitch of clothing and bedding is,

facing: PLAN

EAMER TYPE)

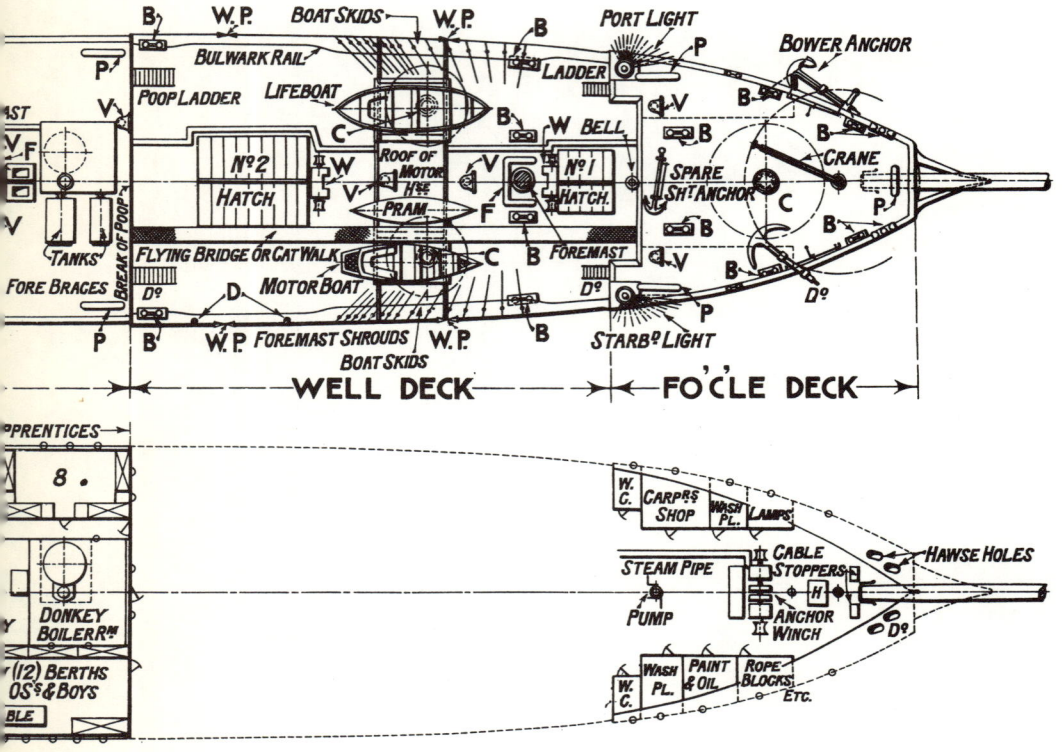

WELL DECK ← →   ← **FO'CLE DECK** →

SLE DECKS OF

CILIE"

1933

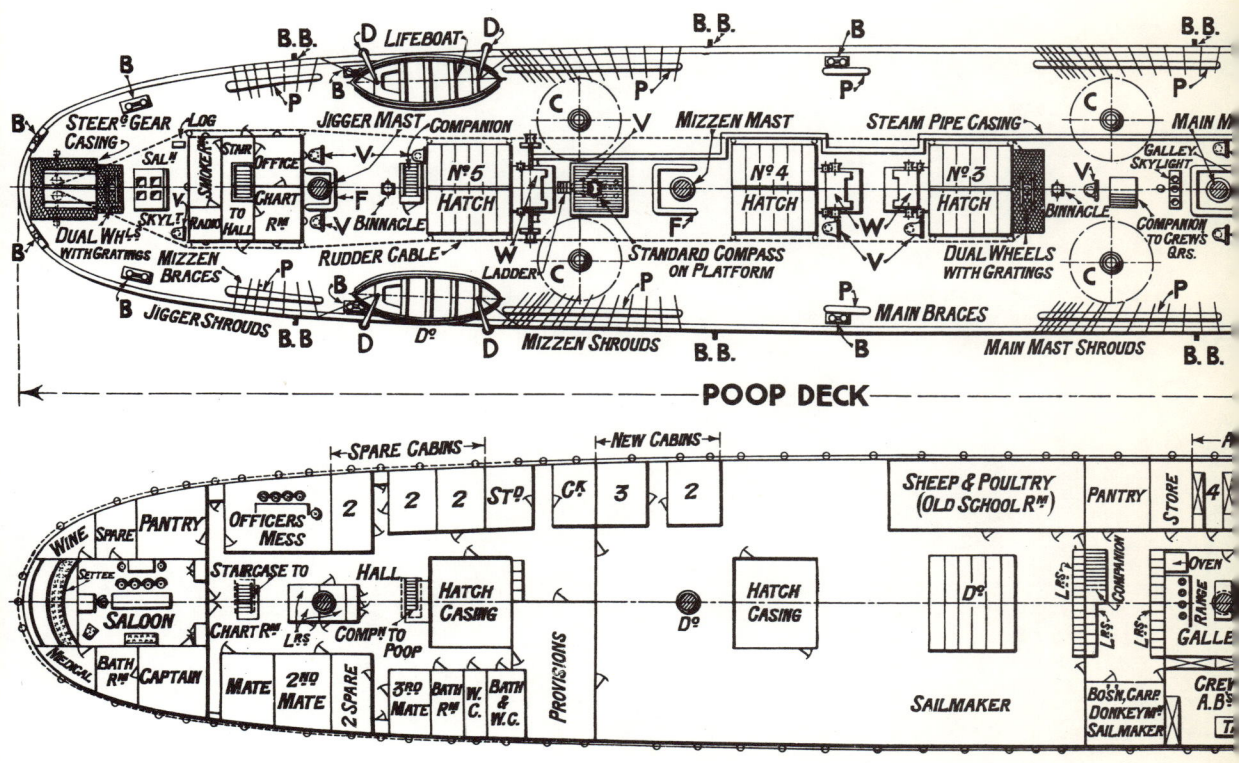

POOP DECK

THE MAIN, POOP AND FO'C

"HERZOGIN CE

AS THEY WERE IN

and will remain, wet, and where the steel floor, as like as not, is inches deep in icy water.

It is, likewise, wellnigh impossible for *Herzogin Cecilie's* galley to be put out of action, and, however rough or unpalatable the food may be, hot food and drink can always be prepared.

In 1921, when *Herzogin Cecilie* was converted from cadet-ship to tramp sailer, considerable changes were made below the poop-deck in view of the greatly reduced personnel which she was thereafter to carry.

The crew's quarters

Rickmers' plan shows a transverse, steel bulkhead running 'thwart-ships between Nos. 3 and 4 hatches. This division was removed, probably at the time of the poop extension, and a wooden partition, well forward of No. 3 hatch, now takes its place. The area of main-deck between this wooden bulkhead and the break of the poop contains the crew's quarters, the galley and the donkey-room, and is the first of the four sections into which, for descriptive purposes, I have divided the 'tween-deck space.

On the starboard side of this section is the roomy fo'c'sle, furnished *The fo'c'sles* with a long mess-table and benches. It contains twelve bunks in two tiers, eight along the full length of the port wall and two in each of the starboard corners. The bo'sun and the three 'idlers' — carpenter, donkey-man and sail-maker — occupy a smaller room just outside the fo'c'sle door and opening into a 'thwartship alleyway behind the galley. This alley is fitted with two rows of tall lockers for oilskins, etc., and the crew's companion-way leads from it to the poop-deck.

On board *Herzogin Cecilie* the so-called apprentices live in a double fo'c'sle on the port side. Except for the nominal segregation of quarters, the apprentices form an integral, though unpaid, part of the crew, being one body in regard to work and watches.

The forward and larger of their two compartments was, in German days, a school-room for the cadets. It has eight bunks, in two tiers, placed as shown in the sketch-plan. Four tall lockers fill up the spaces between the bunks; a table and two benches complete the furnishing.

The second cabin can accommodate four more apprentices, should so many be carried. Adjoining this are two other compartments, marked as store and pantry on the plan because they are so used; actually, the forward of these two cabins is fitted for a couple of bunks.

Amidships and in between the crew and the apprentices are the donkey-room and the galley, an arrangement which, although uncomfortable in the Tropics, is all to the good during those long periods of cold weather in our northern and, especially, in far southern latitudes. The commodious and well-protected galley — sometimes called the caboose — has changed but little. It is fitted with a long cooking-range, a bread oven, a sink, dresser and cupboards, and is pierced in the centre by the butt of the mainmast.

In Rickmers' plan two rooms are shown in the centre of the vessel abaft the galley. One was the carpenter's shop and the other the sail-maker's sanctum, and they were lit by a large, glass skylight in the poop-deck. Nowadays the site of this skylight is occupied by the weather-proof, sliding top of the companionway which descends to the alleyway behind the galley, the aforesaid two cabins having been dismantled.

This first section of the poop-'tween-deck area is quite a self-contained little colony, dry, warm and convenient. A mess-boy aboard *Herzogin Cecilie* does not need to run the gauntlet of cold, wet, slippery decks, carrying tepid food from an exposed galley either to poop or fo'c'sle, oft-times being flung, with his precious cargo, headlong into the scuppers by a wild lurch as 'she takes it green over the rail'. No, there is much to be said for the roofed-over, compact lay-out of a big poop.

The old half-deck, now the sail-loft

Through a sliding door at the after end of the port alley-way is the old half-deck, a space which suffered more severely than any other part of *Herzogin Cecilie* in the transition from German to Finnish ownership. In former days this spacious area accommodated the sixty cadets and the petty officers in charge. It was fitted with tables, forms and nests of lockers, above which at night were slung orderly lines of hammocks. Here also were cabins for the petty officers, lavatory accommodation, and a commodious washing-room with rows of basins. The cadets' school-room was farther forward, level with the galley on the port side. During the day the hammocks were stored away in the square casing of No. 4 tonnage-opening.

Except for a row of locker cupboards against the wooden bulkhead, all this equipment was ruthlessly stripped away in 1921 by *Herzogin Cecilie's* new owner. Captain Erikson naturally had little use for a fully-furnished half-deck, and everything marketable was sold. Even the midship companion-way, by which the cadets reached the poop-deck, disappeared, and all that remained *in situ* were No. 3 hatch, the closed-in shaft of No. 4 hatch, the butt of the mizen mast, and a few air-shafts (for hold ventilation) connected to cowls on the poop. So this big, barren, totally-enclosed space became just a sail-loft, a place where the sail-maker plies his needle and palm in solitude when inclement weather drives him from the deck above.

The old wash-room compartment on the port side is now utilized for live stock. A space has been partitioned off to form a hencoop (*Herzogin Cecilie's* poultry no longer being housed, as in German days, in the fore-'tween-deck) and sheep are penned alongside.

Mr. Villiers describes, in *Falmouth for Orders*, how this deserted, echoing half-deck recaptured, just for one night, some semblance of its former life and bustle, and once more resounded with cheerful young voices. On the Saturday night before she was due to leave Port Lincoln, South Australia, for the long homeward passage to England, a dance was given aboard in reciprocation for the general hospitality which the boys had enjoyed ashore.

A dance in the sail loft

'Rough seats were erected', he writes, 'around the steel sides of the large sail-loft; the flags of the International Code draped from the stringers and beams. Gay streamers of the pale blue-and-gold of Sweden and the blue-and-white of Finland made the well-scrubbed deck look something like a dance hall. Among the guests were the entire crew of the Swedish four-masted barque *Beatrice*, a ship which was also loading grain at Port Lincoln. Everybody had a great time: the ship's own orchestra, in the shape of four of her boys, supplied the music which was very good, and a real Scandinavian supper was served. The whole affair passed off very well, and the presence of two uninvited guests in the shape of two rats, who made themselves known in the middle of a waltz, added considerably to the noise and the excitement. Everybody was there from the Mayor of Port Lincoln to the cabin boy from *Beatrice*. Everybody danced and all enjoyed themselves.'

Two new cabins at the after end, port side, of the half-deck area, are shown on the 1933 sketch-plan. They are of very recent construction, being part of the many minor alterations commenced in 1933 by *Herzogin Cecilie's* present Master, in order to increase the accommodation available for the carriage of passengers. The foremost of these two

Three new cabins

cabins is occupied by the cook and the steward, the other and larger cabin, built against the bulkhead at the end of the half-deck, will take three passengers. A third cabin was added in 1934, and, at the same time, the Master constructed the new companion-way from the half-deck to the poop, opening out on deck between mizen mast and standard compass.

The lower deck and the holds

In the notes on the hull I mentioned that *Herzogin Cecilie* was a two-deck ship. This description had no reference to the poop-deck which, like the fore-deck, is considered, technically, as being merely a superstructure. It refers to (*a*) the main or upper deck and to (*b*) a lower deck which extends the full length of the hull at about ten feet below the main-deck and which, in the plans, is called the 'tween-deck.

Lower-deck hatches

This lower-deck is pierced by five tonnage openings corresponding exactly to those in the main-deck and possessing the same type of hatch coverings, beams running across high coamings and battened down by cross-bars and wedged tarpaulins. Consequently, any water which should penetrate the main-deck hatches enters an upper tier of holds, and yet another set of hatches must give way before it can flood the larger holds which lie between the lower-deck and the ballast-tank tops.

Deck planking

Some idea of the lavish scale on which *Herzogin Cecilie's* original specification was based is given by the fact that not only her poop-deck, fore-deck, and main-deck, but the lower deck and even the floor of the lower hold (i.e. the ceiling of the tank tops) are all completely planked throughout above their plating, a most unusual and expensive feature for a modern commercial windjammer.

The fore-peak and after-peak

The whole area between tank tops and main-deck is cargo space with three exceptions:

(*a*) The triangular fore-peak, forward of No. 1 hold, where in Germans days were the bo'sun's store, the potato bin and the chain locker;

(*b*) The lazarette and after-peak, comprising a series of store-rooms, including, in German days, a cold-store, several big bread-tanks and a 'bottom drawer' of linen, etc. The big, forward compartment, which runs the full width of the barque and was formerly the storage place for spare suits of sails and rolls of new canvas, is now used for cargo. The after-peak is reached, by a ladder, through a small hatch below the stairway which leads from the officers' quarters to the chart-house on the poop. There was at one time a separate entry to the lazarette by another hatchway in the main-deck just forward of the jigger-mast;

(c) An enclosed area beneath the donkey-room. Here are situated, between main and lower decks, the coal-bunkers and, at lower-deck level, the fresh-water tanks. The latter extend the full width of the hull, and the water is piped to a pump in the galley. *Herzogin Cecilie* can carry 168 tons of fresh water, far more than sufficient for her moderate, present-day requirements. An allowance of one ton of water for each member of her personnel is the rough and ready basis on which her needs for each single outward or homeward Australian passage are calculated. This means a total consumption of about eighty tons for a round voyage, and her tankage gives her ample reserve for all eventualities.

Bunkers, fresh-water tanks and pumps

Finally, below these all-important tanks is the steam-driven bilge pump. It is of the greatest importance that no sodden grain or other bilge refuse be allowed to seep into this locality, because it may clog the rose-boxes and so render the pumps inoperative.

While on the subject of holds, it may be pointed out that one benefit derived from the employment of metal in place of wood for shipbuilding is that the internal volume of the hull can be subdivided into separate compartments by more efficient bulkheads, which, where necessary, can be water-tight.

Bulkheads

This form of construction strengthens the hull, lessens the risk of sinking after collision, and localizes, to a great extent, the seat of a fire. A further advantage, particularly in a sailing vessel, is to mitigate the risk of her cargo shifting in heavy weather. Wooden bulkheads were, of course, just as efficacious for the last-mentioned purpose, but otherwise their practical value was small.

The officers' quarters.

The next and third section of the 'tween-deck space to be dealt with, namely, the officers' quarters, is reached through a steel doorway in the port side of the cross bulkhead which cuts off the afterguard from the rest of the vessel. The doorway opens into a short alley, somewhat similar to that other alley, farther forward, in the crew's section. I shall tabulate the cabins and rooms of this third area, because, in that form, the alterations can be shown more clearly than by a running commentary of text alone.

The list commences at the entrance to the alleyway, deals (*a*) with the cabins down the port side of the barque, then (*b*) with those on the starboard side, and, finally (*c*) going aft again, with the central block between the two alleys.

Alterations in accommodation	1902–20 (German)	1921–33 (Finnish) As Sketch Plan	1934–35 Alterations
(A) *Port side, going aft*			
Cabin	Chef	Cook	⎰ New dining saloon
Cabin	2 Stewards	Steward	⎱ for Mates and
Cabin	4th Officer	2 Passengers	passengers
Cabin	3rd Officer	2 Passengers	2 Passengers
Cabin	2nd Officer	2 Passengers	2 Passengers
Messroom	Officers	Mates and Passengers	2 new cabins for 5 passengers in all
Pantry		Unaltered	Large cabin for 2 passengers
(B) *Starboard side, going forward*			
Cabin	1st Officer	Mate	Unaltered
Cabin	Doctor	2nd Mate	Unaltered
Cabin	Senior Instructor	2 Passengers	Unaltered
Cabin	Assistant Instructor	3rd Mate	Unaltered
Bathroom	Officers', etc.	Mates	Unaltered
w.c.	Officers', etc.	Mates	Unaltered
Bath and w.c.	For hospital use	Passengers'	Unaltered
Hospital		Provision Store	Unaltered
(C) *Central, going aft*			
Empty recess facing chef's cabin		Unaltered	New Pantry
No. 5 hatch casing with door into port side alley		Unaltered	Unaltered
Poop companion-ladder		Unaltered	Lounge skylight
Central hall		Unaltered	Lounge
Butt of jigger-mast surrounded by lockers, wine-bins, etc.		Unaltered	Mast-butt now surrounded by settee
Stairway to chartroom		Unaltered	Unaltered

When *Herzogin Cecilie* passed to the Finns, her new owner left this part of the barque, which, in effect, might be called the poop proper, almost unaltered, and thereby preserved much of her inward attractiveness. Only five of the nine cabins were retained in regular use, the other four being idle unless occupied by passengers.

facing: Top. THE MASTER'S SALOON, 1931. THE AFTER EN

Bottom. FORWARD HALF OF THE SALOON (STAIRWAY T THE CHART-HOUSE IN BACKGROUND)

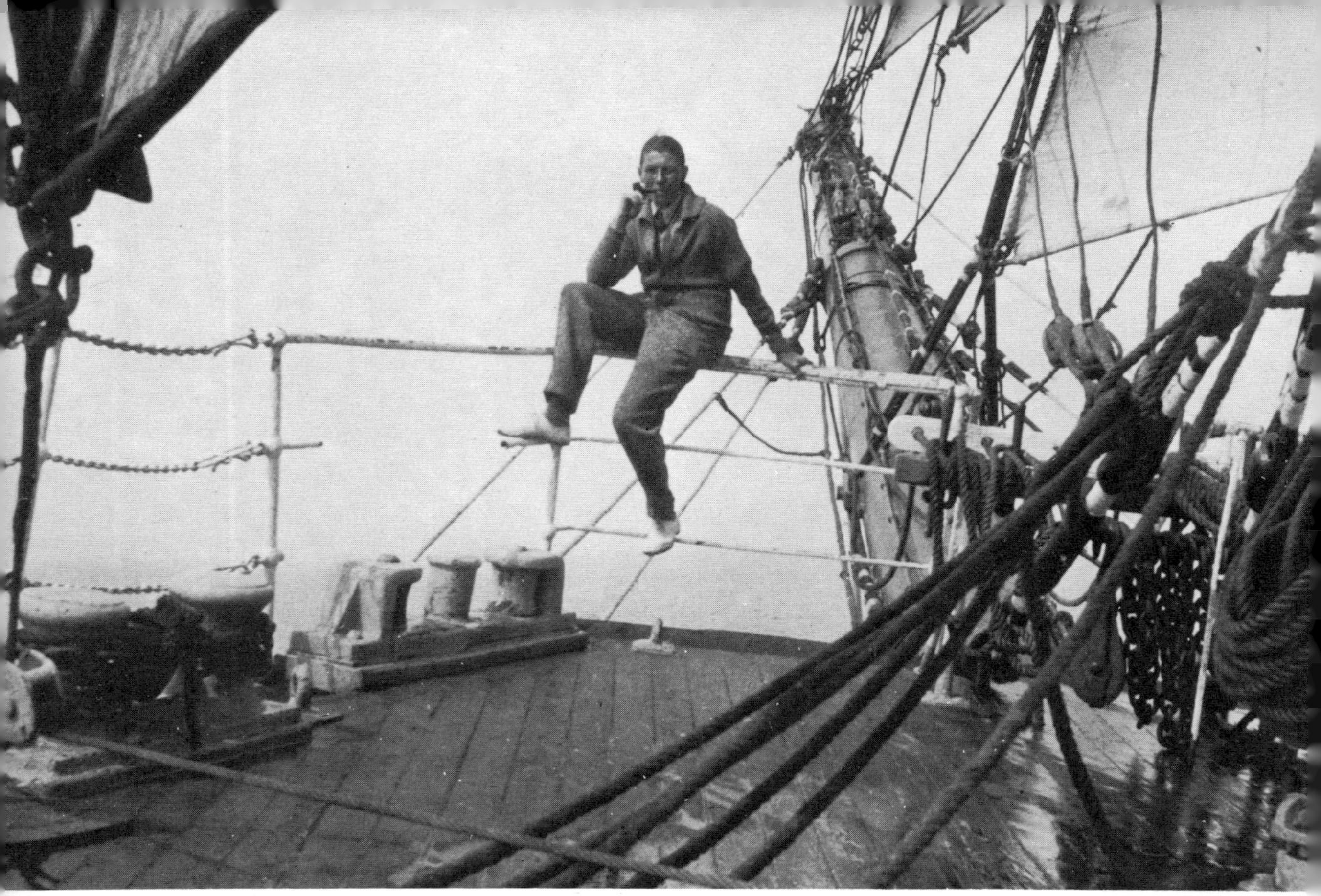
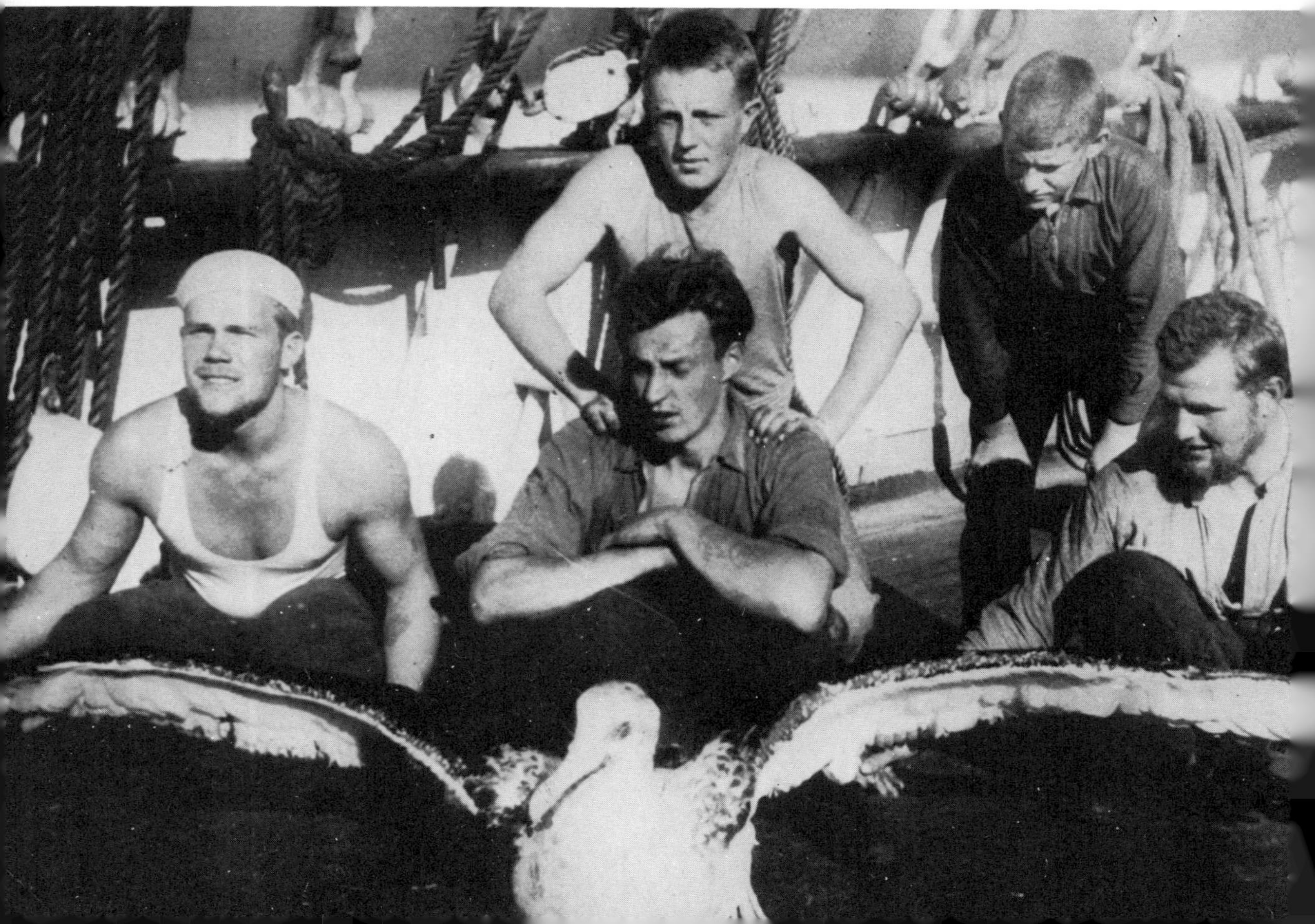

UNDER DECK

Medical provision

The one definite alteration was the conversion of the hospital into a storeroom for provisions. The trading windjammer carries no doctor: medical attention and first-aid supplies depend upon the Master, whose knowledge of both medicine and surgery, naturally, is limited. Should a man be too sick or too badly hurt to carry on, he can expect but little in the way of comfort, nursing, or alleviation. Whether it be due to the healthiness of the life or to the youth and toughness of those concerned, cases of serious illness, accident, or injury are, however, comparatively rare.

Accommodation for passengers

In both the 1921 and 1934 columns above, I have given the maximum number of passengers who can be accommodated in the respective cabins by using a settee, when needed, as a bunk, i.e. some of the so-called two-berth cabins are actually single-berth cabins having a settee.

Prior to 1933 *Herzogin Cecilie* could carry, in all, nine passengers, eight as shown in the table of cabins, and one in a spare berth in the Master's suite. As a result of the subsequent alterations undertaken by Captain Sven Eriksson, this number was increased to a possible nineteen (including settee-berths), circumstances and regulations permitting. He made the old pantry and messroom (by subdividing the latter) into three staterooms, and built the aforementioned three new cabins on the port side of the disused half-deck. The cook and steward were banished to one of these half-deck cabins; their former cabins, plus an adjacent passenger cabin and part of the alleyway, were thrown into a new and more spacious dining saloon. The empty recess, just forward of No. 5 hatch-shaft casing, became a convenient pantry, with direct access into the saloon.

The lounge

To supplement the increased facilities for sleeping and eating, some form of lounge, in addition to the little smoke-room in the chart-house, was essential if a possible nineteen people were to be provided for. Captain Eriksson cleverly contrived this amenity by altering the hall which centres around the butt of the jigger-mast. By building the new poop companion-way in the half-deck he was able to dispense with the narrow ladder which led to the deck from this hall just forward of the jigger.

He also removed the binnacle, which still marked the original site of the forward wheels, and filled the poop-deck space between No. 5 hatch and the jigger-mast with a fine new skylight, having six hinged

acing: Top.   THE AUTHOR ABOARD 'HERZOGIN CECILIE', 1933

Bottom.   AN ALBATROSS ON 'PONAPE'

flaps, each pierced by two glass ports. This made the hall below light and airy, and, refurnished with a long settee against the hatch casing, an oval table under the skylight, and with basket chairs, it became a roomy and completely enclosed lounge. The final alteration was the conversion of the square nest of cupboards at the butt of the jigger-mast into a circular settee. With well-scrubbed deck-planking, partly hidden by two long runners of red carpet, white walls fitted with a waist-high teak handrail, white ceiling, and, at the after end, the balustraded, branching stairway to the chart-room, the whole forms a bright and attractive ensemble.

Furniture and fittings

Owing to the remarkable state of preservation apparent even to-day in the furnishings and fittings of *Herzogin Cecilie's* staterooms, she is particularly well suited to accommodate long-voyage passengers. As this part of the vessel was left intact by the Finns, most of the furniture is the original, solid, handsome German equipment. Expense was of little object to the Norddeutscher Lloyd in 1902 when they commissioned Rickmers to produce a smart cadet-ship, and, by windjammer standards, the results were lavish in the extreme.

Herzogin Cecilie shows every mark of having been well cared for throughout her long and active sea life, and down in her cosy after quarters little sign of thirty-four years' wear and tear is apparent.

Fond as I am of *Herzogin Cecilie*, I have also a very soft spot in my heart for another old tall ship — Erikson's graceful, three-masted, steel barque *Penang*.

A cabin in 'Penang'

My cabin aboard *Penang* belonged, in the ordinary way, to the Third Mate, who had been left behind in Australia suffering from appendicitis: it was so small that the proverbial swinging cat would have undergone a severe bruising therein.

It had a coffin-like bunk along the outer wall, immediately below a somewhat leaky port: my head touched steel plating at one end of the bunk, my feet likewise at the other end. The 'coffin' was bottomed by rough boards on which were spread a 'donkey's breakfast' (a straw-stuffed sack mattress). A tin paraffin lamp was fixed to the wall near the head of the bunk, and beside it, over the washstand, a little looking-glass.

The washstand, contrived from a packing-case, was ingenious: a hole cut in the top held a tin bowl, while on a shelf below the bowl was fixed a large margarine can into which to tip the slops. The stand and its hinged lid were, of course, painted, and the whole was not only crudely efficient but served as a table when the lid was shut down.

A long drawer below the bunk, a (very!) collapsible carpet-stool, a wall-rack holding a water-jug and glass, a row of hooks, and a roof of deck-planking (which in wet weather leaked abominably through the seams just above my bunk) completed the tally of this suite de luxe.

I am not being needlessly sarcastic or scathing, for rarely have I been more contented than during those delightful weeks aboard *Penang*, but the description serves to show the wide difference between a purely trading windjammer and a vessel of *Herzogin Cecilie's* class and design.

Contrast the above with my cabin aboard *Herzogin Cecilie*—a roomy, square compartment with a large, adjustable port-hole. It was fitted with electric light, and had also a big, brass oil-lamp swung in gimbals over the table. The furniture was all of polished mahogany, and a crimson settee ran the full cabin-width below the port-hole. Facing the settee was a high, six-foot bunk with box-spring mattress, new linen sheets, and fine-quality, cream, wool blankets. At the head of the bunk was a folding netting-rack. Below the bunk were three tiers of long drawers, while a tank-type washing compendium, of steamer pattern, having a large mirror, shelves and a rack for glasses and carafe, occupied the space between the bunk and a commodious wardrobe. A bookshelf above the table, a folding chair, a mirror, a radiator, and, finally, a red carpet completely covering the deck area, such is the inventory of a typical cabin aboard *Herzogin Cecilie*.

A cabin in 'Herzogin Cecilie'

At the time of my own sojourn therein the radiator was for ornament rather than for use, dependent, like the hot salt-water supply in her three bathrooms, on the operation of the donkey-boiler. Under this system the only hope of getting a hot bath when at sea was by obtaining buckets of water from the galley range.

Central heating and hot water supply

With a fair amount of breeze a sailing vessel heels well over to lee-ward and stays there. A bath can then be a precarious business, for the water, naturally, finds its own level. In practice, one had a cold douche rather than bother about the bucket method, knowing that most of the hot water would certainly be ejected on to the zinc floor of the bathroom.

All this is now altered, for Captain Eriksson has completed his improvements by renovating the heating arrangements. He has linked up both the central-heating system and the piping from the bathrooms to a newly installed 'Ideal' pattern boiler. This is situated in the old half-deck, against the after bulkhead and just abaft the new companion-way, and its vent is the thin chimney, close to the mizen, mentioned in the deck survey. Under summer conditions the new system is not, of course, maintained in continuous operation; in colder weather, it is possible for the whole of the poop accommodation to be permanently heated and to ensure a constant flow of hot salt-water from the taps.

Even in the last days of the passenger sailing vessel, a bathroom denoted great luxury, and such provision was a point of pride to both the builder and the owner of a vessel thus equipped.

It may be thought, by some, that these amenities are a whit incongruous when applied to that relic of the bygone, a trading windjammer. So indeed they may be, but to others, like myself, these very definite indications that the condition of *Herzogin Cecilie* is being improved upon rather than allowed to fall into a state of disrepair and neglect, outweigh any such criticism.

The Norddeutscher Lloyd monogram is visible still on many of the fittings in the poop accommodation. The cabin walls and ceilings are repainted periodically with glossy, white enamel, and, needless to say, everything is spotlessly clean.

The Master's quarters.

The fourth, last, and most fascinating part of *Herzogin Cecilie's* accommodation below decks is that 'holy of holies', the Master's private sanctum. Immediately abaft the staircase a richly-panelled, teak bulkhead runs completely athwartships, isolating the suite from the rest of the barque, entry being through double doors in the centre.

No other sailing vessel and few steamers below the rank of liner provide finer quarters for their Captain than does this thirty-four-year-old windjammer. Furnished and decorated with Victorian solidarity and rich heaviness, the central saloon and its surrounding cabins preserve to perfection the homely, nautical atmosphere of bygone days, tempered in a delightful fashion by the quaint 'shore' effect of trailing ferns and scarlet flowers in the window-boxes around the big, arched skylight in the roof.

The saloon

This overhead lighting, together with the three portlights in the curved contour of the after end, make the saloon very light and airy by day. At night, glass-globed electric lamps at the four corners of the skylight, or, when the lighting plant is inoperative, a large, handsome, brass

230

facing: Right. CAPSTAN GRIND. RAISING 'PENANG'S' ANCHO

Left. NOCTURNE

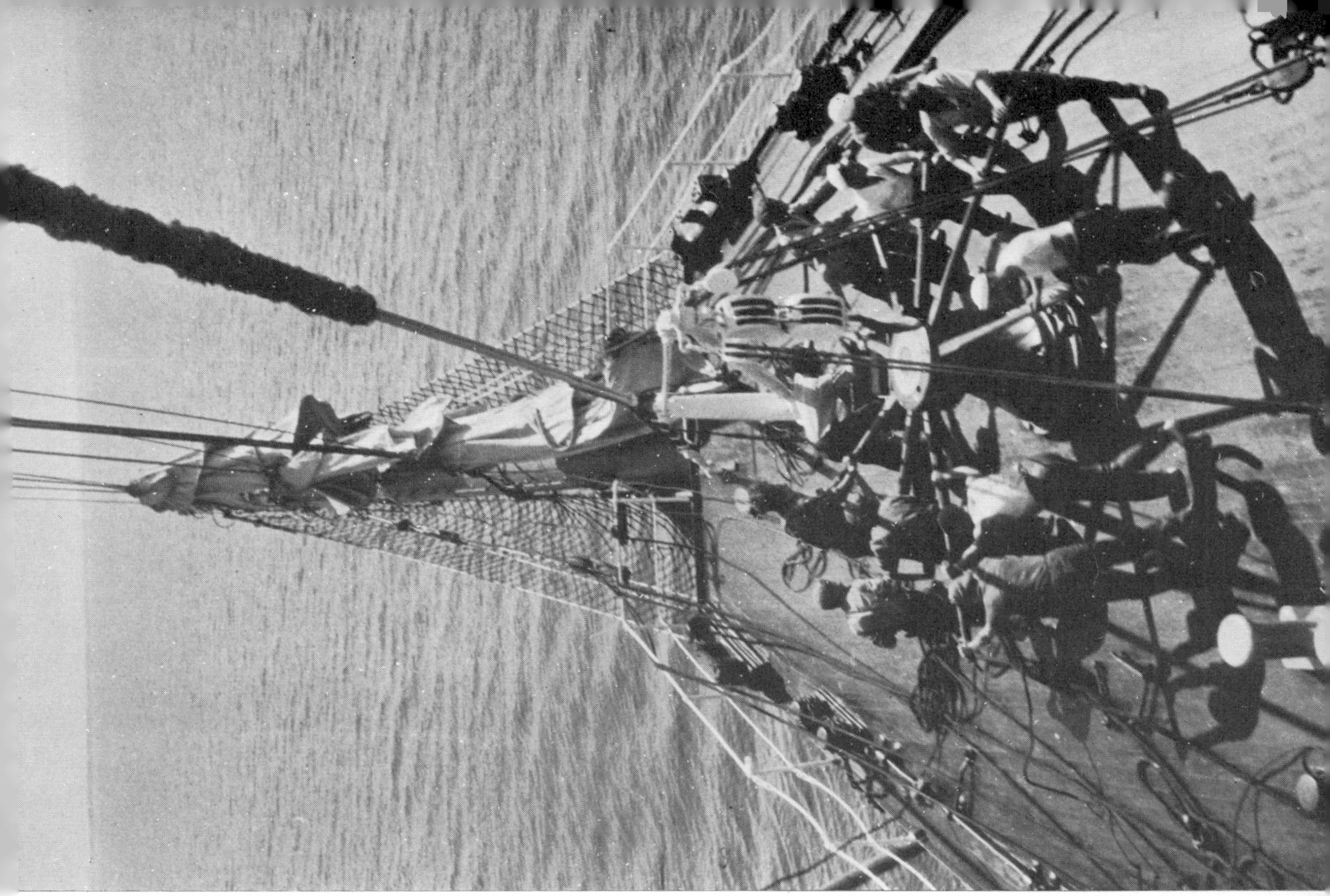

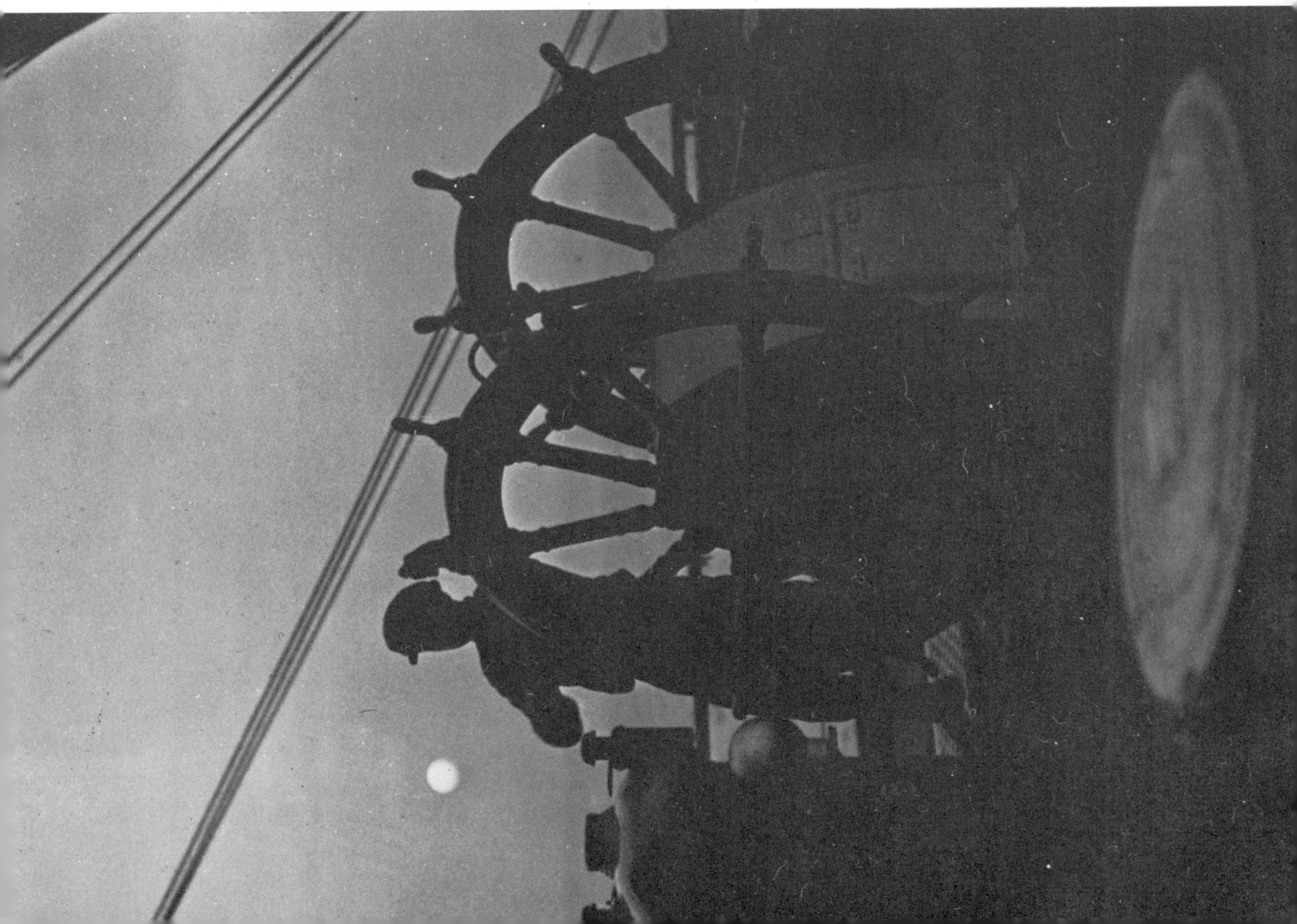

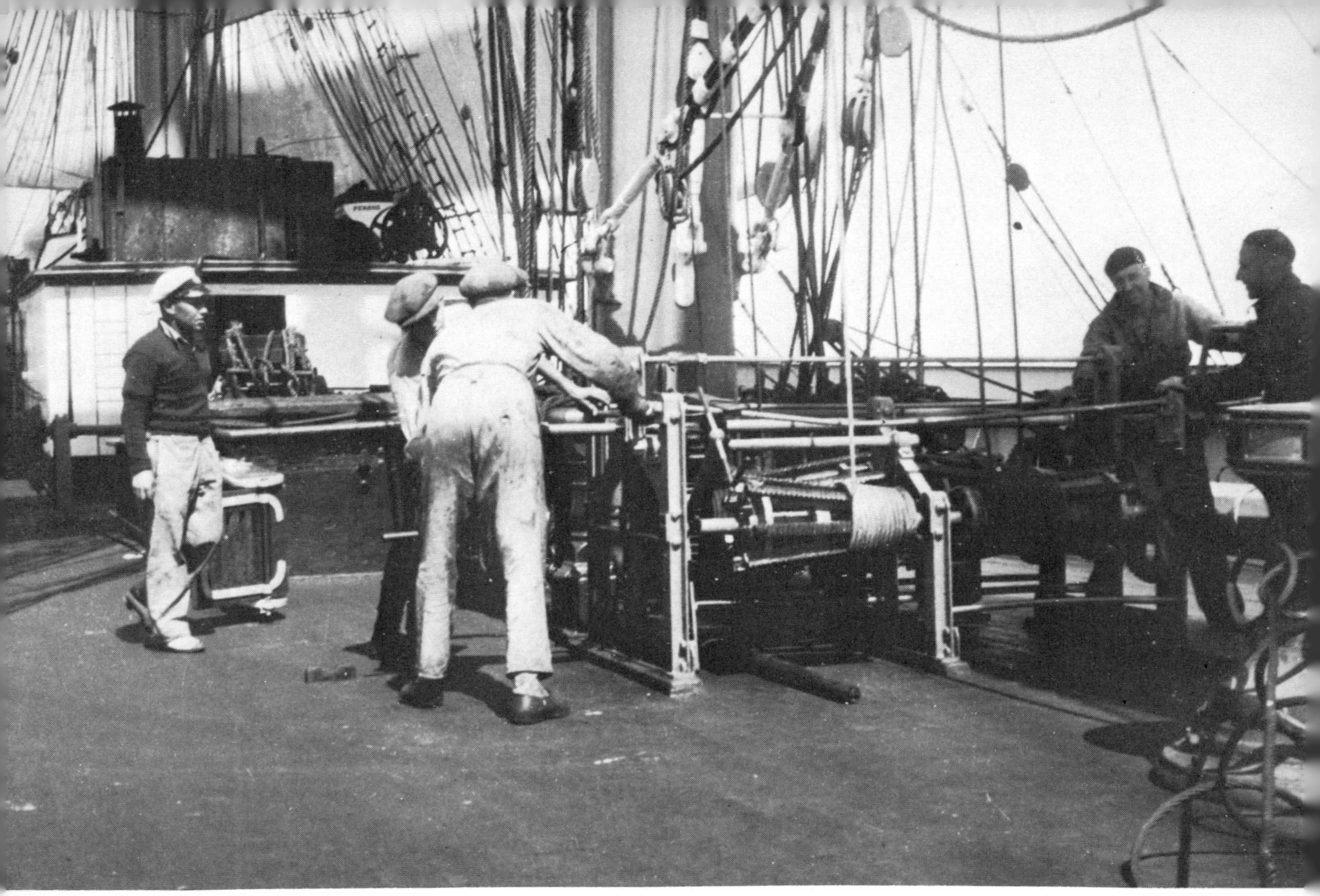

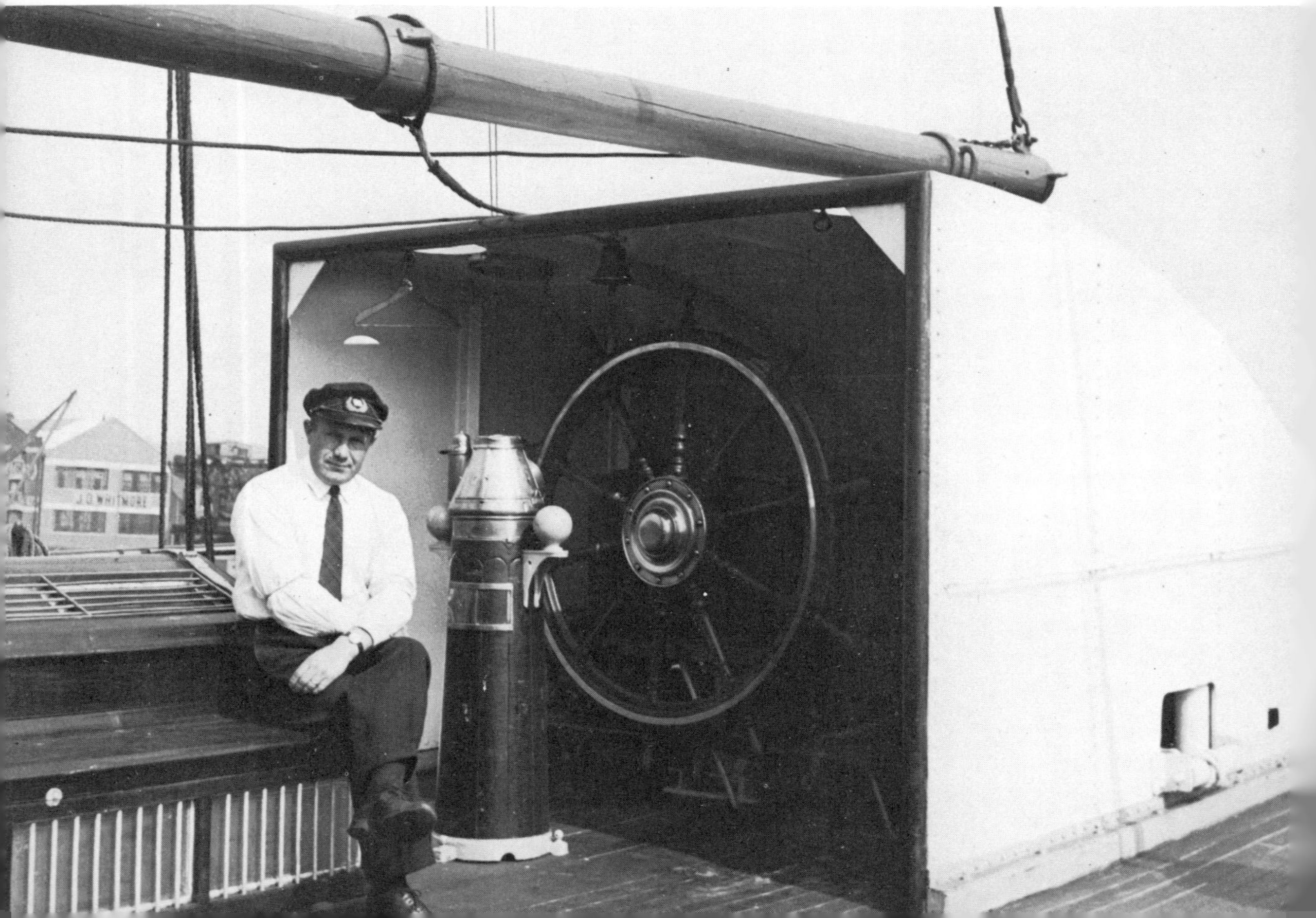
J.O. WHITMORE

lamp hanging in ornamental gimbals, make it both cosy and cheerful. The ceiling and cornices are enamelled white, and the entire wall area is panelled in dark, highly-polished mahogany.

Rickmers' plan and Mr. Herring's photographs show a long, central dining-table flanked by swivel-chairs, but when this old sea-parlour became the floating home of the Master and his English wife, the big table was replaced by a smaller one against the port wall and a round one at the after end. In each forward corner of the saloon, i.e. on either side of the double entrance-doors, stands a brass-railed sideboard, with upper and lower cupboards, and having mirrors inlaid in its top section. Behind the circular table rises, from deck to ceiling, the square casing of the rudder-post, panelled to match the walls. At the back of this casing, on a platform or dais raised one step above the main deck level, is a deep, half-moon-shaped settee upholstered in dark red velvet. It extends the full width of the saloon, its curve following the contour of *Herzogin Cecilie's* shapely counter; its back, being only about four feet in height, does not in any way obstruct the light from the three stern port-lights. Two leather arm-chairs flank the round table, and the side table has its accompanying screwed-down swivel-chairs. In the photographs it will be noticed that the back-piece of each such chair is embossed with the monogram of the Norddeutscher Lloyd. Table covers and deck carpet are dark red, and on the walls hang photographs of the Owner and his wife and pictures of past and present sailing vessels. Facing the small table and running along the starboard wall is a big, comfortable settee.

A large and realistic oil-painting of *Herzogin Cecilie* is a prominent feature of the decoration: it depicts her driving strongly, close-hauled, under full canvas, and is painted as if by an observer aboard another vessel riding close on her weather port quarter.

The raised after end of the saloon can be shut off altogether by thick, full-length curtains, which run on rings along a rail across the front of the rudder-casing.

Such is the Master's saloon, from which open four doors, two on either side.

The saloon cabins

To starboard is his sleeping cabin, a luxurious and roomy dwelling, with fine old mahogany furniture, and with a communicating bathroom and lavatory. A speaking-tube from the chart-room is fitted alongside the bunk.

On the port side, a space corresponding in area to the Master's cabin

231

is taken up by the old pantry (now a stateroom) which, in order that complete privacy may be assured, has no direct entry into the saloon. Facing the bathroom, on the port side, is a spare, single-berth cabin, occasionally used nowadays by a privileged guest. On either side of the steering casing is a tiny, triangular compartment, one serving as a medicine chest and dispensary, the other for the storage of the Master's private stock of beer, whisky, schnapps, etc.

I presume that not even the most ambitious maker of models will attempt to reproduce any under-deck detail: therefore, these notes on accommodation are included mainly because I am wishful to preserve for the future the complete picture of a past era, and also because of their close association with the history of *Herzogin Cecilie*, both in cause and effect.

The comfort and convenience to be found in and about *Herzogin Cecilie's* poop are almost unique among big sailing craft to-day, and the observer is carried back many decades in nautical practice, to the time when a ship was a permanent dwelling rather than a mere conveyor of cargo or a floating hotel.

In regard to the hull, nothing remains for further comment, so it's up and away aloft, even to the main-truck two hundred feet above deck, to learn something of the great top-hamper and mighty spread of canvas which drive *Herzogin Cecilie*.

CHAPTER IV

'LAYING ALOFT'

Just the old round of sailorizing that all us shellbacks know,
The old hauling of sheets and braces in the doldrums to and fro,
The odd jobs aloft in the Tropics when the good trade-winds blow,
Reefing and furling, wheel and look-out, shifting and bending sail,
Tallying on to the topsail halyards, snugging down in a gale.

THE origin of the sail as a means of propulsion is lost in the mists *The origin of the sail* of antiquity. Credit for the innovation has been accorded to Dædalus, who, so legend has it, attached wings to himself. The first pictured sailing craft dates from about the year 6300 B.C., fifteen hundred years before the building of the Ark. Early sails were made of papyrus fibre or of flax, bound and roped with skin. The skins of the hyena and the seal were especially favoured because they were credited with the ability to avert lightning!

It would serve no purpose, in fact a whole book would be needed, to trace the development and design of sail from papyrus to modern No. 1 storm-canvas.

So, the reasons which brought about the evolution of the steel four-masted barque from the wooden full-rigger having been dealt with in Book One, Chapter 1, the present Chapter is concerned not with development but with barque-rig as it exists to-day, and with its manipulation.

I have been faced in this Chapter, to a greater extent than in any other, with the problem of omission. Since 1902 there has been so little change in the lay-out aloft of *Herzogin Cecilie* that Rickmers' plan of her top-hamper is, in itself, an adequate description. Again, in the matter of spars, sails and gear, any one four-masted barque is, in broad outline, much like any other. It would not only make a wearisome catalogue to go over the whole ground rope by rope and sail by sail, but would be almost completely redundant.

Whereas some part of the ensuing text may appear elementary to the knowledgeable reader, other portions may, perforce, be somewhat indigestible fare for the non-technical layman. I hope to combine the necessary technical details, where *Herzogin Cecilie* differs from other vessels, with much generalization, intended to make the plans themselves more intelligible to the uninitiated. Finally, I shall explain briefly the theory of sail propulsion, and describe one or two common manœuvres.

Technical terms

The free use of technical terms is unavoidable in a survey such as this because without their employment the text would become complicated to the point of tedium. Such expressions came into being, often quite fortuitously, as a method of simplification. They contain a whole wealth of meaning compressed into the briefest possible form. The late Mr. Joseph Conrad, master of English prose, expresses in his *Mirror of the Sea* the view that 'to take a liberty with technical language is a crime against the clearness, precision, and beauty of perfected speech'.

To all who, like myself, have sought a sound text-book on square-rig, I recommend *Dana's Seaman's Manual*. Written many years ago by R. H. Dana, Junr., it was revised and corrected by a Registrar-General of Shipping and Seamen, and republished by Messrs. Ward, Lock & Company. It claims, modestly, to be 'a plain treatise on practical seamanship', but it covers the whole field of rigging work and design, the making, bending and handling of square-sail, working ship in every condition of weather, and the duties of all aboard; in fact it is a veritable encyclopædia of sail and its glossary, compiled in the days of the tall ships, is almost unique.

'Tall Ship'

By the opening years of the twentieth century a long, full-lined, steel hull with four masts and barque-rig comprised the popular specification for a new sailing vessel. In the case of *Herzogin Cecilie*, the Norddeutscher Lloyd naturally chose the most up-to-date, orthodox, and, at the same time, safest type of big windjammer for their purpose. Expense was of secondary importance; manual labour was to be provided in abundance by her calling; while strength, good looks, cargo capacity, and sailing qualities above the average were the prime stipulations.

'Tall ship', like 'clipper', is a term which is often all too carelessly employed by writers of romantic fiction or pseudo-fact. It is, however, in the case of *Herzogin Cecilie* a well-deserved epithet. Her main-truck, the topmost point of her highest mast, is 200 feet above her keel and 170 feet above the main-deck. In other words, when sailing fully-loaded her extreme height above the water-line is almost two-thirds of her water-line length of 310 feet.

Such figures are apt to have little significance unless they can be made comparative: if Nelson's Column could be placed on the main-deck of *Herzogin Cecilie*, Nelson's head would be on a level with the barque's main-truck. Again, suppose *Herzogin Cecilie* and *Queen Mary* to be placed in juxtaposition on the floor of the same dry-dock, then, although the barque from bowsprit end to taffrail is just one-third the registered length of the great liner, her main-truck would reach 20 feet above the latter's highest funnel, and be only 34 feet short of the liner's masthead.

Although *Herzogin Cecilie* is a very strongly-rigged vessel, with abnormally heavy top-hamper, her sparring is in no way ungraceful. *Dimension and material of top-hamper* The height and spacing out of her masts and the graduated spread of her yards are well-proportioned, being in keeping with the dimensions of her hull and avoiding the stunted appearance imparted by excessive square-ness. Her sparring, with the exception of the three royal yards and the spanker and double gaff-booms which are of solid wood, is of tubular steel from deck to trucks. The main-yard, her longest horizontal spar, is 94 feet in length, over twice the greatest breadth of the hull; it weighs more than five tons, and would fail to span the extreme width of *Queen Mary* by 12 feet at either end.

The six yards mounted on each of the three square-rigged masts taper upward symmetrically in length to the wooden royal yards, the main-royal being 49 feet long, slightly over half the length of the main-yard.

When the yards are trimmed exactly square, that is, at right angles to the keel line, this main-royal yard outspans, by $1\frac{1}{2}$ feet on either side, the poop-deck, 150 feet below.

All yards, whether they be of wood or of steel, have their greatest diameter in the centre, and taper slightly thence toward either yard-arm.

The model-maker can work with confidence from Rickmers' rigging *Modelling from the plans* plan, because, in all essentials, *Herzogin Cecilie* conforms, still, to the original specification. I except, of course, the leading of the fore-braces to pin-rails at the forward end of the poop, when that deck was lengthened, and certain extra fore-and-aft sails, whose innovation will be dealt with later.

The value of a model, be it considered as a record for the future, as a memory of time spent aboard, or as a work of art alone, depends to a great extent on its accuracy, not only of dimension and rig but also in its more intimate details. The correct placing of such fittings as companions, capstans, pin-rails, etc., makes all the difference to the reality of the finished replica, for it is then possible to visualize the life and work, even the habits, of the personnel of the real vessel.

No less important is the accurate reproduction of rigging detail. For example, unless the scale adopted be too small to permit such inclusions, foot-ropes (slung in proper stirrups) and jack-stays should never be omitted, for a yard without these appendages appears to a sailor as incomplete and useless as a horse without reins and bit, or as a bicycle without saddle and pedals.

I shall have the needs of the modeller in view throughout this concluding chapter of descriptive matter, for, although the plans and the photographs cover the entire subject, there are many minor points which can be supplemented in the text, and which if embodied in a facsimile will make all the difference to its value as an historical record.

Rake of masts

Meticulous artists should note, for instance, that the main-truck is two feet above the equal height of fore and mizen trucks. The slight backward rake of the masts, a feature which is so great an asset to the appearance of a sailer, is five-eighths of an inch to the foot: in other words, a plumb-line from the main-truck would, in the total drop of 200 feet, rest $10\frac{1}{2}$ feet aft of the butt of the mainmast.

The maze of rigging

Neither the rigging of a sailing vessel nor the manipulation of her sails fall, rightly, into the category of 'black arts', comprehensible alone to those who have made themselves over body and soul to the service of the sea. Admittedly this complicated tracery of spars enmeshed in a network of rigging must present to the uninitiated a truly Gordian Knot, but one which I will attempt to cut by a short and simple digression.

Starting from the bows, the names of the three masts on which square-sail is set aboard a four-masted barque are the fore, the main, and the mizen. Although the maze of ropes and wires by which they are supported and controlled appear in their very multiplicity to be complicated to a degree, the key to the puzzle lies in the fact that the rigging of each of these three masts is precisely similar: the relative position of any one rope is the same, whether it serve the spars and sails of fore, main, or mizen.

Mast support

Each mast is supported in four directions: on either side by heavy wires called shrouds, from in front by wire forestays, and from the rear by stronger and more numerous back-stays which deal with the great lateral and after-stresses set up by wind propulsion. If a vessel be driven onward by wind-pressure against canvas, the obvious impulse is for the masts to be forced or bent forward, whereas, except when altering course or if taken aback by a sudden change of wind, there is little tendency for the masts to fall backward. Hence the need for the greater and more widespread support afforded by the several back-stays.

Herzogin Cecilie's masts are not, of course, one-piece spars, for, to *Mast division* stand the strain put upon it in heavy weather, a 200-foot, tapering, steel tube would need to be of impracticably large dimension. In a sectional spar the 'whip' can be controlled, strength obtained without undue girth, and a new upper-section replaced in the event of breakage. Her fore, main, and mizen masts are three-sectioned, while the aftermost mast — the schooner-rigged jigger — is in two parts.

The generic term foremast, therefore, embodies the foremast proper (the lowest section), the fore-topmast and the fore-topgallant mast. Each section has a set of standing-rigging — shrouds, stays, etc. — of its own, which derive their names from the particular division which they serve.

Each of the three square-rigged masts mounts six one-piece yards. *Yard* From deck to truck they are called respectively the course yard, the *nomenclature* lower and upper topsail yards, the lower and upper topgallant yards, and, highest of all, the royal yard. Prefix these names by the name of the mast, as, for example, fore royal yard or mizen lower topgallant yard, and you have the key to the nomenclature of spars, sails, and gear, because the sails, and the ropes which control them, take their titles from the yards from which they depend, e.g. fore lower topgallant sail, main upper topsail halliards, mizen royal braces, etc.

The course yards are not called fore-course yard, etc., but shortened to fore-yard, main-yard, and cross-jack (or cro'jick) yard respectively, their sails being the foresail, mainsail, and cross-jack.

The derivation of these ancient terms, which have served unchanged through many centuries of sail history, merits some explanation.

Mizzen, mizen, or mison as it was formerly spelt, comes from the *Mizen and* Arabic *mizan* or *misan*, meaning a balance. The original term denoted *cross-jack* a sail at either bow or stern, since either position gave balance to the rig. In England it came to mean the after mast, and in France, as *misaine*, the foremast, but both uses are somewhat corrupted.

In the second part of Chapter 1 (Book One) was described how, when the bonaventure or fourth mast of Elizabethan days fell into disuse, the 'mison' was equipped with a square topsail. This necessitated the provision of two square yards, between which the new sail could be spread. As the existing lateen-type mizen-boom, carrying a big fore-and-aft sail, was retained, it followed that the lower of the two fresh yards served merely as a spreader for the foot of the new-fangled topsail.

'Cross' had, in those days, the same nautical meaning as was later to be implied by 'square'. 'Jack', in the phraseology of the sea, has always denoted a small fitting: hence the composite term cross-jack — the insignificant, square yard on the 'mison'. The French called this unused spar *la vergue séche* — the dry or barren yard.

Upon the advent of full or ship rig, the long, lateen mizen-boom disappeared, and a big, square course was set from the enlarged cross-jack yard, the sail itself receiving the name of cross-jack.

In German days *Herzogin Cecilie's* four masts were called *fock* (fore), *gross* (big), *kreuz* (cross) and *besan* (mizen), their mizen being the equivalent of our jigger. The Swedish mast-names, which are to-day in use in the Erikson Fleet, are rather similar to the German: they are *fockmast*, *stormast*, *kryssmast* and *mesanmast*, the mizen-course, or cross-jack, being known as the *begin*.

Actually, the gaff boom, from which the full-rigger set the head of her spanker, was a relic of the lateen yard of the galleon.

The lateen, or the sail of the Latin peoples, was so-called because it continued to characterize Mediterranean (and also Oriental) fighting and trading craft long after square-rig had displaced fore-and-aft rig aboard the larger, deepwater vessels of the northern maritime nations.

'Course' 'Course' is, likewise, an ancient term. It was, originally, 'corse' or 'body' — the main body of the single sail set by the one-masted vessel of the early Middle Ages, and to the foot of which, in fine weather, a 'bonnet' was laced. The ship in Shakespeare's *Tempest* set her 'two corses' in a desperate attempt to claw off a lee shore. The complete area of a medieval square-sail was the fore (or main) corse and bonnet, and sail was reduced, not by the later device of reefing, but by the removal of the bonnets. As masts multiplied and topsails came into being, the old name was retained to denote the large main 'body' of the lower canvas.

Topsail The term 'topsail' did not originate in the fact that it was the sail

238

above or on top of the course, but because it was the sail of the enclosed top-castle which crowned the lower masthead of the fighting craft of the Middle Ages, and which served as a station for picked archers.

About the end of the fifteenth century a second and smaller 'top' *Topgallant* was placed at the head of an upper mast, and was called the topgallant, gallant being a contemporary adjective meaning adventurous or daring. The third yard, then set above the course and topsail, became the topgallant sail yard.

The royal, introduced in the seventeenth century, was then known *Royal* as the topgallant-royal, that is, the sail of the very adventurous top, the new double adjective further qualifying the original term topsail in regard to height above deck. This cumbrous title was soon shortened to royal, and has so remained, although in clipper days two additional square-sails, the skysail and the moonraker, were set at times above it. As a point of interest, the greatest number of yards ever crossed on any one mast by an iron or steel sailing vessel was seven, the seventh being a skysail yard.

The landsman, should he be fortunate enough in these days to be *Fixed and* vouchsafed the unusual sight of a big windjammer in port under bare *sliding yards* poles, may have wondered why her six yards, instead of being spaced out evenly between deck and truck, appear as one single yard, two pairs, and, finally, near the masthead, another single yard.

The explanation is that three of the six yards carried by each square-rigged mast are trussed permanently in position by iron crutches or goosenecks, added support being given by a short, heavy chain. The other three yards are attached to crance-irons or collars around the mast, which allow these yards to be hoisted or lowered a certain distance up or down the mast, movement being controlled by halliards and lifts.

In port, these movable yards are dropped to their lowest position, the halliards having been slacked off. Then, when sail is to be set, the course and the lower topsail are stretched downward from fixed yards; the upper-topsail yard is hoisted half-way to the next fixed yard (the lower topgallant) so permitting two sails to be set, one below and one above it. The upper-topgallant yard and the royal yard are hoisted in turn until, finally, the symmetrical tower of swelling canvas is complete. To sum up (I purposely use non-technical language) it is by pulling three sails down from their yards and by stretching the other three upward (by hoisting three adjustable yards) that square-sail is set.

cing: Top. A WEB OF RIGGING; THE MIZEN-MAST

Bottom. WILD WORK. MAKING FAST THE MIZEN
UPPER-TO'GALLANT IN HEAVY WEATHER

The reason for such an apparently complicated and laborious procedure is that, in bad weather, the lowering of these three movable yards spills the wind rapidly from the sails in question, so rendering the subsequent furling and gasketing a speedier and an easier task.

Furling and setting a sail

It must always be borne in mind that going aloft is only the final part of the job of taking in canvas. To furl a sail the sheets are slacked off, the clews or lower corners of the sail drawn up to the yard-arms by clew-lines, and the bunt or body of the sail hauled upward by bunt-lines attached to its foot. All this is done from the deck, before any man, unless part of the gear aloft be fouled, sets foot on the ratlines to gather in and secure the bunched canvas.

(In former days it was usual to 'clew up to the bunt'; the clews were carried up to the centre of the yard instead of to the yard-arms, thus transforming a rectangular sail into a triangle of canvas, which, when furled, formed a tapering roll whose thickest part was in the centre of the yard. This method yielded an extremely neat and trim appearance.)

On the other hand, when a sail is to be set the first proceeding is to send a man aloft to cast off the gaskets which bind the furled sail to the yard. He stays aloft, by the yard-slings (while the watch on deck stretch or sheet home the sail) to 'overhaul' the bunt-lines and leech-lines by pulling such length of spare tackle through the blocks as will ensure the lines running slackly down the belly of the sail, without chafage. Finally, he 'stops' the lines at the blocks with a strand of rope-yarn, so fastened that a sharp tug on the lines from below will free them at once.

This overhauling and stopping process is a daily task, and, in changeable weather, is sometimes necessary even more frequently. Gaskets, when not in use, must be 'made-up' into neat coils and 'stopped' to the jackstay with sail-twine.

Bracing and trimming yards

In case the term 'fixed', as applied to three yards on each mast, may have been misleading, it must be explained that all yards can be swung from side to side, pivoting on the mast, the angle or trim being controlled by ropes known as braces. By slacking off the braces on the port side and hauling in an equivalent amount of the starboard braces, or vice versa, the sails can be trimmed to the most favourable angle for the prevailing wind. If the wind shifts ahead the usual command is 'Lee fore-brace': if it shifts astern, 'Square cro'jick yard' is ordered.

When close-hauled, i.e. when the course yards have been slewed right round until they touch the back-stays on one side, each upper-yard is braced back a little less than the one below it. There are two reasons for this adjustment: first, that the strain on the lighter, upper rigging shall be lessened gradually in proportion to its relative strength; secondly, so that, with the barque sailing close up into the wind, the helmsman may be warned by the shivering of the weather royal-clew that she is too much 'up' and in danger of 'griping', that is of being taken aback. His job when steering 'by the wind' is to keep the royals just full, for then the more back-braced sails below the royals will be doing their full work.

To steer 'Full and by' is to keep a windjammer in such a relative position to the direction of the wind that none of her canvas shall 'shake', whereas a 'Clean-full' indicates that she must be a fraction farther from the wind, where there is no risk at all of anything 'shaking'.

At the point on the stays where the course yards touch them (in this process of bracing hard round) it is usual to fit a batten to the stay. This takes the chafage of the yard and, in British vessels, was known as a 'Scotchman'.

Herzogin Cecilie's course yards can be braced back through an angle of approximately 50° from the squared position before they touch the back-stays. When thus close-hauled her royal yards should be so trimmed that they are only backed by about 25°.

Yards are well-trimmed if, when standing below the course yard, the weather yard-arms of all the upper yards are visible abaft the course yard.

Access to all the various parts of the top-hamper of a sailing vessel is *Ratlines* obtained by and from ladders in the standing-rigging, contrived by seizing rungs — or ratlines as they are called — to the shrouds at regular intervals. Ratlines differ in length, strength and material, according to the amount of wear and tear which they must undergo; the farther above-deck they are situated the lighter they become.

Taking any one set of lower-mast shrouds aboard *Herzogin Cecilie*, it will be found that the first five ratlines, which begin at the level of the top-gallant rail, consist of iron bars. They extend from the swifter, that is, the foremost shroud of a group, across the full span of four shrouds. Next comes a thick, square-sectioned, wooden spreader, known as the sheer-batten, which is slightly longer than the iron bars, and is pierced with holes for belaying-pins. Above this batten a succession of ever-narrowing wooden rungs are seized across two centre shrouds. As each group of shrouds ultimately converge on a common point at the mast-doublings, it follows that the last few bar-ratlines must be very short: actually, near the head of the lower shrouds, they will barely allow the insertion of one foot at a time.

The wooden rungs are extended to either side by additional rope ratlines, spanning one shroud on one side and two on the other. This provides a quadruple set of steps, permitting several men to get aloft simultaneously, and giving passage to others who may be descending.

The lower rigging naturally gets the most use, because, once the height of the course yards is reached, a body of men going aloft disperse to various points, either out along the yards or into the upper rigging. Consequently, above this point the ratlines of the topmast rigging, except for an occasional short iron spreader, are made of wire or thin rope seized across three adjacent shrouds only. They are subject to frequent breakages, and they are, in general, not renewed until they show obvious signs of wear, or have actually parted. The true sailor, therefore, when going aloft, grips the shrouds, never the ratlines, in order that, should the latter carry away, he still has a secure handhold. The rope ratlines leading up the top-gallant mast are even narrower, just a single ladder across the standing-rigging. The final stage, to the royal yard itself, is up a short, swinging, wooden-runged Jacob's-ladder.

Some ex-training-ships have wooden bar-ratlines right up to the head of their standing-rigging. *Viking* is a case in point; the system is indubitably safer, more durable, and reduces the time taken in getting right aloft.

Foot-ropes

Beneath every yard, and extending the full length of the spar, are wire foot-ropes, rove through thimbles at the end of vertical stirrup-irons. Work on the yards is carried out by men standing on these wires, or, rather, lying across the yard with outstretched legs braced backward against the wires.

The bowsprit is fitted with two long foot-ropes, one on either side, and as *Herzogin Cecilie* does not possess the triangular safety-netting below her bowsprit, which characterized most of her German contemporaries, work on these exposed wires is a dangerous business in heavy weather. The older and very descriptive name for a foot-rope was a 'horse', although it is not on record that the riders were ever dubbed 'horsemen!'

Other pairs of foot-ropes run 'thwartships between the port and starboard shrouds of each lower mast, crossing the after side of the mast itself about half-way between the deck and the mast-cap. Their purpose is to enable men, by sidling along the lower wire and holding on to the upper, to reach a position on the mast itself, where the topgallant stay-sail can be made fast, these sails and the royal stay-sails being stowed by binding them in a vertical roll up the after face of a mast.

Course and tops'l yards have two parallel, steel handrails, known as *Jack-stays* jack-stays, running along the upper side. The head of the sail is bent to the forward jack-stay by closely-spaced lashings called robands. The inner jack-stay provides secure handhold for the workers. Many big sailers have only single jack-stays fitted to all yards, a detail which adds to the danger of work aloft: it is much more difficult to keep a safe hold, since, with the sail bent in position, the obstructed rail cannot be gripped properly.

I have already touched upon the decease of the bonaventure, the *The* fourth mast of galleon times and the predecessor of the schooner-rigged *jigger-mast* jigger-mast of a barque. *Herzogin Cecilie's* jigger-mast carries three booms, which extend aft toward the taffrail. The lowest of the three, set parallel to the deck, is the spanker-boom; the other two, angled upward at 45° from the mast, are the lower and upper gaff-booms.

The setting of three sails on the jigger instead of the more usual two — gaff-topsail and spanker — was a peculiarity common to several of the bigger German four-masters of *Herzogin Cecilie's* generation. The full spanker was subdivided into a lower sail, of somewhat stunted cut, and a smaller, rectangular upper-spanker, the pair being capped by a triangular gaff-topsail.

Four-mast barque-rig can be seen to-day on the River Thames, for *'Arethusa',* the present *Arethusa*, the training-ship of the Shaftesbury Homes, is *ex 'Peking'* actually a German built, nitrate-carrying 'Cape Horner', of 3,152 tons gross, launched at Hamburg in 1911 as the *Peking*, for the great Laeisz 'P' Line. Since 1933 she has been moored at Upnor, near Rochester; she replaces her famous, old, wooden forerunner, the first *Arethusa*.

Peking has been considerably cut down aloft for her new employ-ment; she now crosses only four yards per mast instead of six, all upper-topsail and upper-topgallant yards having been removed. She was, like *Herzogin Cecilie*, fitted with double gaff-booms, but the lower one has now been dispensed with. Incidentally, she is another vessel having the unusual feature of dual steering positions: her forward wheel is on the island midship-section, which, as pointed out in Book Two, Chapter II, was a structure much favoured by Laeisz; the after wheel stands just below the break of her short poop, housed in a glass-windowed wheel-house, and connected to the poop by a speaking-tube.

A climb to the main-truck

In the Preface of this book I suggested that, for the purpose of these four descriptive chapters, the reader might imagine himself to be visiting *Herzogin Cecilie* in the company of a guide. In keeping with that idea, I now propose to set him the task of going right aloft to her main-truck. She is lying peacefully in dock, moored against the quay: there will be no reeling, lurching gait, no thunder of canvas or screaming gale to add reality to the adventure; nevertheless, for a landsman, it is a long and toilsome climb.

The first stage is simple: up the well-spaced but ever-narrowing bar-ratlines of the lower main-shrouds, no more difficult than the ascent of a builder's ladder.

The 'top'

Just short of the cap of the lower mast, where it is overlapped or doubled by the butt of the topmast, is a triangular platform, still known as the 'top'. The days are long past when, first, archers, and then topmen with muskets, filled the painted top-castles of the galleons or the roomy fighting-tops of the wooden frigates. The use has departed, but the name remains.

Herzogin Cecilie's three 'tops' — fore, main, and mizen — are protected by waist-high netting, but they are innocent of 'lubber's holes': that is, being completely floored over with teak gratings, the only access into the top is over the projecting edge. The lower ratlines end a few feet below the 'top', but sagging rope footholds span the steel struts (known as futtock shrouds) which brace the platform to the mast. It is 'out and over' if you wish to go farther aloft; and so with your back to the deck below, your free foot pawing for a thin, stringy, futtock ratline, one hand groping for a safe grip on the 'top' rim above your head, you may feel for a few, long seconds like a fly on a ceiling. But, one more step outward, a heave, a knee on the rim, and you will be standing on the platform ready to tackle the farther ascent of the topmast shrouds, whose narrow wire or hemp ratlines, giving under your weight, will cut painfully into lightly-shod feet.

The cross-trees

The second stage of the climb finishes at the cross-trees, an open, triangular, steel framework at the heel of the topgallant mast. It can be negotiated either through the framing or out and over the edge. It is

244

facing: UNBENDING THE MAIN-ROYAL AND TO GALLANT

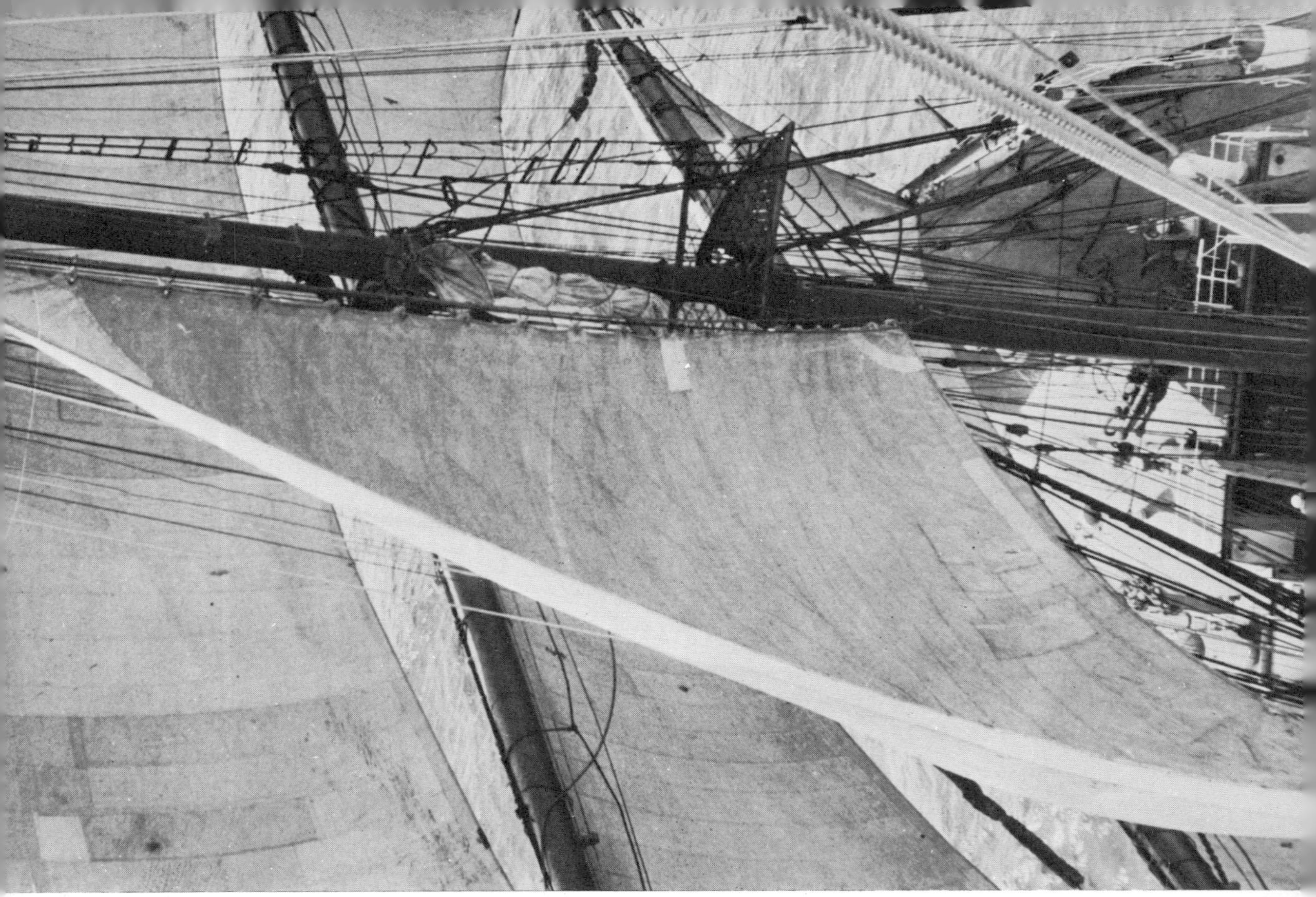

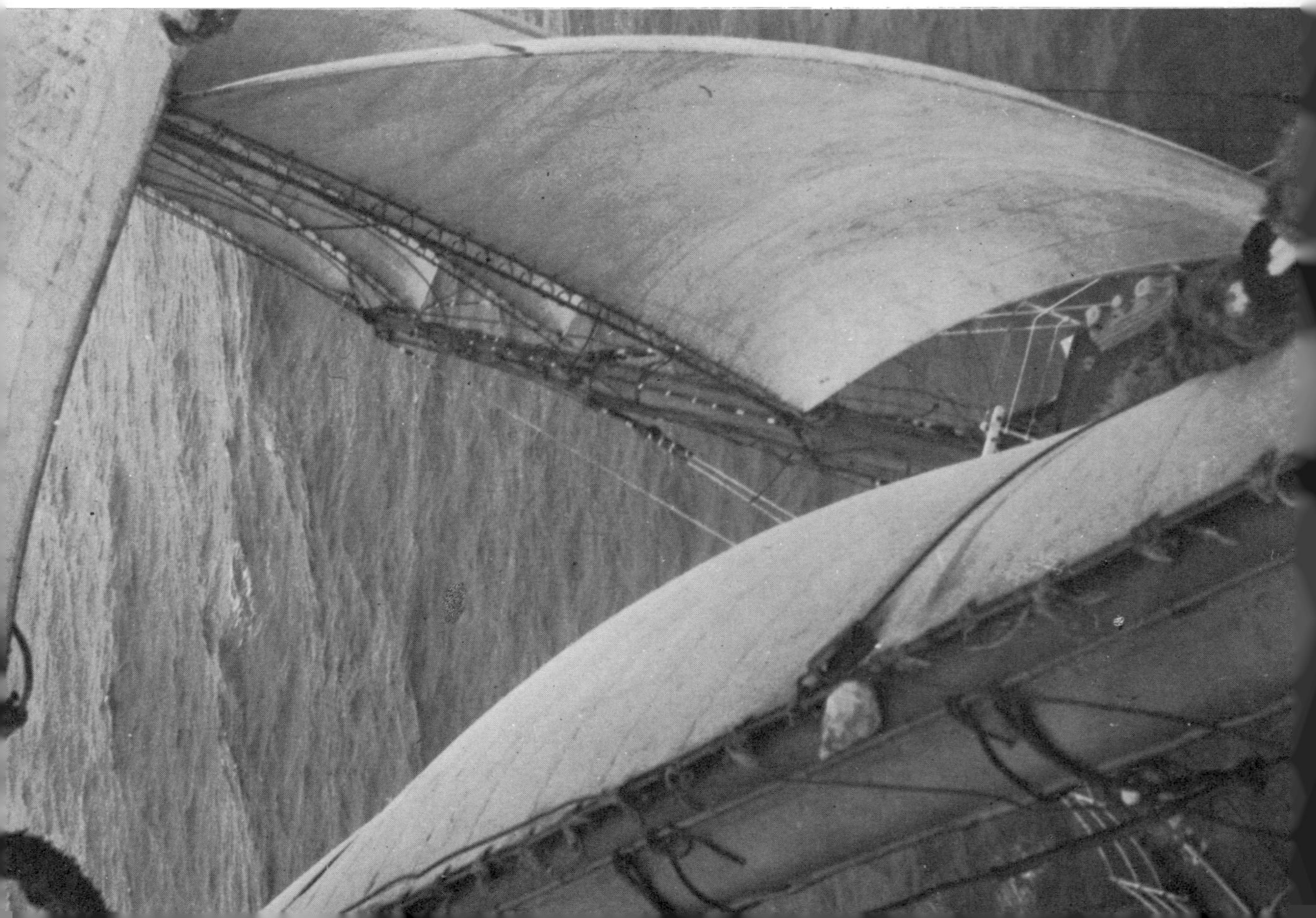

ALOFT

cross-braced for strength, and has no platform, but two long arms extend aftward and act as spreaders for the royal back-stays. Now, after clambering up the few, narrow, rope ratlines between the cross-trees and the head of the topgallant shrouds (several broken or even missing ratlines may be noticed hereabouts) you launch out on to the short, swinging Jacob's-ladder, at the head of which is the royal yard, supposing that spar to be hoisted by its halliards into the working position.

The truck

The final stage of all, if the complete ascent is attempted, is to shin up the last, few, bare, tapering feet of the topgallant mast, past the spreader of the wireless aerial, to a circular, bevelled, bun-like cap, the main-truck itself. Thin signal halliards are rove through narrow sheaves in this wooden cap.

From this dizzy height, nearly two hundred feet above the water, *Herzogin Cecilie's* slim length has the appearance of a mere canoe, but given the need, the skill and the nerve, the deck can be regained in half a minute by sliding down a back-stay. A more orthodox descent by the ratlines is recommended, because, although some among the crew are adept at these spectacular acrobatics, the slightest miscalculation or loss of control means hands and thighs burned and cut to the very bone, or may even mean death should the pain result in loss of grip.

Standing and running rigging

The standing-rigging of *Herzogin Cecilie's* top-hamper is of wire throughout. The majority of the lighter running-gear is Manila rope, but the sheets (the tackle controlling the two lower corners or clews of a sail when it is set) are of heavy-gauge chain, at the outer end, shackled on to wire rope. In view of the terrific strain imposed by her big areas of canvas, hempen sheets would need to be of unworkably large diameter. The lifts and halliards, which control the hoisting and lowering of the movable yards, are also of wire.

Wear and tear aloft

Apart from normal wear and tear, renewals and replacements of rigging are constantly in progress, either for safety or in anticipation of a reclassification survey. The snapping of a ratline is an everyday event, in itself of little consequence, for, as I have explained, a seaman always grips the shrouds. Foot-ropes, shrouds, stays and running gear are, however, perilous details to carry away in times of stress or danger. Constant attention, testing and renewal are essential if accidents are to be minimized.

As a most vital part of the top-hamper, foot-ropes in particular demand great care and vigilance. Any one foot-rope below a long,

245

acing: Right. FORE-MAST CANVAS FROM MAIN CROSSTREES

Left. SAILING 'BY THE WIND'; HEAD CANVAS AND BRACED-UP FOREYARD lower yard of a big barque may have to bear, at times, the weight of an entire watch: if the wire should part, luck alone could prevent fatality.

Captain Söderlund of *Lawhill* recounted to me an experience which happened in the autumn of 1934. When outward bound, in ballast, from London to Australia, his vessel met with a heavy gale in the Channel. At two in the afternoon, when the storm was at its height, the mizen lower-topgallant sail began to split down one seam: three boys went out on the yard to furl it, and had almost completed a safe stow when the foot-rope snapped. No lives were lost, but it was a close call.

Captain Söderlund, who was making his first voyage in *Lawhill*, had all the foot-ropes, in turn, unbent and brought to deck at the first opportunity. He was assured that they had been carefully inspected only a few months before; but, unhappily, it appeared that they were not tested in the proper fashion, that is, beaten with an iron bar while stretched taut by capstan power. No less than seven foot-ropes now broke under this rigorous strain, and were replaced by new wire. It is a process which hardly falls within the province of the surveyor to a classification society, nevertheless, one which any prudent shipmaster should undertake periodically and conscientiously.

Two actual examples of 'what might have been' may serve to emphasize the importance of sound gear. On one occasion, when she was driving hard, close-hauled, *Herzogin Cecilie's* fore-braces carried away. Fortunately, she answered her helm, and paid off (that is, fell away from the wind) before the wildly-swinging, uncontrolled foremast yards could sever the shrouds and back-stays, but for a short while it was touch and go.

At another time, when running under almost full canvas in a moderate gale, one of her long steering wires parted, and she came up into the wind too rapidly for the emergency after-wheels to be manned. As she broached, beam to wind, a large area of her canvas blew bodily away. This involuntary sacrifice saved her from being taken aback, that is, from receiving the full force of the wind on the wrong side of her sails. Had that happened, and had the forestays then parted under the unaccustomed strain, the ultimate outcome might well have been complete dismasting.

The proving of a mighty top-hamper

The stupendous strength of *Herzogin Cecilie's* top-hamper was never more fittingly demonstrated, nor stood her in better stead, than during the last few weeks of its thirty-four years of service.

ALOFT

The tragic story of those weeks will be told in Book Two, Chapter VI; sufficient here, therefore, to say that, having driven hard ashore on rock, she underwent for many hours the grinding force of a heavy swell. She remained fast for nearly a month before being refloated and towed to a seemingly safer berth near by. Bad weather some weeks later, however, exposed hidden rocks beneath her, and, finally, broke her back. Throughout this long period of stress her sparring and rigging withstood most severe and unusual strains without a single breakage or weakening, notwithstanding the amazing fact that when she first struck she was carrying almost full canvas.

The rigging of a big sailing vessel is, to me, a constant source of wonder and admiration. Try to realize the pressure required to propel by wind-power alone a 300-foot steel hull, containing over four thousand tons of cargo, at a speed of, say, 12 knots.[1] That, and even more, is the strain put on the rigging of a barque of the type of *Herzogin Cecilie*, day in, day out, year after year, as she ranges the great oceans of the world. Yet, so scientifically is the driving power harnessed, that perfect distribution of stress is obtained under almost every condition of weather.

The stresses engendered in sailing

Misapplied, however, those stresses could bring driving forces to bear in an inverse direction. If the unfair strain carried away only one stay, the complex network is so interdependent that the resultant collapse might be far-reaching. The powerful forestay may be considered as the keystone of the whole edifice: should it part, it is not inconceivable that the whole top-hamper might crumple up like a house of cards.

In his recent novel, *Victorious Troy*, Mr. John Masefield gives a graphic and seamanlike account of the chaos and peril caused by dismasting. A steel four-poster, homeward-bound with grain, is dismasted when south of the Horn. The mizen topgallant mast is the first to give way: then the mainmast, weakened by the loss of support, goes by the board, and, finally, the unstayed foremast snaps off at deck level. Magnificent as is his description of the storm and the casualty, it is in the wealth of technical detail which he employs to describe the heart-breaking aftermath that Mr. Masefield excels. It was several weeks before *Hurrying Angel* was cleared of the chaotic raffle of broken,

[1] Mr. Maurice Denny of Dumbarton recently established, by trials in an experimental tank, that about 3000 h.p. would have been needed to drive *Cutty Sark* at 16 knots when she was fully loaded (*vide* Doctor Longridge's *The Cutty Sark*).

twisted and tangled gear which cluttered her decks, and dragged over-side like a gigantic sea-anchor. In the very strength of her steel top-hamper and wire rigging lay the crux of the problem: lacking the proper tools, it could neither be cut, chopped, nor sawn away, as was the custom in the old days of wooden spars and rope gear.

The book is a splendid piece of reconstruction, and its careful perusal will well repay any reader who seeks to know something of the technical aspects of sail-handling.

The song of the labouring windjammer

The tautness and power of steel and wire top-hamper will combine, in bad weather, to produce a diapason such as can nowhere be heard except aboard a big, heavy-laden sailer. She becomes, as it were, a giant organ played by the heavy hands of wind and sea. Powerful gusts pluck at the tensed shrouds and straining back-stays like fingers at harp-strings. Where some stays give forth a deep, booming note, others hum wildly, like telegraph wires, under the stress. Halliards twang like banjo-gut, and a continuous and plaintive moaning comes from the rigging-screws. The gale roars through the slacker running-rigging, whose heavy blocks beat a mad tattoo against the steel spars. As she rolls, scuppers under, the steel wash-ports clang to and fro, and all the while the great seas break alongside or crash aboard to swirl from poop to fo'c'sle, battering at the deck-house doors and striving to wrench off the hatch tarpaulins. Every strake and frame of the labouring hull groans with her travail; while the thunder of wet, storm canvas, and the staccato patter of squalls of driven hail add to that almost indescribable cacophony, the song of driven sail.

Annual consumption of new tackle

Every round voyage, that is, every year, approximately two tons of new, best, English Manila rope is consumed by ordinary wear and tear aboard *Herzogin Cecilie*.

1½ inch to 3½ or 4 inch (circumference) Manila comprises the main stock, plus a supply of what is known as 'small stuff' — marline, tarred spun-yarn, ratline (1¼ inch tarred hemp), and wire seizing. If (by a rough calculation) those two tons of rope are averaged into, say, 1 ton of one-inch Manila (breaking strain about 10 cwt., and weight about 23 lbs. for a coil of 120 fathoms), and 1 ton of three-inch (breaking-strain 4 tons, and weight of coil about 206 lbs.), they represent some-thing like 80,000 feet or fifteen miles of miscellaneous cordage.

Herzogin Cecilie's 90-fathom towing-hawsers are of eight-inch Manila, and weigh round about half a ton apiece.

248

facing: ON THE MAIN UPPER-TOPSAIL YARD
THERE ARE SIX MEN, NOT FIVE!

In addition to the fibre gear, something like one ton of new wire rope, in length nearly one and a half miles, is used during a like period.

These are, of course, average figures. Exceptional circumstances, as, for instance, a major casualty, would naturally increase the annual consumption; whereas if no renewals of standing-rigging take place during a particular voyage, a considerable surplus of new wire would be left in hand. Wire rope varies in diameter in accordance with the nature of its employment. Stays in the lower rigging, for example, would call for $3\frac{1}{2}$ to 4 inch tackle (having a breaking stress of nearly thirty tons), whereas royal stays would necessitate only $2\frac{1}{2}$ inch material (breaking stress thirteen tons).

Spare spars

While on the subject of wear and tear, it may be repeated that should any unit of the Erikson Fleet be so badly damaged as to be irreparable, or reach the stage when she is fit only for the breaker's yard, any fittings and spars suitable for further service in other vessels are dismantled and distributed among the Fleet. It is common to see one or more such spare yards cleated down to the deck, either below the hatch-coamings or in the scuppers.

In addition, rough-hewn baulks of Oregon pine, say, seventy feet long and eighteen inches square, are kept in reserve aboard, ready to be shaped up by the carpenter if and when a need arises. To-day, a new, steel spar would have to be made specially to order, and its cost would be quite three times that of a wooden 'home-made' equivalent.

Rigging-screws supersede chain-wales and lanyards

The picturesque outboard channels, a prominent feature on the 'tumble-home' sides of galleons, on old-time whalers and, in a modified form, on the wooden, the composite, and the earlier iron clippers, have no prototype on the more modern steel sailing freighter.

All *Herzogin Cecilie's* heavier standing-rigging, such as her lower shrouds and back-stays which lead up from the hull, is shackled to scupper ring-bolts (or, in the case of the fore-shrouds, shanked to the hull plating) and tautened by massive rigging-screws. These screws are parcelled, i.e. protected, by laced-on leather jackets, and it is customary to paint this part of her rigging in contrasting bands of black and white. Ring-bolts, dead-eyes, strops, shrouds and parcellings are black, and all seizings are picked out in white. Perhaps no other single detail has more effect on the trimness and smartness of a windjammer's appearance than this old-fashioned but pleasing custom.

The ancient term 'channel' is actually a shortened form of 'chain-

249

wale', wale, as in gunwale, denoting any side-planking projecting beyond the ordinary. Chain-wales widened the spread of the old hempen shrouds, which were set up by lanyards, dead-eyes and chains. The introduction of wire standing-rigging, hove taut by screws and set inboard at a less acute angle to the masts, rendered the channel system quite obsolete.

The only 'wales' on *Herzogin Cecilie's* smooth, steel-plated sides are the brace-bumpkins — short, unobtrusive purchase-booms, to which are shackled the lower brace-blocks.

Control of running gear

The ease with which running gear can be handled in an emergency depends first and foremost on its accessibility. Rope gear is, in the main, secured to belaying-pins: the slack is coiled down on the pin in such fashion that, by casting off the coil, instant control is obtained for hauling or for letting go on the run. As a general rule, where gear is belayed to pin-rails the maxim of 'the higher the gear, the farther aft' is observed, i.e. the royal gear is the farthest aft of all running-gear pertaining to a particular mast.

Slung between the stanchions which support the shroud pin-rails are large, single, revolving drums, painted white: on them are coiled down the long falls and slack of the lighter gear. Beneath each pin-rail a narrow foot-rail, having a deck clearance of about six inches, is bolted to the deck.

Wire running-gear, by reason of its toughness and its propensity to kinking, cannot be belayed to or coiled down on the pins. Nor can the requisite degree of tautness be obtained by hauling alone, and *Herzogin Cecilie's* course-sheets, for example, are always led to the capstans.

'Boarding the fore-tack'

When running before the wind with squared yards, the chain and wire gear which controls the clew of a course is referred to as the 'sheet'. So soon as the yards are braced up, and the vessel sails close-hauled, the weather clew is controlled by the 'tack', not by the 'sheet'. 'Boarding the foretack', therefore, indicates that the fore-yard has been braced on to the shrouds, with the weather yard-arm over the foredeck instead of above the well-deck bulwarks. The weather clew of the fore-sail has been stretched by leading the tack forward to the foredeck capstan through a block hooked on to one of the heavy, iron ring-bolts let into the foredeck. At the same time, the sheet of the lee clew of the foresail is led aft and hauled taut to a capstan on the forward end of the poop, the sheet of the weather clew being left slack.

250

ALOFT

The last job for the watch after any sail-handling is to clear up the raffle of running-gear heaped around the pin-rails. The various falls are coiled down on their proper pins or, in fine weather, should subsequent handling be anticipated, set out on the deck in neat 'Flemish coils' or 'French fakes'.

The perusal of much of the more lurid type of sea fiction has led *Belaying-pins* many people to imagine that the main use for a belaying-pin is as a handy weapon for the inevitable 'bucko' Mate. In modern practice, at any rate aboard the hard-worked, sparsely-manned Finnish sailers, it is doubtful whether a pin has ever been put to such use. 'Hazing' is a thing of the past, and one man incapacitated by wilful bullying is far too serious a loss in vital man-power for such treatment to be worth while in the long run. There are many score of iron and wooden belaying-pins in the long pin-rails at the foot of *Herzogin Cecilie's* shrouds, in the fife-rails around each mast, in the wooden sheer-battens of the lower shrouds, and in brass-rimmed holes at intervals along the poop topgallant-rail.

The long lengths of woolly, caterpillar-like covering frapped *Chafing-gear* around many of the stays, and which show up so prominently in the photographs, are known as chafing-gear. This is provided to minimize wear and tear in places where a bellying sail might fret against wire rope.

Square-sails are not square, nor even rectangular. It will be noticed, particularly in the case of the lower topsails and lower topgallants, that the foot of a sail is cut in a curved arc, known as the roach. This arc is designed (and so varies in depth) to allow free passage, when the sail is set and drawing, to the heavy, steel forestays, which, otherwise, would bite into the foot of a sail cut to more generous proportions.

Sail tailoring is passing into the limbo of the lost arts. It is an exact *Sail making* science, and demands an expert workman, for in the cut of a sail lies much of its subsequent serviceableness and the whole of its appearance. Well-cut sails made from good-quality canvas last a very long while. As a true artist, a sail-maker always initials and dates his handiwork, and Mr. Villiers records that in 1928 he found, still in use aboard *Herzogin Cecilie*, an old lower-topsail of German cut dated 1908.

Captain Gustaf Erikson favours British products in the matter of gear and canvas, because of their superior quality. Canvas is an item which bulks large in the upkeep budget of a fleet of sail.

Wear and tear and replacement of canvas

To reclothe *Herzogin Cecilie* completely to-day would cost Captain Erikson about £2,000. Her annual bill for the replacement of sails works out, on an average, to between £300 and £500, although occasions have arisen when that sum has been largely exceeded.

As recently as May 1935, for example, she lost nineteen sails within a period of thirty hours, when off the Scillies homeward-bound from Australia. In the log the wind-force was recorded as 8-10 on the Beaufort Scale (see Appendix A) and conditions were worsened by driving snow. All three Mates were injured, and the crew suffered severely from cold and cramp. Three sails stood throughout the blow, and by the time she arrived at Falmouth, late on the following day, the lost canvas had been replaced 'from stock' and she was then under all square-sail, except the fore-royal and fore upper-topgallant. The lost sails were numbers 2, 3, 4, 8, 9, 12, 14, 15, 16, 17, 19, 22, 23, 24, 25, 27, 28, 29, 30 on the numbered diagram-photographs, facing page 253.

Herzogin Cecilie loads an annual replenishment of Webster's Standard Flax Canvas, made at Arbroath, Scotland, sufficient to enable her to be refitted completely at sea. The average yearly depletion of her canvas reserve, by ordinary wear and tear, is between 8,000 and 10,000 square feet.

Torn or damaged sails are not wasted but, repaired and patched, they form a fine-weather suit of 'tropical rags'. This suit is bent in place of the newer, heavier storm canvas required by the rigours of North or South Atlantic gales.

Complete sail-changing takes place twice on each outward or homeward Australian passage. On the nitrate run, via the Horn, it was customary to make four changes per trip, because in that trade the tropical suit was substituted during the passage of both Atlantic and Pacific equatorial latitudes. The old-time clippers were equipped with three complete suits of canvas of varying grade — storm, medium, and fine-weather — but the economic side of windjamming permits of no like extravagance to-day.

'*Herzogin Cecilie's*' increased sail-plan

Many an old tall ship, sold foreign, has spent her last years under a reduced sail-plan. In the cause of economy, full-riggers have become barques, and barques have been 'bald-headed' by the loss of their royals. 'Jubilee-rig', which came into being in 1887, was a standard type of cut-down top-hamper: it implied a four-masted barque, setting nothing above her topgallants, and having the topgallant yards extended

facing: FROM THE BOWSPRI

until they almost equalled the length of the course yards. The whole effect was one of extreme, almost squat, squareness, and lacked entirely the symmetrical grace achieved by the tapering span of the 'tall ship'.

To-day, however, *Herzogin Cecilie* still retains her full original sail-plan as drafted in 1902. Actually, she sometimes sets a bigger spread of canvas than was specified by Rickmers, for each of her two Finnish Masters have introduced additional 'kites'. Rickmers' plan shows a suit of thirty-one sails; in *Falmouth for Orders* Mr. Villiers gives a total of thirty-four; while in my numbered diagram-photographs a quota of thirty-five is evidenced in actual use, making a spread of 45,000 square feet, or slightly over one acre, of sail area. Of these thirty-five sails only eighteen come under the heading of square-sail.

Bent to a series of rings, or travellers as they are called, which run up and down the topmast, topgallant mast and royal stays, are triangular fore-and-afters known as staysails. These staysails, plus the jibs, the two spankers and the gaff-topsail, a total of seventeen fore-and-afters, make up the tally of thirty-five separate sails now set by *Herzogin Cecilie*.

The later innovations took the form of additional staysails, set, one to each mast, on the uppermost, or royal, forestay: they are numbered 32, 33, 34, and 35 in the diagrams.

Herzogin Cecilie's first Finnish Master, Ruben de Cloux, did not set No. 32 — the fore-royal staysail: hence the single discrepancy between the tally of Mr. Villiers, who sailed under Captain de Cloux, and my figure of thirty-five as used by de Cloux's successor, Captain Sven Eriksson.

In practice, the royal staysails as well as the flying jib (No. 1 in the plan) are set under fine, summer-weather conditions only, and are utilized solely for the purpose of getting every ounce of benefit from light and fickle winds.

The bowsprit, a single, steel spar with no jib-boom extension, sets in all five head sails, a fore-topmast staysail, the inner and outer jibs, a flying jib and, to-day, high up on the fore-royal stay, the unorthodox staysail introduced by Eriksson.

Mr. Basil Lubbock, in Volume 2 of his epic *Last of the Windjammers*, states that *Herzogin Cecilie* set a suit of thirty-six sails when she was a German training-ship. I venture to suggest that as he, at the same time, only allots to her a sail area of 37,000 square feet, he may have been misinformed.

A 'moonsail'

253

One cannot visualize any extra, single sail beyond the present thirty-five as being in keeping with her rig, although, on her last run from Australia, Captain Eriksson set a small, triangular 'moonsail', as he called it, above the main royal yard. This, however, must have been more of a pleasing gesture than a practical or permanent innovation. As far as I can trace, no such 'kite' was ever used in her German days.

Reef-points

To-day *Herzogin Cecilie* has not a single reef-point anywhere in her sail-plan. Her sails are either set or furled; their area cannot be reduced by the old-fashioned process of taking in one or more reefs. When the big, single topsails and single topgallants were divided into upper and lower sections, each section being set from its own yard, reef-bands passed out of general use. Rickmers' sail-plan shows, however, that they fitted a single band of reef-points to each of *Herzogin Cecilie's* courses and upper topsails.

The part furling of big sails by the method of reefing was an arduous undertaking, and when sailing vessels, at the behest of economy, were forced to ship smaller crews, reefing became impracticable: it was superseded by narrower sails, improved running gear and by mechanical devices. For instance, it would be unreasonable to expect *Herzogin Cecilie's* small, boyish crews of to-day to reef her courses and topsails.

The fore-course or fore-sail, one of the largest and strongest of her thirty-five sails, is 87 feet in width and 33 feet deep. There are 2,500 square feet of board-hard No. 1 storm canvas in that sail, and often enough, in bad weather, both watches are required to stow it after it has been gathered up to the fore-yard by the buntlines and clew-lines.

In pre-War days, when *Herzogin Cecilie* housed a big complement of cadets, reefing was not only practicable but was considered to be excellent training for the boys. The reef-bands were probably still *in situ* when she passed to the Finns in 1921; all new sails cut since that date, however, are of perfectly plain pattern. There is an old cross-jack still on board on which traces of reef-cringles can be seen.

Comparisons in top-hamper

The table opposite shows how *Herzogin Cecilie's* top-hamper compares with that of three other big sailing vessels (length and tonnage as per *Lloyd's Register*).

It would appear that *Herzogin Cecilie* can hold her own in relative height, span and spread. A testing period of thirty-four years' sea-service without being dismasted, or even suffering any serious damage aloft, is sufficient to disprove any suggestion of over-sparring or of setting too great an area of canvas. For her type and generation, *Herzogin Cecilie* is perfectly proportioned aloft, a factor which, allied with a graceful hull, sets her sailing qualities well above the average.

Name	'Preussen'	'France'	'L'Avenir'	'Herzogin Cecilie'
Type of vessel	5-masted, steel, full-rigged ship	5-masted steel barque	4-masted steel barque	4-masted steel barque
Year of build	1902	1890	1908	1902
Registered length (feet)	407	361	278	334
Registered gross tonnage	5,081	3,784	2,776	3,111
Sail area* (square feet)	59,000	49,000	33,700	45,000
Keel to main truck (feet)	223	190	192	200
Royal yard (feet)	52½	48	45	49
Course yards (feet)	102	85	90	94

* NOTE. The net sail area is given. The gross area of canvas, i.e. including the 'doublings', would be anything from 25 to 30 per cent greater.

'Preussen'

The giant *Preussen*, launched in the same year as *Herzogin Cecilie*, and bearer of 8,000 tons of cargo, carried forty-five sails in all to complete her immense sail-area of 59,000 square feet. Being a five-masted full-rigger (the only ship of such type ever built) she was able to set twelve more square-sails than a four-masted barque like *Herzogin Cecilie* can carry. Every inch of her sparring was of steel, and it is said that eighteen miles of tackle were employed in rigging her out.

'L'Avenir'

L'Avenir is included in the foregoing table because of her resemblance to *Herzogin Cecilie*, both vessels having the long poop-superstructure peculiar to sailing cadet-craft. By comparison, her performances under the Finnish flag have been quite mediocre, perhaps because her hull is less shapely than that of *Herzogin Cecilie*, being blunter about the bows. She is the easier vessel for a small crew to handle as she is equipped with electric winches and capstans for manipulating all her heavy running-gear, except the braces. She is readily distinguishable at sea from either of the other long-pooped Finnish barques, *Herzogin Cecilie* and *Viking*, owing to her unorthodox, triangular, single-clew mainsail and cross-jack. This peculiar rig still further lightens work, but is one of the reasons why *L'Avenir*'s total area of canvas is so much smaller than that of *Herzogin Cecilie*.

'Viking' – a memory

No lovelier sight can be seen at sea than one of these big, white windships under all sail in a stiff breeze. Fifty years ago scores of such craft voyaged, anchored or berthed in company: a head-wind would bottle up great companies of outward-bound windjammers in the Downs, and the ocean highways of the world were crowded with fine sailers. Now, however, it is but rarely that two deepwatermen sail in close proximity, or even sight one another at sea.

It was my privilege to be aboard *Herzogin Cecilie* when, throughout the best part of twelve hours, *Viking* was in view. Both barques were engaged in beating to the eastward, making long tacks under full canvas, and it so happened that for one considerable period their routes lay parallel and close together. It was a sight I shall never forget. In a stiffish north-easter, with a short-pitched, smoking sea running, both of them heeled well over under their big spreads of canvas. *Viking* was ultimately left, hull down, astern, but, as I watched her driving along at a good twelve knots about a mile abeam of us with a great 'bone in her teeth', sometimes glistening in a stray shaft of sunshine, more often practically blotted out by a squall of rain, she looked, in very truth, a worthy survivor of that countless armada of tall ships which Mr. R. A. Fletcher has eulogized as 'the stateliest and most beautiful creations for which the mind of man has ever been responsible in the whole of his history'.

Grand as *Viking* appeared, *Herzogin Cecilie* must have made an even finer sight, for, a bigger vessel, she was being driven so hard that one 'leg' of that beat cost us four fine-weather sails.

'Herozogin Cecilie' compared with the American clippers

The towering glory of the old-time, true clipper can perhaps be visualized by comparing the ever-famous, American, wooden full-rigger *Lightning* with our modern steel barque. Although there is little difference between the two vessels in regard to extreme beam and depth, *Herzogin Cecilie's* tonnage, because of her fuller section and greater length (she is about seventy feet the longer), is roughly half as much again as that of *Lightning*. The clipper, with her net registered tonnage of 1,468, was 164 feet in height from deck to main-truck, just six feet short of *Herzogin Cecilie*. *Lightning's* main-yard, at 95 feet, was a foot the longer of the two, and was extended by studding-sail booms to an additional 65 feet overall. Under all plain sail, without the stu'nsails but with a moonsail at the main above her three skysails, she set thirty sails. *Herzogin Cecilie*, with a fourth mast and a far bigger hull, carries thirty-five sails when under all sail, but she has double topsails and double topgallants where *Lightning* had only big single sails.

256

Another of McKay's famous 'flyers', the full-rigger *James Baines*, whose tonnage was about 500 tons less than that of *Herzogin Cecilie*, had a main-yard of 100 feet in length, and her complete suit of sails, including stu'nsails, a main-moonsail, and undivided topsails and topgallants, numbered thirty-four.

McKay's ill-fated *Great Republic*, the largest wooden sailing vessel ever built (her dimensions of 325 by 53 by 38 feet gave a registered tonnage of 4,555), had a main-yard of 120 feet in length. In several ways she was an unorthodox vessel: she had four decks, the uppermost of which made her flush-decked. Besides being the pioneer, among big craft, of double topsails, she was the first to be fitted with a deck-engine for halliard-winches and pumps. She was launched in 1853 as a four-masted barque, at a time when ship-rig was almost universal, and her sail plan took 15,653 running yards of canvas. Gutted by fire at New York when loading for her maiden voyage, her immense sail-plan was somewhat cut down when she was rebuilt. Her registered tonnage was reduced to 3,357 by dispensing with the spar-deck; 20 feet were clipped from her course-yards, and the masts were shortened. In 1862 the jigger was removed, and she became a three-masted full-rigger.

Except for a brief survey of the principles and practice of handling square-rig, this concludes the description of *Herzogin Cecilie*. The model-maker will find little more in the remainder of the book to aid him in his delightful hobby, and so I here suggest that the completed model be decorated in seamanlike fashion by the finishing touch of correct bunting:

Bunting, etc.

From her upper gaff-boom *Herzogin Cecilie* spreads the Merchant Ensign of Finland — a white field divided into four quarters by a broad, sky-blue cross.

Her signal-code-flags are set from a spreader halfway up the jigger topmast. The numbered photo-diagrams of the barque under full sail show the signal-flags *in situ*, but as the pictures were taken in 1933 they read TPMK. To-day, under the New International Code (1934) the letters are as follows:

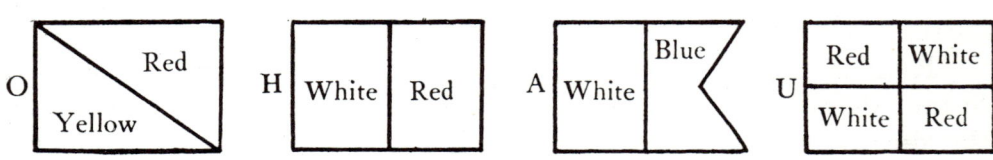

257

A small wind-arrow is fixed above the truck of each square-rigged mast, and, in addition, a long wind-stocking or vane flies from a swivel fitting at the mizen truck.

To give the miniature an air of realism, set Captain Gustaf Erikson's house-flag at the main-truck: it is a simple insigna, just 'G.E.' in black, block letters on a rectangular white ground.

The science of sailing at an angle to the wind

The two principles of wind acting on sails and of water acting on a rudder are the foundation and the whole science of working a sailing vessel. It is the conflict between wind-force and water-resistance that makes it possible to sail at an angle to the direction of the prevailing wind, because the resistance set up by water deflects a floating body obliquely in relation to wind-pressure. A sailing vessel exploits this resistance in two ways: first, in that by reason of the design of the hull she is more easily moved forward than sideways; secondly, by the balance of her sail-power being established at or about the centre of lateral resistance.

In regard to hull design, it should be obvious that a completely round vessel could only be blown along the path of the prevailing wind. Conversely, the longer and narrower a vessel, the greater, in theory, is her capacity to sail up into the wind, i.e. at an angle to the path of the wind.

It is likewise evident that, with a following wind, if square-sail be set at right-angles to the line of the keel, the vessel will be blown ahead, and will utilize to the full the driving power of the wind. If, however, the wind be on the beam, i.e. at right-angles to the keel, or blowing from a point even farther ahead, then, if the sails be trimmed at an angle to the wind, part of its force can still be used to advantage, because water-resistance will prevent the long hull from being merely blown sideways, or down wind. Under such conditions the actual course maintained will be a compromise between the direction in which the vessel's head is pointing and the direction of the wind, providing, of course, the wind be sufficiently strong to propel her against water-resistance. (I omit, for the sake of brevity, the complication of adverse currents, tides, etc.)

Rudder action

Rudder action brings into play extra water-resistance to one side or the other of the central axis of the vessel, forcing the stern away from the direction in which the rudder is turning. When the rudder is centralized, the water flows evenly by it, and has no effect on the vessel's course. So soon as the rudder is put at an angle to the axis of the vessel the water strikes against it and deflects the stern. In other words, if, by putting the wheel itself over to port, both the rudder and the ship's head be ported, then the stern is swung away to starboard.

The arc of this stern-swing is wider than the arc described by the bows, since the pivotal point or rotation centre from which the vessel, so to speak, skids sideways, is not situated amidships, but is more toward the bows. *Pivotal turning point of hull*

A big four-masted barque is always heavy on the helm, but the correct balance of her top-hamper has a far-reaching effect on her handiness. When the centre of cumulative effort is applied perpendicularly over the pivotal turning-point of the hull she is at her best and liveliest, for the entire art and practice of sailing is based on pivotal leverage.

Suppose a vessel to be rigged with three sails only, one forward, one amidships and one aft, and that she is sailing with the wind on the beam, that is, blowing at right-angles to her keel. *Effect of head and stern canvas*

If the head sail, alone, were set she would travel forward slightly, but her bows would tend to fall away from the wind, and her stern would come up until she was pointing more or less down wind.

If the after sail, alone, were set the opposite effect would develop, and she would tend to come up into the wind.

The effect of setting sail amidships only would be the same as if all three sails were used together, that is, the vessel would forge ahead in a straight line although, naturally, more slowly than under full canvas.

However many sails are carried, they all fall into one of the three classes:

(*a*) head sails, i.e. those forward of the centre of rotation, tending to send the craft's head off before the wind;

(*b*) stern sails, i.e. those aft of the centre of rotation, which bring the vessel up into the wind; and, lastly,

(*c*) midship sails, which act equally on either side of the centre of rotation, and do not alter the course.

The quickest method of turning a rowing-boat round, single-handed, is to pull with one oar and to back-water with the other. The same principle applies to the square-rigger, for the turning effect of

259

either the head or of the stern sails is augmented should one or other be set aback, and their driving effect so reversed.

Also, the farther a sail is situated away from the centre of rotation, the greater leverage it exerts, and the greater its tendency to swing the vessel from the line of her keel. Therefore, jibs and spanker have a remarkable influence on manœuvring, notwithstanding their comparatively small area.

Influence of trim on the centre of rotation The centre of rotation is not established amidships but forward of the mainmast at a point, by the way, where the tapering hull of an extreme clipper attained its maximum beam.

This pivotal point is dependent on trim. If the vessel be loaded too deep by the stern it will be established farther aft, or, if she be down by the head, farther forward. This is because the turning proclivity of either the stern or the head sails, as the case may be, is largely negatived by extra water-pressure against the unduly submerged stern or bow. At the same time the opposite tendency is encouraged by lack of water-resistance at the other extremity.

A vessel should be so stowed and have her canvas so balanced that a minimum amount of helm correction is required to maintain a true course. The more the rudder swings away from the line of the keel, the greater its retarding effect on the vessel's speed. In other words, if she tends to fly up into the wind, obliging her to carry considerable weather helm, her speed will suffer in consequence. Such proclivity can be remedied either by reducing the area of her after canvas or by adding to her head sails. A tall ship, holding on to her upper canvas in a strong wind, may develop weather-helm by reason of excessive wind-leverage forcing her bows down to leeward, and so raising her stern.

Leeway Leeway is a factor which the Master of a sailing vessel must always take into account. It is the margin of lateral divergence, or bodily drift down wind. The sideway resistance of water is lessened by waves, and, in consequence, leeway is more pronounced in rough weather. A square-rigger is able to sail closer up to the wind in smooth water than she can in a heavy sea. *Herzogin Cecilie* cannot sail nearer to the wind than about $5\frac{1}{2}$ points, or 60°, on the average. In calm weather she will come up a little more, but in a bad sea the margin is considerably greater.

A square-rigger is unable to work as close up into the wind as a schooner, but, on the other hand, she gains a great advantage over the latter in a leading wind, that is, when running free before a fair wind.

The square-rigger should make little leeway when close-hauled under full sail, but the divergence increases in proportion to the reduction in sail-area. When wind-pressure on a big area of canvas makes her heel over to leeward, thus submerging an abnormal area of the lee-side of the hull, water-resistance is increased and leeway, in consequence, minimized.

The quality of working well to windward, with little leeway, varies considerably between one windjammer and another, and is known as 'being weatherly', but a well-designed sailing vessel always carries some weather-helm, that is, has a tendency to come up into the wind.

In this connection it is interesting to note that the word 'windjammer' was coined as a description of a sailing vessel which, because of her fine lines and general weatherliness, could be jammed close up into the wind. When 'steam come up and sail went down' the term embraced, in a rather contemptuous fashion, all deepwater sailing craft. Now that the windjammer has, by her very rarity, become an object of general interest, the word has become a title of affection. *'Windjammer'*

In reading these notes on the handling of a square-rigger, it should be borne in mind that, as a Finnish vessel, direct wheel-orders are customary aboard *Herzogin Cecilie*. This practice, standardized abroad for years, has only been adopted recently by Great Britain. *Wheel orders*

In sail, the expressions 'Up' and 'Down' ('Looa' and 'Falla' aboard the Erikson vessels) have always been in more general use, for helm orders, than 'Port' and 'Starboard'. The helmsman stands on the weather side of a windjammer's wheel, which, if he pull it, comes 'down' (or 'to') him: if he pushes it, the wheel goes 'up' (or 'off') from him.

Herzogin Cecilie's steering cables and gearing are so assembled that, if the order to 'Port' be given, the wheel is ported and the vessel's head goes to port. The old order 'Port your helm', a legacy of the days when ships were steered by tillers, implied turning the wheel, the rudder, and the vessel's head to starboard; whereas the modern commands mean what they say.

There are two ways in which a windjammer can be put on to a fresh course: one is by coming up into and passing the wind, and is known as 'tacking'; in the other, known as 'wearing', the vessel is allowed to run off before the wind, in a wide arc, until the new direction is attained. *Changing course*

In very heavy weather tacking is an unwise procedure, because of the unusual strain imposed on the forestays for the brief but unavoidable period during the tack when the foremast sails are aback, i.e. receiving the full force of the wind on the wrong side. The surer but longer manœuvre of 'wearing ship' is preferable under such circumstances. Not only does wearing demand greater sea-room than tacking, but, in a heavy sea, it is apt to mean dangerous work for the men at the main-braces of a 'wet' vessel.

Some of the big windjammers of this century were so unwieldy and 'slack in stays' that they were forced to wear round in order to go about. This limitation of handiness proved fatal to many a vessel caught on a lee-shore without adequate sea-room, because, in wearing, she was bound to finish up well to leeward of her former position. Wearing should be an infallible method of altering course, but failure to tack successfully can result in one of two predicaments: either the vessel 'misses stays' and remains up into the wind 'in irons' (a very hazardous position in strong winds), or else she pays off again on her former course. Then the attempt has to be repeated or recourse made, instead, to wearing.

'Tacking ship'

Nice judgment is required to tack a big four-poster, and all hands, even to the cook, are needed aboard a lightly-manned, modern windjammer. Even then it is an arduous task, calling for every ounce of available strength. On the part of the Master it necessitates a sympathetic understanding of the particular vagaries of his vessel.

Suppose that *Herzogin Cecilie* be running close-hauled in a fresh breeze on the starboard tack, her yards braced hard round on the port back-stays, and that it is desired to put her quickly on to the opposite tack.

The Master takes his post near the helmsman, the port watch stand by at the weather main-braces, the starboard watch at the mizen-braces. A couple of hands are stationed on the fore-deck to tend jib-sheets and fore-tack. The slack of the braces is lifted from the pins and coiled down carefully on the deck, all clear for free running, the Mates standing by to cast off the turns.

Since tacking is more expeditious when the vessel has sufficient way on her to keep her under control throughout the operation, she is kept a 'good full', that is, she is allowed to pay off a further point or so until about seven points off the wind. To minimize the subsequent labour it is nowadays the practice to clew up both cross-jack and mainsail, leaving them loose in their bunt-lines. At the Master's order the wheel is spun round until it is hard over, and the big barque begins to come up into the wind, assisted by the spanker, which has been trimmed amidships to promote stern-swing. Jib-sheets are overhauled and the weather fore-brace slightly eased. As the sails begin to come aback, the canvas booms and flaps and the head-sails thrash madly, thumping their heavy blocks on the foredeck planking. Then when the vessel is only about two points $(22\frac{1}{2}°)$ or less off the wind the Master gives the order to brace round. The Mates cast off from the pins the turns of the main and mizen lee-braces, which fly through their blocks as the giant yards begin to swing. The crew tail on to the slack of the weather-braces, and bring main and cross-jack yards round as rapidly as may be, the falls being gathered in hand over hand. If the moment has been calculated to a nicety, the sails on main and mizen should be just sufficiently blanketed by the foremast canvas (which is still braced hard-a'port) to let the yards come round almost of their own accord. Should the order be premature the yards may swing so violently as to threaten the safety of the starboard back-stays. On the other hand, should it be dilatory and, in consequence, no help be forthcoming from wind-power, the subsequent task of man-handling round the heavy yards may become so slow a procedure as to imperil the success of the entire operation.

By reason of wind action on the foreside of the foremast sails, *Herzogin Cecilie* continues to swing up into the eye of the wind. Im-mediately her head passes that point the jib-sheets are put over the stays and sheeted home; as the after sails begin to draw, with the wind three or four points on the other bow, the fore-tack is let go and the fore-yards hauled round. While the barque was head to wind the helm was righted, and from that point should be used as the demands of her coming up or falling off may dictate.

Bracing round the fore-yards is the most laborious part of the whole manœuvre of tacking, and usually necessitates both watches tailing on the fore-brace, and running it down the length of *Herzogin Cecilie's* long poop. They start with a rhythmic stamp, which deteriorates into a mad, pellmell rush as the power begins to tell.

The remaining fore-and-afters are now shifted across, their heavy sheets being passed above the stays: mainsail and cross-jack are reset, tacks boarded, yards trimmed, and everything hauled taut again. Lastly, the heterogeneous raffle of falls and slack gear has to be coiled down before the free watch can go below. It should take about six or seven minutes to get the vessel actually round on the new tack, but, from start to finish, a full hour may be occupied in completing the entire undertaking.

'Heaving-to' With a long vessel, especially one which, like *Herzogin Cecilie*, combines the extra free-board of an extensive poop with the benefits of a short waist, it is rarely necessary to resort to the procedure of heaving-to, that is, taking the way off the vessel and letting her ride, as it were, at moorings. But now and again to every sailing vessel there come times when wind and sea attain to such menacing proportions that, if she continue to scud before their joint violence, she may become unmanageable. A Master who, under such circumstances, holds on to his course and his canvas too long, is in imminent peril of either broaching-to, driving bows-under, being pooped or being dismasted, any one of which happenings can involve total loss. If, however, the manœuvre of heaving-to be undertaken at the right time, while the vessel is still under control, it presents a practicable measure of safety in even the worst of weather.

The vessel has probably been scudding before the gale under her foresail and fore and main lower-topsails only. The first and hardest task is to make fast the foresail. It is clewed up by its gear, and then in all probability, both watches are needed to get it under control and to stow it securely. They start with the weather yard-arm, for, once those gaskets are passed, the lee-side is less formidable. Now, with her yards braced sharp round, the vessel is run dead before the wind until some slight lull in the wildness of the gale, or a momentary easing of the big following seas, allow the wheel to be eased over.

With the coincident setting of a storm spanker, and perhaps of a mizen staysail as well, she is coaxed round, probably shipping it 'green and heavy' the while, until she lies six or seven points off the wind. The wheel is lashed hard over, and the big seas run diagonally under her weather shoulder. Held so, she may drift bodily down wind, may heel over steeply to leeward and take a good deal of water over her weather rail; but, if all her gear holds, she should ride out almost any weather.

In exceptionally bad conditions, all sail can, if not blown out, be made fast when the vessel is once hove-to, because the windage of masts and spars alone is equivalent to that of a single topsail, and is just sufficient to prevent her from gathering stern-way.

To complete this chapter on sails and sailing there is appended the record of three days intensive sail-manœuvres which took place aboard *Herzogin Cecilie* in 1932. She was homeward-bound from Australia, and on the 16th of March was approaching Cape Horn in fairly heavy weather. Intermittent snow-squalls and a biting wind made labour aloft a miserable, dangerous job; the big, confused sea running at the time caused the barque to labour heavily and to ship much icy water. By midnight on the 17th she had rounded 'Cape Stiff', having sailed 403 miles in forty-eight hours, but having in that period only made 352 miles on her true course.

Twelve days later, on the 31st, she underwent another 'dusting': the log (see Appendix A) stating that heavy seas were coming aboard solidly over the foredeck, and that the vessel was pitching badly. There was nothing exceptional about those particular three days; indeed, for that part of the world, conditions were not severe. As evidenced by the log, the whole passage was uneventful and of mediocre duration. They were just days typical of many, both before and since, which *Herzogin Cecilie* has spent time and again in those same stormy latitudes. Studied in conjunction with the sail-diagrams, they should, however, give some idea of the herculean labours which fall to the lot of the young crews who in these days handle, so well, these big, heavily-sparred, old windjammers.

'Herzogin Cecilie' off Cape Horn, 1932

17/3/1932. (*Variation* 23° E. *Deviation* 7° W. *No Leeway*.)

Time	Wind force and direction. (Beaufort scale – see Appendix A)	General (True) Course	Initial Compass Course	Canvas handled during period (see numbered sail-diagram on page 253)
1 a.m. to	NW 6	S. 89° E.	N. 75° E.	*All sail set except* 10, 18, 26, 32, 33, 34, 35 3 *a.m.*, Set 10, 18, 26
4 a.m. to	NW. 4	S. 89° E.	N. 75° E.	*Took in* 1, 2, 3, 4, 11, 12, 19, 20, 27, 28, 29, 30, 31
8 a.m. to	WSW. 4	S. 89° E.	N. 75° E.	*None*

Time	Wind force and direction. (Beaufort scale – see Appendix A)	General (True) Course	Initial Compass Course	Canvas handled during period (see numbered sail-diagram on page 253)
12 noon to	SW. 5-6	S. 89° E.	N. 74° E.	*None*
4 p.m. to	S. 6-8	N. 88° E.	N. 55° E.	*Set* 1, 2, 3, 4, 11, 12, 19, 20, 27, 28, 29, 30, 31 *Took in* 31, 28, 20, 12 *Blown out* 18, 9, 24
8 p.m. to Midnight	S. 8	N. 69° E.	N. 70° E.	*Took in* 30, 26, 21, 18, 10, 1 25, 27, 9, 17 (Shortened down to storm canvas)

18/3/1932. (*Variation* 21° E. *Deviation* 7° W. *No Leeway*.)

Time	Wind force and direction.	General (True) Course	Initial Compass Course	Canvas handled during period
1 a.m. to	S. 6-8	N. 84° E.	N. 70° E.	*None*
4 a.m. to	S. 7-6	N. 84° E.	N. 75° E.	*Set* 1, 9, 10, 17, 20
8 a.m. to	S. 5-6	N. 89° E.	E.	*Set* 21, 24, 25, 26, 27, 30, 31
12 noon to	S. 5 SSW. 4	S. 76° E.	S. 70° E.	*All sail set except* 18, 28, 32, 33, 34, 35
4 p.m. to	SSW. 4	S. 66° E.	S. 85° E.	*Took in* 1, 2, 3, 4, 11, 12, 19, 20
8 p.m. to Midnight	SSW. 4	S. 81° E.	S. 85° E.	*Passed Cape Horn* *Set all sail except* 32, 33, 34, 35

31/3/1932. *(Variation 15° W. Deviation 7° W. No Leeway.)*

Time	Wind force and direction. *(Beaufort scale – see Appendix A)*	General *(True)* Course	Initial Compass Course	Canvas handled during period *(see numbered sail-diagram on page 253)*
1 a.m. to	E. 3-4	N. 2° W.	N. 20° E.	*Full sail except* 32, 33, 34, 35
4 a.m. to	ESE. 6	N. 2° W.	N. 25° E.	*Blown out* 5, 9, 18 *Took in* 5, 9, 10, 18, 26, 21, 27, 28, 29, 31
8 a.m. to	ESE. 7	N. 3° E.	N. 30° E.	*Blown out* 17, 25 *Took in* 1, 12, 30, 17, 25
12 noon to	Variable 4-6	N. 8° E.	N.	*Torn* 16, 20 *Took in* 16 *Set* 29, 30, 21, 16, 17
4 p.m. to	Variable 6	N. 22° W.	S. 70° E.	*Took in* 13, 21, 12
8 p.m. to Midnight	E. 6-7	N. 88° E. S. 52° E. N. 7° W.	S. 30° E.	*Took in* 17 Wore ship on to starboard tack

CHAPTER V

'UNDER TWO FLAGS'

THE STORY OF *HERZOGIN CECILIE*

PART ONE. 1902-21. THE GERMAN TRAINING-BARQUE

Ho, let her rip — with her royal clew a-quiver,
And the long miles reeling out behind —
For the Trade's got a hold of her and every rope's a-shiver,
With the strong and steady urging of the wind.
All the gleaming white of her, all the sun and shade
Leaning, swaying to the seas,
All up the height of her the South-east Trade
Humming like a swarm of bees.

THE whole subject of comparative voyaging bristles with difficulties and abounds in controversial points. Many factors must be taken into account before it can be held with justice that one passage or one burst of speed is better or worse than others. The most logical method lies in generalization rather than in claiming extreme accuracy for individual figures. As matters of speed and distance will enter very frequently into this Chapter, it may be as well to mention some of the many discrepancies which beset their presentation.

The limits of a passage It is sometimes impossible to tell whether an historian, in quoting the length of a passage by sea, is taking its limits as from pilot to pilot, from tug to landfall, or from anchorage to anchorage. In the case of a windjammer, does the orders port determine the end of the particular passage under discussion, or are the extra days to a port of discharge included? By giving the length of a passage as from pilot to pilot a bad trip may be considerably minimized: a London-bound windjammer, having picked up her Channel Pilot off Dungeness, may take as much as a week to reach her final berth up-river. Again, if a vessel be windbound for several days in the immediate vicinity of her loading berth it is sometimes claimed that the final departure therefrom denotes the commencement of the passage, whereas, surely, the intention to sail, as indicated by clearance from port or anchorage, constitutes the only true guide to the inclusive length of the passage. This initial delay is a frequent occurrence in Spencer Gulf.

In calculating the number of days between departure and arrival some authorities allow for the alteration in date entailed by a crossing of the 180° Meridian. The International Date or Calendar Line is a modification of the 180° Meridian, so arranged as to include all the islands of any one group on the same side of the Line. If this particular longitude be traced on a map it will be found that, except for a portion of Siberia and a few small groups of Pacific islands, it cuts only through vast areas of open sea, and, therefore, its choice as a Date Line causes a minimum of dislocation of time. When crossing the Calendar Line on a westerly course the date must be advanced by one day; on an easterly course the opposite applies, and the date must be put back one day.

The Calendar Line

When Noon at Greenwich, the time in South Australia is 9.30 p.m.: hence, to be absolutely accurate, the measure of time occupied by a passage from Spencer Gulf to Falmouth can only be obtained by correcting the Australian sailing-time to its equivalent in Greenwich Mean Time. The difference between G.M.T. Spencer Gulf and G.M.T. Falmouth plus twenty-four hours (for the crossing of the Date Line) is the exact duration of the passage. Such pedantry, however, is uncalled for, and, in the passage-tables of the Grain Trade and the other statistics which are to follow, no allowance is made for variations in time or for Meridian days. On the other hand, Leap years have been taken into account, a detail which is very often overlooked, and both day of departure and day of arrival are counted. The latter point yields a passage one day longer than the more general method of subtraction of dates, but, in calculating all *Herzogin Cecilie's* voyagings, I have adopted it as being the fairest presentation.

The amount of marine growth which accumulates on the under-water surface of a hull varies with the region of the vessel's trading. If, for example, one of the Erikson square-riggers carries a cargo of Baltic timber to South Africa, proceeding thence to Australia in ballast, or sails out via the Seychelles to New Zealand, her sojourn in tropical waters is more protracted than that of a vessel voyaging direct, in ballast, to Spencer Gulf. The fouling consequent upon such visits to the Indian Ocean would, to use trade terms, be largely an encrustation of 'shell'; whereas on the homeward passage from Australia her bottom would

Bottom fouling

collect 'grass'. Iron and steel hulls can foster an extraordinary conglomeration of weed and barnacles during a year at sea, despite the ameliorating effect of modern anti-fouling compounds.

In *The Last of the Windjammers* Mr. Lubbock cites the instance of the iron Blackwaller *Carlisle Castle* homeward bound from Calcutta in 1869: before reaching the Equator she was so sluggish, through the presence of bottom-growth, that she could only be tacked in smooth water. Ribbon-weed was present in such quantities that all efforts to dislodge it at sea were unavailing, and the tendrils grew to a length of four feet and to a width of half an inch. After being posted 'Overdue' for a month at Lloyd's, the *Carlisle Castle* docked at Blackwall, 169 days out from Calcutta.

The oil-carrying windjammer *Daylight* in 1908, after a passage of 145 days from Vizagapatam to Philadelphia, had forty tons of barnacles scraped from her bottom. These barnacles averaged $4\frac{1}{2}$ inches in length.

Adherence, however, was far less rapid on the copper sheathing of the wooden and composite clippers of bygone days, and the condition of a vessel's bottom must be taken into account in criticizing or comparing her performances, because fouling, in any quantity, exercises a considerable retarding effect on her sailing qualities.

Ballast passages   This is one of the reasons why the grain fleet, fresh from dry-docking, make, in the main, shorter passages out to Australia than they do when returning home from Australia. Also, the outward journey is, nowadays, usually made in ballast; all other things being equal, although subject to greater drift and leeway, a windjammer can sail faster in light trim than when fully laden, water resistance being minimized and total weight being reduced by three or four thousand tons.

Season   In considering the merits of a passage the period of the year during which it takes place must not be disregarded. Under sail, January and February are the best months to run eastward from the Antipodes to the Horn, whereas April, May and June are the worst. Thus, the earlier departures, among the grain-fleet, from Spencer Gulf are at an advantage over the later vessels, and this benefit is augmented by the fact that the former vessels should arrive in the North Atlantic before fine summer weather spoils that area from the view-point of the big windjammer. At any time the precincts of the Horn are never likely to offer other than hardship to the few sailers who now round that fearsome

Cape. Occasionally a short fine spell, with good visibility and a moderate sea, will enable one or two of them to carry full canvas off the pitch of the Horn, but such conditions are exceptional. Even in the summer months, November — January, those latitudes have an average rainfall of not less than seven hours per day; while, in winter, snow, sleet or rain, accompanied by winds of gale force and by big seas, are almost continuous.

A misconception of distance can arise by the confusion of nautical miles with statute miles. The length of a sea-mile, representing 1/60th of a degree of latitude, varies, according to latitude, from 6,046 feet on the Equator to 6,092 feet in Latitude 60°. For convenience, however, a sea-mile is standardized at 6,080 feet, this being the exact length of the Admiralty Measured Mile for trial purposes, and equalling 1.1515 land-miles.

Mileage

It must also be remembered that when running eastward, in those southerly latitudes where so many sailing records have been set up, a day, noon to noon, does not imply 24 hours' sailing but only about 23½ hours. Likewise, if distance be reckoned on the basis of so many degrees of longitude traversed in a specified period, it is fallacious to found such calculation on 60 miles to each degree, for when running the Easting down this method would give the vessel the benefit of as much as 100 miles during her day's progress.

It is, of course, only at the Equator that each degree of longtitude represents 60 nautical miles. At Latitude 40° this figure drops to 46 miles, at 50° to 38½ miles, and at 60° to 20 miles to each degree of longitude.

It has been said that many of the wonderful clipper passages of former days were produced, on paper, by some such inaccuracy of fact. In *The Colonial Clippers* Mr. Lubbock deals with such charges, and produces interesting proof in refutation. He prints, for instance, a letter written by Captain Anthony Enright upon the occasion of *Lightning's* 430 mile run in one day, when making her Easting outward-bound to Australia in 1857. Therein are quoted not only the distance made, but the actual time, the knottage, and the number and length of degrees of longitude crossed between noon and noon. (See note, page 51).

The measurement of sea speed

The term knot is subject to much misuse, for it is a measure of sea-speed in nautical miles per hour, not of distance covered in any given period. It is incorrect to state that a vessel sailed, say, 10 knots in an hour when meaning that, having run at a speed of 10 knots, she had covered 10 nautical miles during the hour.

The phrase 'reeling off the knots' had its origin in the old-fashioned, rough and ready method of estimating speed at sea by means of a sand-glass and a marked line, known as a log-ship. A small float attached to a line was thrown overboard: the line, which was spaced out at regular intervals by knots, ran freely from a big reel held over the head of one of the three men executing the manœuvre. A certain number of seconds, measured by the sand-glass, elapsed before the line was stopped by a man at the taffrail, who counted the number of knots which had passed over-side. The distance between any two knots bore the same relation to a nautical mile as the time the turning of the sand-glass bore to one hour. With a 28-second sand-glass the knots were 47 feet apart, and from the number of knots let out the vessel's speed in nautical miles per hour was deduced. The patent log — a small spinner towed at the end of a long line, rotation being converted, by counter-gearing, into mileage run, and registered on a dial at the stern — has now superseded the old hand log, even aboard the unchanging windjammer.

Dead-reckoning   To conclude this rather abstruse and somewhat sketchy explanatory prologue to the more interesting data about *Herzogin Cecilie*, dead-reckoning must be mentioned, as it is still a constant resort of the navigator under sail, when positioning by observation is impossible. It is the most ancient method of establishing a vessel's whereabouts when out of sight of land. Dead-reckoning, or the 'Day's Work' as it is called, is an estimation arrived at by the amalgamation of several factors.

During a given period the courses steered, and the estimated distances run on those courses, can, if allowance be made for currents, leeway, compass error, etc., be worked up into a single course and distance. This, if applied to the last known position on the chart, yields the new position of the vessel.

Dead-reckoning is something more than mere guesswork, for much skill, experience and exactitude are necessary to produce a dependable result. This is especially true in the case of a windjammer. A steamer runs at a relatively steady speed, and maintains an unvarying course for long periods at a time. On the other hand, the windship is affected by every alteration in wind-strength and by every type of weather. She may be unable to steer a compass course at all, and be forced to sail 'by the wind'; she can make several degrees of leeway by being forced bodily to leeward by pressure of wind or sea; often her log-line is carried away, and her speed becomes a matter of judgment. Consequently, positioning based on such changeable factors is of necessity, in her case, only an approximation.

Leeway can be ascertained by measuring, with a bearing-compass, the angle made by the vessel's wake with her keel line.

The greatest sea-speed under sail ever recorded was shown in the log-book of the wooden clipper-ship *James Baines* (of the Liverpool Black Ball Line) on June 18th, 1856. She was running her Easting down at the time, and the entry read: 'Lat. 42°47′S; Long. 115°54′E. Barometer 29.20°, Wind, W. to SW. First part. Breeze freshening. At 6 p.m. Wind SW. and freshening. At 8.30 p.m. In all starboard studding-sails; ship going 21 knots with main skysail set. Midnight. Fresh gale and fine clear night. 8 a.m. Wind and weather the same. Noon. Less wind, attended with snow squalls. Distance 420 miles.'

Effective speed under sail

In December, 1856, the American clipper *Great Republic*, when on passage from New York to 'Frisco, is said to have averaged 19 knots for 19 hours of sailing, her total distance for the day's work being 413 nautical miles.

All such speeds under sail are, however, indicative of the successful utilization of exceptional weather-conditions by exceptional vessels, handled by exceptional Masters, rather than of the effective speed of sail-propulsion.

The fastest homeward passages of the 'China birds' yielded a mean rate of about 6½ knots for the total distance run. When *Cutty Sark* was transferred from the tea trade to the Australian wool trade she improved upon her earlier averages. In the season of 1888, for instance, for a record passage of 70 days, Newcastle, New South Wales to Dungeness, her mean speed was 8 knots, notwithstanding the fact that her sail-area had been reduced since her China days. There was, however, so great a difference between the weather conditions peculiar to those two trades that such comparisons are of little real value. The total of the twenty-nine passages made during that season, by the entire wool fleet, worked out to an average speed of 6 knots.

During the five years 1927-1931 inclusive *Herzogin Cecilie* averaged 100 days for her five homeward passages from Spencer Gulf to an orders port in this country. This gave her a mean effective speed, in the desired direction, of a little under 6 knots.

273

The great strength of top-hamper embodied in the best grade of big steel square-riggers of this century has enabled the better-designed among them to carry canvas to advantage in very strong winds. In that power aloft lies the secret of the fact that *Herzogin Cecilie*, the Laiesz vessels, and others of their generation have, at times, accomplished feats of sailing which vie with any that have gone before.

The benefits of sail-carrying are apt to be exaggerated. The vessel which is most likely to produce good passages is the one in which 'cracking-on' is combined with judicious reduction of sail-area when advisable, no time being lost, however, in resetting canvas in accordance with every improvement in weather conditions.

Such firms as Devitt and Moore, Aitken and Lilburn, and other first-class owners of passenger-carrying fleets in the heyday of the Australian trade under sail, never allowed the safety or the comfort of their passengers to be imperilled for the sake of the advertisement obtained by making record passages. In those flourishing days of sail a vessel's reputation was founded on three factors — the popularity of her Master, the regularity and freedom from casualty of her voyaging, and the standard of her accommodation and table.

Although, in that era, scores of magnificent, medium clippers and barques set a consistent standard of fine sailing, sheer speed, regardless of other issues, was not always a prime motive. Hence the frequent adoption of the Cape of Good Hope route, in preference to the Horn, by many of the crack sailers of the eighties. Devitt and Moore's *Sobraon* always broke her homeward passage to England by calls at Cape Town and St. Helena, making a regular stay of about three days at the latter place.

The wool fleet, racing home for the London sales with valuable cargo as their main source of revenue, were, of course, in a somewhat different case, and for them the old 'Sailor's Way', past the Horn, was the quickest, though hardest, road.

Square-rigger, steamer and yacht

It can be accepted, however, that the mean effective speed of square-rig, if taken over a distance sufficient to include varying climatic conditions, has never reached 10 knots.

On her maiden voyage in 1936 the Union-Castle liner *Stirling Castle* (26,550 tons gross) steamed out to Cape Town at an average speed of 18·94 knots, and came home again at 18·8 knots, setting up new records in each direction. These were not isolated bursts of speed,

274

for she was fulfilling a schedule which is to be within the compass of her sister mail-boats when they have been re-engined. In October, 1935, the cargo-liner *Waiwera*, a motor-vessel of 10,800 tons gross, built in 1934 for the Shaw, Savill and Albion Line by Harland, Wolff, Ltd., made a record passage home from Melbourne, via Suez: notwithstanding a stop at Port Said to load fruit, she arrived at Hull within a month, her actual steaming time, for 11,046 miles, being 28 days 12 hours. The best day's run was on October 18th, nine days after leaving Melbourne, when for twenty-four hours, she maintained a speed of 18 knots, covering 432 nautical miles.

These speeds by steam are capable of being sustained regardless of normal variations in weather conditions, a quality never possessed by the sailer.

In these days, when public interest in the big, ocean-racing yachts is so keen, it is not generally realized that most of the barques of the Erikson Fleet can sail considerably faster than even the largest and strongest sailing yacht. The greatest day's run made by a yacht was on May 24th, 1905, when the schooner-yacht *Atlantic* ran 341 miles in the North Atlantic at an average speed of 14·2 knots. Not only is the yacht shorter than the barque on the water-line but she is unable to carry canvas under the weather conditions in which the big windjammer revels. 'Wind, wind, and still more wind' is the cry of the grain fleet, and *Herzogin Cecilie* could storm along at 15 knots in a gale, and in a sea, which would spell disaster to the most seaworthy yacht ever constructed.

Record times for various passages under sail will be quoted frequently in this chapter. Much of the information has been extracted from a list compiled by Mr. Lubbock for *Lloyd's Calendar*. It must, however, be remembered that an outstanding passage, for which luck in the matter of weather is often responsible, is only one of the thousands which have been sailed on the route in question, and, therefore, any near approach to the record is, of necessity, a passage well out of the common. The windjammer with a series of good performances to her credit has always been a better proposition than a vessel whose reputation is based on a single superlative effort.

Some well-informed readers may find cause for disagreement with one or other of the figures which follow. Any contentious and unprofitable argument may perhaps be avoided if some of the foregoing

Record passages

reasons for variation are considered and borne in mind. A discrepancy of a day more or less, in a wide subject such as this, is not of vital importance.

The object of the chapter is to combine with the story of *Herzogin Cecilie* an idea of the general trend of performance under canvas during this century, without claiming academic exactitude for every supporting fact.

The life-time of 'Herzogin Cecilie'

On June 27th, 1902, *Herzogin Cecilie* sailed from Bremen, under the command of Captain M. Dietrich, for her maiden voyage. From July 25th, 1914, until October 1st, 1920, she lay idle in Chilean waters as an internee. On April 25th, 1936, she drove ashore near Bolt Head, South Devon, and, four months later, was abandoned as a wreck. That life-time of thirty-four years falls, naturally, into two periods, in accordance with which this account has been subdivided.

The first twelve years of continuous trading were spent as the cadet-manned cargo-carrier of the Norddeutscher Lloyd Company. In those days she was the pride of her country's merchant service, and the windjammer 'par excellence'. Then followed the six dismal years of enforced inaction (recorded in the addendum). *Herzogin Cecilie* sailed back from Chile after the War under the German flag. By the action of Reparations she passed to the French Government, from whom, on December 10th, 1921, she was purchased by Captain Gustaf Erikson.

Thenceforward, for the fifteen years that form the second part of this biography, she tramped the seas under the Finnish Ensign. They were years of hard and unbroken servitude as a wage-earner, a carrier of rough cargoes spending much of her time in ballast, facing bitter competition, falling freights and the ever-present threat of economic failure. Yet she remained to the end a fine, handsome, powerful barque. As late as 1931 she accomplished a short burst of sailing at one of the highest speeds attained by a windjammer. Her final passage — Port Lincoln to Falmouth in 1936 — was one of the finest performances of her entire career.

Within the limited scope possible under present-day conditions, she was maintained in good condition, below and aloft, and the smart-ness of her German days was never sacrificed to the utility of her later employment.

In making comparison between the two periods of *Herzogin Cecilie's*

facing: AT BREMERHAVEN, 1902 — THE MAIDEN VOYAGE BEGIN

life at sea, it is necessary to bear in mind that before the War she was heavily manned, independent, to a great extent, of her freight-earning capacity, and, because of her position, very much in the public eye. Under Finnish management she had to be worked by the barest minimum of youthful personnel, and had, at all costs, to avoid undue expense for wear and tear. Her later work was done in comparative obscurity, for the news value, at any rate in this country, of the survivors of square-rig has only manifested itself during the last few years. In point of fact, viewed in the light of these differences, her later life makes a more meritorious showing than the somewhat spectacular, but less competitive, voyaging of her early days.

No attempt will be made to describe individual passages in detail. It is proposed to group the voyages of *Herzogin Cecilie* according to trades, and to intersperse them with various happenings of note. This method will allow comparison to be made with her contemporaries and with her forerunners, and will embrace the performances of some of the Laiesz vessels and of the Erikson Fleet in general.

It was rather extraordinary that, although the twenty-eight years during which *Herzogin Cecilie* was in active commission were practically devoid of serious casualties, some of the worst damage she ever sustained through heavy weather occurred on her maiden passage from Bremen to Astoria, via the Horn.

An inauspicious maiden voyage

South-bound vessels crossing the Tropic of Capricorn during the months of July, August and September are prone to encounter, off the coast of Southern Brazil, sudden, violent, and dangerous squalls. From the fact that such storms sweep seaward over the great Pampas areas of South America, they are known as Pamperos. They gather with little warning, and, blowing up usually from the south-west, are felt as far seaward as 48° W., and are particularly dangerous to a sailing vessel running for the Horn.

On August 22nd, 1902, *Herzogin Cecilie* limped into Monte Video, crippled after an encounter with a Pampero. The earliest reports stated that she had been partly dismasted, but the *Weser Zeitung*, of Bremen, corrected this, at a later date, to the breakage of three spars, and summarized the position as not being serious. Six weeks, however, were occupied in refitting, the journey being resumed on October 9th. From Monte Video to Astoria took only sixty-nine days, an excellent passage.

acing: THE BEAUTY OF A DEEPWATER SQUARE-RIGGER, 1930

AN ABRIDGED LOG
of the movements of the
GERMAN FOUR-MASTED BARQUE
HERZOGIN CECILIE
Training-ship and cargo-carrier for the
NORDDEUTSCHER LLOYD COMPANY
between
1902 and 1921
Compiled, by the Author, from the Records at Lloyd's

Year	Sailed		Intermediate Reports	Arrived	
	Date	Port		Date	Port
1902	June 27	Bremen (Capt. M. Dietrich)	June 30 Passed Lizard Aug. 20 Arrd. Monte Video, in distress, for repairs Oct. 9 Sld. Monte Video	Dec. 17	Astoria
1903	Feb. 20	Astoria	June 2 Arrd. Falmouth, f.o. (for orders) June 8 Sld. Falmouth	June 9 June 10	Barry Cardiff
	July 13 Aug. 27 Sept. 19	Cardiff Bremen Shields	Sept. 28 Passed Dungeness	July 17 Aug. 31 Jan. 19 (1904)	Bremen Shields San Francisco
1904	Mar. 18 Aug. 17 Sept. 9	San Francisco London Bremen	July 16 Passed Beachy Head	July 18 Aug. 20 Nov. 18 Nov. 30	London Bremen Taltal Iquique
1905	Dec. 16 (1904) Apl. 10 June 17 Aug. 26	Iquique Antwerp Bremen Delaware	Feb. 28 Off Lizard	Mar. 4 July 26 Dec. 29	Antwerp Philadelphia Japan

278

Year	Sailed Date	Sailed Port	Intermediate Reports	Arrived Date	Arrived Port
1906	Mar. 2	Kobe	Mar. 16 Arrd. Singapore Mar. 19 Sld. Singapore Apl. 3 Arrd. Rangoon Apl. 23 Sld. Rangoon Aug. 2 Passed Prawle	Aug. 8	Hamburg
1907	Oct. 27 (1906)	Bremen			
	Nov. 18 (1906)	Leith		Mar. 3	Honolulu
	Apl. 10	Honolulu		May 23	Geelong
	June 13	Geelong	Sept. 2 Arrd. Falmouth (f.o.) Sept. 10 Sld. Falmouth	Sept. 12	Liverpool
	Sept. 28	Liverpool		Oct. 4	Bremen
	Oct. 24	Bremen		Jan. 10 (1908)	Adelaide
1908	Feb. 28	Adelaide	May 31 Arrd. Queenstown (f.o.)	June 4 —	Barry Cardiff
	June 30	Cardiff		July 10	Bremen
	July 31	Bremen		Nov. 19	Astoria
	Nov. 21	Astoria		Jan. 25 (1909)	Melbourne
1909	Mar. 7	Port Augusta	Mar. 31 In 49° 40′ S.–135° W. pooped in heavy gale June 15 Arrd. Falmouth (f.o.)	June 19	Antwerp
	July 10	Antwerp		July 12	Bremerhaven
	Aug. 6	Bremerhaven (Capt. O. Walter)		Oct. 12 Oct. 18	Taltal Antofagasta
	Nov. 24	Mejillones	Jan. 26 Off Scillies (1910)	Jan. 30 (1910)	Nieuw Waterweg (Rotterdam)
1910	Feb. 27	Nieuw Waterweg		Mar. 16	Fayal
	Mar. 19	Fayal	Apr. 4 Passed Dungeness	Apr. 8 Apr. 30	Bremerhaven Hamburg
	May 15	Hamburg		May 22	Leith
	June 8	Leith		Oct. 7	Honolulu
	Nov. 9	Honolulu		Dec. 3	Sydney

Year	Sailed		Intermediate Reports	Arrived	
	Date	Port		Date	Port
1911	Jan. 6 (about)	Sydney	Apr. 17 Arrd. Falmouth (f.o.) Apr. 26 Sld. Falmouth Apr. 28 Grounded Dunkirk Rds.	Apr. 29	Dunkirk
	May 28	Dunkirk		May 31 June 21	Bremerhaven Cuxhaven
	July 13 July 17	Cuxhaven Leith		Dec. 13	Honolulu
1912	Jan. 16 Mar. 28	Honolulu Sydney	July 11 Arrd. Queenstown (f.o.)	Feb. 23 July 17 Aug. 11	Sydney Havre Bremerhaven
	Sept. 14	Bremerhaven	Sept. 19 Passed Beachy Head Sept. 27 Passed Madeira	Nov. 24	Valparaiso
1913				Feb. 6	Antofagasta
	Feb. 22	Antofagasta	May 3 Off Old Head of Kinsale May 5 Arrd. Queenstown (f.o.) May 13 Collision with s.s. *Sausenberg* when entering Hamburg	May 10 May 13	Cuxhaven Hamburg
	July 26	Bremerhaven	Aug. 11 Passed Cape Verde	June 6 Oct. 14 Nov. 3	Bremerhaven Gatico Tocopilla
1914	Dec. 19 (1913)	Tocopilla	Mar. 6 25 miles S. of Land's End Mar. 7 Passed Dungeness	Mar. 10	Bremerhaven
	May 5	Bremerhaven (Capt. D. Ballehr)	May 13 Passed Ushant May 29 Passed Cape Verde	July 25	Guayacan
1915 1916 1917 1918		At Guayacan			
1919		At Coquimbo			
1920	Aug. 12 Oct. 1	Coquimbo Antofagasta	Dec. 22 Passed Lizard, and arrd. Falmouth (f.o.) Dec. 23 Sld. Falmouth	Aug. 14 Dec. 26	Caleta Coloso Ostend
1921	June 20		Taken over by the French Government		

The only other bad accident in which *Herzogin Cecilie* was involved during her twelve years of service for the Norddeutscher Lloyd, took place in 1909. Although it entailed no loss of spars or gear, this damage, happening as it did two thousand miles or more from the nearest land, might have terminated her career and added her to that tragic roll, Lloyd's record of 'Missing' vessels. Brief mention has already been made of this incident. She was on her way from Port Augusta to Europe with a cargo of grain, this being the first of her many visits to Spencer Gulf. Twenty-four days out, on March 31st, in 49.40 S., 135 W., she was driving hard, under storm canvas, toward the Horn. A heavy westerly gale was raging, and piling up behind her came the succession of great seas which in 'Fifty South' roll endlessly eastward across the vast tracts of that lonely waste of the South Pacific Ocean. The vertical height from trough to crest of these 'Cape Horn greybeards', as they are called, has been calculated to average between twenty and forty-three feet, and they travel at an estimated speed of from 23 to 27 miles per hour.

Mention was made in Chapter 11, Book Two, of the importance of a whale-back wheel-house for windjammers whose steering-control is placed close to the taffrail. At certain intervals when a big following sea is running, a gigantic roller, far bigger than its predecessors, comes rearing up astern, its smoking ridge capped by a dozen feet of boiling surf. Such abnormal waves have been measured, by sextant, as attaining to a vertical height of over sixty feet. To the unprotected helmsman, even though he be handling the most seaworthy of sailers, wallowing deep-laden in the mile-long trough between giant seas, this occasional, monstrous wave, towering high over the poop, seems certain to engulf his labouring charge.

Herzogin Cecilie, however, as was pointed out when surveying her decks, had two pairs of dual wheels, and steered, normally, from the midship position. This fact undoubtedly saved her in 1909, for she was pooped over the stern by one of these tremendous seas. It fell full upon the after end of her long poop-deck, and swept forward, burying the chart-house in a seething maelstrom of many tons of icy water. Fortunately the steering-cables held. The helmsmen — probably four men were on the midship wheel-gratings at the time — kept the vessel to her course. Without any high, steel-plated bulwarks to impede it, the inundation dispersed from the open-railed poop as her natural

The pooping of 'Herzogin Cecilie'

buoyancy asserted itself. Had the cables snapped or the backlash of the big wheels, set up by the immense leverage exerted by the rudder, caused loss of control, without doubt the barque would have broached-to, fallen away from the wind, taken the next wave over the length of her topgallant rail, and — this book would never have been written.

When the full damage could be ascertained it was discovered that the unprotected pair of wheels at the after end of the poop had disappeared completely, the long skylight abaft the chart-house had been demolished, and the saloon and cabins below were flooded. Worst of all, the after end of the steel chart-house, recipient of the full force of that mighty blow, had been driven inward as though it were a crushed match-box. The interior, central, steel bulkhead of the house had shared the same fate. The chart-room was completely gutted, and a very cataract had poured down the stairway into the central hall of the quarters of the afterguard. Of one of the big lifeboats on the poop no trace remained except the bent and twisted legs of its high cradle. Apart from some minor damage about the poop, that was the sum total of a casualty which few vessels have undergone and yet lived to tell the tale.

Minor casualties

Herzogin Cecilie's name appeared at Lloyd's as a casualty on two subsequent occasions before the War, but, in each case, the damage was trivial and the delay occasioned negligible. On March 28th, 1911, at the close of another trip from Australia, she grounded when approaching Dunkirk Roads but refloated, without assistance, on the same day. In 1913, when entering port at Hamburg, homeward-bound from Antofagasta with nitrate, she came into collision with the anchored German steamer *Sausenberg*, the combined damages being slight.

Germany and the pre-War nitrate trade

The participation of *Herzogin Cecilie* in the pre-War nitrate trade produced some of the most notable passages of her whole sea-life, although it is difficult to draw fair comparison between the conditions under which she carried nitrate and those which prevail in the grain trade of these last days of sail. In the opening decade of this century German tonnage was pre-eminent among the numerous sailers on the Chile run. Although they were in competition with large numbers of British and other European windjammers, the regularity of the sailing of the German square-riggers was never equalled. Not even Dom Bordes, Laeisz's great rivals in the trade, well as that big French fleet was operated, could lower the records of the 'P' vessels. Germany, it seemed, produced the most suitable and best-manned square-riggers for this arduous work, and *Herzogin Cecilie* was true to type. Well found, well manned, enormously strong aloft and shapely below, she proved to be eminently suitable for a voyage which involved a double rounding of the Horn for every cargo imported.

In the table on page 284, based partly on statistics compiled by a member of the staff of Messrs. F. Laeisz, comparison is made between the best feats of two widely divergent types of sailing vessel: the performances of the big, American, soft-wood clippers, the fastest sailing craft ever built, are tabulated with those of the great, steel, 'Flying P' windjammers of half a century later. Both types knew well the stormy seas of 'Fifty South', and both were driven, consistently, to the limit of their possibilities by the finest Masters of sail then living.

The 'P' Fleet versus the American clippers

One striking fact emerges from this tabulation, namely the preponderance of maiden voyages in the tally of American clipper records. As already stated, these soft-wood hulls soon became strained by the intensive driving to which they were subjected, and after a few voyages such vessels lost much of their birthright of speed. The German vessels never succeeded in logging a day's run of 400 nautical miles, but allowance must be made for the fact that great capacity and lasting serviceability were required of them. The wooden clippers, in whom speed was the essential quality, were light-laden and short-lived by comparison with the Laeisz freighters, whose performances, nevertheless, make a fine showing against those of the old-timers.

The best authentic day's sailing made by *Herzogin Cecilie*, which I have been able to trace, was 365 nautical miles in $23\frac{1}{2}$ hours on December 5th, 1930, under the command of Captain Sven Eriksson. This took place to the south of the Cape of Good Hope during a passage of 85 days from Copenhagen to Port Lincoln, in ballast, and it followed upon two other remarkable performances, 326 miles on October 1st and 336 on November 21st.

'Herzogin Cecilie's' best recorded day and week

To accomplish the 365 miles on December 5th the barque averaged $15\frac{1}{2}$ knots under full sail, the wind-force being logged as NW. 6-7 (Beaufort scale). On November 27th she ran 65 miles in four hours, at an average speed of 16·3 knots, wind-force being NW. 8-9. During this period the log showed $17\frac{3}{4}$ knots for two consecutive hours.

In 1922, when on a ballast passage from Melbourne to Taltal, *Herzogin Cecilie* covered 2,210 nautical miles in the seven days from October 5th—11th, during which she ran 326 miles in one day (October

BEST DAY'S SAILING

Vessel	Master	Passage	Length passag
A. THE AMERICAN CLIPPERS:			
Champion of the Seas	Newlands	Liverpool—Melbourne	72 day
Lightning	Forbes	Boston Light—Liverpool	13¾
Lightning	Enright	Liverpool—Cape Otway (Melbourne)	69
James Baines	McDonnell	Liverpool—Melbourne	63½
Donald McKay	Warner	Boston—Liverpool	18
Red Jacket	Eldridge	Sandy Hook—Liverpool	13
Sovereign of the Seas	McKay	Honolulu—New York	82
N. B. Palmer	Low	New York—San Francisco	106
Flying Cloud	Cressy	New York—San Francisco	89¾
Marco Polo	Forbes	Melbourne—U.K.	68
B. THE LAEISZ FLEET:			
Potosi	Hilgendorf	Isle of Wight—Valparaiso	55
Preussen	Petersen	Ushant—Iquique	57
Padua	Jürs	Hamburg—Spencer Gulf	66
Priwall	Clauss	Hamburg—Spencer Gulf	66
Pisagua	Nissen	Port Pirie—Taltal	—
Potosi	Nissen	Tocopilla—Lizard	56

ECORDED

day, utical	Date	Notes	Notable performances, during periods of consecutive days, on various passages		
			4 days	7 days	11 days
5	12/12/1854	On maiden passage (see page 51)			
36	1/3/1854	On maiden passage (see page 31)	1,446	2,188	2,791
30	19/3/'57	From 43° 07' S.—7° 17' W., onwards			
23	6/2/'55	On first Australian passage. In 50° S., making Easting	1,436	2,276	2,969
21	27/2/'55	On maiden passage	—	—	—
7	19/1/'54	On maiden passage	1,501	—	3,185 (10 days)
1	18/3/'53	On first homeward passage; between 48° S.— 143° W. and Diego Ramirez	1,474	2,323	3,457
6	1852	On maiden passage	—	—	—
4	31/7/'51	On maiden passage, when running northward, 2 days from Cape Horn	1,256	—	—
4	4/7/'52	On second voyage, when running northward to Cape Horn	1,344	2,152	—
8	11/5/1900	On eighth voyage, when near Cape Horn	1,328	1,998	2,957
8	23/4/'03	On second voyage, when beyond Cape Horn	1,279	2,085	3,019
1	28/12/'33	Between Cape of Good Hope and Australia	1,193	2,042	3,123
2	25/12/'33	Between Cape of Good Hope and Australia	1,251	2,044	3,025
0	10/9/'01	—— ——	1,251	2,014	2,984
7	19/12/'08	On twentieth voyage, when 5 days from the Lizard			

11th). Probably these performances had been eclipsed in her German days, the logs of which, unfortunately, are not available for reference, but such records do, at least, serve to show that she was, on occasion, quite the equal of the Laeisz 'cracks'.

'Preussen'
and 'Potosi'

No finer square-riggers have ever sailed the seas than *Preussen* and *Potosi*. The statement takes into account not speed, beauty nor any other individual trait alone, but the combination of such qualities allied with strength, capacity and seaworthiness to produce a splendid utilitarian mean. These two vessels set up records for the West Coast run which were unsurpassed under sail. Mr. Lubbock in *The Nitrate Clippers* gives their voyages in full detail, and the following list of outstanding passages is taken from his facts:

Outward:

Potosi	Wight—Valparaiso	55 days	1900
Preussen	Ushant—Iquique	57 ,,	1903
Potosi	Lizard—Valparaiso	59 ,,	1896
Potosi	Wight—Valparaiso	59 ,,	1905

Homeward:

Potosi	Tocopilla—Lizard	56 ,,	1908
Potosi	Iquique—Prawle	57 ,,	1903
Preussen	Iquique—Lizard	61 ,,	1904

Tocopilla and Iquique lie 700 and 750 miles, respectively, north of Valparaiso, Iquique to the Channel representing something between ten and eleven thousand miles of windjamming. To-day, very few people can judge the worth of any given passage under sail, and, in consequence, such times may convey little idea of a vessel's quality. Messrs. Laeisz, however, kept a careful record of the exploits of their fleet by dividing the passages into sections. The addition of the best time in which each section was ever covered by a 'P' sailer gives the minimum possible period for the whole passage, thus:

Out		*Home*	
Lizard—Equator	15 days	Iquique—Horn	15 days
Equator—Horn	21 ,,	Horn—Equator	18 ,,
Horn—Valparaiso	10 ,,	Equator—Lizard	16 ,,
or Horn—Iquique	15 ,,		
		i.e. Iquique—Lizard	49 days
i.e. Lizard—Valparaiso	46 days		
and Lizard—Iquique	51 days		

It appears, therefore, that *Preussen's* 57 days from Ushant to Iquique was only 6 days, and *Potosi's* 57 days from Iquique to Prawle only 8 days, outside the attainable minimum.

The machine-like regularity of the steel five-masted barque *Potosi* was little short of miraculous. Between her launch in 1895 and her internment in 1914 she made 27 round voyages (plus one single outward passage) in the nitrate trade, for she did not enter any other trade during her lifetime. For the 27 outward passages up to and including 1913 she averaged 68 days, the best trip being 55 and the worst 86. No less than 17 of these passages were equal to or less than the average. The 27 homeward runs produced an average time of 76½ days, 56 being the quickest and 88 the slowest; 13 were 76 days or under. These periods are calculated to or from landfall in United Kingdom, i.e. the outward runs are from the Isle of Wight, Lizard, Prawle, etc.; the homeward are to the same points or, in the few cases where no earlier report was registered, to Cuxhaven or Hamburg.

Potosi's maximum effective speed was said to be about 17 knots, and on many occasions she ran for long periods at a 16 knot average, this with a carrying capacity of just over 6,000 tons of nitrate.

On July 4th, 1914, *Potosi* sailed from Hamburg, and on September 23rd arrived at Valparaiso, where she remained throughout the War. In 1918 Laeisz sold her to Vinnen, but under the terms of the Treaty of Versailles she became French property. In 1923 she was purchased by Chilean owners, and renamed *Flora*. She brought her last cargo of nitrate to Hamburg in 1924, and then, after loading coal, coke and patent fuel at Cardiff, sailed for Mejillones. She caught fire in the South Atlantic, and was sunk by gun-fire from an Argentine cruiser.

To-day the Laeisz tradition is carried on by the four-masted barques *Padua* and *Priwall*, which again re-entered the nitrate trade in 1935, after a period of carrying Australian grain.

In 1928, under the command of Captain B. Petersen, who had been Master of *Preussen* before the War, *Padua*, then only two years of age, ran from Hamburg to Talcahuano in 76 days, and returned from Mejillones to Terneuzen in 72 days. In 1930 she was 72 days from the Lizard to Talcahuano, and, in 1931, 70 days from Hamburg to Talcahuano. In 1935 *Priwall* sailed from the Scillies to Talcahuano in 74 days. So it would appear that Germany still has the gift of building, and sailing, big deepwater square-riggers.

'Potosi' the sailing liner

'Padua' and 'Priwall'

Herzogin Cecilie made five outward and four homeward passages in the nitrate trade between 1904 and 1914. The results redounded to her credit, and the following table shows her sailings in comparison with those of *Potosi* during a roughly similar period. In this case it should be noted that the times are given as from port to port, i.e. from Germany to Chile and back to a European port of discharge, instead of from and to landfall:

Outward:	Average	Best	Worst
Herzogin Cecilie, 5 passages, 1904-14	74	68	81
Potosi, 8 consecutive passages, 1909-14	75	66	84
Homeward:			
Herzogin Cecilie, 4 passages, 1905-14	76	68	81
Potosi, 9 consecutive passages, 1909-14	81	66	96

Curiously enough *Herzogin Cecilie's* two best performances on the Chilean run took place in the same year, and were passages of precisely equal length. She left Bremerhaven on August 6th, 1909, under a new Master, Captain O. Walter, and arrived at Taltal, half-way between Valparaiso and Iquique, on the 68th day. After completing her cargo at Mejillones, situated between Taltal and Iquique, on November 24th she sailed for home; 64 days out she reported at the Scillies, and on January 30th, 1910, berthed at Nieuw Waterweg, Rotterdam, after a passage of 68 days.

These two runs of 68 days, berth to berth, are inclusive of day of departure and day of arrival, and the total of 136 days at sea for the round voyage represents the finest sustained sailing which she ever achieved.

Another noteworthy visit to the West Coast was her outward passage of 67 days from Beachy Head to Valparaiso in 1912.

Referring back to the Laeisz records, it will be found that their best outward passage was *Preussen's* 57 days from Ushant to Iquique in 1903, and that their best homeward was 57 days Iquique to Prawle by *Potosi*, also in 1903. If, however, these two splendid runs be calculated as to and from Germany instead of the Channel, it appears that *Preussen* was 74 days from Hamburg, and *Potosi* 64 days to Hamburg: in consequence, *Herzogin Cecilie's* 68 days each way is thereby enhanced.

288

facing: OUTWARD BOUND FROM KOTKA, 1931; TIMBER-LADE:

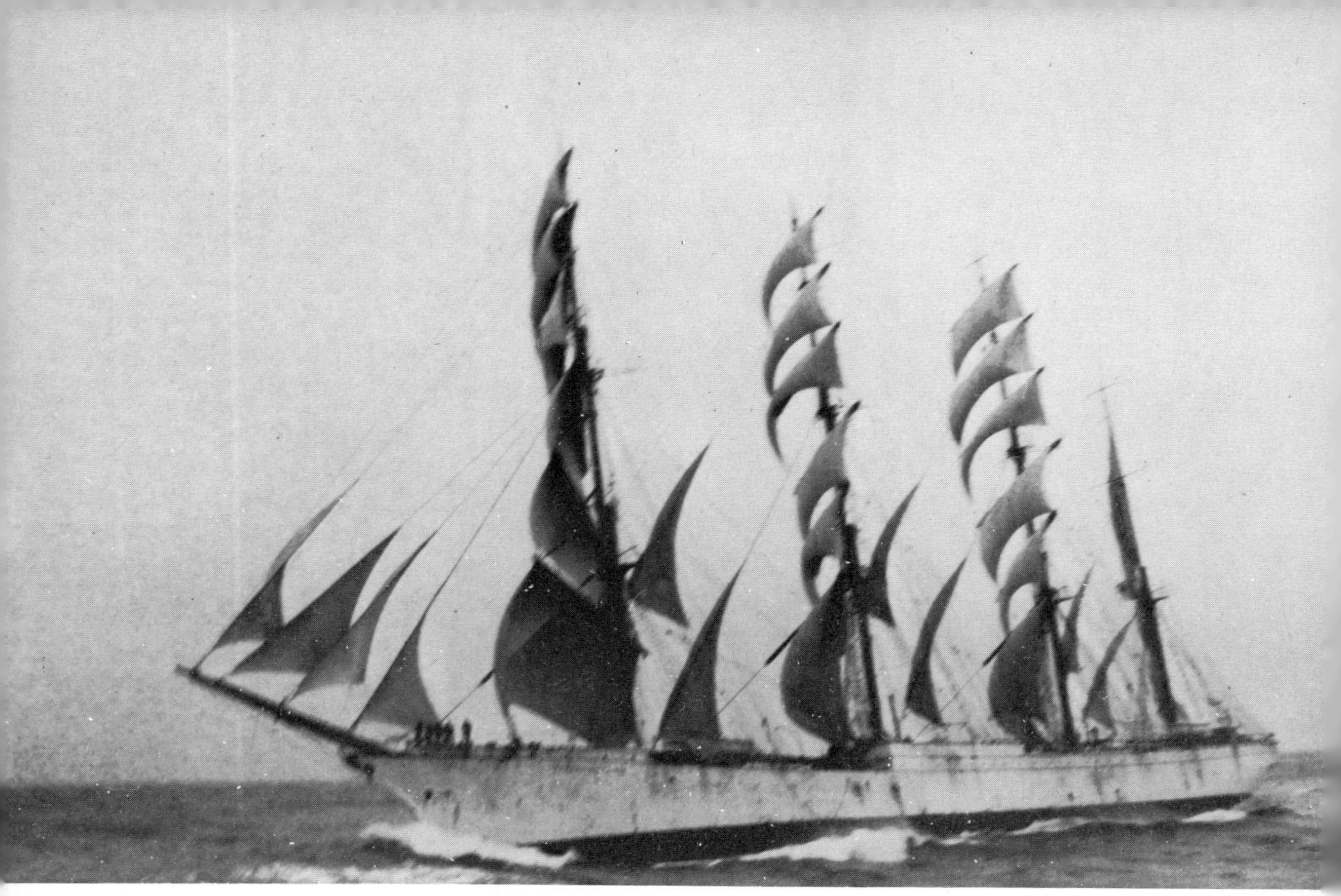

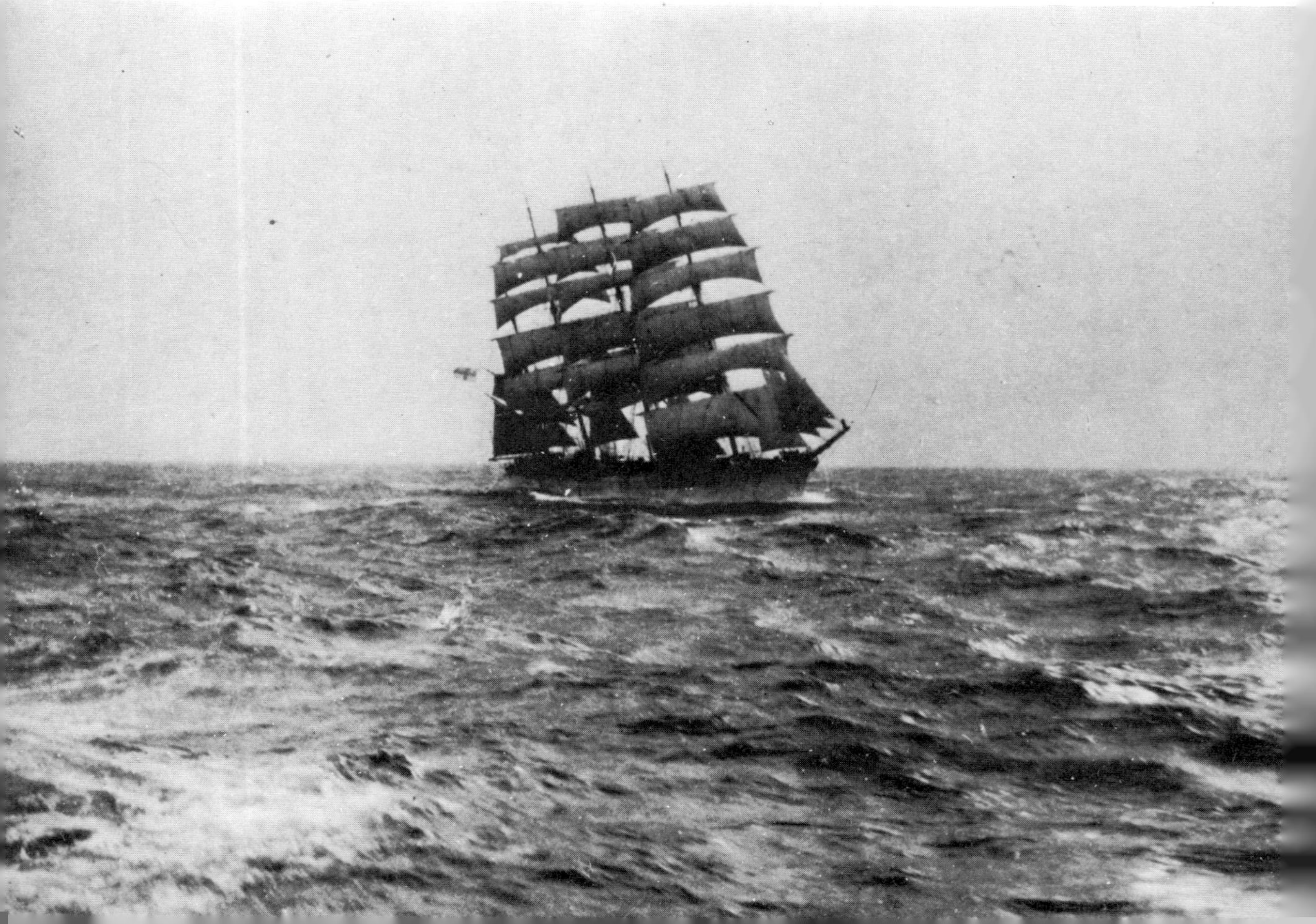

Cape Horn to the Channel under sail

To close this dissertation on the nitrate trade under sail a list is given of the record laps of the Laeisz Fleet, because such data have a bearing on the post-war Australian grain passages (to be dealt with in the Second Part of this Chapter), the homeward routes of the two trades being coincident from the Horn to England:

Cape Horn — Equator:

Potosi (five-masted barque)	18 days —	1903
Potosi	19 ,, —	1898
Potosi	19 ,, —	1909

Equator — Lizard:

Potosi	16 days —	1908
Pampa (full-rigged ship)	17 ,, —	1898
Potosi	18 ,, —	1896
Pangani (four-masted barque)	18 ,, —	1910

It would seem that the huge, five-masted barque had it all her own way on the lap northward from the Horn, but that in the more temperate last section of the homeward passage she was on an equality with smaller vessels.

On the outward run from the Lizard to the Equator, the record for which is 15 days by *Placilla*, *Pisagua* and *Pampa*, neither *Preussen* nor *Potosi* appear among the record makers. On every other stage of the complete round voyage *Preussen* and *Potosi*, between them, carry off practically all the laurels, showing that the bigger and stronger the windjammer the greater the advantage she holds in regions of heavy weather, always providing that she is neither unwieldy nor over-sparred.

This deduction was very apparent in the case of *Herzogin Cecilie*, for she was at her splendid best under conditions of almost gale force, when her ability to carry canvas stood her in good stead. She was never a 'ghoster' of light breezes, for some vessels to whom she could show a clean pair of heels in 50°S., were her equal under milder circumstances.

4,410 miles in 23 days

In reminiscence about a voyage which he made aboard *Herzogin Cecilie* between 1910 and 1911 (Hamburg — Honolulu — Sydney — Dunkirk) Captain A. Schroder stated, in *Sea Breezes*, that during a passage of 25 days from Honolulu to Sydney the barque logged 4,410 nautical miles in 23 consecutive days. *Inman's Nautical Tables* give the direct distance between the two ports as 4,380 nautical miles, and show that a steamer, running at a steady 12 knots, could accomplish the

acing: Top. OFF THE HORN UNDER ROYALS, 1933 (FROM 'OLIVEBANK')

Bottom. A CAPE HORN WINDJAMMER, 1933 (FROM 'OLIVEBANK')

passage in 15 days 5 hours. Many tramp steamers, with a 'steady twelve' well outside their utmost capacity, would be satisfied to equal *Herzogin Cecilie's* time for the run. Captain Schroder went on to say that on the way home, between Sydney and the Horn, in that vast stretch of lonely stormswept sea where two years before she had so narrowly escaped destruction when pooped, *Herzogin Cecilie* ran for many hours at the great speed of 17 knots.

Bremen to Adelaide, 79 days

Although *Herzogin Cecilie* made four homeward trips from Australia under the German flag, she only sailed out direct to Australia on one occasion before the War. This latter passage of 79 days from Bremen to Adelaide in 1907-8, was better by 4 days than the fastest of her many like passages after the War (83 days from Copenhagen to Port Lincoln in 1935). As a point of departure, however, Copenhagen entails at least one day's more sailing than does Bremen.

Geelong— Falmouth, 82 days

The best of the four homeward passages from the Antipodes was 82 days, Geelong to Falmouth, with wool, in 1907, Liverpool being reached two days later. This eclipsed by 4 days the shortest of her eleven grain passages in the Australian trade under Finnish colours — 86 days Port Lincoln to Falmouth in 1936, the last passage she made.

As the Australian trade under sail is to be covered in some detail in the Second Part of this Chapter, no comparative passages need be given at this stage.

Bremen—Astoria, 112 days

In addition to her ill-fated maiden voyage, *Herzogin Cecilie* made two visits to the West Coast of North America on behalf of the Norddeutscher Lloyd. The better passage was in 1908, when she was 112 days from Bremen to Astoria. In Mr. Lubbock's list the nearest comparative record is 100 days, Liverpool to San Francisco, by the iron ship *Archibald Fuller*, in 1871, or the 90 days, Cardiff to 'Frisco, in 1889 of the iron ship *Senator*.

Going still further back in the long history of sail two other fine passages can be found: the American wooden clippers *Young America* and *Glory of the Seas* were, respectively, 96 days in 1872, and 94 days in 1874, from Liverpool to San Francisco. Astoria (Oregon), however, is nearly 700 miles to the north of 'Frisco, and Bremen is several days' sail farther from the Atlantic than is Liverpool.

Astoria—Barry, 109 days

Two homeward passages were made by *Herzogin Cecilie* from the West Coast of North America, the first from Astoria to Barry in 1903, and, a year later, 'Frisco to London. The former was the shorter by several days, Falmouth being reached in 109 days from Astoria.

The best time for this long traverse round the Horn stands to the credit of Hogarth's *Machrihanish* an iron full-rigger of 1,758 tons which in 1892 sailed from Astoria to Queenstown in 91 days.

During *Herzogin Cecilie's* early years, when her elder sister, *Herzogin Sophie Charlotte*, was still in commission, a strong spirit of rivalry was fostered between the two windjammers, which were often engaged in like trades. In 1906-7, for instance, when *Herzogin Cecilie* sailed from Leith to Honolulu in 107 days, the other vessel made identically the same trip in 117 days.

This particular period witnessed some amazing discrepancies in the passages of sailers outward-bound to the Pacific. Weir's *Inverneill* took no less than 177 days from Leith to Honolulu, while *Medea* made the terrible passage of 223 days from Christiannsand to 'Frisco.

The two Norddeutscher Lloyd training-barques made it their practice, whenever possible, to leave port without the assistance of tugs. With their big, well-schooled, cadet personnel keeping station at the braces, the handling of their top-hamper was mechanical in its precision.

It is said that the grand sight which they presented, when beating out of such harbours as Sydney and San Francisco, aroused the admiration of all seamen, for they were manœuvred like great yachts.

Mediocre voyaging

A sailing vessel which never made a bad passage would indeed be a miracle, in fact one doubts whether such a phenomenon ever existed, although *Potosi* might be considered as the exception proving the rule.

Herzogin Cecilie was not by any means a consistent maker of fine voyages. It is pleasant to be able to stress the many excellent performances which stood to her credit, but the log of her 28 sea-going years evidences many mediocre and a few definitely bad passages.

Two of her pre-War return runs from Australia were unimpressive: Port Augusta to Falmouth took her 105 days in 1909 (this was the passage during which she was so badly pooped on the way to the Horn), while in 1912 she was 106 days from Sydney to Queenstown.

Between 1907 and 1911 she made three passages from Leith to Honolulu, the times taken being 107, 122, and 150 days respectively. A difference of 43 days on a basis of 107 shows how poor was the third passage.

On each of these occasions a visit to Australia ensued. The 25 day run from Honolulu to Sydney in 1910 has been referred to already. In 1907, however, she was 44 days between Honolulu and Geelong, a time as bad as the former was good.

Another undistinguished traverse of the Pacific was her 66 days from Astoria to Melbourne in 1908-9, for, in 1888, the iron full-rigger *British Ambassador* ran from 'Frisco to Newcastle, New South Wales, in 39 days.

A visit to the Far East

Although the official and almost ambassadorial status of a school-ship assured for her a ready welcome at all ports of call, none the less *Herzogin Cecilie* was a tramp in that, apart from her nitrate-carrying, she had no fixed itinerary, but travelled all over the world to obtain cargo. Steam was firmly established, for its unquestionable supremacy was never again to be seriously challenged by sail, and the windjammer could no longer rely on any one trade for regular freights.

These joint roles both played a part in a gargantuan voyage, which commenced in June, 1905, included a circumnavigation of the globe and ended, after fourteen months, in August, 1906. No single section of the leisurely voyage can be deemed meritorious. It opened with an Atlantic crossing of 40 days, from Bremen to Philadelphia: from the Delaware *Herzogin Cecilie* went down to the Horn, and clear across the width of the Pacific to Japan, being 125 days at sea. This was the only visit she paid to the Far East, and she saw much of that fascinating quarter of the world. Leaving Kobe early in March, 1906, a few days were spent at Singapore and several weeks at Rangoon, before she turned homeward via the Cape of Good Hope, Hamburg being reached on the 108th day.

The German Masters

1914. Internment at Guayacan

During the twelve years between 1902 and 1914, three Masters commanded *Herzogin Cecilie*. Captain M. Dietrich had her until 1909, Captain O. Walter until 1914, and on the 5th May, 1914, she left Bremerhaven, to load a nitrate cargo on the West Coast, under the command of Captain D. Ballehr. She arrived at Guayacan on July 25th, after quite a fair passage of 81 days (73 from Ushant), although this was the longest of her five similar runs. Discharge was still in progress when War broke out, and she lay idle for six long years as an internee. More fortunate than many of the large quota of vessels in similar plight, *Herzogin Cecilie* was well looked after and suffered comparatively little deterioration, even the unavoidable pitting of her bottom-plating proving, in after years, to be of little consequence.

On July 14th her sister vessel, *Herzogin Sophie Charlotte*, had arrived at the adjacent nitrate port of Caleta Buena. She shared a like fate, and both vessels appeared in Lloyd's *Official List of Enemy Vessels taking shelter in Neutral Ports*, which was published in October, 1914. In February, 1917, a supplement to this list stated that 89 German vessels, of an aggregate tonnage of 318,383, were, by that time, held up in Chile.

In 1920 the last passage, under the German flag, of the two Norddeutscher Lloyd barques took place. Having loaded nitrate at Caleta Coloso, *Herzogin Cecilie* sailed from Antofagasta on October 1st. She signalled the Lizard 83 days later and, the following day, received orders at Falmouth to proceed to Ostend. *Herzogin Sophie Charlotte* made a very bad passage. Leaving Caleta Buena on September 1st, a month before *Herzogin Cecilie's* sailing, she was off the Lizard on the same day as her companion in misfortune, logging a passage of 113 days. Unlucky in her orders, she lay off Falmouth for 11 days before being instructed to discharge at Aalborg. She did not put to sea again until April, 1924, when, under Finnish colours, she bore the name of *Gjertrud*.

1920. *The Norddeutscher Lloyd barques return to Europe*

On December 26th, 1920, *Herzogin Cecilie* reached Ostend, but it was not until the following June that she was taken over by France under the Reparations Agreement. At that time many of the big European ports were congested by laid-up sailing vessels, and for a further six months *Herzogin Cecilie* lay at Ostend, idle, forlorn and unwanted.

During a November gale she broke adrift from her moorings and came into collision with the Norwegian steamer *Svinta*, which was also struck by the French barque *Mimi*. The steamer sustained serious injury. Before they could be made fast again the two barques had caused injury to another sailer, *Gluckstadt*, and to two harbour cranes and a water-tank, their own hulls being damaged in the process.

By the courtesy of the Norddeutscher Lloyd Company an account has been compiled, from their Year Books, of *Herzogin Cecilie's* internment in Chile. This data was not available in time to give it its proper place in this chapter, and it appears, therefore, in the form of an Addendum.

LATE in 1921 Captain Gustaf Erikson instructed Captain Ruben de Cloux to journey to Marseilles for the purpose of inspecting Laeisz's big barque *Passat*, then French property, which was on offer for £11,000. Passing en route through Ostend, de Cloux saw *Herzogin Cecilie*, found that, except for the aforementioned collision damage, she was in good condition, well-rigged and equipped, and that her price was less than half the figure demanded for *Passat*. He went no farther in his search for sail tonnage, and ten years were to elapse before *Passat* became part of the Erikson Fleet. In the interim, although it was said that France had refused to sell *Herzogin Cecilie* back to Germany, *Passat* reverted to her old trade, and once again flew the house-flag of Ferdinand Laeisz.

It is understood that an inquiry for the purchase of *Herzogin Cecilie* was set on foot on behalf of another Åland owner, who, fearing that the four-master would prove too costly to run, bought *Mozart* instead.

Mozart, a British-built steel barquentine of 1,987 tons gross, launched in 1904, was for many years to be the only barquentine in the grain trade. She was scrapped in 1935. Because of her rig she was undoubtedly an economical and handy vessel to operate, but, although her purchase price was little different from that of *Herzogin Cecilie*, her carrying-capacity was far smaller, and, in practice, the latter vessel proved to be the more profitable investment.

Captain Erikson paid £4,250 for *Herzogin Cecilie*, and took her over on December 10th, 1921. Her full inventory was still on board, but, as explained in Chapters II and III (Book Two), several alterations were made, some ornamentation being removed and the half-deck cadet-accommodation dismantled.

In January, 1922, she was towed from Ostend to Christiannsand. By the end of April she had been refitted, dry-docked, provisioned and manned, and had completed loading a full cargo of timber at Fredrikstadt, whence, on April 28th under the command of Captain de Cloux, she cleared for Melbourne.

During her fifteen years of continuous employment for Erikson, *Herzogin Cecilie* made the following passages:

Synopsis of post-War trading

In ballast:
   Seven times from Europe to Australia
   Twice from Africa to Australia
   Once each from Australia to West Coast of South America
                  Europe to West Coast of South America
                  West Coast of South America to Australia

With cargo:
   Eleven wheat cargoes from Australia to Europe
   Three timber cargoes from Europe to Australia
   Two timber cargoes from Europe to Africa
   Three nitrate cargoes from West Coast of South America to Europe
   One coke cargo from England to West Coast of South America
   One wheat cargo from Australia to West Coast of South America

In all that long period she only went home five times, the first occasion on which she visited Mariehamn being in 1928, seven years after she set the Finnish flag at her gaff. Those seven years give a good indication of her success as a freighter. Perhaps a spice of luck was added to good chartering, but the fact remains that she, carrying her cargo without serious casualty, was able to secure sufficient employment to keep her in constant commission.

Although only twice in her whole lifetime did *Herzogin Cecilie* visit London (July 1904 and June 1933), she was often in English waters. While she was Finnish property, she went three times to the Mersey, twice to Belfast, twice to the Bristol Channel, and made a dozen calls at Falmouth, besides one at Queenstown, for orders.

Herzogin Cecilie's post-War entry into the nitrate trade made poor showing by comparison with her excellent Chilean passages of earlier days. Three cargoes were brought home, two to Ostend and one to Dunkirk. The passages (to order ports) were 95, 100, and 105 days respectively and, in view of the fact that her best German passage (right to a port of discharge) was 68 days, and the worst 81, no one of the trio of Finnish passages can be considered even passable.

Chile again

It is more than likely that the deterioration was due to a lack of 'driving'. Captain de Cloux was a fine seamen, but with only a small crew to handle her, and under compulsion to avoid loss of gear, the big barque was handicapped for a hard trade like nitrate. As a crack cadet-barque, in keen rivalry with the Laeisz flyers and with her own sister-

AN ABRID
of the movements of the
HERZOGIN
Trading for Captain Gustaf Erikson of
Compiled, by the Author, from copies of the barque's log-books
Owner's office, from the Records at Lloyd's,

| Year | Sailed | | Cargo | Arrived (F.O. = for orders) | |
	Date	Port		Date	Port
1921	In port at Ostend, as the property of the French Government				
1922	Jan. 25	Ostend	Ballast	Feb. 2	Christiannsand
	Mar. 10	Christiannsand	Ballast	Mar. 17	Fredrikstadt
	Apr. 28	Fredrikstadt (Captain Ruben de Cloux)	Timber		
				Aug. 1	Melbourne
	Sept. 16	Melbourne	Ballast		
	Oct. 24	Taltal	Ballast	Oct. 20 Oct. 25	Taltal, f.o. Mejillones
1923	Nov. 15 ('22)	Mejillones	Nitrate		
				Feb. 17	Falmouth, f.o.
	Feb. 24	Falmouth	Nitrate	Feb. 27	Ostend
	Mar. 26	Ostend	Ballast	Mar. 30	Grangemouth
	May 12	Grangemouth	Coke		
				Aug. 22	San Antonio

ED LOG

Finnish four-masted barque

CECILIE

Mariehamn, Åland, between 1921 and 1936

made by Mr. W. L. Leclercq, from particulars supplied by the
and from other sources of information.

Intermediate Reports and Notes

aken over by Captain Gustaf Erikson on December 10th

tow

tow

ay	5	Passed Butt of Lewis
ay	23	Picked up NE. Trades in 23° 40′ N.—20° 51′ W.
ne	5	Crossed 'Line' in 24° 48′ W.
ly	29	Passed Cape Nelson
ly	30	Passed Cape Otway and entered Bass Strait
ct.	6	Made 309 miles
ct.	11	Made 326 miles (2,120 miles sailed in the 7 days Oct. 5 to Oct. 11)

ec.	12 ('22)	Passed Cape Horn under full sail, wind SSW, force 3
a.	22	Crossed 'Line'
b.	11	Passed Fayal

tow

tow

ay	23	Passed Lizard
ne	9	Passed Cape Verde
ne	21	Crossed 'Line'
g.	2	50° S.—65° W.
g.	5	Passed Cape Horn (full sail. Wind W.)
g.	10	55° S.—79°W.

| Year | Sailed | | Cargo | Arrived (F.O. = for orders) | |
	Date	Port		Date	Port
1923	Sept. 12	San Antonio	Ballast	Sept. 18	Caleta Buena
	Oct. 4	Caleta Buena	Nitrate		
				Jan. 11 ('24)	Falmouth, f.o.
1924	Jan. 17	Falmouth	Nitrate	Jan. 22	Ostend
	Mar. 19	Ostend (Captain F. Grönlund)	Ballast		
				July 9	Taltal, f.o.
	July 12	Taltal	Ballast	July 16	Mejillones
	Aug. 13	Mejillones	Nitrate		
				Nov. 29	Dunkirk
1925	Jan. 5	Dunkirk (Captain Ruben de Cloux)	Ballast		
				Apr. 16	Albany, f.o.
	Apr. 18	Albany	Ballast	Apr. 25	Port Lincoln
	June 1	Port Lincoln	Grain	July 22	Callao
	Sept. 9	Callao	Ballast	Nov. 11	Port Lincoln
1926	Feb. 1	Port Lincoln	Grain		
				June 20	Falmouth, f.o.
	June 23	Falmouth	Grain	July 4	Hamburg

Intermediate Reports and Notes

v.	2	In 56° S.—72°W.
v.	3	Passed Cape Horn under full sail
c.	6	Crossed 'Line'
ı.	3	Called Fayal
ı.	10	Off Lizard

tow

ır.	20	Passed Beachy Head
ır.	21	Crossed 'Line'
ıe	6	54° S.—64° W.
ıe	7	Passed Staten Island
ıe	22	54° S.—81° W.

t.	13	Passed Cape Horn
t.	24	Crossed 'Line'
v.	25	Off Lizard
v.	27	Anchored in the Downs

.	6	Passed Dungeness
.	9	Passed Start Point
.	13	Wind S. by W., force 10-11 (under lower-topsails only)
ı.	14	Crossed 'Line'
r.	8	Made 300 miles
r.	11	Made 313 miles

.	1	Passed Cape Horn
y	7	Crossed 'Line'

| Year | Sailed | | Cargo | Arrived (F.O. = for orders) | |
	Date	Port		Date	Port
1926	Sept. 4	Hamburg	Ballast		
				Dec. 10	Port Lincoln
1927	Jan. 24	Port Lincoln	Grain		
				May 2	Queenstown, f.c
	May 4	Queenstown	Grain		
				May 16	Hamburg
	June 16	Hamburg	Ballast		
				June 30	Sundsvall Sld. Sundsvall 21/ Arrd. Gefle 21/
	Aug. 12	Gefle	Timber		
				Nov. 16	Melbourne
	Dec. 15	Melbourne	Ballast	Dec. 19	Port Lincoln
1928	Jan. 19	Port Lincoln	Grain		
				Apr. 24	Falmouth, f.o.
	Apr. 24	Falmouth	Grain	Apr. 27	Cardiff
	June 2	Cardiff	Ballast		
				June 13	Mariehamn

Intermediate Reports and Notes

ept. 11	Anchored in the Downs
ept. 13	Passed Dover
ept. 18	Passed Lizard
ov. 9	(39° S.—14° W.) Made 311 miles
ov. 24 to ec. 8	3,834 miles sailed in 14 days—279, 295, 253, 225, 230, 299, 296, 283, 299, 310, 267, 283, 249, 266. From 44° S.—57°E. to 36° S.—136° E., the barque averaged 12·2 knots for 5 consecutive days
Iar. 9	Passed Cape Horn
pr. 1	Crossed 'Line'
Iay 1	Off Bull Point
Iay 8	Passed Cap d'Antifer (fog)
Iay 9	Abeam Dungeness
ine 18	Stranded 16 miles S. of Hanstholm
ine 19	Towed off by *Svitzers*
ne 20	Arrd. Frederikshavn (in tow)
ne 23	Sailed Frederikshavn
ne 26	Anchored in the Sound
ne 28	Proceeded
ıg. 22	Anchored Frederikshavn Roads
ıg. 27	Passed N. Foreland
ıg. 29	Passed Beachy Head
pt. 8	Passed Finisterre
ct. 1	Crossed 'Line'
ec. 17	Passed Cape Otway
b. 20	Made 304 miles
b. 21	Passed Cape Horn
ar. 27	Crossed 'Line'
r. 24	Off Lizard
ne 6	Passed St. Catherine's Point
ne 11	Passed Elsinore

| Year | Sailed | | Cargo | Arrived (F.O. = for orders) | |
	Date	Port		Date	Port
1928	Aug. 31	Mariehamn	Ballast		
				Dec. 4	Port Lincoln
1929	Jan. 18	Port Lincoln	Grain		
				May 3	Falmouth, f.
	May 9	Falmouth	Grain	May 12	Liverpool
	May 28	Liverpool	Ballast	June 5	Fredrikstadt
	July 30	Fredrikstadt (Captain Sven Eriksson)	Timber		
				Nov. 20	Melbourne
	Dec. 24	Melbourne	Ballast	Dec. 28	Wallaroo
1930	Jan. 25	Wallaroo	Grain		
				May 15	Falmouth, f.
	May 23	Falmouth	Grain	May 31	Liverpool
	June 7	Liverpool	Ballast	June 26	Mariehamn

Intermediate Reports and Notes

pt.	6	Passed Copenhagen
pt.	10	Passed Ronaldsay (North Orkneys)
pt.	15	S.W gale. Lost all sails then set. Ballast shifted. Bad deck damage
pt.	20	Again under sail
ct.	20	Crossed 'Line'
ov.	10	5,422 miles sailed in 20 days—324, 300, 108, 278, 256, 225, 260, 300, 267, 327, 294, 274,
	to	173, 246, 289, 290, 261, 234, 260, 216
ov.	30	

eb.	18	Passed Cape Horn
eb.	20	Off Falklands
Iar.	29	Crossed 'Line'
Iay	1	Sighted Bishop Rock

Iay	29	Off Scillies
ne	2	Off Goodwins

ug.	6	Abeam N. Foreland (head wind)
ug.	8	Off Beachy Head (fog)
ug.	14	Passed Lizard
pt.	7	Passed Cape St. Vincent .
pt.	22	Crossed 'Line'

n.	27	Passed Cape Borda
eb.	25	Passed Cape Horn
or.	9	Crossed 'Line'
ay	15	Off Lizard

ne	11	Passed Ronaldsay
ne	21	Proceeded after anchoring in the Sound
ne	21	Passed Elsinore

| Year | Sailed | | Cargo | Arrived (F.O. = for orders) | |
	Date	Port		Date	Port
1930	Sept. 9	Mariehamn	Ballast		
				Dec. 13	Port Lincoln
1931	Jan. 23	Wallaroo	Grain		
				Apr. 26	Falmouth, f.o.
	April 28	Falmouth	Grain	May 1	Barry
	May 21	Barry	Ballast		
				June 6	Mariehamn
	June 28	Mariehamn	Ballast	June 30	Trangsund
	July 9	Trangsund	Part cargo of timber	July 10	Kotka
	July 30	Kotka	Timber		
				Nov. 2	Lourenco Marq
	Nov. 19	Lourenco Marques	Part cargo of timber	Nov. 23	Beira
	Dec. 12	Beira	Ballast	Jan. 17 ('32)	Port Lincoln,

Intermediate Reports and Notes

pt. 15   Docked at Copenhagen
pt. 20   Sailed Copenhagen and passed Skaw
pt. 24   Passed Ronaldsay. N.E. gale, force 9–10
ct. 1   Made 326 miles (Wind NE., force 6–7)
ct. 29   Crossed 'Line'
ɔv. 21   Made 336 miles
ɔv. 27   65 miles made in 4 hrs. Average 16·3 knots, log showing 17¾ knots for 2 consecutive hrs.
              Wind NW., force 8–9
ɛc. 5   365 miles in 23½ hrs. Average over 15 knots. Full sail. Wind NW., force 6–7

1. 27   Passed Neptune Island
ar. 4   Passed Cape Horn
ar. 31   Crossed 'Line'
ɔr. 16   Passed Azores
ɔr. 24   Made 299 miles. Wind NW., force 6 (under full sail)
r. 25   Passed Lizard

ay 30   Passed Dover
ɪe 2   Passed Skaw at 5.0 p.m. and Laeso Trindel at 6.15 p.m.; sailing at over 20 knots, log reading
              19¾ knots
ɪe 3   Passed Falsterbo at 6.0 a.m.

g. 7   Docked Copenhagen
g. 14   Sailed Copenhagen
g. 15   Passed Skaw

ɔunded in leaving port — refloated unassisted

| Year | Sailed | | Cargo | Arrived (F.O. = for orders) | |
	Date	Port		Date	Port
1932	Jan. 20	Port Lincoln	Ballast		
				Jan. 25	Port Augusta
	Feb. 9	Port Augusta	Grain		
				May 26	Falmouth, f.o
	May 27	Falmouth	Grain	June 2	Liverpool
	June 14	Liverpool	Ballast	June 28	Mariehamn
	Sept. 6	Mariehamn	Ballast		
				Dec. 16	Port Adelaide
1933	Jan. 25	Port Adelaide	Grain	May 20	Falmouth, f.o
	May 25	Falmouth	Grain		
				May 29	London
	June 28	London	Ballast		
				July 14	Mariehamn
	July 20	Mariehamn	Ballast	July 23	Kotka
	Aug. 9	Kotka	Part cargo timber	Aug. 10	Uuras
	Aug. 17	Uuras	Timber		
				Dec. 5	Lourenco Marques
	Dec. 30	Lourenco Marques	Part cargo timber	Jan. 8 ('34)	Beira

Intermediate Reports and Notes

n. 22   Arrived Port Pirie
n. 24   Left Port Pirie (in tow)

ar. 18   Passed Cape Horn
or. 22   Crossed 'Line'
ay 18   Off Flores
ay 25   Off Lizard

ne 26   Passed Copenhagen

ot. 10   Put into Visby to land the body of a boy
ot. 18   Arrived Copenhagen
ot. 23   Sailed Copenhagen

uch Ice encountered in 56° S.

ıy 26   Passed Prawle
ıy 27   Passed Beachy Head
ıy 29   Passed Dover

y   5   Passed Skaw
y   8   Passed Elsinore

ʒ. 27   Arrived Copenhagen
ʒ. 30   Sailed Copenhagen
t. 29   In 37° N.—23° W. off Azores
.   9   In 22° N.—22° W. off Cape Verde

| Year | Sailed | | Cargo | Arrived (F.O. = for orders) | |
	Date	Port		Date	Port
1934	Jan. 16	Beira	Ballast	Mar. 1	Port Lincoln, f
	Mar. 3	Port Lincoln	Ballast	Mar. 4	Wallaroo
	Apr. 4	Wallaroo	Grain		
				Aug. 3	Falmouth, f.o.
	Aug. 3	Falmouth	Grain	Aug. 9	Belfast
	Sept. 7	Belfast	Ballast		
				Dec. 7	Port Lincoln
1935	Jan. 22	Port Lincoln	Grain		
				May 18	Falmouth, f.o.
	May 24	Falmouth	Grain	June 1	Belfast
	July 10	Belfast	Ballast	July 29	Nystad
	Sept. 30	Nystad	Ballast		
				Jan. 5 ('36)	Port Lincoln
1936	Jan. 28	Port Lincoln	Grain	Apr. 23	Falmouth, f.o
	Apr. 24	Falmouth	Grain		

1939

Intermediate Reports and Notes

May 14	Heavy gale. Lost lifeboat and several sails
May 16	Passed Cape Horn

Sept. 9	Sailed Belfast Lough and passed Skulmartin Light
Nov. 11	} 1,127 miles sailed in 4 days
Nov. 14	
Nov. 24	} 1,880 miles sailed in 7 days (341 miles made on Nov. 27)
Nov. 30	

May 2	Spoken by Swedish barque *Abraham Rydberg* 33° 21′ N.—39° 4′ W.
May 17	Lost 19 sails, off Lizard. Wind force 8–10
May 26	Passed Lizard
June 12	At Belfast. 2 men killed by donkey-boiler explosion

July 19	Passed Elsinore
Oct. 7	In Copenhagen Roads
Oct. 15	Sailed Copenhagen
Oct. 18	In collision, off Anholt, with German steam trawler *Rastede*

Mar. 24	Spoken in 5° 30′ N.—29° W.
Mar. 25	At 3.0 a.m. Went ashore at Sewer Mill Cove, near Bolt Head, Devon
June 19	Refloated, towed to Starehole Cove, Salcombe, and beached
July 17	Vessel's back broken by heavy weather. Salvage abandoned
Oct. 24	Wreck sold as scrap

Masts collapsed, hull capsized and broke up

vessel, she was driven, probably to the limit of her capacity, in order to produce those splendid passages which resulted.

The couple of outward passages from Europe to Chile after 1921 were equally undistinguished.

Below 50° S. in 1923

In 1923 she was 103 days from Grangemouth to San Antonio with a cargo of coke, but on this trip she had one excellent period of sailing. From 50°S. in the Atlantic, on August 2nd, she ran west-about round the Horn, reaching 55°S. in the Pacific by August 10th, having rounded Cape Horn under full sail. The American wooden clippers of the fifties, beating westward past the Horn in their rush to the gold-fields of California, reckoned seven days to be about the best possible time from 50°S. to 50°S., and that anything up to ten days was very satisfactory, the months of June, July and August being the most propitious for a quick traverse.

In January, 1924, *Herzogin Cecilie* sailed out again to Chile, this time in ballast from Ostend, and arrived at Taltal 113 days out. Captain de Cloux was taking a well-earned holiday, and his Mate, F. Grönlund, was Master for this lengthy passage, on which she was 34 days to the Line, 47 from the Line to Staten Island, and a further 32 to Taltal.

De Cloux rejoined her again at Dunkirk at the end of the year, upon the completion of her last and worst homeward passage in the nitrate trade, 109 days from Mejillones. She had taken 32 days to the Horn, 41 from the Horn to the Line, and thence 32 to the Lizard.

Melbourne— Taltal, 35 days, in 1922

A trio of journeys between Australia and the West Coast of South America completed *Herzogin Cecilie's* acquaintance with the 'Flaming Coast'. They were:

1922.	Melbourne—Taltal, in ballast	35 days
1925.	Port Lincoln—Callao, with wheat	52 „
1925.	Callao—Port Lincoln, in ballast	64 „

In 1896 the iron, four-masted full-rigger *Wendur*, of 2,046 tons, sailed from Newcastle, New South Wales, to Valparaiso in 29½ days. In the same year the famous, four-masted, iron barque *Loch Torridon*, 2,081 tons, accomplished this traverse in a fraction over 30 days. David Bruce's 1,500 ton clipper, *Duntrune*, built by A. Stephen & Sons in 1887, sailed in that year from Port Augusta to Valparaiso in 31 days. The total distance covered by *Duntrune* was 6,920 miles, an average of 223½ miles per day for the passage. Mr. Lubbock gives these as record passages. Taltal being several hundred miles to the north of Valparaiso, and

Melbourne well south of Newcastle, *Herzogin Cecilie's* passage of 35 days in 1922 was certainly very good indeed, although she was in ballast, whereas the other two vessels were, presumably, deep-laden with coal.

Comparatively few like passages have been made under sail during the closing era of the deepwater square-rigger, but a few can be quoted to emphasize the merits of *Herzogin Cecilie's* run:

1922.	*Grace Harwar*	Newcastle—Tocopilla,	37 days
1926.	*Mozart* (barquentine)	Peru—Port Lincoln,	110 ,,
1930.	*Ponape*	Port Lincoln—Callao,	50 ,,
1930.	*Viking*	Geelong—Callao,	64 ,,
1931.	*Winterhude*	Port Lincoln—Callao,	71 ,,
1931.	*Winterhude*	Callao—Sydney,	83 ,,

It was during that same passage in 1922 that *Herzogin Cecilie* accomplished what de Cloux always held to be her best performance while under his command. On leaving Melbourne the weather was so unfavourable that, failing to enter Bass Strait, de Cloux ran the barque south-about round Tasmania, a great contrast to the direct, easterly courses of *Wendur* and *Loch Torridon* from Newcastle. Not until the 14th day at sea did *Herzogin Cecilie* leave Campbell Island astern, but from that point she was only 21 days to Taltal. During the latter period she ran 2,120 nautical miles in the seven days (noon to noon) between October 5th and 11th, her log showing consistent stretches of 14-knot sailing. On the second of these seven days she ran 309 miles, and on the last day 326 miles.

2,120 miles in 7 days

According to *Inman's Tables*, a vessel steaming at a steady 12 knots would take 7 days 8 hours to cover 2,120 nautical miles.

This episode was mentioned in Part One of this Chapter; if reference is made to the table of Clipper versus Laeisz performances given therein a number of outstanding seven-day periods of sailing will be found, the greatest being 2,323 by the *Sovereign of the Seas* and 2,276 by the *James Baines*, while the best Laeisz week was *Preussen's* 2,085 in 1903. *Herzogin Cecilie's* 2,120 can, therefore, take a rightful place among the finest bouts of sustained sailing in the annals of windjamming.

Owing to its importance in this story of the passing of square-rig, I propose to leave the Australian grain trade until last in the recital of *Herzogin Cecilie's* employments. Before dealing with her post-War casualties there are, however, a few other classes of passage to be mentioned.

Herzogin Cecilie's two timber cargoes to South African ports did not produce anything remarkable in the way of sailing. In 1931, having loaded at Finnish ports, she was 81 days from Copenhagen to Lourenco Marques, and in 1933 she took 98 days over a like passage. These, however, were summer trips, both commencing in August, and the weather, delightful enough to passengers pleasure-cruising in northern waters, was of little use to the fully-laden windjammer. During the 1931 passage, for instance, her best day's sailing was only 216 miles; in 1933 it took her over a month to reach the Azores, and a further 11 days to Cape Verde.

Incidentally, for anyone wishful to travel in sail without undergoing its more rigorous aspects, the South African trip is ideal; but timber cargoes are becoming more and more rare, and the opportunity may not recur.

Herzogin Cecilie earned three other freights by the carriage of Scandinavian timber, on each occasion transporting a cargo to Melbourne. While one of these passages was quite good, the other two, each of which marked the first voyage of a new Master, were rather protracted.

On April 28th, 1922, under Ruben de Cloux, she left Fredrikstad on her initial passage for Gustaf Erikson. She went north-about round Scotland, and, 93 days out, sighted Cape Nelson. On the following day she passed Cape Otway, arriving at Melbourne on the 96th day after leaving Sweden.

In July, 1929, when, by coincidence, *Herzogin Cecilie* was again at Fredrikstadt, Captain Sven Eriksson took over the command from de Cloux, to whom for a year he had acted as Mate. Although in later days under his command she was to make her finest post-War passage in the Australian trade, Eriksson's regime had an inauspicious start, for *Herzogin Cecilie* took 114 days from Fredrikstadt to Melbourne; August weather in the North Sea and the Channel delayed her over two weeks, for she met with head-winds off the North Foreland and encountered fog near Beachy Head.

Between these two mediocre outward runs, however, there was a better passage, in 1927, of 87 days from Frederikshavn to Melbourne. On this occasion the barque had loaded her timber in the Baltic, at Gefle. After anchoring for a time at Frederikshavn, she took a week to reach Beachy Head and then made a good run of 80 days to Melbourne.

Among the records of clipper days there are ample comparisons with this particular passage, but they are reserved for the discussion of the outward, ballast passages of the grain fleet.

At intervals throughout her life *Herzogin Cecilie* made some extremely good round-the-land passages. In July, 1903, she ran from Cardiff to Bremen in just over 4 days, although in the same month of 1910 she took 10 days for an identical trip; such is the luck of the weather to a windjammer. In May, 1913, she reached Cuxhaven on the 6th day after receiving orders at Queenstown, and in June, 1928, was only 11 days from Cardiff to Mariehamn, in ballast. On this latter passage she had the extraordinary time of under 3 days from Elsinore to Mariehamn.

Good coast-wise sailing

In 1929, having discharged at Liverpool, she set off for Fredrikstadt to load timber. This was Captain de Cloux's last passage in *Herzogin Cecilie*, and as a farewell she gave him of her best. The day after leaving Liverpool she passed the Scillies; four days later she sighted the Goodwin, and from there ran up the North Sea to Fredrikstadt in 3 days.

The most remarkable of all these coastwise journeys, however, took place in 1931. *Herzogin Cecilie* left Barry, in ballast, on May 21st, made slow progress up Channel, and was off Dover on the 30th. Exactly a week later she berthed in Mariehamn harbour. This final lap challenged, very closely, the record set up in 1927 by the little iron barque *Oaklands*, which ran from Gravesend to Viborg, pilot to pilot, in 5 days 21 hours.

'Herzogin Cecilie' exceeds 20 knots

During that week *Herzogin Cecilie* accomplished a bout of sailing at a speed greater than any other ascertainable in her whole history. Earlier in this Chapter it was mentioned that the greatest sea-speed ever claimed by a sailing vessel was the 21 knots of *James Baines* in 1856. Early on the morning of Tuesday, June 2nd, 1931, *Herzogin Cecilie* encountered fog in the North Sea, but by 8.30 a.m. wind had freshened and she stood up toward the Skaw at about 10½ knots, speed increasing in the afternoon to 13 knots. A gale warning, picked up by wireless, gave intimation of the approach of strong winds from a westerly quarter. A great horn of flat, dune-fringed land pointing to the north-east forms the northern extremity of Denmark. It is known as Skagen, or the Skaw, and round its tip must pass all sea-traffic using the Kattegat and Copenhagen Sound. A short distance ENE. from the point, and marking the outer edge of the Skaw Reef Shoal, is moored the Skagens Rev Lightship, to the seaward of which runs the main channel for vessels turning the corner. Precisely at 5 p.m. *Herzogin Cecilie* passed this position, and at 6.15 p.m. she was directly abeam another prominent mark, the Laesö Trindel Lightship. On the chart, the distance between these two lights is 26 nautical miles, the Laesö bearing approximately S.35°E. from the Skagens Rev. To cover 26 miles in 75 minutes necessitates a speed, over the ground, of 20¾ knots, or 34 feet per second.

The above data were provided by Mr. A. S. Herring, who was aboard at the time, and who, during this episode, took the magnificent photograph reproduced herewith. He described that first great hour and a quarter, and much of the night which followed, as being the most thrilling period of all the nine passages which he had made in square-rig. Much of his windjamming experience was obtained aboard *Herzogin Cecilie*.

I understand that the patent-log registered a maximum speed, through the water, of 19¾ knots, and that the greatest angle to which the flying barque lay over was recorded as a list to port of 32°.

The sea was moderate, and obviously *Herzogin Cecilie* had no adverse current with which to contend in her magnificent rush southward through the Kattegat.

From the Laesö Trindel to Anholt Knob Light is 46 miles, and the direct course alters to about S.16°E. On this lap, although sailing somewhat closer into the wind, *Herzogin Cecilie* averaged 17 knots for the distance. Later, as she approached Cape Kullen, where the coasts of Sweden and Denmark converge, the advisability of anchoring under the lee of the eastern shore of Kullen was under consideration, for it was near to dusk. To continue meant navigating the narrow and congested waters of Copenhagen Sound by night, a hazardous and nerve-racking job with the wind-force as it then was. All too often these homeward-bound windjammers spend several days in the negotiation of the 164 miles of land-locked sea which lie between the Skaw and Falsterbo Lighthouse: the latter stands at the extreme south-west of Sweden, and marks the eastward turning-point for vessels entering the Baltic. Captain Sven Eriksson, however, decided to carry on, and, sending up

314

facing: SAILING AT 20 KNOTS; OFF THE SKAW, JUNE 2ND, 193

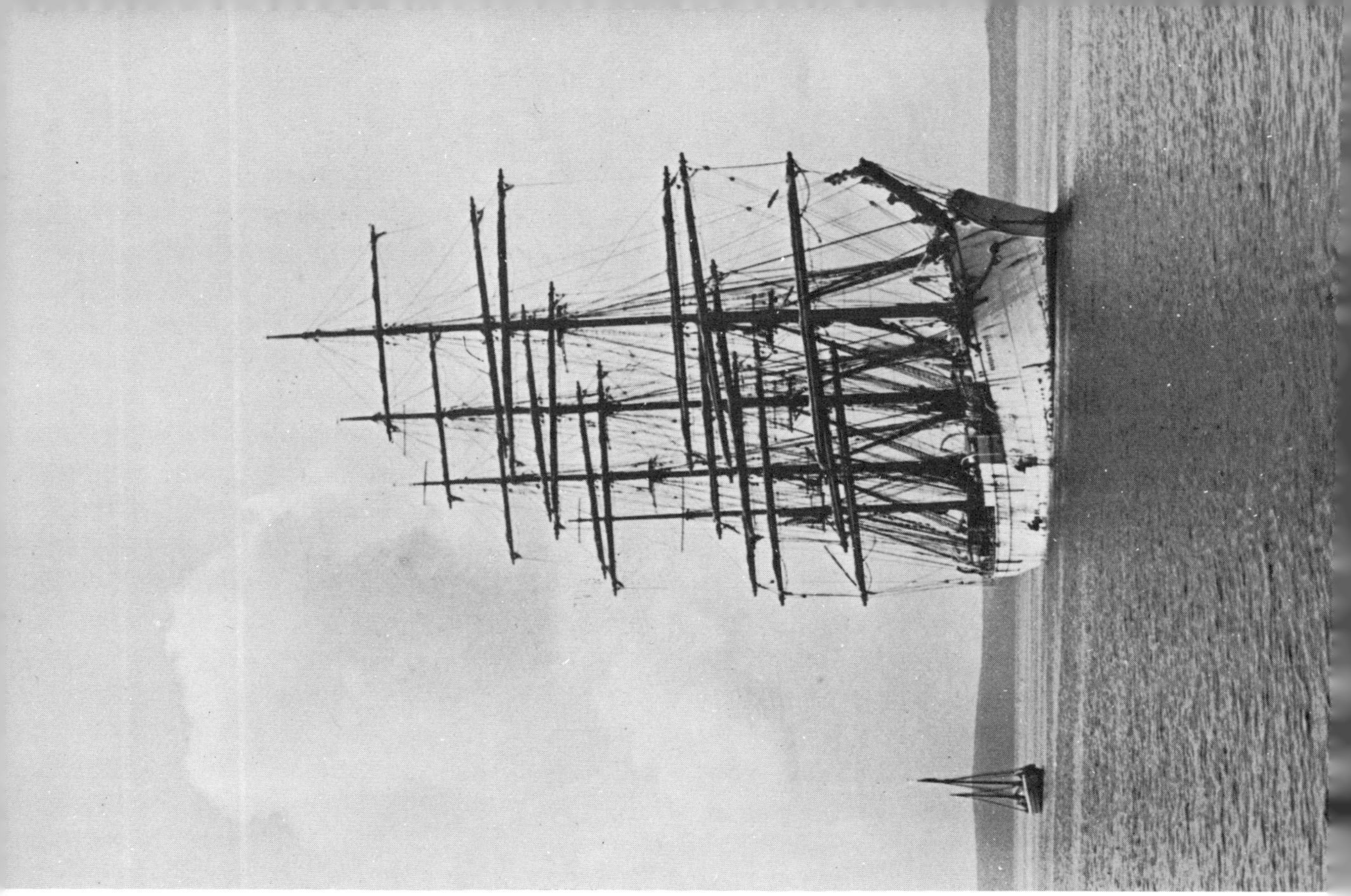

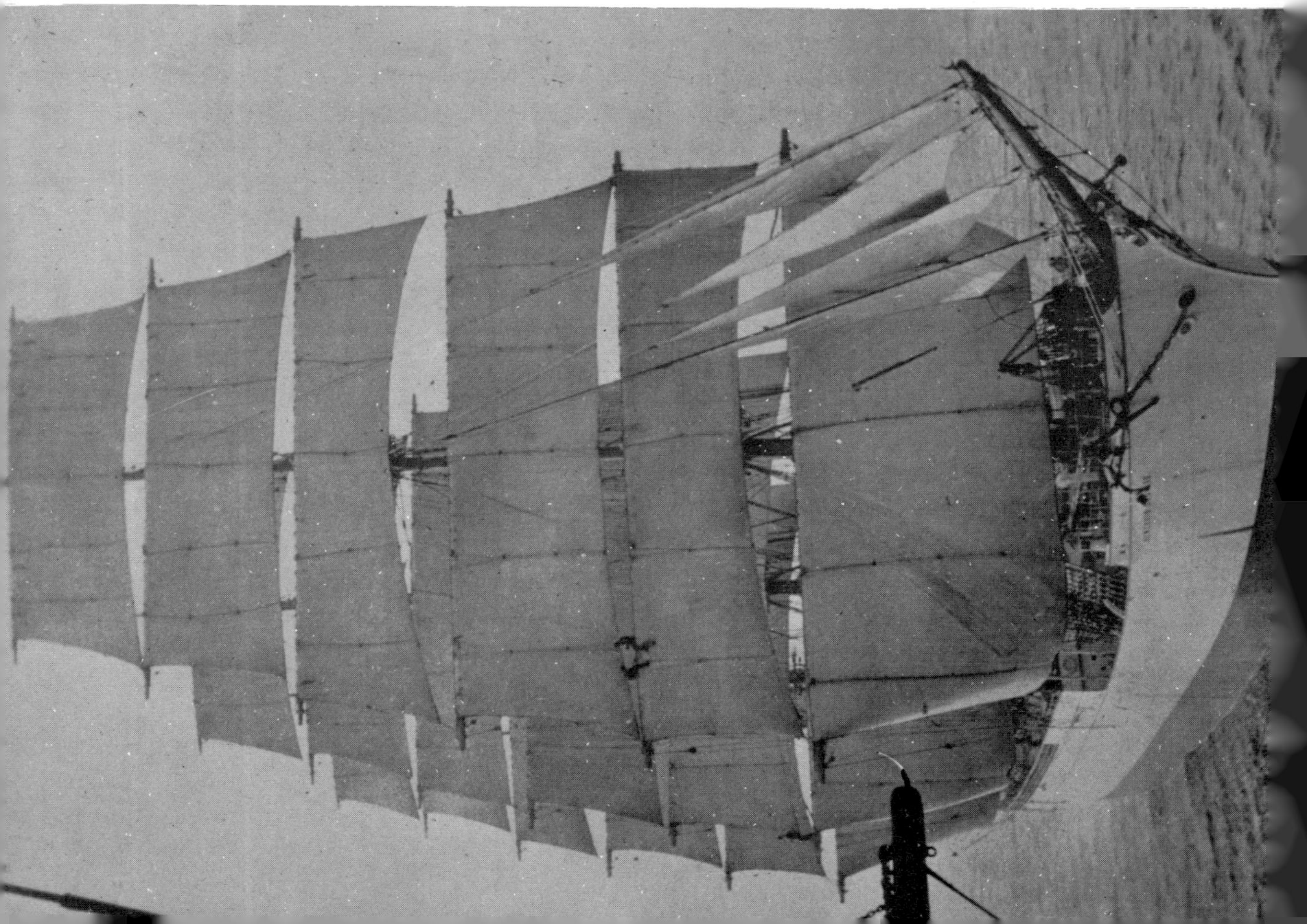

blue flares as a warning to steamers in the vicinity, he drove his vessel into the ever-narrowing approach to Elsinore, where a ferry connects the Danish island of Zealand with Helsingborg, on the Swedish coast, a couple of miles away. Not a soul on board turned in that night: normal watches were abandoned and all hands stood by, unable to do other than watch the great white barque tear madly southward, wondering, no doubt, whether her lighter canvas would withstand the strain of such driving. She fled through the Sound, past Hven Island, overtaking steamers, bound in the same direction, as though they were anchored. Owing to the shelter of the Danish coastline, the sea was comparatively smooth, and the wind, blanketed by the proximity of land, was somewhat less violent. Copenhagen was passed just after dawn, and at 6 a.m. on June 3rd *Herzogin Cecilie* rounded Falsterbo. She had taken just 13 hours from the Skaw, at a mean speed of 12·6 knots, on courses which brought her closer up to the wind the farther south she went.

Although, at the time, *Herzogin Cecilie* was in ballast trim, she was foul below the water-line, for it was nine months since she had last been dry-docked, at Copenhagen. She docked there again in the following August (1931), when, having spent three weeks refitting at Mariehamn, she was outward-bound from Kotka, with timber.

Between those two dockings she had not only made her finest recorded speed but also, as already recounted, the best day's sailing traceable to her account — 365 miles in 23½ hours. Given the requisite amount of wind and sea-room, *Herzogin Cecilie* would always respond to every extra sail set upon her, and, to use a motoring term, her best touring speed, with a strong, steady wind one point or so abaft the beam, was an easy 15 knots.

In addition to the performances mentioned, the following were some of her best efforts while under the command of de Cloux and Eriksson (details of the respective passages can be obtained from the log pages):

Other days and periods of good progression

Outstanding day runs:

27/11/'34	341 nautical miles		9/11/'26	311 nautical miles
19/11/'28	327 ,,		3/12/'26	310 ,,
10/11/'28	324 ,,		6/10/'22	309 ,,
11/ 3/'25	313 ,,			

Periods of fine sailing, representing a mean speed of between 11–12 knots

11/11/'34–14/11/'34	1,127 nautical miles in	4 days; average	282 miles per day
24/11/'34–30/11/'34	1,880 ,, ,,	7 ,, ,,	269 ,, ,,
24/11/'26– 8/12/'26	3,834 ,, ,,	14 ,, ,,	274 ,, ,,
10/11/'28–30/11/'28	5,422 ,, ,,	20 ,, ,,	271 ,, ,,

acing: Right. THE 'FLYING ANGEL' (MISSIONS TO SEAMEN) PAYS A CALL; FALMOUTH, 1930

Left. YARDARM TO YARDARM. FROM THE MAIN-YARD OF 'ARCHIBALD RUSSELL', 1928

It is rather remarkable that all these four sustained bursts of speed took place in the month of November, and in approximately the same locality. On each occasion *Herzogin Cecilie* was running her Easting down, toward the close of an outward passage to Australia in ballast.

In 1875, when bound for Melbourne, the British, iron full-rigger *Melbourne* (1,865 tons register) sailed 5,100 miles in 17 days, an average of 300 miles per day. She, also, was making her Easting under gale conditions: the best day of the 17 showed 374 miles, the equivalent of a steady $15\frac{1}{2}$ knots throughout a 24-hour day.

'Herzogin Cecilie' versus 'Beatrice', 1927

An interesting contest took place, in December 1927, between *Herzogin Cecilie* and the beautiful Swedish, four-masted, iron barque *Beatrice*, built in 1881 as the *Routenburn* by Robert Steele of Greenock. Since 1922 *Beatrice* had been owned by the same concern as *C. B. Pedersen*, and had served the like purpose of a commercial training-vessel for Swedish cadets.

Herzogin Cecilie had brought a cargo of timber out to Melbourne: *Beatrice*, after carrying guano from Assumption Island to New Zealand, had crossed to Melbourne in ballast. Both vessels were then chartered to load wheat at Port Lincoln. On Thursday, December 15th, *Herzogin Cecilie* cleared from the port and was towed down the Yarra River into Port Phillip Bay and toward the open sea. She passed *Beatrice*, at anchor in Hobson's Bay at the mouth of the Yarra, and then dropped her pilot off Melbourne Heads at 10 p.m. *Beatrice* left her anchorage at 9 a.m. on the Friday, and, after passing Queenscliff, found the Finnish barque still in the offing, the night having been almost windless.

During the morning both vessels got under way in a light breeze, which continued throughout that day. By nightfall on Friday *Herzogin Cecilie* was some seven miles ahead, to windward of the Swede, but, once round Cape Otway, the rival barques picked up a good wind which prevailed until evening. Although the wind on the following day was fresh and fair, it was not strong enough for *Herzogin Cecilie* to show her true worth, whereas the smaller Swedish barque, always a good performer in moderate weather, was in her element. She passed the big Finn, which in the morning had been some hours ahead, at 3 p.m. on the Sunday, and then a great tussle took place, for, in a squally wind and high sea, both vessels drove onward at a great pace.

From midnight on Saturday to midnight on Sunday *Beatrice* logged

312 nautical miles; *Herzogin Cecilie* kept abeam of her throughout the evening, and, at one period, made 61 miles in four hours.

As they approached Kangaroo Island *Beatrice* stood farther out to sea than her competitor, and *Herzogin Cecilie* led her into Spencer Gulf, anchoring at Port Lincoln seventeen minutes before the Swede.

Herzogin Cecilie had taken 81 hours from Melbourne as against *Beatrice's* 70 hours from Port Phillip, but there was little to choose between the respective periods under-way. *Beatrice* had come straight out of dry-dock at Melbourne, whereas the Finnish barque had been many months at sea since her last docking, at Hamburg in the previous June. *Beatrice* was commanded by Captain Harald Bruce, who for many years had been her Mate: *Herzogin Cecilie* was under Captain de Cloux.

De Cloux twice drove *Herzogin Cecilie* from Fayal, in the Azores, to England in the excellent time of a week. It so happened that these two successive cargoes of nitrate arrived within twelve months, for she passed Fayal, homeward-bound, on February 11th, 1923, entering Falmouth on the 17th, and was again off Fayal on January 3rd, 1924, this time making the Lizard on the 11th. No doubt winter North Atlantic weather was responsible for these fine runs on the part of a heavily-laden vessel.

The Lizard in 7 days from Fayal, and 26 from the Line

The first of these two passages also produced a 27-day run from the Line to Falmouth. In 1931 Captain Eriksson bettered this by one day (to the Lizard). Although I have already stated that the German record was 16 days for that section of the homeward passage (by *Potosi* in 1908), it is apposite to note that, for the ten consecutive passages of each vessel between 1901 and 1907, *Preussen* and *Potosi* averaged 26 and 28 days, respectively, from the Line to the Lizard.

During the fifteen years of trading for Gustaf Erikson *Herzogin Cecilie's* name appeared six times on the Marine Casualty Board in what has been called 'The Chamber of Horrors' at Lloyd's.

Casualties and fatalities

The first five of those years passed without incident, but on June 18th, 1927, two days after leaving Hamburg, in ballast, for Sundsvall, she stranded on the west coast of Denmark, 16 miles to the south of Hansholm Light. On the following day she was refloated by the aid of a Svitzer salvage-vessel, which towed her to Frederikshavn Roads. She was detained there for three days while her bottom-plating underwent examination by a diver, who pronounced it to be uninjured.

Shortly afterwards, having loaded a timber cargo in Sweden, *Herzogin Cecilie* left for Australia. On this passage one of her crew lost his life. While at work aloft, he unshackled a heavy block without, first, taking the precaution of securing it to the yard. As the shackle was released, the block slipped and caused him to overbalance: in falling he struck his head on the side of the hull, dropped into the water and was never seen again. Five years later there was a similar but even more tragic fatality. On September 8th, 1932, two days after leaving Mariehamn for Australia, a young Swede, who was undertaking his first voyage in sail, fell from the main-yard on to the poop, at a point just forward of the donkey-house. He was killed instantly, the accident, unfortunately, being witnessed by his Mother, who was on board as a passenger to Copenhagen. At the time *Herzogin Cecilie* was in the vicinity of the large Baltic island of Gothland: she put into Visby, the principal town, to land the body.

The luck with which *Herzogin Cecilie* had for so long been blessed seemed to desert her during the last three years of her life. Weather damage, explosion, collision and stranding followed each other in quick succession, although, admittedly, none of these happenings, except, of course, the final stranding, interfered with her trading activities.

The second 'paragraph' at Lloyd's was in August, 1934, when Captain Sven Eriksson reported from Falmouth that, in a heavy gale two days before rounding Cape Horn, he had lost several sails and one lifeboat. It had been a trying passage for the old barque, and was her second longest in the grain trade. She had taken 43 days to reach the Horn from Spencer Gulf, and, in all, was 121 days at sea. Unusually protracted Doldrum calms and, later, a succession of head-winds, were followed by unseasonably severe weather at the entrance to the Channel.

The next homeward journey from Australia resulted in an even greater loss of canvas. This time the damage occurred between the Scillies and Lizard Point, the day before she arrived at Falmouth. Nineteen sails were destroyed in, to employ the Beaufort notation, a strong gale, which, although it was the middle of May, was accompanied by blinding snow-squalls. At one time *Herzogin Cecilie* was forced to heave-to, and for thirty hours in all she battled with big seas. Other particulars of this casualty were given in Chapter IV (Book Two).

The explosion at Belfast in 1935

For the best part of a week *Herzogin Cecilie* lay at Falmouth before receiving orders to proceed to Belfast, where a most extraordinary and fatal accident took place. Discharge had been proceeding for some days by means of a steam-derrick, power being supplied by the barque's donkey-engine. Suddenly, shortly after 4 o'clock on Wednesday, June 12th, 1935, the donkey-boiler exploded with a terrific roar. The casing shot upward like a projectile from some immense gun, tore its way through the steel roof of the house and crashed into the yards of the mainmast. It ascended over 150 feet into the air, and then, describing an arc, dropped on to the roof of a shed on the adjoining quay. The heavy roofing was shattered like matchwood and the metal cylinder landed on some bags of wheat inside the shed. Portions of the wrecked donkey-house were found, later, two hundred yards from *Herzogin Cecilie*, and debris was deposited over a wide area. The main topsail and topgallant yards were buckled and twisted in a most extraordinary fashion, for, afterwards, these four, heavy, steel tubes looked like great crumpled straws. The explosion was heard half a mile away, and the force generated was so great that the steel plating of the forward end of the poop-deck was transformed into a triangular arch, on one side of which hung the two feed-tanks and, on the other, the remains of the riven house.

All the dock labourers who were working on board at the time escaped unhurt, except James Croughan, who, while running for shelter, was struck by splinters and gashed about the head and legs. Boris Lendholm, the Second Mate, was hit in the body by the flying wreckage but was not severely hurt. The cook, Karl Laine, also received injuries. Two of the crew, however, lost their lives in this tragic affair, Oiva Mustonen, aged 21, and Bror Hellstrom, aged 22, both of Helsingfors. It is uncertain whether both men were in the donkey-house at the time of the explosion, for, although one of them was afterwards found on the deck, the other had, apparently, been blown down a companion-way. They were shockingly injured: Mustonen succumbed before the ambulance reached the Mater Infirmorum Hospital, and Hellstrom died soon afterwards.

The cook had been busy in the galley all that afternoon, preparing food for a party which was to have been held aboard in the evening in honour of the Master's birthday. This celebration was, of course, cancelled.

Had work been in progress at the large No. 2 hatch in the well-deck, the loss of life would, undoubtedly, have been far greater, but, at the time, these hatch-coverings had not been disturbed.

Herzogin Cecilie sailed from Belfast four weeks later. She looked a strange sight, for her erstwhile symmetrical sail-plan was shorn of much of its beauty and power. On the mainmast nothing was set above the topsails, no replacement having been made of the main-topgallant and royal yards. Instead of, as usual, visiting Mariehamn, the barque went direct to Nystad, where repairs were undertaken at Captain Erikson's shipyard, her full classification being renewed upon their completion.

The 'Rastede' collision

The year 1935 was indeed unlucky for *Herzogin Cecilie*, her Master and her Owner, as, on October 19th, she was, for the third time in twelve months, 'on the board' at Lloyd's. She had sailed from Copenhagen three days before, but was still within the confines of the Kattegat. On the night of the 18th she ran down the German steam-trawler *Rastede* of Wesermunde, which was fishing to the north of Anholt Island. The trawler received stern damage, and was towed into Elsinore harbour by the motor-vessel *British Pluck*. The damage to the barque was repaired, months later, at Port Lincoln.

As a sequel to a claim for damages instituted by the owners of the trawler, *Herzogin Cecilie* was arrested, by order of the Admiralty Marshal, when she arrived at Falmouth on April 24th, 1936, at the conclusion of her final voyage. She was released, however, within a short while, discussion of the claim being deferred until a later date.

On April 25th *Herzogin Cecilie* made her last appearance in the 'Chamber of Horrors', for, early that morning, the first of a long series of telegrams concerning her went up 'on the board'. It announced that she was badly ashore near Salcombe, a stranding which was to develop into total loss. The recital of the events of those fateful months, however, will have a chapter to itself.

'Herzogin Cecilie' on her beam ends, 1928

Although officially unrecorded elsewhere than in her log-book, *Herzogin Cecilie* underwent an experience in 1928 which, but for the iron nerve and seamanship of Captain de Cloux and the endurance of those who worked under his leadership, might have caused her to be posted as 'Missing'. Leaving Mariehamn at the beginning of September *Herzogin Cecilie* made an auspicious start to the passage by logging a speed of 15 knots on the first day out. Shortly after sailing from Copenhagen, de Cloux gave an exhibition of the wonderful control which he could exercise over the big barque. In the Kattegat she overhauled *Archibald Russell*, also outward-bound for Australia. It was a day of calm sea and light, following breeze, and de Cloux sailed so closely past

facing: Top.   THE WRECKED DONKEY-HOUSE   }   AFTER THE EXPLOSION A
Bottom. HAVOC ALOFT   }   BELFAST, 1935

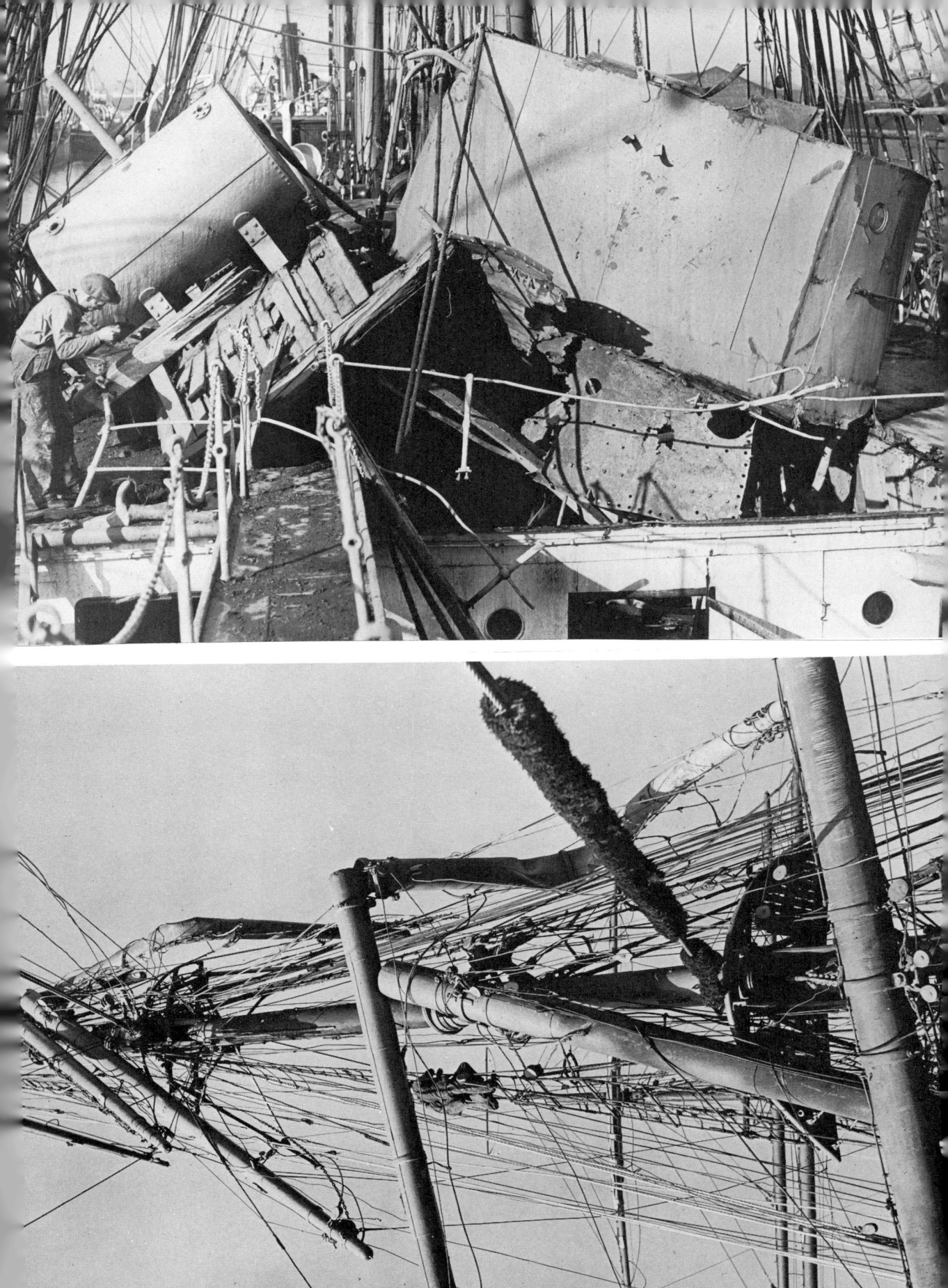

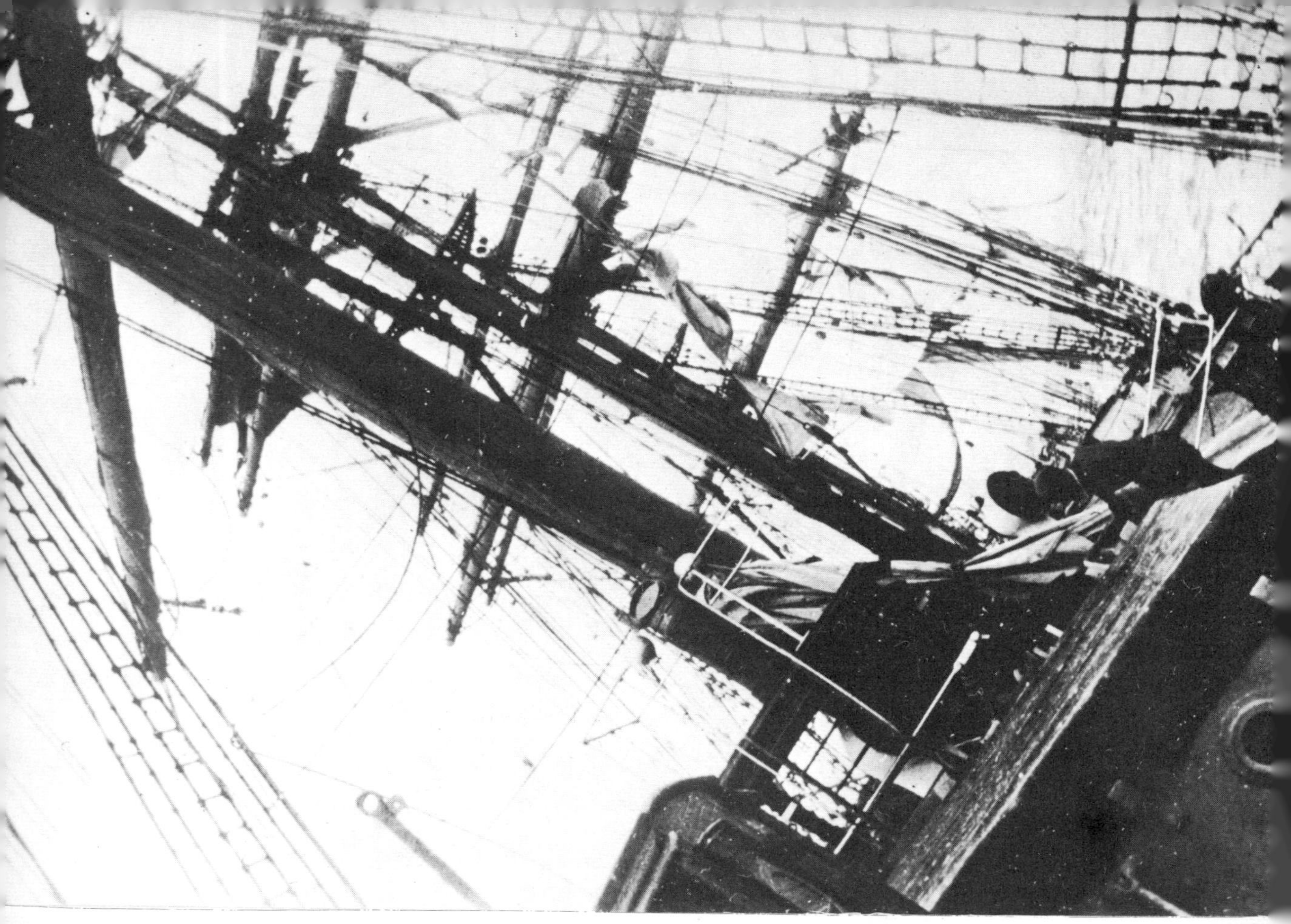

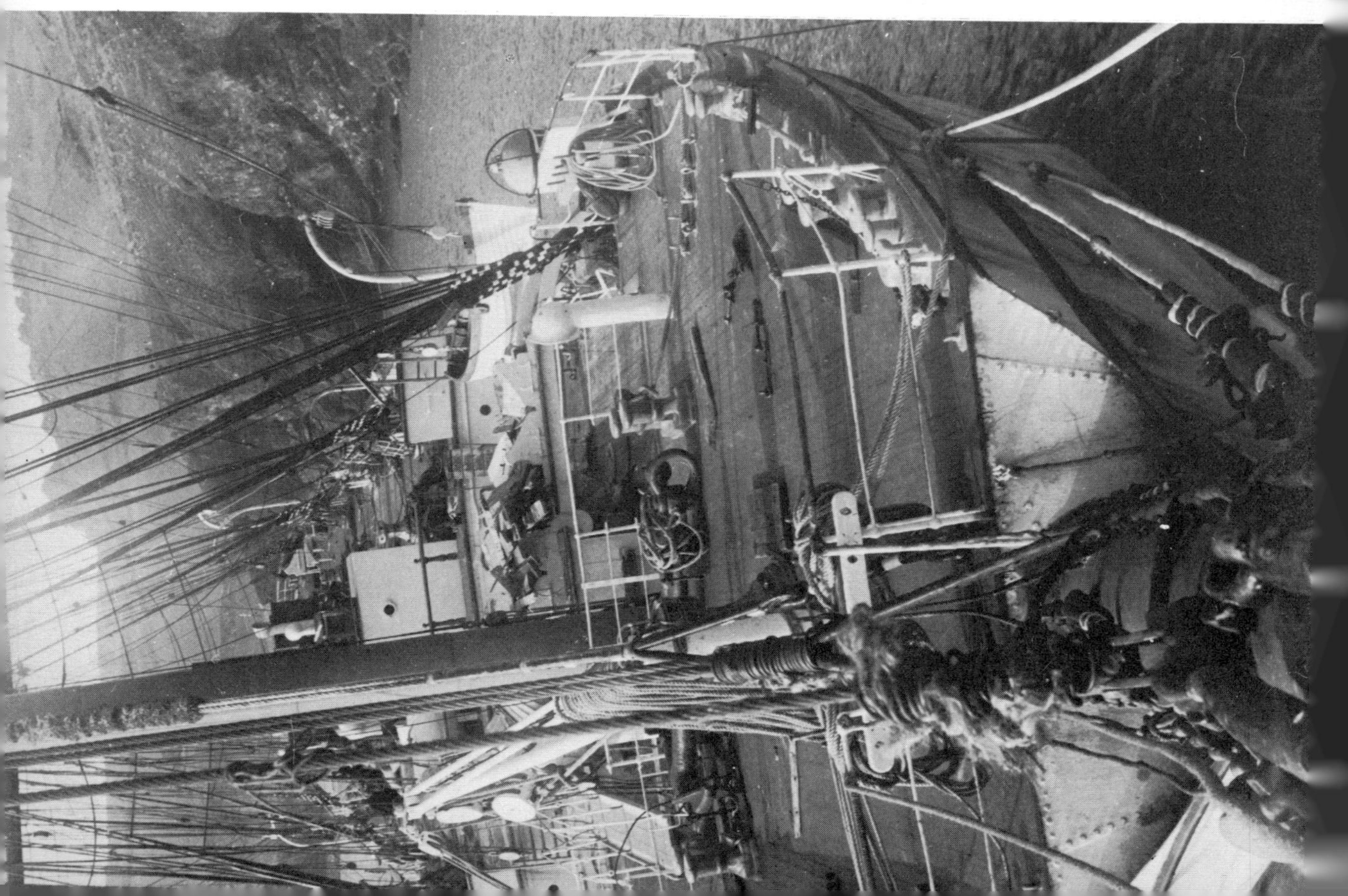

the other Erikson barque that only the matter of a dozen feet separated the respective yard-arms. As photographs afterwards demonstrated, the two vessels were in close proximity for some minutes, and de Cloux, from his own yard-arm, threw a newspaper on to the deck of *Archibald Russell*. Since each vessel had her yards squared, the clearance between two hulls was something like 20 yards. (See photograph, page 315.)

A few days later, however, the fine autumn weather gave place to strong and unfavourable winds, forcing *Herzogin Cecilie* to abandon any idea of entering the Atlantic via the English Channel. Instead, she ran northward, and on September 10th, was off Ronaldsay, in the Orkneys. Four days later she met with a series of fierce gales, and, on September 15th, at the height of a particularly violent south-westerly squall, her 800 tons of solid ballast shifted without any previous warning, rolling her right down to starboard until she lay over to an angle of 70° on her beam-ends. This was more than double the maximum angle to which she would ever heel during the most severe conditions of sailing. The lee coamings of her hatchways were now under several feet of water, and wave-crests were slapping her topgallant yard-arms. All her boats were smashed or swept overboard, the davits being badly twisted, and the top-gallant rail on the lee side was almost demolished.

The degree to which a fully-laden windjammer can lie over, without capsizing, is almost unbelievable. In January 1915, *Inverclyde*, bound home from Seattle round the Horn, was being hove-to on the port tack during a veritable hurricane, when she listed over and her whole cargo shifted. The canvas blew out, and all hands were set to retrim the grain from starboard to port. At one period her *lower-topsail yard-arms* and some feet of her main hatch were under water. It took two days to get her upright, and a further day before she was under sail and again manageable.

So with *Herzogin Cecilie*, which, luckily, had been running under shortened canvas. Such sails as were set blew bodily out of their bolt-ropes: all the sheets were let run, and the loose canvas soon thrashed itself to ribbons. This relief from further leverage aloft, plus the presence of 600 tons of water-ballast, saved her from turning turtle. At times the seas were making a clean sweep over the decks, and, in consequence, it was impossible to open up the main hatches. Through the small lazarette hatch, at the after end of the 'tween-decks, all hands gained access to the lower holds. Fortunately there happened to be a good supply of planking on board, which was intended to serve for renewing the worn parts of the poop-deck. These planks were set fore and aft across the stanchions which supported the deck above, and a series of terraces were formed, up which the ballast could be shovelled, stage by stage. Master, Mates, cook and crew alike toiled as madmen for their lives in the hot darkness of that steel prison. After many hours of grim endeavour, however, some of the planks snapped under the weight of sand, and the striken barque lurched back again to starboard, losing what buoyancy she had regained. Once again the wooden steps were built up, and almost without food, rest or sleep, the crew laboured on, never knowing whether, at any minute, another squall might send their vessel right over, drowning them like rats in a trap. Far from abating, the gale seemed to increase in violence, and, at times, the working of the barque sent little avalanches of ballast cascading down to leeward. Plank barricades, however, were formed as the trimming progressed, and, bit by bit, *Herzogin Cecilie* rose toward the perpendicular.

It is said that, for some time subsequent to the accident, the Mates were compelled to eat their hurried and occasional meals on the *starboard wall* of their mess; while the easiest way to get from one end of the barque to the other was along the *outer* plating of the hull on the weather side. The strain on the standing rigging, particularly on the weather shrouds, must have been terrific, and the fact that nothing carried away speaks volumes for the strength of the top-hamper.

After over 48 hours of continuous, herculean toil, the vessel was once again on a more or less even keel, and the job of clearing the debris on deck and aloft was begun. It was found that the unchecked swinging of the yards, which were no longer controlled by the braces, had fractured or distorted the crance-irons around the masts, and, when spare parts were exhausted, wire lashings had to be improvised as substitutes.

By September 20th the barque was again under sail. There had been no worth-while salvage from the blown-out canvas, and in many cases fresh sails had to be cut and sewn before her full suit could be set. She sailed on, however, to accomplish, seven weeks later at the opposite end of the world, the 5,422 sea miles in 20 days (to which reference has already been made), and to reach Port Lincoln 90 days out from Copenhagen.

Laeisz's 66 days to Spencer Gulf, 1933   On October 31st, 1933, the two remaining Laeisz windjammers quitted Hamburg in company, outward-bound, in ballast, to Spencer

Gulf. The ensuing dual passages, of 66 days to landfall at the Gulf, represent one of the most remarkable achievements under sail since the far-off days of the passenger clippers. Admittedly, weather conditions are more advantageous, to the sailer in the Australian trade, on the outward passage than on the homeward half of the round voyage, because the former includes greater distances wherein the prospect of strong, favourable, prevailing winds may be anticipated. *Padua* and *Priwall* were also benefited by the date of their departure, summer conditions having, by then, given place to what might be called 'windjammer weather'.

In Captain Granith's narrative of a round voyage in *Pommern*, 1932-33 (see Book One, Chapter III) many references are made to the way in which the course of a sailer is affected by belts of wind and calm.

Weather conditions affecting the southward-bound sailer

Each Master of sail has his individual ideas as to the best routes, and such conceptions are guarded jealously. With typical thoroughness the Masters of the German square-riggers tabulated in full detail all such data as winds, currents, ice, etc., encountered by them, and no doubt such records contributed in great measure to the regularity exhibited by the German nitrate-carriers.

In the case of the European windjammer making for the Antipodes, the wind decides whether she shall proceed through the English Channel, or around the north of Scotland. Once clear of home waters, the usual track lies close to Madeira, and then between the Cape Verde Islands and Dakar. The Line is crossed in about 20°W., after which the vessel may be carried by the South-East Trades quite close to the coast of South America. Then follows the long southerly trek through the South Atlantic, landfall sometimes being made at lonely Tristan da Cunha. Generally the square-riggers stand well to the south of the Cape of Good Hope until they pick up the powerful and continuous Westerlies which drive them to their destination. It was for these latitudes of the 'Roaring Forties' that the phrase 'running the Easting down' was coined, and it was there that so many brilliant runs have been accomplished.

Joseph Conrad says, in *The Mirror of the Sea*, that, 'There are no north and south winds of any account upon this earth. They are but small princes in the dynasties that make peace and war upon the sea. They never assert themselves upon a vast stage. They depend upon local causes ... and in the polity of winds, as among the tribes of the earth, the real struggle lies between East and West. In the orientation of winds that rule the sea, the north and south direction are of no importance.'

Very roughly, the prevailing wind-belts affecting the Australian grain sailers are:

North Atlantic – Westerlies.
Tropics, north of the Line – NE. Trades.
Tropics, south of the Line – SE. Trades.
Great Southern Ocean – Westerlies, blowing with increasing strength the more southerly the latitude.

Between the two Trade-wind belts, and also between the SE. Trades and the Westerlies, lie regions of light, variable winds and long periods of calm. The areas of the Trades provide the most idyllic conditions of both the outward and homeward passages under sail. Trade-winds blow from tropic belts of high pressure, and are experienced between about 35° N. and 28° S. The term 'trade' is derived from the old word 'tread', meaning course or direction, and in big stretches of ocean not subject to continental interference these winds are usually dependable.

The following is a brief summary of the wonderful outward passages of *Padua* and *Priwall* in 1933, taken from details provided by Messrs. Laeisz, and published in *Lloyd's List*:

'Padua' (Captain J. Jurs)		'Priwall' (Captain R. Clauss)	
Left Hamburg	Oct. 31	Left Hamburg	Oct. 31
52° 38' N.—2° 56' E.	Nov. 3	52° N.—3° E.	Nov. 3
Passed Lizard	Nov. 4	Passed Isle of Wight	Nov. 4
43° N.—14° W.	Nov. 8		
35° 36' N.—17° 47' W.	Nov. 10	34° 27' N.—17° 26' W.	Nov. 10
21° 40' N.—24° 35' W.	Nov. 14		
1° 31' S.—26° 26' W.	Nov. 24	On the Line in 25° W.	Nov. 23
44° S.—20° E.	Dec. 15	46° S.—21° E.	Dec. 15
44° 30' S.—37° 30' E.	Dec. 18	48° 0' S.—41° 38' E.	Dec. 18
Arrived Spencer Gulf	Jan. 5	Arrived Spencer Gulf	Jan. 5
Arrived Port Broughton	Jan. 6	Arrived Port Victoria	Jan. 6

On the tenth day out *Priwall* was over a degree farther south and on slightly the more easterly of the two courses. She reached the Equator from the Isle of Wight in nineteen days, and was then a day ahead of *Padua*, which took twenty days from the Lizard to the Line.

As the most westerly longitude shown above is 26° 26' W., it would appear that, on this occasion, the SE. Trades did not drive these vessels far to the west of a more or less direct southerly course from the Equator. Both barques rounded the Cape about December 15th, *Priwall* being a little to the south of *Padua*, and still, apparently, ahead of her sister-vessel.

From this point the two competitors sailed to Spencer Gulf in twenty-one days. During those three weeks some grand sailing was achieved by the heavily-manned, modern, light-trimmed barques. Messrs. Laeisz record the following figures:

'Running the Easting down'

	Padua	*Priwall*
December 18th, 1933	287	312 sea miles
,, 19th ,,	305	311 ,,
,, 20th ,,	280	300 ,,
,, 21st ,,	312	273 ,,
,, 22nd ,,	236	245 ,,
,, 23rd ,,	202	93 ,,
,, 24th ,,	308	240 ,,
,, 25th ,,	283	342 ,,
,, 26th ,,	309	312 ,,
,, 27th ,,	250	280 ,,
,, 28th ,,	351	317 ,,
,, 29th ,,	257	277 ,,
,, 30th ,,	284	276 ,,

In thirteen days, therefore, *Padua* sailed 3,664 miles and averaged 282 miles per day, while *Priwall* ran 3,578 at an average of 275. During the last seven days of that period the two barques covered an almost equal distance, *Priwall* sailing 2,044 miles to *Padua's* 2,042; the latter, however, with 351 miles against 342, accomplished the best 'day's work'.

In his account of the 1932 outward voyage of *Pommern* to Australia, Captain Granith stated that for the final twenty-four consecutive days before his barque arrived at Port Victoria, she averaged 265 miles per day, running 6,360 miles in all during that period. The best day, from noon to noon, was 330 miles, measured by log and, therefore, excluding the prevailing easterly set of the current. *Pommern* arrived at Port Victoria on the seventy-sixth day after leaving Copenhagen, this being the eighty-second day out of Mariehamn, a very excellent performance considering that she lay for two days at Copenhagen taking in stores.

For comparison with the foregoing figures the best performances of *Herzogin Cecilie* in similar latitudes may be restated:

November/December 1926. 3,834 sea miles in 14 days. An average of 274 per day.
(On this occasion *Herzogin Cecilie* was only 19 days from the longitude of the Cape of Good Hope to Port Lincoln.)
October 1922. 2,120 sea miles in 7 days.
December 5th, 1930. 365 sea miles in 23½ hours.

Padua and *Priwall* made the entrance to Spencer Gulf in such thick weather that visibility was practically negligible. From their last Channel landfall to the Gulf they had each taken sixty-two days; on the sixty-third day they berthed at their respective loading ports in the Gulf, sixty-seven days out from Hamburg, a truly amazing coincidence in meritorious sailing.

Clipper passages to Australia

It is interesting to make an incursion into the sailings of bygone days in search of record passages for comparative purposes.

The English, composite, clipper ship *Thermopylae*, built in 1868, and of a gross tonnage of 991 tons, holds the record for the London-Melbourne run under sail. On two occasions, 1868-9 and 1870-1, this former tea-carrier took her Australian pilot aboard sixty days after she had dropped his English colleague. On December 13th, 1868, during the first of the above passages, she ran 324 nautical miles during a burst of speed which, starting on December 11th, gave her a total mileage of 3,051 in eleven days.

Cutty Sark's best passage from London to Sydney was sixty-eight days, in 1877-8.

The big, American-built, wooden, Black Ball clipper *James Baines*, signalized her debut in the Australian passenger trade, in 1854, by sailing 14,034 nautical miles from London to Melbourne in sixty-three and a half days. She carried 700 passengers (of whom only 80 were travelling first class), 1,400 tons of general cargo and 350 mail-bags containing 180,000 missives. *James Baines* subsequently returned to England in the excellent time of sixty-nine and a half days.

In the later days of the iron, medium clippers, *Ben Voirlich* equalled *James Baines* with sixty-three days London-Melbourne (pilot to pilot) in 1874-5. In 1883 another iron full-rigger, *Maulesden*, made a fine passage of 69 days from Greenock to Maryborough, Queensland: when running down the Easting, her best day was 335 miles, and the best week's run 1,929 miles.

The passenger routes, such as London to Melbourne, are perhaps not quite a kind basis on which to compare the outward, ballast journeys of the grain fleet of to-day, although the joint feat of *Padua* and *Priwall* was equal to any passage of the clipper era. Another record in Mr. Lubbock's list, however, is a more suitable introduction to the deeds of the Erikson Fleet. This was made in 1896 when the British, four-masted, iron ship *Wendur* sailed from Fredrikstadt to Melbourne in eighty-one days. In *The Last of the Windjammers* Mr. Lubbock states that, in 1907, the famous *Lancing* carried a cargo of Norwegian timber from Langesund, a port near the Skaw, to Melbourne in seventy-five days.

During her Finnish period *Herzogin Cecilie* went, in ballast, seven times from Europe to Australia to load grain, her shortest passage being 83 days from Copenhagen to Port Lincoln in 1935. This was better by four days than the fastest of her three timber-laden runs (Frederikshavn to Melbourne in 1927).

The best outward windjammer passages of recent years follow, in order of merit. In some cases they show considerable improvement on the quoted times of *Wendur* and *Lancing*, but it must be remembered that most of them were made in ballast trim:

Good and bad outward passages, 1930-6

Padua and *Priwall*	Hamburg—Spencer Gulf	67 days in	1933
C. B. Pedersen	Gothenburg—Port Germein	71 ,,	1936
Parma	Barry—Port Victoria	73 ,,	1936
Pommern	Copenhagen—Port Victoria	76 ,,	1932
Pamir	Copenhagen—Port Lincoln	77 ,,	1932
Pamir	Dublin—Port Lincoln	78 ,,	1936
L'Avenir	Helsingborg—Port Victoria	82 ,,	1932
Priwall	Hamburg—Port Victoria	83 ,,	1935
Herzogin Cecilie	Copenhagen—Port Lincoln	83 ,,	1935
Herzogin Cecilie	Copenhagen—Port Adelaide	84 ,,	1932
Viking	Copenhagen—Port Lincoln	84 ,,	1932
Pommern	Elsinore—Port Victoria	84 ,,	1936
Herzogin Cecilie	Copenhagen—Port Lincoln	85 ,,	1930
Padua	Hamburg—Port Victoria	85 ,,	1935
Archibald Russell	Skaw—Port Lincoln	85 ,,	1936
Olivebank	Copenhagen—Port Lincoln	86 ,,	1935
Pommern	Elsinore—Port Lincoln	86 ,,	1935
Killoran	Gothenburg—Port Victoria	86 ,,	1936
Lawhill	Copenhagen—Port Lincoln	86 ,,	1936
Penang	Copenhagen—Port Victoria	86 ,,	1932

This list gives sufficient evidence of the fact that most of the post-War square-riggers have, on occasion, been able to make a good showing.

Strangely enough, *C. B. Pedersen*, a barque which in the normal course of her voyaging has exhibited no pretentions to speed, comes next to the Laeisz 67 day dual passages, with which her 71 days for a more extended journey compares very favourably.

The luck of the wind is instanced by the fact that, out of the twenty-one passages given, seven took place in 1936, six in 1932, and five in 1935, whereas no unit of the 1934 outward-bound fleet makes an appearance.

In 1935 some good times were made from last landfall, *Padua* being 74 days from Beachy Head, *Pommern* 76 from Dungeness and *Priwall* 77 from Dover.

To glance at the other side of the picture: in 1935 *Abraham Rydberg* was 115 days from Gothenburg, *Killoran* 109 from Elsinore, and *Viking* 107 from the Skaw; in 1936 *Penang* was 109 days from Elsinore and *L'Avenir* 108 from Copenhagen, while, in 1932, it took *Priwall* no less than 138 days from Hamburg, four days more than the aggregate time of the two Laeisz barques in the year which followed.

The 'Grain Race' fallacy

This concludes the notes on the first half of the round voyage entailed by participation in the Australian trade, and leaves only an account of the much publicized homeward run with grain to complete the odyssey of *Herzogin Cecilie*. It was as a direct result of her successes in the latter category that she first attracted the attention, it might almost be said the affection, of that vast body of sea-minded and ship-loving people, the British general public.

Sufficient has been said already of the fallacy of describing the little annual armada of homeward-bound square-riggers as a 'Grain race', to prevent undue significance being accorded to the competitive element, which, however, does play some part in that last trade under sail.

About the time when the home-coming of these vessels had become a head-line topic in the Press, *Herzogin Cecilie* received much un-warranted adulation. It so happened that in the six years 1926-1931 she was on four occasions the first square-rigger to reach England (in the other two seasons she was the second arrival). Although in only two of the four years did her passage prove to be the fastest of its year, she was hailed in some quarters as 'the winner' of all four 'races'.

Naturally the two things do, to a degree, march together, but, apparently, no account was taken of the fact that in those four seasons she was the first, second, second, and third vessel, respectively, to leave Spencer Gulf. The same misapprehension has been commented upon and explained in respect of *Abraham Rydberg*.

In these days it is the windjammer with the best passage average which deserves the most credit, and as such *Herzogin Cecilie* reigned supreme. During the 11 consecutive years (1926-36 inclusive) in which she carried home an annual cargo of grain she made, on four occasions, the quickest run of the year to an order port in the United Kingdom. Her shortest, and last, passage of 86 days was eclipsed only once in the post-War Australian trade under sail — in 1933, when *Parma* made Falmouth 83 days out from Port Victoria.

'Herzogin Cecilie's' regularity in the grain trade

The average of *Herzogin Cecilie's* 11 passages works out to 107 days. *Archibald Russell*, the only windjammer to make a greater number of post-War grain passages than *Herzogin Cecilie*, has, to date, averaged 115 days for 12 runs. So far, *Lawhill* has participated for 11 seasons, and her mean is 120 days. *Pommern* has been one of the steadiest of the Erikson Fleet. Her 8 grain-laden journeys give her, at 107 days, the same average time as *Herzogin Cecilie's* 11 passages; *Pommern's* shortest trip to date has been 94 days, and her longest 129. Since *Pamir* came under Finnish control she has carried 5 grain cargoes in an average time of 104 days, her passage limits falling between 92 and 118 days. Strangely enough *Parma*, holder of the post-War record, had the quite mediocre average of 115 days for her quota of 5 passages.

At the other end of the scale come the barquentine *Mozart* and the little, Finnish, three-masted barque *Favell*, both now broken up. The former made 8 grain trips: the quickest was 110 days, and the average 132. *Favell's* 10 passages produced a mean 135 days, the longest being 210 days in duration; but in 1921 she ran from Melbourne to London in the excellent time of 98 days.

For much of the ensuing summary of the grain trade (and for many of the above statistics) I am indebted to Mr. A. A. Hurst, now serving as an apprentice on *Moshulu*. It is the result of much painstaking research on his part, and I believe it to be a complete and authentic record. He has based his calculations as from departure from Australian anchorage to arrival at an English orders port; failing that, to landfall, or to discharge port when reached direct without a call for orders, although the latter is now a very rare occurrence. He has made a straightforward subtraction of dates and allowed for leap years, but not for Meridian days.

A complete résumé of the grain trade from 1921, onwards

The original summary covered sixteen years, 1921-1936, but, for this new edition, three further years have been added as the outbreak of war virtually ended the Australian grain trade under sail.

THE AUSTRALIA—EUROPE GRAI

Vessel	1921	1922	1923	1924	1925	1926	1927	192
Abraham Rydberg								
Alfhild				126				
Alonso					153			
Archibald Russell	115				130		124	I
Atlantique					114			
Audny				160				
Beatrice (ex Svithiod)	115		88		103	118		I
Bellands	157	105			121			
Bellpool				113				
Carl Vinnen (auxiliary)						125		
C. B. Pedersen							154	I
Elfrieda						145		
E. R. Sterling							286	
Favell	98				125		156	2
Garthpool	130					188	121	I
G. D. Kennedy	120	109	126					
Grace Harwar	129				125		136	
Greif				110			126	
Gullmarn			131					
Hamburg					144			
Herzogin Cecilie						139	98	
Hippalos				116				
Hougomont	139						120	
Killoran	157						147	
Kobenhavn (auxiliary)				90			109	
L'Avenir			241			110		
Lawhill	114	127					120	
Lisbeth (ex Pendragon Castle)					113		120	
Lisbeth (ex Renée)					137			
Magdalene Vinnen (auxiliary)								

RADE UNDER SAIL, 1921—1939 *(See also page 338)*

929	1930	1931	1932	1933	1934	1935	1936	1937	1938	1939
			125	125	107	147	130	112	109	117
93	110	98	136	119	130	111	104	98	133	121
23	109									
07	107	117	120	108	128	137	117			
8	115	111	121	144	148					
30										
38			132	127	129	98				
4	110	93	106	115	121	116	86			
7		139								
	120	130	111	125	131	120		116	128	139
								129		
				120	137	105	107			
0	122	106	121	121	122	124	118	107	131	140
			96	96	91	99		118		

Vessel	1921	1922	1923	1924	1925	1926	1927	1928
Marlborough Hill	91		151					
Mayotte			142					
Melbourne (ex Gustav)			146		127		123	138
Milverton		90						
Moshulu								
Mozart			136		151		158	
Olivebank (ex Caledonia)				113	147		167	
Padua								
Pamelia					139			
Pamir								
Parchim					146			
Parma								
Passat								
Penang	152							155
Phyllis					165			
Pommern								
Ponape (ex Bellhouse)	102						107	121
Port Caledonia		127						
Port Stanley				134				
Priwall								
Rajore			138					
Richelieu					109			
Skaregrom					130	131		
Svarvanut	163				123			
Sylfid		199						
Toni				128				
Viking	107			119	149			
Werner Vinnen (auxiliary)			137					
Winterhude								
Woodburn	117	129						

1929	1930	1931	1932	1933	1924	1935	1936	1937	1938	1939
	125	109	Sunk							
							112	102	121	91
9	93		150	113	122	110				
7		122	108	104	115	118	108	106	135	119
					109	100				96
			103	92	118	109	98	140	104	96
			103	83	138	136	117			
				110	106	99	87	94	98	98
20	101	115	112	123	115	111	113	138	210	
22	105	105	129	98	110	95	94	94	119	117
98		99	118	121	130	120	114			
				106	108	91				
		121	122	108	137	97	116	103	117	119
			146	144	126	105	117	126	165	134

Owing to exceptional circumstances, six of the passages shown have little comparative value, and it would be unfair to class them as normal sailings. They are:

L'Avenir – 1923   After encountering heavy weather in the Indian Ocean, *L'Avenir* spent a couple of months refitting at Port Natal.

Garthpool – 1926   She put into Rio de Janeiro on May 13th, leaking and with damage to steering gear. She sailed again on·June 27th, and was 70 days from Rio to Falmouth.

E. R. Sterling – 1927   The story of this disastrous journey was related in Book One, Chapter 11.

Mozart – 1930   A ballast passage.

Penang – 1930   A ballast passage.

C. B. Pedersen – 1935   A ballast passage.

The fastest annual passage under sail

From the tabulation on pages 330-333, I have extracted a summary (on pages 336-337) of the best passage of each year, placing the auxiliary sailing vessels separately for purposes of comparison.

The vessels listed on page 338 participated in 1921, but in no other year.

The average of the fastest annual passage under sail during the sixteen years works out to 96·6 days. For the four consecutive passages which comprised her service in the trade, the auxiliary sailer *Magdalene Vinnen* averaged 95·5 days, six of the sixteen windjammer runs being equal to or less than (in one case by 8 days) her fastest trip of 91 days.

'Breaking the hundred days'

Ample proof is forthcoming of the truth of the dictum that any windjammer 'breaking the hundred' between Australia and England has made an exceptional passage. Out of the 272 passages made between 1921 and 1936 by square-riggers (including auxiliaries) only 29 were of less than 100 days. Of these, *Magdalene Vinnen* (auxiliary) and *Herzogin Cecilie* each accounted for four, *Pommern* for three, and *Archibald Russell*, *Pamir*, *Passat*, and *Ponape* for two each. Of the 68 vessels sailing home from Australia in the season of 1921 only three arrived in less than 100 days. Although for her total of 11 homeward runs *Herzogin Cecilie* averaged 107 days, this figure was raised from 104 to 107 by her first post-War grain cargo which was at sea for 139 days. For the five consecutive passages 1927-31, inclusive, she averaged exactly 100 days, the fastest of these trips being 93, and the slowest 110.

Under 90 days

Four passages of under 90 days were accomplished during the 16 years tabulated, 83 days by *Parma*, 86 days by *Herzogin Cecilie*, 87 days by *Passat* and 88 days by *Beatrice* (to London), *Passat* being unlucky in making her best passage in the same year as *Herzogin Cecilie's* 86, and so losing the contest by a day.

A few notes concerning the earlier square-riggers which appear in the list of winning passages may be of interest. *Marlborough Hill* was a fine iron, four-masted barque, a skysail-yarder, built in 1885 by W. H. Potter & Sons, at Liverpool. Her Finnish owner was R. Mattson of Mariehamn, who maintained her in splendid trim until, in 1925, she went to Italian shipbreakers.

Milverton, an iron full-rigger, was one of the fine fleet of sailers owned by John Stewart & Company of London. She was launched, in 1866, by Oswald, Mordaunt & Company at Southampton. In 1921 Stewart's sold her to B. B. Gronblom of Åbo.

Greif, a steel full-rigger built at Sunderland in 1892, had served under three flags. Originally the *Wiscombe Park*, she became in 1921 the Frenchman, *Edouard Bureau*. Two years later the Stettiner Dampfer, A.G. purchased her and gave her the German title of *Greif*.

The other vessels in the list have been referred to elsewhere in this book.

A short discursion into the realms of the feats of noted, bygone windjammers will provide some standard of values by which to judge the post-War grain passages.

Homeward clipper passages

Cutty Sark's best runs home with Australian wool were:

1883–4	82 days	Newcastle, N.S.W.—London
1884–5	80 ,,	Newcastle, N.S.W.—London
1885	72 ,,	Sydney—The Downs
1888	70 ,,	Newcastle, N.S.W.—Dungeness

Thermopylae, although never equalling 70 days, was very consistent in her homeward sailings:

1879–80	81 days	Sydney—London
1882	77 ,,	Sydney—London
1884	78 ,,	Sydney—Prawle Point
1887–8	79 ,,	Sydney—London

Over a period of about ten years *Cutty Sark* and *Thermopylae* averaged, respectively, 82 and 88 days. These ex-China extreme clippers appear definitely to have been faster than the true wool clippers of fuller section and greater strength, and they made better sailing under the more severe weather of the wool run than they had done in their earlier Eastern employment. The wool-clip for the season 1887-8,

THE WINNERS O

Year	Sailing vessel	Flag	Time	Passage
1921	*Marlborough Hill*	Finn	91	Port Lincoln—Queenstown
1922	*Milverton*	Finn	90	Melbourne—London
1923	*Beatrice*	Swede	88	Melbourne—London
1924	*Greif*	German	110	Port Lincoln—Falmouth
1925	*Beatrice*	Swede	103	Adelaide—Falmouth
1926	*L'Avenir*	Belgian	110	Geelong—Lizard
1927	*Herzogin Cecilie*	Finn	98	Port Lincoln—Queenstown
1928	*Herzogin Cecilie*	Finn	96	Port Lincoln—Falmouth
1929	*Archibald Russell*	Finn	93	Melbourne—Queenstown
1930	*Pommern*	Finn	105	Wallaroo—Falmouth
1931	*Herzogin Cecilie*	Finn	93	Wallaroo—Falmouth
1932	*Parma*	Finn	103	Port Broughton—Falmouth
	Pamir	Finn	103	Wallaroo—Queenstown
1933	*Parma*	Finn	83	Port Victoria—Falmouth
1934	*Passat*	Finn	106	Wallaroo—Lizard
1935	*Priwall*	German	91	Port Victoria—Queenstown
1936	*Herzogin Cecilie*	Finn	86	Port Lincoln—Falmouth
1937	*Passat*	Finn	94	Port Lincoln—Falmouth
	Pommern	Finn	94	Port Victoria—Falmouth
1938	*Passat*	Finn	98	Port Victoria—Falmouth
1939	*Moshulu*	Finn	91	Port Victoria—Queenstown

HE 'GRAIN RACE'

passage of any iary sailing vessels cipating	Flag	Time	Passage	Number of vessels participating
				68
				7
ner Vinnen	German	137	Adelaide—Dungeness	10
nhavn	Dane	90	Port Victoria—Bordeaux	10
				20
Vinnen	German	125	Albany—Hamburg	7
nhavn	Dane	109	Port Adelaide—Falmouth	17
				9
				14
				7
				13
dalene Vinnen	German	96	Port Victoria—London	19
dalene Vinnen	German	96	Sydney—Niton (I.O.W.)	21
dalene Vinnen	German	91	Port Victoria—Plymouth	22
dalene Vinnen	German	99	Port Lincoln—Falmouth	21
				17
odore Johnsen (Magdalene Vinnen)	German	118	Port Lincoln—Falmouth	14
				11
odore Johnsen	German	107	Port Lincoln—Queenstown	13

ADDITIONAL 1921 SAILINGS

Bellhouse — see *Ponape*
Svithiod — see *Beatrice*
Caledonia — see *Olivebank*
Alice — 138
Alcyon — 119
Amiral Cécilie — 137
Amiral Halgan — 148
Andre Theodore — 143
Bellas — 159
Bohus — 104
Bonchamp — 132
Bonneveine — 143
Bossuet — 111
Bragdo — 150
Chateau d'If — 114
Clevedon — 126
Clyde — 136
Colonel de Villebois Mareuil — 118
Cornil Bart — 137
Crillon — 133
Derwent — 115
Desaix — 202
Dieppedalle — 117
Duquesne — 132
Edmund Rostand — 120
Elginshire — 144
Eugène Schneider — 151
Falkirk — 129
Garthgarry — 128
Garthsnaid — 110
General Foy — 158
General de Negrier — 197
Geneviève Molinos — 150
Germaine — 123
Glenard — 154
Glitre — 131
Inverclyde — 177
Janna — Went missing
Kensington — 111
Kilmallie — 126
Kilmeny — 98
Manicia — 132
Mannheim — 136
Marechal de Turenne — 116
Mimosa — 142

Mount Stewart	123
Port Patrick	112
Prompt	101
St. Louis	133
Skomvaer	127
Susanne	142
Terpsichore	145
Thiers	154
Versailles	156
Vincennes	143

NOTE. – The 1921 grain sailings commenced on January 1st with the departure of the *Bellands* from Melbourne for St. Nazaire, and continued until the sailing of the *Janna* from Sydney on December 3rd. There were twenty-two sailings during April and May.

---

when both ships made such good showing, was carried to London by 29 British square-riggers, most of whom were of the beautiful medium-clipper type which will always be remembered for its association with the greatest days of that trade under sail. The average passage of the fleet worked out at 95 days, 19 vessels being under 100 days, and no less than 8 under 90 days. The longest run was 130 days.

The wool-clip of 1882 gave employment to 38 sailing vessels; the average of their passages from the ports of New South Wales and Victoria to the United Kingdom was just 100 days.

The fastest passage made home from Australia under sail stands to the credit of *Lightning*, for that ever-famous big clipper ran from Melbourne to Liverpool, pilot to pilot, in 63 days. In 1869 the iron full-rigged Britisher *Patriarch* was 68 days from Sydney to London.

Barclay Curle's *Loch Torridon* and *Loch Moidart*, built in 1881 for Messrs. Aitken and Lilburn, were considered to be the most perfect examples of four-masted barques ever constructed. The former's fine passage of 81 days from Sydney to the Lizard, the best performance of all the great fleet of 77 sail which brought home the 1891-2 wool, was remarkable in that, although she took 40 days from Sydney to the Horn, she ran from the Horn to the Line in 20 days, and to the Lizard in another 21. Her Master, Captain Pattman, believed that 41 days from the Horn to the Lizard was a record for the run; it makes interesting comparison with the figures already given for the Laeisz vessels of later date.

In a way, however, it is unfair to instance these remarkable wool passages because, not only were the vessels and their crews entirely

339

different from the massive, lightly-manned freighters of post-War days, but the wool ports of Sydney, Melbourne and Newcastle were five or six days' run nearer to the Channel than are the grain ports of Spencer Gulf; in addition to which, the Gulf has always been a notoriously difficult point of departure for sailing vessels.

'Swanhilda's' 66 days home from Spencer Gulf, 1894

For the finest passage recorded in the South Australian grain trade one must go back to 1894, when the steel four-masted barque *Swanhilda* reached Queenstown for orders on April 18th, 66 days out from Wallaroo, Spencer Gulf.

Swanhilda, British-built in 1890, was owned by the Nova Scotian firm of J. W. Carmichael & Company, and made many fine passages under her first 'Blue-nose' Master, Captain Colin Fraser. Her end was stark tragedy. On May 5th, 1910, she drove ashore on the inhospitable coast of Staten Island when outward-bound from Cardiff to the West Coast. Her young master, Captain Pine, was on his honeymoon trip. He and his bride, with half *Swanhilda's* crew, were drowned, the bodies of the young couple being found, later, awash in the surf, locked in each other's arms.

The quickest passage since the War, 'Parma's' 83 days

As the shortest grain passage since the War, *Parma's* 83 days at sea (excluding the extra Meridian day) between Port Victoria and Falmouth, in 1933, deserves some mention in this chronicle of the doings of the last of the windjammers:

Stage	Days	Average per day	Mean speed for the period
Kangaroo Island—Cape Horn	27	210	9 knots
Cape Horn—Equator	28	165	7 ,,
Equator—Falmouth	27	147	6 ,,

Parma spent some while in beating out of Spencer Gulf but passed Tasmania on the sixth day, and New Zealand on the tenth. From the Horn to the Falklands took four days, easterly weather forcing the barque to landward of the Jason Islands. The SE. Trades were poor, and five days were spent in the near vicinity of the Line. She lost the NE. Trades in 28° N., but ran from the Azores to Bishop Rock, in the Scillies, in six days. The best day's run during this passage was 263 miles on March 18th, in 52° S.

Mr. Villiers states that Captain de Cloux, who was then part-owner and Master of *Parma*, did not spend a whole night in his bunk throughout the journey, but dozed, fitfully, on a settee in the chart-room. The Mate, who had been injured by a fall at Port Victoria, was partly incapacitated, and this added much to de Cloux's burden and responsibility.

In all, *Parma* made 14,555 miles on her true course, the actual distance sailed being nearer 15,000 miles. This gave an average daily distance made of 175 miles throughout the passage. She was only 79 days at sea between her last Australian landfall, Kangaroo Island, and her first European landfall at the Scillies.

Sixty-six days is an almost incredibly short passage from Spencer Gulf, and will always redound to the credit of *Swanhilda* as one of the most remarkable efforts in long-distance sailing ever achieved: but it certainly makes even *Herzogin Cecilie's* figures look very mediocre. Sufficient has, however, been said about the doings of the Finnish barque, when in competition with her contemporaries, to render to her the modest laurels which she so well deserves. It may be remembered that her best homeward run from Australia under the German flag was 82 days, from Geelong to Falmouth with wool in 1907, and that her only pre-War cargo from Spencer Gulf was 105 days en route between Port Augusta and Falmouth in 1909 (the occasion when she was pooped so destructively).

The following is a list of her eleven Antipodean grain runs for Captain Gustaf Erikson:

The 11 grain passages of 'Herzogin Cecilie', 1926—1936

1926	Port Lincoln—Falmouth	139 days	Captain R. de Cloux
1927	Port Lincoln—Queenstown	98 ,,	,,
1928	Port Lincoln—Falmouth	96 ,,	,,
1929	Port Lincoln—Falmouth	104 ,,	,,
1930	Wallaroo—Falmouth	110 ,,	Captain S. Eriksson
1931	Wallaroo—Falmouth	93 ,,	,,
1932	Port Augusta—Falmouth	106 ,,	,,
1933	Port Adelaide—Falmouth	115 ,,	,,
1934	Wallaroo—Falmouth	121 ,,	,,
1935	Port Lincoln—Falmouth	116 ,,	,,
1936	Port Lincoln—Falmouth	86 ,,	,,

Although Captain de Cloux averaged 109 days for four passages as against Captain Eriksson's 107 for seven, his figures were completely spoilt by *Herzogin Cecilie's* first grain run of 139 days in 1926. It was a year of protracted passages, for *Garthpool* took 188 days (including a distress call at Rio), *Elfrieda* 145 days from Port Germein to Queenstown, and *Skaregrom* 131 from Geelong to the Lizard.

1926. 139 days at sea

Only seven windjammers secured grain freights for that season. *Herzogin Cecilie* was the first to leave, on February 3rd. Five of the others sailed before March was out, but *L'Avenir*, never a maker of fast passages (her best grain run up to the present being 105 days), did not get away from Geelong until May 4th, and she, with 110 days to the Lizard, won the undistinguished 'race' of 1926.

Captain de Cloux found that *Herzogin Cecilie's* cargo had been loaded badly, in that, instead of her usual trim of an extra foot by the stern, his vessel was down slightly by the head. Added to this drawback was the fact that, owing to labour trouble in Australia, he set out with a crew of only nineteen all told. These reasons induced him to start home by the slower and easier route of Good Hope instead of the Horn. Ten days were spent, in the Bight, in an abortive endeavour to weather the Leeuwin against heavy westerly gales, until, at last, de Cloux went about and ran eastward for the Horn. Five days later *Herzogin Cecilie* was back again, abreast of Kangaroo Island, off the entrance to Spencer Gulf, and, ultimately, she passed Cape Horn on the 59th day after leaving Port Lincoln. She took 36 days from the Horn to the Line, experienced unusually moderate trade weather, got a severe dusting from a heavy sou'wester in the Bay of Biscay, and did not make Falmouth Roads until June 20th, 44 days from the Line.

The '88 day' mistake, 1927

Owing to an error in the telegram announcing her departure, *Herzogin Cecilie* has been credited, both by Mr. Lubbock and Mr. Villiers, with a grain passage of 88 days in 1927, but, actually, she took 98 days. Her log states that she left Port Lincoln on January 24th, not February 3rd as has been given elsewhere. This erroneous transmission caused her sailing to be posted incorrectly at Lloyd's, a very rare occurrence. It seems likely that the confusion may have arisen over the fact that ten days after sailing she was still within sight of Cape Borda, for, once more, *Herzogin Cecilie* had tried, unsuccessfully, to make westing toward the Leeuwin. Although 88 days from Borda to Queenstown was a remarkably fine run, the facts remain that her actual passage was 98 days from Port Lincoln, and that she took, in all, 45 days to reach the Horn. Therefrom, however, all went well, for from the Horn to the Line she was only 22 days; a further 30 days brought her to landfall at Bull Point, Queenstown being entered on the following day.

Stages of the Horn route

So far as I can ascertain (for the transcription of *Herzogin Cecilie's* log made by Mr. W. L. Leclercq, which has been the medium for much of my information, ends with 1932) 22 days from Cape Horn to the Equator is the shortest time in which the barque covered that lap in post-War days. In 1931 she accomplished it in 27 days, and in 1923, with a nitrate cargo, she took 33 days, but, in general, the stage occupied nearer 40 days of her homeward passages.

Usually, however, one good lap is insufficient to produce an out-standing passage. In most cases it needs to be linked with at least one other lap of like quality, as witness *Loch Torridon's* 40 + 20 + 21 day passage in 1891-2, with wool. In both 1929 and 1930 *Herzogin Cecilie* reached Cape Horn just one month after leaving a Spencer Gulf port. This was indeed first-class driving, but the resultant passages were quite mediocre. In 1929, although she ran up to the Falklands in two days from the Horn, she was another 37 to the Line, and then 33 days elapsed before she made landfall at the Scillies. In 1930 the Horn to the Line took 43 days, and she sighted the Lizard 36 days after crossing the Equator. By the analysis of two recent fast passages to Queenstown, *Priwall's* 91 days in 1935 and *Passat's* 87 days in 1936, it is found that they each contained two excellent laps. *Priwall* was only 28 days from Cape Borda to the Horn, and the same time from there to the Line; *Passat*, with 32 days from Port Victoria to the Horn, passed the Line after a further 27 days. (See also page 340.)

No matter how strong a sailing vessel may be, how numerous and efficient her crew, or how ambitious her Master, her movements are at all times at the mercy of the wind. The remarkable dual outward passages of 67 days from Hamburg to Spencer Gulf ports by *Padua* and *Priwall* were followed by a race home again.

Priwall cleared from Port Victoria on February 15th, 1934, and *Padua* from Port Broughton on the following day. Both vessels took 35 days to the Falklands and 77 days, in all, to the Line. When nearing England, nearly three weeks later, they were still neck and neck, for in each case they reported themselves by wireless from latitude 43° N., *Priwall* on May 19th, and *Padua* on May 21st. *Padua* made her English landfall at Barry Island, after 108 days of sailing; *Priwall* was 109 days to Queenstown, her Master, Captain Clauss, stating that light winds and protracted calms throughout the passage were responsible for its length.

These two round voyages of 175 and 176 days at sea, a unique

'Padua' and 'Priwall' race back, 1934

example of rivalry under canvas, serve to show that unless favoured by the requisite weather conditions a homeward passage of under 100 days is outside the compass of even the fastest sail freighter of a full cargo of grain, no matter how great may be the incentive to quick passage-making.

In the same year (1934) *Passat*, formerly a colleague of the two Laeisz barques, left Spencer Gulf one day later than *Padua* and arrived, at Falmouth, on the same date as *Priwall*. She thus accomplished a passage of 106 days, the quickest of a remarkably consistent season, for *Abraham Rydberg* (an early departee, via the Cape of Good Hope) took 107 days, and *Pommern* 110.

'*Falmouth for Orders*', 1928

Herzogin Cecilie's passage of 96 days from Port Lincoln to Falmouth in 1928 forms the subject of a book of which some mention has already been made, *Falmouth for Orders*. Mr. Villiers shipped before the mast for that passage, and he describes the journey, the crew and the barque in some detail.

On this occasion *Herzogin Cecilie* had to beat out of the Gulf against a fresh head-wind; then, for 16 days, luck seemed to be against her, for she encountered fog, calms, heavy rain and adverse winds. She successfully negotiated, however, the difficulties of Backstairs Passage and the Bass Strait, but was then forced southward past Campbell Island, until, in 55° S., she found, at last, her good west wind and started the eastward drive to the Horn.

By common consent the bad luck had been attributed to the presence of a woman stowaway, who was discovered on the second day out. She was Miss Jeanne Day, aged 22, a schoolmistress from Adelaide, who had been on holiday at Port Lincoln while *Herzogin Cecilie* was there loading grain. At first, great was the general consternation aboard, but, after a time, things appear to have settled down. By the kindness of Captain de Cloux, a niche was found, for which, very wisely, the unwelcome visitor adapted herself, to become, in due course, absorbed into the general life and routine of the barque's company.

In the lonely area between Campbell Island and Cape Horn, which was so well suited to her capabilities, *Herzogin Cecilie* made some grand sailing, frequently logging between 12 and 15 knots. On one occasion she sailed 116 miles between midnight and 8 a.m. (a speed of $14\frac{1}{2}$ knots) and then, on the 32nd day out, between noon and noon, ran 304 miles, including a great four-hour burst of 60 miles. The following day she rounded Cape Horn in a strong westerly wind and bright sunshine, running the while at a steady 13 knots with royals set. The SE. Trades were picked up on the 60th day: under their influence the barque ran 1,200 miles in the five days between March 19th and 23rd, crossing the Line four days later. On arrival at Falmouth the final log-reading was 15,900 miles, evidencing a rough mean speed of 7 nautical miles per hour throughout the passage.

The short coastwise race from Melbourne to Port Lincoln against *Beatrice* (which has already been described) preceded this passage, and it is said that Captain de Cloux and Captain Bruce had agreed upon a race home. Both barques left Port Lincoln on the same day, but this time *Herzogin Cecilie* beat her rival handsomely, by 18 days, for, having chosen the Good Hope route in preference to the Horn, Captain Bruce made a passage of 114 days to Falmouth

Herzogin Cecilie, however, was not always the right 'horse' to back, even for those who knew her best. In 1930 Captain Sven Eriksson wagered Captain Granith that *Herzogin Cecilie* would beat *Pommern* home by a clear fortnight. She sailed from Spencer Gulf 12 days before *Pommern*, but only arrived at Falmouth a week ahead of the smaller barque. The latter's passage occupied 105 days against the 110 days of *Herzogin Cecilie*.

A wager lost – 1930

On October, 15th, 1935, *Herzogin Cecilie* sailed from Copenhagen on what was to prove her final voyage. Apart from the collision, three days later, with the trawler *Rastede*, the outward journey was uneventful, Port Lincoln being reached on the 83rd day out. This was the quickest of her seven outward ballast passages to Australia for Gustaf Erikson. On this occasion the barque made a rapid turn-about, for on January 28th, just three weeks after arrival, she cleared from Port Lincoln for England. Within a few days of leaving Spencer Gulf she met with heavy weather, but, after finding Cape Horn conditions unusually fair, she crossed the Line 53 days out from Port Lincoln. This indicated that two of the three major stages, into which the homeward run can be divided, had been covered in splendid time. Had the final stage been anything like as good *Herzogin Cecilie* would have established a record for the 'grain race' which might have stood unbeaten to the end of deepwater sail. It may be recalled that *Parma*, on her 83-day record passage, was 56 days to the Line and then 27 days to Falmouth.

The last round voyage

On March 24th, three days after reaching the Equator, *Herzogin*

Cecilie was 'spoken' by a steamer. She was then about 500 miles NNE. of the Brazilian island of Fernando de Noronha, and had just passed close to that isolated sea-mark, St. Paul Rocks. It was, however, another thirty days before she reached Falmouth, for she was delayed, and her passage spoilt, by head-winds encountered in the neighbourhood of the Azores. She hung about for a long and dreary eight days before beginning the last drive to England. When only two days away from Falmouth *Herzogin Cecilie* met with some of the most severe weather of the whole trip, two of the crew being injured.

In 1935, in accordance with her usual practice, the Swede, *Abraham Rydberg*, had made an early departure from Europe: in consequence, she had loaded, and sailed from Wallaroo by New Year's Day, 1936. Four weeks later *Herzogin Cecilie* left Port Lincoln, the leader of the sixteen windjammers then loading in the Gulf. *Abraham Rydberg* came home via the Cape of Good Hope, putting into Port Natal on the way. She reported at Start Point, South Devon, on May 11th, when 130 days out, this being 19 days after the arrival of *Herzogin Cecilie* at Falmouth. Hence this concluding journey made by *Herzogin Cecilie* was meritorious on three counts: she was the first arrival of that season's grain fleet under sail; her passage of 86 days was the fastest of the year; lastly, it was the best passage she ever made in the trade.

The log of the 1932 passage home

Although, in all probability, it will have little practical appeal for the non-technical reader, I have included, as an Appendix, an abridged copy of the log of *Herzogin Cecilie* for her homeward passage of 1932. It is based upon a transcription by Mr. Leclercq, who, on that occasion, was a passenger. It was an undistinguished journey, providing no sailing pyrotechnics, but because in days to come when the tall ships have passed for ever, such a record may possess some historic value, I feel that it should be incorporated in this chronicle of the closing phase of windjamming.

CHAPTER VI

'SIC TRANSIT GLORIA MARIS'

THE LOSS OF *HERZOGIN CECILIE*

B Y 1886 the carriage of tea from China had passed so completely into the hands of steam that only two clipper ships, Joseph Somes' *Leander* and John Willis's *Hallowe'en*, took part in the transport of that year's crop.

John Willis & Son of Leadenhall Street, in the City of London, were among the most noted of clipper owners, for they numbered in their fine fleet such famous and beautiful ships as *Cutty Sark*, *Blackadder*, *Whiteadder*, *Dharwar*, *Taitsing* and *The Tweed*.

Hallowe'en, built by Maudslay, Son, and Field, was an iron full-rigger of 920 tons gross, with lines said to have been taken off from *The Tweed*. At any rate she proved to be a clipper of outstanding quality. In the three successive years (1873-5) she ran home from Shanghai, under favourable monsoon conditions, in 89, 92 and 92 days, respectively, pilot to pilot.

Mr. Lubbock awards the laurels of the China trade to the composite clipper ship *Sir Lancelot* for her 89 days from Foochow, against the monsoon, in 1869.

On August 13th, 1886, *Hallowe'en*, under Captain Dawton, left Foochow for London. She passed Anjer on October 4th, Ascension Island on November 26th, and entered the English Channel on January 17th, 1887, 96 days out. At 7.30 p.m. on the same day she drove ashore at Sewer Mill Sands, between Bolt Head and Bolt Tail, to the west of Salcombe, South Devon. Her bottom was ripped open, and she filled almost at once, becoming badly hogged amidships. Heavy seas swept the doomed vessel and, before twenty-four hours had elapsed, her main-mast had snapped six feet from the deck, the mizen topmast had gone overside, and her back had broken. Only one life was lost, the remainder of her crew of 22 getting ashore safely. A week later she broke completely in half, and the little bay was soon strewn with her wreckage, and with lead-covered chests of tea.

Just fifty years after *Hallowe'en* left the China coast on that last, fateful passage, another proud windjammer, likewise one of the finest and

The wreck of 'Hallowe'en', 1887

Half a century later – the stranding of 'Herzogin Cecilie'

347

fastest of her day, quitted Spencer Gulf on her final journey. In the humbler annals of the grain trade, *Herzogin Cecilie* had been the prototype of the bygone tea-clipper. By a sad and remarkable coincidence she was to share the self-same grave, for, early on the morning of Saturday, April 25th, 1936, *Herzogin Cecilie*, with her bottom holed by striking the Ham Stone Rock, drove onshore at Sewer Mill Cove, a hundred yards or so from where *Hallowe'en* had found her last resting-place.

The causes contributing to the loss of *Herzogin Cecilie* are somewhat obscure. Why should a well-found barque, in capable hands, deviate so far from her intended course that, after logging less than fifty miles, she found herself in dire distress almost ten miles to the north of her calculated position? Such a happening would seem to be attributable only to some undiscovered error in navigation, or to one of those inexplicable strokes of ill-fortune which are among the many hazards of the sea. In his deposition to the Receiver of Wreck, the Master gave his opinion of the cause of the loss: he thought it was due to a combination of fog and possible magnetic attraction, plus the presence of sufficient tidal impulse to set the vessel right off her course.

Having received her orders to proceed from Falmouth to Ipswich, where the grain would be discharged, *Herzogin Cecilie* got under way at 8.20 p.m. on Friday, April 24th. Since the previous day she had been lying in Falmouth Bay, outside the spacious harbour, and about a mile and a half south-west of St. Anthony's Head.

A south-west breeze, force 2-3, was blowing, and there was a moderate sea, misty weather, and patches of light fog. She stood out to sea on the starboard tack, setting a course which was given in the Master's deposition as S.24°E. (true), and passing a few miles to the east of the dreaded Manacles Rocks, near Lizard Head. By 10.40 p.m. she had sailed 12 miles on this tack.

The following alterations of course are stated to have been made during the night. The true courses are given, together with the estimated distance sailed on each course:

10.40 p.m.	Course altered to	S.35½° E. then sailed	2½	miles
11.10 p.m.	,,	,,	S.46½° E.	,,	2	,,
11.30 p.m.	,,	,,	N.74° E.	,,	17½	,,
2.0 a.m.	,,	,,	N.79° E.	,,	10	,,
3.30 a.m.	,,	,,	N.83° E.	,,	5	,,

At 3.50 a.m. the barque struck the Ham Stone Rock.

By 11 p.m., although the wind had not varied, the haze had thickened and, half an hour later, the fog was sufficiently dense to necessitate the use of fog signals. At that time the barque was running free before a light WSW. wind. By 2 a.m., when she was hauled out a further 5°, *Herzogin Cecilie* was said to be sailing at a speed of 7 knots in thick fog.

If the above courses are plotted on a chart it will be found that those in charge of the barque intended that, before she turned through a considerable angle to head E. by N. up-Channel, she should be in a position, after allowing for tidal set and leeway, to pass many miles south of any landfall hazard that lay before her.

Save that her Master had, apparently, hauled her out a further 5°, and then, as the fog thickened, another 4°, *Herzogin Cecilie* held to her new direction for five and a half hours. Then, just before 4 a.m., she went ashore at a spot which was many miles off her destined course.

The total distance sailed through the water, according to the above estimate, was 49 miles in 7½ hours, giving a mean sailing speed of 6½ knots.

The direct route between St. Anthony's Head and Sewer Mill Cove is 46 miles, passing, some 30 miles from the former point, just north of the Eddystone. It was expected that this warning would be seen or heard about two in the morning. Eddystone Light is a group light, consisting of two flashes every 30 seconds, having a field of visibility of 17 miles radius in clear weather. It also shows a fixed, white, lower light, visible for 15 miles, and is fitted with a fog-explosive warning. No indication of its presence was, however, recorded by those on board *Herzogin Cecilie* as she sailed onward, unknowingly, to her doom. Fog signals are notoriously inconsistent in their receptive range, and it is conceivable that the barque passed through a 'dead' area for reception, even, perhaps, relatively near to the lighthouse.

Eddystone and Start?

The next important warning to vessels bound up-Channel is at Start Point, just eastward of Prawle Point, and 24 miles from Eddystone. On a clear night the white flash (every twenty seconds) of the Start Light is visible 20 miles away, and the lighthouse is equipped with a powerful fog-siren.

Following, on the chart, the events of that foggy spring night, it will be seen that *Herzogin Cecilie* should have passed many miles to seaward of Start Point, instead of which, at 3.50 a.m., the Mate saw a dark mass

'Herzogin Cecilie' strikes the Ham Stone Rock

loom out of the fog on the port side of the barque. The Master was informed, and the helm put hard-a-starboard in an effort to clear the obstruction. At the same time the starboard braces were let run, but, almost immediately, *Herzogin Cecilie* crashed into the Ham Stone, holing herself in the fore-hold and pump-room and flooding three compartments. The force of the impact, aided by wind and sea, swung her clear of the rocks: both anchors were let go, but they found no holding ground and she slewed round broadside-on to the precipitous cliffs, a thousand yards a-lee.

The stranding   The heavy swell carried her inshore, to ground at the mouth of Sewer Mill Cove. She came in stern first, but, on striking rock near her stern, swung broadside again, and remained fast 50 yards or so from the base of the 300 feet cliff which forms the west face of Bolt Head.

The barque's distress flares and rockets were observed by a coastguard at Hope Cove, some miles to the west of the scene of the stranding.

Shortly afterwards, a young Danish seaman named Larsen swam ashore to seek assistance, a brave deed under the intimidating conditions of darkness, rough sea and an inhospitable, unknown landing-place.

The questions of tide set and magnetic interference   In regard to the possible causes which can be advanced in respect of the casualty, one, fog, has already been detailed. The question of the action of tides on the course of the barque is interesting. According to the tide-tables, she had, until about 10.30 p.m., a favourable tide running under her in a direction, roughly, north-east. This tide would tend to set her in towards the Eddystone, but, in the two hours before the tide turned against her, under normal conditions the barque should not have been set more than three miles in a north-easterly direction. An hour after the tide had turned came the change of course which took *Herzogin Cecilie*, ostensibly, up-Channel, and well clear of all danger. From this point, on her proper course, she should have had the tide slightly on the starboard bow, tending again to set her in towards the land, but now to a far lesser degree. On the other hand, the nearer she drew toward Bolt Head, the more the tide, following, as it would do, the bight of the land, tended to divert her toward the north-west, and, consequently, off her course and toward the coast.

Herzogin Cecilie stranded some five hours before high water, four days before neap tides, and at a period when the rise and fall (on Salcombe Bar) was about 17 feet.

350

facing: SEWER MILL COVE, 25TH APRIL, 19

THE WRECK

It has been stated that compass trouble was experienced during the later stages of the homeward passage from Australia. The theory, which was advanced, subsequently, by local opinion, that *Herzogin Cecilie's* compasses were affected by the magnetic properties attributed to the ironstone promontory of Bolt Head, is, however, hardly tenable. Her compasses had been checked at frequent intervals, and, only two days earlier, a compass deviation of 1°E. had been ascertained over an easterly course. The needles did, it was said, oscillate violently just before she hit the Ham Stone, but, to bring her so far inside Start Point, she must, of necessity, have been holding a false course for some considerable time. In other words, the suggested magnetic local influence, of which no mention is made in Admiralty publications, must have exerted its baleful effect at what was, surely, an incredible distance seaward.

The question of magnetic interference

It so happened that, although Captain Sven Eriksson had sailed out of Falmouth Bay on *Herzogin Cecilie* on five previous occasions, only once had he travelled to the eastward. This was in 1933, when, under orders for London, she was reported off Prawle on the first day out of Falmouth, and docked three days later at Millwall. His other four departures were all westward, to Liverpool, Barry or Belfast; on the first of these passages Captain Eriksson was acting as Mate of the barque which he was later to command.

So much for a commentary on the available information relative to the stranding; now to return to the scene of the casualty.

The Salcombe lifeboat put to sea shortly after 4 a.m., and, although hindered by fog, reached *Herzogin Cecilie* in just over an hour. The arrival of the boat coincided with the lifting of the fog, and communication was established with the coastguards, on the cliff-top above, by means of a Morse-lamp.

The work of the Salcombe lifeboat

There were thirty-one people on board the stricken barque, including two women, Mrs. Eriksson and a friend who had joined her at Falmouth for the trip to Ipswich. Mrs. Eriksson (formerly Miss Pamela Bourne, daughter of the late Sir Ronald Bourne of South Africa) came home from Australia aboard *Herzogin Cecilie* in 1934. Subsequently she became engaged to the Master, and the tragedy of this final round voyage of the old barque was heightened by the fact that it was their honeymoon journey.

Despite the big swell and a fresh south-west wind, the rescue work

ing: BELOW THE FROWNING CLIFFS OF BOLT HEAD

was carried on without great difficulty; at 8 a.m. the lifeboat, with 21 of the crew of *Herzogin Cecilie* and the solitary passenger, left the barque, Salcombe being reached at 9.30 a.m. Later in the day the men were sent to Plymouth, from whence two Finns returned to *Herzogin Cecilie*. Captain and Mrs. Eriksson, the Mate, the Second Officer, and three Danes and an Ålander from the crew elected to remain on board when the option of leaving was offered. The lifeboat returned in the afternoon and stood by until about 3 p.m., the sea being too rough for it to get alongside again. Rocket apparatus was, therefore, brought from a station between Sewer Mill and Hope, and a line was shot from the cliff. It was made fast to the mizen mast, and a temporary breeches-buoy rigged in order that the eight people on board could be taken off, if and when the need arose. Two days later the breeches-buoy was replaced by a proper bosun's-chair, which could be operated from the barque. Various personal effects were landed by means of the breeches-buoy, and its first human freight was Captain Eriksson. At the earliest opportunity he went ashore, in order to get in touch with the vessel's London Agents, but soon returned aboard again.

Captain Eriksson's pet Alsatian, Paik (see photograph, page 169), remained on board for some days, but then had to go into quarantine kennels to await reshipment to Finland. Paik, although unfriendly toward most people, is extraordinarily attached to his master, whose control over the dog is uncanny.

During the day on which *Herzogin Cecilie* left Falmouth, I had arranged with the Agents to sign on again, upon completion of her discharge at Ipswich, for the ballast passage to Mariehamn. The suggestion was put forward that I should proceed forthwith to join her at Falmouth, and sail round to London. To my lasting regret, that was not possible, but my feelings can be better imagined than described when on arrival at Lloyd's the following morning I found *Herzogin Cecilie's* name blazoned large on the 'Losses Book', and the first of the many telegrams, which were to retail the sequence of events, posted on the Casualty Board.

The opinion of salvage experts   The first step taken by the underwriters interested in the grain cargo was to instruct the Salvage Association to act in their interests, and a Special Officer was at once dispatched to the scene of the stranding. In his first report, dated April 26th, he stated that the barque was broadside on to the shore, 50 yards out, with her foredeck awash at high tide. She was drawing 18 feet aft, soundings outside the hull showing 25-30 feet of water. Slight straining was apparent in her plating in the way of the main-mast. The forepeak and two holds were flooded, and there was 13 feet of water in the after hold, increasing. The wind was still south-west, but the swell was moderating.

By the following day the position had worsened; the Salvage Association Officer reported that the water in the after holds had risen to 17 feet, practically the whole of the cargo being water-damaged, and he feared that there was no hope of saving the hull.

At the top of the tide on April 28th there was 20 feet of water in the after holds, and the depth of water under the stern indicated that *Herzogin Cecilie* was held fast, by rocks, forward from a point below the mizen mast. Owing to this suspended position she worked with the swell at high water, grinding on her rocky bed.

Immediately they received news of the casualty the Compagnie de Remorquage et de Sauvetage les Abeilles (of Havre) dispatched two of their tugs to the spot on the chance of securing a salvage contract. *Abeille No.* 24 went from Brest and *Abeille No.* 26 from Havre, the latter being equipped with pumps and diving-gear, and having a salvage expert on board. The famous and powerful German salvage tug *Seefalke* came from her station at Queenstown, and on the 26th her Master went aboard *Herzogin Cecilie*.

As explained in Chapter 11, Book One, however, a 'no cure, no pay' basis of contract was out of the question, and the tugs, deeming that, in her present position, salvage of the hull of the barque was impracticable, left again within a short while, the Frenchmen advising their owners that owing to heavy seas the position was hopeless.

A vital change of weather

It seemed impossible, therefore, that *Herzogin Cecilie* would again float upon the sea, but the luck, which had apparently deserted her for ever, now changed. The alteration took the form of an improvement in weather conditions. As she lay, fully exposed to the south-west, suspended on rock for two-thirds of her length and with thousands of tons of sodden, swelling grain inside her, any continuance of heavy weather from that quarter must, undoubtedly, have meant the end. From that time onward, however, for all those further seven weeks that she lay inert at Sewer Mill Cove, she received little further outward damage; fine weather set in from the east and north, and week after week she rested undisturbed, sheltered by the frowning height of Bolt Head. Now and again, notably on June 15th, she had to withstand a certain amount of south-westerly weather, but it was never severe, and her position remained unchanged throughout.

As it transpired, the principal danger was from within rather than without. One of the reasons which had, from the first, made the experts take a pessimistic view of the situation was the likelihood of the shell bursting under the great pressure set up by the expansion of the cargo. Such was the strength of that old hull, however, that these forebodings were quite unfounded, and once the work of cargo removal was started *Herzogin Cecilie* showed comparatively little sign of further straining.

Salvage of undamaged cargo The cargo consisted of 52,514 bags of South Australian grain. The gross weight was 4,295 tons; the net, after deduction of tare (i.e. weight of bagging), being about 4,240 tons. The stowage plan was, approximately, three-eighths in the forward holds (Nos. 1 and 2) and five-eighths in the three after holds.

For her last cargo of grain *Herzogin Cecilie* had been fixed at 25s. 6d. per net ton, i.e. the total freight worked out at £5,400 sterling.

It is the practice in the Australian trade for the Master of a vessel to be paid a proportion of the freight in advance, upon completion of loading. This advance, which is limited to one-half the total freight, is to offset the expenses and disbursements incurred by the vessel while in Australian waters. Usually it represents between one-quarter and one-third of the entire freight, and, not being returnable, becomes an integral part of the arrived market value of the cargo. As such, it is included in the insurance of the cargo, and so, taking the then current price of Australian wheat, and allowing, say, £1,400 for advanced freight, *Herzogin Cecilie's* last cargo was worth, in round figures, £27,500.

The question of the non-application, under English law, of the principle of 'distance freight' has already been discussed in Book One, Chapter II. The whole of the balance of the freight (about £4,000), being unearned by reason of failure to deliver the cargo at its proper destination, was not collectible and represented a dead loss to the owner of the vessel.

On behalf of the underwriters concerned, a contract was arranged by the Salvage Association with the Risdon Beazley Marine Trading Company Limited of Southampton. This resulted in a refund to underwriters of about one-third of the value of the 464 tons of undamaged grain rescued from the after holds. Suitable gear was rigged, and work commenced on April 29th. By the end of the first week in May all the sound cargo had been recovered and transported to Plymouth aboard the motor-vessel *Roselyne*. The salvors then reported that the great mass of sodden grain left in the holds was swelling, heating and giving off gases.

Owing to the difficulty of the handling and disposition of this un-savoury bulk, a fresh contract was entered into, whereby the salvors paid the underwriters a fixed sum per ton of cargo salved, and them-selves disposed of the wet grain to their best advantage. After about 450 tons had been dealt with, difficulties increased still further, and underwriters accepted a lower rate for any subsequent realization.

Dealing with the wet grain

This wet, salty grain was sold to Dutch buyers as pig-food, and fetched quite a good price, but the expense of extracting it, and of shipping it by small Dutch motor-craft from the barque to the Continent, ate up much of its cash value and left little in the way of recovery for the underwriters.

In the meantime an Examination on Oath had been instituted by the Receiver of Wreck at Plymouth, under the powers vested in Receivers by the Merchant Shipping Act of 1894. The circumstances of the stranding were attested by the Master, and copies of the deposition were forwarded, as is usual in such cases, to the Board of Trade and to Lloyd's. As there was no loss of life involved by this accident to a foreign vessel within our three-mile limit, no further action was anticipated.

Official inquiries

The Finnish Consul at Plymouth took a Maritime Declaration on board the barque, and also held an Official inquiry into the cause of the stranding.

All over the country, and especially in the sea-minded West, public interest had been aroused to an extraordinary extent by the misfortune of this well-known windjammer. Thousands flocked to the adjacent cliffs to view her, and at week-ends the congestion in the narrow lanes of the vicinity was so great that police were drafted to improvise a one-way system. Farmers converted their grazing-land into vast car-parks; the Automobile Association produced bright yellow signs lettered 'TO THE WRECK', and the quiet little town of Salcombe will not soon forget what came to be known as the 'Cecilie Summer', for a brisk trade was car-ried on in photographs, small boats, and parking space. A substantial contribution was made to the Royal National Lifeboat Institution by

Public interest in 'Herzogin Cecilie'

the owners of private property in the neighbourhood of Sewer Mill Cove, as the proceeds of a charge levied upon people crossing the fields to see the stranded barque.

The barque is offered to the Admiralty

On April 28th a start was made in the dismantling of *Herzogin Cecilie*, her sails being taken ashore, but, a day or two later, a dramatic offer to save her was announced. On condition that the Admiralty would use the barque as a naval training-ship, Lady Houston was prepared to finance the whole task of salvage and repair. Lord Monsell, First Lord of the Admiralty, replied, however, that, while fully appreciative of such a generous and patriotic offer, it was not, at that time, our policy to provide training in sail for the officers and men of the Royal Navy. In consequence, not being in a position to make the requisite use of the vessel if and when she might be salved, he was compelled to decline the proffered gift.

Hopes were entertained that Sir William Garthwaite's Sea Lion Sail-Training Society might be interested, but these negotiations broke down.

The cost of another and more regularized offer to salve proved too high to be practicable, and it seemed that *Herzogin Cecilie's* fate was sealed.

Constructive total loss and its effect on salvage

As already explained (see pages 132-133), it was not a sound economic proposition for Gustaf Erikson to join, *pari passu*, with the cargo interests in a combined attempt to save the entire venture. According to the experts, and also from every commercial view-point, *Herzogin Cecilie* was already a constructive total loss, and, as such, financially unsalvable. Ninety per cent of her cargo was damaged irretrievably, in that it now had no value for human consumption. Even were the hull insured for anything like the low market value possessed to-day by sail tonnage, it is doubtful whether the underwriters concerned would have contemplated the considerable expenditure involved by extensive, and apparently futile, salvage operations.

No one, of course, could have anticipated the luck of the weather with which *Herzogin Cecilie* was to be blessed. A prompt start followed by favourable conditions were the two factors most necessary to any possible success in salvage operations. If, at the outset, any party had come forward who, for sentimental reasons and regardless of expense, was desirous of saving the vessel, *Herzogin Cecilie* might now be sailing the seas.

Although no offer had been forthcoming to work on a 'no cure, no pay' basis, one or other of the big concerns specializing in difficult salvage jobs would, doubtless, have been willing to undertake the task of re-floating the barque, providing that their expenses had been guaranteed by the parties concerned in the property, and, in the light of after events, in all probability they would have succeeded.

Herzogin Cecilie, however, was to be an 'unconscionable long time a'dying', and that she ever left Sewer Mill Cove at all was entirely due to private enterprise; but much precious time had elapsed before such aid materialized.

Ever since the accident scores of letters to Captain and Mrs. Eriksson had been arriving daily, for, although it was but a 'nine days' wonder', the fate of *Herzogin Cecilie* seemed to have awakened that innate love of the sea and ships which centuries of sea-faring has instilled into the British nation. Many such communications expressed sympathy in a concrete form, by enclosing or proffering donations to any fund which might be inaugurated for an attempt to save the famous old sailer.

The repair fund

By the co-operation of a Sunday newspaper, a scheme was launched about the middle of May. It took the form of an appeal for contributions to a salvage and repair fund, and, couched in the following terms, it was broadcast through the general medium of the Press:

'By hundreds of letters and telegrams the British public have made it clear that their interest in sail is genuine and their sympathy for the "Duchess" profound. Only through sentiment and rigid economy has the owner of *Herzogin Cecilie* been able to maintain his fleet of sailing ships. A loss such as the "Duchess" he is unable to meet. With him and his wife the British people have mourned the fate of the *Herzogin*. She can be saved. It is only lack of money that keeps her on the rocks. We have already received unsolicited contributions towards the cost of her salvage. This has encouraged us to appeal to a wider public. Should the public help the "Duchess" to sail the seas again, Captain Sven Eriksson guarantees that the owner, Gustaf Erikson, will take not less than six and up to ten British apprentices yearly, free of all fees, to gain their experience in sail before the mast. This will, we hope, in time, repay the British people for their generosity and sympathy.

'Contributions should be sent to the "Duchess Cecilie", Lloyds Bank Limited, Salcombe, Devon.'

The moving spirit behind this scheme was the Master's wife, for never, even when prospects seemed most hopeless, had she accepted the general dictum that *Herzogin Cecilie* must, of necessity, remain to break up where she lay. Mrs. Eriksson pursued indefatigably every possibility which held out the slightest hope of saving a vessel of which she was intensely proud and fond.

The subscription list, which was to reach a total of about £800, was augmented by a charge made for visiting the barque. Many people availed themselves of this opportunity of inspecting one of the last surviving square-riggers, and *Herzogin Cecilie* was, as far as was possible under the circumstances, maintained in her former meticulous trim. Unfortunately the depredations of unscrupulous hunters of souvenirs, who could not respect even private property, marred these visitations. In the sideboard cupboards of the Master's saloon, for instance, was a quantity of glass and china bearing the insignia of the Norddeutscher Lloyd Company. Naturally this had a considerable sentimental value to its owners, but, during those weeks on the Devon coast, nearly all this ware, as well as many other things, disappeared.

The anonymous benefactor

While the fund was in its infancy, however, a proposal was made by a gentleman, said to be a naval officer who desired to remain anonymous, to shoulder the risk of financing salvage operations, the fund to act as a reserve for subsequent repairs. It is understood that Captain Gustaf Erikson was prepared to spend up to £2,000 on the repair of the barque once she was safely docked.

The generous private gesture to salve *Herzogin Cecilie* was, I believe, qualified to the extent that failure was to entitle the donor to a share in whatever sum the hull might realize subsequently, if and when it was sold. Such refund, however, was not to exceed his outlay. In the event of success it was left to the owner, if he so wished, to recoup the anonymous benefactor for out-of-pocket expenses. As it turned out, those expenses were to amount to something like £1,200, and although the venture so nearly succeeded, it is feared that, as the ultimate break-up value was infinitesimal, the financial loss must have been as severe as it was undeserved.

The sale of the remaining cargo

Once the underwriters had settled a total loss on the cargo policies, the grain and its proceeds became, under the principle of subrogation, their property, and all rights were vested in them. Consequently, their consent had to be obtained before the mixture of grain and water could

facing: A TALL SHIP PASSE

be sacrificed in an attempt to lighten *Herzogin Cecilie* sufficiently to lift her from the rocks. A price for the sale of the 3,000 odd tons of cargo still in the holds was mutually agreed between the parties, underwriters being satisfied to receive even a nominal sum for what, otherwise, was likely to prove an unrealizable asset.

Pumping commences

On May 10th divers from Plymouth examined the lower hull, and then two 12-inch and one 6-inch salvage pumps, besides a 4-inch submersible pump and generator, were sent from Plymouth and installed on board the barque. Pumping tests took place on May 28th, and, soon, steady streams of grain-laden water were shooting overside, the lightening process being accelerated by jettisoning cargo in large baskets slung outboard by tackle rigged above the hatches.

The question of endangering the stability of the vessel by unequal discharge needed careful attention, and it was necessary to proceed always with great caution. It must be remembered that, at that time, no one knew how much bottom-damage had been sustained, or whether, even if *Herzogin Cecilie* were lifted free of the impaling rocks, the pumps could cope with the inrush of water. The size of the orifices in the double-bottom could not be calculated either from outside by divers, or from inside until the lower holds were cleared. The whole proposition, therefore, was in the nature of a gamble, with, from the view-point of the barque, everything to gain and nothing to lose; nothing that is except her break-up value should she sink in deep water.

The first attempt to refloat

The first attempt to refloat *Herzogin Cecilie* was made nearly seven weeks after she had gone ashore: on June 10th two tugs, *Trevol*, of 600 h.p., and *Alexandra*, of 350 h.p., connected up with the stern of the barque. Prior to high water (10 a.m.) repeated attempts were made to heave her clear. A heavy mist shrouded the operations. All three pumps were working continuously, two forward and a third well aft. Presently the towing-hawsers were shifted to the bow of the barque, and fresh efforts were made. A hawser was led to the big anchor-capstan on the foredeck, and fourteen men manned the bars in an abortive attempt to help ease her seaward. Several long pulls were then made in unison by the tugs, but, although slight tremors were felt aboard the barque and observers said that she became a shade more vertical, all efforts failed as the tide fell away.

Further salvage operations were postponed until the next spring tides, when a 15 feet 5 inch tide was calculated to give about two

acing: Top. REFLOATED AND IN TOW (HAM STONE ROCK IN BACKGROUND)

Bottom. THE END. STAREHOLE BAY, 1937

feet more water. In the meantime jettison of cargo went on continuously.

On June 19th when, only some 1,700 tons of grain remained, *Herzogin Cecilie*, despite all jeremiads, was refloated with comparative ease. The same two tugs were employed as at the first attempt. For fully fifteen minutes on that fateful afternoon they strained at the cables without any sign of movement from the barque. Suddenly she shuddered, assumed a slightly more upright stance, and then moved forward about 15 feet, only to take ground again with an ominous jar. The tugs, however, renewed their efforts, and she slid gently seaward, free at last to start eastward around Bolt Head to a safer berth. A heartfelt cheer went up from the little band who had stuck to their charge so devotedly and for so long. The hopes of all on board soared high. In this short passage they visualized the first stage toward ultimate reconditioning. Anxiety, however, was tense. Would the pumps be able to counteract the leakage or would *Herzogin Cecilie* go farther and farther down by the head, to founder in a depth of water which would make work impossible? But all went well, and, in half an hour, the barque was towed safely into Starehole Bay, a rock-bound inlet on the eastern face of Bolt Head, just outside Salcombe Bar.

This venue had been selected for three reasons: it promised, at that time of year, reasonable shelter and security; it was presumed to possess a safe, gently-shelving, sandy floor; and it was at a sufficient distance from human habitation to prevent the noxious fumes given off by the rotting cargo from becoming a public nuisance. Owing to the unknown state of the under-water hull it was not considered expedient to risk a tow of nearly fifty miles to Falmouth, where the barque could have been dry-docked. Instead it was decided to place her for the time being in this local berth, where, after further discharge, temporary patching could be done, and the vessel so rendered more seaworthy for the passage to a place of permanent repair.

When she left Sewer Mill Cove *Herzogin Cecilie* had no yards in situ above her topsail yards, the topgallants and royals having, by then, been dismantled and sent ashore. All such stripping helped to lighten her, and, although down by the head, she had several feet of free-board at the well-deck. She approached Starehole Bay bows on, the tugs then transferring their pull to the stern, swinging her round and running her inshore stern first. She took the ground, on a level bottom, so close to the apex of the cove that, later on, a rope-bridge spanned the gap between the vessel and the cliffs. Once she was securely berthed and moored, the pumps, which had been working at full pressure for some hours, were stopped, and, as the water found its level in the holds, she settled down in an upright position.

At low tide a considerable area of the hull was exposed: an examination by diver revealed that, apart from a certain denting and a bent rudder-post, the stern section was undamaged. It was fairly certain, however, that the double-bottom was set up and pierced further forward, but survey was impossible until the holds were cleared.

The damage estimated

Neither the shock of striking the Ham Stone under full canvas, nor the stress and strain of subsequent events, had caused any real damage or weakening aloft, a truly remarkable tribute to the quality and condition of the sparring and the standing-rigging.

Captain and Mrs. Eriksson, who had been living on board for most of the eight weeks since the stranding, settled down in their new surroundings in a far more contented and optimistic frame of mind, for they could see a reasonable prospect of being again under sail before the year was out.

Besides the nucleus of officers and crew, several ratings from Plymouth were on board in charge of the salvage pumps and gear. There were also eight Cambridge undergraduates, recruited by Mr. J. Stevens: these young men had volunteered to help in the unpleasant task of discharge, and, in the ensuing weeks, they were to render yeoman service.

Volunteer labour

Because of her more accessible position, many visitors came aboard *Herzogin Cecilie* in Starehole Bay. One and sixpence per head was charged for admission, the money being added to the repair fund.

Prospective purchasers of wet grain also visited the scene, and by June 26th the Dutch motor-vessel *Apollinaris IV* was alongside, loading a cargo of what, when dried, would make excellent fodder.

Although the weather was clement, work proceeded slowly, it being hindered by the presence of noxious gas in the holds. It was largely due to this factor that the high expectations of ultimate success were never realized. So virulent were the fumes that, on the last occasion upon which I trod the decks of *Herzogin Cecilie*, only a short while before hope had been abandoned, the gas had eaten away every vestige of paint and varnish on deck and in the 'tween-decks, while her once spotless, white hull was pitted, corroded and almost completely blackened.

The gas problem, and labour troubles

Gas masks and goggles were advisable for workers in the lower holds, and much optical trouble was endured by all concerned. Ventilation was improved by the provision of long, tubular, canvas wind-funnels, which were suspended from the rigging and hung down through the hatches into the holds. It was heavy work down there in those fetid holds. The bags of grain scaled, in their water-logged condition, two hundredweight apiece, about a third heavier than in a dry state. The bags had to be slit around the middle with knives, the halves man-handled into capacious baskets, and loose grain shovelled in afterwards. The baskets, hoisted by tackle operated from the winches, were swung outboard and tipped above the hatches of the craft alongside.

It may be that the accounts which reached Salcombe of the unattractive conditions of work aboard the barque became, in the telling, somewhat exaggerated, but it soon proved difficult to obtain local labour. In the end, further discharge became dependent upon volunteer effort and the pace became slower and slower. Not only were the workers few in number, but, in the interests of health, the length of the shifts had to be reduced.

On July 14th, while exploring the lower holds, Captain Eriksson was overpowered by gas fumes, and was found lying in water. Fortunately, although not at the time wearing a mask, he soon recovered.

The gas seemed to emanate from the lower tiers of bags, and to penetrate the water-logged areas in the form of bubbles, which burst on reaching the air.

About this time the last of the undergraduates left the vessel. They had done fine work under trying circumstances, and had been forced to eat and rest in great discomfort. Many minor injuries and painful symptoms had been endured with stoicism, but it was all of no avail, for, within a few days, the fate of *Herzogin Cecilie* was sealed by most unseasonable weather.

'Herzogin Cecilie' breaks her back Under the influence of a violent ground-swell from the south-east she worked her way deeper into the sand. In itself this was not too serious, but, by a crowning stroke of misfortune, she found rock again beneath her keel where only sand had been anticipated. This time she was held amidships, while the eddies sucked away the sand from both bow and stern. The two ends of the hull sagged downward several feet below the level of the central portion, and a terrific strain was placed upon the latter area, causing its rivets to fly in all directions.

362

THE WRECK

On the night of July 17th a severe gale from an entirely unexpected quarter broke upon the doomed barque and completed the havoc. Heavy seas damaged her so severely that all hope of saving her was abandoned. The poop-deck lifted; the lower deck rose, amidships, by two feet; *Herzogin Cecilie's* back was broken.

For 84 days, almost as long as she had taken for her last passage home from Australia, she had fought for her life on Devon's shores. Although 34 years old, she had withstood stresses under which many younger craft would have succumbed. As it was, sentiment did its best to save her, only to be beaten by rotting cargo, lack of labour, a hidden rock and, for the time and place, exceptionally inclement weather.

All that was now left to be done was to salve every item which could *Stripping the wreck* conceivably benefit the Erikson Fleet. Under the direction of Captain Eriksson and Mr. Elis Karlsson (the Mate) a skeleton crew stripped the hull bare of its fittings. Teakwork, capstans, winches, piping, wheels, donkey-boiler, cabin fittings, heating and lighting plants, the figure-head, bells, and seventy brass port-lights were removed and loaded on board the little vessel *Vera*, which Gustaf Erikson had sent to transport the salvaged articles to Mariehamn.

It is reported that a motion-picture concern made overtures on behalf of some of the gear for the purpose of making up studio sets, but the Owner decided that the entire residue could be employed to greater advantage in his business.

Who knows how long the remnants of *Herzogin Cecilie* may continue to travel that storm-swept seaway off the Horn, which she, in her prime, knew so well and rode so royally? I understand that the figurehead of the German Duchess, in company with the big bronze bell, is to grace Captain Erikson's private collection. The log-books of the barque will join other archives of deepwater sail in the Mariehamn Maritime Museum; but, scattered among the last of the square-riggers, such items as her capstans, winches and the like may yet see years of service, perhaps until square-rig is no more.

The public subscriptions were returned to the donors, anonymous and collective sums being divided between the two bodies who had aided the crew on the morning of the stranding — The Royal National Lifeboat Institution and The Shipwrecked Fishermen and Mariners' Royal Benevolent Society.

Offers were invited for the wreck of *Herzogin Cecilie* 'as she now lies', for any demolition had, of necessity, to be undertaken in Starehole Bay. The complete chart-house and staircase were sold privately to a local buyer, as they stood, for £25.

On September 24th an offer of £225 was accepted for the vessel, and what remained of the once proud barque became the property of a firm of scrap-merchants at Kingsbridge, near Salcombe. To-day the cost of building a replica of *Herzogin Cecilie*, with material and fittings of a like quality, could not be much below £40,000.

Such was her strength that, four months later when the last picture in this book was taken, the stout old barque, stripped and hogged though she was, showed little sign of succumbing to the winter gales which had battered and flooded her: her four tall 'sticks' were, even then, as erect as on that evening, years before, when they had lured me down to Millwall to make her acquaintance.[1]

'Vale!' On August 9th, 1936, in a letter to *The Times*, Captain Sven Eriksson wrote — 'As Master, and on behalf of Sjöfartrodet[2] Gustaf Erikson, I wish to thank all those who have given of their help and sympathy in the effort to save *Herzogin Cecilie*. That her destiny was written otherwise must be the regret of everyone who has known her and served in her.'

To me, he wrote as follows:

'. . . as things are now, she will end her days in Starehole Bay. It is sadder than I can say, especially for me who have been on board for eight years and, every year, have come to love her more and more. You will be able to give a real ending to your story of *Herzogin Cecilie*.'

---

[1] *In April, 1937, twelve months after the stranding, all her masts were still intact.*
[2] A term denoting Director or Controller.

L'ENVOI

All coiled down, an' it's time for us to go;
Every sail's furled in a neat harbour stow;
Another ship for me, an' for her another crew —
An' so long, sailorman . . . good luck to you!

IT was a night of unclouded and brilliant moonlight. The sea was almost calm. Just sufficient breeze was blowing to let *Herzogin Cecilie* carry to advantage every stitch of canvas which could be set. With yards braced part round, all her fore-and-aft canvas was drawing well, and the course headed her directly into the eye of the new-risen moon.

I went out along the foot-ropes of the bowsprit to a favourite perch at the foot of the royal forestay. Out there, high above the water, one felt almost on a level with the fore-yard. Under the high arch of the great foresail, the deserted decks were clearly visible.

On such a night, the watch were standing-by in the well-deck; only the look-out man on the fore-deck, a hand at the midship wheel, and the distant figure of the Mate pacing the weather side of the poop, were to be seen.

Herzogin Cecilie, heeling a few degrees to starboard, was slipping through the water at about seven knots. So steady was the big barque that her progression was almost soundless. Only a faint, but continuous, hissing 'frou-frou' could be heard, and she raised but little bow-wave as her sharp cut-water clove forward.

As the moon rose higher, the whole, white, lovely height of her foremast sails became moulded in gleaming silver against a dark sky. There was not a quiver in that canvas: wind-pressure extended every sail to a rigid convexity, beautiful to behold, which might have been carved in purest marble.

With gracious dignity and unruffled calm, a few feet below me, the wooden 'Duchess' swam serenely onward. The moonlight was kind to those ageing features, for, that night, she almost smiled. Neither she, gazing always toward the distant horizon, nor I, feasting on the glory which towered above her, dreamt that her long years of roaming were drawing to a close.

We seemed to be borne forward in an effortless, mystical progression, until the unbroken peace, and that stillness which is engendered by moving with the wind, created the fantasy that the old tall ship was but a giant statue, the very Spirit of Sail, set in running water.

Such is one of my own most vivid and unforgettable impressions of *Herzogin Cecilie*.

Now, she is gone! Never again will her like be launched. Surely, the Sea is the poorer for her passing?

FINIS

APPENDICES

ADDENDUM
AND
EPILOGUE

APPENDIX A

THE technical account of a mediocre passage: no records were broken, no noteworthy feats accomplished; the weather was neither very good nor very bad, nor were any untoward perils encountered. *Herzogin Cecilie* had just completed an outward journey, via East African ports, of 180 days, and her bottom was foul after the long sojourn in tropical waters.

Owing to a slight grounding between Lourenco Marques and Beira, a minor leak developed in her bottom-plating during the homeward passage. It was controlled with ease by the pumps, but this also detracted from her sailing qualities. The length of the passage includes, in this instance, the extra 'Meridian' day.

For reasons of clarity the degree sign has been omitted in the 'Course', 'Position', 'Variation', and 'Deviation' columns of this abridged copy of the logbook.

'D.R.' in the 'Noon Position' column indicates a figure arrived at by dead-reckoning instead of by observation.

Only the principal happenings and sail-handling are given under 'Notes', and in a shortened form.

The figures under 'Wind and Weather' indicate wind-strength on the Beaufort Wind Scale, as follows:

Admiral Beaufort's numerals	Average velocity of wind in knots (nautical m.p.h.)	Seaman's description of wind	Deepsea criterion for a steel-full-rigged ship, deep-loaded, clean-bottom, steering 'full and by'
0	0	Calm	—
1	2	Light air	Steerage-way only
2	5	Light breeze	2 knots under full sail
3	9	Gentle breeze	3–4 knots under full sail
4	14	Moderate breeze	5–6 knots under full sail
5	19	Fresh breeze	Can just carry royals and light staysails
6	24	Strong breeze	
7	30	Moderate (half) gale	
8	37	Fresh gale	
9	44	Strong gale	
10	52	Heavy (whole gale)	Main lower topsail only
11	60	Storm	Storm staysail or trysail only
12	Over 80	Hurricane	No canvas can stand

Date	Days on Passage	General (True) Course	Distance made between noon positioning	Noon Position	Estimate of total distance sailed to date	Wind and Weather	
1932							
9/2	0	S.	—	—	15	Light N. wind	Clear
10/2	1	S.	—	—	68	Light variable wind 8 p.m. W. 4-5	Slight rain
11/2	2	S.	—	—	170	W. 3-5	Overcast
12/2	3	S.	—	—	278	W. 3	Clear
13/2	4	S. 34 E.	124	S. 37.24 E. 137.59	422	W. 3–SW. 4	Clear
14/2	5	S. 58 E.	129	S. 38.44 E. 140.11	518	SW. 3–S. 1	Clear
15/2	6	S. 80 E.	61	S. 38.57 E. 141.26 (D.R.)	572	S. 1	Clear
16/2	7	S. 68 E.	41	S. 39.7 E. 142.14 (D.R.)	704	SE. 2-3	Clear
17/2	8	S. 67 W.	83	S. 39.50 E. 140.37	751	SE. 1 later WSW. 1	Calm at Noon Clear
18/2	9	S. 23 E.	81	S. 40.4 E. 141.18	826	SW. 1-2	Overcast
19/2	10	S. 39 E.	87	S. 42.26 E. 143.11	985	NW. 1 to NW. 4	Overcast

Locality	Notes		Variation	Deviation
...encer Gulf	8 a.m., left in tow of tugboat *Yacka* Loaded with 53,174 sacks of wheat Carrying 4,171 tons net, 4,225 tons gross Drawing 23½ feet forward, 23.7 aft Slight list to starboard Set sails 1 p.m. Cast off tug 2 p.m. and dropped pilot. Proceeded under full sail		4 E.	
...encer Gulf	Ship steering badly, down by the head Shortened down 8 p.m.		4 E.	
...ncer Gulf	Tacked ship three times	5° leeway	4 E.	
...ncer Gulf	Shifted cargo from No. 1 to No 5 hold to trim by the stern Secured anchors at catheads Log carried away twice to-day Reset royals	5° leeway	4 E.	
...sman Sea	Set new log, and oiled decks Full sail	5° leeway	4 E.	
...man Sea	Full sail	5° leeway	5 E.	10 W.
...man Sea	Wore ship twice. Full sail	5° leeway	6 E.	12 W.
...man Sea	Full sail. Moonlight Head bearing NE. by N. at 8 a.m.	5° leeway	6 E.	12 W.
...nan Sea	Full sail. No steerage way on ship between 8 a.m. and 1 p.m.	5° leeway	6 E.	6 W.
...nan Sea	Full sail		6 E.	6 W.
...nan Sea	Nearly full sail		6 E.	10 W.

Date	Days on Passage	General (True) Course	Distance made between noon positioning	Noon Position	Estimate of total distance sailed to date	Wind and Weather	
1932							
20/2	11	S. 32 E.	202	S. 45.17 E. 146.31	1,188	NW. 4-5 NW. 5-6	Clear
21/2	12	S. 39 E.	186	S. 47.36 E. 149.52	1,352	NW. 5-6 Moderating	Clear
22/2	13	S. 45 E.	162	S. 49.31 E. 152.30 (D.R.)	1,493	NNE. 5-6 to WNW. 3-5	Overcast Rain squalls Clear later
23/2	14	S. 63 E.	100	S. 50.17 E. 154.47 (D.R.)	1,607	NW. 2 to S. 2, later SW. 3-5	Clear
24/2	15	S. 63 E.	201	S. 51.50 E. 158.32 (D.R.)	1,816	W. 6-8 NW. 7-8 W.4	Overcast Steady rain
25/2	16	S. 88 E.	194	S. 51.14 E. 167.34	2,047	W. 5-8 WNW. 7-8	Clear
26/2	17	S. 86 E.	232	S. 51.31 E. 173.43 (D.R.)	2,217	W. 6-7 W. 4-5	Overcast Rain and hail squalls
27/2	18	S. 84 E.	163	S. 51.41 E. 178.13	2,355	W. 3-4	Clear, rain la
27/2	18	S. 84 E.	137	S. 51.52 W. 178.52	2,469	W. 4-1	Very clear
28/2	19	S. 79 E.	94	S. 52.29 W. 176.35	2,629	NNE. 2-3 NNE. 6-7	Rain squalls l
29/2	20	S. 70 E.	161	S. 53.26 W. 173.10 (D.R.)	2,764	NE. 6-7 NW.4 W.3	Steady rain ar squalls
1/3	21	S. 84 E.	143	S. 54.31 W. 166.33	2,921	W. 4	Clear Hail squalls

Locality	Notes	Variation	Deviation
...tered South Pacific	Took in all stays'ls and jibs 8 a.m. 8 p.m., big sea running	8 E.	5 W.
...th Pacific	Set all sail at midnight	10 E.	5 W.
...th Pacific	Full sail	13 E.	5 W.
...th Pacific	Full sail	16 E.	8 W.
...th Pacific	Took in stays'ls and jibs at 5 p.m.	16 E.	8 W.
...th Pacific	Same canvas. At 5.30 a.m., Auckland Island, bearing NNE. ¼ E. and 20 miles distant	18 E.	16 W.
...th Pacific	All square-sail set, spanker and gaff taken in Drifting weed. Ship pitching badly	20 E.	16 W.
...th Pacific	All square-sail	22 E.	16 W.
...th Pacific	Extra day (180° Meridian) All square-sail	22 E.	16 W.
...th Pacific	Full sail at noon. Between 4 and 8 p.m. took in royals, upper-t'gallants and cro'jick 5° leeway in evening	22 E.	16 W.
...th Pacific	Set all sail during day 5° leeway	22 E.	16 W.
...th Pacific	Full sail	22 E.	16 W.

Date	Days on Passage	General (True) Course	Distance made between noon positioning	Noon Position	Estimate of total distance sailed to date	Wind and Weather	
1932							
2/3	22	S. 82 E.	142	S. 54.34 W. 161.49	3,044	W. 2-4	Clear Rain squalls
3/3	23	S. 84 E.	224	S. 54.55 W. 156.4 (D.R.)	3,327	W. 5-6 NW. 6-9 WNW. 6-7	Overcast Heavy rain Confused sea
4/3	24	S. 85 E.	312	S. 55.21 W. 148.1 (D.R.)	3,547	NW. 6-8 NW. 5-4	Overcast Rain Fog later
5/3	25	E.	208	S. 56.38 W. 140.29	3,721	NW. 3-4 W. 4	Clear
6/3	26	E.	155	S. 56.34 W. 135.40	3,867	W. 3 WNW. 3 N. 3	Clear Light rain : hail squalls
7/3	27	S. 77 E.	153	S. 57.37 W. 130.38	4,027	N. 3 ENE. 5-7 ENE. 7-9	Overcast Steady rain Later full gale
8/3	28	N. 28 E.	75	S. 57.15 W. 129.34 (D.R.)	4,108	E. 6-8 E. 1 WSW. 1 SE. 1-2 SE. 4-5	Fog and drizz Nearly calm midday
9/3	29	E.	130	S. 57.15 W. 125.34 (D.R.)	4,310	SE. 4 S. 7	Fog lifted Overcast and squally
10/3	30	S. 89 E.	191	S. 57.18 W. 119.31 (D.R.)	4,475	S. 3-4	Squally and drizzle
11/3	31	E.	120	S. 56.56 W. 114.37	4,558	S. 2 SE. 2 SW. 3	Overcast Heavy snow, hail squalls

Locality	Notes	Variation	Deviation
South Pacific	Full sail	24 E.	16 W.
South Pacific	Full sail — later took in royals and cro'jick Ship rolling heavily; seas coming over	24 E.	16 W.
South Pacific	Set royals 1 a.m. Full sail at noon Log carried away Repaired torn main-royal	24 E.	16 W.
South Pacific	Full sail. Set new log	26 E.	16 W.
South Pacific	Took in fore-and-aft canvas 10 a.m. Full sail again by noon	26 E.	16 W.

South Pacific	Full sail all morning, shortened down 1 p.m. By 7 p.m. reduced
	   to inner jib, lower stays'ls, tops'ls and foresail
	Seas coming over, ship jammed into the wind
	                5°-15° leeway during day
		26 E.
		
		26 E.
			11 W.
			
			11 W.

South Pacific	Visibility at 8 a.m. only 200 yards Log hauled in 15° leeway	29 E.	11 W.
South Pacific	Carrying all square-sail, three jibs and upper and lower spanker Steep sea coming over in afternoon	29 E.	11 W.
South Pacific	Full sail till noon Later took in jibs and stays'ls	29 E.	11 W.
South Pacific	Full sail by midday Fore-and-aft canvas taken in later but ultimately reset	30 E.	11 W.

APPENDIX A

Date	Days on Passage	General (True) Course	Distance made between noon positioning	Noon Position	Estimate of total distance sailed to date	Wind and Weather	
1932 12/3	32	E.	144	S. 56.56 W. 110.19 (D.R.)	4,743	SW. 5 NW. 5-6 NNE. 6-7 NW. 6-5	Squally with heavy rain and hail
13/3	33	S. 83 E.	137	S. 57.51 W. 104.57	4,899	NW. 5 SE. 1-3 S. 5-6 SE. 8-9	Calm Squally
14/3	34	N. 84 E.	254	S. 58.15 W. 97.54 (D.R.)	5,229	SW. 9-10 SSW. 9-8 SW. by S. 8-9	Gale Rain squalls Snow later
15/3	35	E.	226	S. 56.41 W. 89.39	5,529	SW. 8-7 S. 7-6	Squally
16/3	36	E.	270	S. 56.34 W. 81.53	5,714	S. 6-4 NW. 3 NW. 6-7	Clear and fine later
17/3	37	S. 89 E.	190	S. 56.50 W. 76.55	5,939	NW. 6-4 WSW. 4 S. 6-8	Overcast
18/3	38	N. 85 E.	215	S. 56.30 W. 70.39 (D.R.)	6,117	S. 6-8 S. 5-6 SSW. 4	Rain later

Locality	Notes	Variation	Deviation
outh Pacific	Seas coming over. Shortened down in afternoon; finally, furled cro'jick and mainsail	30 E.	11 W.
outh Pacific	No steerage-way between 5-7 a.m. Confused high sea, no wind. Centre of cyclonic disturbance Full sail (except gaff tops'l) at 1 p.m., but shortened down by evening Heavy seas then coming over	30 E.	11 W.
outh Pacific	Blowing full gale. Running under foresail, tops'ls and lower t'gallants Seas coming over. 1 a.m., main lower t'gallant sheet carried away. Sail blew out. Three helmsmen Log carried away 6 a.m. 4 p.m., ship labouring heavily Bent new main lower-t'gallant Seas coming aboard heavily 8 p.m., set fore and upper-t'gallant, mizen upper-t'gallant and cro'jick	30 E.	7 W.
uth Pacific	Gradually made sail all day, almost under full canvas again by evening	30 E.	7 W.
uth Pacific	2 a.m., heavy snow squall At 1 p.m. set new log. Carrying all sail until midnight when royals taken in	26 E.	7 W.
ar Cape Horn	Set royals again 4 a.m. Took in all fore-and-aft canvas during morning but reset at 4 p.m. 7 p.m., main royal blew out; fore upper-t'gallant split 10 p.m., mizen lower-t'gallant blew out Heavy seas coming over. Ship labouring heavily. Sundry damage on deck Shortened down to storm canvas	23 E.	7 W.
uth Pacific hted Tierra del ego 5 a.m. Cape rn 11 p.m.	Heavy seas coming over. Slight list to port 4 p.m., Diego Ramirez Is. bearing S. by E. $\frac{1}{4}$ E. Carrying all sail at noon except main royal, shortened down fore-and-aft canvas at 3 p.m. but under full sail by midnight	21 E.	7 W.

Date	Days on Passage	General (True) Course	Distance made between noon positioning	Noon Position	Estimate of total distance sailed to date	Wind and Weather	
1932 19/3	39	N. 84 E.	162	S. 55.33 W. 64.18	6,328	WSW. 3 NW. 3-4	Exceedingly clear
20/3	40	N. 72 E.	220	S. 54.23 W. 58.13 (D.R.)	6,538	NW. 4-5 N. 5-6	Overcast Heavy rain
21/3	41	N. 70 E.	169	S. 53.26 W. 53.44 (D.R.)	6,678	W. 2 S. 3	Overcast Clear
22/3	42	N. 57 E.	106	S. 52.5 W. 51.19 (D.R.)	6,761	S. 2-1 NNE. 3-4	Clear, calm Rain
23/3	43	S. 80 E.	120	S. 52.14 W. 48.3 (D.R.)	6,919	NE. by N. 3. NW. 3 SW. 4	Fog
24/3	44	N. 41 E.	134	S. 50.33 W. 45.53 (D.R.)	6,979	SW. 4 SW. 1	Light fog
25/3	45	N. 41 E.	54	S. 49.14 W. 44.10	7,097	SW. 1 W. 3	Overcast
26/3	46	N. 35 E.	192	S. 46.31 W. 41.6	7,308	W. 3-4	Clear
27/3	47	N. 30 E.	195	S. 43.25 W. 38.24	7,457	W. 3 WSW. 3 SW. 2	Overcast
28/3	48	N. 29 E.	124	S. 41.37 W. 37.14 (D.R.)	7,578	SW. 2-3	Overcast Clear later
29/3	49	N. 40 E.	74	S. 39.54 W. 35.19	7,621	SW. 2-1 Variable	Clear and fine

Locality	Notes	Variation	Deviation
uth Atlantic ssed Staten land	Under full sail	18 E.	7 W.
uth Atlantic	Port main t'gallant back-stay carried away and repaired. Main lower-t'gallant split and taken in Afternoon visibility 200 yards 5° leeway	12 E.	7 W.
uth Atlantic	NW. swell, ship pitching heavily Later, heavy confused swell Took in fore-and-aft canvas at midday Full sail again by midnight	8 E.	7 W.
uth Atlantic	Mid-morning — no steerage-way. Small school of whales alongside Clewed up courses at 8 a.m. Full sail at night	6 E.	7 W.
uth Atlantic	Constant sail work	6 E.	7 W.
uth Atlantic	All sail except stays'ls and jigger-mast canvas	6 E.	7 W.
uth Atlantic	Set all sail at noon	6 E.	7 W.
ith Atlantic	Full sail	5 W.	5 W.
ith Atlantic	Full sail	8 W.	7 W.
ith Atlantic	Took in fore-and-aft canvas 1 p.m.	12 W.	7 W.
ith Atlantic	Calm sea — no swell Under full sail at 10 p.m.	15 W.	7 W.

Date	Days on Passage	General (True) Course	Distance made between noon positioning	Noon Position	Estimate of total distance sailed to date	Wind and Weather	
1932							
30/3	50	N. 38 E.	30	S. 39.31 W. 34.54 (D.R.)	7,708	SW. 1 E. 1 ENE. 2-4	Overcast
31/3	51	N. 4 W.	145	S. 37.6 W. 35.7 (D.R.)	7,833	E. 3-4 ESE. 6-7 Variable 4-6 E. 6-7	Steady rain an squalls Visibility only 250 yards
1/4	52	N. 23 E.	52	S. 36.9 W. 34.46	7,912	SE. 3 E. 2 S. 1-3	Clearing Clear and fine
2/4	53	N. 37 E.	135	S. 34.2 W. 33.24	8,097	SSE. 4-3	Clear and fine Cloud and rai later
3/4	54	N. 33 E.	161	S. 31.43 W. 31.57	8,210	S. 2 SE. 2-1	Clear and fine
4/4	55	N. 22 E.	70	S. 30.20 W. 31.22	8,275	SE. 1 E. by N. 1 NE. 1	Clear and fine
5/4	56	N. 1 E.	41	S. 29.9 W. 31.35	8,408	ENE. 2 NW. 3	Clear and fine Heavy NW. r squalls later
6/4	57	N. 44 E.	116	S. 28.22 W. 30.4 (D.R.)	8,465	NW. 3 SW. 1	Overcast Drizzle Clear later
7/4	58	N. 37 E.	54	S. 26.57 W. 29.23	8,521	SW. 1 SSE. 1 S. by E. 1	Very clear an fine Overcast later

Locality	Notes	Variation	Deviation
South Atlantic	Full sail. Variable wind	15 W.	7 W.
South Atlantic	4 a.m., took in royals, cro'jick, spanker and gaff. Foresail, fore-upper t'gallant, and main-royal blew out Unbent foresail. Ship taking seas solid over fo'c'slehead. Pitching and labouring heavily Main and mizen upper-t'gallants blew out. Main lower-t'gallant and mizen t'gallant-stays'l torn 2 p.m., gale moderating, wore ship on port tack Ship jammed up into wind and making no headway. Log hauled in. Took in mainsail 11 p.m., wore ship on to starboard tack	15 W.	7 W.
South Atlantic	Heavy easterly swell Set all sail during day	18 W.	7 W.
South Atlantic	Swell from SE. Heavy sea and rain squalls in afternoon	18 W.	7 W.
South Atlantic	Full sail except mizen t'gallant stays'l	18 W.	7 W.
South Atlantic	Full sail except mizen t'gallant stays'l	18 W.	7 W.
South Atlantic	4 a.m., wore ship port tack. Bent extra flying jib. Wireless aerial carried away 6 p.m. Fore and mizen royals blew out. Mizen lower-t'gallant and gaff tops'l blew out. Took in cro'jick and royals. 12 p.m., set cro'jick and main and mizen royals	18 W.	7 W.
South Atlantic	Bent fore royal. Under all square-sail	18 W.	7 W.
South Atlantic	Under full sail by noon 8 p.m., clewed up cro'jick	20 W.	7 W.

Date	Days on Passage	General (True) Course	Distance made between noon positioning	Noon Position	Estimate of total distance sailed to date	Wind and Weather	
1932							
8/4	59	N. 27 E.	53	S. 26.9 W. 29.58 (D.R.)	8,635	ENE. 1 Variable 0 NW. by W. 1-3	Rain Clear later
9/4	60	N. 38 E.	159	S. 23.45 W. 27.17 (D.R.)	8,779	NW. by N. 3	Clear Rain squalls
10/4	61	N. 39 E.	120	S. 21.57 W. 25.3	8,879	NW. by N. 2 NW. 1	Clear and fine
11/4	62	N. 34 E.	74	S. 20.20 W. 24.27	8,956	NW. 2-1	Clear and fine
12/4	63	N. 27 E.	53	S. 19.15 W. 23.52	9,000	N. 1 NW. 1	Clear and fine
13/4	64	N. 35 E.	38	S. 18.21 W. 22.27	9,029	NW. 1 Calm	Clear and fine
14/4	65	N. 16 E.	16	S. 18.14 W. 23.32	9,036	Calm	Clear and fine
15/4	66	N. 25 W.	22	S. 17.55 W. 23.15	9,072	NE. 1	Clear and fine
16/4	67	N. 9 W.	48	S. 17.59 W. 23.39	9,166	E. by S. 1-2	Clear and fine
17/4	68	N. 7 W.	115	S. 14.50 W. 24.41	9,315	ESE. 2-3	Clear and fine Light rain squa
18/4	69	N. 10 W.	172	S. 11.56 W. 25.32	9,501	ESE. 3-4	Fine
19/4	70	N.	196	S. 8.39 W. 25.26	9,685	ESE. 4-3	Fine
20/4	71	N.	176	S. 5.35 W. 26.49	9,870	ESE. 3-4	Fine

Locality	Notes	Variation	Deviation
South Atlantic	8 a.m., tacked ship port tack. Set cro'jick	20 W.	7 W.
South Atlantic	Full sail	20 W.	7 W.
South Atlantic	Full sail	20 W.	7 W.
South Atlantic	Full sail	20 W.	7 W.
South Atlantic	Full sail	22 W.	7 W.
South Atlantic	Full sail. Mains'l and cro'jick clewed up twice during day. SE. swell Tacked ship to starboard tack 6 p.m.	22 W.	9 W.
South Atlantic	Tacked ship twice	22 W.	7 W.
South Atlantic	Shifted some cargo from port to starboard. Slight starboard list	22 W.	7 W.
South Atlantic	Full sail. Picked up SE. Trade	22 W.	7 W.
South Atlantic	Full sail	22 W.	7 W.
South Atlantic	Full sail	22 W.	7 W.
South Atlantic	Fore royal blew out. Repaired and reset	22 W.	5 W.
South Atlantic	Full sail	22 W.	5 W.

Date	Days on Passage	General (True) Course	Distance make between noon positioning	Noon Position	Estimate of total distance sailed to date	Wind and Weather	
1932							
21/4	72	N.	180	S. 2.20 W. 26.20	10,025	SE. by E. 3	Overcast and damp
22/4	73	N.	139	N. 0.69 W. 26.27	10,152	SE. by E. 3	Fine
23/4	74	N.	99	N. 1.49 W. 26.46	10,224	E. 1-2 SE. 1 ENE. 1-0	Overcast Rain squalls
24/4	75	N.	80	N. 3.9 W. 26.46 (D.R.)	10,292	ESE. 1 Calm	Overcast
25/4	76	N.	43	N. 3.53 W. 27.37	10,340	NNE. 1 Calm NNE. 1-3	Overcast
26/4	77	N. 47 W.	69	N. 4.53 W. 28.0	10,417	NE. by N. 2 NE. 3 NE. 2-1	Overcast
27/4	78	N. 46 W.	102	N. 6.1 W. 29.19	10,551	NE. 3	Overcast
28/4	79	N. 27 W.	131	N. 8.4 W. 30.30	10,699	NE. 3	Clear and fine
29/4	80	N. 28 W.	145	N. 10.21 W. 31.54	10,840	NE. 3	Clear and fine
30/4	81	N. 32 W.	142	N. 12.30 W. 33.48	10,976	NE. 3-2	Overcast, rain
1/5	82	N. 29 W.	114	N. 14.0 W. 34.53	11,096	NE. 2	Overcast
2/5	83	N. 26 W.	120	N. 15.48 W. 35.97 (D.R.)	11,197	NE. 2-1	Slightly overca

Locality	Notes	Variation	Deviation
South Atlantic	Full sail	22 W.	5 W.
North Atlantic	Crossed the Line	22 W.	5 W.
North Atlantic	Full sail. Lost SE. Trades	22 W.	5 W.
North Atlantic	Heavy N. swell and heavy rain Full sail. Steamer heading N. 25 miles to port. No steerage-way after 9 p.m.	22 W.	5 W.
North Atlantic	Heavy rain. Clear later Mains'l and cro'jick clewed up twice to-day No steerage-way 9 a.m.–4 p.m.	22 W.	5 W.
North Atlantic	Large steamer heading N. 15 miles to port NNE. swell later and rain squalls. Full sail. Picked up NE. Trades 5° leeway	22 W.	5 W.
North Atlantic	12 p.m., swell lessening. Rain squalls Lee sheet fores'l carried away and sail split. Outer flying-jib halliard carried away 5° leeway	22 W.	5 W.
North Atlantic	Full sail. Reset fores'l and flying-jib	18 W.	3 W.
North Atlantic	Full sail	18 W.	3 W.
North Atlantic	Full sail	18 W.	3 W.
North Atlantic	Full sail	18 W.	3 W.
North Atlantic	Full sail	18 W.	3 W.

Date	Days on Passage	General (True) Course	Distance made between noon positioning	Noon Position	Estimate of total distance sailed to date	Wind and Weather	
1932 3/5	84	N. 29 W.	93	N. 17.6 W. 36.34 (D.R.)	11,293	NE. 2	Overcast Clear later
4/5	85	N. 32 W.	93	N. 18.32 W. 37.34	11,380	NE. 2-1	Clear and fine
5/5	86	N. 33 W.	70	N. 19.42 W. 38.53	11,432	NE. 2-1 Calm	Clear and fine
6/5	87	N. 16 W.	25	N. 20.19 W. 39.17	11,497	Calm E. 1-2	Clear and fine
7/5	88	N. 16 W.	105	N. 22.5 W. 39.51	11,650	E. 2 ENE. 3	Clear and fine
8/5	89	N. 27 W.	138	N. 24.21 W. 41.1	11,772	ENE. 3-2	Clear and fine
9/5	90	N.	136	N. 26.49 W. 41.13	11,929	SE. 3	Clear and fine
10/5	91	N. 18 E.	149	N. 29.7 W. 40.29	12,093	SSW. 3-4	Overcast Some rain
11/5	92	N. 21 E.	166	N. 31.43 W. 39.21 (D.R.)	12,228	SW. by W. 3-4 WSW. 3-2 Variable	Overcast, squally
12/5	93	N. 4 W.	77	N. 32.37 W. 39.52	12,343	NE. by N. 3 NE. by E. 3-1	Overcast Clear
13/5	94	N.	33	N. 32.53 W. 39.50	12,392	NE. by E. 2-1 E. 1	Clear and fine
14/5	95	N.	24	N. 33.35 W. 39.34	12,428	E. by N. 1 SW. 1	Clear and fine

Locality	Notes	Variation	Deviation
orth Atlantic	Full sail	18 W.	3 W.
orth Atlantic	Full sail	18 W.	3 W.
orth Atlantic	Swell from N. Drifting weed No steerage-way at night Clewed up mains'l and cro'jick	18 W.	3 W.
orth Atlantic	No steerage-way before 8 a.m. Swell increasing. Full sail afternoon	18 W.	7 W.
orth Atlantic	Log fouled by weed and hauled in Full sail	18 W.	7 W.
orth Atlantic	Swell decreasing. Full sail	18 W.	7 W.
orth Atlantic	Full sail	20 W.	3 W.
orth Atlantic	Took in all fore-and-aft canvas 3 a.m.	20 W.	3 W.
orth Atlantic	2 a.m., took in cro'jick after it had blown out. Wore ship to star- board tack Steady and heavy rain midday Reset all canvas at noon Shifted cargo in fore-hold to port	21 W.	3 W.
rth Atlantic	Passenger steamer passed ahead, 3 miles off, bound W. Later steamer bound E. passed, 3 miles astern Wore ship on port tack. 8 p.m., full sail	21 W.	3 W.
rth Atlantic	NE. swell. Wore ship starboard tack	21 W.	3 W.
rth Atlantic	Oil tanker passed astern bound E. Motor tanker *Beth* of Oslo passed close astern bound W. Took in fore-and-aft canvas when wind veered to SW.	21 W.	5 W.

Date	Days on Passage	General (True) Course	Distance make between noon positioning	Noon Position	Estimate of total distance sailed to date	Wind and Weather	
1932							
15/5	96	N. 30 E.	51	N. 34.28 W. 39.2	12,507	SW. 1-2	Clear and fine
16/5	97	N. 36 E.	114	N. 36.1 W. 37.17	12,664	SW. 2-4 WSW. 4 NNW. 3	Squally
17/5	98	N. 42 E.	174	N. 38.2 W. 34.36	12,837	NNW. 3 W. 3	Clear
18/5	99	N. 54 E.	180	N. 39.56 W. 30.58	13,022	WNW. 7-5 W. 5-6 NW. 6-7	Squally
19/5	100	N. 54 E.	188	N. 41.22 W. 27.25	13,226	N. 5	Squally
20/5	101	N. 55 E.	188	N. 43.4 W. 24.27	13,392	N. 4-3 NW. 3	Squally
21/5	102	N. 50 E.	145	N. 44.31 W. 20.50	13,519	WNW. 2-3 WSW. 3	Overcast
22/5	103	N. 52 E.	124	N. 45.46 W. 18.6	13,671	W. by S. 3 WNW. 3-5	Rain Clear
23/5	104	N. 53 E.	193	N. 47.44 W. 13.47	13,906	NW. 5	Squally
24/5	105	N. 71 E.	212	N. 49.19 W. 8.34	14,098	N. 5 NNE. 6-4	Squally
25/5	106	N. 17 E.	143	N. 49.27 W. 4.47	14,189	NNE. 3-2 ENE. 1 N. by E. 1	Clear
26/5	107	—	—	—	14,244*	NNE. 1	Clear and fine

*14,244 corrected = 14,15

Locality	Notes	Variation	Deviation
North Atlantic	Steamer bound NE. passed 20 miles off to port. No more seaweed All square-sail, but cro'jick and mains'l clewed up	22 W.	3 W.
North Atlantic	Full sail at 8 p.m. Midnight, flying-jib halliard carried away	23 W.	5 W.
North Atlantic	Heavy sea. Full sail. Later all square-sail only	23 W.	5 W.
North Atlantic Midday: Corvo 30° E. Flores 26° W.	Set all sail 4 a.m. Steamer ahead bound E.	23 W.	2 W.
North Atlantic	Heavy beam sea. All sail except flying jib. Barquentine passed close on port beam bound W.	22 W.	3 W.
North Atlantic	Full sail except flying-jib	22 W.	3 W.
North Atlantic	Took in all fore-and-aft canvas when wind went round to WSW.	22 W.	3 W.
North Atlantic	Under full sail by noon	21 W.	3 W.
North Atlantic	Heavy beam sea 5° leeway	20 W.	5 W.
North Atlantic	Mizen t'gallant-stays'l and main upper-t'gallant torn. Repaired and reset Several trawlers in sight. Heavy squalls Large steamer bound W. to port at 1 p.m. 5° leeway	19 W.	4 W.
English Channel	Thunder squalls. Tacked ship starboard tack 8 a.m. Full sail. Both anchors prepared 11 p.m. Lizard Light bearing NE. by E. ¾ E. Wolf Rock N. ½ E. 5° leeway	19 W.	4 W.
English Channel	Set course to landmarks and light bearings. Full sail Took pilot 4 a.m. Tacked ship twice. Dropped anchors in Falmouth Roads 8 a.m.	—	—

Distance made by observations: 13,851

APPENDIX B

A BIBLIOGRAPHY OF LATTER-DAY SAIL

THE following list in no way claims to be exhaustive. It is comprised of books and periodicals which have proved helpful, informative, inspiring and interesting aids to the study of the vessels, the men and the trades of the last days of sail. Those marked * contain an extensive glossary of sail terminology.

A. TECHNICAL

Lloyd's Register (Volume I)
All the World's sail-tonnage in technical detail.
Lloyd's Daily Index
of Sailings, Speakings, Arrivals and Casualties.
Lloyd's Calendar.
A maritime encyclopædia of wide scope and usefulness.
Dana's Seaman's Manual. R. H. Dana, Jun. (Ward, Lock)
*An invaluable text-book on square-rig.
A Seafarer's Harvest. Commander R. L. Dearden, R.N. (Blackie)
Enough about navigation, seamanship and weather to turn a landsman into a sailor without sending him to sea.
Old Sea Wings, Ways and Words. R. C. Leslie (Chapman & Hall)
*Sea-lore, and windjammer development.
How to make Clipper Ship Models. E. W. Hobbs, A.I.N.A. (Brown, Son & Ferguson)
The standard work on this subject.
Sailing Models, Ancient and Modern. E. Keble Chatterton (Hurst & Blackett)
The evolution of sail, superbly illustrated.
Ships and Ship Models. (Percival Marshall)
A monthly technical magazine.
**A Dictionary of Sea Terms.* A. Ansted (Brown, Son & Ferguson)

B. HISTORICAL AND REFERENCE WORKS

The Last of the Windjammers (2 volumes); *The Colonial Clippers; The Nitrate Clippers.* Basil Lubbock (Brown, Son & Ferguson)
Three classics by the foremost living writer on sail matters.
In the Days of the Tall Ships. R. A. Fletcher (Brentano's)

Ocean Racers. Cicely Fox Smith (Philip Allan)
  The story of the Clippers.
Seamen All. E. Keble Chatterton (Philip Allan)
Ships and Seamen. Geoffrey Rawson (Thornton Butterworth)
  A pocket survey of maritime history.
Sailing Ships, Their History and Development. G. S. Laird Clowes,
  M.A., A.I.N.A. (H.M. Stationery Office)
Sail (3 volumes). Basil Lubbock and Jack Spurling (*Blue Peter*)
  The history of many famous vessels, beautifully illustrated by
  paintings.
The Last of a Glorious Era. Ronald Pearse (*Syren & Shipping*)
The Last Survivors in Sail. John Anderson (Percival Marshall)
A Short History of the World's Shipping Industry. C. Ernest Fayle
  (Allen & Unwin)
The Last Days of Mast and Sail. Sir Alan Moore, BT. (Oxford
  University Press)
  *A technical exposition on rig, fully illustrated by sketches.
Sea Breezes (The P.S.N. Company, Liverpool)
  An illustrated monthly, entirely devoted to reminiscences of sail.

POETRY

Sea Songs and Ballads; *Full Sail*; *Sailor's Delight*. Cicely Fox
  Smith (Methuen)
Songs and Chanties. Cicely Fox Smith (Elkin Mathews)
The Poems of John Masefield. (Heinemann)
Wind in the Topsails. Bill Adams (Harrap)

BOOKS ABOUT *HERZOGIN CECILIE*

Falmouth for Orders. Alan J. Villiers (Bles)
  Australia to England in 1928.
Wind in de Zeilen. W. L. Leclercq (Van Kampen, Amsterdam)
  Australia to England in 1932.
Out of the World. Pamela Bourne (Bles)
  Australia to England in 1934.

VOYAGES IN OTHER POST-WAR WINDJAMMERS

Fair Winds and Foul. Heinrich Hauser (Hurst & Blackett)
  Hamburg to Chile in *Pamir*.
Windjammer. Shaw Desmond (Hutchinson)
  Vancouver to Durban in *Hougomont*.

By Way of Cape Horn. Alan J. Villiers (Bles)
   Before the mast in *Grace Harwar*, 1929.
Voyage of the 'Parma'. Alan J. Villiers (Bles)
   1932 — written from the poop.
Strange Sea Road. Warren Bednall (Jonathan Cape)
   Melbourne to Gothenburg, *via* Torres, aboard *C. B. Pedersen*
   in 1935.
Rolling Round the Horn. Claude Muncaster (Rich & Cowan).
   An artist in *Olivebank's* foc'sle, 1931.
White Sails Crowding. Commander C. M. Butlin, D.S.C., R.N.
    (Jonathan Cape)
   A scholarly account of *L'Avenir's* 1933 homeward voyage.
Cape Horn Passage. W. M. Hutton (Blackie)
   A passenger in *Viking*, 1934.
Heavenly Hell. Richard Brinsley Sheridan (Putnam)
   A round voyage, before the mast, in *Lawhill*, 1934.
Under Sail in the Last of the Clippers. Frederick W. Wallace
    (Brown, Son & Ferguson)
   Montreal to Liverpool in 1920, in the old clipper *Hesperus*, then
   under Russian colours.
Horizon. Ken Attiwill (Jonathan Cape)
   The fo'c'sle of *Archibald Russell* in 1929.

F. MAINLY PICTORIAL

   The Sea in Ships. Alan J. Villiers (Routledge)
     Pictures aboard *Herzogin Cecilie* and *Grace Harwar*.
   The Last of the Windships. Alan J. Villiers (Routledge)
     200 photographs of life in the Grain Fleet.

G. MISCELLANEOUS

   Round the Horn before the Mast. Basil Lubbock (Murray)
     Home from 'Frisco in 1899.
   Sea Dogs of To-day. Alan J. Villiers (Harrap)
     Captains, crews, and craft.
   Victorious Troy. John Masefield (Heinemann)
     *A fictional account of the dismasting of a steel full-rigger,
     down south of the Horn.
   The Seagoer (Seagoer Publishing Co. Ltd.)
     A quarterly containing many narratives and pictures of square-rig.

APPENDIX C

A.B. Able-bodied seaman, as distinct from the less experienced ordinary seaman (o.s.).

ABACK. The position of sails when, instead of being distended, they are pressed against the mast by a head wind, and so tend to force the vessel astern.

ABAFT. Toward the stern.

ABEAM. At or from a point level with the centre of the hull.

ABOUT (to go). To change the direction of a vessel by putting her on to the opposite tack.

ACCOMMODATION LADDER. A set of railed steps, with one or more platforms, giving easy access from deck to quay (or boat).

AFTER. In a position nearer, relatively, to the stern.

AFTERGUARD. The Master and officers. Derived from the fact that, in sail, their quarters were, almost invariably, under the poop.

AFTER PEAK. The stern-most compartment below the main-deck, and, therefore, of irregular shape.

ALOW. On or under deck; the opposite of Aloft.

AMIDSHIPS. Actually a point midway along the centre-line of a hull, but used, broadly, for the central part of a vessel.

ATHWART. Across; at right-angles to the centre-line of the hull.

BACK (to). To trim a sail in such fashion that it receives the wind on its fore side; a method of checking the forward progress of the vessel.

BACKING. Of the wind when it veers in an anti-clockwise direction.

'BALD-HEADED'. Rigged without royal yards, the topgallants being the uppermost square-sails.

BALLAST. Heavy substances (or water, if tanks are fitted) carried, low down in the hull, to stabilize an empty vessel. 'In ballast' denotes an entire absence of cargo.

'BARE POLES'. Having no canvas set.

BEAM. The width of a hull at its widest part.

'BEAM ENDS'. A vessel is said to be 'on her beam ends' when forced completely over on her side.

BEAMS. Internal cross-supports of a hull.

BEAM WIND. A wind blowing at right-angles (roughly) to the length of a vessel.

BEARING. The direction of one object in relation to another.

BEAR UP (OR BEAR AWAY). To turn a vessel's head away from the wind, causing her to go to leeward and bringing the wind more abaft the beam.

BEAT. To advance toward the wind by a series of alternate tacks.

BECKET. A rope handle (often ornamental) to a sea-chest, etc.

BELAY. To make fast a rope by hitching it to a cleat or a belaying-pin.

BELAYING-PINS. Short, thick, round bars, of wood or iron, fitting loosely into holes in a rack or rail.

BEND. To attach or to fit into position.

BILGE. That part of the bottom and lower sides of a vessel on which she would rest if aground.

BILGE-KEEL. A strip, or flange, running along the outside of the turn of the bilge. Fitted to minimize rolling and to act as a true keel when, in sailing, the vessel heels over.

BILGE-WATER. Foul water, caused by slight leakage or condensation, which collects in the bilges.

BINNACLE. The stand and case housing a compass.

BITTS. Short, massive uprights, bolted through the deck, to which cables or wires are secured.

'BLACKWALLER'. A famous and beautiful type of passenger-carrying sailing vessel, built at Blackwall, River Thames, for the Colonial trades.

BLOCK. A sheaved pulley of wood or iron.

BOLLARD. *See* BITTS.

BOLT ROPE. Rope, running along the edge of a sail, round which the canvas is stitched.

BOOM. Spar spreading the foot of a fore-and-aft sail, or, in the old days, of a studding-sail.

BOSUN (Boatswain). The senior member of the crew; a link-man between officers and men.

BOSUN'S CHAIR. A short, plank seat, slung in a rope bridle, and travelling along a fixed wire or rope.

BOWER. The anchor(s) used at the head of a vessel.

BOWSPRIT. Spar projecting from the bows, and setting the head-sails, i.e. jibs and staysails.

BRACE. Rope, wire, or chain attached to the extremity of a yard, whose position it adjusts and controls.

'BRASS-BOUNDER'. An old and somewhat derisive term for a sea-apprentice. It referred to the wearing of uniform.

BREECHES BUOY. A canvas funnel, its mouth spread by a hoop, which can be hauled along a cable between ship and shore.

BROACH-TO. Said of a vessel which, when uncontrolled by her helm, has fallen away from her course, and lies broadside to high seas, in danger of capsizing or being dismasted.

BULKHEADS. Partitions dividing the interior area of a vessel into compartments.

BUNKERS. Vessel's supplies of fuel; also, the compartment where such fuel is stored.

BUNTLINE. Ropes attached to the lower part of the bunt, or body, of a sail. They lead up the sail and, through blocks on the yard and blocks on the mast, down to the deck. When hauled up they bunch the canvas below the yard, preparatory to the furling of the sail.

BY THE WIND (*see* CLOSE-HAULED). To sail with the wind ahead of the beam, course being set in relation to wind-direction instead of steering by compass.

CABLE LOCKER (or CABLE TIER). A compartment, in the bows below the main-deck, in which anchor-chains are coiled down as they come in through the hawse-pipes and round the windlass-drum.

'CAPE HORNER'. A sailing vessel trading regularly on routes which bring her past Cape Horn.

'CAPE STIFF'. Cape Horn.

CAPSTAN. A revolving drum, mounted perpendicularly to the deck, turned by long levers (capstan-bars) inserted into slots round its upper edge. Used for heavy haulage, especially of wire gear. Sometimes steam-driven.

CARRY AWAY. To snap a rope, spar, or lashing, or to lose canvas in bad weather.

CATHEAD. A metal or timber projection, at the bows, to which an anchor is raised before it is fished or stowed.

CATWALK. Railed foot-bridge connecting the superstructures on a vessel's main-deck.

CHARTER. A contract for the hire or use of a vessel or of any or all of her cargo-space.

'CHINA BIRDS'. Clipper-ships in the China tea trade.

CLEAT. Fixed peg or bar to which ropes are belayed. To cleat down is to lash to a ring-bolt or other similar hold.

CLEWS. The two lower corners of a square-sail.

CLEW LINES. Ropes, leading from the deck through blocks at the yard-arms, by which the clews are hauled up to the yard preparatory to furling the sail.

CLOSE-HAULED (*see* BY THE WIND). Describes a windjammer when she is sailing as nearly as possible toward the wind, her canvas being so trimmed that she is able to work to windward.

COAMING. The raised sill of a hatch or of a doorway; designed to prevent the entry of water.

COCK-BILL. To cant a yard at an angle to the deck; also, to leave an anchor hanging at the hawse.

COMPANION. A stairway leading below from the deck and having an enclosed, weatherproof entrance.

COUNTER. The curve of a vessel's stern, which projects beyond the sternpost.

CRINGLE. A rope ring worked into the bolt-rope of a sail. A reef-cringle is a similar loop on the body of a sail.

CROSS-TREES. V-shaped spreaders, near the head of the topmast, to brace and give purchase to the upper shrouds.

DAVITS. Curving, metal uprights fitted with tackle for hoisting or lowering a vessel's boats.

DEAD-EYE. A circular block of wood pierced by three holes through which are rove the lanyards by which shrouds and back-stays are set up taut. The circumference of the dead-eye has a deep groove.

DEEPWATERMAN. A vessel engaged in ocean trading, in contradistinction to coasting or local work.

DOG WATCH. Half-watch, of two hours, designed to break the continuity of 'four on and four off'.

DOLDRUMS. Belts of calm, with fickle winds and heavy rain-squalls, lying between the Trade-wind regions.

DONKEY ENGINE. Light steam-engine for driving winches, pumps, anchor-windlass, etc.

DOUBLING. The overlap of one section of a mast with another; also an underlying bolt of canvas fitted to strengthen the outer cloths at foot, head or leech of a sail.

DOWNHAUL. Rope for hauling jibs or staysails quickly down the stays, when taking in canvas.

DRAUGHT. Depth of water required to float a vessel; variable according to her load.

EASTING. A sailing vessel bound to Australia via the Cape of Good Hope traverses, below about latitude 45° S., a great area of open sea where strong, westerly winds prevail. Fast and continuous eastward sailing is, therefore, possible to such vessels between South Africa and Australia, and is known as 'running the Easting (or Eastern, as it used to be called) down'.

ENTRY. The narrowing of the lower part of a vessel's hull as her sides converge on the stem or cut-water.

EYES. The extreme forward part of the bows, where the plating is pierced by eye-like hawse-holes.

FAIRLEAD. A ring, sheave-hole or other contrivance by which rigging is led in a required direction or free of obstruction.

FALL. That rope, in a tackle, which is free or hauled upon.

FIDDLE. Strips of wood bisecting and surrounding the surface of a table as a safeguard against sliding crockery, etc.

FIFE-RAIL. Baulk of timber surrounding a mast, at deck-level, and housing the belaying-pins to which lead much of the running-rigging.

FLARE. The outward overhang of the sides of a vessel where they converge toward the bows.

FLEMISH COIL. A neat method of coiling down the slack of a rope on the deck in such fashion that it will not entangle when let run.

'FLYING KITES'. Fanciful, fair-weather additions to plain sail, augmenting the total area of canvas to a considerable degree, but of small relative power-value.

FORE-PEAK. The foremost compartment below the main-deck; a wedge-shaped space in the bows.

FORWARD (pronounced 'forrard'). Toward the bows of a vessel. Used as the opposite of abaft.

'FOUR POSTER'. A four-masted square-rigger, nowadays always a four-masted barque.

FREE. Sailing with a fair wind, i.e. with the wind abaft the beam.

FREEBOARD. Strictly, the distance between the lower-deck level and the water-line, but used to denote the entire amount of clearance above the surface of the water.

FRENCH FAKE. *See* FLEMISH COIL.

FULL-RIGGER. A sailing ship with three or more masts, all of which are square-rigged.

FURL. To gather up and lash a sail into a tight roll along the yard.

FUTTOCKS. Outward-sloping metal bars, crossed by rope ratlines and bracing the 'top' platform (or futtock-plate) to the mast.

GALLEY. Kitchen.

GAFF. A spar set at an angle to a mast and extending the head of a fore-and-aft sail. In the case of a gaff-topsail the foot of the sail is extended by the gaff.

GASKET. A length of light line passed round a sail (after the canvas has been gathered into a roll) to secure it to the yard.

'GHOST'. To maintain steerage-way in a faint breeze.

'GREEN'. To 'ship it green' is to take heavy seas aboard over the rail.

GRIPE. The tendency of some sailers to come up into the wind, and so to require much weather-helm.

GUNWALE. Or topgallant rail; the massive, upper rail running round the circumference of a vessel's open deck-space. *See* TAFFRAIL.

HALF-DECK. That part of a vessel's accommodation in which the apprentices live.

'HALF TIDE ROCK'. Used to describe a heavy-laden vessel when, in bad weather, her decks are continually inundated or swept by heavy seas.

HALLIARD. Or halyard; rope or wire by which yards, and sometimes sails, are hoisted.

HARNESS CASK. Brine vat for storing salt meat.

HAUL OUT. To give a vessel more sea-room by altering course away from the proximity of land.

HAWSE-HOLE. An aperture in the bows through which runs the anchor cable.

HAZING. Bullying.

HEAD. The upper edge of a square-sail; also, the fore part of a hull.

HEAD SAILS (or HEAD CANVAS). The jibs and staysails set between fore-mast and bowsprit; the expression may include, also, the square-sails on the foremast.

HEAVE-TO. To put a vessel, in bad weather, with her weather bow facing wind and sea, her sails being so trimmed that she rides in that position; also, to set part of her canvas aback in order to check forward progress.

HELM ORDERS. Steering commands based on the ancient method of operating a rudder by means of a tiller (i.e. lever); the tiller was put in the opposite direction to which the rudder and the head of the vessel turned.

HOGGED. A vessel which, through lack of equalized support, sags at bow and stern or subsides amidships, so buckling her plating and straining her framing.

HOLYSTONE. Large, abrasive block for scouring deck-planking.

'IDLERS'. Those members of a crew who, by reason of their duties (e.g. carpenter, sailmaker, etc.), work by day and sleep at night instead of sharing in the watch rota.

'IN IRONS' (or 'MISSED STAYS'). Said of a vessel which, having failed to go about on a fresh tack, is left head to wind, unable to pay off.

JACOB'S LADDER. Rope-ladder with wooden rungs.

JETTISON. To sacrifice cargo or gear by throwing it overside.

JIB. A triangular sail set between foremast and bowsprit.

JIBBOOM. A spar rigged as an extension to a bowsprit.

JIGGER. The aftermost mast of a four-masted barque.

JURY-RIG. Temporary and, usually, unorthodox gear, improvised to replace lost spars, sails or rudder.

'KETTLE-BOTTOMED'. A vessel having a flat floor and bulging lower sides.

KNIGHTHEADS. Heavy beams, to either side of the stem, flanking the bowsprit. In bygone times the crown of such a beam was carved to the likeness of a head.

LABOURING. Pitching and rolling violently in heavy seas.

LANDFALL. The extremities of an ocean passage, i.e. the last proximate coastline visible at departure and the first land sighted upon arrival.

LANYARDS. Short ropes, rove through dead-eyes, by which heavier gear is set up taut.

LATEEN. A large, triangular sail bent to a long, cock-billed, curving yard.

LAZARETTE. Secure storage-place for provisions; usually in proximity to the officers' quarters.

LEAD. A weight with a recessed base: used for sounding the depth of water and for ascertaining the composition of the sea-bed.

LEADING WIND. A fair wind, i.e. blowing from abaft the beam or from astern.

LEE. That side of a vessel which is away from the wind; the opposite of WEATHER.

LEE HELM. Corrects any tendency in a vessel to fall away from the wind.

LEE SHORE. A vessel which is being blown onshore is said to have the land 'under her lee', and the coast becomes, to her, a 'lee shore'.

LEEWARD (pronounced 'loo'ard'). On the lee side, i.e. down-wind; the opposite of WINDWARD.

LEEWAY. Bodily drift down-wind; sideway divergence from a steered course.

LEECH-LINES. Ropes, running from the deck, over the yard, to the leeches (or vertical edges) of square-sails; used, like buntlines and clewlines, for furling sail.

LEG. Distance sailed between changes of course when beating against the wind by a series of tacks.

LIFT. Rope, chain or wire gear for supporting, raising and lowering a yard.

LIGHT-LINE. The water-line of a vessel in ballast trim.

'LIME-JUICER'. A derisive term applied to British sailing vessels; it arose from the custom of serving lime-juice as an anti-scorbutic.

LINE (THE). The Equator.

LINES. The contour, or shape, of a hull.

LOAD-LINE. The mark to which a vessel sinks when fully laden.

LOG. An automatic recorder of distance run — a towed spinner register-
ing on a dial. The ship's official journal, recording progress,
weather, and general happenings.

LUBBER'S HOLE. Vent between futtock-plate and mast, giving access to
higher rigging without using the futtock-shrouds.

MISSED STAYS. *See* IN IRONS.

MOONSAIL and MOONRAKER. Small, light square-sails set above skysails.
Now obsolete.

'NO CURE, NO PAY'. A form of salvage contract, under which remuneration is dependent upon the success of the operations.

O.S. Ordinary (i.e. relatively unskilled) seaman.

OUTBOARD CHANNELS. Ledges, projecting outward from the side of the
hull, to spread the lower rigging. Now obsolete.

OVERHAUL. To examine and loosen light running-gear so as to ensure
its free operation and to avoid chafage.

PACKET. A passenger vessel engaged in a regular mail-carrying service.

PARCEL (or SERVE). To fit any form of protective covering or binding to
rigging.

PARREL. Device for confining a yard to a mast.

PASSAGE. A journey between two ports, as distinct from a round, i.e.
out and home, voyage.

PAWL. A loose, metal arm which clanks over the toothed ratchet at the
base of a capstan-drum, but which engages with the teeth when the
drum ceases to revolve, so locking it and preventing it from reversing.

PAY OFF. To allow a vessel's head to turn away from the wind by the
action of the wind.

PLAIN SAIL. Full, normal spread of orthodox canvas.

PORT. The left-hand side of a vessel (facing forward). A vessel sailing
on the port tack has the wind blowing on to her port side.

PORT-LIGHT (or PORTHOLE). Circular, brass-rimmed scuttle or window;
the glazed portion is hinged, and opens inward. 'Painted ports'
were imitation gun-ports painted, as black squares on a white band,
along the side of a merchantman.

PUMP ROOM. Under-deck compartment containing the bilge-pumps.

QUARTER. That section of the circumference of a hull which lies between the counter and the midship mark. Quarter-boats are the lifeboats mounted on either quarter, i.e. usually on the poop.

RAKE. The sternward inclination of a mast from the perpendicular. The forward slope, from keel to bowsprit, of a vessel's stem.

REEFING. To decrease the area of a square-sail by furling only its upper section, or reef.

REEF-POINTS. Short, loose lengths of rope fastened at regular intervals across the body of a sail, forming a reef-band and enabling the reef itself to be bound to the yard.

RIDE. To remain (at anchor or when hove-to) in a given position despite wind, sea, or tide.

RIG. The style in which a vessel's masts and sails are fitted; also, to equip with rigging, spars, sails or gear.

RING-BOLT. Heavy iron ring bolted to the deck.

ROADS. A sheltered, offshore anchorage.

ROBANDS. Short lengths of rope-yarn by which the head of a square-sail is secured to the jack-stay of the yard.

ROSE-BOX. A pierced cap, at the suction end of a pump, acting as a strainer.

RUN. To sail before a following wind. The sternward convergence of a vessel's sides.

RUNNING RIGGING (or RUNNING GEAR). Comprises all *moving* ropes controlling sails or spars, e.g. sheets, braces, halliards, buntlines, etc.

'SAILOR'S WAY'. The route, to or from the West Coast of North or South America, past Cape Horn.

SCUD. To run before a gale under minimum canvas.

SCUPPERS. Gully, or open drain, running round the outer edge of a deck at the foot of the bulwarks or rails.

SCUTTLE. Covered vent, in a deck, to admit light or air, or to provide entry; also, to sink a craft by foul means.

SEA-ANCHOR. A heavy, improvised raft, enabling a vessel moored to it to remain head to sea and so to ride out bad weather in safety.

SEA-ROOM. A sufficiency of open sea to enable a vessel to manœuvre without fear of stranding.

SEIZE. To fasten or bind by lashings of light stuff, such as marline, spun-yarn, etc.

SEIZINGS. Spaced-out bindings round the lower end of the shrouds. Usually picked out with white paint.

SERVE. *See* PARCEL.

SET UP. To tauten rigging.

SHARP UP (or SHARP ROUND). Describes a yard when it is hauled round, by braces, to the maximum extent.

SHEAVE. A grooved pulley-wheel.

SHEET. Rope, wire or chain controlling the clew of a sail. *See* TACK.

SHEET ANCHOR. The largest of a vessel's several anchors.

'SHELLBACK'. An old sailor who has spent most of his life at sea, especially if he has served in sail.

SHROUDS. Heavy-gauge wires from mast-head to deck, giving lateral support and, where crossed by ratlines, providing a means of getting aloft.

SKIDS. Parallel, arched rails running thwartships and joined by a platform on which rest boats.

'SKYSAIL-YARDER'. A square-rigger crossing a skysail yard above the royal on one or more of her masts.

SNUB. To check suddenly the run of a rope.

SPANKER. Large, lower, fore-and-aft sail set, by boom and gaff, on the aftermost mast of a barque or ship.

SQUARED. Describes yards when they are trimmed at right-angles to the centre-line of a vessel.

SQUARE-RIGGER. A sailing vessel whose masts carry yards from which square-sail is set, in contradistinction to a schooner or other fore-and-aft type whose sails are set, along the centre-line, on booms.

STANCHION. A fixed upright, supporting bulwarks, etc.

STANDING RIGGING. Comprises all that part of the rigging which is permanently 'in situ', such as shrouds, stays, footropes, etc., and which plays no part in the handling of sails or spars.

STARBOARD. The right-hand side of a vessel (facing forward).

STAYSAILS. Triangular sails set on the forestays of each mast.

STEERAGE-WAY. A vessel maintains steerage-way when she makes controlled progress, however slight.

STEM. The foremost upright beam in a hull, marking the junction of the bows.

STERN DELIVERY. The contour of the lines of a hull where the stern leaves the water.

STOCK. The crosspiece at the head of an anchor.

STOP. To fasten temporarily in such fashion that a strong pull will free the rope or sail.

STRAKE. Any one of the tiers of plating along the length of a hull.

STUDDING SAIL (pronounced 'stuns'l'). Light, fair-weather set sail on a boom rigged as an extension to a yard. Now obsolete.

SUBROGATION. The right of an insurer to take over, if he so desires and after he has paid a loss, the rights and remedies of the assured in the subject-matter in question.

SUPERCARGO. A member of the personnel of a vessel who takes no part in working her. In earlier days a supernumerary clerk in charge of the trading side of a sea-venture.

TACK. To put a vessel about by bringing her head across the wind; a series of tacks produce a zig-zag course toward the wind, each side of the vessel becoming, alternately, weather and lee.

The weather clew of a course (i.e. of a lower square-sail) is controlled by a tack when it is carried right forward, the lee clew being led aft by its sheet.

TAFFRAIL. That part of the topgallant rail which encircles the stern.

THWARTSHIPS. Across the breadth of a hull.

TOPGALLANT RAIL. *See* GUNWALE and TAFFRAIL.

TOP-HAMPER. The whole of the motive power of a sailing vessel, e.g. masts, spars, sails, rigging, etc.

TRICK. A spell, or period, of work; usually associated with the duty of helmsman.

TRIM. The adjustment of cargo or ballast; also, the resultant position of a vessel in the water, governed by the amount and situation of her contents.

TRUCK. A circular wooden cap at the extreme mast-head; the highest point of the top-hamper.

'TUMBLE-HOME'. When the sides of a hull incline inward as they rise to deck-level, the breadth of the hull being less there than at the water-line; the opposite of FLARE.

VOYAGE. Used generally in this book to denote a double passage, i.e. a round voyage — out and home.

WAIST. That part of the main deck which is exposed between poop and fo'c'sle. The area where a vessel has her lowest freeboard.

WATCH. At the outset of a passage the crew are divided into two working parties, under the Mates, known as the Port and Starboard watches.

WEAR. To alter course by turning a vessel's head away from the wind so that she describes a wide arc in attaining her new direction.

WEATHER. That side of a vessel upon which the wind is blowing; the opposite of LEE.

WEATHER HELM. Corrects the tendency of a sailing vessel to gripe, i.e. to run up into the wind and be taken aback.

WINDLASS. A large capstan, usually steam-driven and having auxiliary hand-power; employed for hoisting anchor. *See* CAPSTAN.

WINDWARD. On the weather side, i.e. up-wind; the opposite of LEE-WARD.

YARDS. Spars crossing the masts of a square-rigged vessel. They are attached to the mast at their centre-point, some as fixtures, others capable of being hoisted and lowered. All, however, can be swung from side to side. A yard spreads the head of a square-sail.

YARD-ARM. Either extremity of a yard.

YAW. To make small deviations from a set course owing to faulty steering, to badly set canvas, or to some innate idiosyncrasy of the vessel herself.

ADDENDUM

CHILE 1914–1920

(From an account published in the Year Books of the Norddeutscher Lloyd Company)

SOME two hundred miles to the north of Valparaiso lies the sheltered Bay of Herradura, which takes its name from a small fishing village, a holiday resort of the nearby seaport of Coquimbo. On the south shore of the bay are the smelting works of Guyacan, with an anchorage for vessels importing fuel.

On July 25th, 1914, *Herzogin Cecilie* entered Herradura Bay and commenced to deliver her part-cargo of 2,500 tons of coke. A few days later the news of the outbreak of War gave rise to labour difficulties, and the remaining 1,800 tons of coke was discharged by the personnel of the barque.

In addition to her officers and a small crew, *Herzogin Cecilie* was carrying seventy-five cadets, and, although temporary internment in neutral waters was preferable to almost certain capture on the high seas, no one on board visualized the possibility of a confinement of six years, or that, before their vessel again set sail, three would die, seventeen escape, and many of the rest settle down as residents in Chile.

In the early days of that dreary period, local feeling was strongly anti-German, and by July, 1915, when, following numerous insults, stones were thrown at shore-going parties, all leave from the barque was suspended.

Late in 1914 representations had been made to the authorities that *Herzogin Cecilie's* wireless was being utilized to transmit information to Admiral Graf von Spee's squadron. It was afterwards understood that a German secret agent in Chile informed von Spee of the whereabouts of Admiral Cradock, who was then awaiting the arrival of the battleship *Canopus*.

Von Spee annihilated Cradock off Coronel (500 miles south of Herradura Bay) on November 1st, only to be decimated in turn, a short while later, at the Battle of the Falklands. The light cruiser

Dresden, the sole German survivor, returned to the Pacific, but was trapped and sunk by H.M.S. *Kent* at Juan Fernandez (Robinson Crusoe's island), which lies off the Chilean coast near Herradura.

Herzogin Cecilie was proved to be innocent of complicity in these naval events, for, when the Harbour Commandant of Coquimbo investigated the charges, he found that the seals which had been placed on her wireless installation were still intact. At the request of the British Consulate, however, further precautions were instituted. Guard-posts were set up on either bank of the quarter of a mile wide channel which forms the entrance to Herradura Bay. Their object was to prevent any attempt to reach the open sea in small boats; at the same time, the use and practice of Morse signalling on the barque was forbidden.

Captain Ballehr maintained unbroken discipline aboard *Herzogin Cecilie*; the training of the cadets continued so far as circumstances would permit, boat-drill and theoretical work being supplemented by a survey of the bay and district; the charts which resulted were presented to the Chilean Government.

As the weary months passed and local opinion, fostered by German propaganda, became less hostile and more tolerant, sports on shore and in the water became a feature of the life, and parties were organized to give concerts, entertainments, and gymnastic displays ashore. By like means, and by the sale of the products of hobbies and handicrafts, a total of over $13,000 was raised by the personnel of the barque; it was given to such charities as the Red Cross and the Relief Fund for destitute Germans in Chile.

A party of cadets was allowed to undertake a long explorative expedition into the Chilean hinterland, a journey which involved good mountaineering.

Two deaths occurred while *Herzogin Cecilie* lay at her moorings at Guyacan anchorage. In October 1914 a cadet was killed by diving into shallow water; while in January 1916 the steward, Reinecke, succumbed to inflammation of the lungs. They were both buried in the little European cemetery at Guyacan settlement.

Immediately upon the outbreak of war, four of the barque's officers had left, by permission of Captain Ballehr, to try to reach Germany.

In 1917, a daring and successful escape was planned and executed by one officer and thirteen cadets. To avoid suspicion they divided into two parties, going ashore in uniform and there changing into civilian disguises provided by sympathizers. The first party reached their objective, Calbuco in the south of Chile, but they had been recognized, when in a train, by their fair colouring. Representations were thereupon made to the Master to take every precaution against further desertion, but, a few days later, the second party slipped away, and, ultimately, joined forces with their comrades at Calbuco.

The little band set sail in the old barque *Tinto* of Chilean registry, whose owner, and also the former master of *Tinto*, were, subsequently, punished for their complicity in the plan. A Chilean naval vessel was badly damaged during the search for the fugitives, who, months later, safely reached the Norwegian port of Drontheim. The affair caused much trouble, for it was suggested that, by its failure to apprehend the party, the Chilean Government had committed a breach of neutrality; conditions were therefore imposed which negatived any further chance of escape from *Herzogin Cecilie*.

When, in April 1917, the United States of America entered the War, the Allies endeavoured to induce Chile to break diplomatic relations with Germany in order that the large quota of shipping sheltering in Chilean waters might be confiscated.

A rumour became current that there was a possibility of interned vessels being forcibly towed out of their havens of refuge, and, as a result, certain precautions were taken by Captain Ballehr. *Herzogin Cecilie*'s rudder, weighing three and a half tons, was unshipped and suspended overside by tackle in order that it could be dropped into deep water at a moment's notice. The steering-gear was dismantled, the component parts being laid on a prepared shute, so arranged that its contents could be tipped into the sea. Measures for scuttling the barque, by means of sea-cocks, were rehearsed in secret, and containers of sulphuric acid were placed in readiness for destroying the sails, which had already been stowed away below.

Towards the end of the War, local feeling again became strongly pro-Ally, and, in November 1918, a large guard of armed Chilean sailors was quartered aboard *Herzogin Cecilie*. They conducted an intensive search for concealed explosives, and, although their number was decreased as time went on, the barque remained under resident supervision for the rest of her stay in South America.

With peace in sight at last, preparations for a homeward passage were carried on with feverish activity. Much of the tophamper had been dismantled but, now, yards were sent aloft again and rigging re-installed. Bitter was the disappointment on board, however, when it was realized that Germany's shipping had become the spoil of her victors and that *Herzogin Cecilie* must, therefore, languish in captivity pending her disposition.

About this time the unfortunate vessel was swept by an epidemic of influenza, which resulted in the death of another cadet.

On November 15th, 1918, arrangements were completed, by the Chilean Naval Authorities, for a cruiser to tow *Herzogin Cecilie* to Coquimbo, where she would be more under their control. Owing to the speed at which she was towed, the barque was several times in great danger during the short passage. On one occasion the towing-hawser snapped, and she drifted, helplessly, toward a rocky coast. The broken rope fouled the screw of the cruiser, and all she could do was to send away her boats to succour the Germans from an apparently unavoidable wreck. As *Herzogin Cecilie* neared the shore, however, a tug, which had followed from Guyacan but which had been out-distanced by the fast tow, managed to pass a rope, and the barque was gradually hauled off-shore and brought safely to anchorage in Coquimbo Roads. She was not allowed to fly German colours during the shift as that would have rendered her liable to seizure as a prize.

Her fate hung in the balance for another eighteen months, but in June 1920 came the definite news that German sailing vessels in Chile could proceed to Europe. By this time many changes had taken place among the personnel. By escape and by death her complement had shrunk to less than seventy-five per cent of its former strength and, one by one, as hope of return waned, her cadets had requested to be discharged in order to take up positions ashore as engineers, surveyors, officers in local vessels, farmers, and so forth, to which end many of them took out naturalization papers. Finally, only eleven cadets were left on board, and, during the last year of detention, all instruction was discontinued.

At last, in July, Captain Ballehr received orders to load a cargo of nitrate for Europe at Caleta Coloso, a small, bleak port near Antofagasta, and about 350 miles north of Coquimbo.

No dry-dock was available in which the tremendous encrustation of bottom-growth could be scraped away, but, before she was fit to sail, these huge barnacles had to be removed. They were likened to cauliflowers, for, in the six years of idleness, thick, sprouting stalks had grown out from the plating. Working from a raft, the crew, with long-handled scrapers, cut the growth away as far as the turn of the bilges. Then a sleigh-like appliance, the size of a table and having cutting edges, was hauled along the barque's bottom by special tackle. Finally she was listed over by shifting her ballast and trimming her tanks, and the plating thus exposed was repainted.

For the two-day passage to Caleta Coloso the crew was augmented by five sailors from the German windjammer *Niobe* and by some Chileans. There, she discharged ballast, loaded 3900 tons of nitrate and went on to Antofagasta, where a diver completed the bottom-cleaning and where nine more Germans, who had been brought from Europe by the steamer *Lucie Woermann*, joined for the homeward run.

On October 1st, 1920, *Herzogin Cecilie* sailed from Antofagasta for Falmouth. Cape Horn was rounded on the twenty-first day out, and the Line was crossed thirty days later. This was fine sailing, but head-winds and calms in the North Atlantic delayed the barque, and it was almost Christmas before she made her Channel landfall. As related in Book Two, Chapter v, she received orders to proceed to Ostend for discharge, where all members of the crew who could be spared were given immediate leave. They arrived at Bremen on the last day of 1920, and, led by Captain Ballehr, were received by the Directorate of the Norddeutscher Lloyd.

TWENTY YEARS LATER

THE DEMISE OF THE TRADING WINDJAMMER

The grave of the 'Duchess'

'C. B. Pedersen' sunk in collision 1937

By the end of 1957 not one of the big sailing ships which have been the subject of this book, was still at sea for during that year, of the three still in commission, *Abraham Rydberg*, by then Portuguese and renamed *Foz de Douro*, was scrapped, *Pamir* had foundered with the loss of eighty lives and *Passat*, after carrying the last trans-ocean cargo shipped in square-rig, was permanently laid up.

Two decades earlier, the last vestige of *Herzogin Cecilie* had disappeared. The end came almost three years after her stranding in Sewer Mill Cove. She had lain in Starehole Bay throughout the rigours of two winters after the ship-breakers to whom Erikson had sold the wreck had abandoned their partial demolition. Bulwarks, fo'c'sle-head and much of the poop-deck, rails and fittings had been removed, but her four great masts were still erect with taut shrouds, and it seemed she might remain, a sad monument to a past era of maritime history, for years to come.

But on January 19th, 1939, during the second day of a protracted and severe gale, the masts went by the board, the hull capsized and broke into four parts and, by the next day, the wreckage of the proud white 'Duchess' was completely submerged.

The tabulation on pages 102–3 shows that at the end of 1936 sixteen big trading square-riggers were still actively employed. Twelve were then owned at Mariehamn by Gustaf Erikson, two by F. Laeisz of Hamburg and two in Gothenburg.

Four months later on April 25th, the Swedish four-mast barque *C. B. Pedersen* was sunk in collision with Elders & Fyffe's steamer *Chagres* 600 miles south-west of the Azores. It was a fine, moonlit night and lights were clearly visible. *Pedersen* was struck on the starboard quarter between the mizzen and jigger masts, and went down within twenty minutes. *Chagres*, outward bound from Swansea to Puerto Cortes, put into the Azores for repair carrying *Pedersen's* complete complement of thirty-two. The Master of *Chagres* died from heart-failure caused by the shock of the casualty, which was later to involve his Owners in a costly reimbursement.

Another four-mast barque was more tragically lost the following year. Erikson had sold *L'Avenir* to the Hamburg-Amerika Line for conversion to a school ship for, it is said, almost six times the £3,000 he had paid for her in 1932. Renamed *Admiral Karpfanger*, she sailed from Port Germein in Spencer Gulf, with bagged grain, early in February 1938 and was in wireless touch on March 12th. Later a fragment of identifiable wreckage was found on Navarino Island but, despite a thorough search of the vicinity of Cape Horn by Chilean ships, no other trace could be found of the barque or of her complement of sixty, about half of them cadets. It was presumed that either she had struck an iceberg or that she had broached-to in heavy weather and capsized. In the September of that year, Lloyd's posted her as missing. So, at the onset of the second great war of this century, the world's active deep-water sail tonnage comprised fourteen barques: eleven Finnish, two German and one Swedish.

'Admiral Karpfanger' ex 'L'Avenir' posted 'missing' 1938

In the spring of 1939 eleven of the fourteen had loaded South Australian grain and all reached their European port of discharge in safety. *Moshulu* made the best passage of the year by calling at Queenstown for orders ninety-one days out from Port Victoria.

Gustaf Erikson (whose greatest loss by war was to be that of his youngest son, drowned when Third Mate of the Finnish steamer *Argo*, when she was sunk in the Baltic) lost three of his sailing-ships through enemy action.

'Olivebank' mined 1939

Within five days of the outbreak of war, his forty-seven-year-old *Olivebank* struck a mine off the Danish coast and sank with the loss of her Master, Captain Granith, the Mate and twelve of the crew. Seven survivors were picked up by an Esbjerg trawler after they had clung to the rigging of a projecting spar for fifty hours without food or drink.

Olivebank, after a long passage of 119 days from Port Victoria to Queenstown, had discharged her grain at Barry and sailed south-about in ballast for Mariehamn.

The only three three-mast barques still afloat were Erikson's *Penang*, *Winterhude* and *Killoran*; two of them were lost by war perils almost at the same time.

Penang had not participated in the 1939 Australian grain-fleet because in the previous year she had spent sixty-three days repairing at Dunedin where she had put in for refuge after extensive weather damage which included the loss of her main top-mast. In consequence it was 210 days in all before she reached England.

In July 1939 she sailed from Middlesbrough for Mauritius arriving at the end of October. She loaded guano at Juan de Nova for Auckland and discharged in March 1940. On June 27th she sailed from Port Victoria with a cargo of grain and, months later, enemy radio announced that she had been torpedoed off Ireland and that there were no survivors of her complement of eighteen. As this statement could not be confirmed, Lloyd's, in March 1941, posted *Penang* as 'Untraced'.

The last pre-war cargo of Australian grain to arrive in Europe by sail was carried by *Killoran*. She had been 139 days at sea when, after running the submarine blockade, she made Queenstown for orders and discharged at nearby Cork in November 1939. From there, in January 1940, she was towed to Cardiff to load coal for Buenos Aires, where she arrived in May. On June 15th, laden with 2,500 tons of maize and 500 tons of sugar, she sailed for Las Palmas.

On the morning of August 10th, in latitude 32.30° N., longtitude 34° W., an unidentified steamer fired a shot across her bows. She was ordered to heave-to and to send a boat across. Captain Leman went with four men and found himself aboard a German auxiliary cruiser. He was interrogated about his cargo, its consignors and consignees, and a German officer went aboard *Killoran* to verify his statements. Nevertheless the Captain of the raider maintained that the ultimate destination of the cargo was England and that therefore *Killoran*, a neutral vessel trading between neutral ports with non-contraband cargo, must be sunk. Part of the sugar cargo and all spirits and tobacco found aboard were transferred to the raider before three time-bombs were set and the crew ordered to the boats: *Killoran* sank within a minute and a half of the explosion.

Captain Leman and his crew were aboard the cruiser for forty-one days, then transferred to another vessel in which, on October 9th, they reached St. Nazaire. They were sent to an internment camp at Montreuil-sur-Saumur but, after efforts by the Finnish Consulate, all except one New Zealander were transferred to Paris and, in January 1941, were repatriated to Finland.

Lloyd's had, in November 1940, posted *Killoran* as 'Missing', but a few days before this, a copy of *Deutsche Allegemeine Zeitung* had come into the hands of Gustaf Erikson and, in its illustrated supplement, he had recognized, in a photograph of the sinking of a sailing-ship, his own *Killoran*.

The foregoing three war losses leave the fate of eight Erikson tall ships to be recounted. *Viking*, *Passat* and *Pommern* all berthed safely at Mariehamn in 1939 after discharging their Australian grain in the United Kingdom. They lay in their home port until July 1944 when they were towed across to Stockholm to serve as floating grain-stores. After the armistice between Russia and Finland they were towed back to Abö with relief cargoes of wheat.

Pommern never went to sea again because Gustaf Erikson presented her to his home town of Mariehamn to be a reminder to future genera- *'Pommern' at Mariehamn for posterity* tions of Ålanders of the old Tall Ships. She is permanently moored and is maintained as a museum and nautical club.

Viking refitted at Mariehamn in the summer of 1946 and in Decem- *'Viking' now a school-ship* ber loaded a full cargo of Baltic timber for South Africa. It was a tough voyage, for she encountered severe North Atlantic winter gales, but she arrived safely. Some voyaging in the Southern Hemisphere followed before, in 1949, *Viking* loaded grain in Spencer Gulf for the United Kingdom. She arrived in July and was then towed from London to Antwerp where she carried out repairs and was laid up. Later, Sweden purchased her from Erikson and berthed her at Gothenburg to serve as a maritime school-ship.

Passat had many years of seafaring ahead and was destined to be, in 1957, the last active survivor of the Tall Ships of this book, so she will be the subject of the closing section of this Epilogue.

Archibald Russell discharged her final grain cargo at Hull in August *'Archibald Russell' scrapped 1949* 1939. She was still in the Humber when hostilities opened between England and Finland and was then taken over and used for food storage. To obviate her presenting a sighting mark for German bombers, her topmasts, to'gallant masts and all her yards were dismantled. In 1948 she was shifted to Newcastle before being handed back to Erikson who, in October 1949, sold her to a United Kingdom scrapyard.

Winterlude, the last and oldest of the three-mast barques, was a late *'Winterhude' hulked 1945* arrival in the United Kingdom from Australia in 1939. Having discharged her grain, she sailed to Stavanger under time-charter to Norway as a granary for the State Grain Control. During their occupation of Norway, the Germans shifted her to Copenhagen to serve as a floating barracks, the object apparently being to segregate certain of their naval personnel from shore contacts. In October 1945 she was towed to Hamburg to end her days as a coal hulk.

'Lawhill's' four years of service to the Allies

'Lucky' *Lawhill*, the oldest surviving windjammer, built at Dundee in 1892, the same year as the Clyde-built veteran *Olivebank*, made a poor homeward passage of 140 days from Australia to Falmouth in 1939. She discharged at Glasgow and was laid-up in Rothesay Bay until May 1940 when she sailed from Troon for Montevideo. This was an excellent voyage of fifty-four days, and was followed by an equally good thirty-eight day run round the Cape of Good Hope to Mahé in the Seychelles where she loaded guano for Auckland, discharging there early in 1941.

Her next cargo was grain from Spencer Gulf for South Africa. Loading in May 1941, she reached East London in July but, while discharging, was seized as a prize by the South African Government, actually before war had been declared between England and Finland. It was not until April 1942 that the Prize Court at Cape Town granted the Union Government's application for an Order condemning the barque as a lawful prize of war.

The Union decided to keep her at sea under their management and, insured for S. Afr. £28,000, she sailed from East London in September 1943 for Bunbury, West Australia. This was quite a remarkable passage for a sailing-ship of over fifty years of age, for she arrived in twenty-three days. The direct steamer route is 4,700 miles so *Lawhill*, 'running her Easting down' logged an average of at least 200 miles per day.

She continued to voyage between the two continents and when on one occasion she berthed at Sydney, she was said to be the first of her kind for twenty-one years to berth in that superb harbour which had housed so many famous wool-clippers in the heyday of trade under sail.

The Union Government had maintained *Lawhill's* Finnish Master, Captain Soderlund, in command with part of his original crew supplemented by a sprinkling of Danes, Norwegians, British and Australians, and she carried a 'half-deck' of eight cadets. Captain Soderlund has stated that in her four years of service to the Allies this fine vessel, the last trading square-rigger owned in the British Empire, had transported 55,000 tons of cargo. He recalled that on her first round voyage under the Blue Ensign of the Union, when returning to South Africa from Australia round Cape Horn loaded right down to her marks with grain, her deck was continuously awash for eighteen hours, during which skylights and companionways were swept away; but after eighty days at sea, 'lucky' *Lawhill* delivered her cargo intact.

This grand old ship ended her days derelict at Lourenco Marques. She surely deserved a better fate than abandonment to the ravages of rust and rot.

Moshulu was Gustaf Erikson's last sail purchase, four years before the war. After her winning ninety-one-day passage from Port Victoria to Queenstown in the 1939 so-called grain race, she loaded grain again in January 1940, this time at Buenos Aires. She approached the south coast of Norway, unwittingly, on the very night of the German invasion. Threatened by a minefield she put into Farsund on April 10th and was captured there, taken to Christiannsund for discharge and then towed to Kirkenaes, a northern Norwegian port, where later she was found and seized by Russia. *'Moshulu' now a store ship*

When Erikson regained possession of *Moshulu* she had been roughly handled and was in poor condition. He sold her to Norway and later she was re-sold to Sweden for grain storage, but ultimately she came back into Finnish hands and is in use as a storeship at Nådendahl.

Priwall, owned by Laiesz of Hamburg, was outward bound from her home port to load nitrate in Chile in 1939. She arrived at Valparaiso on the actual day of the outbreak of war and was interned there until 1941 when Chile, then being at war with the Axis, converted her to a motor-ship, renamed her *Lautaro*, and manned her with 300 cadets. Like so many nitrate-carriers in the past, *Lautaro's* cargo combusted when in March 1945 she was burned out with the loss of twenty lives. *'Priwall' burnt 1945*

The other Laiesz four-master, *Padua*, sailed for Germany from the Clyde on the eve of war, after discharging her grain cargo. She berthed at Hamburg on August 9th, survived our intensive bombing of that port, and was found there after Germany capitulated. *Padua* later served for a spell in the Baltic as a training-ship for the Mercantile Marine, but was refitted at Rostock and, in January 1946, was handed over to the Russian Navy as a school-ship to accommodate several hundred naval personnel. She is now named *Krusenstein*. *'Padua' now a Russian school-ship*

EPILOGUE

'Abraham Rydberg' re-named 'Foz de Douro' broken up 1957

The only Swedish four-master still trading in 1939 was the cargo training barque *Abraham Rydberg*. On the eve of war she left Gothenburg for Buenos Aires and then sailed homeward for Denmark. Being, unlike most of her contemporary sailers, equipped with wireless, she was diverted to American waters but, sustaining heavy weather damage, put into Barbados. The cargo was sold to American consignees and in March 1940 she discharged at New York.

For two years *Rydberg*, still under the Swedish flag, plied between U.S. Atlantic ports and the East coast of South America before being laid up at Baltimore during the height of the U-boat activities in American waters. She was bought by Portugal, renamed *Foz de Douro* and, until March 1945 when she was converted into a diesel auxiliary, sailed regularly between Portugal and the Americas, often with Red Cross cargoes. She was then laid up at Philadelphia but in 1951 was purchased by the Sociedade Industrial Ultramarina of Lisbon. *Foz de Douro* was broken up at Spezia in February 1957.

So to the last two survivors of the sixteen Tall Ships to be dealt with in this Epilogue, both of them being under the German flag.

'Pamir' foundered 1957

Pamir was built in 1905 by Blohm & Voss at Hamburg for the Flying P Line of nitrate-carriers owned by Ferdinand Laiesz of that port. The 1914-18 war had cost Laiesz the whole of his fleet of fourteen windjammers but, between the wars, he rebuilt it by repurchasing six of his ships and building two new ones, *Priwall* and *Padua*.

When the nitrate trade under sail ceased to be a financial proposition Laiesz gradually disposed of all his sailers except the two new ones. Gustaf Erikson bought *Penang*, *Ponape*, *Pommern*, *Passat* and, in 1931, *Pamir*. As was his pleasing custom, he retained their original names.

Pamir was a typical German nitrate sailer. Slightly smaller than *Priwall* and *Padua* built in the Twenties, she was given the great strength of hull and tophamper and the large mid-ship bridge-deck typical of the Laiesz vessels destined for the arduous West Coast trade via Cape Horn both ways. Her tragic loss in 1957, after forty-two years of seafaring, was in no way due to weakness or condition alow or aloft. As Alan Villiers said in a BBC interview after the loss, when asked how *Pamir* would stand up to a hurricane, 'Why, she was built to take hurricanes.'

Having discharged her grain at Southampton in June 1939 after a

facing: PAMIR

EPILOGUE

passage of ninety-six days from Australia to her orders port, *Pamir* was laid up at Gothenburg until March 1940, when she sailed to Bahia Blanca. Later that year she loaded guano at Mahé for New Zealand, returning to the Seychelles for a second cargo which she delivered at Wellington in July 1941.

During the latter passage Finland had become a combatant, and on arrival *Pamir* was arrested, the first time New Zealand had ever exercised prize jurisdiction. Her case was similar to that of *Lawhill* in South Africa, for the first writ was followed, in 1943, by a formal writ based on the official Proclamation of a State of War between the Dominions and Finland, and the Supreme Court condemned the barque as a lawful prize although this ruling was without prejudice to any claim Erikson might formulate on the grounds that the original writ was premature.

In March 1943, completely overhauled and refitted, *Pamir*, officered and manned by New Zealanders, commenced a series of transpacific cargo voyages under the flag of the Southern Cross. She shuttled between New Zealand and San Francisco, under charter to the Union Steamship Company, carrying wool and tallow northbound and grain southbound. By September 1945 she was stated to show a credit trading balance of about £30,000.

In 1951 *Pamir* came back to the German flag having been, like *Passat*, purchased by Herr Schliewen of Lübeck. He equipped both barques with supernumerary auxiliary power, by installing an ex-U-boat diesel in each, because of his intention to use the ships in a training-trading rôle. By 1952 they were again at sea, but within a year Schliewen went bankrupt and his ships passed into the hands of the Banks concerned.

In 1954 some forty German shipowners formed, with Federal backing, a combine whose aim was to acquire and operate two big sailing-ships in which to revive sea-training for their cadets, combined with commercial trading. The venture was called the Foundation Pamir-Passat but it proved economically short-lived for, in 1957, the Foundation's chairman stated that, because grain freights had fallen so low, a subsidy was entailed by every voyage and the venture was therefore no longer a commercial proposition.

On September 21st, 1957, *Pamir*, on passage home with 4,000 tons of Argentine barley, was caught in hurricane 'Carrie' when 600 miles

facing: PASSAT, THE LAST SURVIVOR

south-west of the Azores and was blown down and foundered with a loss of eighty lives. Fifty-four of her complement of eighty-six were cadets, two of whom were among the six survivors in a lifeboat which was sighted by the American freighter *Saxon* during an extensive sea and air search. Apart from one other derelict and badly damaged boat, this was the only vestige ever found of *Pamir*.

The lifeboat had only been kept afloat by constant baling and was completely waterlogged when picked up. Torrential rain and tempestuous seas had been endured for fifty-four hours, there was no drinking water, and five men had died. *Pamir* had capsized so quickly that no boats had actually been launched. The one picked up by *Saxon*, and a rubber life-raft, had been torn loose as she went down. The survivors said that about fifteen men reached the raft and then, seeing the lifeboat, tried to swim to it but only eleven reached it. Had *Pamir's* radio operator not been able to send an SOS which was picked up by the British freighter *Manchester Trader*, her fate would, in all probability, have never been known.

The survivors were transferred to the American steamer *Gieger* and were taken to Casablanca where all recovered from their frightful ordeal. A Board of Enquiry was convened but was postponed until January 1958 in order that certain tests might be carried out on *Passat* which might cast light on the capsizing of *Pamir*.

Passat's arrival had been delayed because, having encountered similar weather in the same area, she had been almost on her beam-ends and had taken in much water, but had righted herself by flooding her starboard ballast tanks. She still had a $7\frac{1}{2}$-degree list when she put into Lisbon for repairs. The area where all this happened was not one ordinarily subject to hurricanes, for only seven had crossed it in the previous fifty years!

Several factors emerged at the Enquiry at Lübeck. When *Pamir* had loaded at Buenos Aires the local dockers were on strike so the crew stowed the bulk barley cargo and it was suggested that, in consequence, the holds were not trimmed as fully as if they had been loaded professionally. Barley is a particularly volatile grain which can settle considerably during passage, and can readily shift, especially in a sailing-ship subject to considerable heel by wind-pressure.

Earlier in this book it was stated that Spencer Gulf grain was always bagged, but that during loading, a modicum of the bags were slit so that their contents could fill the crevices between the mass of stowed bags and so weld the cargo into a virtually immovable whole.

Her usual Master being ill, *Pamir* was commanded for this voyage by a Master aged sixty-one who, although having extensive sail experience, had not served in *Pamir* or in other cargo-carrying sailers and consequently was unfamiliar with his ship's factor of stability. The Board considered that the First Officer, although an efficient seaman, was also not sufficiently experienced, and that crew-wise the vessel was undermanned.

Pamir was close-hauled on the starboard tack when the first squall, of force 9, hit her. She was then carrying foresail, some topsails and several staysails and, although it was not clear how much notice the Master had of the approaching hurricane, the Board considered that this amount of canvas had a most adverse effect on stability. Evidence was given that even under bare poles she could have listed $17\frac{1}{2}$ degrees in a force 12 wind but if carrying canvas, this could have increased to 40 degrees.

Her ballast tanks, with a capacity of 750 tons of water, had been filled with 450 tons of barley. It was said that had she been fully water-ballasted the maximum list would have been reduced to 20 degrees which should have meant survival instead of capsizing. In fact, after all her canvas had been blown away and her foremast had snapped, she failed to right herself. The last the survivors saw of her was keel upward.

The Chairman of the Board said that its function was not to apportion blame but to elicit the contributory factors of the loss and to draw constructive conclusions therefrom. They thought that grain in a sailing-ship should always be in bags rather than bulk. They criticized the waterproofing of the distress flares in the lifeboats because, had those in the surviving boat been usable, other lives might have been saved. In their opinion the weather was no more severe than *Pamir* had withstood before during her long sea-life, but her earlier Masters had had a better knowledge of the stability factors of a loaded windjammer and would have shortened down her canvas at an earlier stage.

These findings and recommendations were, however, to be of little practical purpose since, with the cessation of the Foundation Pamir-Passat, deepwater cargo trading under square-rig combined with the sea-training of cadets, is unlikely ever to be revived.

EPILOGUE

Passat, a four-master of 3,137 tons gross launched in 1911, was, like *Pamir*, built at Hamburg by Blohm & Voss for Laiesz. She had the bridge-deck midship section and the full requisite strength for her intended Chilean trade. Erikson bought her in 1932 and she was the youngest vessel in his fleet of windjammers.

After discharging her 1939 cargo of Australian grain in the United Kingdom, *Passat* sailed to Mariehamn where she lay until July 1944 when she, like *Viking* and *Pommern*, was towed across the Baltic to Stockholm and used there for grain storage. When war between Russia and Finland ended, the three ships were towed back to Åbo with relief cargoes of wheat.

Having refitted at Mariehamn in the summer of 1946, *Passat* and *Viking* loaded Baltic timber for South Africa. Sailing in December, both ships caught the North Atlantic at its winter worst but both arrived safely. They voyaged in the Southern Hemisphere until, in 1949, they loaded grain in Spencer Gulf for the United Kingdom. *Passat's* arrival in October gained her the distinction of completing the last deepwater voyage of an Erikson windjammer, terminated her Owner's thirty-six years of sail operation and ended the carriage of Australian grain by sail.

Erikson sold *Passat* to Belgian ship-breakers, but she was reprieved, as was *Pamir*, by being purchased by Schliewen of Lübeck in 1951. She was back at sea by 1952 but in 1954 was sailing with *Pamir* for the Foundation Pamir-Passat.

When *Pamir* foundered, *Passat* was loading bulk barley at Buenos Aires. It was an eventful passage because, after encountering a severe gale in the South Atlantic, she had to put into Lisbon for repairs and restowage of cargo. For economic reasons, coupled with the adverse publicity of the loss of *Pamir*, this was to be the final voyage of *Passat's* forty-six years of seafaring, and her cargo was the last ever to be shipped deepwater under square-rig.

'Passat' the last of the Tall Ships

In bringing to an end this chronicle of the final era of the Tall Ships, it is pleasant to record that *Passat*, after being accorded a permanent berth at Travemuende, was purchased by the Hansestadt of Lübeck to serve as a headquarters for sailing clubs.

THE INSURANCE OF CARGOES SHIPPED IN *PAMIR* AND *PASSAT* IN 1952

My thanks are due to an old friend at Lloyd's, Mr. Miles Illingworth, a Director of Anthony Gibbs & Sons (Insurance) Limited, who, on learning of the re-publication of this book, offered their kind permission for the inclusion therein of the document appearing overleaf. It is almost historic in that it was one of the last insurances to be placed in London on cargo carried by the ships which have been my subject, of which *Pamir* and *Passat* were then the only sea-going survivors.

Mr. Illingworth, as a marine broker, placed this coverage himself, and he recalls my subscribing the $8,000 which appears therein against A.L.S., the patronymic of the Lloyd's firm for whom I was marine underwriter.

A brief outline of the method of negotiating insurances in the London Market may make the document more understandable to the layman.

Upon receiving an enquiry from a client, the broker prepares what is known as a 'slip' embodying an outline of the venture and the client's requirements. This he submits to several underwriters likely to be interested and obtains their terms and quotations. He submits to his client what he considers to be the most suitable proposition and, on receiving instructions to proceed, gets the underwriter who so quoted to 'lead' the risk by subscribing his 'line', i.e. the proportion of the value which he wishes to have.

The broker then goes round the Market showing the risk to companies and to Lloyd's underwriters for their acceptance or refusal, each acceptor 'under-writing' his 'line' until the 'slip' totals the coverage required, or more as in this case where approximately 50 per cent was written by Lloyd's and 50 per cent by companies.

Subsequently the policy is prepared in accordance with the 'slip' and is signed on behalf of all participants.

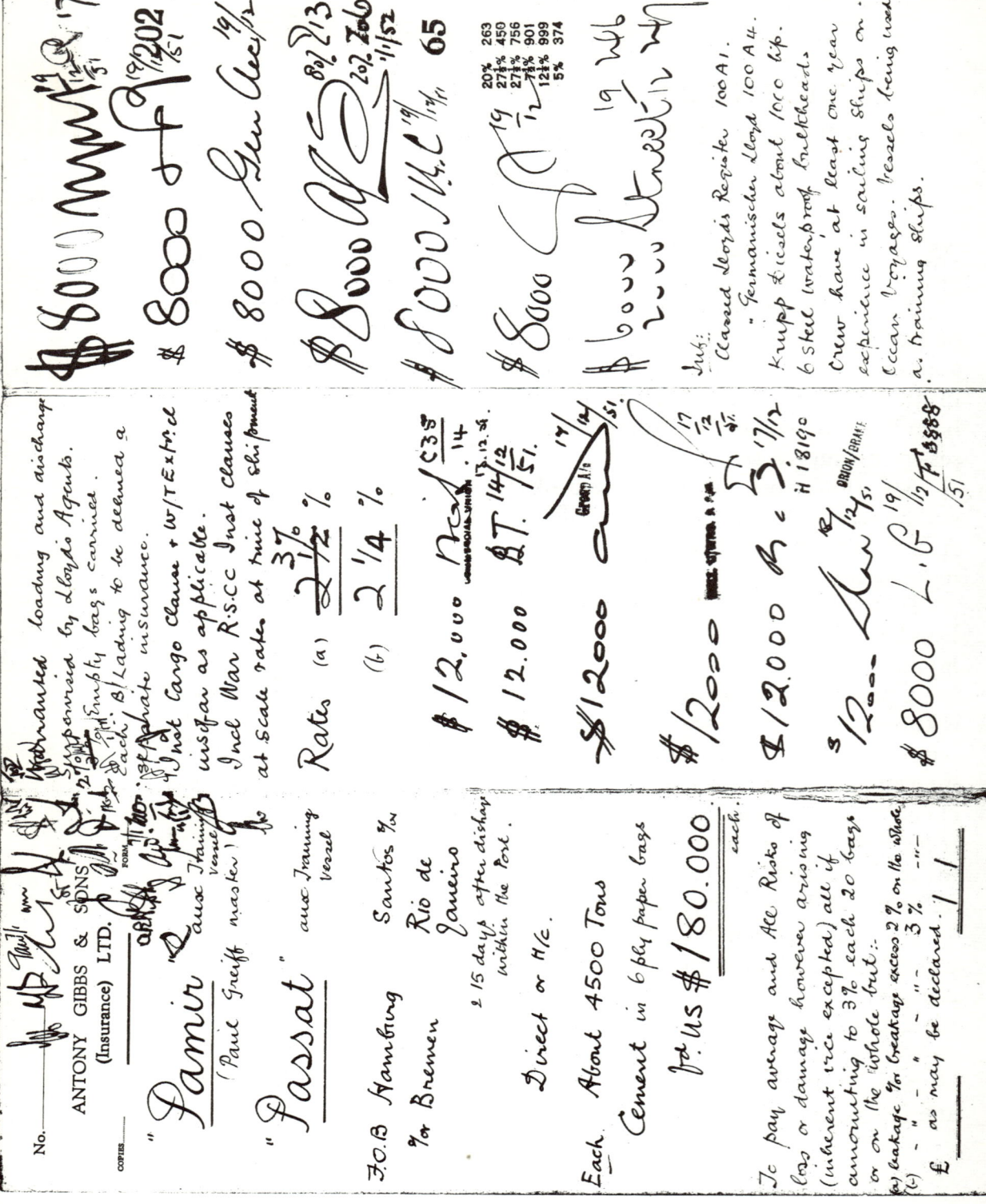

$3000 [signature] 115

$5000 [signature] 20/12/51 448
$12.000 [signature] W/N
$5000 [signature] 20/12/51
$3000 [signature] 25/7/53
$4 [signature] 707
$2000 [signature] 20/4/51 358

$5000 [signature] 16/11/51
$5000 [signature] 10/12/51 298
$5000 Cash 19/12/51 304
$5000 [signature] 19/12
$5000 [signature] 725 19.12.51
$5000 [signature] 19/12 50% 632 50% 633
$5000 [signature] 19/12
$5000 [signature] 19.12.51
$4000 [signature] 80% 165 20% 168 19/12
$4000 [signature] 20/12/51 2500 590 1500 592
$4000 [signature] 16/12

[signature] 156

P12/70